D1384190

BENEDICT DE SPINOZA

THE POLITICAL
WORKS

BENEDICT DE SPINOZA

THE POLITICAL
WORKS

THE TRACTATUS THEOLOGICO-POLITICUS
IN PART AND THE
TRACTATUS POLITICUS IN FULL

EDITED AND TRANSLATED
WITH AN INTRODUCTION AND NOTES
BY

A. G. WERNHAM

REGIUS PROFESSOR OF MORAL PHILOSOPHY
IN THE UNIVERSITY OF ABERDEEN

OXFORD
AT THE CLARENDON PRESS

Oxford University Press, Amen House, London E.C.4

GLASGOW NEW YORK TORONTO MELBOURNE WELLINGTON
BOMBAY CALCUTTA MADRAS KARACHI LAHORE DACCA
CAPE TOWN SALISBURY NAIROBI IBADAN ACCRA
KUALA LUMPUR HONG KONG

FIRST PUBLISHED 1958
REPRINTED LITHOGRAPHICALLY AT THE
UNIVERSITY PRESS, OXFORD,
FROM CORRECTED SHEETS OF THE FIRST EDITION
1965

PRINTED IN GREAT BRITAIN

PREFACE

SPINOZA's political writings have attracted few students in this country; not because they are unimportant, but because there is no satisfactory edition of them in English. The present work is an attempt to remedy this deficiency. In order to achieve my object within the compass of a single volume I have edited the *Tractatus Theologico-Politicus* only in part, and have omitted most of Spinoza's excursions into Biblical criticism; for although his views on the nature and extent of the authority of Scripture play a vital part in his political thought, it is hardly necessary to peruse his detailed examination of prophecy and the Pentateuch in order to understand them. On the other hand I have been careful to retain passages which throw light on his moral doctrines.

By restricting the scope of the work I have made my task easier, but still not easy; and I have often had to invoke the help of friends in order to remedy my ignorance. Dr. D. ter Haar, formerly Lecturer in Theoretical Physics in the University of St. Andrews, has looked over my citations from the *Nagelate Schriften*. Dr. E. Ullendorff, of the Department of Hebrew and Oriental Languages, has checked some of Spinoza's references against the verse numbering of the Hebrew Bible. Members of the Departments of German and Spanish have freely placed their knowledge at my disposal, and Mr. L. J. Woodward has also introduced me to Dr. A. M. Salazar, with whom I have had a profitable corre-, spondence over the interpretation of the passage about King Pedro in *Tractatus Politicus* vii, 30. In addition, Emeritus Professor W. L. Lorimer has helped me with some difficulties in the Latin text, Mr. G. P. Henderson has cast a critical eye over my attempt to summarize the *Ethics* in Part II of the Introduction, and Mr. J. Kemp has not only made valuable comments on my discussion of the political theory, but has also helped to render the translation more accurate and idiomatic. These friends have saved me from many errors, and are in no way responsible for those which remain. I am also indebted to the staff of the University Library in St. Andrews for helping me to obtain the editions I required; and to the staff of the Clarendon Press, who have carried out a difficult task with admirable care and skill. But my greatest debt is to my wife, who has borne my long devotion to Spinoza with patience and understanding, and in a household containing two vigorous youngsters has miraculously maintained sufficient peace and order to enable me to complete my work.

Preface

Since this book is the result of research done as Croom Robertson Fellow of Aberdeen University, it is fitting that it should be dedicated to the memory of George Croom Robertson; and with his name I should like to couple that of the late John Laird, who was chairman of the Committee which awarded me the Fellowship in 1939. I hope that the surviving members of that Committee, who have waited so long for this publication, will find that in the end I have justified their confidence.

A. G. W.

The United College,
St. Andrews
July 1956

PREFACE TO THE SECOND IMPRESSION

In this impression I have corrected errors on pp. 26 and 43; I have altered the translation on pp. 291, 315, 343 and 345; and on p. 238 I have added to the apparatus criticus a reading suggested to me some years ago by my late teacher and friend, Professor A. Cameron. Apart from these changes this impression is a reprint of the first.

A. G. W.

King's College,
Aberdeen
August 1964

CONTENTS

ABBREVIATIONS

APPARATUS CRITICUS

I   *Tractatus Theologico-Politicus. Hamburgi, apud Henricum Künraht.* 1670. The first edition.

II
III } Later quarto editions bearing the same date.
IV

O   *Tractatus Theologico-Politicus, Cui adjunctus est Philosophia S. Scripturae Interpres. Ab Authore longè Emendatior. Anno Dom. 1674.* The second edition.

Mr   The Latin text of Spinoza's notes on the *Tractatus Theologico-Politicus* in Murr's edition of 1802.

ML   The Latin text of these notes preserved in the Leiden MS.

StG   The French version of these notes appended to St Glain's translation of the *Tractatus* (1678).

OP   The Latin text of the *Tractatus Politicus* in *B.d.S. Opera Posthuma,* 1677.

NS   The Dutch text of the *Tractatus Politicus* in *De Nagelate Schriften van B.d.S.,* 1677.

P   *Benedicti de Spinoza Opera quae supersunt omnia. Iterum edenda curavit . . . Henr. Eberh. Gottlob Paulus. Jenae,* 1802–3.

Gf   *Benedicti de Spinoza Opera Philosophica omnia edidit . . . A. Gfrœrer. Stuttgardiae,* 1830.

B   *Benedicti de Spinoza Opera quae supersunt omnia. Ex editionibus principibus denuo edidit et praefatus est Carolus Hermannus Bruder. Lipsiae. Tauchnitz,* 1843–6.

V–L   *Benedicti de Spinoza Opera quotquot reperta sunt. Recognoverunt J. van Vloten et J. P. N. Land. Hagae Comitum, apud Martinum Nijhoff,* 1882–3.

M   *Benedictus de Spinoza — Staatkundig Vertoog. Uit het Latijn door W. Meijer. S. L. van Looy, Amsterdam,* 1901.

L   *Ad Spinozae Opera Posthuma scripsit Dr. J. H. Leopold. Hagae Comitis, apud Martinum Nijhoff,* 1902.

G   *Spinoza Opera im Auftrag der Heidelberger Akademie der Wissenschaften herausgegeben von Carl Gebhardt. Heidelberg, Carl Winters Universitätsbuchhandlung,* 1924–6.

Abbreviations

THE NOTES

KV   *Korte Verhandeling van God, de Mensch, en deszelfs Welstand.* English translation: *Short Treatise on God, Man, and his Wellbeing,* by A. Wolf, A. and C. Black, 1910.

CPP   *Renati des Cartes Principiorum Philosophiae Pars I & II,* with an appendix entitled

CM   *Cogitata Metaphysica.* English translation: *The Principles of Descartes' Philosophy,*[1] by H. H. Britan, Open Court, 1905.

DIE   *Tractatus de Intellectus Emendatione.* English translation: *On the Improvement of the Understanding,* by R. H. M. Elwes, in *Spinoza's Works,* vol. ii. My references here are to the paragraph numbers in Bruder's text.

TT-P   *Tractatus Theologico-Politicus.*

E   *Ethica.* English translation: *Ethics,* by W. H. White and A. H. Stirling, Oxford, 1927.

TP   *Tractatus Politicus.*

Ep.   *Epistolae.* English translation: *The Correspondence of Spinoza,* by A. Wolf, Allen and Unwin, 1928.

---

[1] This title is a mistranslation; the work is an exposition *more geometrico* of Descartes's *Principia Philosophiae* Parts I and II.

GENERAL INTRODUCTION

SPINOZA is a systematic thinker. His political theory is linked to his moral theory, for he regards the state as a necessary precondition of man's salvation;[1] and both are based on his conception of human nature, which in turn depends on his metaphysical views. But his interest in politics is not confined to general theory; if a theory is to make an effective contribution to human welfare it must be embodied in definite political institutions.[2] Again, although the geometrical presentation of the *Ethics* gives that work an appearance of remoteness from the burning questions of the day, Spinoza's political writings are obviously related to a particular historical background. These considerations determine the shape of this Introduction, which is divided into four parts, as follows:

I. A brief account of the historical background against which Spinoza wrote.

II. A sketch, necessarily inadequate, of his metaphysical, psychological, and moral doctrines.

III. A survey of his political theory. Since his theory is most easily understood in relation to the theory of Hobbes, and is to some extent the product of critical reflection on Hobbes's theory, I have cast this survey in the form of a comparison between their views.

IV. A discussion of the model constitutions in which Spinoza sought to give his theory concrete embodiment.

I

THE HISTORICAL BACKGROUND

For after the Bible was translated into English, every man, nay, every boy and wench that could read English, thought they spoke with God Almighty, and understood what he said. . . . Every man became a judge of religion, and an interpreter of the Scriptures to himself.

HOBBES, *Behemoth*

FROM earliest times rulers have tried to control their subjects by enlisting the aid of religion,[3] and religious conformity has often been regarded as so vital to political loyalty that heresy has been taken as a sign, if not a proof, of disaffection.[4] The effectiveness of religion as a means

---

[1] *TT-P* v, p. 93, and xvi, p. 129; *TP* ii, 15, p. 277.   [2] *TP* vii, 2, p. 335.

[3] *TT-P* v, pp. 97–99; xvii, pp. 155–7.

[4] As, for example, at the trial of Socrates.

of political control obviously depends on two conditions: (*a*) all or nearly all the subjects must recognize the same religious authority, and (*b*) the ruler must be supported by that authority. In medieval Europe both conditions were often satisfied. But when the Reformation replaced a single universal church by a number of different churches they ceased to be satisfied in many European states. Not only did subjects recognize different religious authorities, but these various authorities regarded each other with such hostility that it was extremely difficult for a ruler to conciliate one without antagonizing the others. Yet religion had been a prop to civil government for so long that kings could not feel secure on their thrones without its support: witness the remark of James I, 'No Bishop, no King.' Hence his attempt, paralleled in many European states, to impose religious uniformity upon his subjects.

The position, in fact, was still more serious, for in claiming divine inspiration for their views the Reformers set an example which undermined all religious authority whatsoever. If God had spoken to Martin Luther, why not to every man? Thus in England the Divine Right of Kings was opposed by the divine right of the individual to follow God's guidance. Buffe-coate asserts this right in an extreme form during the debates at Putney in 1647: 'Whatsoever hopes or obligations I should be bound unto, if afterwards God should reveal himself, I would break it speedily, if it were an hundred a day.'[1] Ireton saw the danger: 'When I hear men speak of laying aside all engagements to consider only that wild or vast notion of what in every man's conception is just or unjust, I am afraid and do tremble at the boundless and endless consequences of it.'[2] And Hobbes saw the danger too. When one considers the claims of Buffe-coate it comes as no surprise to find Hobbes asserting that 'covenants, without the sword, are but words',[3] and rejecting the idea that nothing more is needed for the preservation of peace and the government of mankind 'than that men should agree to make certain covenants and conditions together, which themselves should then call laws'.[4] Buffe-coate is not 'a political animal by nature'; he needs a sovereign to keep him in order, and his sovereign must control religious doctrine and education, judging which doctrines are fit to be taught,[5] and prescribing *Leviathan* as a university textbook.[6] Such was Hobbes's solution. His doctrine of sovereignty can be viewed

---

[1] *The Clarke Papers*, Camden Society, vol. i, p. 273.
[2] Op. cit., p. 264.   [3] *Leviathan* 17.   [4] *De Cive* i, 2.
[5] *Leviathan* 18.   [6] Ibid., Review and Conclusion.

as an answer to the religious individualism rife among his contemporaries.

Hobbes's solution was not new; it had already been tried in England with unfortunate results. It could expect even less success in the Netherlands, which had a vigorous tradition of religious toleration and freedom of worship. The revolt of the northern provinces from Philip II was partly due to the latter's attempt to impose a single religion upon all his subjects: and the parties to the Union of Utrecht in 1579 duly agreed 'that every citizen should remain free in his religion, and no man be molested or questioned on the subject of divine worship'. This was the manifesto which attracted the persecuted Jews of Spain and Portugal, including the forbears of Spinoza, to the infant state. The Dutch Republic, then, was founded in the faith that stable civil government need not be based on religious uniformity.[1] Yet, as Spinoza notes,[2] it did not always remain true to the faith of its founders, for as the Calvinist church grew in strength it began to claim authority over the civil power in the sphere of religion, and to assume the role of persecutor in its turn. It thus came into conflict with republican statesmen like Oldenbarneveldt and De Witt, who regarded the authorization of forms of worship as a matter for the civil power, and supported toleration as a necessary condition of economic prosperity.[3]

Since the Princes of Orange allied themselves with the Calvinists in order to regain the position of stadtholder,[4] the advocates of persecution and intolerance in the Netherlands tended to be supporters of monarchy also. Spinoza sided with the republican statesmen on both issues, but his opposition to monarchy is mild in comparison with his opposition to attempts at enforcing religious uniformity. He is by no means a diehard opponent of monarchy like Van Hove;[5] he may even have come to believe that a stadtholder was inevitable in the Netherlands.[6] But his hatred of persecution and intolerance is rooted in the ancient sufferings of his race. The depth of his feelings on this issue is

---

[1] p. 227, n. 1. [2] *TT-P* xx, p. 241.

[3] Cf. *TT-P* xx, p. 241. Spinoza's support for the liberal religious policy of these statesmen did not go unmarked: a contemporary pamphlet describes the *TT-P* as a work 'produced in Hell by the renegade Jew in collaboration with the Devil, and published with the connivance of Mr. Jan and his accomplices' (Freudenthal, *Lebensgeschichte*, pp. 194–5).

[4] Cf. p. 241, n. 1. [5] *TP* vii, 31, p. 365.

[6] In *TP* ix, 14, p. 427, Spinoza appears to have given up the view expressed in *TT-P* xviii, p. 203, and to hold that sovereignty in the Netherlands originally lay with the counts. If so, the principle enunciated in the latter passage will lead to a conclusion which is precisely the opposite of the one drawn. And the fact that Spinoza thought it worth while to sketch a model monarchy in the *TP* is not without significance.

shown by the concluding chapter of the *TT-P*, which is written with an eloquence seldom attained in the rest of the work, and in this respect is worthy to be set beside the last chapter of *The Prince*.

Between the Ages of Faith and of Reason comes the Age of Fanaticism,[1] with Buffe-coate as its political problem child. This was the age in which Hobbes and Spinoza lived. Hobbes for his part has some sly remarks to make about the 'horrid thing'[2] which was the cause of the trouble—'to say God hath spoken to him in a dream is no more than to say he dreamed that God spake to him',[3] and so on—but he never actually denies the existence of supernatural revelation.[4] To do so would undermine the authority of Scripture, and as a professed Christian Hobbes is unwilling to do that; he therefore takes refuge in the distinction between knowledge and faith. All we can *know* of God is that God exists: that the laws of nature are his commands and that he inspired the Hebrew prophets are matters of *faith*, and not to be too curiously investigated. 'For it is with the mysteries of our religion as with wholesome pills for the sick; which swallowed whole have the virtue to cure; but chewed, are for the most part cast up again without effect.'[3]

II

A. METAPHYSICS

Ab Jove principium, Musae: Jovis omnia plena.   VIRGIL, *Eclogue* iii

Vulgus philosophicum incipere a creaturis, Cartesium incepisse a mente, se incipere a Deo.   SPINOZA

There is no power but of God.   ST. PAUL

THE God of Hobbes, a first cause for science and philosophy, but a legislator, and therefore a person, for faith and morals, did not satisfy Spinoza. Nor was he content with Descartes's God, who predestined

---

[1] The words 'fanatic' and 'fanaticism' (often with the spelling 'ph') come into common use in the seventeenth century. The abbreviation 'fan' has a curious history. Used in the seventeenth century to refer to an enthusiastic devotee of some religious sect, it vanishes from the English language until modern times. Its current meaning suggests that in the interval there has been a considerable change in the object of the common man's devotion.

[2] Cf. the remark which Bishop Butler is said to have made to Wesley: 'Sir, the pretending to extraordinary revelations and gifts of the Holy Ghost is a horrid thing, a very horrid thing.'

[3] *Leviathan* 32.

[4] It was no doubt Spinoza's critique of revelation, and of faith in general, which caused Hobbes to say that the author of the *TT-P* 'had cut through him a bar's length, for he durst not write so boldly'. See John Aubrey, *Brief Lives*, edited by A. Clark, Clarendon Press, Oxford, 1898, vol. i, p. 357.

all things, yet still left men free will. Descartes might regard the problem as something beyond the power of human understanding to resolve,[1] but Spinoza had no love for mysteries.[2] Inspired not only by a desire for theoretical consistency but by the practical need to find a means of salvation, he attempted to reconcile the God of science and the God of religion. Naturally he had to recast or reinterpret a great deal of the traditional theology. But the assertion that God is infinite, omnipotent, and immutable he took very seriously indeed.

If God is infinite, there is nothing outside God, nothing whose existence is separate from his. Genesis rightly suggests that God is the cause of all things; but wrongly describes him as a craftsman, for the products of a craftsman are external to him, whereas all God's products must be in God.[3] But in what sense can the effects be 'in' the cause? Spinoza answers by giving an analogy. The relation of God to finite things is like the relation of the understanding to its ideas.[4] The understanding is thinking power; and although it is the cause of its ideas it is not something separate from them, for each idea is a determinate expression of thinking power. Finite things, then, are 'in God' in the sense that they are determinate expressions or 'modes' of God. But they are also 'in God' in a secondary sense. By the very fact that finite bodies, for example, are modes of God qua physical energy, they are parts of the whole which is the infinite expression of God qua physical energy, i.e. the extended universe, and in this sense too they may be said to be 'in God'. It is important to distinguish these senses:[5] for, as we shall see below, that man is 'in God' in the second sense is the reason for his predicament; that he is 'in God' in the first sense is the key to his salvation.

Although Spinoza often speaks, *more humano*, of the power of God,[6] he holds in fact that God is not omnipotent but omnipotence, that God *is*, rather than *has*, infinite power.[7] The infinite power which is God acts in accordance with eternal and inviolable laws, the laws of its own nature alone.[8] Now finite things are determinate expressions or forms of this power; consequently they too act in accordance with laws, and if

---

[1] *Principia Philosophiae* i, xxxix–xli.

[2] See Meyer's Preface to the *CPP*, referred to in *Ep.* xxi; cf. also *Epp.* xliii and lviii.

[3] *E* i, 15.   [4] For the analogy see *KV* i, First Dialogue.

[5] Spinoza distinguishes between the mode–substance relation and the part–whole relation in *Ep.* xxxii.

[6] Cf. *TT-P* xvi, p. 125; *TP* ii, 2–3, p. 267.   [7] *E* i, 34.

[8] *TP* ii, 18, p. 279; *E* i, 17. If God had a 'lawless freedom' knowledge and science would be impossible; cf. *E* i, 33 Sch. 2.

not in accordance with the laws of their own nature *alone*, then at least in accordance with the laws which govern their intercourse with other finite things, i.e. the laws of the nature of the whole in which they and the other finite things exist as parts.[1] All such laws we may call laws of nature or God's decrees as we please,[2] provided we remember that they are scientific laws, and not the commands of a legislator.[3] It follows:

1. That there is no human thought, feeling, volition, or action which does not occur in accordance with laws of nature (its causes),[4] and consequently,

2. That there is no such thing as supernatural inspiration.[5] To say that a man is guided by God is merely to say that his conduct is determined by laws of nature:[6] if we do not mean this we are simply evincing our ignorance of the laws which actually determine it.[7] Spinoza's conception of God leaves no room for the claims of Buffe-coate.

B. PSYCHOLOGY AND MORALS

(i) *Of Human Bondage, or the Strength of the Passions*

O miseras hominum mentes, o pectora caeca!
LUCRETIUS, *De Rerum Natura* ii, 14.

As part of the extended universe man's body is affected through its sense organs by other bodies external to it. In the first instance the actual presence of another body is necessary to produce an affection of the human body, but once an affection has been produced it tends to persist even when its cause is removed.[8] It may even recur later in the absence of its cause; for if the human body has often been affected by two objects together, it will tend to be affected by one of these objects in the same way as it was originally affected by both. Now although there is no causal connexion between physical and mental events, whenever an affection occurs in the body an idea simultaneously occurs in the mind. Spinoza thus correlates the association of ideas and memory with the persistence of bodily dispositions.[9]

---

[1] *Ep.* xxxii.   [2] *TT-P* iii, p. 53.   [3] *TP* ii, 18, p. 279, and 22, pp. 281–3.
[4] Cf. *TP* i, 4, p. 263. By the 'cause' of a passion Spinoza sometimes means the law in accordance with which it occurs.
[5] *TT-P* v, p. 107.   [6] *TT-P* iii, p. 55.
[7] For God as the *asylum ignorantiae* see *E* i, App.
[8] *E* ii, 17 Cor. Dem.   [9] *E* ii, 18.

The ideas which occur as the mental counterparts of bodily affections involve awareness of external objects,[1] but they may also involve awareness of an increase or decrease in the power of the human body.[2] Awareness of an increase in power is joy; of a decrease, sorrow;[3] and when joy and sorrow are referred to external causes they respectively constitute love and hatred of these causes.[4] Now suppose that a human body has been affected by two external objects, x and y, and that x diminished its power while y neither increased nor diminished it. When on a later occasion y alone acts on the body, the latter will tend to be affected by y alone in the same way as it was previously affected by the joint action of x and y. In being aware of y the mind will also be aware of a decrease in the body's power, i.e. it will feel sorrow, refer its sorrow to y, and so hate y.[5] We have now brought to light one of the 'causes' of the passions, one of the laws in accordance with which passions occur. This law—let us call it the law of transference—may be formulated thus: when ideas are connected the emotion involved in one tends to be transferred to another, no matter how accidental or superficial the connexion may be.

The scope of this law is tremendous. It explains how hatred for the few men who caused the death of Christ was extended to the whole Jewish race,[6] and is thus one of the 'causes' of intolerance and persecution. It explains many inner conflicts, conflicts of emotion: an object may affect a man with joy, yet, because it is like something else, simultaneously affect him with sorrow, so that he both loves and hates it.[7] Moreover, since the ways in which different men associate ideas will differ according as their bodies have acquired different habits through the action of external objects,[8] the emotional attitudes of different men to the same object may be very different. A may associate y with x, which he hates; B may associate y with z, which he loves. If so, A will hate y and desire to destroy it, while B will love y and desire to preserve it.[9] The law of transference is not only the explanation of many inner conflicts of emotion; it also accounts for many conflicts between man and man.

There is, however, another psychological law which might seem at first sight to mitigate the effects of the law of transference. This second law, the law of imitation or sympathy, states that when one man

---

[1] *E* ii, 16 Cor. 1.   [2] *E* iii, Def. 3.   [3] *E* iii, 11 Sch.
[4] *E* iii, 13 Sch.   [5] *E* iii, 15.
[6] *E* iii, 16 and 46. These two propositions reveal the ethical bearing of Spinoza's attack on universals in *E* ii, 40 Sch. 1.
[7] *E* iii, 17.   [8] *E* ii, 18 Sch. and 40 Sch. 1.   [9] *E* iii, 28.

imagines that another is affected by a certain emotion he will tend to feel that emotion himself:[1] for example, a man who sees another sorrowing will tend to feel sorrow himself and to pity the sufferer. Although passion usually divides men it can on occasion unite them,[2] and Spinoza makes use of this fact in *TP* vi, 1 when he discards the social contract as an explanation of the historical origin of the state. But in many cases the effect of the law of imitation is merely to increase conflict. Let us revert to our previous example, and suppose that *A* and *B* are aware of one another's emotions. Then *A*, hating *y*, will also tend to love it in sympathy with *B*, while *B*, loving *y*, will also tend to hate it in sympathy with *A*. Both will be torn between love and hatred of *y*, and neither will have inner peace until one of the conflicting emotions is destroyed. In such a case each will endeavour to maintain his own original emotional attitude, *A* trying to make *B* hate *y* so as to confirm and not disturb his own hatred for *y*, *B* trying to make *A* love *y* so as to confirm and not disturb his own love for *y*. Once more the result is intolerance and persecution.[3] If *A* succeeds in making *B* hate *y* the conflict is resolved: but if *B* succeeds in making *A* love *y*, and *y* is an object which only one of them can possess, a contest for possession is likely to arise between the lovers, and the winner will be hated and envied by the loser. Thus the law of imitation is the cause of ambition and envy as well as of pity and benevolence:[4] ambition being defined as the attempt to make others love what we love or hate what we hate.[5] Men are often dimly aware that 'ambition' may recoil upon their own heads, and so it comes to pass that 'while they delight to sing the praises of what they love, they fear lest they should be believed'.[6] Few cardinals could have extolled their worldly goods to the Borgia Pope with whole-hearted enthusiasm.

We have now seen how man's predicament arises from the fact that his body is a part of the extended universe which is acted upon by the other parts and reacts upon them in its turn. We have seen how he is torn by conflicting passions, how he is led to love or hate things which do him neither good nor harm, and how he is driven to misguided efforts by such emotions. As parts of nature men are in bondage to passion, and the normal relationship between them is one of hatred and warfare. In his analysis Spinoza is not only explaining why the minds of men are 'like the troubled sea, when it cannot rest':[7] he is

---

[1] *E* iii, 27.   [2] Contrast the formulation of *E* iv, 34 with that of *E* iv, 35.
[3] *E* iii, 31 and Cor.   [4] *E* iii, 32 and Sch.   [5] *E* iii, 31 Cor.   [6] *E* iv, 37 Sch. 1.
[7] Isaiah 57, 20, referred to in *TT-P* iv, p. 85.

also laying the foundation for his account of the state of nature in the political works.

(ii) *Of the Power of Understanding, or Human Freedom*

Deus Illuminatio Mea[1]

In considering man's predicament we saw how ideas arose in his mind as correlates of the affections of his body, and how these ideas were connected in the same way as the affections of his body. In treating of his salvation we must start from his mind, not from his body, and view him as a mode of God under the attribute of thought, i.e. as an intellect or thinking power.

As an intellect man is the source of adequate ideas connected in a logical chain; so that his mind contains adequate ideas which are logically connected as well as inadequate ideas linked by association.[2] If by reflection on his ideas he clearly distinguishes between these two kinds,[3] he will never again rest content with the second, but will try to form adequate ideas of things he has so far conceived inadequately, ideas which can be linked up with others in the logical chain. Although success in this will not eliminate his original inadequate ideas,[4] it will weaken the associative linkage between them. But when the connexion between two ideas is weakened, the tendency for an emotion involved in one to be transferred to the other is weakened also: and this tendency, as we saw, is one of the main causes of inappropriate and conflicting emotions. Thus the weakening of the associative connexion will at once render the man less liable to such emotions. But this is only the negative result of the formation and 'concatenation' of adequate ideas: the positive result is a rational reorganization of the whole emotional life. For just as the emotion involved in an inadequate idea tends to be transferred to another inadequate idea accidentally associated with the first, so the emotion involved in an adequate idea tends to be transferred to the adequate idea which is logically connected with the first. The law which was formerly a cause of chaotic passions is now a cause of emotional stability.[5]

---

[1] With apologies to the University of Oxford.

[2] Spinoza distinguishes between the *ordo imaginationis* (which is based on the *communis ordo naturae*) and the *ordo intellectualis* in *E* ii, 18 Sch. and 29 Sch.

[3] The process is discussed in the *DIE*. The difficulty of translating the title of this work is due to the fact that understanding needs purification or emendation only in the sense that it requires to be distinguished from imagining. See H. H. Joachim, *Spinoza's Tractatus de Intellectus Emendatione*, Clarendon Press, Oxford, 1940, p. 1, n. 1.   [4] *E* ii, 35 Sch.

[5] Cf. *E* v, 10 and Sch. But in the last half of this paragraph I am concerned to follow up

'No remedy for the passions', says Spinoza, 'is more excellent than that which consists in true knowledge of them.'[1] Then part iii of the *Ethics* is not only an account of man's predicament but a remedy for it. This remedy, like the others, depends on his ability to distinguish logical connexion from association, and on his love for the former. But since logical connexion, the intellectual order, is the expression of God qua thinking power, love of the intellectual order is love of God. And this is both the beginning and the end of man's salvation.

I shall conclude my brief sketch of Spinoza's moral theory by making some general remarks. The question which he seeks to answer is the question asked of Jesus in the Gospels, 'What shall I do to inherit eternal life?'[2] But Spinoza's answer is not a command; the *Ethics* contains no 'oughts',[3] no imperatives, only 'eternal truths'.[4] The moral fervour which inspires it may remind us of the Hebrew prophets of old, but Spinoza is not a prophet. He does not exhort or castigate his readers—that, he thinks, is not a philosopher's task[5]—but tries to give them a 'clear and distinct' understanding of themselves and their emotions, secure in the assurance that he who has this has also love of God and salvation.[6] The transition from 'is' to 'ought' which Hume thought fatal to 'all the vulgar systems of morality'[7] is never made by Spinoza: the very notion of duty is alien to his thought. While he speaks of 'the dictates of reason',[8] he holds in fact that the 'dictates' of a man's own reason are not prescriptions at all:[9] here, as elsewhere, an old linguistic bottle proves quite inadequate to contain his new philosophical wine. Certainly a desire springing from passion may conflict with a desire which springs from reason,[10] and if we think of this situation as a case of 'rebellion' in the soul we may easily pass to the notion of duty by conceiving reason as 'laying down the law' to insubordinate subordinates. But for Spinoza reason is no more a legislator than God is, and political metaphors are as much out of place in moral psychology as they are in philosophical theology. The crux of the situation is a conflict of desires, and in this conflict the stronger wins.[11] But which *is*

hints given in *E* ii and iii rather than to expound the obscure and difficult propositions at the start of *E* v.

[1] *E* v, 4 Sch.   [2] Matthew 19, 16; Mark 10, 17; Luke 18, 18.
[3] But the best of translators may nod. White and Stirling do so in *E* v, 16, where the meaning is not that love of God *ought* to occupy the mind, but that it *must* occupy the mind, *sc.* if the man clearly understands himself and his affects.
[4] *TT-P* iv, pp. 77–83.   [5] *TP* i, 1, p. 261, and 4, p. 263.
[6] *E* v, 15–16.   [7] *Treatise* iii, i, 1.   [8] See *E* iv from 18 Sch. onwards.
[9] Spinoza's treatment of the dictates of reason is discussed on pp. 19–20 below.
[10] For the expression see *TP* ii, 5, p. 269.   [11] *E* iv, 7 and 14–15.

the stronger depends on the agent's degree of enlightenment: in a 'free man' the desires which spring from reason are seldom troubled by opposition.[1] Laird's remark that Spinoza 'had no appreciation of duty at all'[2] would not be regarded by the philosopher as a slur on his moral character, but as a tribute to its excellence.

III

THE POLITICAL THEORY

Gratias agamus Machiavello et hujusmodi scriptoribus qui aperte et indissimulanter proferunt quid homines facere soleant, non quid debeant.   BACON, *De Augmentis Scientiarum*

SINCE civil life, in Spinoza's view, is a necessary precondition of the attainment of salvation,[3] political theory, like moral theory, must start from the predicament of unregenerate men;[4] and must show how they can be made to live together in settled peace in spite of their emotional instability and mutual enmity.[5] A political theory which assumes that men are saints is quite superfluous from a practical point of view,[6] 'for if men desired most what was most to their advantage there would be no need of artifice to promote loyalty and concord'.[7] Those who conceive men 'as they would like them to be'[8] evade, and do not solve, the problem of politics. Spinoza thus adopts the starting-point of Machiavelli and Hobbes. And his handling of the problem owes something to both writers. In laying down the outline of his solution he is influenced by the method of Hobbes, who treated the problem as if it were a problem in geometry[9]—given that men have a certain nature, it is required to determine, by the aid of reason alone, the broad conditions under which they may live together in peace. But when he goes on to test and even to qualify his conclusions by reference to practical experience[10] the influence of Machiavelli's empiricism begins to appear: and it becomes predominant when he proceeds to recommend particular institutions.[11]

---

[1] *E* v, 42 Sch.

[2] J. Laird, *Hobbes*, Ernest Benn Ltd., 1934, p. 303.

[3] *TT-P* v, p. 93, and xvi, p. 129; *TP* ii, 15, p. 277.

[4] *TP* i, 5, pp. 263–5.   [5] *TP* vii, 2, p. 335.   [6] *TP* i, 1, p. 261.

[7] *TP* vi, 3, p. 315.   [8] *TP* i, 1, p. 261.   [9] *Leviathan* 20.

[10] As in *TT-P* xvii, pp. 149–53, where he concludes that absolute sovereignty is a theoretical ideal to which practice can only approximate: cf. *TP* viii, 3–5, pp. 369–73.

[11] *TP* i, 3, p. 263, suggests that the institutions recommended in *TP* vi–xi are all based, at least to some extent, on political practice, and I have done my best to find historical precedents for them in my notes.

At present, however, we are concerned with his general theory. This I propose to introduce by comparing it with the theory of Hobbes, which has influenced its content and terminology as well as its method. But Spinoza is no mere follower of Hobbes. He borrows much, but he also finds much to criticize: he uses the same terms, but he gives them a new sense. In order to show this my comparison of the two theories will take the form of a comparison between the meanings attached by Hobbes and Spinoza to their basic terms. And first I shall consider 'the right of nature'.

(i) *The Right of Nature*

> Spinoza, more consistently naturalistic than Hobbes, relinquishes the distinction between might and right and teaches the natural right of all passions: Hobbes, on the other hand, . . . asserts the natural right only of the fear of death.
>
> LEO STRAUSS, *The Political Philosophy of Hobbes*

Hobbes and Spinoza commence their political arguments with an account of the state of nature, an account of the condition of men who are not subject to civil government; and they agree that this condition is one of mutual hostility and war.[1] But whereas Spinoza's account of the state of nature is purely 'an inference made from the passions',[2] Hobbes distinguishes man's natural right from his natural passions, and holds that both factors play a part in making the state of nature a state of war.[3] His account of the right of nature proceeds on the following lines. Man is led by his passions, in particular by his vanity, into a conflict with his fellows which endangers his life, and, seized by an overwhelming fear of death, seeks to avoid destruction 'by a certain impulsion of nature no less than that whereby a stone moves downward'. Now one cannot reasonably say that he ought not to do what he cannot help doing: his conduct, then, is not contrary to reason. 'But that which is not contrary to right reason, that all men account to be done justly, and with right.' Man has therefore a natural right to try to preserve life and limb.[4] Moreover, since the right to pursue an end involves the right to use any means necessary to achieve that end, man has a natural right to attempt any action necessary for his own preservation.[5] And he has also a natural right to judge and decide what *is* necessary, i.e. it is

---

[1] *De Cive* i, 12; *TP* ii, 14, pp. 275–7.   [2] Hobbes's phrase in *Leviathan* 13.
[3] *De Cive* i, 12: cf. *EL* i, 14, 11.
[4] *De Cive* i, 7: cf. *EL* i, 14, 6, and see *De Cive*, The Epistle Dedicatory, p. ii.
[5] Ibid. i, 8; *EL* i, 14, 7.

unreasonable to say that he ought not to do this. For if we say that *B* ought to judge what is necessary for *A*'s preservation, then, since men in the state of nature are equal, we must allow *A* to judge whether the means decided by *B* are necessary for his (*A*'s) preservation or not; and this is to make *A* the ultimate judge of the means to his own preservation.[1]

Hobbes now goes on to assert that man's natural right is 'a right to all things'.[2] This statement, which occurs in *The Elements of Law* and *Leviathan* as well as in *De Cive*, leads Oakeshott to contrast man's absolute natural right with his limited natural power, and to say that 'nothing a man does can exceed what he has a natural right to do'.[3] Now certainly man's natural right to *decide* which actions are necessary for his preservation is absolute; but his natural right to *do* such actions is limited by his power to do them. Hobbes does not believe that man has a natural right to jump over the moon, even to save his life. A man may not even have a natural right to do actions which are within his general physical capacity: this is so when he is prevented from doing them by external impediments.[4] Strictly speaking, man's natural right is not even a right to defend life and limb, but only a right to do so as far as he *can*;[5] even as a right to all things it is no more than a right to possess, use, and enjoy all that he will, and *can* get.[6] But we must not conclude that the natural right to do is co-extensive with the power to do, for in many passages Hobbes implies that man's power is wider than his natural right. In *Leviathan* 13, for example, he contrasts those who aggress from vanity with those who aggress in order to protect themselves from the vain, and remarks that 'such augmentation of dominion over men being necessary to a man's conservation, it ought to be allowed him': which suggests that the second kind of aggressor acts *jure naturali*, but not the first.[7] In *De Cive* i, 10, n. he says that 'if any man pretend somewhat to tend necessarily to his preservation, which yet he himself doth not confidently believe so, he may offend against the laws of nature'. But what *transgresses* the laws of nature, i.e. the laws of natural reason, is not done by natural right.

[1] *De Cive* i, 9; *EL* i, 14, 8.

[2] *De Cive* i, 10; *EL* i, 14, 10; *Leviathan* 14.

[3] See Hobbes' *Leviathan*, edited with an Introduction by Michael Oakeshott (Blackwell, Oxford, 1946), pp. lviii–lix. It seems to me that Oakeshott confuses natural right with what Strauss calls natural appetite: see Leo Strauss, *The Political Philosophy of Hobbes* (Clarendon Press, Oxford, 1936), pp. 8 and ff. Strauss himself draws a clear distinction between them (op. cit., p. 155, n. 2).

[4] *Leviathan* 14.

[5] *De Cive* i, 7; *EL* i, 14, 6.

[6] *De Cive* i, 10; *EL* i, 14, 10.

[7] Cf. *De Cive* i, 4.

Again in *De Cive* iii, 27, n. we find him asserting that 'in the state of nature what is just and unjust is not to be esteemed by the actions but by the counsel and conscience of the actor. That which is done out of necessity, out of endeavour for peace, for the preservation of ourselves, is done with right (recte).' This implies that actions which do not fall under these heads are not done *jure naturali*. And finally in *EL* i, 19, 2, he says that 'nothing but fear can justify the taking away of another's life'.

I conclude that in Hobbes's view an agent has no natural right to do an action unless (*a*) he is able to do the action, (*b*) his aim is the preservation of his own life, and (*c*) he regards the action as necessary for the achievement of that aim. Then in what sense is the right of nature a right to all things? It is a right to all things in the sense that it excludes no *type* of external action taken against other men:[1] it is a right to aggress, to appropriate, to enslave, and even to kill. But it exists only when the above conditions are satisfied, and these conditions are not always satisfied even in the state of nature, where *A* often tries to overcome *B* merely to assert his own superiority. In such a case *A* has no natural right to aggress: but *B* has a natural right to take what measures he thinks necessary for his own defence. Suppose that *B*, in order to strengthen himself against *A*, thinks it necessary to attack *C* and make him subject: he has then a natural right to try to do so.[2] Now suppose that *C*, realizing *B*'s danger, suspects that *B* is going to attack him: then he in turn has a natural right to defend himself against *B* if he can, and to forestall *B*'s attack by getting his blow in first.[3] This illustration shows how possession of the right of nature creates suspicion and hostility even between moderate men, and why Hobbes conceived it as one of the factors which make the state of nature a state of war.

Hobbes holds, then, that man's natural right does not extend as far as his natural power, but covers only some of his actions. Unfortunately, the limits which he set on the right of nature can be removed by the consistent application of his own principles. According to Hobbes, everything a man does is determined by antecedent causes. Now it is unreasonable to say of a man[4] that he ought not to do what he is causally

---

[1] This, perhaps, is the view adopted by Strauss (op. cit., pp. 23–24); but he does not make his meaning very clear.

[2] See the passage from *Leviathan* 13 quoted above.

[3] Ibid.: 'there is no way for any man to secure himself so reasonable as anticipation.'

[4] But not '*to* him': Hobbes successfully refutes Bramhall's assertion that his determinism makes consultations and admonitions to be in vain (*EW* v, pp. 153–4).

determined to do, for he cannot do anything else:[1] consequently he has a natural right to do everything he is causally determined to do, i.e. his right of nature covers all his actions. Besides, it follows from Hobbes's account of human physiology[2] that all man's actions are efforts to preserve himself: therefore man's right to preserve himself again covers all his actions, those motivated by vanity as well as those motivated by fear of death. Spinoza accepts both these points, and so maintains that a man has a natural right to do everything he does do.[3] At the same time he extends the possession of natural right to everything that exists,[4] holding that since all things in nature always act to preserve themselves, and cannot do anything else, all things in nature always act by natural right.

This right of nature, which is possessed by everything that exists, is derived by Spinoza from the basic principles of his metaphysics. God and nature are identical; the power of God and the right of God are identical;[5] therefore the power of nature and the right of nature are identical. Moreover the power of God or nature is simply the law of God or nature in action: therefore the right of nature and the law of nature are identical.[6] Now everything in nature exists and acts, i.e. preserves itself, by the power of God:[7] therefore it exists and acts, or preserves itself, by the right of nature. Of course, the fact that all things in nature exist and act by the power of God, by the right of nature, or in accordance with natural law, does not mean that they all exist and act in the same way. Though all bodies, for example, act in accordance with the general laws which apply to bodies as such, particular kinds of bodies act in accordance with particular forms of these general laws. In so far as this is so a human body does not act in the same way as a log of wood:[8] though both act by natural right, their natural right is different because their power is different. Similarly, a human mind does not act in the same way as the mind of a horse.[9] Thus the fact that Spinoza conceives everything in nature to possess natural right in no way prevents him from recognizing a natural right peculiar to man:[10] man exists and acts, i.e. preserves himself, by the right of his

[1] As Bramhall says, Hobbes maintains that all things are 'extrinsically predetermined to one' (*EW* v, p. 84).

[2] *EL* i, 7, 1–4.   [3] *TT-P* xvi, pp. 125–7; *TP* ii, 4–5, pp. 267–9.

[4] Hobbes appears to restrict the possession of natural right to God, men, and beasts. For the natural right of beasts see *De Cive* viii, 10.

[5] *TP* ii, 3, p. 267.   [6] *TP* ii, 4, p. 267.   [7] *TP* ii, 2, p. 267.

[8] *Ep.* xxi; cf. *E* ii, 13 Sch. and iii, 2 Sch.   [9] *E* iii, 57 Sch.

[10] This is clear from *TT-P* xvi, p. 125, where he starts from 'the laws of each individual thing's nature'; contrast *TP* ii, 4, p. 267.

own nature. In particular, he decides on the means to his preservation by the right of his own nature,[1] and Spinoza, like Hobbes, regards this right to decide as of vital importance.

A striking feature of Spinoza's account of natural right is his use of the idiom 'does by natural right' rather than the idiom 'has a natural right to do'. One reason for his preference is the fact that the former idiom, unlike the latter, obviates any temptation to divorce right from power. But there is another reason. Although man always acts by the right of his own nature, or in accordance with the laws of his own nature,[2] he does not necessarily act in accordance with the laws of his own nature *alone*, or by the right of his own nature *alone*, i.e. he is not necessarily *sui juris*;[3] for since he is part of a whole his actions may be partly determined by the nature of the other parts which affect him. This distinction between acting or deciding by the right of one's own nature and acting or deciding by the right of one's own nature *alone* would be difficult to express in Hobbes's idiom, and is in fact alien to his thought. But for Spinoza it is vital: it is the distinction between slavery to the passions and freedom. Hobbes in contrast defines freedom as the absence of external impediments,[4] and holds that a man is free as long as he can do what he wills,[5] no matter how his will, or rather his volition,[6] is determined.

(ii) *The Law of Nature*

Necessitas dat legem, non ipsa accipit.
PUBLILIUS SYRUS

As we saw, Hobbes holds that in the state of nature it is sometimes not unreasonable for a man to aggress, appropriate, enslave, and even kill. Such actions, however, necessary and justifiable in an emergency, afford at best only a temporary security, and in the long run merely increase the agent's danger; for he who successfully employs anticipation against others will inevitably find his own weapon turned against himself, and since men are roughly equal, he must soon succumb to

---

[1] *TP* ii, 12, p. 275; *E* iv, 37 Sch. 2.

[2] For Spinoza, who identifies natural right and natural law, the idiom also provides a convenient means of passing from one to the other; cf. *TP* ii, 5, p. 269.

[3] See *TP* ii, 8 and 11, pp. 273 and 275.

[4] *Leviathan* 14.   [5] Ibid. 21.

[6] In *Leviathan* 6 he says that the will is 'the act, not the faculty, of *willing*' (cf. Spinoza, *E* ii, 48 Sch.). Hence Oakeshott's statement (op. cit., p. lviii) that for Hobbes natural right 'is inherent in the will, which is limitless in its claims' is doubly misleading.

unexpected attack.[1] Accordingly, when a man apprehends no danger to himself it is reasonable for him to act peaceably, and unreasonable to commit aggression. In turning from what is not unreasonable to what is reasonable or unreasonable, from what a man may do to what he ought or ought not to do, from what reason permits to what reason advises or counsels against, we turn from 'blameless liberty'[2] to obligation,[3] from natural right to natural law.

Hobbes's laws of nature, when conceived as based on reason alone, are 'conclusions or theorems concerning what conduceth to the conservation and defence of (men) themselves'.[4] The fundamental theorem states that peace, when possible, is the means to preservation,[5] and since he who wills the end ought to will the means it follows that men ought to seek peace. Subordinate theorems state that certain dispositions,[6] and certain kinds of overt action, are the means to, or conditions of, peace; and from these theorems it follows that men ought to have these dispositions and perform actions of these kinds. The theorems of reason thus give rise to rules or precepts of reason, or alternatively, to obligations. It is, for example, a rule of reason that men should be disposed to keep covenants, and this rule has no exceptions. It is also a rule that they should keep covenants, but this rule is binding only when they think they can do so with safety: when they are not sure that they can, as is often the case in the state of nature, it is not unreasonable for them to break their covenants, i.e. they have a natural right to do so. 'The laws of nature oblige *in foro interno*; that is to say, they bind to a desire they should take place: but *in foro externo*, that is, to the putting them in act, not always.'[7]

Because Hobbes claims originality for this deduction of moral rules[7] he cannot maintain that the just man's motive is fear of death. When Strauss says that Hobbes identifies conscience with fear of death, and believes the just man to obey the laws of his state for fear of the state of nature,[8] he is taking Hobbes's theoretical deduction of moral rules for an account of the actual motive of the just man: and this is a mistake. Hobbes explicitly says that the just man is one 'who doth just things because the law commands it',[9] and appears to hold that moral rules, though logically hypothetical, are psychologically categorical for the just man.

[1] *De Cive* i, 13 and 15.   [2] Hobbes's phrase in *EL* i, 14, 6.
[3] Cf. *De Cive* xiv, 3: 'law is *a fetter*, right is *freedom*.'
[4] *Leviathan* 15; cf. *De Cive* iii, 33.
[5] Ibid. ii, 2; *Leviathan* 14.   [6] *De Cive* iii, 29; *Leviathan* 15.
[7] Ibid.   [8] Strauss, op. cit., pp. 25–26.   [9] *De Cive* iii, 5.

Since laws are properly commands, the moral rules which Hobbes has deduced are not yet laws: but they become laws in the strict sense when they are conceived as commands of God.[1] This is how they are conceived by those who accept the authority of Scripture. However, the belief that they are God's commands need not depend on the acceptance of Scripture.[2] A man need not be acquainted with Scripture in order to believe that God exists and has given him reason 'for the rule of his actions';[3] and if he believes this he may easily conclude that the dictates of his reason are God's commands. Whether Hobbes himself really believed that moral rules are commands of God is not easy to determine. His acceptance of the view may be merely formal—a sop to the religious, or a duty imposed on him by his sovereign. Certainly his account of God's will makes it hard to conceive that will as a direct source of commands: 'when we ascribe to God a *will*, it is not to be understood, as that of man, for a *rational appetite*; but as the power by which he effecteth everything.'[4] Yet according to Taylor[5] Hobbes 'meant quite seriously what he so often says, that the natural law is the command of God'.

Whether genuine or not, Hobbes's acceptance of this view proved embarrassing when confronted with his determinism. Bramhall argued that God was deceitful if he openly commanded men to do one thing while secretly determining them to do another;[6] and unjust if he punished them for transgressing commands which he had determined them to transgress.[7] He concluded that determinism was false—'God's chiding proves man's liberty.'[8] Hobbes answered the second point by saying that conduct unjust in man was not unjust in God, since 'the power of God alone, without other help, is sufficient justification of any action he doth'.[9] Moreover, determinism did not necessarily make God's chiding 'to be in vain', for divine admonitions and commands—like human ones—might be causally efficacious.[10] But in spite of all his ingenuity Hobbes could do little with the first point. He was left with a paradox—a God with two wills, one of which might conflict with the other; and even the authority of the Protestant doctors to whom he appealed[11] was hardly sufficient to commend such a monster.

---

[1] *EL* i, 17, 12; *De Cive* iii, 33; *Leviathan* 15.

[2] See J. M. Brown, 'Hobbes—A Rejoinder', in *Political Studies*, vol. ii, pp. 170–1.

[3] Hobbes's phrase in *De Cive* iv, 1.

[4] *Leviathan* 31.

[5] A. E. Taylor, 'The Ethical Doctrine of Hobbes', in *Philosophy*, vol. xiii, 1938, p. 418.

[6] Hobbes, *EW* v, pp. 98–99.   [7] Ibid. p. 114.   [8] Ibid. p. 99.

[9] Ibid. p. 115.   [10] Ibid. pp. 151–5.   [11] Ibid. p. 103.

Spinoza's conception of God enabled him to eliminate this paradox: 'God is not a legislator or king who lays down laws for men.'[1] The laws of God or nature are scientific laws, not commands or prescriptions;[2] they operate whether men apprehend them or not; and they are inviolable.[3] It is, for example, a law of nature that men necessarily do what they think to be in their own best interests. Then to say that they ought not to act in this way is absurd. Suppose that a man, having made a promise, comes to the conclusion that it would be in his own best interests to break it. Because he thinks so, he cannot keep it: so to say of him that he ought to keep it is again absurd.[4] Where there is no 'can' there is no 'ought'; no obligation can stand against a law of nature in Spinoza's sense.[5]

It is true that he often speaks of 'the dictates of reason', and that in these dictates we find some sort of parallel to Hobbes's laws of nature. But when we consider the sense in which Spinoza conceives his dictates of reason to oblige we soon see that he has taken great pains to reconcile his account of them with his determinism. Unlike Hobbes, he thinks it important to know whose reason is dictating; for the sense in which reason 'obliges' a man depends on whether we are speaking of his own reason or not. Let us first consider the sense in which a man's own reason 'obliges' him.

For Spinoza reason is the power to form adequate ideas[6] and to grasp necessary connexions.[7] Then to say that a man's own reason dictates a certain action to him is to say that he has an adequate idea of his own interest and sees that the action in question is the necessary means to it. Now since men necessarily do what they think to be in their own best interests, it follows that he is bound to do the action. And in this 'is bound' we have the 'obligation' which his reason imposes: an 'obligation' which is not an 'ought' but a 'must'.[8]

It follows that to speak of a man's reason as issuing commands or

---

[1] *TT-P* iv, pp. 77–83.

[2] *TT-P* iv, p. 67, and xvi, pp. 125–7; *TP* ii, 4, p. 267, and 8, p. 273.

[3] *TT-P* iv, pp. 77–83; *TP* ii, 18, p. 279, and 22, pp. 281–3. Cf. *Ep.* xix: 'it would argue a great imperfection in God if something were to happen against his will.'

[4] *TT-P* xvi, pp.129–31; cf. *TP* ii, 12, p. 275. For another sense of 'ought', in which it is not absurd—but may even be true—to say that he ought to keep it, see p. 20.

[5] It is significant that Spinoza commences the *TP* with an assertion of his determinism; see *TP* i, 1, p. 261, and 4, p. 263.

[6] *E* ii, 41.

[7] *TT-P* iv, pp. 77–83; cf. *E* ii, 44.

[8] Cf. the use of 'bound' in *TT-P* xvi, p. 131: 'since by natural law I am bound to choose the lesser evil.'

counsels to him is to use a misleading metaphor. When we conceive the relation between a man and his reason as similar to that between a subject and his sovereign we are apt to suppose that the rational life is a life of obedience, and that a man is free to transgress his reason's dictates.[1] To conceive the relation as similar to that between the recipient of advice and his adviser makes it impossible to draw the first conclusion: on the other hand it leads us to suppose that a man's freedom against his own reason is even greater than the command metaphor allows. And a man has no freedom of this kind whatsoever— he who is said 'to sin against the light' has, at the moment of action,[2] no light to sin against. But if, to speak strictly, a man's reason neither commands nor advises him, the 'dictates' of his reason are not really prescriptions at all, and Spinoza accepts this conclusion. 'As for the natural divine law, whose main precept, I said, was to love God, I have called it a "law" in the sense in which scientists apply the word to the universal rules of nature in accordance with which all things necessarily come to pass.'[3] The dictates of reason are thus identified with the laws of the rational man's nature:[4] and unenlightened men 'are no more bound to live by the laws of a sound understanding than a cat is bound to live by the laws of a lion's nature'.[5]

Let us now consider the second sense in which reason 'obliges'. We sometimes say that a man is obliged by the dictates of reason to do something even when his own reason does not dictate at all, and he in fact feels no obligation or inclination whatsoever to do the action in question. In this sense an unenlightened man *is* bound to order his life wisely, and a commonwealth *is* bound to maintain the conditions of fear and respect.[6] But to say that *A* is bound or obliged by the dictates of reason to do *x* in this sense is simply to say that *x* is in fact the necessary means to the true welfare of *A*: and, of course, one may say this even if *A* is causally determined to do something other than *x*. This sense of 'ought' or 'is obliged' does not presuppose 'can'.

---

[1] *TP* ii, 20, pp. 279–81.

[2] The qualification is necessary, since a man who sees that action *x* is most to his advantage may shortly afterwards do action *y* instead: but this merely means that his grasp of what is in his own best interests is intermittent and unstable. Since a man always uses all the power he has in order to preserve himself (*TP* ii, 6, pp. 269–71), the fact that he acts irrationally always implies a weakness in his reason.

[3] *TT-P*, n. 34, p. 247.

[4] See *TT-P* iv, p. 75, n. 3.

[5] *TT-P* xvi, p. 127.

[6] For this sense see *TP* iv, 4–5, pp. 301–5.

The Political Theory

(iii) *The State of Nature*

Hobbes and Spinoza agree that the state of nature is a state of war, but there are differences in their accounts. According to Hobbes, nothing can be unjust in the state of nature; the notions of right and wrong, justice and injustice, have there no place.[1] But it is clear from other passages that he is speaking here of injustice towards men, i.e. breach of covenant with them,[2] for he admits that in the state of nature a man can commit injustice in the wide sense, i.e. break the laws of nature or sin against God.[3] Now this Spinoza denies. Men cannot break the laws of nature in his sense, for these laws are inviolable.[4] Nor can they sin against God, for God is not a king who lays down laws which men can break.[5] They can transgress the dictates of reason in the sense that they can do actions which a spectator knows to be harmful to them:[6] but since in the state of nature no man's reason is a law for another,[7] in doing such actions they 'sin' only against themselves. As for their own reason, it either dictates to them or it does not: if it does, they cannot transgress its dictates; if it does not, they do not transgress them. Spinoza accordingly concludes that sin, in the strict sense of transgression of law, does not exist in the state of nature.

A second difference between their accounts of the state of nature arises from their different conceptions of liberty. Although Hobbes admits that in the state of nature men are impediments to one another,[8] he conceives it as a state of liberty, since no man is subject to another's commands.[9] Spinoza agrees that the state of nature is a state of liberty in this sense,[10] but holds that in another important sense it is a state of slavery. In the state of nature a man cannot live by the right of his own nature alone, or in accordance with the laws of his own nature alone, for he is enslaved by his passions, and in particular by his fear of

---

[1] *Leviathan* 13.

[2] Hobbes's statements about injustice in this sense are notoriously inconsistent. In *Leviathan* 14 he says that there are valid covenants—which it is possible for men to break—in the state of nature; in *Leviathan* 15 he says that 'the validity of covenants begins not but with the constitution of a civil power'.

[3] *De Cive* i, 10, n.; cf. *EL* ii, 2, 3 and *Leviathan* 21 (the killing of Uriah).

[4] *TP* ii, 18, p. 279.   [5] *TT-P* iv, pp. 77–83.

[6] *TP* iv, 4–5, pp. 301–5.   [7] *TP* ii, 18, p. 279.

[8] *EL* i, 8, 4; *De Cive* v, 4; *Leviathan* 17.

[9] *De Cive* i–iv are headed 'Of Liberty'; v–xiv 'Of Dominion'.

[10] *TP* ii, 9, p. 273.

other men.[1] The life of reason, the life of moral liberty and blessedness, is impossible. Now this assertion is important for the following reason. Like Hobbes, Spinoza derives from his account of the state of nature his conception of the end of the state, and he agrees with Hobbes that this is peace and security of life.[2] But in Spinoza's view peace is hardly worth the name if it is achieved in ways which debar the individual from attaining the life of reason and living by the right of his own nature alone.[3] Certainly a state cannot legislate men into blessedness,[4] but a good state will maintain the conditions which make it possible for them to attain blessedness. In particular, it will respect that independence of thought and judgement on which the attainment of blessedness depends.[5]

(iv) *The Contract*

Ex quibus concludimus pactum nullam vim habere posse nisi ratione utilitatis.   SPINOZA

I have said above[6] that Hobbes's account of the state of nature is an inference from man's nature and man's natural right, and not a description of an historical condition. Historical evidence may support Hobbes's account, but can never justify it entirely: it can furnish approximations to the state of nature, but it never provides us with instances of the ideal limit of anarchy which is the war of all against all. And the reason is plain: before the ideal limit is reached men see their danger, and cling more closely together for mutual protection. As soon as they discover that self-assertion is inimical to survival they are prepared to abate their claims to superiority. Thus even an approximation to the state of nature brings to light a value which all men recognize:[7] and to realize this value is the end of the state. Hobbes's problem is now clear, and can be formulated thus: given human nature, how can a state be constructed which will provide men with the maximum peace? His version of the social contract gives the construction required.

The contract described by Hobbes is not something that has taken place or is taking place, but something which *ought* to take place, i.e.

---

[1] *TP* ii, 15 and n. 2, p. 277.

[2] *TP* v, 2, p. 309; cf. *TT-P* iii, pp. 55–59.

[3] *TP* v, 4–5, p. 311, and vi, 4, p. 317; *TT-P* xx, pp. 229–31.

[4] *TT-P* vii, p. 109.   [5] *T T-P* xx, *passim.*   [6] p. 12.

[7] *Leviathan* 15: 'and consequently all men agree on this, that peace is good.' Hobbes regards this valuation as part of the given: though he agrees with it, he does not advance it as a personal moral judgement.

must take place if men are to have permanent peace. Consequently, it is irrelevant to point out that many historical states do not embody his principles of construction, and therefore do not possess a sovereign in his sense: Hobbes would regard this as a criticism of these states rather than of his theory. There are some, he says,

> that maintain that there are no grounds, nor principles of reason, to sustain those essential rights which make sovereignty absolute. For if there were they would have been found out in some place or other; whereas we see there has not hitherto been any commonwealth where those rights have been acknowledged or challenged. Wherein they argue as ill as if the savage people of America should deny there were any grounds or principles of reason so to build a house as to last as long as the materials, because they never yet saw any so well built. Time and industry produce every day new knowledge. And as the art of well building is derived from principles of reason, observed by industrious men that had long studied the nature of materials, and the divers effects of figure and proportion, long after mankind began, though poorly, to build: so, long time after men have begun to constitute commonwealths, imperfect and apt to relapse into disorder, there may principles of reason be found out, by industrious meditation, to make their constitution, excepting by external violence, everlasting. And such are those which I have in this discourse set forth.[1]

In order to discover the correct construction Hobbes starts from the end, peace, and argues to its necessary conditions. The steps of his argument are these:[2]

1. For peace observance of the laws of nature is necessary.
2. For observance of the laws of nature security is necessary.
3. For security it is necessary (*a*) that men should combine on a large scale, and (*b*) that their actions should be constantly directed to peace.
4. That their actions may be constantly directed to peace it is necessary that they should be kept in awe by a common power.[3]
5. To create a common power it is necessary for each man to promise his fellows to place his power at the disposal of a representative (one man or a body) who will use it for the general peace

---

[1] *Leviathan* 30. Cf. 29: 'they (men) cannot without the help of a very able architect be compiled into any other than a crazy building.'

[2] *De Cive* v, 3–7; cf. *EL* i, 19, 3–7 and *Leviathan* 17.

[3] For the second, third, and fourth steps in Hobbes's argument see J. Ebbinghaus, 'The Law of Humanity and the Limits of State Power', in *The Philosophical Quarterly*, vol. iii, pp. 16–17. Although this article never mentions Hobbes, it illuminates several features of his theory.

and defence: and in *Leviathan* Hobbes proceeds to quote a form of words by which this may be done.[1]

The fourth step is the vital one, and Hobbes stresses its importance by pausing to criticize Aristotle's view that man is a political animal by nature: a view which led the latter to suppose that 'for the preservation of peace . . . there were nothing else necessary than that men should agree to make certain covenants and conditions together, which themselves should then call laws'.[2] Having thus made clear that his own construction is based on the given, i.e. on his own conception of human nature, Hobbes thinks it unnecessary to prove its adequacy. Accordingly the means whereby the sovereign acquires his power has seldom been understood.[3]

As we saw, each individual contracts with each of his fellows to give some person agreed upon the right to use his power. He thus incurs a double obligation, (*a*) to his fellows, and (*b*) to the sovereign.[4] The contracts he makes with each of his fellows are strictly covenants, for he does not immediately place his power at the sovereign's disposal but only gives him the right to use it when he requires. Now such covenants create a motive for fulfilling them which is distinct from the obligation they impose qua covenants. They do so because when *A* promises his fellows to give the sovereign the use of his power, his fellows promise *A* to give the sovereign the use of theirs, so that *A* must expect all his fellows to support the sovereign when the latter requires. And this gives *A* a motive for supporting the sovereign which is independent of his obligation to fulfil his covenants with his fellows, a motive which is fear of the sovereign's power. In short, the contract immediately creates a belief in the sovereign's power in the minds of the contractors, and 'reputation of power is power'.[5] It is important to note here that in Hobbes's ideal state the sovereign is the sole centre of unity, and the subjects are a 'dissolute multitude'.[6] We can now see that it is necessary for Hobbes to hold this view; for the power of the sovereign to compel his subjects to keep their covenants depends on their disunity.[7] As soon as the subjects tell one another that they feel no obliga-

---

[1] *Leviathan* 17.   [2] *De Cive* i, 2.

[3] See Oakeshott, op. cit., p. xxxviii, and the articles by J. M. Brown and Dorothea Krook in *Political Studies*, vol. i, pp. 53–64, 216–27, vol. ii, pp. 168–72. Here Brown is obviously in the right, but even he does not explain how 'the political covenant' creates a power sufficient 'to keep men in awe'.

[4] *De Cive* vi, 20; *Leviathan* 18.   [5] Ibid. 10. Cf. *De Cive* xv, 13.

[6] *EL* ii, 2, 7, and 11; ii, 8, 9. *De Cive* vi, 1, and n.; vii, 5, 7, 9, and 11; xii, 8. *Leviathan* 19.

[7] Cf. Hume, *Of the Original Contract*: 'When an artful and bold man is placed at the head

tion to obey the sovereign, and would like to be rid of him, his power, and their fear of it, are automatically destroyed; for his power depends on their belief in it, and their belief in it depends on their failure to communicate. In so far as Hobbes's contract is deliberately designed to inspire belief in the sovereign's power it may aptly be called a confidence trick.

In the *TT-P* Spinoza conceives the state of nature not only as 'an inference made from the passions' but also as an historical condition which existed prior to the formation of the state; he says, for instance, that 'the state of nature is prior to religion both in nature and in *time*'.[1] In consequence he regards his contract as an historical fact, as something which men actually made in founding a state. In this contract each individual did two things: he promised to observe the dictates of reason,[2] and he transferred all his right or power to the society as a whole, which means or implies that he promised to obey any decision which the society might take.[3] Spinoza, however, does not merely say that he did this; he says that he must have done this. He regards the contract as embodying the essential conditions which must be satisfied if a state is to be created, i.e. if *any* state is to be created. It follows that his contract is not, like Hobbes's, a recipe for constructing an ideal.

In the *TP* this contract is never mentioned.[4] There Spinoza asserts that 'the causes and natural foundations of the state are not to be sought in the precepts of reason';[5] that 'men's natural motive for uniting and being guided as if by one mind is not reason but some common passion, common hope or common fear or a common desire to avenge some common injury'.[6] It remains true that the state confers great benefits on men by making possible economic, intellectual, and spiritual development;[7] that it can be rationally justified;[8] but it was not created by any contract undertaken through rational foresight of these benefits,

---

of an army or faction, it is often easy for him, by employing, sometimes violence, sometimes false pretences, to establish his dominion over a people a hundred times more numerous than his partisans. *He allows no such open communication that his enemies can know with certainty their number or force.* He gives them no leisure to assemble together in a body to oppose him. *Even all those who are the instruments of his usurpation may wish his fall; but their ignorance of each other's intention keeps them in awe, and is the sole cause of his security.* By such arts as these many governments have been established; and this is all the *original contract* which they have to boast of.'

[1] *TT-P* xvi, p. 143.   [2] *TT-P* xvi, p. 129.   [3] *TT-P* xvi, p. 133.

[4] In the *TP* Spinoza uses the colourless word *convenire* (*TP* ii, 13, p. 274, l. 26; ii, 15, p. 276, l. 19; vi, 1, p. 314, l. 3) as opposed to *pacisci* (*TT-P* xvi, p. 128, l. 19, and p. 132, l. 19).

[5] *TP* i, 7, p. 265.   [6] *TP* vi, 1, p. 315.

[7] *TP* ii, 15, p. 277; cf. *TT-P* v, p. 93.

[8] *TP* iii, 6, pp. 287–9; cf. *TT-P* xvi, pp. 133–5, and n. 33, p. 247.

but by the blind desire to survive against aggression. Individuals, of course, must be prepared to observe the dictates of reason in their dealings with one another, and to obey their sovereign, if they are to continue united; and in so far as Spinoza's contract is simply the assertion that these are the essential conditions required for the maintenance of the state we may say that he still accepts it. But he no longer regards it as an historical event by which the state was created.

His reasons for abandoning the hypothesis of an historical social contract are not difficult to discover. The making of such a contract implies an exercise of rational foresight which is hardly possible in the state of nature.[1] At the same time it suggests the assumption by individuals of an obligation which is independent of utility, and Spinoza emphatically denies that there is any such obligation.[2] This provoked Hallam to indignation: 'In his treatise of Politics, especially in the broad assertion that good faith is only to be preserved so long as it is advantageous, Spinoza leaves Machiavel and Hobbes at·some distance, and may be reckoned the most phlegmatically impudent of the whole school.'[3] But Spinoza, who is not making a recommendation but stating a corollary of one of his laws of nature,[4] the law that an agent's conduct is always determined by what he personally thinks to be most advantageous to himself. It is because Spinoza never forgets this law that he is able to claim that he always keeps natural right (i.e. the individual's right or power to decide for himself) intact.[5] In a sense a man can give up his right or power to decide for himself; he may, for example, let a sovereign decide for him. But only if he decides for himself that it is to his advantage to let the sovereign decide for him,[6] and only for as long as he believes that this *is* to his advantage. As soon as he decides that it is not, he will cease to let the sovereign decide for him.[7]

Now this doctrine renders an historical social contract utterly superfluous. It means that the right of the sovereign to decide does not depend on any promise to let it decide made by the subjects in the past,

---

[1] *TP* ii, 15, p. 277.

[2] *TP* ii, 12, p. 275; cf. *TT-P* xvi, pp. 129–31.

[3] Henry Hallam, *Introduction to the Literature of Europe in the Fifteenth, Sixteenth, and Seventeenth Centuries* (John Murray, MDCCCXXXIX), vol. iv, p. 362.

[4] As is clear from *TT-P* xvi, p. 129, and *TP* iii, 18, p. 299. See above, p. 19.

[5] *Ep.* l.   [6] *TP* iii, 3, pp. 285–7.

[7] Cf. Laird, *Hobbes*, p. 302 : 'Every one *had* to do precisely what seemed to suit him. If he thought civil disobedience paid, he *had* to be disobedient; and Spinoza did not perceive these utterly devastating consequences.' I agree that the consequences are devastating—for the historical social contract; I do not agree that Spinoza failed to perceive them.

but on their recognition in the present that it is advantageous to let it decide. Its right, in fact, depends on its power to convince the subjects that it is in their interest to let it decide. As soon as it fails to do so, as soon as someone persuades them that it is more to their advantage to let *him* decide, he has gained the sovereign power or right, and the old sovereign is sovereign no longer.[1] By abandoning the historical social contract Spinoza shifts the main responsibility for preserving the state from the subjects to the sovereign.[2] He saddles the sovereign with the task of continually showing its subjects that it is more to their advantage to obey than to disobey. Failure in this task means rebellion:[3] the state of nature is a threat to sovereigns as well as to subjects.

It remains to discuss the contract which Spinoza *does* mention in the *TP*, namely the contract whereby a people transfers its right either to a king or to an aristocratic council.[4] Such a transfer was also envisaged by Hobbes,[5] who maintained in his early works that democracy was the original form of commonwealth by institution.[6] Hobbes, however, held that as soon as a people transferred its sovereignty to a king it ceased to exist, i.e. it became a 'dissolute multitude',[7] and so any covenant which the king might have made with it was rendered null and void.[8] The sovereignty possessed by the king was thus as absolute as that formerly held by the people.[9] Now, as we have seen,[10] it is necessary for Hobbes's ideal that the subjects of a king should have no unity except in and through their king. Spinoza, however, is not concerned with ideals but with facts, and in rejecting Hobbes's argument it is to the facts that he appeals. It is not the case that a people entirely dissolves when it transfers its right to a king. For suppose it were: then, if the king died without providing for a successor the society would be completely destroyed.[11] Now this never happens;[12] in such a case 'sovereignty reverts to the people, which has therefore the right to make new laws and repeal the old'.[13] But if the people retains a

---

[1] *TT-P* xvi, pp. 133 and 135.　　　　　[2] Cf. *TP* v, 2–3, pp. 309–11.

[3] *TP* iii, 9, p. 291; iv, 4, pp. 303–5.

[4] *TP* iv, 6, p. 305. It is clear from this and other passages (e.g. *TP* vii, 5, p. 339, and vii, 25, p. 357) that a *multitudo* in Spinoza's sense can do things which are impossible for a *multitudo* as conceived by Hobbes (*De Cive* vi, 1, n.); hence I have here—and elsewhere—rendered Spinoza's *multitudo* by 'people'.

[5] *EL* ii, 2, 7, and 9; *De Cive* vii, 8 and 11.　　　　　[6] *EL* ii, 2, 1; *De Cive* vii, 5.

[7] *EL* ii, 2, 10; *De Cive* vii, 11. Cf. Rousseau, *Social Contract* ii, 1.

[8] Cf. *De Cive* vii, 9.　　　[9] *EL* ii, 1, 18; *De Cive* vi, 13, and n.　　　[10] pp. 24–25.

[11] As Hobbes argued in *Leviathan* 19.　　　　　[12] Cf. *TP* vi, 1–2, p. 315.

[13] *TP* vii, 25, p. 357. Spinoza actually says that the king's death causes a return from the political to the natural condition. But only 'in a sense' (*quodammodo*); *status naturalis* in this

certain unity, a king is not as free as Hobbes supposes to break a covenant made with it to rule in accordance with certain fundamental laws.[1] He is not, and cannot be, as absolute in practice as the original democratic sovereign.[2] He may in fact be a constitutional monarch; in which case Spinoza reconciles theory with practice by supposing that the fundamental laws of the state emanate from the king's will.[3]

The senses in which a king may be bound to keep a covenant made with his people can be discovered from our previous analysis.[4] He may be bound in the sense of being determined to keep it by the thought that to keep it is necessary for his own preservation. If he does not think that it is necessary for his own preservation to keep it he is not bound in this sense. But in the second sense he *is* bound if breach of the covenant is in fact going to lead to general indignation and rebellion.[5] This, however, may not be so. In some cases a rigid adherence to his coronation oath may be contrary to the interests of the people, and the people may see that it *is* contrary; under such circumstances to break his covenant is a better means to his preservation than to keep it, and he is therefore not bound to keep it in the second sense.[6]

(v) *The Sovereign*

Naturae ... non imperatur, nisi parendo.
BACON, *Novum Organum*

As T. H. Green remarked, Hobbes's contract gives the sovereign an absolute right to the obedience of all its subjects, irrespective of its actual power against them.[7] The contract once made, individuals have, in general,[8] a duty to obey the sovereign's commands. The sovereign in turn has the right to provide for their peace and defence—to make laws and enforce them, settle disputes, censor doctrines, and handle foreign affairs.[9] The laws it makes must be good laws, i.e. clear, and necessary for its subjects' good; and their good is not merely preservation, but also 'all other contentments of life'.[10] To do all this is not only

---

passage refers to a loose primary democracy (*multitudo*)—we must remember that in Spinoza's view democracy is *maxime naturalis* (*T T-P* xvi, p. 136)—and not to a condition of war.

[1] Spinoza believes that such a covenant is always made; see *TP* vii, 1, p. 335.

[2] According to Spinoza aristocracy is more absolute than monarchy (*TP* viii, Rubric, p. 367; viii, 7, p. 373), and democracy the most absolute of all (*TP* viii, 3, p. 371; xi, 1, p. 441).

[3] *TP* vii, 1, p. 335.　　　　[4] pp. 19–20.　　　　[5] Cf. *TP* iv, 4, pp. 301–5.

[6] *TP* iv, 6, p. 305; cf. Locke on prerogative, *Second Treatise*, §§ 159–64.

[7] *Principles of Political Obligation*, p. 60.

[8] The duty may be destroyed by the individual's right to preserve his own life.

[9] *De Cive* vi; *Leviathan* 18.　　　　　　　　[10] Ibid. 30; cf. *De Cive* xiii, 4.

its right but its duty: and not only its duty in the sense of its function, but also its moral duty, a duty it owes to God, the author of the law of nature.[1] The sovereign, then, is bound by the law of nature to promote the welfare of its subjects in a wide sense.

To be consistent with Hobbes's egoistic psychology the subjects' duty to obey and the sovereign's duty to promote the common welfare must both be founded on self-interest. Hobbes, however, sometimes suggests a more 'respectable' account.[2] We need not be too impressed by his suggestion that these duties derive from the duty to obey God, for he bases this primary duty on fear of punishment or hope of reward.[3] But his assertion that injustice involves a contradiction in the will[4] does tend to convey the impression that there is a duty which is independent of self-interest. Perhaps it is difficult for a contract theorist not to suggest this view: in the *TT-P* Spinoza himself sometimes appears to hold that a subject is bound to obey a tyrant by the mere fact that he has contracted to do so.[5] But this is simply a sign that he has not yet fully worked out the implications of his explicit assertion that a contract can have no binding force but utility. It is his explicit assertion which is important: and when this is set alongside Hobbes's attempt to reduce injustice to self-contradiction, it is easy to conclude that Hobbes shows a proper respect for covenants which is lacking in his 'wickeder' and 'more impudent' successor.

But instead of indulging in facile moralizing, let us consider the political consequences which follow from Hobbes's flirtation with respectability, and compare them with those which follow from Spinoza's more disreputable doctrine. Hobbes's insistence on the duty of the sovereign to promote the welfare of its subjects certainly shows that in intention at least he was on the side of the angels: but it is possible to doubt whether he in fact gave his sovereign sufficient motive to act as he intended. If a sense of duty is inadequate to keep subjects to their covenants[6] it is also inadequate to make the sovereign rule decently, especially since the sovereign, as Spinoza noted,[7] is particularly exposed to temptation. Machiavelli had already said that 'a

---

[1] *Leviathan* 30. In maintaining that the sovereign's duty is to God alone (cf. 21) Hobbes joins hands with those who believed in the divine right of kings.

[2] For an attempt to make Hobbes 'respectable' see A. E. Taylor, 'The Ethical Doctrine of Hobbes', in *Philosophy*, vol. xiii, 1938, pp. 406–24.

[3] *De Cive* xv, 7.

[4] *EL* i, 16, 2 and *De Cive* iii, 3; contrast the more cautious statement in *Leviathan* 14.

[5] *TT-P* xvi, p. 147; xix, p. 215. In this connexion it is interesting to compare the account of treason in *TT-P* xvi, pp. 141–3, with that in *TP* iv, 3, p. 301.

[6] *EL* i, 19, 4; *De Cive* v, 4–5; *Leviathan* 17.   [7] *TP* vi, 3, p. 315.

prince who knows no other control but his own will is like a mad-man';[1] and Locke was later to point out that absolute power is not apt 'to purify men's bloods' or 'correct the baseness of human nature'.[2] Then a subject in Hobbes's state might well be 'exposed to all the misery and inconveniences that a man can fear from one who, being in the unrestrained state of nature, is yet corrupted with flattery and armed with power'.[3] Hobbes, of course, argued that it was not in the interest of sovereigns to oppress their subjects, 'in whose vigour con-sisteth their own strength and glory';[4] but a sovereign might not be sufficiently enlightened to see where its own true interest lay. In any case, for all Hobbes's appeals to God, duty, and enlightened self-interest, he admitted that a prince might 'sometimes have an inclination to do wickedly'; but this, he said, was an inconvenience that just had to be accepted, 'for he that hath strength enough to protect all, wants not sufficiency to oppress all'.[5] Hobbes's monarch, then, may be a tyrant: nevertheless the subjects, having made a contract, are in duty bound to maintain him. Those who applaud Hobbes for suggesting that there is a duty independent of self-interest may well baulk at this unattractive conclusion.

By keeping natural right intact Spinoza eliminated all obligations that were not founded on self-interest, all 'moral obligations' in the deontologist's sense, and so made it impossible to appeal to such obligations in order to bolster up tyranny. Men can never give up their right to decide so entirely that they cease to be men and can be treated like sheep:[6] if a king rules badly his subjects will soon conspire to destroy him,[7] in spite of any promises to obey they may have made. And in fear of rebellion Spinoza can appeal to a powerful motive which even the most unenlightened ruler is capable of appreciating. An unenlightened ruler, of course, may be led by this fear merely to intensify his oppressive measures;[8] but this will simply increase in-dignation against him and accelerate his downfall. Sovereign power misused is self-destructive. A tyrant may survive by the aid of his army, but only if he furthers the interests of his army.[9] He may oppress one section of the population, but only if he conciliates another and stronger part.[10] Even so, although his state may be free from war, it is not at peace; for in Spinoza's view peace is not mere absence of war, but a

---

[1] *Discourses* i, 58. [2] *Second Treatise*, § 92. [3] Op. cit., § 91.
[4] *Leviathan* 18; cf. *De Cive* x, 2. [5] Ibid. vi, 13, n.
[6] TP vii, 25, p. 357; cf. TT-P xvii, p. 149. [7] TT-P v, p. 95, and xvi, p. 135.
[8] Cf. TT-P xviii, p. 201. [9] TP vii, 12, p. 345.
[10] Cf. TP vii, 25, pp. 355–7.

union or agreement of minds.[1] The enlightened sovereign will try to promote the interests of all his subjects so as to unite them solidly and whole-heartedly behind him:[2] this is his task and this his toil. The prize is a great one—the absolute authority of which Hobbes spoke.[3] But it can be gained and kept only by the sovereign's constant and obvious devotion to the common welfare; no formal contract on the part of the subjects can possibly bestow it.

Here, however, an objection arises.

I agree [says the objector] that Spinoza abandoned the social contract and eliminated the moral obligation to obey a tyrant. His abandonment of the contract has an important consequence. It makes it unnecessary for him to credit men in the state of nature with the exercise of reason and foresight, and so enables him to conceive the state as making possible the moral development of man to an extent that Hobbes never envisaged. According to Hobbes the state simply enables men to perform without risk the actions which they have always known to be right; according to Spinoza it is only in the state that men can discover what these actions are.[4] Spinoza, in fact, lays as much stress as Aristotle and Rousseau on the state's contribution to man's moral development. Admittedly we must be wary of the word 'development' in referring to Spinoza, who explicitly rejects a teleological view of man;[5] but the word can be justified if we remember that although man does not acquire a new nature in the state,[6] and his natural powers are the same as before, his reason has little chance of exercise in the state of nature, and can come into play only when the influence of the passions, and particularly of fear, is weakened by the achievement of security. Now my objection is this. Spinoza insists that the enlightened man will recognize the massive contribution which the state makes to his welfare. 'The whole teaching of reason', he says, 'is that men should seek peace. But peace cannot be achieved unless the common laws of the commonwealth are kept inviolate; and so the more a man is guided by reason, i.e. the more free he is, the more steadfastly will he observe the laws of the commonwealth and carry out his sovereign's commands.' Even if 'the rational man has sometimes, by order of the commonwealth, to do what he knows to be opposed to reason, this inconvenience is far outweighed by the advantage which he derives from the actual existence of the political order'.[7] From such statements it appears that the enlightened man will not rebel, even against a tyrant; and if this is so Spinoza has removed moral obligation as a buttress of tyranny merely to set up enlightened self-interest in its place.

To this objection the following answer may be made. Certainly Spinoza says that 'peace can never be bought too dearly':[8] but he also

[1] *TP* v, 4, p. 311, and vi, 4, p. 317.   [2] *TP* vii, 11, pp. 343–5.
[3] *TT-P* xvii, p. 149, n. 1.   [4] *TT-P* xix, p. 207; cf. *TP* ii, 23, p. 283.
[5] *E* i, App.   [6] Cf. *TP* iv, 4, p. 303.   [7] *TP* iii, 6, p. 289.   [8] *TP* viii, 31, p. 395.

says, as we have seen, that 'peace is not mere absence of war, but a union or agreement of minds'. The tyrant creates devastation and calls it peace:[1] Spinoza calls it 'the greatest misfortune that men can suffer'.[2] Now reason cannot possibly bid men maintain a 'peace' which is their 'greatest misfortune': if it is to bid men support a tyrant he must provide something better than 'slavery, barbarism, and desolation'. As long as he does so, it may well be reasonable to support him, for revolution involves misery and bloodshed, and is apt to produce a new tyrant who is no improvement on his predecessor.[3] Even so, enlightened self-interest is a feeble support for tyranny, for though all men are self-interested, few are enlightened.[4] This is especially true in a tyranny: tyranny, in fact, is inimical to the attainment and maintenance of enlightenment, which require freedom from fear as their necessary condition.

I have said above that in Spinoza's view the sovereign can maximize his power only by promoting the common welfare.[5] But phrases like 'the common welfare' and 'the common good' may refer to very different things. For instance, if a ruler increased the material prosperity of his subjects we should say, other things being equal, that he promoted the common welfare. But if he improved the quality of their social relations, replacing mutual distrust by friendship and voluntary co-operation, we should again say that he promoted the common welfare.[6] It is in the sovereign's interest to promote the common welfare in both senses, but here we are concerned only with the second. Now according to Spinoza there is only one way in which the sovereign can promote the common welfare in this sense. Human nature is so intractable that men will co-operate willingly only on certain conditions, which are embodied in the dictates of reason (Hobbes's laws of nature). In so far as a ruler fails to make laws in conformity with these dictates he fails to unite his subjects, and so fails to achieve the maximum power.[7] The foolish ruler, then, is like an unskilful carpenter;

---

[1] *TP* v, 4, p. 311.   [2] *TP* vi, 4, p. 317.   [3] *TT-P* xviii, pp. 201–3; *TP* v, 7, p. 313.
[4] *TT-P* v. p. 93.   [5] *TP* vii, 5, p. 339.
[6] It is difficult to find appropriate labels for these two senses, but the difference may be made clearer if we consider Rousseau's assertion that 'the general will is always right and tends to the public advantage' (*Social Contract* ii, 3). The general will is always right, i.e. just, because it embodies the principle of equal freedom, the only principle on which a union—as opposed to an assemblage—of men is possible. This union is itself the common good (in my second sense); cf. Plato's belief that the good of a state is its unity. But, of course, when men are united they achieve prosperity more easily; thus the general will tends, i.e. leads, to the public advantage or common good (in my first sense).
[7] *TP* ii, 21, p. 281; iii, 7, p. 289; v, 2, p. 309.

ignorant of the nature of his materials, and of the only glue by which they can be fixed together, he constructs a throne which creaks and is liable to collapse under his weight. In contrast the wise ruler, by knowing and respecting his materials, and using the proper glue, builds himself a throne on which he can sit secure. He understands and observes the conditions on which the successful maintenance of power depends. Spinoza believes that there are certain things a ruler must do if he is to keep a firm grip on his power, and certain things he cannot do without losing it.

In addition to enacting and enforcing rational civil laws a sovereign must avoid arousing the indignation or contempt of a large number of its subjects. In laying down this condition Spinoza is obviously following Machiavelli. Machiavelli attempted to formulate political laws of the form 'if a ruler does *x* then *y* happens'; and one of these laws stated that if a ruler aroused the hatred or contempt of his subjects he destroyed his own power.[1] For Machiavelli, however, this law was a generalization founded on experience and supported by historical examples; although it appeared to have no exceptions he did not regard it as a necessary truth. Spinoza accepts Machiavelli's law, but by basing it on his own scientific account of human nature he converts it into a natural law which is eternal and inviolable.[2] In comparison with this law, and the law that a sovereign weakens itself if it undermines the unity of its subjects by irrational legislation, human conventions are of little significance. A king may sometimes violate his coronation oath with impunity: but if he acts in ways which arouse the indignation or contempt of his subjects his downfall is inevitable. If his oath is binding at all, it is binding only because it has a sanction in one of the laws of nature which apply to sovereigns, and are the real arbiters of their destinies.[3]

I shall conclude this section by discussing Spinoza's treatment of the sovereign's right or power in the field of religion. He uses the word 'religion' to cover three different things:

1. 'Inward religion' or 'the means by which the mind is inwardly led to worship God',[4] i.e. the individual's beliefs about God. These beliefs vary considerably from individual to individual,[5] but there are certain basic beliefs which are essential to 'inward religion' or

---

[1] *Prince* xix; cf. *Discourses* iii, 21. In *The Myth of the State* (Oxford University Press, 1946), ch. xii, p. 161, E. Cassirer cites *oderint dum metuant* as a maxim approved by Machiavelli. Wrongly; Machiavelli's maxim is *metuant dum ne oderint*.

[2] See the emphatic statement in *TP* iv, 4, p. 303.

[3] *TP* iv, 6, pp. 305–7.   [4] *TT-P* xix, p. 205.   [5] *TT-P* xiv, pp. 117–19.

faith.[1] Over inward religion the sovereign has no direct control,[2] for men cannot believe to order,[3] and the attempt to make them do so must always lead to disaster.[4]

2. 'Outward religion.' This is divided into:

(*a*) the performance of just and charitable actions, and

(*b*) participation in sacred rites and ceremonies.

Moral and religious practice can and must be controlled by the sovereign, since they must be adapted to the public welfare.[5]

Hobbes held that observance of his laws of nature was 'the greatest worship of all',[6] and Spinoza followed him by regarding the practice of justice and charity as the true form of outward religion.[7] In *TT-P* xix he is more concerned to show that the sovereign has the right to control outward religion in this sense, i.e. to determine which actions are just and charitable, than to show that it has the right to lay down a single form of public worship. He did not explicitly reject Hobbes's assertion that 'seeing a commonwealth is but one person, it ought also to exhibit to God but one worship';[6] he could hardly fail to see the advantages of religious uniformity. Machiavelli had already shown how much the religion of the Romans contributed to the cohesion of their state,[8] and the national religion of the Jews was obviously a tremendous unifying force.[9]

But in prescribing for the conditions of his own day Spinoza set his face against the imposition of religious uniformity. In his model monarchy there appears to be no established church:[10] and the established church is not the only one which exists in his aristocracies.[11] The others, of course, exist by the permission of the sovereign, but this permission is to be liberally bestowed. Here it should be noted that in requiring all the patricians to belong to the established church[12] Spinoza is not imposing uniformity but utilizing the measure of uniformity which already exists. Since the creed of the established church is the lowest common denominator of all creeds,[13] members of other churches who are co-opted to the patriciate are not required to believe anything which they did not believe before, or to discard any of their previous beliefs: and we may suppose that the ritual of the established church is as inoffensive as its creed.

---

[1] *TT-P* xiv, pp. 119–21.
[2] He may have indirect control; cf. *TT-P* xvii, pp. 151–3, and xx, p. 227.
[3] *TP* iii, 8, pp. 289–91.   [4] *TT-P* xx, pp. 237–9.   [5] *TT-P* xix, pp. 211–17.
[6] *Leviathan* 31.   [7] *TT-P* xix, p. 207.   [8] *Discourses* i, 11.
[9] *TT-P* xvii, pp. 175–81.   [10] *TP* vi, 40, p. 333.   [11] *TP* viii, 46, p. 411.
[12] Loc. cit.   [13] *TT-P* xiv, pp. 119–21.

There seem to be two main reasons for Spinoza's refusal to prescribe religious uniformity in his model states. Certainly the national religion of the Jews helped to keep them internally united, but it also cut them off from the rest of the world by encouraging intolerance and hatred of foreigners.[1] Their peculiar form of church-state 'could only be expedient for men who wanted to live their own lives behind their own frontiers, with no foreign trade or contact with the rest of the world, and not for men who must have dealings with others'.[2] Uniformity of religion, then, had economic disadvantages:[3] it tended to hinder trade with foreigners who practised a different religion. In the second place, attempts to enforce it in contemporary European states had proved dangerous, if not disastrous. Spinoza, of course, did his best to convince his readers that since rites and ceremonies made no contribution to blessedness it was not worth while disturbing the public peace because of them;[4] but he knew that most of his contemporaries were deaf to such arguments, and that if a ruler attempted, for instance, to impose Roman Catholicism on Protestant subjects, he would inevitably arouse their hatred and indignation. If the Protestant subjects were sufficiently numerous he might even destroy his own power, as Philip II had done in the Netherlands.

(vi) *Summary and Conclusion*

> By uniting determinism with the doctrine of calculating selfishness, Hobbes, in a way that ultimately ruined the consistency of his political theory, maintained roundly that every man *must* choose his own apparent good, that is to say, what seemed to him to be *his own greatest good*. JOHN LAIRD, *Hobbes*

As far as political theory is concerned, Spinoza is often described as a follower of Hobbes, and it is true that he borrowed many ideas and arguments from his great predecessor. But when he remarked that, unlike Hobbes, he kept natural right intact, he was not pointing to a minor deviation, but to a disagreement on fundamentals. In fact, by keeping natural right intact, i.e. by insisting on Hobbes's own principle that a man, in so far as he can be said to act at all, necessarily does what he personally thinks to be in his own best interests, he demolished the basic concepts of Hobbes's political theory. This principle—a law of

---

[1] *TT-P* xvii, p. 177.   [2] *TT-P* xviii, p. 191.

[3] The benefits of religious diversity and toleration are illustrated by the prosperity of Amsterdam; see *TT-P* xx, p. 241.

[4] *TP* iii, 10, p. 293; cf. *TT-P* v, p. 99.

nature in Spinoza's sense—released the right of nature from the limits within which Hobbes had sought to confine it, and gave every man a natural right to do whatever he thought to be most advantageous to himself. It eliminated all obligation which was not based on self-interest, and—except in a Pickwickian sense of the word—all obligation which was not based on the agent's conception of his own interest: it thus reduced Hobbes's laws of nature to dictates of the enlightened man's reason, not really binding on the majority of mankind. Moreover, by eliminating the obligation to keep any promise which the agent thought he could break with advantage, it struck at the roots of Hobbes's social contract. Certainly the right of the sovereign depended on the subjects' obligation to obey: but a subject's obligation to obey did not depend on the fact—if fact it was—that he had made a covenant to obey, but on his own belief that it was more advantageous for himself to obey: and this belief in turn depended on the sovereign's power to induce it. It followed that the sovereign's right was not, as Hobbes suggested, independent of its power.

But his demolition of Hobbes's theory left Spinoza with a problem. He had kept the right of nature intact; he had insisted that men are individualists of the most ruthless and uncompromising kind. At the same time he had suggested that Hobbes's conception of the end of the state was too low. On the one hand 'men are by nature enemies':[1] on the other hand the state is 'a union or agreement of minds'. In theory it is the task of the sovereign to make men see that it is in their own interests to obey its laws, and so to create 'a union or agreement of minds' among men who are 'enemies by nature': but in practice few sovereigns are capable of performing such a task without assistance. And this, in Rousseau's phrase, 'makes a legislator necessary'.[2]

IV

THE MODEL CONSTITUTIONS

Nec ostendisse sufficit quid oporteat fieri, sed apprime quî fieri possit ut homines, sive affectu sive ratione ducantur, jura tamen rata fixaque habeant.   SPINOZA

STUDENTS of Spinoza's political thought often dismiss his model constitutions as unworthy of serious attention. Laird remarks that 'in the later part of the book Spinoza . . . took to constitution-building, an exercise in which he was not conspicuously proficient'.[3] Hampshire

---

[1] *TP* ii, 14, p. 277.   [2] *Social Contract* ii, 6.   [3] Laird, *Hobbes*, p. 301, n.

calls Spinoza's discussion 'naïve',[1] and says that it shows a 'radical lack of the idea of history'.[2] This last assertion is particularly unfortunate, since it is apt to convey the erroneous impression that Spinoza was quite oblivious to the importance of historical factors. In reality he knew perfectly well that the constitution of any actual state was affected by the history[3] and nature[4] of its people. He was careful to remind his readers that the institutions of his model monarchy could be of service only to a free people, 'for a people accustomed to another form of government will not be able to uproot the accepted foundations of their whole state, and to change its entire construction, without great danger of destroying it completely'.[5] He by no means imagined that his institutions were suited to the Turks.[6] He held that it was extremely dangerous for a people accustomed to monarchy to set up a republic, and vice versa, since it was difficult, perhaps even impossible, for a people to escape from its constitutional past.[7] He obviously realized that only a limited number of peoples could profitably adopt his proposals; peoples which were still 'capable of being given laws',[8] or peoples like the Dutch which had already made some progress towards his constitutional ideals.

But although Spinoza's models are certainly intended to suggest practical improvements in existing constitutions, and especially in the constitution of the Netherlands, they have also a theoretical purpose. Green maintained that there was in Spinoza's theory an 'impassable gulf' between the *status naturalis* and the *status civilis*,[9] and if men have natural right in Spinoza's sense the creation and maintenance of a decent political order, in fact of any sort of political order, is certainly very difficult indeed. Now the model constitutions are intended to illustrate by concrete examples the principle on which this difficulty is to be solved. In so far as this is their purpose, the criticism that Spinoza shows a 'radical lack of the idea of history' is quite irrelevant: and so is the charge that he is not a very proficient constitution-builder. It may be true that some of the institutions he describes are not very effective means to the ends which he desires to achieve: but even if this *were* true it would cast no doubt on the principle of his solution.

---

[1] Stuart Hampshire, *Spinoza*, Faber & Faber, 1956, p. 147.
[2] Op. cit., p. 145.   [3] *TP* viii, 18, p. 383.
[4] *TP* viii, 37, p. 403.   [5] *TP* vii, 26, pp. 357–9.
[6] Who had long been accustomed to absolute rule; cf. *TP* vi, 4, pp. 315–17.
[7] *TT-P* xviii, pp. 199–203. Cf. *Discourses* i, 16, where Machiavelli notes that a people which has got rid of a tyrant finds difficulty in preserving its new-found liberties.
[8] Rousseau, *Social Contract* ii, 10.   [9] *Principles of Political Obligation*, pp. 55–56.

But before we come to the principle of his solution we must first take the full measure of his difficulty. The end of the state is peace, and peace consists in 'a union or agreement of minds', i.e. in *voluntary* co-operation. This means that 'the ultimate purpose of the state is not to subject men to tyranny, or to restrain and enslave them through fear',[1] for 'as long as men act from fear alone they act *most unwillingly*';[2] they 'should really be governed in such a way that they do not regard themselves as being governed, but as following their own bent and their own free choice in their manner of life'.[3] Freedom from oppression, then, is part of the end of a good state: as the sub-title of the *TP* proclaims, Spinoza's aim is to secure 'the peace and freedom of the citizens'.[4] And so to secure them that they *'remain* intact'; for 'the virtue of a state is stability'.[5]

Concord, freedom, and a stable political order are obviously to the advantage of every man, and 'if human nature were such that men desired most what was most to their advantage'[6] there would be no difficulty in realizing these ends. But although 'all men certainly seek their own advantage', they seldom do so 'as sound reason dictates'; 'in most cases appetite is their only guide, and in their desires and judgements of what is beneficial they are carried away by their passions, which take no account of the future or anything else'.[7] *And this is true of rulers, as well as of ruled.*[8] No doubt, as we saw above, an enlightened ruler will understand and observe the conditions on which the successful maintenance of power depends,[9] and knowing that his own interests are inseparable from those of his subjects will do his utmost to promote their welfare.[10] But Spinoza has started from the predicament of unregenerate men:[11] in addition, he is well aware of the temptations to which the possession of power gives rise.[12] In consequence he refuses to put his trust in the enlightenment of rulers.[13] 'Kings are not gods, but men, who are often enchanted by the Sirens' song';[14] and

---

[1] *TT-P* xx, p. 229.   [2] *TT-P* v, p. 95.   [3] *TP* x, 8, pp. 435-7.

[4] p. 257. I agree with M. Francès (*Œuvres Complètes de Spinoza*, Gallimard, 1954, pp. 1471-4) that this sub-title is by one of Spinoza's editors. But it gives an accurate description of the contents of the work as left by Spinoza, whose aristocracy is designed to secure the rule of the 'best' men in a literal sense (*TP* viii, 2, p. 369; 30, p. 393), and not only to safeguard the plebeians from oppression by the patricians or 'citizens' (*TP* viii, 11, p. 377; 41, p. 407; 46, p. 411; ix, 14, p. 425), but also to prevent the 'citizens' themselves from falling prey to a tyrant (*TP* viii, 2, p. 369; 9, p. 375; 12, p. 379; 18, p. 383; x, 2, pp. 431-3).

[5] *TP* i, 6, p. 265.   [6] *TP* vi, 3, p. 315.   [7] *TT-P* v, p. 93.

[8] *TT-P* xvii, p. 153; *TP* x, 1, p. 429.

[9] p. 33.   [10] p. 31.   [11] p. 11.   [12] *TP* vi, 3, p. 315.

[13] *TP* i, 6, p. 265.   [14] *TP* vii, 1, p. 335.

'those who believe that a people, or men divided over public business, can be induced to live by reason's dictate alone, are dreaming of the poets' golden age or of a fairy-tale'.[1] The gulf between Spinoza's political ideals and his account of human nature seems 'impassable' indeed.

Naturally he claims that the gulf can be bridged: but he also contends that the average political theorist does little or nothing to show how these ideals, or indeed any other ideals, can be realized. Such a man starts by neglecting the problem, and ends by giving it up in despair. He usually produces an excellent paper constitution, which would certainly ensure concord and freedom if only men would accept and observe it. He insists, of course, that they 'ought' to accept and observe it: and his 'ought' implies 'can', for he conceives human passions 'as vices into which men fall through their own fault'. In consequence, when men because of their passions either will not accept or will not observe his constitution, he gets angry[2] with them for what he can only regard as voluntary wickedness, and retires in frustration to denounce the depravity of human nature. He can, indeed, do little else; for by assuming free-will he has made wickedness completely unintelligible, and by making it completely unintelligible he has destroyed all hope of preventing or curing it. Since his constitution makes no appeal to ordinary human nature it is doomed to remain an impracticable ideal.[3]

The correct procedure is very different. The political thinker must realize from the start that men necessarily do what they personally think to be in their own best interests: in Spinoza's phrase, he must 'keep the right of nature intact'. He will then realize that if they do things which are wicked it is because they think it in their own best interests to do them. He will also realize that it is of little use to tell them that they ought not to do these things, and ought to do something else: this is true in a sense, but to say it is seldom effective. People accustomed to dealing with real human beings have long since discovered this from experience. Little Michael has a tummy-ache, and he ought, i.e. it would in fact be in his best interests, to take some castor-oil. Unfortunately he does not see this: he is not determined to take his castor-oil by the thought that it would be in his own best interests to do so. On the contrary, he is determined to avoid taking it by the thought

---

[1] *TP* i, 5, p. 265.
[2] Notice the irony; on the theorist's principles his own anger is as much a vice as the passions which occasion it.   [3] *TP* i, 1, p. 261.

that it has a very nasty taste. In such a situation Michael's mother does not waste her breath in telling him that he ought to take it. She either says, 'Michael, I shall smack you if you don't drink your castor-oil': this induces Michael to drink it, but not to drink it willingly. Or else she conceals the castor-oil in a glass of orange-juice, which Michael likes: and since he then drinks his castor-oil willingly, this is a better way of dealing with the situation.

The methods used by Michael's mother for dealing with Michael are in principle the methods used by statesmen for influencing unenlightened men: and they must be employed by any thinker whose proposals are to be of practical use.[1] If his aim is concord, i.e. voluntary co-operation, he will naturally avoid the first method as far as possible, and will try to appeal to motives other than fear. But he will always appeal to the motives which men have, to their own conception of their own interests, inadequate though that conception may be; because it is only through their own conception of their own interests that they can be 'bound', i.e. determined, to do what he wants, and it is only if they are 'bound' in this sense that his constitution will be a good one. For a constitution which does not provide ordinary human beings with effective incentives to observe it is not in fact a good constitution, however exalted its aims may be. Such a constitution may have 'a specious appearance of benevolence';[2] but 'if civil right, or public liberty, has no basis but the slender support of legal prescriptions, it will not only be very difficult for the citizens to maintain, but will actually prove their undoing'.[3] A good constitution, then, must be based not only on reason but also on 'the common passions of men'.[4] Certainly avarice and ambition are low-grade motives when compared with love of God, but to purify human motives is the task of the moral teacher: the task of the political thinker is to show 'how men, even when led by passion, may still have fixed and stable laws'.[5]

In order to illustrate how Spinoza devises his constitutions so as to enlist 'the common passions of men' in the service of sound political ends, I shall briefly consider the basis of freedom in his monarchy. Machiavelli had argued in *The Prince* that a citizen army was more dependable than a force of mercenaries,[6] and had therefore advised the future saviour of Italy to employ native troops.[7] Naturally he did not emphasize that an armed people could not easily be oppressed, and would tend sooner or later to claim political power: but his *Discourses*

---

[1] *TP* i, 2–3, pp. 261–3. [2] Aristotle, *Politics* 1263[b] 15. [3] *TP* vii, 2, pp. 335–7.
[4] *TP* x, 9, p. 437. [5] *TP* vii, 2, p. 335. [6] *Prince* xii–xiii. [7] Ibid. xxvi.

show that he was not unaware of these consequences.[1] He was in fact a more subtle 'republican' than Rousseau imagined.[2] Spinoza incorporates Machiavelli's advice in a law: the army of his monarchy is to consist of citizens, of all the citizens, and there are to be no mercenaries.[3] This will prevent the king both from oppressing the citizens as a whole[4] and from using one section of the citizens to oppress the rest.[5] If we now ask what motives the citizens have for maintaining this law, Spinoza gives us two: their desire for freedom,[6] and their avarice.[7] Mercenaries are more expensive than citizen soldiers.[8]

Consider now how the citizens are safeguarded against oppression by the king's council and judges. In the first place Spinoza has bound all members of the state so closely together by ties of economic interest that most counsellors and judges will probably see that their own prosperity is dependent on the prosperity of the ordinary citizens.[9] But if they do not, there is always the fear of reprisals from their successors to restrain them from oppression,[10] for no counsellor or judge is to hold office for more than four years.[11] If we now ask what motive the citizens have for maintaining the laws which govern the appointment and tenure of counsellors, the answer is ambition: for the large number of counsellors and the brevity of their period of office gives everyone a high hope of attaining the position when he reaches the statutory age.[12] And the laws governing the appointment and tenure of judges are supported in their turn by the ambition of the lawyers.

I propose to say no more about the details of Spinoza's model constitutions. One may admire the ingenuity with which he uses 'the common passions of men' to support and stabilize his laws: but many of these laws are now of academic interest only. Like the constitution of the ancient Jewish state they have ceased to be practicable under altered conditions.[13] What is of permanent and vital importance for practice is the principle on which they are based.

---

[1] *Discourses* i, 4–6. Aristotle had already noted the connexion between military and political power: as the hoplite phalanx replaced the body of cavalry as the main weapon of war, Greek cities tended to change from aristocracies into moderate democracies (*Politics* 1297^b 16–25; cf. 1321^a 9–14).　　　　　[2] Cf. *Social Contract* iii, 6.

[3] *TP* vi, 10, p. 319. According to Spinoza this law was in force in the ancient Jewish state; see *TT-P* xvii, pp. 165 and 173.

[4] *TP* vii, 12, p. 345; 17, p. 349; cf. *TT-P* xvii, p. 173.

[5] *TP* vii, 22, p. 353.　　　　　　　　　　[6] Ibid.

[7] *TP* vii, 17, p. 349.　　　　　　　　　　[8] Cf. *TP* vi, 31, p. 331.

[9] *TP* vii, 8, pp. 341–3; 21, p. 353.　　　　[10] *TP* vii, 13, p. 345; 21, p. 353.

[11] *TP* vii, 13–14, pp. 345–7; 21, p. 353.

[12] *TP* vii, 10, p. 343.　　　　　　　　　　[13] *TT-P* xviii, p. 191.

INTRODUCTION TO THE
TEXT, TRANSLATION, AND NOTES

I. THE TEXT AND APPARATUS CRITICUS

THE *Tractatus Theologico-Politicus* was published anonymously in 1670, ostensibly at Hamburg by Henricus Künraht, but in fact at Amsterdam by Spinoza's friend Jan Rieuwertsz.[1] Its rise to notoriety was meteoric, and after frequent condemnations by religious bodies it was finally banned by the civil authorities in July 1674.[2] The *Tractatus Politicus* first appeared in *B.d.S. Opera Posthuma* (1677), a volume which also contained Spinoza's *Ethics*, his *Tractatus de Intellectus Emendatione*, a selection from his correspondence, and his *Hebrew Grammar*. Since this volume was edited by Spinoza's friends, and prepared for the press with considerable haste,[3] its text has not the same authority as that of the earlier work.

The main problem concerning the text of the *Tractatus Theologico-Politicus* was solved by J. P. N. Land in 1881.[4] Whereas earlier editors had assumed that any quarto copy dated 1670 was a first edition, Land showed that such copies fell into four different groups, which I shall follow Gebhardt in calling *I*, *II*, *III*, and *IV*. These could be distinguished by the following marks. On the title-page of *I* and *II* the publisher's name appeared as *Künraht*; whereas *III* and *IV* had *Künrath*. *I* could be distinguished from *II* by comparing the list of corrections at the end of the copy with the text; in the text of *II* some of these corrections had already been incorporated. *III* could be distinguished from *IV* by the fact that like *I* and *II* it had a list of corrections at the end; whereas *IV* had not. *II* was derived from *I*, *III* from *II*, and *IV* from *III*; and *II*, *III*, and *IV* had been antedated to 1670 in order to make it appear that they had been published before the ban. By his careful collation of the texts of *I*, *II*, *III*, and *IV* Gebhardt[5] confirmed Land's conclusions; he also showed that the early octavo edition of 1674, which I shall call *O*, was the true second

---

[1] W. Meijer, *De Veris et Fictis Tractatus Theologico-Politici Editoribus*, in *Chronicon Spinozanum MCMXXI*, pp. 264–7.

[2] J. Freudenthal, *Die Lebensgeschichte Spinoza's*, Leipzig, 1899, pp. 121–41.

[3] Spinoza died on 21 Feb. 1677. In July Schuller wrote to a friend as follows: 'Omnia posthuma Dni Spinozae opera typographo tradita sunt, in illorum editione sedulo pergitur; edentur autem in idiomate Latino et Belgico simul' (Freudenthal, op. cit., p. 205).

[4] See J. van Vloten et J. P. N. Land, *Benedicti de Spinoza Opera*, vol. i, pp. v–vi.

[5] *Spinoza Opera*, vol. iii, pp. 364–6.

edition,[1] although he rejected its claim to be *Ab Authore longè Emendatior*. He thus gave the following account of the relations between these various editions:

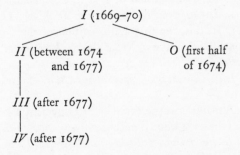

Gebhardt also investigated two early Dutch translations of the work.[2] He found that the first, ostensibly published at Hamburg by Henricus Koenraad in 1693,[3] was made from the printed text of *I*; and that the second, ostensibly published at Bremen by Hans Jurgen von der Weyl in the following year, was made from either *III* or *IV*. Neither, therefore, is of any importance for establishing the Latin text.

It remains to say something of Spinoza's notes on the *Tractatus Theologico-Politicus*. In 1675 he told Oldenburg[4] that he wished to remove prejudices against the book by adding explanatory notes; and although he was unable to carry the project very far, we know that he did write a few notes on the margins of his own copy of the *Tractatus*,[5] and also on copies presented to his friends. One of the latter, formerly in the University Library at Königsberg,[6] bears the following inscription: *Nobilissimo Dº Dº. Jacobo Statio Klefmanno Dono D. Autor, et nonnullis notis illustravit illasque propria manu scripsit Die 25. Julii Anno 1676.* This copy, however, contains only five notes, and these on passages which I

---

[1] Ibid. pp. 366–8. This had already been suggested by Land in his Introduction to Meijer's Dutch translation (*Godgeleerd-Staatkundig Vertoog*, Amsterdam, 1894, p. 15).

[2] *Die alten holländischen Übersetzungen des Tractatus Theologico-Politicus*, in *Chronicon Spinozanum MCMXXIV–VI*, pp. 271–8.

[3] This is the translation mentioned in *Ep.* xliv (17 Feb. 1671), where Spinoza forbade its publication. A comparison of its rendering of *I*, pp. 176–7, with the *NS* rendering of the parallel passage in *TP* ii, 8, suggests that it was made by the translator of the *Opera Posthuma*, Jan Hendriksze Glazemaker. See the catalogue of Spinoza's works appended to the Lucas Biography, Freudenthal, op. cit., p. 25.

[4] *Ep.* lxviii. Cf. *Ep.* lxix.

[5] Freudenthal, op. cit., p. 226.

[6] Now in the possession of the Spinozaeum at Haifa, Israel.

have omitted from my selections. The notes with which I am concerned are extant in three main sources:

1. *Mr Benedicti de Spinoza Adnotationes ad Tractatum Theologico-Politicum. Ex autographo edidit ac praefatus est, addita notitia Scriptorum Philosophi, Christophorus Theophilus de Murr. Hagae-Comitum. MDCCCII.* In this, the first Latin edition of the notes, the text is headed *Benedicti de Spinoza Notae Ms^{tae} Marginales ad Tractatum Theologico-Politicum* (edit. in 4to 1670) descriptae ex originali, quod possidebat Joh. Rieuwertsz, Typographus Civit. Amstelod.* It contains 33 notes.

2. *ML* A manuscript preserved in the University Library at Leiden, bearing the following title: *Animadversiones, seu Additiones ad Tractatum B. De S. cui titulus est Tractatus Theologico-Politicus: Exscriptae ex Exemplari hujusce Tractatûs, cujus margini propria manu illas ipse scripserat Autor. Non mihi videntur Additiones, quod quidam volunt; Textum enim malè secant: sed potiùs Animadversiones et Notae. Hîc etiam occasione Errata quaedam restituenda curavi.* This manuscript was originally attached to a copy of the *Tractatus* which was presented to the Library by Prosper Marchand (1675–1756). It seems to have been written by Marchand himself. It contains 35 notes.

3. *StG* At the end of his translation of the *Tractatus* (*La Clef Du Sanctuaire*, 1678) Gabriel de Saint Glain published a French version of the notes, under the heading *Remarques curieuses, et necessaires pour l'intelligence de ce livre.* This version contains 31 notes. *StG* gives some of the notes in a fuller version than either *Mr* or *ML*, and must therefore be derived from a different original.[1] *Mr* and *ML* preserve substantially the same text; they differ mainly in details like spelling and word-order, and have several errors in common. Gebhardt therefore argued that they derived from the same original:[2] he also showed that *Mr* was not based directly on Spinoza's autograph notes, but on a manuscript copy of them which Murr had in his library. But although I agree that *Mr* and *ML* have a common original, I suggest that their original was not Spinoza's autograph, but another copy; that this copy claimed to be derived from the autograph; and that in copying it the writer of *ML* and the writer of Murr's manuscript reproduced its claim in different ways. This seems to me the easier way of accounting for the errors which are common to *Mr* and *ML*.

Spinoza's posthumous works, unlike his *Tractatus Theologico-Politi-*

[1] As Murr himself remarked: see p. 38 of his edition.
[2] *G*, vol. iii, pp. 383–8.

cus, were published simultaneously in Latin and in Dutch:[1] thus the Dutch versions contained in *De Nagelate Schriften van B.d.S.* must have been made from Spinoza's own manuscripts, and not from the Latin texts printed in the *Opera Posthuma*. This was pointed out by Land in 1881,[2] but the full importance of the Dutch versions was not realized until 1902, when J. H. Leopold made use of them to emend several passages in the Latin.[3] In the Heidelberg edition of 1924–6 Gebhardt followed Leopold's lead: on the other hand he maintained that the Dutch versions were made long before Spinoza's death,[4] and that after they were made Spinoza subjected his Latin manuscripts to constant revision.[5] But neither of these statements is very plausible when applied to the *Tractatus Politicus*, for this work was composed in the last years of Spinoza's life,[6] and although there is evidence that Spinoza made a few changes and insertions in his Latin manuscript, his revision was very superficial.[7] Thus in the case of the *Tractatus Politicus* we may confidently use the Dutch text to emend the Latin: and Gebhardt in fact did so, making fuller use of it than any previous editor. But his claim to have cited every variant in the Dutch[8] will not bear examination. Not only has he failed to cite all the variants: he has failed to cite some which are obviously correct, e.g. *Het verdrach*, i.e. *Contractus* (for *Contractûs*) in iv, 6; *de zelfden voor onwettig houden*, i.e. *illi illegitimi habeantur* (for *illegitimi habeantur*) in vi, 14; *uit het negende Lid*, i.e. *ex Art. 9* (for *Art. 9*) in viii, 7; and *Hollant*, i.e. *Hollandia* (for *Hollandiae*) in ix, 14.

---

[1] Freudenthal, op. cit., p. 205 (the letter from Schuller quoted above).

[2] See *V–L*, vol. i, p. vii.

[3] *Ad Spinozae Opera Posthuma*, Hagae Comitis apud Martinum Nijhoff, MCMII.

[4] *G*, vol. ii, p. 315.   [5] Ibid. p. 317.

[6] *Opera Posthuma, Praefatio*, p. 30: *Tractatum Politicum Auctor noster paulo ante obitum composuit*. Cf. the remark appended to the letter which prefaces the *Tractatus* (p. 258).

[7] For changes see *TP* ix and x, where the phrase used in *NS* to refer to a federal aristocracy is consistently emended in *OP*, probably by Spinoza himself. For insertions see v, 7; vi, 26; vii, 5; and viii, 1. But no argument for revision can be based either on the pleonastic style of the Dutch text or on the Latin glosses in its margins. Glazemaker's version of the *TT-P* (which was certainly made from *I*) is equally pleonastic. The Latin glosses inspire little confidence. Misprints are common (e.g. *discreptantes* for *discrepantes* in vi, 17; *molimenta* for *emolumenta* in vi, 29), and sometimes the glossator can be convicted of giving his own rendering of the Dutch instead of consulting the Latin manuscript (e.g. *syndici* in viii, 19, and *imperia aristocratica* in x, 7 and 9). That Spinoza's revision of his Latin manuscript was superficial is shown by the fact that the Latin and Dutch texts sometimes agree in obvious errors, e.g. *ducendi* (*te geleiden*) for *conducendi* in iv, 2; *sedeat* (*zal zitten*) for *praesideat* in viii, 34; and *habet* (*heeft*) for *habent* in x, 3. The first and third of these errors are corrected in the list of Errata at the end of *OP*; but if these corrections had been made by Spinoza himself they would surely have been incorporated in the text.   [8] *G*, vol. iii, p. 421.

Introduction

The text of the parts of the *Tractatus Theologico-Politicus* here printed is a corrected version of *I*. Most of the corrections have been culled from earlier editors, but I have added a few of my own. Not being a Hebrew scholar I have omitted Spinoza's quotations from the Old Testament, printing only his Latin translations of such passages. In dealing with Spinoza's notes I have followed *Mr*,[1] correcting it where necessary with the help of *ML* and *StG*: but where *StG* preserves a note in a fuller form I have given the French version after the Latin text. The text of the *Tractatus Politicus* is based on a careful collation of the Latin and Dutch texts, and only in one or two cases have I ventured to depart from both. In matters of orthography I have mostly followed Gebhardt; but I have modernized the punctuation and abolished most of the accents and capitals.

In order to keep the apparatus criticus within reasonable bounds I have usually cited later editions only when the text in the first editions appeared to be wrong or doubtful. I have thus refrained from pursuing the divagations of *II*, *III*, and *IV* in my notes on the *TT-P*, but have quoted freely from *NS* in my notes on the *TP*. I have attempted throughout to attribute corrections to their original authors, and the fact that a correction is attributed to Paulus does not mean that it has not been accepted by later editors. Anonymous corrections are due to myself.

II. THE TRANSLATION

MY main object here has been to give an accurate, brief, and straightforward rendering of Spinoza's Latin. The chief problem which faces a translator into English arises from the ambiguity of the word *jus*: sometimes 'right' is clearly the correct rendering, sometimes 'law', but often it is extremely difficult to choose between them. *Sui juris* is also difficult: prima facie 'independent' seems the best rendering, but since it obscures the connexion between *sui juris* and *jus* I have generally preferred the rather clumsy phrase 'possessed of one's own right'. When in doubt about the meaning of the Latin I have consulted with profit the work of modern translators like Meijer,[2] Gebhardt,[3]

---

[1] The choice between *Mr* and *ML* is a difficult one, but in general the word-order of *Mr* is superior to that of *ML*, and more consistent with Spinoza's practice elsewhere.

[2] W. Meijer, *Godgeleerd Staatkundig Vertoog*, S. L. van Looy and H. Gerlings, Amsterdam, 1894; and *Staatkundig Vertoog*, S. L. van Looy, Amsterdam, 1901.

[3] Carl Gebhardt, *Theologisch-politischer Traktat*, Verlag der Dürr'schen Buchhandlung, Leipzig, 1908; and *Abhandlung vom Staate*, Felix Meiner, Leipzig, 1922.

Appuhn,[1] Misrahi,[2] and Francès,[2] although I have not always agreed with their renderings. The English version of the *Tractatus Theologico-Politicus* by Elwes[3] is frequently inaccurate, and the version of the *Tractatus Politicus* made for Elwes by A. H. Gosset is disfigured by several 'howlers' (e.g. his rendering of *volent* in iv, 4). In addition, both versions were made from the text of Bruder, which has long since been superseded.

III. THE NOTES

My notes owe a great deal to the work of previous editors, and particularly to that of Gebhardt. Sometimes I use them to explain difficulties or historical allusions in the text; sometimes to give references to relevant passages, either in the same work or in other works by Spinoza; sometimes to indicate where he has borrowed or adapted phrases or sentences from classical Latin authors; and occasionally to illustrate his doctrines by reference to other political thinkers. But their main purpose is to trace the sources of his political ideas and of the institutions which he recommends. His favourite political authors were Machiavelli and Hobbes, but he knew the latter only from *De Cive*, and not from *Leviathan*.[4] Hence most of my references to Hobbes are to the earlier work. As regards institutions, Spinoza's main source-book is Van Hove's *Polityke Weegschaal*, to which I have given numerous references. But many of his proposals are based on the Dutch constitution, with which he had a first-hand acquaintance. Here the British editor is fortunate in being able to illustrate his borrowings and adaptations by reference to Sir William Temple's *Observations upon the United Provinces of the Netherlands*. Of course, since Spinoza explicitly says that he proposes nothing which is 'new and unheard of' (see *TP* i, 3-4), it should be possible to find sources in history for every one of the institutions described in *TP* vi-xi; but such an undertaking is far beyond my powers.

---

[1] Ch. Appuhn, *Œuvres de Spinoza*, vols. ii and iii, Garnier, Paris, 1929.

[2] *Œuvres Complètes de Spinoza*, Gallimard, 1954.

[3] *Spinoza's Works* translated by R. H. M. Elwes, vol. i, 2nd edn., revised, Bell & Sons, London, 1889. *Benedict de Spinoza's Writings on Political Philosophy*, edited by A. G. A. Balz, Appleton-Century, 1937, reprints selections from Elwes's first edition (1883), and is still more inaccurate.

[4] I can find no internal evidence to suggest that Spinoza had read *Leviathan*; and it is not listed among the books from his library which were offered for sale after his death.

TRACTATUS
THEOLOGICO-POLITICUS,

Continens

Dissertationes aliquot,

Quibus ostenditur Libertatem Philosophandi non tantum
salva Pietate et Reipublicae Pace posse concedi; sed
eandem nisi cum Pace Reipublicae ipsaque
Pietate tolli non posse.

Johann. Epist. I Cap. IV vers. XIII.

Per hoc cognoscimus quod in Deo manemus, et Deus manet
in nobis, quod de Spiritu suo dedit nobis.

A TREATISE ON
RELIGION AND POLITICS,

Containing
several Discussions

Which show that Freedom to Philosophize not only can be
granted without detriment to Piety and Public Peace;
but cannot be destroyed
without destroying them as well.

John, Epistle I, Chapter IV, verse XIII.

Hereby we learn that we abide in God, and God in us,
because he hath given us of his Spirit.

CAPUT III

De Hebraeorum vocatione

VERA felicitas et beatitudo uniuscujusque in sola boni fruitione consistit, non vero in ea gloria, quod solus scilicet et reliquis exclusis bono fruatur; qui enim se propterea beatiorem aestimat, quod ipsi soli,
5 caeteris non item, bene sit, aut quod reliquis sit beatior et magis fortunatus, is veram felicitatem et beatitudinem ignorat, et laetitia quam inde concipit, nisi puerilis sit, ex nulla alia re oritur quam ex invidia et malo animo. Ex. gr. vera hominis felicitas et beatitudo in sola sapientia et veri cognitione consistit, at minime in eo, quod sapientior reliquis
10 sit, vel quod reliqui vera cognitione careant; hoc enim ejus sapientiam, hoc est, veram ejus felicitatem, nihil prorsus auget. Qui itaque propter hoc gaudet, is malo alterius gaudet, adeoque invidus est et malus, nec veram novit sapientiam neque verae vitae tranquillitatem. Cum igitur Scriptura, ut Hebraeos ad obedientiam legis hortetur, dicit Deum eos
15 prae caeteris nationibus sibi elegisse (vide Deut. Cap. 10 vers. 15), ipsis propinquum esse, aliis non item (Deut. Cap. 4 vers. 4, 7), iis tantum leges justas praescripsisse (ejusdem Cap. vers. 8), ipsis denique tantum, caeteris posthabitis, innotuisse (vide ejusdem Cap. vers. 32 etc.), ad eorum captum tantum loquitur, qui, ut in superiore Capite
20 ostendimus, et Moses etiam testatur (vide Deut. Cap. 9 vers. 6, 7), veram beatitudinem non noverant. Nam sane ipsi non minus beati fuissent, si Deus omnes aeque ad salutem vocavisset; nec ipsis Deus minus foret propitius, quamvis reliquis aeque prope adesset; nec leges minus justae, nec ipsi minus sapientes, etsi omnibus praescriptae fuis-
25 sent; nec miracula Dei potentiam minus ostendissent, si etiam propter alias nationes facta fuissent; nec denique Hebraei minus tenerentur Deum colere, si Deus haec omnia dona omnibus aequaliter largitus fuisset. Quod autem Deus Salomoni dicit (vide Reg. Lib. 1 Cap. 3 vers. 12) neminem post eum aeque sapientem ac ipsum futurum, modus
30 tantum loquendi videtur esse ad significandam eximiam sapientiam:

17–19. *I* omits the brackets round these two references.

50

CHAPTER III (in part)

In what sense the Jews were a chosen people

MAN's true happiness and blessedness lies solely in the enjoyment of good. Not in feeling elated because such enjoyment is his alone, and others are excluded from it; for he who thinks that his blessedness is increased by the fact that he is better off, or happier and more fortunate, than the rest of mankind, knows nothing of true happiness and blessedness, and the pleasure he derives from such thoughts, unless merely childish, arises only from spite and malice. Let me elaborate. A man's true happiness and blessedness lies simply in his wisdom and knowledge of truth,[1] and not in the belief that he is wiser than others, or that others lack true knowledge; for this adds nothing whatever to his wisdom, i.e. to his true happiness. Hence the man who is pleased by such thoughts is pleased by the misfortune of another; he is therefore spiteful and wicked,[2] and knows nothing either of true wisdom or of the peace of mind which true living involves.[3] Accordingly, when Scripture tries to encourage the Jews to obey the law by saying that God has chosen them as his own before all other peoples (see Deuteronomy, Chapter 10, verse 15), that he is nigh unto them and not unto others (Deuteronomy, Chapter 4, verses 4 and 7), that he has given just laws only to them (verse 8 of the same Chapter), and, finally, that he has revealed himself to them alone, preferring them to the rest (see the same Chapter, verses 32 and ff.), the words are merely a concession to the understanding of the Jews, who, as I have shown in the previous Chapter, and as Moses in fact confirms (see Deuteronomy, Chapter 9, verses 6 and 7), knew nothing of true blessedness. For would they have been less blessed themselves had God called all men equally to salvation? Would God be less gracious to them were he equally nigh to the rest? Would their laws have been less just, and they themselves less wise, had such laws been given to all? Would miracles have revealed God's power less clearly, had they been wrought for other peoples as well? And finally, would the Jews have been less bound to worship God if he had vouchsafed all these gifts to all alike? As for God's promise to Solomon that no one in time to come would be as wise as he (see 1 Kings, Chapter 3, verse 12), it seems to be merely a metaphorical way of signifying extraordinary wisdom: at any rate we

---

[1] *TT-P* iv, p. 71; *E* iv, 26–28.   [2] *E* iii, 24 Sch.   [3] *E* v, 42 Sch.

quicquid sit, minime credendum est quod Deus Salomoni ad majorem ejus felicitatem promiserit se nemini postea tantam sapientiam largiturum fore; hoc enim Salomonis intellectum nihil augeret, nec prudens rex, etsi Deus se eadem sapientia omnes donaturum
5 dixisset, minores pro tanto munere Deo ageret gratias.

Verum enimvero, etsi dicamus Mosen in locis Pentateuchi modo citatis ad Hebraeorum captum locutum fuisse, nolumus tamen negare quod Deus ipsis solis leges illas Pentateuchi praescripserit, neque quod tantum iis locutus fuerit, nec denique quod Hebraei tot miranda
10 viderint qualia nulli alii nationi contigerunt; sed id tantum volumus, Mosen tali modo, iisque praecipue rationibus, Hebraeos monere voluisse ut eos ex ipsorum puerili captu ad Dei cultum magis devinciret: deinde ostendere voluimus Hebraeos non scientia neque pietate, sed plane alia re caeteras nationes excelluisse; sive (ut cum Scriptura ad
15 eorum captum loquar) Hebraeos non ad veram vitam et sublimes speculationes, quanquam saepe monitos, sed ad aliam plane rem electos a Deo prae reliquis fuisse. Quaenam autem ea fuerit, ordine hic ostendam.

Verum antequam incipiam, explicare paucis volo quid per Dei
20 directionem, perque Dei auxilium, externum et internum, et quid per Dei electionem, quidque denique per fortunam in sequentibus intelligam. Per Dei directionem intelligo fixum illum et immutabilem naturae ordinem sive rerum naturalium concatenationem: diximus enim supra, et in alio loco jam ostendimus, leges naturae universales, secundum
25 quas omnia fiunt et determinantur, nihil esse nisi Dei aeterna decreta, quae semper aeternam veritatem et necessitatem involvunt. Sive igitur dicamus omnia secundum leges naturae fieri, sive ex Dei decreto et directione ordinari, idem dicimus. Deinde, quia rerum omnium naturalium potentia nihil est nisi ipsa Dei potentia, per quam solam
30 omnia fiunt et determinantur; hinc sequitur, quicquid homo, qui etiam pars est naturae, sibi in auxilium ad suum esse conservandum parat, vel quicquid natura ipso nihil operante ipsi offert, id omne sibi a sola divina potentia oblatum esse, vel quatenus per humanam naturam agit, vel per res extra humanam naturam. Quicquid itaque natura humana
35 ex sola sua potentia praestare potest ad suum esse conservandum, id Dei

are not to suppose that the promise never to bestow such wisdom on anyone again was made to increase Solomon's happiness; for this promise could add nothing to Solomon's understanding, and even if God had promised to endow all men with the same wisdom a wise king would not thank him any the less for so great a gift.

Yet although I hold that in the passages just cited from the Pentateuch Moses used expressions adapted to the understanding of the Jews, I have no wish to deny that God ordained the laws in the Pentateuch for them alone, or that his words were addressed to them only, or, finally, that the Jews witnessed many marvels such as no other people has seen; all I mean is that Moses used these expressions, and these particular methods of exhortation, in order to appeal to the childish understanding of the Jews and attach them more firmly to the worship of God. I also wanted to show that it was not in knowledge or piety, but in something quite different, that the Jews excelled the other peoples; in other words (to follow Scripture in adapting my language to their understanding) that the Jews were not chosen by God above all others to live the true life and to think sublime thoughts, although they were often exhorted to do so, but for quite a different purpose. What this was I shall duly show.

But before I begin I wish to explain briefly what is meant in the following discussion by the guidance of God, by God's help, external and internal, by the election of God, and finally by fortune. By the guidance of God I mean the fixed and immutable order of nature, or the coherent system of natural things: for, as I said above, and have already shown in another place,[1] the universal laws of nature, in accordance with which all things come to pass and are determined, are simply the eternal decrees of God, which always involve eternal truth and necessity. Hence it is all one whether we say that all things come to pass in accordance with the laws of nature, or that they are governed by God's decree and guidance. Again, since the power of everything in nature is simply the power of God,[2] by which alone all things come to pass and are determined; and since man too is a part of nature;[3] it follows that everything a man procures for himself to help in preserving his own existence, and everything he gets from nature without any effort of his own, is given him by God's power alone, working either through human nature or through things external to it. Thus all that human nature can do by its own unaided power to preserve its own

---

[1] *CM* ii, 9; cf. *KV* ii, 24.
[2] *TT-P* xvi, p. 125; *TP* ii, 2–3, p. 267.
[3] *E* iv, 4, and App. 7.

auxilium internum, et quicquid praeterea ex potentia causarum externarum in ipsius utile cedit, id Dei auxilium externum merito
vocare possumus. Atque ex his etiam facile colligitur quid per Dei
electionem sit intelligendum. Nam cum nemo aliquid agat nisi ex
5 praedeterminato naturae ordine, hoc est, ex Dei aeterna directione et
decreto, hinc sequitur neminem sibi aliquam vivendi rationem eligere,
neque aliquid efficere, nisi ex singulari Dei vocatione, qui hunc ad hoc
opus, vel ad hanc vivendi rationem, prae aliis elegit. Denique per
fortunam nihil aliud intelligo quam Dei directionem quatenus per
10 causas externas et inopinatas res humanas dirigit. His praelibatis ad
nostrum intentum revertamur, ut videamus quid id fuerit propter quod
Hebraea natio dicta fuerit a Deo prae reliquis electa. Ad quod ostenden-
dum sic procedo.

Omnia quae honeste cupimus ad haec tria potissimum referuntur:
15 nempe, res per primas suas causas intelligere; passiones domare, sive
virtutis habitum acquirere; et denique, secure et sano corpore vivere.
Media quae ad primum et secundum directe inserviunt, et quae tanquam causae proximae et efficientes considerari possunt, in ipsa humana
natura continentur; ita ut eorum acquisitio a sola nostra potentia, sive
20 a solis humanae naturae legibus, praecipue pendeat. Et hac de causa
omnino statuendum est haec dona nulli nationi peculiaria, sed toti
humano generi communia semper fuisse; nisi somniare velimus naturam
olim diversa hominum genera procreavisse. At media quae ad secure
vivendum et corpus conservandum inserviunt in rebus externis prae-
25 cipue sita sunt; atque ideo dona fortunae vocantur, quia nimirum
maxime a directione causarum externarum, quam ignoramus, pendent:
ita ut hac in re stultus fere aeque felix et infelix ac prudens sit. Attamen ad secure vivendum et injurias aliorum hominum, et etiam
brutorum, evitandum, humana directio et vigilantia multum juvare
30 potest. Ad quod nullum certius medium ratio et experientia docuit
quam societatem certis legibus formare, certamque mundi plagam
occupare, et omnium vires ad unum quasi corpus, nempe societatis,
redigere. Verum enimvero ad societatem formandam et conservandam
ingenium et vigilantia non mediocris requiritur; et idcirco illa societas
35 securior erit, et magis constans, minusque fortunae obnoxia, quae
maxime ab hominibus prudentibus et vigilantibus fundatur et dirigitur;
et contra, quae ex hominibus rudis ingenii constat, maxima ex parte a

2. *P cadit.*

54

existence, we can rightly call the inward help of God; and everything else that turns out to its advantage through the power of external causes, the outward help of God. From these same premises we can readily discover the true meaning of God's election. For if everything a man does is governed by the predetermined order of nature, i.e. by God's eternal guidance and decree, then no one chooses any way of life for himself, or does anything whatsoever, unless he has been specially called and chosen by God before all others to perform that task or to live that manner of life. Finally, by fortune I simply mean the guidance of God in so far as he directs human affairs through unforeseen external causes. After this preamble let us return to our subject, and try to discover the reason why the Jewish people was said to have been chosen by God before all others. To make this clear I proceed as follows.

Generally speaking, all legitimate objects of human desire fall under three heads: knowledge of things through their primary causes; control of the passions, or the formation of a virtuous disposition; security and physical health. The direct means to the first two goods, their proximate and efficient causes if you like, are contained in human nature itself; so that their attainment largely depends on our own unaided power, i.e. on the laws of human nature alone. We must therefore insist that these gifts are not peculiar to any people, but have always been common to the whole human race; unless, perhaps, we are prepared to indulge in the dream that nature once created men of different species. But the means to security and physical survival lie mainly in things outside us. Accordingly, these goods are called gifts of fortune, because they are largely dependent on the unknown operation of external causes; so much so that in these matters a man's folly or prudence may make very little difference to his lot. Still, human guidance and vigilance can do a great deal to help men live in safety and avoid injury from other men and wild animals: and the surest means to this end, the means prescribed by reason and experience, is to form a society with definite laws, to occupy a particular stretch of territory, and to concentrate the strength of all the members in a single body, the body of the society.[1] But to form and maintain a society requires ability and vigilance of no mean order.[2] Hence a society formed and guided in the main by prudent and vigilant men will be more secure, more stable, and less at the mercy of fortune; while one composed of men whose ability is small is largely dependent on fortune,

---

[1] *TT-P* xvi, p. 133.   [2] *E* iv, App. 13.

fortuna pendet, et minus est constans. Quod si tamen diu permanserit, id alterius directioni, non suae debetur; imo, si magna pericula exsuperaverit, et res ipsi prospere successerint, non poterit ipsa Dei directionem (nempe quatenus Deus per causas latentes externas, at non 5 quatenus per humanam naturam et mentem agit) non admirari et adorare, quandoquidem ipsi nihil nisi admodum inexpectatum et praeter opinionem contigit; quod revera etiam pro miraculo haberi potest.

Per hoc igitur tantum nationes ab invicem distinguuntur, nempe 10 ratione societatis et legum sub quibus vivunt et diriguntur; adeoque Hebraea natio non ratione intellectus neque animi tranquillitatis a Deo prae caeteris electa fuit, sed ratione societatis, et fortunae qua imperium adepta est, quaque id ipsum tot annos retinuit. Quod etiam ex ipsa Scriptura quam clarissime constat: si quis' enim ipsam vel 15 leviter percurrit, clare videt Hebraeos in hoc solo caeteras nationes excelluisse, quod res suas quae ad vitae securitatem pertinent feliciter gesserint, magnaque pericula exsuperaverint, idque maxime solo Dei externo auxilio; in reliquis autem caeteris aequales fuisse, et Deum omnibus aeque propitium. Nam ratione intellectus constat (ut in 20 superiori Capite ostendimus) eos de Deo et natura vulgares admodum cogitationes habuisse; quare ratione intellectus non fuerunt a Deo prae caeteris electi. At nec etiam ratione virtutis et verae vitae; hac enim in re etiam reliquis gentibus aequales fuerunt, et non nisi paucissimi electi. Eorum igitur electio et vocatio in sola imperii temporanea 25 felicitate et commodis constitit; nec videmus quod Deus patriarchis aut eorum successoribus aliud praeter hoc promiserit.[4] Imo in Lege pro obedientia nihil aliud promittitur quam imperii continua felicitas et reliqua hujus vitae commoda; et contra pro contumacia, pactique ruptione, imperii ruina maximaque incommoda. Nec mirum; nam 30 finis universae societatis et imperii est (ut ex modo dictis patet, et in sequentibus fusius ostendemus) secure et commode vivere; imperium autem non nisi legibus quibus unusquisque teneatur subsistere potest;

and less stable. If such a society has nevertheless lasted a long time, its survival is due to another's guidance, not to its own; what is more, if it has surmounted great dangers, and prospered in its enterprises, it will inevitably regard the guidance of God (in so far, that is, as he acts through hidden external causes, and not through the nature and mind of man) with wonder and reverence, since all its successes have been entirely unexpected and unforeseen. Indeed it may even regard them as miraculous.

Peoples, then, are distinguished from one another by one thing only—the nature of the society in which they live and of the laws by which they are governed.[1] Thus the election of the Jewish people by God did not consist in its superior understanding and peace of mind, but in its social organization, and the good fortune whereby it achieved its independence as a state and maintained it for so many years. This is also shown conclusively by the actual words of Holy Writ: for even a cursory reading makes it plain that the only respect in which the Jews surpassed the rest of the world was their success in handling matters concerning security of life and in surmounting great dangers—a success due almost exclusively to God's external aid; in other respects they were no better than the rest, and God was equally gracious to all. As far as understanding went they had obviously very crude ideas about God and nature (as I have shown in the previous Chapter[2]); so it was not in this respect that they were chosen by God above the rest. Nor indeed were they chosen in respect of virtue and true living; for here again they were no better than the Gentiles, and the number of those chosen was very small. It follows that their election and vocation consisted simply in the temporal prosperity and advantages of their state, and I cannot see that God promised anything more than this to the patriarchs or their successors.[3] In the Law, indeed, the only reward promised for obedience is the continuing prosperity of the state, and other worldly goods; while the penalty threatened for disobedience, and the breaking of the covenant, is the destruction of the state, and great misfortunes. Nor is this surprising. It is obvious from what I have just said (and it will be shown at greater length below[4]) that the purpose of every society and state is secure and comfortable living. But a state cannot survive without laws binding on each member, for if all the

---

[1] *TT-P* xvii, p. 181.

[2] Moses, for example, worshipped an anthropomorphic God who dwelt in the heavens: Isaiah believed that the sun moved round the earth.

[3] n. 4, p. 247.   [4] *TT-P* v, p. 93.

quod si omnia unius societatis membra legibus valedicere velint, eo ipso societatem dissolvent et imperium destruent. Hebraeorum igitur societati nihil aliud pro constanti legum observatione promitti potuit quam vitae securitas[5] ejusque commoda, et contra pro contumacia 5 nullum certius supplicium praedici quam imperii ruina, et mala quae inde communiter sequuntur, et praeterea alia quae ex eorum singularis imperii ruina ipsis peculiariter suborirentur. Sed de his non est opus impraesentiarum prolixius agere. Hoc tantum addo, leges etiam Veteris Testamenti Judaeis tantum revelatas et praescriptas fuisse: nam cum 10 Deus ipsos ad singularem societatem et imperium constituendum tantum elegerit, necessario singulares etiam leges habere debebant.

. . . .

Superest jam tantum ut quorundam rationibus respondeamus, quibus sibi persuadere volunt Hebraeorum electionem non temporaneam, et 15 ratione solius imperii, sed aeternam fuisse. Nam, ajunt, videmus Judaeos post imperii amissionem tot annos ubique sparsos, separatosque ab omnibus nationibus, superstites esse, quod nulli alii nationi contigit: deinde, quod Sacrae Literae multis in locis docere videntur Deum Judaeos in aeternum sibi elegisse; adeoque, tametsi imperium per- 20 diderunt, nihilominus tamen Dei electos manere. Loca quae hanc aeternam electionem quam clarissime docere putant sunt praecipue: I. vers. 36 Cap. 31 Jeremiae, ubi Propheta semen Israëlis in aeternum gentem Dei mansuram testatur, comparando nimirum eos cum fixo coelorum et naturae ordine. II. Ezechiëlis Cap. 20 vers. 32 etc., ubi 25 videtur velle quod, quamvis Judaei data opera Dei cultui valedicere velint, Deus tamen eos ex omnibus regionibus in quibus dispersi erant recolliget, ducetque ad desertum populorum sicuti eorum parentes ad Aegypti deserta duxit, et tandem inde, postquam eos a rebellibus et deficientibus selegerit, ad montem ejus sanctitatis, ubi tota Israëlis 30 familia ipsum colet. Alia praeter haec adferri solent, praecipue a Pharisaeis; sed omnibus me satisfacturum puto ubi hisce duobus

---

5. *O supplicium; I suplicium.* Cf. p. 208, l. 10, where *I* has *suplicio* and *O supplicio.*
23. *G mansurum.*   31. *O duobus; I duobis.*

58

members of a society are prepared to abandon the laws they will thereby disrupt the society and destroy the state. Hence the Jewish community could have been promised no other reward for constant observance of the laws than secure and comfortable living,[1] and, conversely, no surer punishment for disobedience could have been foretold than the destruction of the state, the suffering to which this generally leads, and the additional suffering likely to befall the Jews in particular through the destruction of their particular state. But there is no need to elaborate this now. I shall merely add that the laws in the Old Testament were also revealed to, and ordained for, the Jews alone; for since God chose them to form a society and state of their own, though for nothing else, it was necessary that they should have laws of their own as well.

.   .   .   .

It only remains now to answer the arguments by which some try to convince themselves that the election of the Jews was not temporary, and concerned only with their political independence, but everlasting. First they point to the fact that the Jews, although scattered all over the world, and not incorporated in any other nation, have long survived the loss of their state; and they claim that no other people has done this. Secondly, they say, Holy Writ appears to teach in many places that God chose the Jews as his own people for ever; so that even although they have lost their state they still remain God's chosen people. The passages which they take as most clearly teaching this everlasting election are chiefly: I. Jeremiah, Chapter 31, verse 36, where the Prophet testifies that the seed of Israel will remain God's people for ever, actually comparing them with the fixed order of the heavens and of nature in general. II. Ezekiel, Chapter 20, verses 32 and ff., where the meaning seems to be this: that although the Jews are determined to forsake the worship of God, he will gather them together again out of all the countries wherein they are scattered, will lead them to the wilderness of the peoples even as he led their fathers to the wildernesses of Egypt, and, in the end, after he has purged them of rebels and back-sliders, will bring them to the mountain of his holiness, where the whole house of Israel will worship him. Further arguments are frequently adduced, especially by the Pharisees; but I think I shall satisfy everyone if I answer these two.[2] And this I shall

---

[1] n. 5, p. 247.

[2] Most translators have gone astray here: *hisce duobus* does not refer to the two passages from Scripture, but to the two arguments outlined at the start of the paragraph.

respondero. Quod levi negotio faciam, postquam ex ipsa Scriptura ostendero Deum Hebraeos in aeternum non elegisse, sed tantum eadem conditione qua ante Canahanitas elegerit; qui etiam, ut supra ostendimus, pontifices habuerunt qui Deum religiose colebant, et quos tamen
5 Deus propter eorum luxum et socordiam et malum cultum rejecit. Moses enim in Levitico Cap. 18 vers. 27, 28 monet Israëlitas ne incestis polluantur veluti Canahanitae, ne ipsos terra evomat, sicuti evomuit illas gentes quae illa loca inhabitabant. Et Deut. Cap. 8 vers. 19, 20 ipsis expressissimis verbis totalem ruinam minatur. Sic enim ait:
10 *Testor vobis hodie quod absolute peribitis; sicuti gentes quas Deus ex vestra praesentia perire facit, sic peribitis.* Et ad hunc modum alia in Lege reperiuntur, quae expresse indicant Deum non absolute neque in aeternum Hebraeam nationem élegisse. Si itaque prophetae iis novum et aeternum foedus Dei cognitionis, amoris, et gratiae praedixerunt, id
15 piis tantum promitti facile convincitur. Nam in eodem Ezechiëlis Capite quod modo citavimus expresse dicitur quod Deus ab iis separabit rebelles et deficientes; et Tsephoniae Cap. 3 vs. 11, 12 quod Deus superbos auferet e medio, et pauperes superstites faciet; et quia haec electio veram virtutem spectat, non putandum est quod piis Judaeorum
20 tantum, caeteris exclusis, promissa fuerit, sed plane credendum gentiles veros prophetas, quos omnes nationes habuisse ostendimus, eandem etiam fidelibus suarum nationum promisisse, eosque eadem solatos fuisse. Quare hoc aeternum foedus Dei cognitionis et amoris universale est, ut etiam ex Tsephoniae Cap. 3 vs. 9, 10 evidentissime con-
25 stat; adeoque hac in re nulla est admittenda differentia inter Judaeos et gentes, neque igitur etiam alia electio iis peculiaris praeter illam quam jam ostendimus. Et quod prophetae, dum de hac electione quae solam veram virtutem spectat, multa de sacrificiis et aliis caeremoniis, templi et urbis reaedificatione misceant, pro more et natura prophetiae
30 res spirituales sub talibus figuris explicare voluerunt, ut Judaeis, quorum erant prophetae, imperii et templi restaurationem, tempore

---

7. *I ut,* corrected to *ne* in the list of Errata.
17. *B v. 11. 12; I vs. 12, 13.*   21. *O eandem; I eandum.*
24. *B v. 9. 10; I vs. 10, 11.*   28. *Gf* inserts *loquuntur* after *spectat.*

do without much difficulty, once I have proved from the actual words of Scripture that God did not choose the Jews for ever, but only on the same condition as he earlier chose the Canaanites; who also had priests devout in the worship of God, as I have shown above, yet were rejected by God because of their sensuality, sloth, and depraved manner of worship. In Leviticus, Chapter 18, verses 27 and 28, Moses warns the Israelites not to defile themselves with abominations like the Canaanites, lest the land vomit them out even as it vomited out the peoples who used to dwell within it. And in Deuteronomy, Chapter 8, verses 19 and 20, he threatens them with utter destruction in the plainest of terms: 'I swear unto you this day that ye shall perish utterly; even as the peoples which the Lord maketh to perish before your presence, so shall ye perish.' And we find other passages in the Law to the same effect, which plainly show that God did not choose the Jewish people unconditionally or for ever. So if the prophets foretold to the Jews a new and everlasting covenant based on the knowledge, love, and grace of God, it was promised to the pious only. This is easily shown. For in the very Chapter of Ezekiel just quoted it is expressly stated that God will purge them of rebels and back-sliders, while in Zephaniah, Chapter 3, verses 11 and 12, we are told that God will destroy the proud and leave the poor as a remnant; and since this election refers to true virtue we must not suppose that it was promised only to the pious among the Jews, and that other pious men were excluded, but must assuredly believe that the true prophets of the Gentiles—and I have shown that all peoples had such men[1]—promised the same election to the faithful among their nations also, and gave them the same consolation. Hence the everlasting covenant based on the knowledge and love of God is universal, as is also made abundantly clear by Zephaniah, Chapter 3, verses 9 and 10; so that in this respect we must admit no difference between Jews and Gentiles, and, in consequence, no other election peculiar to the former save that already described. The fact that the prophets, in speaking of the election which concerns true virtue only, intersperse their account with a great deal about sacrifices and other ceremonies, and about the rebuilding of the temple and the city, is easily explained. Their object was to convey a spiritual message; but in accordance with the nature and tradition of prophecy they conveyed it by these figurative expressions, so that they might also reveal to the Jews, whose prophets they were, the restoration of the state and the

---

[1] In the part of the chapter omitted Spinoza cites Noah, Enoch, Abimelech, and Balaam as examples.

Cyri expectandam, simul indicarent. Quare hodie Judaei nihil prorsus habent quod sibi supra omnes nationes tribuere possint. Quod autem tot annos dispersi absque imperio perstiterint, id minime mirum, postquam se ab omnibus nationibus ita separaverunt ut omnium odium 5 in se converterint, idque non tantum ritibus externis, ritibus caeterarum nationum contrariis, sed etiam signo circumcisionis quod religiosissime servant. Quod autem nationum odium eos admodum conservet, id jam experientia docuit. Cum Rex Hispaniae olim Judaeos coëgit regni religionem admittere, vel in exilium ire, perplurimi Judaei ponti-
10 ficiorum religionem admiserunt; sed quia iis qui religionem admiserunt omnia Hispanorum naturalium privilegia concessa sunt, iique omnibus honoribus digni existimati sunt, statim ita se Hispanis immiscuerunt ut pauco post tempore nullae eorum reliquiae manserint, neque ulla memoria. At plane contra iis contigit quos Rex Lusitanorum religionem
15 sui imperii admittere coëgit; qui semper, quamvis ad religionem conversi, ab omnibus separati vixerunt, nimirum quia eos omnibus honoribus indignos declaravit. Signum circumcisionis etiam hac in re tantum posse existimo, ut mihi persuadeam hoc unum hanc nationem in aeternum conservaturum; imo, nisi fundamenta suae religionis eorum
20 animos effoeminarent, absolute crederem eos aliquando, data occasione,—ut sunt res humanae mutabiles—suum imperium iterum erecturos, Deumque eos de novo electurum. Cujus etiam rei exemplum praeclarum habemus in Chinensibus, qui etiam comma aliquod in capite religiosissime servant quo se ab omnibus aliis separant; et ita
25 separati tot annorum millia se conservaverunt ut antiquitate reliquas omnes nationes longe superent. Nec semper imperium obtinuerunt, attamen illud amissum recuperaverunt; et sine dubio iterum

---

1. *IV Cyri; I Ciri.*

temple to be expected in the time of Cyrus.[1] Hence the Jews of today have absolutely nothing to which they can lay more claim than the rest of mankind. As for the fact that they have survived their dispersion and the loss of their state for so many years, there is nothing miraculous in that, since they have incurred universal hatred by cutting themselves off completely from all other peoples; and not only by practising a form of worship opposed to that of the rest, but also by preserving the mark of circumcision with such devoutness. That their survival is largely due to the hatred of the Gentiles has already been shown by experience. When the King of Spain compelled the Jews of bygone days either to accept the religion of his realm or to go into exile,[2] a great number of them embraced the Roman Catholic faith; but since those who did so were admitted to all the privileges of native-born Spaniards, and were regarded as worthy candidates for all positions of honour, they immediately identified themselves so closely with the Spanish that in a few years' time no traces and even no memory of them remained. But precisely the opposite happened to those who were forced by the King of Portugal[3] to embrace the religion of his kingdom; for although they were converted, they continued to live apart from the rest of community, simply because he declared them unworthy of any position of honour.[4] The mark of circumcision is also, I think, of great importance in this connexion; so much so that in my view it alone will preserve the Jewish people for all time; indeed, did not the principles of their religion make them effeminate, I should be quite convinced that some day when opportunity arises—so mutable are human affairs—they will establish their state once more,[5] and that God will choose them afresh. We find a remarkable example of the effects of such a symbol among the Chinese, for in the pigtail they also preserve most devoutly a mark which distinguishes them from the rest of mankind; and through this distinguishing mark they have maintained their national identity for so many millennia that they are a far older people than any other. They have not always kept their political independence either, though they have always recovered it when lost;

[1] For the prophecy see *Jeremiah* 25, 12, and 29, 10: for its fulfilment *Ezra* 1.

[2] A reference to the decree of Ferdinand (and Isabella) in 1492.

[3] Manuel I, in 1496.

[4] It is true that in Spain the converts were quickly absorbed, while in Portugal they remained distinct: but this seems to have been partly due to the fact that many of the more devoted Jews had fled to Portugal from Spain. See Cecil Roth, *A History of the Marranos*, chs. i-iv.

[5] Israel became a state again in 1948.

recuperabunt, ubi Tartarorum animi prae luxu divitiarum et socordia languescere incipient. Denique, si quis velit defendere Judaeos hac vel alia de causa a Deo in aeternum electos fuisse, non ipsi repugnabo, modo statuat hanc electionem, vel temporaneam vel aeternam, quatenus ea
5 tantum Judaeis peculiaris est, non respicere nisi imperium et corporis commoditates (quandoquidem hoc solum unam nationem ab alia distinguere potest); at ratione intellectus et verae virtutis nullam nationem ab alia distingui, adeoque his in rebus nec a Deo unam prae alia eligi.

2. *I vellet.*

and no doubt will recover it again once the character of the Tartars[1] begins to weaken through the enervating effects of wealth and ease. In conclusion, if anyone wishes to defend the view that the Jews were chosen by God for ever, either because of the mark of circumcision or for some other reason, I shall not oppose him, as long as he admits that in so far as this election—whether temporary or everlasting—is peculiar to the Jews alone it is concerned only with their political organization and worldly prosperity (since this alone can distinguish one people from another); and agrees that in respect of understanding and true virtue no people is distinguished from another, and, consequently, that in these respects no one people is chosen by God in preference to another.

[1] The name *Tartar*, originally used of the followers of Genghis Khan who invaded China in the thirteenth century, was later applied to other foreign invaders. The reference here is to the Manchus, who overran China in the first half of the seventeenth century, and established a dynasty which was to survive into the twentieth.

CAPUT IV

De lege divina

LEGIS nomen absolute sumptum significat id secundum quod unumquodque individuum, vel omnia vel aliquot ejusdem speciei, una
eademque certa ac determinata ratione agunt; ea vero vel a necessitate
5 naturae, vel ab hominum placito dependet. Lex quae a necessitate
naturae dependet illa est quae ex ipsa rei natura sive definitione necessario sequitur; ab hominum placito autem, et quae magis proprie jus
appellatur, est ea quam homines ad tutius et commodius vivendum, vel
ob alias causas, sibi et aliis praescribunt. Ex. gr. quod omnia corpora,
10 ubi in alia minora impingunt, tantum de suo motu amittunt quantum
aliis communicant, lex est universalis omnium corporum quae ex necessitate naturae sequitur. Sic etiam, quod homo, cum unius rei recordetur,
statim recordetur alterius similis, vel quam simul cum ipsa perceperat,
lex est quae ex natura humana necessario sequitur. At quod homines de
15 suo jure quod ex natura habent cedant, vel cedere cogantur, et certae
rationi vivendi sese adstringant, ex humano placito pendet. Et quamvis
absolute concedam omnia ex legibus universalibus naturae determinari
ad existendum et operandum certa ac determinata ratione, dico tamen
has leges ex placito hominum pendere. I. Quia homo, quatenus pars est
20 naturae, eatenus partem potentiae naturae constituit. Quae igitur ex
necessitate naturae humanae sequuntur, hoc est, ex natura ipsa quatenus
eam per naturam humanam determinatam concipimus, ea, etiamsi
necessario, sequuntur tamen ab humana potentia; quare sanctionem
istarum legum ex hominum placito pendere optime dici potest, quia
25 praecipue a potentia humanae mentis ita pendet ut nihilominus humana
mens, quatenus res sub ratione veri et falsi percipit, sine hisce legibus
clarissime concipi possit, at non sine lege necessaria ut modo ipsam
definivimus. II. Has leges ex placito hominum pendere etiam dixi,
quia res per proximas suas causas definire et explicare debemus, et illa
30 universalis consideratio de fato et concatenatione causarum minime
nobis inservire potest ad nostras cogitationes circa res particulares
formandas atque ordinandas. Adde quod nos ipsam rerum coordina-
tionem et concatenationem, hoc est, quomodo res revera ordinatae et

CHAPTER IV

Of the divine law

THE word 'law' in the widest sense means a rule in accordance with
which all individual things, or all things of the same species, or some
of them, act in one and the same fixed and determinate way; and this
either by natural necessity or by the will of men. A law based on
natural necessity is one which follows necessarily from the actual
nature or definition of the thing in question; while a law based on the
will of men—more properly called an ordinance—is one which men
prescribe for themselves and others in order to live in greater security
and comfort, or for some other purpose. E.g. that any body impinging
on a smaller body loses as much of its own motion as it imparts to the
other is a law which is common to all bodies and depends on natural
necessity.[1] Similarly, that on thinking of one thing a man immediately
thinks of something else like it, or associated with it in his previous
experience, is a law which follows necessarily from human nature.[2]
But that men should surrender, or be forced to surrender, the right
which they hold from nature, and should bind themselves to follow a
definite rule of life, depends on human volition. And although I fully
admit that all things are determined to exist and act in a fixed and
definite way by universal laws of nature, I still say that laws of the
second type depend on the will of men; and for two reasons. I. Since
man is part of nature, he forms part of nature's power. Everything,
therefore, which follows from the necessity of human nature, i.e.
from nature itself conceived in the determinate form of human nature,
follows, albeit necessarily, from human power. Hence the institution
of these laws may well be said to depend on the will of men, because
they largely depend on the power of the human mind, yet, unlike
necessary law as I have just defined it, need not be contained in an
adequate conception of the human mind as perceiving things under the
form of truth and falsity. II. My second reason for asserting that these
laws depend on the will of men is that we ought to define and explain
things through their proximate causes, since general considerations
about necessity and causal connexion can give us very little help in
forming and arranging our ideas about particular things. Besides, the
actual system and interconnexion of things, i.e. the way in which

[1] *CPP* ii, 20.   [2] *E* ii, 18.

67

concatenatae sunt, plane ignoremus; adeoque ad usum vitae melius, imo necesse est, res ut possibiles considerare. Haec de lege absolute considerata.

Verum enimvero, quoniam nomen legis per translationem ad res 5 naturales applicatum videtur, et communiter per legem nihil aliud intelligitur quam mandatum quod homines et perficere et negligere possunt, utpote quia potentiam humanam sub certis limitibus, ultra quos se extendit, constringit, nec aliquid supra vires imperat; ideo lex particularius definienda videtur, nempe, quod sit ratio vivendi quam 10 homo sibi vel aliis ob aliquem finem praescribit. Attamen, quoniam verus finis legum paucis tantum patere solet, et perplurimum homines ad eum percipiendum fere inepti sunt, et nihil minus quam ex ratione vivunt; ideo legislatores, ut omnes aeque constringerent, alium finem, longe diversum ab eo qui ex legum natura necessario sequitur, sapienter 15 statuerunt, nempe legum propugnatoribus promittendo id quod vulgus maxime amat, et contra iis qui eas violarent minitando id quod maxime timet; sicque conati sunt vulgum, tanquam equum fraeno, quoad ejus fieri potest cohibere. Unde factum est ut pro lege maxime haberetur ratio vivendi quae hominibus ex aliorum imperio praescribitur; et 20 consequenter ut ii qui legibus obtemperant sub lege vivere dicantur, et servire videantur. Et revera qui unicuique suum tribuit quia patibulum timet, is ex alterius imperio et malo coactus agit, nec justus vocari potest; at is qui unicuique suum tribuit ex eo quod veram legum rationem et earum necessitatem novit, is animo constanti agit, et ex 25 proprio, non vero alieno decreto, adeoque justus merito vocatur. Quod etiam Paulum docere voluisse puto, cum dixit eos qui sub lege vivebant per legem justificari non potuisse; justitia enim, ut communiter definitur, est constans et perpetua voluntas jus suum cuique tribuendi;

things are really ordered and interconnected, is quite unknown to us;[1] so for practical purposes it is better, indeed necessary, to regard things as possible.[2] So much for law in the widest sense. _____

But the application of the word 'law' to natural things seems to be metaphorical,[3] and the ordinary meaning of law is simply a command which men can either obey or disobey, since it confines human power within definite bounds which are narrower than its natural limits, and requires nothing that is beyond man's strength. This makes it advisable, I think, to restrict the word to its second meaning, and to define law as a rule of life which man prescribes to himself or to others for some object. Yet the real object of law is seldom obvious to more than a few; most men are practically incapable of seeing it, and do anything but live by reason's guidance. Thus in order to bind all men equally legislators have wisely introduced another motive for obedience —very different from the one which follows necessarily from the nature of law—by holding out the sort of reward for active support, and the sort of penalty for transgression, that appeals most strongly to the hopes and fears of the masses; and in this way they have tried to keep them on the tightest possible rein. In consequence, law is apt to be regarded as a rule of life prescribed for men by the command of others;[4] accordingly, those who obey law are said to live under law, and are thought to be slaves. Now it is true that he who gives every man his own because he fears the gallows acts by the command of another and under compulsion of evil, so that he cannot be called just; still, he who gives every man his own because he knows the real reason and necessity for law acts with constancy of purpose and of his own volition, not another's, and hence is rightly called just. This, I think, is in fact what Paul meant to convey when he said that those who lived under law could not be justified by law,[5] for justice as commonly defined is the constant and permanent will to give every man his own;

---

[1] The argument seems to be this. Prescriptive laws, unlike the 'necessary laws' (Laws of Nature) mentioned above, depend on human thoughts and volitions. The part played by volition is vital, for a prescriptive law does not follow directly from the nature of the human mind *qua* cognitive. Again, although the volition which is the proximate cause of a prescriptive law is in turn determined, the combination of causes by which it is produced is too complex for us to grasp. We must therefore be content to say that prescriptive laws depend on the human will. For the profession of ignorance about how things are interconnected cf. *TT-P* xvi, p. 127; *TP* ii, 8, p. 273, and 22, p. 281; *Epp.* xxx and xxxii.

[2] *E* i, 33 Sch. 1, and iv, Deff. 3 and 4.

[3] The application of the word 'law' to natural objects involves conceiving God as the 'sovereign' of the universe (*TT-P* iv, pp. 77–83; *E* ii, 3 Sch.).

[4] As by Hobbes (*De Cive* vi, 9). Spinoza points out that law may be self-imposed.

[5] *Romans* 3, 19–20. A man who lives 'under law' is *eo ipso* convicted of moral incapacity.

et ideo Salomon Cap. 21 vers. 15 Prov. ait justum laetari cum fit
judicium, iniquos autem pavere. Cum itaque lex nihil aliud sit quam
ratio vivendi quam homines ob aliquem finem sibi vel aliis praescribunt,
ideo lex distinguenda videtur in humanam et divinam. Per humanam
5 intelligo rationem vivendi quae ad tutandam vitam et rempublicam
tantum inservit; per divinam autem quae solum summum bonum, hoc
est, Dei veram cognitionem et amorem, spectat. Ratio cur hanc legem
voco divinam est propter summi boni naturam, quam hic paucis, et
quam clare potero, jam ostendam.

10   Cum melior pars nostri sit intellectus, certum est, si nostrum utile
revera quaerere velimus, nos supra omnia debere conari ut eum quantum fieri potest perficiamus; in ejus enim perfectione summum nostrum
bonum consistere debet. Porro, quoniam omnis nostra cognitio, et
certitudo quae revera omne dubium tollit, a sola Dei cognitione depen-
15 det—tum quia sine Deo nihil esse neque concipi potest, tum etiam
quia de omnibus dubitare possumus quamdiu Dei nullam claram et
distinctam habemus ideam—hinc sequitur summum nostrum bonum
et perfectionem a sola Dei cognitione pendere, etc. Deinde, cum nihil
sine Deo nec esse nec concipi possit, certum est omnia quae in natura
20 sunt Dei conceptum pro ratione suae essentiae suaeque perfectionis
involvere atque exprimere; ac proinde nos, quo magis res naturales
cognoscimus, eo majorem et perfectiorem Dei cognitionem acquirere:
vel (quoniam cognitio effectus per causam nihil aliud est quam causae
proprietatem aliquam cognoscere) quo magis res naturales cognoscimus,
25 eo Dei essentiam (quae omnium rerum causa est) perfectius cognoscere.
Atque adeo tota nostra cognitio, hoc est, summum nostrum bonum,
non tantum a Dei cognitione dependet, sed in eadem omnino consistit.
Quod etiam ex hoc sequitur, quod homo pro natura et perfectione rei
quam prae reliquis amat, eo etiam perfectior est, et contra; adeoque
30 ille necessario perfectissimus est, et de summa beatitudine maxime
participat, qui Dei, entis nimirum perfectissimi, intellectualem cognitionem supra omnia amat, eademque maxime delectatur. Huc itaque
nostrum summum bonum nostraque beatitudo redit, in cognitionem
scilicet et amorem Dei. Media igitur quae hic finis omnium humanarum
35 actionum, nempe ipse Deus quatenus ejus idea in nobis est, exigit,
jussa Dei vocari possunt, quia quasi ab ipso Deo quatenus in nostra
mente existit nobis praescribuntur; atque adeo ratio vivendi quae

1. *B v. 15; I vers. 12.*   17. *O summum; I summam.*

70

and this is why Solomon says in Proverbs, Chapter 21, verse 15 that the just rejoice when justice is done, while the unjust are afraid. Law, then, is simply a rule of living which men prescribe to themselves or to others for some object; and since this is so, it seems necessary to divide it into two categories, human and divine. By human law I mean a rule of living which serves no other purpose than to preserve life and the state; while by divine law I mean one whose sole object is the supreme good, i.e. true knowledge and love of God. I call the latter divine because of the nature of the supreme good, which I shall now explain as briefly and as clearly as possible.

Since the better part of us is our understanding, it follows that, if we really wish to seek our own good, our primary aim must be to make our understanding as perfect as possible; for it is in its perfection that our supreme good must lie.[1] Now since all our knowledge, and the certainty which really removes all doubt, depends wholly on our knowledge of God—not only because nothing can either be or be conceived without God, but also because complete scepticism is possible as long as we have no clear and distinct idea of God[2]—our supreme good and perfection is wholly dependent on our knowledge of God and the consequences of that knowledge. Again, since nothing can either be or be conceived without God it necessarily follows that everything in nature involves and expresses the concept of God in proportion to its essence and perfection; so that the more we learn of things in nature, the greater and more perfect is the knowledge of God we acquire:[3] or (since to understand an effect through its cause is simply to understand a particular property of the cause) the more we learn of things in nature the more perfect becomes our knowledge of God's essence, which is the cause of all things. Hence all our knowledge, i.e. our supreme good, not only depends upon, but wholly consists in our knowledge of God. This also follows from the fact that a man is more perfect as the main object of his love is more perfect, and vice versa; so that the man whose main love and chief delight is the intellectual knowledge of the most perfect being, God, is necessarily most perfect, and shares most fully in supreme blessedness. Our highest good and blessedness, then, is summed up in this—knowledge and love of God. Accordingly, the means required by this object of all human actions, i.e. by God himself in so far as we have the idea of him in our minds, can be called the commands of God, since they are, so to speak, prescribed to us by God himself in so far as he exists in our minds; and so

[1] *E* iv, App. 4.   [2] *DIE*, par. 79.   [3] *E* v, 24.

hunc finem spectat lex divina optime vocatur. Quaenam autem haec media sint, et quaenam ratio vivendi quam hic finis exigit, et quomodo hunc optimae reipublicae fundamenta sequantur, et ratio vivendi inter homines, ad universalem ethicam pertinet. Hic non nisi de lege divina
5 in genere pergam agere.

Cum itaque amor Dei summa hominis felicitas sit et beatitudo, et finis ultimus et scopus omnium humanarum actionum; sequitur eum tantum legem divinam sequi qui Deum amare curat, non ex timore supplicii, neque prae amore alterius rei, ut deliciarum, famae, etc.,
10 sed ex eo solo quod Deum novit, sive quod novit Dei cognitionem et amorem summum esse bonum. Legis igitur divinae summa, ejusque summum praeceptum, est Deum ut summum bonum amare, nempe, ut jam diximus, non ex metu alicujus supplicii et poenae, nec prae amore alterius rei qua delectari cupimus: hoc enim idea Dei dictat,
15 Deum summum esse nostrum bonum, sive Dei cognitionem et amorem finem esse ultimum ad quem omnes actiones nostrae sunt dirigendae. Homo tamen carnalis haec intelligere nequit, et ipsi vana videntur, quia nimis jejunam Dei habet cognitionem, et etiam quia in hoc summo bono nihil repperit quod palpet, comedat, aut denique quod
20 carnem, qua maxime delectatur, afficiat, utpote quod in sola speculatione et pura mente consistit. At ii qui norunt se nihil intellectu et sāña mente praestantius habere haec sine dubio solidissima judicabunt.

Explicuimus itaque in quo potissimum lex divina consistit, et quaenam sint leges humanae; nempe omnes illae quae alium scopum collimant.
25 Nisi ex revelatione sancitae fuerint; nam hac etiam consideratione res ad Deum referuntur (ut supra ostendimus), et hoc sensu lex Mosis, quamvis non universalis, sed maxime ad ingenium et singularem conservationem unius populi accommodata fuerit, vocari tamen potest lex Dei, sive lex divina; quandoquidem credimus eam lumine prophetico
30 sancitam fuisse. Si jam ad naturam legis divinae naturalis, ut eam modo explicuimus, attendamus, videbimus:

I. Eam esse universalem sive omnibus hominibus communem; eam enim ex universali humana natura deduximus.

II. Eam non exigere fidem historiarum, quaecunque demum eae
35 fuerint; nam quandoquidem haec lex divina naturalis ex sola consideratione humanae naturae intelligatur, certum est nos eam aeque

---

3. The correct reading may be *hinc.*   19. *IV reperit.*   22. *O sana; I sane.*

the rule of living which has this object in view is well named the divine law. What these means are, what rule of living this object requires, and how the principles of the best state, and the best way of living among men, are derived from it, are questions for a comprehensive treatise on ethics.[1] Here I shall confine myself to discussing the divine law in general terms.

Since love of God is the supreme happiness and blessedness of man, and the highest object and aim of all human actions, the only man who fulfils the divine law is he who seeks to love God, not from fear of punishment, or through love for other things like pleasure, fame, and so forth, but simply because he knows God, or knows that knowledge and love of God is the supreme good.[2] Hence the sum of the divine law, and its fundamental precept, is to love God as the supreme good; that is—to repeat what I have said already—not from fear of any punishment or penalty, or through love of anything else which we desire to enjoy. For what the idea of God teaches us is that God is our supreme good, i.e. that knowledge and love of God is the ultimate object to which all our actions should be directed. The sensual man cannot understand this, and to him it seems empty talk, because he has too slight a knowledge of God, and also because in the supreme good, which consists entirely in contemplation and purity of spirit, he has found nothing to fondle or eat, nothing, in short, to appeal to the carnal nature which is his chief source of pleasure. But those who know that they have no possessions more precious than understanding and soundness of mind will doubtless regard these blessings as pretty substantial. I have thus explained the main content of the divine law, and shown which laws are human; they are all that have a different aim. Unless, of course, they have been established through revelation; for this too is a reason for ascribing things to God (as I have shown above),[3] and in this sense the law of Moses, although not universal, but primarily adapted to the temperament, and designed for the preservation, of one people in particular, can be called the law of God, or the divine law, in so far as we believe that it was established by prophetic insight. If we now consider the nature of natural divine law in the sense just explained, we shall see:

I. That it is universal, i.e. common to all men; for I have deduced it from human nature in general.

II. That it requires no belief in historical narratives of any kind; for since reflection on human nature is all that is needed to understand

---

[1] They are partly dealt with in *E* iv, 67–73.   [2] *E* v, 42.   [3] In *TT-P* i.

concipere posse in Adamo ac alio quocunque homine, aeque in homine qui inter homines vivit ac in homine qui solitariam vitam agit. Nec fides historiarum, quantumvis certa, Dei cognitionem, et consequenter nec etiam Dei amorem nobis dare potest. Amor enim Dei ab ejus cogni-
5 tione oritur; ejus autem cognitio ex communibus notionibus per se certis et notis hauriri debet; quare longe abest ut fides historiarum requisitum sit necessarium ut ad summum nostrum bonum perveniamus. Attamen, quamvis fides historiarum Dei cognitionem et amorem nobis dare nequeat, earum tamen lectionem ratione vitae
10 civilis perutilem esse non negamus; quo enim hominum mores et conditiones—quae ex nulla re melius quam ex eorum actionibus nosci possunt—observaverimus et melius noverimus, eo inter ipsos cautius vivere, nostrasque actiones et vitam eorum ingenio, quantum ratio fert, melius accommodare poterimus.

15 Videmus III. hanc legem divinam naturalem non exigere caeremonias, hoc est actiones quae in se indifferentes sunt et solo instituto bonae vocantur, vel quae aliquod bonum ad salutem necessarium repraesentant, vel, si mavis, actiones quarum ratio captum humanum superat. Nihil enim lumen naturale exigit quod ipsum lumen non
20 attingit, sed id tantum quod nobis clarissime indicare potest bonum sive medium ad nostram beatitudinem esse. Quae autem ex solo mandato et instituto bona sunt, vel ex eo quod alicujus boni sint repraesentamina, ea nostrum intellectum perficere nequeunt, nec aliud nisi merae umbrae sunt, nec inter actiones quae quasi proles aut fructus intellectus et
25 sanae mentis sunt numerari possunt. Quod hic non opus est prolixius ostendere.

IV. Denique videmus summum legis divinae praemium esse ipsam legem, nempe Deum cognoscere, eumque ex vera libertate et animo integro et constante amare; poenam autem horum privationem et
30 carnis servitutem, sive animum inconstantem et fluctuantem.

His sic notatis inquirendum jam est:

I. Num lumine naturali concipere possumus Deum veluti legislatorem aut principem leges hominibus praescribentem.

II. Quid Sacra Scriptura de lumine et lege hac naturali doceat.

32. *O I. num; I omits I.*

it, this law can certainly be conceived in Adam as easily as in any other man, in a solitary as easily as in a social being. In any case, belief in historical narratives, however well-grounded, cannot give us knowledge of God, and hence cannot give us love for him either. For love of God arises from knowledge of him, and knowledge of him must be derived from common notions which are self-validating and self-evident;[1] hence it is quite untrue that belief in historical narratives is a necessary condition of our attaining our supreme good. Nevertheless, although belief in historical narratives cannot give us knowledge and love of God, I do not deny that a perusal of them gives very useful guidance for living in society; for the more we have observed, and the better we know, men's characters and dispositions—which are best discovered from their actions—the more we shall be able to live discreetly among them, and to make reasonable allowances for their nature in the conduct of our lives.

III. We see that this natural divine law does not require ceremonies, i.e. actions which are indifferent in themselves and are called good only by convention, or symbolize some good necessary for salvation, or, if you like, have a justification which is beyond human understanding.[2] For the light of nature requires nothing that is beyond its own compass, but only what it can clearly show us to be good, i.e. a means to our blessedness. Actions whose only claim to goodness is the fact that they are prescribed by convention, or that they symbolize some good, can do nothing to perfect our understanding, but are simply empty forms, and no part of conduct which is the product or fruit of understanding and sound sense. But there is no need to show this more fully here.

IV. Finally, we see that the supreme reward of the divine law is the law itself,[3] i.e. to know God and love him in true freedom with a pure and constant mind; while its penalty is lack of these blessings and slavery to the flesh, or a troubled and inconstant mind.

Having noted these points we must now inquire:

I. Whether the light of nature allows us to conceive God as a legislator or king who lays down laws for men.

II. What Holy Writ teaches regarding the light of nature and this natural law.

---

[1] *E* ii, 40 Sch. 2, and 45–47.   [2] *TT-P* v, p. 99.

[3] Not 'to know the law itself', as some translate. A man does not achieve perfection until the divine law becomes the law of his nature, *descriptive* and no longer prescriptive (cf. n. 34, pp. 247–9; *KV* ii, 18; *Ep.* xix).

III. Quem ad finem caeremoniae olim institutae fuerunt.

IV. Denique, quid referat sacras historias scire et eis credere.

De primis duobus in hoc Capite; de duobus autem ultimis in sequente agam.

5   Quid circa primum statuendum sit facile deducitur ex natura voluntatis Dei, quae a Dei intellectu non nisi respectu nostrae rationis distinguitur; hoc est, Dei voluntas et Dei intellectus in se revera unum et idem sunt, nec distinguuntur nisi respectu nostrarum cogitationum quas de Dei intellectu formamus. Exempli gratia, cum ad hoc tantum
10 attendimus, quod natura trianguli in natura divina ab aeterno continetur tanquam aeterna veritas, tum dicimus Deum trianguli ideam habere, sive naturam trianguli intelligere. Sed cum postea ad hoc attendimus, quod natura trianguli sic in natura divina continetur ex sola necessitate divinae naturae, et non ex necessitate essentiae et
15 naturae trianguli, imo, quod necessitas essentiae et proprietatum trianguli, quatenus etiam ut aeternae veritates concipiuntur, a sola necessitate divinae naturae et intellectus pendeat, et non ex natura trianguli; tum id ipsum quod Dei intellectum vocavimus Dei voluntatem sive decretum appellamus. Quare respectu Dei unum et idem
20 affirmamus cum dicimus Deum ab aeterno decrevisse et voluisse tres angulos trianguli aequales esse duobus rectis, vel Deum hoc ipsum intellexisse. Unde sequitur Dei affirmationes et negationes aeternam semper necessitatem sive veritatem involvere. Si itaque, exempli gratia, Deus Adamo dixit se nolle ut de arbore cognitionis boni et mali
25 comederet, contradictionem implicaret Adamum de illa arbore posse comedere, adeoque impossibile foret ut Adamus de ea comederet; nam divinum illud decretum aeternam necessitatem et veritatem debuisset involvere. Verum quoniam Scriptura tamen narrat Deum id Adamo praecepisse, et nihilominus Adamum de eadem comedisse, necessario
30 dicendum est Deum Adamo malum tantum revelavisse quod eum necessario sequeretur si de illa arbore comederet, at non necessitatem consecutionis illius mali. Unde factum est ut Adamus illam revelationem non ut aeternam et necessariam veritatem perceperit, sed ut legem, hoc est, ut institutum quod lucrum aut damnum sequitur non

1. P *fuerint.*

76

III. What purpose lay behind the original institution of sacred rites: and finally,

IV. What importance can be attached to knowledge of and belief in sacred history.

The first two questions I shall discuss in this Chapter; the last two I shall reserve for the next.

The answer we must give to the first is easily deduced from the nature of God's will, which is distinguished from his understanding only from the viewpoint of our reason; that is to say, God's will and God's understanding are in themselves really one and the same, and the distinction between them has no basis but our different ways of conceiving God's understanding.¹ For example, when we confine our attention to the fact that the nature of a triangle is eternally contained in the divine nature as an eternal truth, we say that God has an idea of the triangle, or understands the nature of the triangle. But when we afterwards consider that it is only through the necessity of the divine nature that the triangle's nature is thus contained in it, and not through the necessity of the essence and nature of the triangle, indeed, that the necessity of the essence and properties of the triangle, again in so far as they are conceived as eternal truths, depends wholly on the necessity of the divine nature and understanding, and not on the nature of the triangle; then what we called God's understanding we now call God's will or decree. Hence we make one and the same assertion about God in saying that he has eternally decreed and willed the three angles of the triangle to be equal to two right angles, and in saying that he has understood this to be so. It follows that God's affirmations and negations always involve eternal necessity or truth.² Thus if God, for example, had told Adam that he willed him not to eat of the tree of the knowledge of good and evil, it would have involved a contradiction for Adam to be able to eat of that tree, and so it would have been impossible that Adam should eat of it;³ for that divine decree would necessarily have involved eternal necessity and truth. But since Scripture nevertheless relates that Adam did eat of the tree in spite of what God had told him, we must hold that God only revealed to Adam the evil which would befall him if he ate of it, and did not reveal the necessity with which that evil would follow. In consequence, Adam did not regard the revelation as an eternal and necessary truth, but as a law, i.e. as an ordinance involving

¹ *CPP* i, 17 Cor.; *CM* ii, 8; *E* i, 17 Sch.
² *TP* ii, 18, p. 279.   ³ *Ep.* xix.

ex necessitate et natura actionis patratae, sed ex solo libitu et absoluto imperio alicujus principis. Quare illa revelatio respectu solius Adami, et propter solum defectum ejus cognitionis, lex fuit, Deusque quasi legislator aut princeps. Et hac etiam de causa, nempe ob defectum
5 cognitionis, Decalogus respectu Hebraeorum tantum lex fuit; nam quoniam Dei existentiam ut aeternam veritatem non noverant, ideo id quod ipsis in Decalogo revelatum fuit, nempe Deum existere, Deumque solum adorandum esse, tanquam legem percipere debuerunt: quod si Deus nullis mediis corporeis adhibitis, sed immediate iis loquu-
10 tus fuisset, hoc ipsum non tanquam legem, sed tanquam aeternam veritatem percepissent. Atque hoc quod de Israëlitis et Adamo dicimus, de omnibus etiam prophetis qui nomine Dei leges scripserunt dicendum, videlicet, quod Dei decreta non adaequate, ut aeternas veritates, per-ceperunt. Ex. gr. de ipso Mose etiam dicendum est, eum ex revela-
15 tione vel ex fundamentis ei revelatis percepisse modum quo populus Israëliticus in certa mundi plaga optime uniri posset, et integram societatem formare sive imperium erigere, deinde etiam modum quo ille populus optime posset cogi ad obediendum; sed non percepisse, nec ipsi revelatum fuisse, modum illum optimum esse, neque etiam quod ex
20 populi communi obedientia in tali mundi plaga necessario sequeretur scopus ad quem collimabant. Quapropter haec omnia non ut aeternas veritates, sed ut praecepta et instituta percepit, et tanquam Dei leges praescripsit; et hinc factum est ut Deum rectorem, legislatorem, regem, misericordem, justum, etc. imaginaretur; cum tamen haec omnia solius
25 humanae naturae sint attributa, et a natura divina prorsus removenda. Atque haec, inquam, de solis prophetis dicendum qui nomine Dei leges scripserunt, non autem de Christo. De Christo enim, quamvis is etiam videatur leges Dei nomine scripsisse, sentiendum tamen est eum res vere et adaequate percepisse: nam Christus non tam propheta quam os
30 Dei fuit. Deus enim per mentem Christi (ut in Cap. I ostendimus), sicuti ante per angelos, nempe per vocem creatam, visiones, etc., quaedam humano generi revelavit. Quapropter aeque a ratione alienum esset statuere Deum suas revelationes opinionibus Christi accommo-davisse, ac quod Deus antea suas revelationes opinionibus angelorum,
35 hoc est, vocis creatae et visionum, accommodaverit, ut res revelandas

6. I *et*, corrected to *ut* in the list of Errata.   8. *O adorandum*; I *adorarandum*.
26. II *hoc*.

rewards and penalties which do not follow necessarily from the nature of the action performed, but are wholly dependent on the whim and absolute authority of some king. Hence that revelation was a law, and God a legislator or king, only in Adam's eyes, and only because of his lack of knowledge did he conceive them in this way. Similarly, the Decalogue was a law only in the eyes of the Jews; and this for the same reason, lack of knowledge. For since they did not apprehend God's existence as an eternal truth, they had to regard what was revealed to them in the Decalogue, i.e. that God exists and that God alone must be worshipped, as a law: whereas if God had spoken to them directly, without using any physical means, they would have understood this revelation as an eternal truth, and not as a law. What I have just said about the Israelites and Adam applies with equal force to all the prophets who wrote laws in God's name; none of them understood God's decrees adequately, as eternal truths. It applies even to Moses himself. For through revelation, or the fundamental laws revealed to him, Moses merely saw how the people of Israel could be united in a particular strip of territory, could form an independent community, i.e. establish a state, and could be compelled to obedience; he did not see or have revealed to him that the means prescribed were the best, and that the general obedience of the people in such a strip of territory would necessarily lead to the end they sought. He thus conceived all his discoveries, not as eternal truths, but as precepts and ordinances, and commanded them as God's laws; accordingly, he imagined God as a ruler, a legislator, a king, as merciful, just, and so on; although all such characteristics belong to human nature only, and must be eliminated completely from our conception of the divine nature.[1] These remarks, I say, are true only of the prophets who wrote laws in God's name, and must not be applied to Christ.[2] For although he too appears to have written laws in God's name, we must hold that he perceived things truly and adequately, since he was not so much a prophet as the instrument of God's word. For (as I have shown in Chapter I) God made revelations to mankind through the mind of Christ as he had previously done through angels, i.e. through created voices, visions, and so on. It would therefore be as unreasonable to hold that God adapted his revelations to the beliefs of Christ as to hold that he adapted his earlier revelations to the beliefs of angels, i.e. of created voices and visions, in

---

[1] *E* ii, 3 Sch.
[2] Spinoza always speaks of Christ with the highest respect (cf. *Epp.* lxxiii and lxxv). His view is that while the prophets had vivid imaginations Christ had a perfect mind (*TT-P* i).

prophetis communicaret. Quo quidem nihil absurdius statui posset; praesertim cum non ad solos Judaeos sed totum humanum genus docendum missus fuerit, adeoque non satis erat ut mentem opinionibus Judaeorum tantum accommodatam haberet, sed opinionibus et docu-
5 mentis humano generi universalibus, hoc est, notionibus communibus et veris. Et sane ex hoc, quod Deus Christo sive ejus menti sese immediate revelaverit, et non, ut prophetis, per verba et imagines, nihil aliud intelligere possumus quam quod Christus res revelatas vere percepit, sive intellexit; tum enim res intelligitur cum ipsa pura mente
10 extra verba et imagines percipitur. Christus itaque res revelatas vere et adaequate percepit. Si igitur eas tanquam leges unquam praescripsit, id propter populi ignorantiam et pertinaciam fecit; quare hac in re vicem Dei gessit, quod sese ingenio populi accommodavit. Et ideo, quamvis aliquantulum clarius quam caeteri prophetae locutus sit,
15 obscure tamen, et saepius per parabolas res revelatas docuit, praesertim quando iis loquebatur quibus nondum datum erat intelligere regnum coelorum (vide Matth. Cap. 13 vs. 10 etc.). At sine dubio eos quibus datum erat mysteria coelorum noscere res ut aeternas veritates docuit, non vero ut leges praescripsit; et hac ratione eos a servitute legis
20 liberavit, et nihilominus legem hoc magis confirmavit et stabilivit, eorumque cordibus penitus inscripsit. Quod etiam Paulus quibusdam in locis indicare videtur, nempe Epistol. ad Rom. Cap. 7 vs. 6 et Cap. 3 vs. 28. Attamen nec ille etiam aperte loqui vult, sed, ut ipse ait Cap. 3 vs. 5 et Cap. 6 vs. 19 ejusd. Epist., humano more loquitur: quod
25 expresse dicit cum Deum justum vocat. Et sine dubio etiam propter carnis imbecillitatem Deo misericordiam, gratiam, iram, etc. affingit, et ingenio plebis, sive (ut ipse etiam ait Cap. 3 vs. 1, 2 Epist. 1 ad Corinth.) hominum carnalium sua verba accommodat. Nam Cap. 9 vs. 18 Epist. ad Rom. absolute docet Dei iram ejusque misericordiam
30 non ab humanis operibus, sed a sola Dei vocatione, hoc est voluntate, pendere; deinde quod ex operibus legis nemo fiat justus, sed ex sola fide (vide Ep. ad Rom. Cap. 3 vs. 28), per quam sane nihil aliud

---

17. *I et sine dubio.*

communicating to the prophets what had to be revealed to them. No greater absurdity could be maintained; especially as Christ was sent to teach not only the Jews but the whole human race. Thus it was not enough for him to have a mind attuned to Jewish beliefs alone; his mind had to be attuned to beliefs and precepts common to the human race, i.e. to notions which are universal and true. Indeed, in saying that God revealed himself to Christ or to Christ's mind directly, and not through words and images as he did to the prophets, we can only mean that Christ perceived truly, or understood, what was revealed to him: for a thing is understood when it is grasped by pure thought without the help of words and images. Christ, then, perceived truly and adequately what was revealed to him. In consequence, if he ever commanded these revelations as laws, he did so because of the igno-rance and obstinacy of the people, and thus played God's part in adapting his message to their nature. This is why, although he spoke rather more clearly than the prophets, he still veiled his real meaning, and often used parables to convey what had been revealed to him, especially when addressing those who were not yet capable of understanding the kingdom of heaven (see Matthew, Chapter 13, verses 10 and ff.). But doubtless to those who were capable of understanding the mysteries of heaven he taught things as eternal truths, and did not lay them down as laws; thus freeing them from bondage to the law, and yet, by so doing, confirming and strengthening the law, and planting it deep in their hearts.[1] Paul, indeed, seems to suggest this view in some passages, e.g. Romans, Chapter 7, verse 6 and Chapter 3, verse 28. Yet he too is unwilling to speak openly, but, as he says himself in Chapter 3, verse 5 and Chapter 6, verse 19 of the same Epistle, he speaks after the man-ner of men: and he says this explicitly when he calls God just. No doubt the infirmity of the flesh is also his reason for ascribing such qualities as mercy, grace, and anger to God, and adapting his words to the nature of the masses, or (as he actually says himself in Chapter 3, verses 1 and 2 of the First Epistle to the Corinthians) to the nature of sensual men. For in Romans, Chapter 9, verse 18 he says outright that God's anger and mercy do not depend on human works, but simply on the election of God, i.e. on his will; again (see Romans, Chapter 3, verse 28), that no one becomes just by doing what the law prescribes, but only through faith, by which he obviously means no

---

[1] Cf. n. 34, pp. 247–9. The enlightened man is in a state of freedom, not of bondage. Freedom, however, imposes, and does not remove, the necessity of acting (*TP* ii, 11, p. 275): so he *necessarily* acts as the law prescribes (cf. *Romans* 3, 31).

intelligit quam plenum animi consensum; et denique quod nemo fiat beatus nisi mentem Christi in se habeat (vide Epist. ad Rom. Cap. 8 vs. 9), qua scilicet leges Dei ut aeternas veritates percipiat. Concludimus itaque Deum non nisi ex captu vulgi, et ex solo defectu
5 cogitationis, tanquam legislatorem aut principem describi, et justum, misericordem, etc. vocari; Deumque revera ex solius suae naturae et perfectionis necessitate agere et omnia dirigere; et ejus denique decreta et volitiones aeternas esse veritates, semperque necessitatem involvere: idque est quod primo in loco explicare et ostendere constitueram.

10 Ad secundum igitur transeamus, et Sacram Paginam percurramus, et quid ipsa de lumine naturali et lege hac divina docet videamus. Primum quod nobis occurrit est ipsa primi hominis historia, ubi narratur Deum Adamo praecepisse ne comederet de fructu arboris cognitionis boni et mali; quod significare videtur Deum Adamo praecepisse
15 bonum agere et quaerere sub ratione boni, et non quatenus contrarium est malo, hoc est, ut bonum ex amore boni quaereret, non autem ex timore mali. Qui enim, ut jam ostendimus, bonum agit ex vera boni cognitione et amore, libere et constanti animo agit; qui autem ex timore mali, is malo coactus et serviliter agit, et sub imperio alterius
20 vivit. Atque adeo hoc unicum quod Deus Adamo praecipit totam legem divinam naturalem comprehendit, et cum dictamine luminis naturalis absolute convenit. Nec difficile esset totam istam primi hominis historiam sive parabolam ex hoc fundamento explicare; sed malo id missum facere, cum quia non possum absolute esse certus num
25 mea explicatio cum scriptoris mente conveniat, tum quia plerique non concedunt hanc historiam esse parabolam, sed plane statuunt eam simplicem narrationem esse. Praestabilius erit igitur alia Scripturae loca in medium adferre, illa praesertim quae ab eo dictata sunt qui ex vi luminis naturalis, quo omnes sui aevi sapientes superavit, loquitur, et
30 cujus sententias aeque sancte ac prophetarum amplexus est populus; Salomonem puto, cujus non tam prophetia et pietas quam prudentia et sapientia in Sacris commendatur. Is in suis Proverbiis vocat humanum intellectum verae vitae fontem, et infortunium in sola stultitia constituit. Sic enim ait Cap. 16 vers. 22: *Fons vitae* (est) *intellectus sui*

---

5. The correct reading may be *cognitionis*. Cf. p. 78, ll. 3 and 5.
20. The correct reading may be *praecepit*.   34. *B vers. 22; I vers. 23.*

more than full assent of the mind;[1] and finally (see Romans, Chapter 8, verse 9), that no one becomes blessed unless he has within him the mind of Christ, which, of course, enables him to understand God's laws as eternal truths. I conclude then that the stupidity of the masses, and their failure to think, is the only reason why God is described as a legislator or king, and called just, merciful, and so on; that in fact God acts and directs everything by the necessity of his own nature and perfection alone; and, finally, that his decrees and volitions are eternal truths, and always involve necessity. This was the first point which I proposed to explain and prove.

Let us therefore pass to the second question, and run through the pages of Holy Writ to see what it teaches about the light of nature and this divine law. The first thing we find is the story of the first man, which tells how God commanded Adam not to eat the fruit of the tree of the knowledge of good and evil. This seems to mean that God told Adam to do and pursue good as good, and not as the opposite of evil, i.e. to pursue good from love of good, and not from fear of evil.[2] For, as I have already shown, he who does good from true knowledge and love of good acts with freedom and constancy of purpose; while he who does good from fear of evil acts under compulsion of evil, like a slave, and lives under the control of another.[3] Thus this single command laid by God upon Adam comprehends the whole of the natural divine law, and is in complete agreement with the dictate of the light of nature. Nor would it be difficult to explain the whole story or parable of the first man on this basis; but I prefer to say no more on this topic, not only because I cannot be absolutely certain that my interpretation agrees with the intention of the author, but also because most men refuse to admit that this story is a parable at all, and insist that it is a straightforward record of fact. It will therefore be better to cite other passages of Scripture; in particular, the words of a man who speaks from a power of natural reason unequalled by any sage of his day, and whose sayings have been cherished by the people with as much reverence as those of the prophets. I am thinking of Solomon, who is commended in Holy Writ for his prudence and wisdom rather than for piety and prophetic gifts. In his Proverbs he calls man's understanding a well-spring of true life, and makes misfortune consist in folly alone. Here are his words (Chapter 16, verse 22): 'Understanding (is) a well-spring

[1] Contrast the definition in *TT-P* xiv, p. 115, where faith is linked with obedience.
[2] For another discussion of the Genesis myth see *E* iv, 68 Sch.
[3] *E* iv, 63.

domini,* *et supplicium stultorum est stultitia*; ubi notandum quod per vitam absolute Hebraice vera vita intelligatur, ut patet ex Deut. Cap. 30 vers. 19. Fructum igitur intellectus in sola vera vita constituit, et supplicium in sola ejus privatione; quod quidem absolute convenit cum
5 eo quod IV loco notavimus circa legem divinam naturalem. Quod autem hic fons vitae, sive quod solus intellectus, ut etiam ostendimus, leges sapientibus praescribit, aperte ab eodem hoc sapiente docetur; ait enim Cap. 13 vers. 14, *Lex prudentis* (est) *fons vitae*, id est, ut ex modo allato textu patet, intellectus. Porro Cap. 3 vs. 13 expressissimis verbis
10 docet intellectum hominem beatum et felicem reddere, veramque animi tranquillitatem dare. Sic enim ait: *Beatus homo qui invenit scientiam, et filius hominis qui intelligentiam eruit.* Ratio est (ut vers. 16, 17 pergit) quia *directe dat dierum longitudinem,*† *indirecte divitias et honorem; ejus viae* (quas nimirum scientia indicat) *amoenae sunt, et*
15 *omnes ejus semitae pax.* Soli igitur sapientes ex sententia etiam Salomonis animo pacato et constante vivunt, non ut impii, quorum animus contrariis affectibus fluctuat, adeoque (ut Esaias etiam ait Cap. 57 vs. 20) neque pacem neque quietem habent. Denique in his Salomonis Proverbiis maxime nobis notanda sunt quae habentur in secundo
20 Cap., utpote quae nostram sententiam quam clarissime confirmant. Sic enim vs. 3 ejusd. Cap. incipit: *Nam si prudentiam inclamabis, et intelligentiae dederis vocem tuam etc., tunc timorem Dei intelliges, et Dei scientiam* (vel potius amorem; nam haec duo verbum *Jadah* significat) *invenies. Nam* (N.B.) *Deus dat sapientiam; ex ore suo*
25 (manat) *scientia et prudentia.* Quibus sane verbis clarissime indicat, I. quod sola sapientia sive intellectus nos doceat Deum sapienter timere, hoc est, vera religione colere: deinde docet sapientiam et scientiam ex Dei ore fluere, Deumque illam dare; quod quidem nos etiam supra ostendimus, nempe quod noster intellectus nostraque scientia a sola
30 Dei idea sive cognitione pendeat, oriatur, et perficiatur. Pergit deinde vers. 9 expressissimis verbis docere hanc scientiam veram ethicam et

---

* *Hebraismus. Qui rem aliquam habet, vel in sua natura continet, ejus rei dominus vocatur. Sic avis dominus alarum Hebraice vocatur, quia alas habet; dominus intellectus intelligens, quia intellectum habet.*

† *Hebraismus, nihil aliud significans quam vitam.*

---

18. P *neque pacem*; I *pacem.*

84

of life unto its lord,* and folly is the punishment of fools.' Note here that 'life' unqualified means in the Hebrew 'true life', as is clear from Deuteronomy, Chapter 30, verse 19. He thus makes the fruit of understanding consist simply in true living, and punishment simply in lack of true living; which is in full accord with the fourth point I made about the natural divine law.[1] He also teaches explicitly that this well-spring of life, i.e. that understanding by itself lays down laws for the wise, as I have shown too; for he says in Chapter 13, verse 14 that 'the law of the wise (is) the well-spring of life', i.e. is understanding, as is clear from the text just cited. Again, in Chapter 3, verse 13 he declares in the plainest of terms that understanding makes a man blessed and happy, and gives him true peace of mind: 'Blessed is the man that findeth wisdom, and the son of man that getteth understanding.' The reason is (as he goes on to say in verses 16 and 17) that 'it giveth length of days† directly, and indirectly wealth and honour; its ways (the ways revealed by wisdom) are pleasant, and all its paths are peace'. Solomon then agrees that only the wise have calm and steadfast minds; unlike the wicked, whose minds are agitated by conflicting passions, and who thus (as Isaiah says also in Chapter 57, verse 20) have neither peace nor rest.[2] Finally, none of Solomon's Proverbs are more worthy of our notice than those contained in the second Chapter, since they confirm my view in the clearest possible way. In verse 3 of that Chapter he begins as follows: 'For if thou shalt cry after prudence, and lift up thy voice after understanding . . ., then shalt thou understand the fear of God, and find the knowledge of God' (or rather, 'the love of God', since 'Jadah' means both knowledge and love). '*For God giveth wisdom; out of his mouth (cometh) knowledge and prudence.*' These words in fact make it perfectly clear, first that wisdom or understanding alone teaches us to fear God in wisdom, i.e. to worship him with true piety:[3] secondly, that wisdom and knowledge flow from God's mouth, and that God is the giver thereof. This, of course, is precisely what I have shown above, namely, that our understanding and knowledge depends entirely on our idea or knowledge of God, which is at once its source and its culmination. Next, in verse 9 he goes on to declare in the plainest of terms that this knowledge contains the

---

* Ā Hebrew expression. Anything which possesses something, or contains it in its nature, is called lord of that thing. Thus a bird is called lord of wings in Hebrew, because it possesses wings; an intelligent being lord of understanding, because it possesses understanding.

† A Hebrew expression, which simply means 'life'.

[1] p. 75. [2] *E* iv, 33.

[3] For 'true religion' (as distinct from the 'faith' of *TT-P* xiv) cf. *E* iv, 37 Sch. 1.

politicam continere, et ex ea easdem deduci: *Tunc intelliges justitiam,
et judicium, et rectitudines,* (et) *omnem bonam semitam.* Nec his conten-
tus pergit: *Quando intrabit scientia in cor tuum, et sapientia tibi erit
suavis, tum tua providentia* tibi vigilabit, et prudentia te custodiet.*
5 Quae omnia cum scientia naturali plane conveniunt; haec enim
ethicam docet et veram virtutem, postquam rerum cognitionem acquisi-
vimus et scientiae praestantiam gustavimus. Quare felicitas et tranquillitas ejus qui naturalem intellectum colit ex mente Salomonis etiam
non ab imperio fortunae (hoc est, Dei auxilio externo), sed a sua in-
10 terna virtute (sive Dei auxilio interno) maxime pendet; nempe, quia
vigilando, agendo, et bene consulendo se maxime conservat. Denique,
nequaquam hic praetereundus est locus Pauli qui habetur Cap. 1 vs. 20
Epist. ad Rom., ubi (ut Tremellius vertit ex Syriaco textu) sic ait:
*Occulta enim Dei a fundamentis mundi in creaturis suis per intellectum
15 conspiciuntur, et virtus et divinitas ejus quae est in aeternum, adeo ut
sint sine effugio.* Quibus satis clare indicat unumquemque lumine
naturali clare intelligere Dei virtutem et aeternam divinitatem, ex
qua scire et deducere possunt quid iis quaerendum quidve fugiendum
sit; adeoque concludit omnes sine effugio esse, nec ignorantia excusari
20 posse; quod profecto possent si de lumine supranaturali loqueretur, et
de carnali Christi passione et resurrectione, etc. Et ideo paulo infra vers.
24 sic pergit: *Propter hoc tradidit eos Deus in concupiscentias immundas
cordis eorum, etc.,* usque ad finem Capitis; quibus vitia ignorantiae
describit, eaque tanquam ignorantiae supplicia enarrat: quod plane
25 convenit cum Proverbio illo Salomonis Cap. 16 vers. 22 quod jam
citavimus, nempe, *et supplicium stultorum est stultitia.* Quare non
mirum quod dicat Paulus maleficos esse inexcusabiles. Nam prout
unusquisque seminat, ita metet; ex malis mala necessario sequuntur
nisi sapienter corrigantur, et ex bonis bona si animi constantia comi-
30 tetur. Scriptura itaque lumen et legem divinam naturalem absolute
commendat; atque his quae in hoc Capite agere proposueram absolvi.

---

* Mezima *proprie cogitationem, deliberationem, et vigilantiam significat.*

---

1. *I et ex ea deduci.*   20. *II supranaturali; I supra naturali.*
29–30. *O omits et . . . comitetur.*

---

[2] Spinoza speaks here as if ignorance excused: but it becomes clear below that ignorance
does not excuse men from divine punishments, since these are simply the natural and necessary consequences of the actions performed (see my discussion of n. 34, p. 249). Spinoza's view
of divine punishments is adumbrated by Hobbes in *Leviathan* 31.

true principles of morals and politics as deductions from itself: 'Then shalt thou understand justice, and judgement, and righteous deeds, (yea) every good path.' And not content with this he goes on: 'When knowledge shall enter into thine heart, and wisdom shall be pleasant to thy soul, then shall thy discretion* watch over thee, and thy prudence keep thee.' All this applies perfectly to natural knowledge, which teaches morality and true virtue once we have gained understanding of things and tasted the excellence of wisdom. Thus Solomon agrees that the happiness and peace of the man who cultivates his natural understanding depends mainly on his own inherent virtue (or God's internal aid), and not on the control of fortune (or God's external aid); because by his vigilance, initiative, and wise counsel he largely takes care of himself. Finally, we must certainly notice here the passage in Romans, Chapter 1, verse 20, where (according to Tremellius' rendering from the Syriac text)[1] Paul writes as follows: 'For the invisible things of God have been manifest in his works from the beginning of the world, and are perceived by the light of understanding, even his eternal power and divinity; so that men are without excuse.' Here Paul is showing quite plainly that the light of nature gives all men a clear understanding of God's eternal power and divinity, and that from this they can learn and deduce what they must seek and avoid. He therefore concludes that they are all without excuse, and cannot be pardoned because of ignorance;[2] as they certainly could if he were speaking of a supernatural light, and meant by 'works' things like Christ's passion and resurrection in the flesh. This is why he presently goes on to say in verse 24 that 'God therefore gave them over to the filthy lusts of their hearts', and continues thus for the rest of the Chapter. Here he is describing the vices which follow upon ignorance, and listing them as punishments of ignorance; which is in full accord with the saying of Solomon already quoted (Proverbs, Chapter 16, verse 22)—'and folly is the punishment of fools'. No wonder then that Paul says evil-doers cannot be pardoned. For as each man sows, so shall he reap; evil which is not set right by wisdom leads inevitably to evil, and good, if united with steadfastness of purpose, to good. Thus Scripture entirely confirms the light of nature and the natural divine law; and I have now completed the task of this Chapter.

---

* 'Mezima' in its proper meaning combines the notions of thought, deliberation, and watchfulness.

---

[1] Emmanuel Tremellius, *Novum Testamentum ex syriaco latinum*, [Geneva] 1569. See A. J. Servaas van Rooijen, *La Bibliothèque de Bénédict Spinoza*, 1888, p. 120.

[2] *See opposite page.*

CAPUT V

*De ratione cur caeremoniae institutae fuerint; et de fide
historiarum, nempe qua ratione et quibus ea necessaria sit*

In superiore Capite ostendimus legem divinam quae homines vere
beatos reddit, et veram vitam docet, omnibus esse hominibus univer-
5 salem; imo eam ex humana natura ita deduximus ut ipsa humanae
menti innata et quasi inscripta existimanda sit. Cum autem caeremoniae,
eae saltem quae habentur in Vetere Testamento, Hebraeis tantum
institutae, et eorum imperio ita accommodatae fuerint, ut maxima ex
parte ab universa societate, non autem ab unoquoque exerceri potuerint,
10 certum est eas ad legem divinam non pertinere, adeoque nec etiam ad
beatitudinem et virtutem aliquid facere; sed eas solam Hebraeorum
electionem, hoc est (per ea quae in tertio Cap. ostendimus), solam
corporis temporaneam felicitatem et imperii tranquillitatem respicere,
proptereaque non nisi stante eorum imperio ullius usus esse potuisse.
15 Si eae igitur in Vetere Testamento ad legem Dei referantur, id propterea tantum fuit quia ex revelatione vel ex fundamentis revelatis
institutae fuerunt. Verum quia ratio, tametsi solidissima, apud communes theologos non multum valet, lubet hic haec quae modo ostendimus Scripturae etiam authoritate confirmare; et deinde ad majorem
20 perspicuitatem ostendere qua ratione et quomodo caeremoniae ad imperium Judaeorum stabiliendum et conservandum inserviebant. Esaias
nihil clarius docet quam quod lex divina absolute sumpta significet
illam legem universalem quae in vera vivendi ratione consistit, non
autem caeremonias. Capite enim 1 vs. 10 Propheta gentem suam vocat
25 ad legem divinam ex se audiendam, ex qua prius omnia sacrificiorum
genera secludit et omnia festa, et tandem legem ipsam docet (vide vers.
16, 17), atque his paucis comprehendit, nempe in purificatione animi,
et virtutis sive bonarum actionum usu seu habitu, et denique inopi
auxilium ferendo. Nec minus luculentum testimonium est illud Psalmi
30 40 vers. 7, 9. Hic enim Psaltes Deum alloquitur: *Sacrificium et munus
non voluisti; aures* mihi perfodisti; holocaustum et peccati oblationem*

---

* Est phrasis ad significandum perceptionem.

---

30. Verses 7 and 9 in the Hebrew Bible, but 6 and 8 in the A.V.

88

The reason for the institution of sacred rites. Why and for whom belief in historical narratives is necessary

IN the previous Chapter I showed that the divine law which makes men truly blessed, and teaches them true living, is common to all men; indeed, I derived it from human nature in such a way that it must be regarded as innate in the human mind and, so to speak, engraved upon it. Now sacred rites, or at any rate those in the Old Testament, were ordained for the Jews alone, and so adapted to their political organization that for the most part they could only have been practised by the whole community, and not by single individuals. It clearly follows that they have nothing to do with the divine law, and consequently contribute nothing to blessedness and virtue, but relate only to the election of the Jews, i.e. (according to my conclusions in Chapter III) only to their temporal physical welfare and the peace of their state; and for this reason could only have been useful while that state survived. Thus if they are included in God's law in the Old Testament, it was only because they were based on revelation or on principles revealed therein.[1] However, since rational argument, no matter how cogent, carries little weight with the ordinary run of theologians, I now want to reinforce what I have just proved by adding the authority of Scripture, and then to clarify the point still further by showing why and how sacred rites served to strengthen and preserve the Jewish state. Isaiah teaches in the plainest of terms that the divine law in the strict sense has no reference to sacred rites, but means that universal law which embodies the true principle of living; for when in Chapter 1, verse 10 the Prophet summons his people to hear the divine law from his lips, he begins by excluding from it all kinds of sacrifices and all public celebrations, and only then does he teach the law itself (see verses 16 and 17), summing it up in these few points: purification of heart, the habitual practice of virtue or good actions, and, finally, the relief of the poor and helpless. The evidence of Psalm 40, verses 6 and 8 is equally clear. Here the Psalmist addresses God and says: 'Sacrifice and offering thou hast not desired; ears to hear* thou hast given me; burnt offering and sin

---

* A phrase used to signify understanding.

[1] *TT-P* iv, p. 73.

non petiisti. Tuam voluntatem exequi, mi Deus, volui; nam lex tua est in meis visceribus. Vocat igitur illam tantum legem Dei quae visceribus vel menti inscripta est, et ab ea caeremonias secludit; nam eae ex solo instituto et non ex natura sunt bonae, adeoque neque menti-
5 bus inscriptae. Praeter haec alia adhuc in Scriptura reperiuntur quae idem testantur, sed haec duo attulisse sufficit. Quod autem caeremoniae nihil ad beatitudinem juvent, sed quod tantum imperii temporaneam felicitatem respiciant, etiam ex ipsa Scriptura constat, quae pro caeremoniis nihil nisi corporis commoda et delicias promittit, et pro sola
10 lege divina universali beatitudinem. In quinque enim libris qui Mosis vulgo dicuntur nihil aliud, ut supra diximus, promittitur quam haec temporanea felicitas, nempe honores sive fama, victoriae, divitiae, deliciae, et valetudo. Et quamvis quinque illi libri praeter caeremonias multa moralia contineant, haec tamen in iis non continentur tanquam
15 documenta moralia omnibus hominibus universalia, sed tanquam mandata ad captum et ingenium solius Hebraeae nationis maxime accommodata, et quae adeo etiam solius imperii utilitatem spectant. Ex. gr. Moses non tanquam doctor aut propheta Judaeos docet ne occidant neque furentur, sed haec tanquam legislator et princeps jubet;
20 non enim documenta ratione comprobat, sed jussibus poenam addit, quae pro ingenio uniuscujusque nationis variare potest et debet, ut experientia satis docuit. Sic etiam jussum de non committendo adulterio solius reipublicae et imperii utilitatem respicit; nam si documentum morale docere voluisset, quod non solam reipublicae utilitatem,
25 sed animi tranquillitatem et veram uniuscujusque beatitudinem respiceret, tum non tantum actionem externam, sed et ipsum animi consensum damnaret; ut Christus fecit, qui documenta universalia tantum docuit (vide Matth. Cap. 5 vs. 28). Et hac de causa Christus praemium spirituale, non autem, ut Moses, corporeum promittit. Nam
30 Christus, uti dixi, non ad imperium conservandum et leges instituendum, sed ad solam legem universalem docendum missus fuit. Et hinc facile intelligimus Christum legem Mosis minime abrogavisse, quandoquidem Christus nullas novas leges in rempublicam introducere voluerit, nec aliud magis curaverit quam documenta moralia docere, eaque a
35 legibus reipublicae distinguere, idque maxime propter Pharisaeorum ignorantiam, qui putabant illum beate vivere qui jura reipublicae sive legem Mosis defendebat; cum tamen ipsa, uti diximus, nullam nisi

offering thou hast not sought. To do thy will, O my God, has been my delight; for thy law is within my heart.' He thus confines the term 'law of God' to the law written in his heart or mind, and excludes sacred rites from it; for these are not good by nature, but only by convention, and so are not written in men's minds. There are other passages in Scripture to the same effect, but these two quotations will suffice. Again, that sacred rites make no contribution to blessedness, but aim only at the temporal welfare of the state, is also shown by the actual words of Holy Writ, which promises no reward for the performance of sacred rites but physical goods and pleasures, and promises blessedness only for fulfilment of the universal divine law. For in the five books commonly attributed to Moses the only reward promised is, as I said above,[1] this temporal well-being, i.e. honours or fame, victories, wealth, pleasures, and health. And although these five books contain many moral precepts as well as ceremonial rules, these are not included as moral precepts common to all men, but as commands especially adapted to the understanding and disposition of the Jewish people only, and so aimed at the welfare of their state alone. For instance, Moses does not teach the Jews not to kill or steal as a sage or prophet, but forbids them to do these things as a law-giver and king; for he gives, not precepts backed by rational argument, but commands backed by a penalty, which, as experience has amply shown, can and must vary to suit the temperaments of different peoples. Thus even his prohibition of adultery is aimed at the welfare of the community and state alone; for had he wished to teach a moral precept, aimed not merely at the welfare of the community but at the peace of mind and true blessedness of the individual, he would condemn not only the outward act but also the actual volition; as Christ, who taught nothing but universal moral precepts, did in Matthew, Chapter 5, verse 28. And this is why Christ promises a spiritual, and not, like Moses, a temporal reward. For Christ, as I said, was not sent to preserve the state and establish laws, but to teach only the universal law. From this it is easily seen that Christ in no way abolished the law of Moses, for Christ had no wish to introduce any new laws into the state, his main object being to teach moral precepts and to distinguish them from the civil law. His concern with this was largely due to the ignorance of the Pharisees,[2] who thought that the man who observed the laws of the state, i.e. the law of Moses,[3] lived a blessed life; although the aim of

---

[1] *TT-P* iii, pp. 57–59. [2] *TT-P* xviii, pp. 193–5.
[3] *TT-P* vii, p. 109.

reipublicae rationem habuerit, nec tam ad Hebraeos docendum quam cogendum inserviverit.

. . . .

His puto me meam sententiam Scripturae authoritate confirmavisse. 5 Superest jam ostendere quomodo et qua ratione caeremoniae inserviebant ad imperium Hebraeorum conservandum et stabiliendum; quod quam paucissimis potero ex universalibus fundamentis ostendam. Societas non tantum ad secure ab hostibus vivendum, sed etiam ad multarum rerum compendium faciendum perutilis est, et maxime etiam 10 necessaria; nam, nisi homines invicem operam mutuam dare velint, ipsis et ars et tempus deficeret ad se quoad ejus fieri potest sustentandum et conservandum. Non enim omnes ad omnia aeque apti sunt, nec unusquisque potis esset ad ea comparandum quibus solus maxime indiget. Vires et tempus, inquam, unicuique deficerent, si solus deberet 15 arare, seminare, metere, molere, coquere, texere, suere, et alia perplurima ad vitam sustentandum efficere; ut jam taceam artes et scientias, quae etiam ad perfectionem humanae naturae ejusque beatitudinem sunt summe necessariae. Videmus enim eos qui barbare sine politia vivunt vitam miseram et paene brutalem agere, nec tamen pauca illa, 20 misera et impolita, quae habent, sine mutua opera, qualis qualis ea sit, sibi comparant. Jam si homines a natura ita essent constituti ut nihil nisi id quod vera ratio indicat cuperent, nullis sane legibus indigeret societas, sed absolute sufficeret homines vera documenta moralia docere, ut sponte integro et liberali animo id quod vere utile est 25 agerent. Verum longe aliter cum humana natura constitutum est; omnes quidem suum utile quaerunt, at minime ex sanae rationis dictamine, sed perplurimum ex sola libidine, et animi affectibus abrepti (qui nullam temporis futuri aliarumque rerum rationem habent) res appetunt, utilesque judicant. Hinc fit ut nulla societas possit subsistere 30 absque imperio et vi, et consequenter legibus quae hominum libidinem atque effraenatum impetum moderentur et cohibeant. Non tamen humana natura patitur absolute se cogi, et, ut Seneca tragicus ait,

that law, as I said, was purely political, and its function was to restrain the Jews rather than to instruct them.

. . . .

These quotations, I think, have given scriptural authority for my view. It now remains to show how and why sacred rites served to preserve and strengthen the Jewish state; and this I shall do from general principles as briefly as I can. Society enables men not only to live in security from enemies, but also to achieve prosperity with a minimum of effort. For these purposes it is very useful, and indeed absolutely indispensable, since if men were not prepared to help one another they would lack both the skill and the time to obtain the maximum possible security and comfort; for men are not all equally suited to all employments, and no isolated individual could provide himself with what he needs most for his own survival. An individual, I say, would lack both the strength and the time to plough, sow, reap, grind, cook, weave, sew, and do all the many other tasks necessary to support life, for himself;[1] to say nothing here of cultivating the arts and sciences, which are also absolutely necessary for the perfection and blessedness of human nature. Men who live in barbarous fashion without any political organization live, as we see, a miserable and almost brutish existence, and they cannot provide themselves with even the few commodities which they do possess, wretched and crude though these be, without mutual help of some kind or other. Now if human nature were such that men desired nothing but what true reason prescribes, a society would admittedly need no laws whatsoever;[2] for men to do of their own free will what is really for their benefit it would be quite enough to teach them true moral precepts. But in fact human nature is very different. All men certainly seek their own advantage, but seldom as sound reason dictates; in most cases appetite is their only guide, and in their desires and judgements of what is beneficial they are carried away by their passions, which take no account of the future or anything else. The result is that no society can exist without government and force, and hence without laws to control and restrain the unruly appetites and impulses of men.[3] Yet human nature will not submit to unlimited

---

[1] Plato, *Republic* 369–70.

[2] *TT-P* xvi, p. 131; *TP* vi, 3, p. 315. In Hobbes's phrase (*Leviathan* 17), 'there would be peace without subjection'.

[3] On the need for a sovereign cf. Hobbes, *De Cive* v, 4. But Spinoza thinks that Hobbes neglected the practical limitations placed on the actions of the sovereign by human nature, and laid excessive stress on fear as a motive for political obedience. He elaborates both criticisms in *TT-P* xvii, pp. 149–53.

violenta imperia nemo continuit diu; moderata durant. Quamdiu enim homines ex solo metu agunt, tamdiu id quod maxime nolunt faciunt, nec rationem utilitatis et necessitatis rei agendae tenent, sed id tantum curant, ne capitis aut supplicii rei sint scilicet. Imo non possunt malo 5 aut damno imperatoris, quamvis cum suo magno etiam malo, non tamen laetari, ipsique omnia mala non cupere, et ubi poterunt adferre. Homines deinde nihil minus pati possunt quam suis aequalibus servire et ab iis regi. Denique, nihil difficilius quam libertatem hominibus semel concessam iterum adimere. Ex his sequitur: primo, quod vel tota 10 societas, si fieri potest, collegialiter imperium tenere debet, ut sic omnes sibi et nemo suo aequali servire teneatur; vel, si pauci aut unus solus imperium teneat, is aliquid supra communem humanam naturam habere, vel saltem summis viribus conari debet vulgo id persuadere. Deinde, leges in quocunque imperio ita institui debent ut homines non 15 tam metu quam spe alicujus boni quod maxime cupiunt retineantur; hoc enim modo unusquisque cupide suum officium faciet. Denique, quoniam obedientia in eo consistit, quod aliquis mandata ex sola imperantis authoritate exequatur; hinc sequitur eandem in societate cujus imperium penes omnes est, et leges ex communi consensu 20 sanciuntur, nullum locum habere, et, sive in tali societate leges augeantur vel minuantur, populum nihilominus aeque liberum manere, quia non ex authoritate alterius sed ex proprio suo consensu agit. At contra accidit ubi unus solus imperium absolute tenet; nam omnes ex sola authoritate unius mandata imperii exequuntur, adeoque, nisi 25 ita ab initio educati fuerint ut ab ore imperantis pendeant, difficile is poterit, ubi opus erit, novas leges instituere, et libertatem semel concessam populo adimere.

His sic universaliter consideratis, ad Hebraeorum rempublicam descendamus. Hi cum primum Aegypto exiverunt, nullo alterius 30 nationis jure amplius tenebantur, adeoque iis licebat novas leges ad libitum sancire sive nova jura constituere, et imperium ubicunque

---

4–6. *P non possunt non malo . . . non tantum laetari, ipsique omnia mala cupere; Gf non possunt non malo . . . tamen laetari, ipsique omnia mala cupere; B non possunt malo . . . non tamen laetari, ipsique omnia mala cupere.*
8. *O difficilius; I dificilius.* 29. *O ex Aegypto.*

coercion; indeed, to quote Seneca the tragic poet, 'No one has ever maintained a violent despotism for long; but moderate governments last.'[1] As long as men act from fear alone they act most unwillingly, never thinking of the utility and necessity of what they have to do, but simply seeking to avoid being condemned to death or punishment. Moreover they cannot help rejoicing when their ruler suffers misfortune or loss, even although his setback involves great damage to themselves; they cannot help wishing him every misfortune, and inflicting it upon him when they get the chance. Again, there is nothing men can endure less than to be subject to and ruled by their equals. Finally, there is nothing more difficult than to deprive men of a freedom which has once been allowed them. These facts lead me to the following conclusions. First, either all the members of a society should hold sovereignty as a body, if this is possible, so that they may all be bound to obey themselves, and no one need obey his equal; or else, if sovereignty is held by a few men, or by one only, he should have more than ordinary human ability, or at any rate should do his best to make the masses believe this.[2] Secondly, the laws of every state should be so framed that men are restrained less by fear than by the hope of some good which they greatly desire; this will ensure that everyone does his duty with enthusiasm. Finally, since obedience is the performance of commands for no other reason but the authority of a ruler, it follows that in a society where sovereignty is vested in all, and laws are made by common consent, obedience has no place, and the people remains equally free whether the number of laws is increased or diminished, because it acts by its own decision and not by the authority of another. But the opposite is true when one man holds absolute sovereignty by himself, for everyone carries out the government's commands by his authority alone; so that, unless his subjects have been trained from the start to hang on their ruler's lips, he will find it hard to make new laws when necessary, and to deprive the people of the freedom originally allowed them.[3]

Let us now apply these general considerations to the Jewish state.[4] As soon as the Jews left Egypt they were no longer bound by the laws of any other people, and were thus free to establish new laws or make new ordinances as they pleased, to maintain a state wherever they

---

[1] Seneca, *Troades* 258–9, quoted again in *TT-P* xvi, p. 135.
[2] *TT-P* xvii, pp. 155–7. [3] *TT-P* xviii, p. 199.
[4] For a more detailed account of the institution of the Jewish state see *TT-P* xvii, pp. 157 and ff.

locorum vellent tenere, et quas terras vellent occupare. Attamen ad nihil minus erant apti quam ad jura sapienter constituendum, et imperium penes sese collegialiter retinendum; rudis fere ingenii omnes erant, et misera servitute confecti. Imperium igitur penes unum tan-
5 tum manere debuit, qui caeteris imperaret, eosque vi cogeret, et qui denique leges praescriberet, et imposterum eas interpretaretur. Hoc autem imperium Moses facile retinere potuit, quia divina virtute supra caeteros excellebat, et se eam habere populo persuasit, multisque testimoniis ostendit (vide Exodi Cap. 14 vers. ultimo, et Cap. 19 vers.
10 9): is itaque, virtute qua pollebat divina, jura constituit et populo praescripsit. At in iis summam curam gessit ut populus non tam metu quam sponte suum officium faceret; ad quod haec duo eum maxime cogebant, populi scilicet ingenium contumax (quod sola vi cogi non patitur), et instans bellum: ubi, ut res prospere cedant, milites magis
15 hortari quam poenis et minis territare necesse est; sic enim unusquisque magis studet virtute et magnanimitate animi clarere quam supplicium tantum vitare. Hac igitur de causa Moses virtute et jussu divino religionem in rempublicam introduxit, ut populus non tam ex metu quam devotione suum officium faceret. Deinde eos beneficiis obligavit, et
20 divinitus multa in futurum promisit, nec leges admodum severas sancivit; quod unusquisque qui iis studuit facile nobis concedet, praecipue si ad circumstantias quae ad aliquem reum damnandum requirebantur attenderit. Denique, ut populus, qui sui juris esse non poterat, ab ore imperantis penderet, nihil hominibus scilicet servituti assuetis ad
25 libitum agere concessit; nihil enim populus agere poterat quin simul teneretur legis recordari, et mandata exequi quae a solo imperantis arbitrio pendebant. Non enim ad libitum, sed secundum certum et determinatum jussum legis licebat arare, seminare, metere; item nec aliquid comedere, induere, neque caput et barbam radere, neque laetari,
30 nec absolute aliquid agere licebat nisi secundum jussa et mandata in legibus praescripta. Nec hoc tantum, sed etiam in postibus, manibus, et inter oculos signa quaedam habere tenebantur quae eos semper obedientiam monerent. Hic igitur scopus caeremoniarum fuit, ut homines

---

8. *supra* should perhaps be deleted. Cf. p. 52, l. 14.   31. *sed* not in *O*.

wished, and to occupy any lands they desired. Yet they were utterly incapable of framing laws wisely, and of holding sovereignty collectively; for none of them had much experience, and they were worn out by the miseries of slavery. So the sovereignty had to rest with one man only, with someone capable of commanding the others, of compelling them by force, and, finally, of laying down laws and later interpreting them. Now it was easy for Moses to keep the sovereignty, since he not only excelled the rest in divine power, but was able to give the people many convincing proofs that this was so (see the last verse of Exodus, Chapter 14, and Chapter 19, verse 9): so it was he who—by the divine power which he possessed so abundantly—established and laid down laws for the people. Yet in framing his laws he took great pains to see that the people should do its duty willingly and not through fear, and this for two main reasons: the obstinacy of the Jewish character (which will not submit to constraint by simple force), and the imminence of war. For if war is to be waged successfully soldiers need to be heartened, rather than cowed by penalties and threats; then they will all seek to distinguish themselves by courage and heroism, and not simply to avoid punishment. Thus Moses' purpose in using his divine power and authority to introduce religion into the state was to make the people do its duty through devotion rather than fear. He also bound them by the benefits he achieved for them, and by promises, based on revelation, of many more in the future; nor were his laws very harsh, as anyone who has studied them will readily grant me, especially if he has noted the conditions which had to be fulfilled if a defendant was to be convicted.[1] Finally, to ensure that the people, which could not be its own master, should hang on the lips of its ruler, he did not allow his subjects—who were, of course, accustomed to slavery—to do anything at their own good pleasure; they could do nothing without having at once to recall the law and carry out instructions which depended wholly on the will of their ruler. They were not allowed to plough, sow,[2] or reap[3] as they pleased, but had to follow a fixed and definite legal prescription; similarly, they could not eat,[4] dress,[5] shave their heads or beards,[6] make merry, or do anything whatsoever, except as the law instructed and prescribed. What is more, they were even required to have on their doorposts, hands, and foreheads certain signs to recall them continually to obedience.[7] Thus the object of sacred rites

---

[1] See, for example, *Deuteronomy* 19, 15.
[3] *Leviticus* 19, 9.   [4] *Leviticus* 11.
[6] *Leviticus* 19, 27.

[2] *Deuteronomy* 22, 9–10.
[5] *Deuteronomy* 22, 11–12.
[7] *Deuteronomy* 6, 8–9.

nihil ex proprio decreto, sed omnia ex mandato alterius agerent, et
continuis actionibus et meditationibus faterentur se nihil prorsus sui,
sed omnino alterius juris esse. Ex quibus omnibus luce clarius constat
caeremonias ad beatitudinem nihil facere, et illas Veteris Testamenti,
5 imo totam legem Mosis, nihil aliud quam Hebraeorum imperium, et
consequenter nihil praeter corporis commoda spectavisse. Quod autem
ad Christianorum caeremonias attinet, nempe Baptismum, Coenam
Dominicam, festa, orationes externas, et si quae adhuc aliae quae toti
Christianismo communes sunt, semperque fuerunt—si eae unquam
10 a Christo aut ab Apostolis institutae sunt (quod adhuc mihi non satis
constat)—eae non nisi ut universalis ecclesiae signa externa institutae
sunt, non autem ut res quae ad beatitudinem aliquid faciunt, vel quae
aliquid sanctimoniae in se habeant. Quare, quamvis hae caeremoniae
non ratione imperii, ratione tamen integrae societatis tantum institutae
15 sunt; adeoque ille qui solus vivit iis minime tenetur. Imo, qui in imperio ubi Christiana religio interdicta est vivit, is ab his caeremoniis
abstinere tenetur, et nihilominus poterit beate vivere. Hujus rei exemplum in regno Japonensium habetur, ubi Christiana religio interdicta
est, et Belgae qui ibi habitant ex mandato Societatis Indiae Orientalis
20 ab omni externo cultu abstinere tenentur. Nec hoc alia authoritate
jam confirmare puto; et quamvis non difficile foret hoc ipsum etiam ex
fundamentis Novi Testamenti deducere, et forte claris insuper testimoniis ostendere, haec tamen libentius missa facio, quia ad alia festinat
animus. Pergo itaque ad id de quo secundo loco in hoc Capite agere
25 constitui; scilicet, quibus et qua ratione fides historiarum in Sacris
contentarum necessaria sit. Ut autem hoc lumine naturali investigetur,
sic procedendum videtur.

Si quis hominibus aliquid suadere vel dissuadere vult quod per se
notum non est, is, ut id iidem amplectantur, rem suam ex concessis
30 deducere, eosque experientia vel ratione convincere debet; nempe, ex
rebus quas per sensus experti sunt in natura contingere, vel ex axiomatibus intellectualibus per se notis. At nisi experientia talis sit ut clare et
distincte intelligatur, quamvis hominem convincat, non tamen poterit
ipsa intellectum aeque afficere, ejusque nebulas dissipare, ac cum res

12. The correct reading may be *faciant*.
31–32. *G axiomatibus*; *I axiomatis*.

was that men should never act of their own volition, but always by the command of another, and should continually acknowledge by their thoughts and deeds that they were not their own masters but completely under another's control. From all this it is clearer than noonday that sacred rites make no contribution to blessedness, and that those prescribed in the Old Testament, and indeed the whole law of Moses, were concerned only with the Jewish state, and thus with temporal benefits alone. As for Christian rites like Baptism, the Lord's Supper, festivals, public prayers, and any others that are, and always have been, common to the whole of Christendom—if any others were ever instituted by Christ or his Apostles (and so far I have no sufficient evidence for this)—they were instituted only as outward symbols of a universal church, and not as things which make any contribution to blessedness or have any intrinsic sanctity. Thus although these rites were not established for a political end, their sole purpose was the preservation of a united society; so that the man who lives by himself is not bound by them at all. Indeed, the man who lives in a state where the Christian religion is forbidden is bound to abstain from these rites, and will still be able to live a blessed life. For example, the Christian religion is forbidden in the kingdom of Japan, and the Dutch who live there are bound by order of the East India Company to abstain from all outward forms of Christian worship.[1] I do not propose to cite any other authority for my view at present; and although it would not be hard to show that it follows from the principles of the New Testament as well, and perhaps to confirm it by other striking illustrations, I am content to let the matter rest, the more so since I am in a hurry to proceed to other topics. I pass on, then, to the second question which I proposed to discuss in this Chapter, namely for whom and why belief in the historical narratives contained in Holy Writ is necessary. To investigate this problem by the light of nature we must, I think, proceed as follows.

Anyone who wishes to make men believe or disbelieve anything which is not self-evident must win their assent by deducing his doctrine from common ground, and appealing either to experience or to reason; i.e. either to their sense-experience of what happens in nature or to self-evident intellectual axioms. The appeal to experience may convince a man; but unless the experience is such as to be understood clearly and distinctly, it will not in itself be able to influence his understanding and dispel its doubts as effectively as a deduction of the

[1] *TT-P* xvi, p. 147.

docenda ex solis axiomatibus intellectualibus, hoc est, ex sola virtute intellectus, ejusque in percipiendo ordine, deducitur, praesertim si quaestio de re spirituali, et quae sub sensus nullo modo cadit, sit. Verum quia ad res ex solis notionibus intellectualibus deducendum longa per-
5 ceptionum concatenatio saepissime requiritur, et praeterea etiam summa praecautio, ingenii perspicacitas, et summa continentia, quae omnia raro in hominibus reperiuntur; ideo homines ab experientia doceri malunt quam omnes suas perceptiones ex paucis axiomatibus deducere, et invicem concatenare. Unde sequitur quod, si quis doctri-
10 nam aliquam integram nationem, ne dicam universum humanum genus, docere, et ab omnibus in omnibus intelligi vult, is rem suam sola experientia confirmare tenetur, rationesque suas et rerum docendarum definitiones ad captum plebis, quae maximam humani generis partem componit, maxime accommodare, non autem eas concatenare, neque
15 definitiones prout ad rationes melius concatenandum inserviunt tradere; alias doctis tantum scribet, hoc est, a paucissimis tantum hominibus, si cum reliquis comparentur, poterit intelligi. Cum itaque tota Scriptura in usum integrae nationis prius, et tandem universi humani generis revelata fuerit, necessario ea quae in ipsa continentur ad captum plebis
20 maxime accommodari debuerunt, et sola experientia comprobari. Rem clarius explicemus. Quae Scriptura docere vult quae solam specula-tionem spectant, haec potissimum sunt: nempe dari Deum, sive ens quod omnia fecit et summa sapientia dirigit et sustentat, et quod hominum summam habet curam, nempe eorum qui pie et honeste
25 vivant; reliquos autem multis suppliciis punit et a bonis segregat. Atque haec Scriptura sola experientia comprobat, nempe iis quas narrat historiis; nec ullas harum rerum definitiones tradit, sed omnia verba et rationes captui plebis accommodat. Et quamvis experientia nullam harum rerum claram cognitionem dare possit, nec docere quid Deus
30 sit, et qua ratione res omnes sustentet et dirigat, hominumque curam habeat; potest tamen homines tantum docere et illuminare quantum ad obedientiam et devotionem eorum animis imprimendum sufficit. Atque ex his satis clare constare puto quibus et qua ratione fides historiarum in Sacris contentarum necessaria sit. Ex modo ostensis enim evidentissime

1. *G. axiomatibus*; *I axiomatis.*   2–3. *O si quaestio sit . . . cadit.*
6. *O* omits *summa* before *praecautio.*
25. Perhaps the correct reading is *vivunt.*

doctrine from intellectual axioms alone, i.e. a deduction based on the pure power of understanding and following its order of apprehension;[1] especially if the question is a spiritual one and completely outwith the sphere of the senses. But since to deduce points from intellectual notions alone usually requires a long string of propositions, as well as the greatest caution, insight, and restraint—all of which are rarely met with in human beings—men are content to be taught by experience rather than to deduce all their ideas from a few axioms and link them up one with another. The result is that anyone who wants to teach some doctrine to a whole nation—not to mention the whole human race—and wishes it to be understood in all its details by everyone, must establish it from experience alone, and must largely adapt his arguments and definitions of terms to the understanding of ordinary people,[2] who make up the great majority of the human race. He must not link his arguments in a chain, or define his terms as best enables him to do so; otherwise he will write for the learned only, in other words, only a very small proportion of mankind will be able to understand him. Now since the whole of Scripture was revealed originally for an entire nation, and ultimately for the whole human race, the doctrines it contains had necessarily to be adapted to a very great extent to the understanding of the masses, and established from experience alone. Let me explain the point more clearly. The chief theoretical doctrines which Scripture aims to inculcate are these: that there is a God, or a being who has made all things; that he directs and sustains them with consummate wisdom; and that he takes great care of men, or of men who live piously and righteously—the others he chastises with many punishments and separates from the good.[3] These doctrines Scripture establishes from experience alone, i.e. from the historical narratives which it provides; it gives no definitions of the terms employed, but adapts all its expressions and arguments to the understanding of the masses. Now although experience cannot give men clear knowledge of these things, or teach what God is,[4] or how he sustains and directs everything, and takes care of men, it can nevertheless teach and enlighten them sufficiently to inspire them to obedience and devotion. This, I think, shows clearly enough for whom and why belief in the narratives contained in Holy Writ is necessary; for what I have just shown obviously leads to the following conclusions. First,

[1] *DIE*, parr. 19–29.　　　　　　　　　　　　　　[2] *TT-P* iv, p. 81.
[3] For a detailed account see *TT-P* xiv, pp. 119–21.
[4] *TT-P* xiv, p. 121.

sequitur earum notitiam et fidem vulgo, cujus ingenium ad res
clare et distincte percipiendum non valet, summe esse necessariam:
deinde, eum qui eas negat quia non credit Deum esse, neque eum rebus
et hominibus providere, impium esse; qui autem eas ignorat, et
5 nihilominus lumine naturali novit Deum esse, et quae porro diximus,
et deinde veram vivendi rationem habet, beatum omnino esse, imo
vulgo beatiorem, quia praeter veras opiniones clarum insuper et di-
stinctum habet conceptum. Denique sequitur eum qui has historias
Scripturae ignorat, nec lumine naturali aliquid novit, si non impium
10 sive contumacem, inhumanum tamen esse et paene brutum, nec ullum
Dei donum habere. Verum hic notandum nos, cum dicimus notitiam
historiarum vulgo summe esse necessariam, non intelligere notitiam
omnium prorsus historiarum quae in Sacris Literis continentur, sed
tantum earum quae praecipuae sunt, et quae solae sine reliquis doctri-
15 nam quam modo diximus evidentius ostendunt, hominumque animos
maxime movere possunt. Nam si omnes Scripturae historiae necessariae essent ad ejus doctrinam probandam, nec conclusio elici posset
nisi ex universali consideratione omnium prorsus historiarum quae in
ipsa continentur, tum sane ejus doctrinae demonstratio et conclusio non
20 tantum plebis, sed absolute humanum captum et vires superaret. Quis
enim ad tam magnum numerum historiarum simul attendere posset, et
ad tot circumstantias et partes doctrinae quae ex tot tamque diversis
historiis deberet elici? Ego saltem mihi non possum persuadere quod
homines illi, qui nobis Scripturam prout eam habemus reliquerunt,
25 tanto ingenio abundaverint ut talem demonstrationem investigare
potuerint; et multo minus quod doctrina Scripturae non posset intelligi
nisi auditis litibus Isaaci, Achitophelis consiliis Absolomo datis, et bello
civili Judaeorum et Israëlitarum, et aliis ad hunc modum chronicis;
aut quod primis Judaeis qui tempore Mosis vixerunt ipsa doctrina
30 ex historiis non aeque facile demonstrari potuerit ac iis qui tempore
Hesdrae vixerunt. Sed de his fusius in sequentibus. Vulgus itaque eas
tantum historias quae maxime eorum animos ad obedientiam et devotionem movere possunt scire tenetur. At ipsum vulgus non satis aptum
est ad faciendum de iis judicium, utpote quod magis narrationibus

knowledge of them and belief in them are quite indispensable for the masses, whose minds are incapable of perceiving things clearly and distinctly. Secondly, the man who rejects them because he does not believe that God exists, or that he takes care of things and men, is impious; whereas the man who has no knowledge of them, but knows by the light of nature that God exists and takes care of his creatures, and who also follows the true way of life, is wholly blessed—yes, more blessed than the masses, since he has a clear and distinct understanding as well as true beliefs. Lastly, the man who is ignorant of these scriptural stories, and knows nothing by the light of nature, may not be impious or obstinate, but he is inhuman and little more than a brute, and has none of God's gifts. There is, however, one point to be noted here. When I say that a knowledge of historical narratives is quite indispensable for the masses, I do not mean a knowledge of absolutely all the stories contained in Holy Writ, but only of the most important, i.e. of those which are sufficient by themselves to bring out clearly the doctrines which I have just stated, and to have a powerful influence on men's minds. For if all the stories in Scripture were needed to establish its teaching, and no conclusion could be drawn except from a full consideration of absolutely all the stories it contains, it would of course be quite beyond the intellectual powers of any human being, and not only of the masses, to establish its teaching with finality. For who could attend to so many stories at once, and to all the contexts and parts of a doctrine which had to be elicited from so many diverse narratives? I at any rate cannot believe that the men who left us Scripture in its present form were endowed with the great ability required to make any such investigation; still less do I believe that it would be impossible to understand the teaching of Scripture without having heard of the quarrels of Isaac,[1] the advice given to Absalom by Ahithophel,[2] the civil war between the men of Judah and of Israel,[3] and other chronicles of the kind; or that its true teaching could not have been demonstrated from historical narratives to the original Jews, the contemporaries of Moses, as easily as to their descendants in the time of Ezra.[4] But I shall discuss this more fully later. The masses, then, need know only the stories which can best inspire them to obedience and devotion. But the masses are not wise enough themselves to judge which these are, since they take more pleasure in the stories, and

---

[1] *Genesis* 26, 20 and ff.   [2] *2 Samuel* 16, 21 and ff.   [3] *TT-P* xviii, pp. 195–7 and nn.

[4] Who is supposed by Spinoza to have collected and revised the historical books of the Old Testament (*TT-P* viii).

et rerum singulari et inexpectato eventu quam ipsa historiarum doctrina delectatur: atque hac de causa praeter lectionem historiarum pastoribus sive ecclesiae ministris insuper indiget, qui ipsum pro imbecillitate ejus ingenii doceant. Attamen ne a nostro proposito divage-
5 mur, sed id quod praecipue intendebamus ostendere concludamus, nempe fidem historiarum, quaecunque demum eae sint, ad legem divinam non pertinere, nec homines per se beatos reddere, neque ullam utilitatem nisi ratione doctrinae habere; qua sola ratione aliae historiae aliis praestantiores possunt esse. Narrationes igitur in Vetere et Novo
10 Testamento contentae reliquis profanis, et ipsae etiam inter se unae aliis praestantiores sunt, pro ratione salutarium opinionum quae ex iis sequuntur. Quare si quis historias S. Scripturae legerit, eique in omnibus fidem habuerit, nec tamen ad doctrinam quam ipsa iisdem docere intendit attenderit, nec vitam emendaverit, perinde ipsi est ac si
15 Alcoranum, aut poëtarum fabulas scenicas, aut saltem communia chronica ea attentione qua vulgus solet legisset; et contra, uti diximus, is qui eas plane ignorat, et nihilominus salutares habet opiniones veramque vivendi rationem, is absolute beatus est et revera Christi spiritum in se habet. At Judaei contra plane sentiunt; statuunt enim veras opiniones
20 veramque vivendi rationem nihil prodesse ad beatitudinem quamdiu homines eas ex solo lumine naturali amplectuntur, et non ut documenta Mosi prophetice revelata. Hoc enim Maimonides Cap. 8 Regum Lege 11 aperte his verbis audet affirmare: *Omnis qui ad se suscipit septem praecepta,** *et ea diligenter exequutus fuerit, is ex piis*
25 *nationum est, et haeres futuri mundi; videlicet si ipsa susceperit et exequutus fuerit propterea quod Deus ea in lege praeceperit, et quod nobis per Mosen revelaverit quod filiis Noae eadem antea praecepta fuerunt. Sed si ea a ratione ductus exequutus fuerit, hic non est incola, nec ex piis, nec ex scientibus nationum.* Haec sunt verba Maimonidis. Quibus R. Joseph,
30 filius Shem Tob, in suo libro quem vocat Kebod Elohim, seu Gloriam

---

* N.B. Judaeos putare Deum Noae septem praecepta dedisse, et iis solis omnes nationes teneri; Hebraeae autem soli alia perplurima praeterea dedisse, ut eam beatiorem reliquis faceret.

in the curious and unexpected issue of events, than in the actual moral they convey: so that they need pastors or ministers of the church to supplement their reading by giving them instruction suited to their feeble understanding. However, let me not wander from my point, but state the conclusion which it was my main object to prove, namely that belief in historical narratives of any kind whatsoever has nothing to do with the divine law, that it cannot make men blessed by itself, and that its only value lies in the lesson conveyed. On this score alone can some stories be better than others. Thus the narratives contained in the Old and New Testaments are better than secular history, and some of these sacred stories are better than others, in so far as they inspire more salutary beliefs. It follows that anyone who has read the stories in Holy Writ, and placed complete credence in their truth, but has not paid attention to the lesson they are designed to convey, or mended his ways, might as well have read the Koran, or poetic dramas, or at any rate ordinary history with the usual attention given by the masses; whereas, as I said, he who is completely ignorant of them, but has salutary beliefs and a true principle of life, is wholly blessed and has in truth the spirit of Christ in his heart. The Jews, however, take quite a different view. They maintain that true beliefs and a true principle of life make no contribution to blessedness as long as men embrace them by the light of nature alone, and not as precepts revealed to Moses by prophetic insight. In Chapter 8 of Kings, Law 11, Maimonides goes so far as to affirm this openly. 'Everyone who accepts the seven commandments,* and has followed them scrupulously, is among the pious of the Gentiles and an heir of the world to come; if, that is, he has accepted and followed them because God prescribed them in the law, and revealed to us through Moses that the same were formerly laid on the sons of Noah. But if he has been led by reason to follow them he has no place among us, and is not one of the pious among the Gentiles, or one of their wise men.'[1] Such are the words of Maimonides. In his book called *Kebod Elohim* (The Glory of God) Rabbi Joseph, the son of Shem Tob,[2] adds the following: that although

---

* N.B. The Jews believe that God gave seven commandments to Noah, and that these alone are binding on all peoples; but that to the Jews he gave many others besides, so as to make them more blessed than the rest.

---

[1] The passage is from the last book of the *Mishneh Torah*. But the text followed by Spinoza is corrupt: the true text gives '*but* one of their wise men'.

[2] A learned Spanish Jew of the fifteenth century. Though a keen student of Aristotle's *Ethics*, on which he wrote a commentary, he held that only observance of the *Torah* could confer immortality.

Dei, addit quod quamvis Aristoteles (quem summam ethicam scripsisse putat, et supra omnes aestimat) nihil eorum quae ad veram ethicam spectant, et quae etiam in sua Ethica amplexus est, omisisset, sed omnia diligenter exequutus fuisset, hoc tamen ipsi ad salutem prodesse non potuit, quia ea quae docet non amplexus est ut documenta divina prophetice revelata, sed ex solo dictamine rationis. Verum haec omnia mera esse figmenta, et nullis rationibus neque Scripturae authoritate suffulta, unicuique haec attente legenti satis constare existimo; quare ad eandem rem refutandum ipsam recensuisse sufficit. Nec etiam eorum sententiam hic refutare in animo est, qui nimirum statuunt lumen naturale nihil sani de iis quae ad veram salutem spectant docere posse. Hoc enim ipsi qui nullam sanam rationem sibi concedunt, nulla etiam ratione probare possunt; et si aliquid supra rationem se habere venditant, id merum est figmentum, et longe infra rationem; quod jam satis eorum communis vivendi modus indicavit. Sed de his non est opus apertius loqui. Hoc tantum addam, nos neminem nisi ex operibus cognoscere posse; qui itaque his fructibus abundaverit, scilicet charitate, gaudio, pace, longanimitate, benignitate, bonitate, fide, mansuetudine, et continentia, adversus quos (ut Paulus in Epistola ad Galatas Cap. 5 vs. 23 ait) lex non est posita, is, sive ex sola ratione, sive ex sola Scriptura edoctus sit, a Deo revera edoctus est, et omnino beatus. His itaque omnia quae circa legem divinam agere constitueram absolvi.

---

20. *B vers. 23; I vs. 22.*

Chapter V

Aristotle (who in his opinion wrote the finest work on ethics, and was the greatest of moral philosophers) had neglected none of the precepts of true morality which he included in his Ethics, but had scrupulously observed them all, this could make no contribution to his salvation, since he did not regard them as divine precepts revealed by prophecy, but accepted them on the authority of reason alone. But all this is pure invention, supported neither by rational arguments nor by scriptural authority, as is, I think, clear enough to anyone who reads it with care; so that the mere statement of the view is a sufficient refutation of it. Nor need I here refute the view that the light of nature can give no sound guidance about the means to true salvation. This is a view which those who deny themselves all ability to reason soundly have no rational ability to prove; and if they boast of having some supra-rational faculty, it is a mere figment, and far inferior to reason, as their usual manner of living has already shown clearly enough.[1] But of them there is no need to speak more openly. I shall merely add that we can know men only from their works; so that if a man is rich in such fruits of the spirit as love, joy, peace, long-suffering, kindness, goodness, faithfulness, meekness, and temperance, against which there is no law (as Paul says in the Epistle to the Galatians, Chapter 5, verse 23), then, whether he has been taught solely by reason or solely by Scripture, he has in truth been taught by God, and is wholly blessed. I have now dealt with all the questions I proposed to discuss in connexion with the divine law.

[1] The great rationalist will naturally have no truck with the doctrine that human reason is depraved (cf. p. 235, n. 1). According to Gebhardt, the objects of his present attack are the Counter-Remonstrant theologians. See *TT-P* xx, p. 241 and nn.

CAPUT VII

De interpretatione Scripturae

. . . .

Et ne quis exemplo pontificis Hebraeorum deceptus putet religionem catholicam etiam indigere pontifice, venit notandum quod leges Mosis,
5 quia publica jura patriae erant, indigebant necessario, ut conservarentur, authoritate quadam publica; si enim unusquisque libertatem haberet jura publica ex suo arbitrio interpretandi, nulla respublica subsistere posset, sed hoc ipso statim dissolveretur, et jus publicum jus esset privatum. At religionis longe alia est ratio. Nam quandoquidem ipsa
10 non tam in actionibus externis quam in animi simplicitate et veracitate consistit, nullius juris neque authoritatis publicae est. Animi enim simplicitas et veracitas non imperio legum neque authoritate publica hominibus infunditur, et absolute nemo vi aut legibus potest cogi ut fiat beatus; sed ad hoc requiritur pia et fraterna monitio, bona educatio,
15 et supra omnia proprium et liberum judicium. Cum igitur summum jus libere sentiendi, etiam de religione, penes unumquemque sit, nec possit concipi aliquem hoc jure decedere posse, erit ergo etiam penes unumquemque summum jus summaque authoritas de religione libere judicandi, et consequenter eandem sibi explicandi et interpretandi;
20 nam nulla alia de causa summa authoritas leges interpretandi, et summum de rebus publicis judicium, penes magistratum est, quam quia publici juris sunt; adeoque eadem de causa summa authoritas religionem explicandi et de eadem judicandi penes unumquemque erit, scilicet quia uniuscujusque juris est. Longe igitur abest ut ex authoritate
25 pontificis Hebraeorum ad leges patriae interpretandum posset concludi Romani pontificis authoritas ad interpretandam religionem; cum contra hanc unumquemque maxime habere facilius ex illa concludatur.

. . . .

CHAPTER VII (in part)

The interpretation of Scripture

. . . .

AND lest anyone be misled by the example of the Jewish high priest into thinking that the universal religion[1] also requires a high priest, I must point out that since the laws of Moses were the civil laws of his country[2] they necessarily required some civil authority to maintain them. For if everyone were free to interpret civil laws as he pleased, no state could survive;[3] this alone would immediately disrupt any state, and turn public right into private. But with religion[4] the case is entirely different. For since it consists more in simplicity and integrity of spirit than in outward acts, it is not subject to any control by public authority. Simplicity and integrity of spirit are not inspired in men by the command of laws or by public authority, and it is quite impossible to make anyone blessed by force or legal enactments; the means required are pious and brotherly counsel, a good upbringing, and, above all, a judgement that is free and independent. Thus since everyone has a perfect right to think freely, even about religion, and cannot conceivably surrender this right, everyone will also have a perfect right and authority to judge freely about religion, and hence to explain and interpret it for himself. The only reason why the magistrate has supreme authority to interpret laws and take final decisions about public affairs is that these are matters of public right; so for a similar reason everyone will possess supreme authority to explain religion and judge of it for himself, i.e. because it is a matter of individual right. Thus it is quite impossible to argue from the Jewish high priest's authority to interpret the laws of his country to the Pope's authority to interpret religion; on the contrary, it is easier to conclude from it that the authority to interpret religion rests entirely with the individual.

. . . .

---

[1] *T T-P* xiv, pp. 119 and ff.   [2] *T T-P* xvii, p. 159.
[3] *TP* iii, 4, p. 287.
[4] Spinoza is speaking of 'inward religion': the control of 'outward religion' is vested in the sovereign (*T T-P* xix, pp. 211 and ff.).

CAPUT XIV

Quid sit fides; quinam fideles; fidei fundamenta
determinantur, et ipsa a philosophia tandem
separatur

AD veram fidei cognitionem apprime necessarium esse scire quod
5 Scriptura accommodata sit non tantum captui prophetarum, sed etiam
varii et inconstantis Judaeorum vulgi, nemo qui vel leviter attendit
ignorare potest. Qui enim omnia quae in Scriptura habentur promiscue
amplectitur tanquam universalem et absolutam de Deo doctrinam, nec
accurate cognovit quidnam captui vulgi accommodatum sit, non
10 poterit vulgi opiniones cum divina doctrina non confundere, et hominum commenta et placita pro divinis documentis non venditare,
Scripturaeque authoritate non abuti. Quis, inquam, non videt hanc
maximam esse causam cur sectarii tot tamque contrarias opiniones
tanquam fidei documenta doceant, multisque Scripturae exemplis con-
15 firment, unde apud Belgas dudum in usum proverbii abierit *geen ketter*
sonder letter? Libri namque sacri non ab uno solo, nec unius aetatis
vulgo scripti fuerunt, sed a plurimis diversi ingenii diversique aevi
viris; quorum si omnium tempus computare velimus, fere bis mille
annorum et forte multo longius invenietur. Sectarios tamen istos
20 nolumus ea de causa impietatis accusare, quod scilicet verba Scripturae
suis opinionibus accommodant; sicuti enim olim ipsa captui vulgi
accommodata fuit, sic etiam unicuique eandem suis opinionibus accommodare licet, si videt se ea ratione Deo in iis quae justitiam et
charitatem spectant pleniore animi consensu obedire posse. Sed ideo
25 eosdem accusamus quod hanc eandem libertatem reliquis nolunt concedere, sed omnes qui cum iisdem non sentiunt, quanquam honestis-
simi et verae virtuti obtemperantes sint, tanquam Dei hostes tamen
persequuntur; et contra, eos qui iis assentantur, quamvis impotentissimi
animi sint, tamen tanquam Dei electos diligunt: quo nihil profecto
30 scelestius et reipublicae magis perniciosum excogitari potest. Ut igitur
constet quousque ratione fidei uniuscujusque libertas sentiendi quae

CHAPTER XIV (in part)

What faith is. Who the faithful are. The basis of faith is determined, and faith itself finally distinguished from philosophy

To reach a true conception of faith it is above all necessary to realize that Scripture was adapted not only to the understanding of the prophets,[1] but also to that of the fickle and inconstant Jewish people;[2] as no one who pays even the slightest attention can fail to see. For he who accepts everything in Scripture indiscriminately as the universal and ultimate teaching about God, and does not know precisely what has been adapted to the understanding of the masses, will inevitably confound their opinions with the divine teaching, hail the arbitrary inventions of men as the precepts of God, and misuse the authority of Scripture. Who, I ask, can fail to see that this is the main reason why the sectaries teach so many contradictory opinions as articles of faith, and can confirm them with so many scriptural illustrations? Or that this is why 'No heretic without a text' has long since become proverbial among the Dutch? The fact is that the sacred books were not written by one man only, or for the common people of a single age, but by many men of different temperaments and periods; so that if we calculate the time covered by them all we shall find that it amounts to nearly two thousand years and perhaps much longer. Not that I wish to charge the wretched sectaries with impiety for adapting the words of Scripture to their own opinions; for since Scripture was originally adapted to the understanding of the masses, everyone is free to adapt it to his own opinions if he sees that he can thereby obey God with greater conviction in matters of justice and charity. The reason why I accuse them is that they refuse to allow this same liberty to others, and persecute everyone who disagrees with them, no matter how righteous and steadfast in true virtue he may be, as an enemy of God; while those who agree with them, no matter how lacking in character, they cherish as God's elect. A course more wicked and more disastrous for the state it is quite impossible to imagine. In order to show, then, how far everyone's freedom to think what he pleases extends in matters

---

[1] In *TT-P* ii Spinoza argues that God adapted his revelations to the understanding and opinions of the prophets, who were often ignorant of scientific facts.

[2] *TT-P* iv, p. 81, and v, p. 101.

vult se extendit, et quosnam, quamvis diversa sentientes, tanquam fideles tamen aspicere tenemur, fides ejusque fundamentalia determinanda sunt: quod quidem in hoc Capite facere constitui, simulque fidem a philosophia separare, quod totius operis praecipuum intentum fuit.

5 Ut haec igitur ordine ostendam, summum totius Scripturae intentum repetamus; id enim nobis veram normam fidei determinandae indicabit. Diximus in superiori Capite intentum Scripturae esse tantum obedientiam docere: quod quidem nemo inficias ire potest. Quis enim non videt utrumque Testamentum nihil esse praeter obedientiae disci-

10 plinam, nec aliud utrumque intendere quam quod homines ex vero animo obtemperent? Nam, ut jam omittam quae in superiori Capite ostendi, Moses non studuit Israëlitas ratione convincere, sed pacto, juramentis, et beneficiis obligare; deinde populo legibus obtemperare sub poena interminatus est, et praemiis eundem ad id hortatur: quae

15 omnia media non ad scientiam, sed ad solam obedientiam sunt. Euangelica autem doctrina nihil praeter simplicem fidem continet; nempe Deo credere eumque revereri, sive, quod idem est, Deo obedire. Non opus igitur habeo ad rem manifestissimam demonstrandam textus Scripturae qui obedientiam commendant, et quorum perplures in utroque Testa-

20 mento reperiuntur, coacervare. Deinde, quidnam unusquisque exequi debeat ut Deo obsequatur, ipsa etiam Scriptura plurimis in locis quam clarissime docet; nempe totam legem in hoc solo consistere, in amore scilicet erga proximum. Quare nemo etiam negare potest quod is qui ex Dei mandato proximum tanquam se ipsum diligit revera est obediens,

25 et secundum legem beatus; et qui contra odio habet, vel negligit, rebellis est et contumax. Denique, apud omnes in confesso est Scripturam non solis peritis, sed omnibus cujuscunque aetatis et generis hominibus scriptam et vulgatam fuisse; atque ex his solis evidentissime sequitur nos ex Scripturae jussu nihil aliud teneri credere quam id quod ad hoc

30 mandatum exequendum absolute necessarium sit. Quare hoc ipsum mandatum unica est totius fidei catholicae norma, et per id solum omnia fidei dogmata, quae scilicet unusquisque amplecti tenetur, determinanda sunt. Quod cum manifestissimum sit, et quod ex hoc solo fundamento vel sola ratione omnia legitime possunt deduci, judicet

35 unusquisque quî fieri potuit ut tot dissensiones in ecclesia ortae sint, et

10. *P quam ut.*
15. *I scientias.*

14. *V–L hortatus.*
33. *P et quia.*

of faith, and which men—in spite of the diversity of their opinions—we must regard as the faithful, I have to define faith and determine its basis. The purpose of the present Chapter is to do this, and at the same time to distinguish between faith and philosophy, which is the main object of the whole work.

Let us proceed methodically by recalling at the outset the chief object of Scripture as a whole; for that will give us the true touchstone of faith. I said in the previous Chapter that the object of Scripture was simply to inculcate obedience. Now this no one can deny; for who can fail to see that both Testaments are simply a training in obedience, and that the sole object of both is to inspire men to sincere devotion? I need not repeat now what I have proved in the previous Chapter; but Moses, for instance, did not seek to convince the children of Israel by reason, but to bind them by a covenant, by oaths, and by gratitude for services; besides, he threatened the people with penalties for disobeying his laws, and held out rewards to encourage it to observe them.[1] All these devices are means of inculcating obedience only, and not knowledge. Moreover the Gospel teaches men nothing but simple faith, that is, to believe in God and worship him, in other words, to obey him. I have therefore no need to muster the texts of Scripture which commend obedience, and which occur in abundance in both Testaments, to prove such an obvious point. Secondly, Scripture also shows very clearly in many passages what everyone must do in order to obey God; it teaches that the whole law is contained in love of one's neighbour alone. Hence no one can deny either that he who loves his neighbour as himself in accordance with God's commandment is truly obedient, and blessed according to the law; and that he who hates or disregards him is rebellious and disobedient. Finally, it is universally admitted that Scripture was not written and propagated for the learned only, but for all mankind, irrespective of age or race;[2] and from this alone it obviously follows that Scripture does not require us to believe anything more than is absolutely necessary for the performance of its chief commandment. Hence this commandment is in itself the one and only criterion of the whole catholic creed, and the sole canon for determining all the dogmas of faith which everyone is bound to accept. Since this is abundantly clear, and since men can legitimately deduce all these dogmas from this single basis merely by using their reason, let everyone judge for himself whether the many disputes that have arisen

---

[1] *TT-P* v, p. 91.

[2] In *TT-P* iv, p. 81, Spinoza has said that Christ was sent to teach the whole human race.

an aliae potuerint esse causae quam quae in initio Cap. VII dictae
sunt. Eae itaque ipsae me cogunt hic ostendere modum et rationem
determinandi ex hoc invento fundamento fidei dogmata. Nam ni hoc
fecero remque certis regulis determinavero, merito credar me huc
5 usque parum promovisse, quandoquidem unusquisque quicquid velit
sub hoc etiam praetextu, quod scilicet medium necessarium sit ad
obedientiam, introducere poterit; praesertim quando de divinis attri-
butis fuerit quaestio.

Ut itaque rem totam ordine ostendam, a fidei definitione incipiam,
10 quae ex hoc dato fundamento sic definiri debet; nempe, quod nihil
aliud sit quam de Deo talia sentire quibus ignoratis tollitur erga Deum
obedientia, et hac obedientia posita necessario ponuntur. Quae definitio
adeo clara est, et adeo manifeste ex modo demonstratis sequitur, ut
nulla explicatione indigeat. Quae autem ex eadem sequuntur paucis
15 jam ostendam. Videlicet, I. Fidem non per se, sed tantum ratione
obedientiae salutiferam esse, vel, ut ait Jacob. Cap. 2 vs. 17, fidem per
se absque operibus mortuam esse: qua de re vide totum hujus Apostoli
praedictum Caput. II. Sequitur quod is qui vere est obediens necessario
veram et salutiferam habet fidem; obedientia enim posita, et fidem
20 necessario poni diximus. Quod etiam idem Apostolus Cap. 2 vs. 18
expresse ait, nempe his: *Ostende mihi fidem tuam absque operibus, et
ego ostendam tibi ex operibus meis fidem meam.* Et Johannes in Epist. 1
Cap. 4 vers. 7, 8: *Quisquis diligit* (scilicet proximum) *ex Deo natus est,
et novit Deum; qui non diligit, non novit Deum; nam Deus est charitas.* Ex
25 quibus iterum sequitur nos neminem judicare posse fidelem aut in-
fidelem esse nisi ex operibus; nempe, si opera bona sunt, quamvis
dogmatibus ab aliis fidelibus dissentiat, fidelis tamen est; et contra, si
mala sunt, quamvis verbis conveniat, infidelis tamen est. Obedientia
enim posita fides necessario ponitur, et fides absque operibus mortua est.
30 Quod etiam idem Johannes vers. 13 ejusdem Cap. expresse docet. *Per
hoc,* inquit, *cognoscimus quod in eo manemus, et ipse manet in nobis, quod
de spiritu suo dedit nobis,* nempe charitatem. Dixerat enim antea Deum
esse charitatem; unde (ex suis scilicet tum receptis principiis) concludit
eum revera spiritum Dei habere qui charitatem habet. Imo, quia nemo

12. *P et quae hac obedientia posita* etc. But cf. p. 146, ll. 15–17.

in the church can have had any other causes than those stated at the start of Chapter VII.[1] It is precisely these disputes which compel me to explain now the rational method of deriving the dogmas of faith from the basis I have discovered. For unless I do this, and specify definite rules for proceeding, it will justly be thought that I have so far made little headway, since everyone will still be able to introduce any dogma he pleases on the pretext that it is a necessary means to obedience; especially when the point at issue concerns the divine attributes.

To explain the whole matter in an orderly way I shall begin with the definition of faith; which on the basis given must be formulated thus. Faith is simply those beliefs about God without which obedience to him cannot exist, and which necessarily exist when this obedience exists.[2] This definition is so clear, and follows so obviously from what I have just shown, that it needs no explanation. Its corollaries, however, I shall now briefly set out. I. Faith is not a means to salvation in itself, but only because of the obedience it involves; or, as James says in Chapter 2, verse 17, faith by itself, without works, is dead. On this point see the whole of the Chapter cited. II. The man who is truly obedient necessarily possesses a true and saving faith; for, as I said, where obedience exists faith necessarily exists as well. This indeed is expressly taught by the same Apostle in Chapter 2, verse 18: 'Show me thy faith without works, and I by my works shall show thee my faith.' So too John in Epistle 1, Chapter 4, verses 7 and 8: 'Everyone that loveth (i.e. loveth his neighbour) is begotten of God, and knoweth God; he that loveth not, knoweth not God; for God is love.' From which it follows in turn that we cannot judge anyone a believer or an unbeliever except by his works. If his works are good, then, even although he may disagree with other believers on questions of dogma, he is still a believer, while if his works are evil he is an unbeliever, even although he may agree verbally with the others; for where obedience exists faith necessarily exists, and faith without works is dead. This, in fact, is expressly taught by the same Apostle in verse 13 of the Chapter cited. 'Hereby', he says, 'we learn that we abide in him, and he in us, because he hath given us of his spirit';[3] and by 'his spirit' he means love. For he has said above that God is love; and from this (i.e. from the premise which he there accepted as his own) he concludes that the man who has love has in truth the spirit of God. Nay more,

---

[1] Ambition and superstition.
[2] For the form of the definition cf. *E* ii, Def. 2, and 10 Cor. Sch.
[3] This quotation also appears on the title-page.

Deum vidit, inde concludit neminem Deum sentire vel animadvertere nisi ex sola charitate erga proximum, atque adeo neminem etiam aliud Dei attributum noscere posse praeter hanc charitatem, quatenus de eadem participamus. Quae quidem rationes, si non peremtoriae sunt,
5 satis tamen clare Johannis mentem explicant; sed longe clarius quae habentur Cap. 2 vers. 3, 4 ejusdem Epist., ubi expressissimis verbis id quod hic volumus docet. *Et per hoc,* inquit, *scimus quod ipsum novimus, si praecepta ipsius observamus. Qui dicit 'Novi eum,' et praecepta ejus non observat, mendax est, et in eo non est veritas.* Atque ex his iterum
10 sequitur eos revera Antichristos esse qui viros honestos et qui justitiam amant persequuntur propterea quod ab ipsis dissentiunt, et cum ipsis eadem fidei dogmata non defendunt. Qui enim justitiam et charitatem amant, eos per hoc solum fideles esse scimus; et qui fideles persequitur Antichristus est. Sequitur denique fidem non tam requirere vera quam
15 pia dogmata, hoc est, talia quae animum ad obedientiam movent; tametsi inter ea plurima sint quae nec umbram veritatis habent, dummodo tamen is qui eadem amplectitur eadem falsa esse ignoret; alias rebellis necessario esset. Quomodo enim fieri posset ut aliquis qui justitiam amare et Deo obsequi studet tanquam divinum adoret quod a
20 divina natura alienum scit esse? At animi simplicitate errare possunt homines, et Scriptura non ignorantiam sed solam contumaciam, ut jam ostendimus, damnat. Imo ex sola fidei definitione hoc necessario sequitur, cujus omnes partes ex universali jam ostenso fundamento, et unico totius Scripturae intento—nisi nostra placita admiscere lubet—
25 peti debent. Atqui haec non expresse exigit vera, sed talia dogmata quae ad obedientiam necessaria sunt, quae scilicet animum in amore erga proximum confirment; cujus tantum ratione unusquisque in Deo (ut cum Johanne loquar), et Deus in unoquoque est. Cum itaque uniuscujusque fides ratione obedientiae vel contumaciae tantum, et non ratione
30 veritatis aut falsitatis, pia vel impia sit habenda, et nemo dubitet commune hominum ingenium varium admodum esse, nec omnes in omnibus aeque acquiescere, sed opiniones diverso modo homines regere (quippe quae hunc ad devotionem, eae ipsae alterum ad risum et contemtum movent); hinc sequitur ad fidem catholicam sive universalem

from the fact that no one has seen God he concludes that no one has any awareness or consciousness of God save through one thing only, love towards his neighbour; and hence he also concludes that no one can discover any attribute of God except this love, in so far as we participate therein. These arguments, if not conclusive,[1] at least give a fairly plain indication of John's meaning; but this is expressed much more clearly by Chapter 2, verses 3 and 4 of the same Epistle, where he teaches in the plainest of terms the doctrine I am now trying to convey. 'And hereby', he says, 'we are assured that we know him, if we keep his commandments. He that saith "I know him," and keepeth not his commandments, is a liar, and the truth is not in him.' From this it follows in turn that the true enemies of Christ are those who persecute righteous and justice-loving men for disagreeing with their views and not joining them in defending the same dogmas of faith. For if men love justice and charity, that in itself is proof that they are of the faithful; and he who persecutes the faithful is an enemy of Christ. It follows, lastly, that faith does not require true dogmas so much as pious dogmas, i.e. dogmas which inspire the mind to obedience. That there are many such which lack even a semblance of truth is of no consequence, as long as the man who accepts them does not know that they are false. If he did, he would necessarily be rebellious and disobedient; for how could anyone who seeks to love justice, and obey God, worship as divine what he knows to be foreign to the divine nature? Yet men may err through simple-mindedness, and it is not ignorance, but only obstinacy, which Scripture condemns, as I have already shown. Our final conclusion follows necessarily from the bare definition of faith, which—if we are to avoid introducing our own predilections—must be entirely based on the universal foundation already established and the single purpose underlying the whole of Scripture. Now this definition does not expressly require true dogmas, but only such as are necessary to obedience, i.e. such as may serve to confirm the mind in love of one's neighbour; for, in the words of John, it is only through such love that men are in God, and God in men. Since, then, the value of each man's faith is to be judged only by the obedience or obstinacy which it inspires, and not by its truth or falsity, and since no one questions that men differ widely in general disposition, so that they do not all accept the same doctrines with equal readiness, but are influenced by beliefs in different ways—those that move one man to devotion moving another to ridicule and contempt—it follows

[1] The last two conclusions are not accepted by Spinoza.

nulla dogmata pertinere de quibus inter honestos potest dari controversia. Quae enim ejus naturae sunt, respectu unius pia, et respectu alterius impia esse possunt, quandoquidem ex solis operibus sunt judicanda. Ad fidem ergo catholicam ea solummodo dogmata pertinent quae erga
5 Deum obedientia absolute ponit, et quibus ignoratis obedientia est absolute impossibilis; de reliquis autem, prout unusquisque (quia se ipsum melius novit) sibi ad se in amore justitiae confirmandum melius esse viderit, sentire debet. Et hac ratione puto nullum locum controversiis in ecclesia relinqui.

10 Nec jam verebor fidei universalis dogmata sive universae Scripturae intenti fundamentalia enumerare, quae (ut ex iis quae in his duobus Capitibus ostendimus evidentissime sequitur) omnia huc tendere debent: nempe, dari ens supremum quod justitiam et charitatem amat, cuique omnes, ut salvi sint, obedire tenentur, eumque cultu justitiae et
15 charitate erga proximum adorare. Atque hinc facile omnia determinantur, quaeque adeo nulla praeter haec sunt. Videlicet,

I. Deum, hoc est ens supremum, summe justum et misericordem, sive verae vitae exemplar, existere. Qui enim nescit, vel non credit, ipsum existere, ei obedire nequit, neque eum judicem noscere.

20 II. Eum esse unicum. Hoc enim etiam ad supremam devotionem, admirationem, et amorem erga Deum absolute requiri, nemo dubitare potest; devotio namque, admiratio, et amor ex sola excellentia unius supra reliquos orientur.

III. Eum ubique esse praesentem, vel omnia ipsi patere. Si res
25 ipsum latere crederentur, vel ipsum omnia videre ignoraretur, de aequitate ejus justitiae qua omnia dirigit dubitaretur, vel ipsa ignoraretur.

IV. Ipsum in omnia supremum habere jus et dominium, nec aliquid jure coactum, sed ex absoluto beneplacito et singulari gratia
30 facere: omnes enim ipsi absolute obedire tenentur, ipse autem nemini.

that all dogmas which can give rise to controversy among good men are
excluded from the catholic or oecumenical creed. For such dogmas may
be good in respect of one man, and bad in respect of another, since they
are to be judged solely by the works they inspire. Hence to the catholic
creed belong only those dogmas which are absolutely necessary for
obedience to God, and without which obedience is absolutely impossible; of the rest each man (since he knows himself best) must believe
whatever he thinks best adapted to strengthen his love of justice. This
principle, I think, removes all possibility of controversy within the
church.

I shall now make bold to enumerate the dogmas of the oecumenical
creed, or the basic beliefs which Scripture as a whole aims to convey.
These (as is clear from what I have shown in this Chapter and the
last)[1] must all reduce to the following: that there exists a supreme being
who loves justice and charity; that all men must obey him in order to
be saved; and that they must worship him by practising justice and
charity towards their neighbours. From these it is easy to derive them
all, and the following is a complete list.[2]

I. God, a supreme being, supremely just and merciful, i.e. a model
of true living, exists. This is a necessary article of faith, for if a man
does not know or does not believe that God exists he cannot obey him
or recognize him as his judge.

II. There is but one God. No one can doubt that this belief too is
absolutely necessary for the highest devotion, reverence, and love
towards God; for such devotion, reverence, and love will only arise
from the superiority of one being to all others.

III. God is omnipresent, i.e. nothing is hidden from his sight. If
men believed that things were hidden from him, or did not know that
he saw everything, they would be either sceptical or ignorant of the
impartiality and justice wherewith he directs the universe.

IV. God has supreme right and dominion over everything. He is
bound by no obligation, but acts from an untrammelled will and peer-
less grace: for while all men are bound to obey him unconditionally,
he is not bound to obey anyone.

---

[1] Cf. *TT-P* v, p. 101. Although Spinoza bases his discussion on the Jewish-Christian
Scriptures he is in fact attempting to enumerate the dogmas common to all religions. What
follows is therefore a contribution to an 'oecumenical movement' which is not simply Jewish-
Christian.

[2] In *TP* viii, 46, p. 411, Spinoza requires that the patricians in his aristocracy should ad-
here to the simple universal faith here described, and this may have suggested to Rousseau
the idea of a 'civil religion' (*Social Contract* iv, 8).

V. Cultum Dei ejusque obedientiam in sola justitia et charitate sive amore erga proximum consistere.

VI. Omnes qui hac vivendi ratione Deo obediunt salvos tantum esse; reliquos autem, qui sub imperio voluptatum vivunt, perditos. Si
5 homines hoc firmiter non crederent, nihil causae esset cur Deo potius quam voluptatibus obtemperare mallent.

VII. Denique, Deum poenitentibus peccata condonare. Nullus enim est qui non peccet; si igitur hoc non statueretur, omnes de sua salute desperarent, nec ulla esset ratio cur Deum misericordem crederent.
10 Qui autem hoc firmiter credit, videlicet Deum ex misericordia et gratia qua omnia dirigit hominum peccata condonare, et hac de causa in Dei amore magis incenditur, is revera Christum secundum spiritum novit, et Christus in eo est.

Atque haec omnia nemo ignorare potest apprime cognitu necessaria
15 esse, ut homines, nullo excepto, ex praescripto legis supra explicato Deo obedire possint; nam horum aliquo sublato, tollitur etiam obedientia. Caeterum quid Deus sive illud verae vitae exemplar sit, an scilicet sit ignis, spiritus, lux, cogitatio, etc., id nihil ad fidem; ut nec etiam qua ratione sit verae vitae exemplar, an scilicet propterea quod animum
20 justum et misericordem habet, vel quia res omnes per ipsum sunt et agunt, et consequenter nos etiam per ipsum intelligimus, et per ipsum id quod verum, aequum, et bonum est videmus; perinde est quicquid de his unusquisque statuerit. Deinde nihil etiam ad fidem si quis credat quod Deus secundum essentiam vel secundum potentiam ubique sit;
25 quod res dirigit ex libertate, vel necessitate naturae; quod leges tanquam princeps praescribat, vel tanquam aeternas veritates doceat; quod homo ex arbitrii libertate, vel ex necessitate divini decreti Deo obediat; quodque denique praemium bonorum et poena malorum naturalis vel supranaturalis sit. Haec et similia, inquam, nihil refert in respectu

V. Worship of God and obedience to him consists solely in justice and charity (or love) towards one's neighbour.[1]

VI. All who obey God by following this mode of life are saved, and they alone; the rest, those who live as slaves to pleasure, are damned. If men were not firmly convinced of this, they would have no reason for wishing to obey God rather than the promptings of pleasure.

VII. Finally, God forgives the sins of the penitent. All men sin; so if this article were not included, all would despair of their salvation, and would have no reason to believe in God's mercy. But he who is firmly convinced that God forgives the sins of men with the mercy and grace whereby he governs everything, and is thus fired with greater love towards God, has a true knowledge of Christ after the spirit, and Christ is truly in his heart.[2]

Now everyone must see that it is absolutely necessary for all these dogmas to be known if men, without exception, are to be able to obey God as prescribed by the law set out above; for if any of these beliefs is destroyed, obedience is destroyed as well. But what God or our model of true living really is, whether he is fire, spirit, light, thought, or something else, is as irrelevant to faith as the question how he comes to be the model of true living; whether it is because he has a just and merciful spirit, or because, being the ground of the existence and activity of everything, he is also the ground of our understanding, and the source of our grasp of what is true, just, and good. It does not matter what conclusions an individual has reached on such topics. Nor does it matter whether God is believed to be omnipresent actually or potentially; to govern things freely or by natural necessity; to lay down laws as a ruler or to teach them as eternal truths: whether man is held to obey God from free will or by the necessity of the divine decree; or, finally, whether the reward of the good and the punishment of the wicked is regarded as natural or supernatural.[3] On such topics

---

[1] Cf. Kant, *Religion* iv, 2, 2: 'Everything man fancies he can do, over and above good moral conduct, in order to make himself acceptable to God, is mere false worship of the Deity.'

[2] Spinoza is prepared to admit that faith, especially when confined to the simple dogmas he has just set forth, can lead to salvation, i.e. to peace of mind; cf. the story of his conversation with his landlady (Freudenthal, *Lebensgeschichte*, p. 61). Yet the way of philosophy, i.e. of truth and freedom, is superior to the way of obedience. As Kant noted (*Grundlegung*, p. 92), a morality based on the will of God involves heteronomy.

[3] Although Spinoza regards these questions as philosophical, the formulation of some of them is conditioned by the presuppositions of faith. For example, although God's 'laws' are eternal truths and not commands, God cannot be said to 'teach' in the ordinary sense; so that neither of the alternative answers to this question is philosophically acceptable.

fidei qua ratione unusquisque intelligat, dummodo nihil eum in finem
concludat ut majorem licentiam ad peccandum sumat, vel ut minus
fiat Deo obtemperans; quinimo unusquisque, ut jam supra diximus,
haec fidei dogmata ad suum captum accommodare tenetur, eaque sibi
5 eo modo interpretari quo sibi videtur eadem facilius sine ulla haesitatione, sed integro animi consensu amplecti posse, ut consequenter Deo
pleno animi consensu obediat. Nam, ut jam etiam monuimus, sicuti
olim fides secundum captum et opiniones prophetarum et vulgi illius
temporis revelata scriptaque fuit, sic etiam jam unusquisque tenetur
10 eandem suis opinionibus accommodare, ut sic ipsam absque ulla mentis
repugnantia sineque ulla haesitatione amplectatur. Ostendimus enim
fidem non tam veritatem quam pietatem exigere, et non nisi ratione
obedientiae piam et salutiferam esse, et consequenter neminem nisi
ratione obedientiae fidelem esse. Quare non ille qui optimas ostendit
15 rationes optimam necessario ostendit fidem, sed ille qui optima ostendit
opera justitiae et charitatis. Quae doctrina quam salutaris quamque
necessaria sit in republica ut homines pacifice et concorditer vivant,
quotque, inquam, quantasque perturbationum et scelerum causas prae-
scindat, omnibus judicandum relinquo.

20 .   .   .   .

Superest jam ut tandem ostendam inter fidem sive theologiam et
philosophiam nullum esse commercium, nullamve affinitatem; quod
jam nemo potest ignorare qui harum duarum facultatum et scopum et
fundamentum novit, quae sane toto coelo discrepant. Philosophiae
25 enim scopus nihil est praeter veritatem: fidei autem, ut abunde ostendimus, nihil praeter obedientiam et pietatem. Deinde philosophiae
fundamenta notiones communes sunt, et ipsa ex sola natura peti
debet: fidei autem historiae et lingua, et ex sola Scriptura et revelatione petenda, ut in VII Cap. ostendimus. Fides igitur summam
30 unicuique libertatem ad philosophandum concedit, ut quicquid velit de
rebus quibuscunque sine scelere sentire possit; et eos tantum tanquam
haereticos et schismaticos damnat qui opiniones docent ad contumaciam, odia, contentiones, et iram suadendum; et eos contra fideles
tantum habet qui justitiam et charitatem pro viribus suae rationis et
35 facultatibus suadent.

.   .   .   .

32. *P schismaticos*; *I scismaticos*.

as these, I say, an individual's views make no difference to his faith, as long as he does not accept a conclusion in order to give himself greater freedom to sin, or to lessen his obedience to God; in fact, as I have already said above, everyone must adapt these dogmas of faith to his own understanding, and interpret them for himself in whatever way he thinks will best enable him to embrace them unreservedly and with complete conviction, and thus to obey God with all his heart. For, as I have also observed, just as faith was originally revealed and written in a form adapted to the understanding and beliefs of the prophets and the common people of that period, so everyone to-day must adapt it to his own beliefs, that he may thus embrace it without any mental repugnance or hesitation. For I have shown that faith demands goodness rather than truth, that it is good and a means to salvation only because of the obedience which it inspires, and, consequently, that it is obedience alone which makes a man a believer. Hence it is not necessarily the man who produces the best arguments who displays the best faith, but he who produces the best works of justice and charity. How salutary this doctrine is, how necessary it is in a state if men are to live in peace and harmony, and how many potent causes of disturbance and wickedness it cuts off at the source, the reader may judge for himself.

. . . .

It now remains to show in conclusion that between faith or theology and philosophy there is no connexion or relationship; a point that must now be clear to everyone who knows the aims and bases of these two disciplines, which are clearly poles apart. The sole aim of philosophy is truth:[1] the sole aim of faith obedience and piety, as I have abundantly shown. Moreover, philosophy is based on common notions, and must be built on the study of nature alone; whereas faith is based on history and language, and must be derived only from Scripture and revelation, as I have shown in Chapter VII. Thus faith allows everyone complete freedom in the field of philosophy, so that he can blamelessly hold any beliefs he pleases on any question whatsoever; it condemns as heretics and dissenters none but those who disseminate their beliefs in order to foster obstinacy, hatred, strife, and anger, while it regards as believers none but those who commend justice and charity to the best of their intellectual powers.

. . . .

[1] Yet we know from *DIE*, parr. 1–16, that the ultimate aim of Spinoza's own philosophy was salvation. It looks as if he has here deliberately omitted the practical effects of philosophy (love of God, freedom, and blessedness), in order to sharpen the contrast with faith.

CAPUT XVI

De reipublicae fundamentis; de jure uniuscujusque naturali et civili; deque summarum potestatum jure

Huc usque philosophiam a theologia separare curavimus, et libertatem philosophandi ostendere quam haec unicuique concedit. Quare tempus
5 est ut inquiramus quo usque haec libertas sentiendi, et quae unusquisque sentit dicendi, in optima republica se extendat. Hoc ut ordine examinemus, de fundamentis reipublicae disserendum, et prius de jure naturali uniuscujusque, ad rempublicam et religionem nondum attendentes.
10 Per jus et institutum naturae nihil aliud intelligo quam regulas naturae uniuscujusque individui secundum quas unumquodque naturaliter determinatum concipimus ad certo modo existendum et operandum. Ex. gr. pisces a natura determinati sunt ad natandum, magni ad minores comedendum; adeoque pisces summo naturali jure aqua potiuntur, et
15 magni minores comedunt. Nam certum est naturam absolute consideratam jus summum habere ad omnia quae potest, hoc est, jus naturae eo usque se extendere quo usque ejus potentia se extendit; naturae enim potentia ipsa Dei potentia est, qui summum jus ad omnia habet. Sed quia universalis potentia totius naturae nihil est praeter potentiam
20 omnium individuorum simul, hinc sequitur unumquodque individuum jus summum habere ad omnia quae potest, sive jus uniuscujusque eo usque se extendere quo usque ejus determinata potentia se extendit. Et quia lex summa naturae est ut unaquaeque res in suo statu quantum in se est conetur perseverare, idque nulla alterius sed tantum sui habita
25 ratione, hinc sequitur unumquodque individuum jus summum ad hoc habere, hoc est (uti dixi) ad existendum et operandum prout naturaliter determinatum est. Nec hic ullam agnoscimus differentiam inter homines et reliqua naturae individua, neque inter homines ratione praeditos et inter alios qui veram rationem ignorant, neque inter fatuos, delirantes,
30 et sanos. Quicquid enim unaquaeque res ex legibus suae naturae agit, id summo jure agit, nimirum quia agit prout ex natura determinata est, nec aliud potest. Quare inter homines, quamdiu sub imperio solius naturae vivere considerantur, tam ille qui rationem nondum novit, vel qui virtutis habitum nondum habet, ex solis legibus appetitus summo
35 jure vivit quam ille qui ex legibus rationis vitam suam dirigit. Hoc est,

CHAPTER XVI

The basis of the state; the right of the individual, both natural and civil; and the right of the sovereign

So far I have been concerned to distinguish philosophy from theology, and to show that the latter allows everyone to philosophize in freedom. Now it is time to inquire how far this freedom of thought and expression extends in a good state. To examine this question methodically we must discuss the basis of the state; and we must begin with the natural right of the individual, paying no attention for the present to either state or religion.

By the right and law of nature I simply mean the rules of each individual thing's nature, the rules whereby we conceive it as naturally determined to exist and act in a definite way.[1] Fish, for example, are determined by nature to swim, and the large to eat the smaller; so fish occupy the water, and the large eat the smaller, with perfect natural right. For there is no doubt that nature in the absolute sense has a perfect right to do everything in its power, i.e. that the right of nature extends as far as its power; the power of nature being nothing but the power of God, who has a perfect right to do everything.[2] But the universal power of nature as a whole is simply the power of all individual things combined; hence each individual thing has a perfect right to do everything it can, in other words, its right extends to the limit of its power. And since the supreme law of nature is that everything does its utmost to preserve its own condition, and this without regard to anything but itself,[3] everything has a perfect right to do this, i.e. (as I said) to exist and act as nature has determined it to do. Nor do I recognize any difference in this respect between men and other individual things in nature, or between men endowed with reason and others to whom true reason is unknown, or between the foolish, the mad, and the sane: for whatever anything does by the laws of its nature it does with perfect right, simply because it acts as it has been determined by nature to act, and can do nothing else. Hence as long as men are regarded as living under the sway of nature alone, he who is still P. 73, 83. blind to reason, or has still to acquire a virtuous disposition, lives EP. xxiii wholly by the laws of appetite with as perfect a right as he who guides his life by the laws of reason. In other words, just as an enlightened

---

[1] *TP* ii, 4, pp. 267-9.　　[2] *TP* ii, 2-3, p. 267.　　[3] *TP* ii, 7, p. 271.

sicuti sapiens jus summum habet ad omnia quae ratio dictat, sive ex
legibus rationis vivendi, sic etiam ignarus et animi impotens summum
jus habet ad omnia quae appetitus suadet, sive ex legibus appetitus
vivendi. Atque hoc idem est quod Paulus docet, qui ante legem, hoc
5 est, quamdiu homines ex naturae imperio vivere considerantur, nullum
peccatum agnoscit.

Jus itaque naturale uniuscujusque hominis non sana ratione sed
cupiditate et potentia determinatur. Non enim omnes naturaliter
determinati sunt ad operandum secundum regulas et leges rationis; sed
10 contra, omnes ignari omnium rerum nascuntur, et antequam veram
vivendi rationem noscere possunt et virtutis habitum acquirere, magna
aetatis pars, etsi bene educati fuerint, transit, et nihilominus interim
vivere tenentur, seque quantum in se est conservare; nempe ex solo
appetitus impulsu, quandoquidem natura iis nihil aliud dedit, et
15 actualem potentiam ex sana ratione vivendi denegavit: et propterea
non magis ex legibus sanae mentis vivere tenentur quam felis ex legibus naturae leoninae. Quicquid itaque unusquisque, qui sub solo
naturae imperio consideratur, sibi utile vel ductu sanae rationis vel ex
affectuum impetu judicat, id summo naturae jure appetere, et quacun-
20 que ratione, sive vi, sive dolo, sive precibus, sive quocunque demum
modo facilius poterit, ipsi capere licet; et consequenter pro hoste
habere eum qui impedire vult quominus animum expleat suum.

Ex quibus sequitur jus et institutum naturae, sub quo omnes nascuntur et maxima ex parte vivunt, nihil nisi quod nemo cupit et quod nemo
25 potest prohibere; non contentiones, non odia, non iram, non dolos,
nec absolute aliquid quod appetitus suadet aversari. Nec mirum; nam
natura non legibus humanae rationis, quae non nisi hominum verum
utile et conservationem intendunt, intercluditur, sed infinitis aliis quae
totius naturae, cujus homo particula est, aeternum ordinem respiciunt:
30 ex cujus sola necessitate omnia individua certo modo determinantur ad
existendum et operandum. Quicquid ergo nobis in natura ridiculum,
absurdum, aut malum videtur, id inde venit quod res tantum ex parte
novimus, totiusque naturae ordinem et cohaerentiam maxima ex parte
ignoramus, et quod omnia ex usu nostrae rationis dirigi volumus; cum
35 tamen id quod ratio malum esse dictat non malum sit respectu ordinis

18. Perhaps *vivere* should be inserted before *consideratur*.

man has a perfect right to do everything which reason dictates, or to live by the laws of reason, so too an unenlightened and weak-minded man has a perfect right to do everything that appetite suggests, or to live by the laws of appetite.[1] And this is precisely the doctrine of Paul,[2] who admits no sin before the existence of law, i.e. as long as men are regarded as living under the sway of nature.

Thus man's natural right is not determined by sound reason, but by his desire and his power.[3] For men are not all determined by nature to act in accordance with the rules and laws of reason; on the contrary, all men are born in complete ignorance, and, even although they are well brought up, much of their life must pass before they can discover the true way of living and acquire a virtuous disposition. Yet meanwhile they have to live and preserve themselves as best they can; that is, by the prompting of appetite alone, since nature has given them nothing else, and has denied them the effective power to live by sound reason. Hence they are no more bound to live by the laws of a sound understanding than a cat is bound to live by the laws of a lion's nature. Anything, then, that an individual who is considered as subject only to nature judges to be useful to himself—either through the guidance of sound reason or through the impetus of passion—he has a perfect natural right to desire and indeed to appropriate by any means in his power—by force, fraud, entreaty, or however he finds it easiest; and hence a perfect natural right to regard as an enemy anyone who wishes to prevent him from satisfying his desire.

It follows that the right and law of nature, under which all are born and for the most part live, forbids nothing save what nobody desires and nobody can do: it forbids neither strife, nor hatred, nor anger, nor deceit; in short, it is opposed to nothing that appetite can suggest. Nor is this surprising; for nature is not bounded by the laws of human reason, which aim only at men's true interest and preservation, but by other laws of infinite scope governing the eternal order of the whole of nature, in which man is a tiny part: and it is by the necessity of this order alone that all individual things are determined to exist and act in a definite way. Hence if anything in nature seems to us ridiculous, absurd, or bad, this is because we know things only in part, being almost entirely ignorant of how they are linked together in the universal system of nature;[4] and because we wish everything to be directed in conformity with our own reason. Yet what reason declares to be bad is

---

[1] *TP* ii, 5–8, pp. 269–73.   [2] *Romans* 4, 15.

[3] *TP* ii, 5, p. 269.   [4] *Ep.* xxxii.

et legum universae naturae, sed tantum solius nostrae naturae legum respectu.

Verum enim vero quanto sit hominibus utilius secundum leges et certa nostrae rationis dictamina vivere, quae, uti diximus, non nisi
5 verum hominum utile intendunt, nemo potest dubitare. Praeterea nullus est qui non cupiat secure extra metum quoad fieri potest vivere; quod tamen minime potest contingere quamdiu unicuique ad lubitum omnia facere licet, nec plus juris rationi quam odio et irae conceditur. Nam nullus est qui inter inimicitias, odia, iram, et dolos non anxie
10 vivat, quaeque adeo quantum in se est non conetur vitare. Quod si etiam consideremus homines absque mutuo auxilio miserrime, et absque rationis cultu necessario vivere, ut in Cap. V ostendimus, clarissime videbimus homines ad secure et optime vivendum necessario in unum conspirare debuisse; ac proinde effecisse ut jus quod unus-
15 quisque ex natura ad omnia habebat collective haberent, neque amplius ex vi et appetitu uniuscujusque sed ex omnium simul potentia et voluntate determinaretur. Quod tamen frustra tentassent si nihil nisi quod appetitus suadet sequi vellent (ex legibus enim appetitus unus-quisque diverse trahitur), adeoque firmissime statuere et pacisci
20 debuerunt ex solo rationis dictamine (cui nemo aperte repugnare audet ne mente carere videatur) omnia dirigere, et appetitum quatenus in damnum alterius aliquid suadet fraenare, neminique facere quod sibi fieri non vult, jusque denique alterius tanquam suum defendere.

Qua autem ratione pactum hoc iniri debeat ut ratum fixumque sit,
25 hic jam videndum. Nam lex humanae naturae universalis est ut nemo aliquid quod bonum esse judicat negligat nisi spe majoris boni vel ex metu majoris damni, nec aliquod malum perferat nisi ad majus evitan-dum, vel spe majoris boni; hoc est, unusquisque de duobus bonis quod ipse majus esse judicat, et de duobus malis quod minus sibi videtur
30 eliget. Dico expresse quod sibi eligenti majus aut minus videtur, non quod res necessario ita se habeat ut ipse judicat. Atque haec lex adeo *firmiter* naturae humanae inscripta est ut inter aeternas veritates sit ponenda quas nemo ignorare potest. At ex ea necessario sequitur neminem absque dolo[32] promissurum se jure quod in omnia habet

---

10. *P eaque adeo*, but cf. p. 158, l. 9.   17. *I si nisi.*

not bad in relation to the order and laws of nature as a whole, but only in relation to the laws of our nature in particular.[1]

Still, nobody can doubt that it is much more advantageous for men to live by the laws and sure dictates of our reason, which, as I said, aim at nothing but the true interest of men. Moreover everyone desires to enjoy the maximum safety and security (which is impossible as long as each may do anything he pleases, and reason is allowed no more influence than hatred and anger); for everyone lives a life of anxiety when surrounded by hostility, hatred, anger, and treachery, and so does his utmost to escape such things. If we also reflect on what was shown in Chapter V,[2] that without mutual help men live in utter wretchedness, and are inevitably debarred from the cultivation of reason, we shall see very clearly that to live safely and well men had necessarily to join together. They therefore arranged that the right to do everything which each had by nature should be held collectively, and should be determined no longer by the force and appetite of each but by the power and will of all together. But they would not have succeeded in this had they been willing to follow nothing but the prompting of appetite (for by the laws of appetite individuals are drawn in different ways); so each must have firmly resolved and contracted[3] to direct everything by the dictate of reason alone (which no one dares to oppose openly lest he appear to lack understanding), to bridle his appetite when it suggested anything harmful to another, to do to nobody what he would not wish done to himself, and, finally, to defend his neighbour's right as if it were his own.

But we must now inquire how this contract must be made if it is to be permanently binding: for it is a universal law of human nature that no one forgoes anything he thinks good save from hope of a greater good or fear of a greater loss, or tolerates any evil save to avoid a greater, or from hope of a greater good. In other words, of two goods everyone will choose the one which he thinks the greater, and of two evils the one which he thinks the lesser. I say expressly 'which he (the chooser) thinks the greater or lesser'; not that his judgement is necessarily correct. Now this law is graven so deeply upon human nature that it must be set among the eternal truths which everyone must know; yet its necessary consequence is that no one will promise to surrender his

---

[1] This paragraph is repeated with minor variations in *TP* ii, 8, p. 273.

[2] p. 93.

[3] Contrast *TP* i, 7, p. 265, and vi, 1, p. 315, where the idea of an historical social contract is abandoned.

cessurum, et absolute neminem promissis staturum nisi ex metu majoris
mali vel spe majoris boni. Quod ut melius intelligatur, ponatur latro-
nem me cogere ut ei promittam me mea bona ubi velit ipsi daturum.
Jam quandoquidem, ut jam ostendi, meum jus naturale sola mea
5 potentia determinatur, certum est quod si possum dolo me ab hoc
latrone liberare, ipsi quicquid velit promittendo, mihi id naturae jure
facere licere, dolo scilicet quicquid velit pacisci. Vel ponatur me absque
fraude alicui promisisse me spatio viginti dierum non gustaturum cibum
neque ullum alimentum, et postea vidisse me stulte promisisse, nec
10 sine damno maximo promisso stare posse; quandoquidem ex jure
naturali de duobus malis minus eligere teneor, possum ergo summo jure
fidem talis pacti rumpere, et dictum indictum ut sit facere. Atque hoc
inquam jure naturali licere, sive vera et certa ratione videam, sive ex
opinione videre videar me male promisisse; sive enim id vere sive falso
15 videam, maximum timebo malum, quodque adeo ex naturae instituto
omni modo vitare conabor. Ex quibus concludimus pactum nullam vim
habere posse nisi ratione utilitatis, qua sublata pactum simul tollitur
et irritum manet, ac propterea stulte alterius fidem in aeternum sibi
aliquem expostulare, si simul non conatur efficere ut ex ruptione pacti
20 ineundi plus damni quam utilitatis ruptorem sequatur: quod quidem in
republica instituenda maxime locum habere debet. At si omnes homines
facile solo ductu rationis duci possent, summamque reipublicae utilitatem et necessitatem noscere, nullus esset qui dolos prorsus non de-
testaretur, sed omnes summa cum fide ex cupiditate summi hujus
25 boni, nempe reipublicae conservandae, pactis omnino starent, et fidem,
summum reipublicae praesidium, supra omnia servarent. Sed longe
abest ut omnes ex solo ductu rationis facile semper duci possint; nam
unusquisque a sua voluptate trahitur, et avaritia, gloria, invidia, ira
etc. saepissime mens ita occupatur ut nullus locus rationi relinquatur.
30 Quapropter, quamvis homines certis signis simplicis animi promittant
et paciscantur se fidem servaturos, nemo tamen, nisi promisso aliud
accedat, de fide alterius potest esse certus, quandoquidem unusquisque
naturae jure dolo agere potest, nec pactis stare tenetur nisi spe majoris

right to do everything except with intent to deceive,[1] and no one at all will keep promises save from fear of a greater evil or hope of a greater good. To understand this better, suppose a robber forces me to promise that I will give him my goods whenever he wishes. Now since my natural right is determined solely by my power, as I have already shown, obviously, if I *can* get out of the robber's clutches by making a counterfeit promise to do anything he wishes, I have a natural right to do this, i.e. to make a counterfeit promise to do anything he wishes. Or suppose I have made a genuine promise to someone that I will not taste food or take any nourishment for twenty days, but later see that my promise was foolish, and that I cannot keep it without great harm to myself; then, since by natural law I am bound to choose the lesser evil, I have a perfect right to break this promise and take back my word. I may do so, I say, by natural right; and it does not matter whether my idea that I have made a harmful promise is knowledge based on true and certain reasoning, or merely an impression based on conjecture; for whether my idea is true or false, I shall fear the worst, and so, by the law of nature, do my utmost to avoid it.[2] From this I conclude that a contract can have no binding force but utility;[3] when that disappears it at once becomes null and void. Hence it is foolish to require a man to keep faith with you for ever unless you also try to ensure that breach of the contract will bring him more loss than gain. Now this precaution must be given pride of place in the formation of the state. No doubt if it were easy for everyone to be guided by reason alone, and to grasp the supreme utility and necessity of the state, all men would regard perfidy with utter detestation, and, in their desire for this supreme good, the preservation of the state, would abide most faithfully by their contracts and cherish good faith, the chief bulwark of the state, above all else. But for everyone always to be guided by reason alone is far from easy; for each is seduced by his own pleasure,[4] and it is very common for greed, pride, envy, anger, etc. to take such a hold upon the mind that no place is left for reason. Hence even although men give sure signs of honest intentions in promising and contracting to keep faith, no one can be certain of the good faith of another unless his promise is guaranteed by something else,[5] since everyone can make counterfeit promises by the right of nature, and is not bound to abide by his contracts save by

---

[1] n. 32, p. 247.   [2] *TP* ii, 12, p. 275.

[3] Further reflection on this conclusion may have helped to convince Spinoza that the social contract envisaged above was superfluous.

[4] Virgil, *Eclogues* ii, 65 (quoted again in *TP* ii, 6, p. 271).

[5] Hobbes, *De Cive* v, 4–5.

boni vel metu majoris mali. Verum quia jam ostendimus jus naturale
sola potentia uniuscujusque determinari, sequitur quantum unusquisque
potentiae quam habet in alterum vel vi vel sponte transfert, tantum
etiam de suo jure alteri necessario cedere; et illum summum jus in
5 omnes habere qui summam habet potestatem qua omnes vi cogere et
metu summi supplicii, quod omnes universaliter timent, retinere potest.
Quod quidem jus tamdiu tantum retinebit, quamdiu hanc potentiam
quicquid velit exequendi conservabit; alias precario imperabit, et nemo
fortior, nisi velit, ei obtemperare tenebitur.

10　　Hac itaque ratione sine ulla naturalis juris repugnantia societas
formari potest, pactumque omne summa cum fide semper servari, si
nimirum unusquisque omnem quam habet potentiam in societatem
transferat; quae adeo summum naturae jus in omnia, hoc est, summum
imperium sola retinebit, cui unusquisque vel ex libero animo vel metu
15 summi supplicii parere tenebitur. Talis vero societatis jus democratia
vocatur, quae proinde definitur coetus universus hominum qui collegialiter summum jus ad omnia quae potest habet. Ex quo sequitur
summam potestatem nulla lege teneri, sed omnes ad omnia ei parere
debere; hoc enim tacite vel expresse pacisci debuerunt omnes cum
20 omnem suam potentiam se defendendi, hoc est, omne suum jus in eam
transtulerunt; quippe, si aliquid sibi servatum volebant, debuerant
simul sibi cavere quo id tuto defendere possent. Cum autem id non
fecerint, nec absque imperii divisione et consequenter destructione
facere potuerint, eo ipso se arbitrio summae potestatis absolute sub-
25 miserunt. Quod cum absolute fecerint, idque (ut jam ostendimus) et
necessitate cogente et ipsa ratione suadente, hinc sequitur quod, nisi
hostes imperii esse velimus, et contra rationem imperium summis
viribus defendere suadentem agere, omnia absolute summae potestatis
mandata exequi tenemur, tametsi absurdissima imperet; talia enim
30 ratio exequi etiam jubet ut de duobus malis minus eligamus. Adde
quod hoc periculum, se scilicet alterius imperio et arbitrio absolute
submittendi, facile unusquisque adire poterat; nam, ut ostendimus,

2–4. *G sequitur . . . cedere*; *I sequitur quod . . . cedere*; *V–L sequitur quod . . . cedat.*
29. *IV exequi*; *I exiqui.*

hope of a greater good or fear of a greater evil. But since everyone's natural right is determined solely by his power (as I have already shown), it follows that in so far as he transfers his power to another—whether voluntarily or by compulsion does not matter—he necessarily surrenders to the other his right as well; and that the man who has supreme power to coerce all, and to restrain them by the threat of a supreme penalty which is universally feared, has also supreme right over all. Of course he will only retain this right as long as he preserves the power to do everything he wishes; otherwise he will govern by courtesy, and no one stronger will be bound to obey him unless he wants to do so.[1]

In this way, then, a society can be formed without any opposition from natural law,[2] and every contract can always be kept with the greatest good faith; if, that is, everyone transfers all his power to the society. Thus it alone will have a perfect natural right to do everything, i.e. sovereign power, and everyone will be bound to obey it either in freedom of spirit or from fear of the supreme penalty. Now when the right belongs to a society so formed the state is called a democracy; which is accordingly defined as a general assembly of men that possesses in its corporate capacity the supreme right to do everything it can.[3] It follows that the sovereign is bound by no law, and that all citizens must obey it in all things, since they must all have contracted to do so, either tacitly or expressly, when they transferred to it all their power to defend themselves, i.e. all their right. For had they wished to retain any part of their right, they would also have had to provide themselves with some safe way of defending it; but they did not do so, and could not have done so without dividing and hence destroying the state. They therefore submitted unreservedly to the jurisdiction of the sovereign: and this complete submission was (as I have just shown) both forced on them by necessity and advised by reason itself. It follows that, unless we wish to be enemies of the state and to contravene reason's advice to do our utmost to defend it, we are bound to perform all the commands of the sovereign without exception; for no matter how foolish they may be, reason still bids us perform them so as to choose the lesser evil.[4] Besides, the risk involved in submitting completely to the government and jurisdiction of another was one which the individual could lightly

---

[1] *Ep.* l.

[2] In such a society the individual still does what he thinks to be in his own best interests (*TP* iii, 3, pp. 285–7); but he no longer thinks it advantageous to break his covenant, because there is now a sovereign to punish him for doing so.

[3] *TP* ii, 17, pp. 277–9.   [4] *TP* iii, 5–6, pp. 287–9.

summis potestatibus hoc jus quicquid velint imperandi tamdiu tantum competit quamdiu revera summam habent potestatem: quod si eandem amiserint, simul etiam jus omnia imperandi amittunt, et in eum vel eos cadit qui ipsum acquisiverunt et retinere possunt. Quapropter raro
5 admodum contingere potest ut summae potestates absurdissima imperent; ipsis enim maxime incumbit, ut sibi prospiciant et imperium retineant, communi bono consulere et omnia ex rationis dictamine dirigere; violenta enim imperia, ut ait Seneca, nemo continuit diu. Quibus accedit quod in democratico imperio minus timenda sunt
10 absurda. Nam fere impossibile est ut major unius coetus pars, si magnus est, in uno absurdo conveniat: deinde propter ejus fundamentum et finem, qui, ut etiam ostendimus, nullus alius est quam absurda appetitus vitare, et homines sub rationis limites quoad ejus fieri potest continere, ut concorditer et pacifice vivant. Quod fundamentum si tollatur facile
15 tota fabrica ruet. His ergo providere summae tantum potestati incumbit; subditis autem, uti diximus, ejus mandata exequi, nec aliud jus agnoscere quam quod summa potestas jus esse declarat.

At forsan aliquis putabit nos hac ratione subditos servos facere; quia putant servum esse eum qui ex mandato agit, et liberum qui animo suo
20 morem gerit. Quod quidem non absolute verum est. Nam revera is qui a sua voluptate ita trahitur, et nihil quod sibi utile est videre neque agere potest, maxime servus est, et solus ille liber qui integro animo ex solo ductu rationis vivit. Actio autem ex mandato, hoc est, obedientia, libertatem quidem aliquo modo tollit; at non illico servum facit, sed acti-
25 onisratio. Si finis actionis non est ipsius agentis, sed imperantis utilitas, tum agens servus est et sibi inutilis. At in republica et imperio ubi salus totius populi, non imperantis, summa lex est, qui in omnibus summae potestati obtemperat non sibi inutilis servus, sed subditus dicendus; et ideo illa respublica maxime libera est cujus leges sana ratione fundatae
30 sunt. Ibi enim unusquisque ubi velit liber esse potest,[33] hoc est, integro

21–22. The correct reading may be *ut ... possit.*

incur; for, as I have shown, sovereigns only have the right to command everything they wish as long as they actually have supreme power. Once they lose that, they also lose the right to command everything, which falls to the man or the men who have gained and can hold it. Hence it is very rare for sovereigns to issue commands which are utterly foolish, for their main task—if they are to safeguard themselves and retain their sovereignty—is to plan for the common good and direct everything by the dictate of reason;[1] since, as Seneca says, tyrannical governments never last long.[2] In addition, there is less danger of foolish decrees in a democracy: first because it is practically impossible for the majority in an assembly, especially in a large assembly, to agree upon a piece of folly;[3] and secondly because of the basis and aim of democracy, which, as I have also shown, is precisely to avoid the follies of appetite, and to restrain men as far as possible within the bounds set by reason, that they may live in harmony and peace. Destroy this basis and the whole fabric will collapse at a touch. These, then, are the ends which it is the task of the sovereign, and of the sovereign alone, to pursue; the duty of subjects, as I said, is to carry out the sovereign's commands, and not to recognize as law anything but what it declares to be such.

But someone may think that this is to turn subjects into slaves; on the ground that a slave is a man who acts by order, and a free man one who does as he pleases. This, however, is not entirely true; for the man who is captivated by his pleasures, and can neither see nor do anything advantageous to himself, is really the greatest slave of all,[4] and the only free man is one who has a sound mind and lives wholly by the guidance of reason. Admittedly action done by order, i.e. obedience, does destroy freedom in a sense, but it does not of itself make a man a slave; what makes a man a slave is the object of his action. If its object is not the benefit of the agent himself, but of the man who gives the order, then the agent is a slave, and useless to himself. But in a state where the welfare of the whole people, and not of the ruler, is the highest law, he who obeys the sovereign in everything must not be called a slave, useless to himself, but a subject. Thus the state whose laws are based on sound reason enjoys the greatest freedom; for in it everyone can be free whenever he wishes,[5] i.e. can live with a sound

---

[1] *TP* iii, 7, p. 289.
[2] Seneca, *Troades* 258 (also quoted above in *TT-P* v, p. 95).
[3] Spinoza believes that there is safety in numbers; cf. *TP* viii, 6, p. 373.
[4] *E* iv, Pref.   [5] n. 33, p. 247.

animo ex ductu rationis vivere. Sic etiam liberi, tametsi omnibus parentum mandatis obedire tenentur, non tamen servi sunt; nam parentum mandata liberorum utilitatem maxime spectant. Magnam ergo differentiam inter servum, filium, et subditum agnoscimus, qui
5 propterea sic definiuntur: nempe servus est qui mandatis domini quae utilitatem imperantis tantum spectant obtemperare tenetur; filius autem qui id quod sibi utile est ex mandato parentis agit; subditus denique qui id quod communi, et consequenter quoque sibi, utile est ex mandato summae potestatis agit.

10 Atque his imperii democratici fundamenta satis clare ostendisse puto; de quo prae omnibus agere malui, quia maxime naturale videbatur, et maxime ad libertatem quam natura unicuique concedit accedere. Nam in eo nemo jus suum naturale ita in alterum transfert ut nulla sibi imposterum consultatio sit, sed in majorem totius societatis
15 partem cujus ille unam facit. Atque hac ratione omnes manent, ut antea in statu naturali, aequales. Deinde de hoc solo imperio ex professo agere volui, quia ad meum intentum maxime facit, qui de utilitate libertatis in republica agere constitueram. Reliquarum ergo potestatum fundamentis supersedeo, nec nobis, ut earum jus noscamus, scire jam
20 opus est unde ortum habuerint, et saepe habeant; id enim ex modo ostensis satis superque constat. Nam quisquis summam habet potestatem, sive unus sit, sive pauci, sive denique omnes, certum est ei summum jus quicquid velit imperandi competere: et praeterea quisquis potestatem se defendendi sive sponte sive vi coactus in alium transtulit,
25 eum suo jure naturali plane cessisse, et consequenter eidem ad omnia absolute parere decrevisse: quod omnino praestare tenetur quamdiu rex, sive nobiles, sive populus summam quam acceperunt potestatem, quae juris transferendi fundamentum fuit, conservant. Nec his plura addere opus est.

mind under the guidance of reason. By the same argument children, although bound to obey all the commands of their parents, are not slaves either; for the commands of parents are aimed primarily at the benefit of their children. Hence I recognize a great difference between a slave, a son, and a subject, and therefore define them as follows. A slave is one who is bound to obey the commands of a master given solely in the master's interest; a son is one who does what is in his own interest by the command of a parent; and, finally, a subject is one who does what is in the common interest, and consequently in his own interest also, by the command of a sovereign.[1]

This, I think, has made the basis of democracy sufficiently clear; and it was democracy in particular that I wished to discuss, because it seemed to be the most natural form of state,[2] and to come nearest to preserving the freedom which nature allows the individual. For in it no one transfers his natural right to another so completely that he is never consulted again, but each transfers it to a majority of the whole community of which he is a member. In this way all remain equal, as they were before in the condition of nature. The second reason for deliberately confining my discussion to this kind of state is that it best serves my purpose of dealing with the benefits of freedom in a commonwealth. I therefore pass over the bases of other governments; indeed, it is no longer necessary for us to know how they have arisen—and often arise still—in order to discover their right, which is abundantly obvious from what I have just shown.[3] For whoever has sovereign power, whether it be one man, or a few, or all, has undoubtedly a perfect right to command everything he wishes; furthermore, whoever has transferred his power to defend himself to another, whether voluntarily or under constraint, has undoubtedly divested himself of his natural right completely, and in consequence has determined to obey the other in everything without exception; and this obedience he is bound to yield unreservedly as long as the king, aristocracy, or people preserves the supreme power which it has received, and which was the basis of the transfer of right.[4] Nor need any more be said.

---

[1] Spinoza is dealing with the subject of a good state: the subject of a tyrant is little better than a slave (*TP* v, 6, p. 311). Hobbes discusses the same topic in *De Cive* ix, 9.

[2] *TT-P* xx, p. 239. Spinoza is referring to the primary democracy mentioned in *TP* viii, 12, pp. 377–9. He later recognizes types of democracy which are less broadly based (*TP* xi, 1–3, pp. 441–3).

[3] They may arise through a transfer of right by the original assembly (*TP* iv, 6, p. 305), or through conquest (*TP* v, 6, p. 311). But the right of the sovereign is the same in both cases (loc. cit.).   [4] See p. 133.

Imperii fundamentis et jure ostensis, facile erit determinare quid jus civile privatum, quid injuria, quid justitia et injustitia in statu civili sit; deinde quis confoederatus, quis hostis, et quid denique crimen laesae majestatis sit. Per jus enim civile privatum nihil aliud
5 intelligere possumus quam uniuscujusque libertatem ad sese in suo statu conservandum quae edictis summae potestatis determinatur, solaque ejusdem authoritate defenditur. Nam postquam unusquisque jus suum ex proprio beneplacito vivendi, quod sola sua potestate determinabatur, hoc est, suam libertatem et potentiam se defendendi, in
10 alium transtulit, ex sola illius ratione jam vivere tenetur, et solo ejusdem praesidio se defendere. Injuria est cum civis vel subditus ab alio aliquod damnum contra jus civile, sive edictum summae potestatis, pati cogitur. Injuria enim non nisi in statu civili potest concipi; sed neque a summis potestatibus, quibus jure omnia licent, ulla fieri
15 potest subditis; ergo in privatis tantum, qui jure tenentur invicem non laedere, locum habere potest. Justitia est animi constantia tribuendi unicuique quod ei ex jure civili competit; injustitia autem est specie juris alicui detrahere quod ei ex vera legum interpretatione competit: vocantur etiam aequitas et iniquitas, quia qui constituti sunt ad lites
20 dirimendas nullum respectum personarum, sed omnes aequales habere tenentur, et jus uniuscujusque aeque defendere, non diviti invidere neque pauperem contemnere. Confoederati sunt homines duarum civitatum, qui ne belli discrimine in periculum veniant, vel ob aliam quamcunque utilitatem, inter se contrahunt invicem non laedere, sed
25 contra necessitate cogente opitulari, idque unaquaque suum imperium retinente. Hic contractus tamdiu erit validus quamdiu ejus fundamentum, nempe ratio periculi sive utilitatis, in medio erit; quippe nemo contrahit nec pactis stare tenetur nisi spe alicujus boni vel sollicitudine alicujus mali. Quod fundamentum si tollatur pactum ex
30 sese tollitur; quod etiam experientia satis superque docet. Nam quamvis diversa imperia inter se contrahant invicem non laedere, conantur tamen quantum possunt impedire quo minus alterutrum potentius evadat, nec fidem dictis habent nisi utriusque ad contrahendum finem et utilitatem satis perspectam habuerint; alias dolum timent. Nec
35 injuria; quis enim dictis et promissis ejus qui summam potestatem et

8. *I quo.* 25. *I unoquoque.*

138

Chapter XVI

Now that the basis and right of the state have been explained, it will be easy to determine the nature of private civil right, of wrong-doing, and of justice and injustice in the political order; then to define an ally, an enemy, and finally the crime of treason. By private civil right we can only mean the individual's freedom to maintain himself in his own condition, a freedom defined by the edicts of the sovereign and upheld by its authority alone. For as soon as the individual has transferred his right to live at his own good pleasure, which was limited only by his power, i.e. has transferred his freedom and power to defend himself to another, he is bound to live solely by the guidance of the other's reason, and to defend himself solely by the other's protection. Wrong-doing occurs when one citizen or subject is forced by another to suffer some harm contrary to the civil law, or the edict of the sovereign. For wrong-doing can only be conceived in a political order;[1] but no wrong can be done to their subjects by sovereigns, who have a right to do everything; so it can only occur between private citizens, who are bound by law not to harm one another. Justice is the settled disposition to give everyone what belongs to him by civil law; while injustice consists in depriving someone with a false show of legality of what on a true interpretation of the laws is his own.[2] Justice and injustice are also called equity and iniquity, because those appointed to settle lawsuits are bound to have no respect for persons, but to regard all citizens as equals and to uphold the rights of each impartially, without envying the rich or despising the poor. Allies are men of different commonwealths who, to avoid the dangers of war, or to secure some other advantage, make a contract not to harm one another, but to render mutual help when necessity requires, each commonwealth in the meantime retaining its own sovereignty. This contract will only continue in force as long as its basis, i.e. fear of of danger or hope of advantage, remains; since no one makes a contract or is bound to abide by it save by the hope of some good or the apprehension of some evil. If this basis disappears, the contract dissolves of itself; as experience too makes abundantly plain. For although two different states may make a contract not to harm one another, each still does its utmost to prevent its ally from becoming too powerful, and neither puts any faith in verbal assurances unless it has satisfied itself that it understands the aim and object which leads the other to make the contract; otherwise it suspects a trick. And rightly; for who but a fool who knows nothing of the right of sovereigns will take at their face value the words and promises of one who retains full power

---

[1] See p. 127, and cf. *TP* ii, 19, p. 279.   [2] *TP* ii, 23, p. 283.

jus retinet ad quidlibet faciendum, et cui sui imperii salus et utilitas summa lex debet esse, acquiescet, nisi stultus qui summarum potestatum jus ignorat? Et si praeterea ad pietatem et religionem attendamus, videbimus insuper neminem qui imperium tenet absque scelere promis-
5 sis stare posse cum damno sui imperii; quicquid enim promisit quod in damnum sui imperii cadere videt, id praestare non potest nisi fidem subditis datam solvendo; qua tamen maxime tenetur, et quam etiam servare sanctissime promittere solent. Porro hostis est quicunque extra civitatem ita vivit ut neque ut confoederatus, neque ut subditus impe-
10 rium civitatis agnoscat; hostem enim imperii non odium sed jus facit, et jus civitatis in eum qui ejus imperium nullo contrahendi genere agnoscit idem est ac in eum qui damnum intulit, quippe quacunque ratione poterit eundem vel ad deditionem vel ad confoederationem jure potest cogere. Denique crimen laesae majestatis in subditis sive civibus tantum,
15 qui pacto tacito vel expresso omne suum jus in civitatem transtulerunt, locum habet; atque is subditus tale crimen commisisse dicitur qui jus summae potestatis aliqua ratione arripere seu in alium transferre cona-tus est. Dico *conatus est*, nam si non essent condemnandi nisi post factum commissum, sero plerumque post jus arreptum aut translatum
20 in alium id conaretur civitas. Dico deinde absolute *qui aliqua ratione jus summae potestatis arripere conatur*, nullam scilicet agnoscendo dif-ferentiam sive inde damnum sive incrementum totius reipublicae quam clarissime sequeretur; quacunque enim ratione id conatus est, majesta-tem laesit et jure damnatur. Quod quidem in bello omnes fatentur jure
25 optimo fieri; nempe si quis stationem suam non servat, sed inscio im-peratore hostem adit, quamvis bono consilio—sed suo—rem aggressus fuerit, hostemque expugnaverit, capitis tamen jure damnatur, quia juramentum jusque imperatoris violavit. At quod omnes absolute cives hoc jure semper teneantur non aeque clare omnes vident: ratio tamen ea-
30 dem prorsus est. Nam quandoquidem respublica solo summae potestatis

10. *P agnoscat; I agnoscit.*

and right to do anything he pleases, and who must regard the safety and advantage of his own state as the highest law? Besides, if we consider morality and religion we shall also see that no sovereign can keep promises to the detriment of his state without committing a sin; for if he sees any promise he has made to be turning out to the disadvantage of his state, he can only keep it by breaking his pledge to his subjects, although the latter is a pledge which binds him most strictly, and one moreover which men generally promise most solemnly to keep.[1] An enemy is anyone who lives outside a commonwealth in such a way that he does not recognize its sovereignty either as an ally or as a subject. For it is not hatred but right that makes a man the enemy of a state, and the right of a state against the man who does not recognize its sovereignty by any kind of contract is the same as its right against the man who has done it harm, since it has the right to use every means in its power to force him either to submit or to become an ally. Finally, the crime of treason[2] can only be committed by subjects or citizens, who by contract, either tacit or express, have transferred all their right to the commonwealth; and a subject is said to have committed this crime if he has attempted to usurp the sovereign's right or to transfer it to another from any motive whatsoever. I say 'has attempted', for if men were not to be condemned until the deed was done, then, once the right had been usurped or transferred, it would generally be too late for the commonwealth to try to condemn them.[3] Again I say unreservedly 'if he attempts to usurp the sovereign's right from any motive whatsoever': thereby denying that it makes any difference whether his action tended to the detriment or the obvious advantage of the whole state; for whatever the motive behind his attempt, he has committed treason and is rightly condemned. Now in time of war all admit that this punishment is fully justified; i.e. that if a man deserts his post, and attacks the enemy unbeknown to his general, then, no matter how good his intentions were, or how completely he defeated the enemy, he has taken matters into his own hands and is rightly condemned to death for breaking his oath to his general and infringing the latter's right. But not all see with equal clearness that every citizen without exception is always bound by this right: although the principle is precisely the same. For since a state must be preserved and guided solely by the policy

---

[1] *TP* iii, 13–17, pp. 295–9.   [2] *TP* iv, 3, p. 301.
[3] Cf. the old epigram:

> 'Treason doth never prosper: what's the reason?
> For if it prosper, none dare call it Treason.'

consilio debet conservari et dirigi, hocque jus ei soli competere absolute pacti sunt, si quis ergo solo suo arbitrio et inscio supremo concilio negotium aliquod publicum aggressus est exequi, quamvis inde incrementum civitatis, uti diximus, certo sequeretur, jus tamen sum-
5 mae potestatis violavit et majestatem laesit, atque jure merito damnatur.

Superest jam, ut omnem scrupulum amoveamus, respondere an id quod supra affirmavimus, quod scilicet unusquisque qui rationis usum non habet in statu naturali ex legibus appetitus summo jure naturae vivit, non aperte juri divino revelato repugnet. Nam cum omnes
10 absolute (sive rationis usum habeant sive minus) aeque tenerentur ex mandato divino proximum tanquam se ipsum amare, non ergo sine injuria alteri damnum inferre possumus et solis legibus appetitus vivere. Verum huic objectioni, si tantum ad statum naturalem attendimus, facile respondere possumus; nam is et natura et tempore prior est
15 religione. Nemo enim ex natura scit se ulla erga Deum teneri obedientia,[34] imo nec ulla ratione hoc assequi, sed tantum ex revelatione signis confirmata unusquisque id habere potest. Quare ante revelationem nemo jure divino quod non potest non ignorare tenetur. Et ideo status naturalis cum statu religionis minime confundendus, sed absque re-
20 ligione et lege, et consequenter absque peccato et injuria concipiendus; ut jam fecimus, et Pauli authoritate confirmavimus. Nec tantum ratione ignorantiae statum naturalem ante jus divinum revelatum et absque eodem concipimus, sed etiam ratione libertatis qua omnes nascuntur. Si enim homines ex natura jure divino tenerentur, vel si
25 jus divinum ex natura jus esset, superfluum erat ut Deus cum hominibus contractum iniret, et pacto et juramento eosdem obligaret. Quare absolute concedendum jus divinum ab eo tempore incepisse, a quo homines expresso pacto Deo promiserunt in omnibus obedire; quo sua libertate naturali quasi cesserunt jusque suum in Deum transtulerunt,
30 sicuti in statu civili fieri diximus. Sed de his in sequentibus prolixius agam.

---

3. *I consilio.*   8. *O jure; I jurae.*

of the sovereign, and since the citizens have agreed unreservedly that this right belongs to the sovereign alone, then, if anyone has attempted to perform any public function without the knowledge and authority of the supreme council, he has infringed the sovereign's right and committed treason, even although his action, as I said, was certain to lead to the commonwealth's advancement; and his condemnation is fully justified.

It now remains to remove all misgivings by answering the following objection. Is not the assertion made above,[1] that in the state of nature everyone who does not have the use of reason lives by the laws of appetite with perfect natural right, plainly inconsistent with revealed divine law? Surely, since all men without exception (whether they have the use of reason or not) would appear to be equally bound by divine command to love their neighbour as themselves, we cannot do harm to another and live solely by the laws of appetite without doing wrong.[2] But if we confine our attention to the state of nature, this objection can easily be answered, since the state of nature is prior to religion both in nature and in time. For nobody knows by nature that he owes any obedience to God;[3] nor indeed can he attain this knowledge by any exercise of reason,[4] but only through revelation confirmed by signs. Thus prior to revelation nobody is bound by a divine law which must necessarily be unknown to him. And so the state of nature is certainly not to be confused with a condition where religion exists, but must be conceived as without religion and law, and hence as without sin and wrong-doing; which is how I have conceived it, confirming my view by the authority of Paul.[5] Nor is it only because of men's ignorance that I conceive the state of nature as prior to and lacking in revealed divine law, but also because of the freedom which is every man's birthright. For if men were naturally bound by divine law, or if divine law were law by nature, there would have been no need for God to make a contract with men, and to bind them by a covenant and an oath.[6] Hence we must admit unreservedly that divine law only came into force when men made an explicit covenant to obey God in all things; by so doing they so to speak surrendered their natural freedom and transferred their right to God, just as they transfer it to the sovereign in the political order. With this, however, I shall deal more fully later.[7]

---

[1] pp. 125–7.   [2] *TP* ii, 22, pp. 281–3.   [3] n. 34, pp. 247–9.
[4] Because the God revealed by reason is not a prince who lays down laws for men (*TT-P* iv, pp. 77–83).
[5] p. 127.   [6] *TP* ii, 18, p. 279.   [7] *TT-P* xvii, pp. 157 and ff.

Verum instari adhuc potest quod summae potestates aeque ac subditi hoc jure divino tenentur, quas tamen diximus jus naturale retinere, et iis omnia jure licere. Quare ad hanc integram amovendam difficultatem, quae non tam ex ratione status quam juris naturalis oritur, dico 5 quod unusquisque in statu naturali eadem ratione tenetur jure revelato ac tenetur ex dictamine sanae rationis vivere; nempe quia ipsi utilius est et ad salutem necessarium. Quod si nollet, cum suo periculo licet; atque adeo ex solo proprio, non autem ex alterius decreto vivere, neque aliquem mortalem judicem nec jure religionis vindicem agnoscere 10 tenetur. Atque hoc jus summam potestatem retinuisse affirmo; quae quidem homines consulere potest, at neminem judicem agnoscere tenetur, nec ullum mortalem praeter se alicujus juris vindicem, nisi prophetam qui expresse a Deo missus fuerit, quique id indubitatis signis ostenderit. At nec tunc quidem hominem, sed Deum ipsum judicem 15 agnoscere cogitur. Quod si summa potestas nollet Deo in jure suo revelato obedire, id ipsi cum suo periculo et damno licet, nullo scilicet jure, civili vel naturali, repugnante. Jus enim civile ab ejus decreto tantum pendet: jus autem naturale pendet a legibus naturae, quae non religioni, humanum tantum utile intendenti, sed ordini universae 20 naturae, hoc est, aeterno Dei decreto, nobis incognito, accommodatae sunt. Quod quidem alii obscurius concepisse videntur; qui scilicet statuunt hominem contra voluntatem Dei revelatam quidem, sed non contra ejus aeternum decretum quo omnia praedeterminavit posse peccare.

25 Si quis autem jam roget: *Quid si summa potestas aliquid contra religionem et obedientiam quam Deo expresso pacto promisimus imperet? Divino an humano imperio obtemperandum?* Sed quia de his in sequentibus prolixius agam, hic breviter tantum dico Deo supra omnia obediendum quando certam et indubitatam habemus revelationem. Sed quia 30 circa religionem maxime errare solent homines, et pro ingeniorum diversitate multa magno certamine fingere, ut experientia plus quam satis testatur, certum est quod si nemo summae potestati jure teneretur

---

21. *O alii; I Alii.*

But it can still be urged that sovereigns[1] are as much bound by this divine law as subjects; whereas I have said that they retain the right of nature, and have a right to do everything. So to remove this whole difficulty, which is based on the right of nature rather than on the state of nature, I affirm that everyone in the state of nature is bound by revealed law for the same reason as he is bound to live by the dictate of sound reason, i.e. because it is in his own best interests and necessary for his own welfare to do this.[2] But if he will not do this he is free to do otherwise at his own risk; thus he may live entirely as he pleases and is not bound to obey the will of another, or to recognize any mortal as his judge or as a champion of religion by right. And this is the right which I assert that the sovereign has retained. No doubt it can consult men, but it is not bound to recognize anyone as its judge, or to regard any mortal but itself as the champion of any law, unless he be a prophet who has been sent expressly by God, and has proved his authority by unmistakable signs. Even then it is not forced to recognize a human being as its judge, but God himself. And if the sovereign will not obey God in his revealed law, it is free to do otherwise at its own cost and risk; i.e. no right, either natural or civil, stands in its way. For civil right depends entirely on its decree, while natural right depends on the laws of nature, and these have no regard to religion (which aims at human welfare only), but conform to the system of nature as a whole, that is, to the eternal decree of God, to us unknown. This seems to have been dimly apprehended by those who hold that man *can* sin against the revealed will of God, but not against the eternal decree by which he has fore-ordained all things.[3]

But suppose someone now asks: 'What if the sovereign commands something contrary to religion and the obedience we have expressly promised to God? Are we to obey the divine or the human command?'[4] As I shall be dealing with this more fully in a later chapter,[5] I shall content myself here with the brief assertion that God has the first claim on our obedience when we have a sure and unmistakable revelation of his will. But in matters of religion men are particularly prone to err, and because of their different temperaments to conceive and cherish many conflicting prejudices, as experience amply testifies; so that if nobody were bound by right to obey the sovereign in matters which

---

[1] The point is that sovereigns exist in a state of nature which is not prior to revealed religion, so that in their case the argument from ignorance does not apply.

[2] *TP* iv, 5, p. 305.

[3] *TP* ii, 22, pp. 281–3.

[4] *TP* iii, 10, p. 293.

[5] *TT-P* xix.

obtemperare in iis quae ipse ad religionem pertinere putat, tum jus
civitatis a diverso uniuscujusque judicio et affectu penderet. Nam
nemo eodem teneretur qui id contra suam fidem et superstitionem
statutum judicaret; atque adeo unusquisque sub hoc praetextu licentiam
5 ad omnia sumere posset. Et quandoquidem hac ratione jus civitatis
prorsus violatur, hinc sequitur summae potestati, cui soli jura imperii
conservare et tutari tam jure divino quam naturali incumbit, jus
summum competere de religione statuendi quicquid judicat, et omnes
ad ejusdem de eadem decreta et mandata ex fide ipsi data, quam Deus
10 omnino servari jubet, obtemperare teneri. Quod si ii qui summum
tenent imperium sint ethnici, vel cum iis nihil contrahendum, sed
potius quam jus suum in eos transferant extrema pati deliberandum;
vel, si contraxerint, jusque suum in eos transtulerint, quandoquidem eo
ipso se jure se religionemque defendendi privaverunt, iis obtemperare
15 tenentur, fidemque servare vel ad id cogi, excepto eo cui Deus certa
revelatione singulare contra tyrannum promiserit auxilium, vel nomina-
tim exceptum voluit. Sic videmus ex tot Judaeis qui Babylone erant
tres tantum juvenes qui de Dei auxilio non dubitabant Nabucadono-
zori obtemperare noluisse: reliqui autem sine dubio, excepto etiam
20 Daniële, quem rex ipse adoraverat, jure coacti obtemperaverunt;
animo forte reputantes se ex Dei decreto regi deditos, regemque
summum obtinere imperium et divina directione conservare. Contra
Eleazarus, stante adhuc utcunque patria, exemplum constantiae suis
dare voluit, ut eum secuti omnia potius tolerarent quam paterentur jus
25 suum et potestatem in Graecos transferri, et omnia experirentur ne in
ethnicorum fidem jurare cogerentur. Quod etiam quotidiana experientia confirmatur. Qui enim Christianum imperium obtinent, ad majorem
ejus securitatem non dubitant foedus cum Turcis et ethnicis pangere,
subditosque suos qui eo habitatum eunt jubere ne majorem libertatem
30 ad aliquid humanum aut divinum exercendum sumant quam expresse
contraxerunt, vel illud imperium concedit; ut patet ex contractu Belgarum cum Japonensibus de quo supra diximus.

13–14. *P eo ipso se jure se religionemque defendendi privaverunt*; *I eo ipso se religionemque
defendendi privaverunt.*
15–17. Cf. p. 114, ll. 11–12.

he personally thought to be the concern of religion, the civil law would obviously depend on the differing judgements and feelings of individuals. For no one would be bound by it if he thought that it contradicted his own superstitious convictions; so on this pretext everyone would be able to assume a complete liberty of action. And since this destroys the civil law altogether, it follows that the sovereign, which, by both divine and natural law, alone has the function of preserving and safeguarding the laws of the state, possesses a perfect right to make any decrees about religion it thinks fit, and that all are bound to obey these decrees and commands by reason of the pledge they have given it, a pledge which God bids men keep with all scrupulousness. If those who hold the sovereign power are infidels, either no contract should be made with them, and a man should make up his mind to suffer the worst rather than transfer his right to them; or, if he has made a contract, and has transferred his right to them, then, since he has thereby surrendered the right to defend himself and his religion, he is bound to obey them, and to honour his pledge or be compelled to honour it; unless God, by a sure revelation of his will, has promised him particular aid against a tyrant, or has exempted him by name. Thus we see that out of all the Jews in Babylon only three youths who were sure of God's aid refused to obey Nebuchadnezzar:[1] the rest—Daniel, whom the king himself had worshipped,[2] also excepted—were no doubt compelled by right to obey, thinking probably that they had been delivered into the king's hands by God's decree, and that the king held and maintained his sovereign power by divine guidance. (Contrast Eleazar,[3] who, living when his country was still maintaining itself as best it could, wished to set an example of constancy for his countrymen to follow, that they might endure every hardship rather than allow their right and power to be transferred to the Greeks, and might do their utmost to avoid being forced to swear allegiance to Gentiles.) But everyday experience also confirms my view; for to ensure the greater security of their states Christian rulers do not hesitate to make treaties with Turks and infidels, and to command their subjects who go to live in such lands not to assume greater freedom in their ordinary conduct and religious worship than has been expressly stipulated in the treaty, or is permitted by the foreign government; as is clear from the treaty of the Dutch with the Japanese which I have mentioned above.[4]

---

[1] *Daniel* 3.   [2] *Daniel* 2, 46.
[3] Eleazar was martyred during the attempt of Antiochus Epiphanes to hellenize the Jews in the first half of the second century B.C.   [4] *TT-P* v, p. 99.

CAPUT XVII

Ostenditur neminem omnia in summam potestatem trans-
ferre posse, nec esse necesse. De republica Hebraeorum,
qualis fuerit vivente Mose; qualis post ejus mortem ante-
quam reges elegerint; deque ejus praestantia; et denique
de causis cur respublica divina interire, et vix absque
seditionibus subsistere potuerit

CONTEMPLATIO praecedentis Capitis de jure summarum potestatum in
omnia, deque jure naturali uniuscujusque in easdem translato, quamvis
cum praxi non parum conveniat, et praxis ita institui possit ut ad eandem
magis ac magis accedat, nunquam tamen fiet quin in multis mere
theoretica maneat. Nam nemo unquam suam potentiam et consequenter neque suum jus ita in alium transferre poterit ut homo esse desinat;
nec talis ulla summa potestas unquam dabitur quae omnia ita ut vult
exequi possit. Frustra enim subdito imperaret ut illum odio habeat qui
eum sibi beneficio junxit, ut amet qui ei damnum intulit, ut contumeliis
non offendatur, ut a metu liberari non cupiat, et alia perplurima hujusmodi quae ex legibus humanae naturae necessario sequuntur. Atque
hoc ipsam etiam experientiam clarissime docere existimo; nam nunquam homines suo jure ita cesserunt, suamque potentiam in alium ita
transtulerunt, ut ab iis ipsis qui eorum jus et potentiam acceperunt non
timerentur, et imperium non magis propter cives, quanquam suo
jure privatos, quam propter hostes periclitaretur.[35] Et sane si homines
jure suo naturali ita privari possent ut nihil in posterum possent nisi
volentibus iis qui supremum jus retinuerunt, tum profecto impune
violentissime in subditos regnare liceret: quod nemini in mentem
venire posse credo. Quare concedendum unumquemque multa sibi
sui juris reservare, quae propterea a nullius decreto sed a suo solo

---

8. *Gf easdem; I eandem.*

CHAPTER XVII

That nobody can, or need, transfer everything to the sovereign. An account of the Jewish state as it was in Moses' life-time; of its nature after his death, before the institution of kings; and of its excellence. Finally, an account of the reasons why the theocracy was liable to destruction, and could hardly exist without civil strife

THE views I expressed in the previous Chapter about the absolute right of the sovereign, and the transfer to it of the individual's natural right, agree fairly well with actual practice, and practice can be made to conform to them more and more closely;[1] yet they must always remain in many respects purely theoretical. For no one will ever be able to transfer his power and right to another so completely as to cease to be a man;[2] nor will there ever be a sovereign so powerful that it can do everything it pleases. If a sovereign were to command a subject to hate someone who has bound him by a service, or to love someone who has done him harm,[3] if it were to command him not to take offence at insults, not to desire to rid himself of fear, and not to feel the many other emotions of this kind which follow necessarily from the laws of human nature, it would command in vain. And this, I think, is plainly shown by actual experience; for men have never surrendered their right and transferred their power to others so completely that they ceased to be feared by the very rulers who received their right and power, and, although deprived of their natural right, became less dangerous to the state as citizens than its external enemies.[4] Of course if men could be deprived of their natural right so completely that they were unable to do anything thereafter except by the will of the sovereign, it would certainly be possible to exercise the most violent tyranny over subjects with impunity: but no one, I think, can believe this for a moment.[5] Hence we must admit that the individual retains his own right in many of his actions, which therefore depend on nobody's decision but his own.

---

[1] But only if the sovereign convinces his subjects that he has their interests at heart: cf. Locke on prerogative (*Second Treatise of Civil Government*, § 165).

[2] *TP* vii, 25, p. 357.

[3] *TP* iii, 8, p. 291.

[4] n. 35, p. 251: cf. *TP* vi, 6, p. 317.

[5] Cf. the quotation from Seneca on pp. 95 and 135.

pendent. Attamen ut recte intelligatur quousque imperii jus et potestas se extendat, notandum imperii potestatem non in eo praecise contineri quod homines metu cogere potest, sed absolute in omnibus quibus efficere potest ut homines ejus mandatis obsequantur; non enim ratio
5 obtemperandi, sed obtemperantia subditum facit. Nam quacunque ratione homo deliberet summae potestatis mandata exequi, sive ideo sit quod poenam timet, sive quod aliquid inde sperat, sive quod patriam amat, sive alio quocunque affectu impulsus, tamen ex proprio suo consilio deliberat et nihilominus ex summae potestatis imperio agit. Non
10 igitur ex eo quod homo proprio consilio aliquid facit illico concludendum eum id ex suo et non imperii jure agere; nam quandoquidem, tam cum ex amore obligatus quam cum metu coactus ad malum evitandum, semper ex proprio consilio et decreto agit, vel imperium nullum esset nec ullum jus in subditos, vel id necessario ad omnia se extendit quibus
15 effici potest ut homines ipsi cedere deliberent. Et consequenter quicquid subditus facit quod mandatis summae potestatis respondet, sive id amore obligatus, sive metu coercitus, sive (quod quidem magis frequens) ex spe et metu simul, sive ex reverentia, quae passio est ex metu et admiratione composita, sive quacunque ratione ductus, ex
20 jure imperii, non autem suo agit. Quod etiam hinc quam clarissime constat quod obedientia non tam externam quam animi internam actionem respiciat; adeoque ille maxime sub alterius imperio est qui alteri integro animo ad omnia ejus mandata obtemperare deliberat, et consequitur eum maximum tenere imperium qui in subditorum animos
25 regnat. Quod si qui maxime timentur maximum tenerent imperium, tum profecto id tyrannorum subditi tenerent, qui a suis tyrannis maxime timentur. Deinde quamvis non perinde animis ac linguis imperari possit, sunt tamen animi aliqua ratione sub imperio summae potestatis, quae multis modis efficere potest ut permagna hominum
30 pars quicquid vult credat, amet, odio habeat, etc. Adeoque etsi haec non directo mandato summae potestatis fiant, fiunt tamen saepe, ut experientia abunde testatur, ex authoritate ipsius potentiae et ipsius directione, id est, ex ipsius jure: quare sine ulla intellectus repugnantia

4. *O mandatis*; *I mendatis.*   24. *V–L consequitur*; *I consequenter.*

But we cannot form a true idea of how far the right and power of the state extends unless we note that its power is not restricted to the power of coercing men by fear,[1] but includes absolutely every means it has to make men obey its commands; since it is not the motive for obedience which makes a man a subject, but the will to obey. For if a man decides to carry out a sovereign's commands, it does not matter whether his motive is fear of punishment, or the hope of some reward for obedience, or love of country, or any other emotion whatsoever; his decision arises from his own deliberation, yet his action is still determined by the sovereign's authority. We must not therefore jump to the conclusion that because a man's action arises from his own deliberation he does it by his own right and not by the right of the state; for since his actions always arise from his own deliberation and decision, both when he is bound by love, and when he is forced by fear to avoid evil, there would on that view be no sovereignty at all, and no right over subjects whatsoever. The alternative is that sovereignty necessarily includes every means by which it can induce men to decide to obey it; from which it follows that anything a subject does in response to a sovereign's commands, whether he does it from ties of affection, or compulsion of fear, or (and this is more usual) from hope and fear together, or from respect, a passion compounded of fear and admiration, or from any other motive whatsoever, he does by the right of the state and not by his own.[2] My point is also proved conclusively by the fact that obedience is less a matter of the outward act than of the mind's inner activity, so that the man who wholeheartedly decides to obey all the commands of another is most completely under his government; and in consequence he who rules in the hearts of his subjects has the most absolute sovereignty. If those who inspire most fear had the most absolute sovereignty it would undoubtedly belong to the subjects of tyrants, who inspire very great fear in their masters. Besides, although minds cannot be governed to the same extent as tongues,[3] they are to some degree under the control of the sovereign, which has many means of making most of its subjects believe, and feel love, hate, and other emotions towards, anything it wishes. And although this does not happen by the sovereign's direct command, it is quite common for it to happen by its guidance and the authority of its power, i.e. by its right, as experience amply testifies: so

---

[1] *TP* v, 6, p. 311. The passage is directed against Hobbes's emphasis on fear as a motive for political obedience.
[2] He is not *sui juris*: yet he still acts *jure naturali* (cf. *TP* iii, 3, pp. 285–7).
[3] *TT-P* xx, p. 227.

concipere possumus homines qui ex solo imperii jure credunt, amant, odio habent, contemnunt, et absolute nullo non affectu corripiuntur.

At quanquam hac ratione jus et potestatem imperii satis amplam 5 concipimus, nunquam tamen fiet ut ullum adeo magnum detur ut ii qui id tenent potentiam absolute ad omnia quae velint habeant: quod me jam satis clare ostendisse puto. Qua autem ratione imperium formari posset ut nihilominus secure semper conservetur, jam dixi meum intentum non esse id ostendere: attamen, ut ad id quod volo perveniam, 10 ea notabo quae in hunc finem divina revelatio Mosen olim docuit, et deinde Hebraeorum historias et successus perpendemus, ex quibus tandem videbimus quaenam praecipue subditis ad majorem imperii securitatem et incrementum concedenda sunt a summis potestatibus.

Quod imperii conservatio praecipue pendeat a subditorum fide, 15 eorumque virtute et animi constantia in exequendis mandatis, ratio et experientia quam clarissime docent: qua autem ratione iidem duci debeant ut fidem et virtutem constanter servent non aeque facile est videre. Omnes namque, tam qui regunt quam qui reguntur, homines sunt, ex labore scilicet proclives ad libidinem. Imo qui tan- 20 tum varium multitudinis ingenium experti sunt de eo fere desperant, quia non ratione sed solis affectibus gubernatur; praeceps ad omnia, et facillime vel avaritia vel luxu corrumpitur; unusquisque solus omnia se scire putat, et omnia ex suo ingenio moderari vult, et eatenus aliquid aequum vel iniquum, fasque nefasque existimat, qua- 25 tenus in suum lucrum vel damnum cadere judicat; prae gloria aequales contemnit, nec ab iis dirigi patitur; prae invidia melioris laudis, vel fortunae, quae nunquam aequalis est, malum alterius cupit, eoque delectatur. Nec opus est omnia recensere; norunt quippe omnes quid sceleris fastidium praesentium et rerum novandarum cupiditas, quid 30 praeceps ira, quid contemta paupertas frequenter suadeant hominibus, quantumque eorum animos occupent agitentque. His ergo omnibus praevenire, et imperium ita constituere ut nullus locus fraudi relinquatur, imo omnia ita instituere ut omnes, cujuscunque ingenii sint, jus publicum privatis commodis praeferant, hoc opus, hic labor est. 35 Rei quidem necessitas multa excogitare coëgit; attamen nunquam eo

---

25. *O damnum; I damnum.*

that there is no rational objection to our conceiving[1] of men who believe, love, hate, despise, in short, feel every emotion which seizes them, by the right of the state alone.

But although when thus conceived the right and power of the state is pretty great, it will never be possible for any such right to be so great that those who possess it have the power to do absolutely everything they wish: so much, I think, I have already made quite plain. How a state can be organized so that, in spite of this, it is always kept secure, it is not, as I have already said, my intention to show:[2] yet in order to reach the topic I wish to discuss, I shall note the means of achieving this end which Moses learnt of old through divine revelation. Then I shall consider the course of Jewish history; and hence we shall eventually discover the main rights which must be granted to subjects by sovereigns for the greater security and advancement of the state.

That the preservation of a state depends mainly on the loyalty of its subjects, and on their excellence and steadfastness in executing commands, is taught very plainly by both reason and experience: but the means by which they should be led to preserve their loyalty and excellence consistently are more difficult to see. For all, rulers and ruled alike, are men, i.e. are apt to slip from the hard path of duty into the pursuit of pleasure.[3] In fact, those who know the utter fickleness of the people are driven almost to despair, for it is not guided by reason but solely by its passions: it has no self-restraint, and is easily corrupted by greed or luxury; every single man imagines that he has a monopoly of wisdom, and wants to direct everything to suit his own inclinations; he thinks things fair or unfair, right or wrong, only as he believes them conducive to his own gain or loss; through pride he despises his equals and refuses their guidance; through envy of better reputation, or of better fortune—and fortune is never equal—he desires and takes pleasure in the calamities of others. But there is no need to review the whole count, for everyone knows the wickedness which is often inspired in men by dislike of the status quo and desire for revolution, by hasty anger and the slights of poverty, and the extent to which these things occupy and disturb their minds. To forestall all this, and to organize the state in such a way that no room is left for disloyalty, nay more, to arrange every detail of the constitution so that everyone, whatever his disposition, prefers public right to private advantage,[4] this is the task and this the toil.[5] Its urgency has forced men to devise

---

[1] In theory. [2] This topic is discussed in *TP* vi–xi.
[3] Terence, *Andria* 77–78. [4] *TP* vi, 3, p. 315. [5] Virgil, *Aeneid* vi, 129.

perventum est ut imperium non magis propter cives quam hostes periclitaretur, et qui id tenent non magis illos quam hos timerent. Testis invictissima ab hostibus Romanorum respublica, toties a suis civibus victa et miserrime oppressa, ac praecipue in bello civili Vespa-
5 siani contra Vitellium: qua de re vide Tacitum in initio libr. IV Histor., ubi miserrimam urbis faciem depingit. Alexander simplicius (ut ait Curtius in fine libr. 8) famam in hoste quam in cive aestimabat, quippe a suis credebat magnitudinem suam posse destrui etc. Et fatum suum timens amicos haec precatur. *Vos modo me ab intestina fraude et*
10 *domesticorum insidiis praestate securum; belli martisque discrimen im-* *pavidus subibo. Philippus in acie tutior quam in theatro fuit; hostium* *manum saepe vitavit, suorum effugere non valuit. Aliorum quoque regum* *exitus si reputaveritis, plures a suis quam ab hoste interemptos numerabitis.* Vide Q. Curtii lib. 9 § 6. Hac igitur de causa reges qui olim imperium
15 usurpaverant, ad se scilicet securos praestandos, persuadere conati sunt se genus suum a Diis immortalibus ducere; nimirum quia putabant quod, si modo subditi et omnes eosdem non ut aequales aspicerent, sed Deos esse crederent, libenter se ab iisdem regi paterentur, seseque facile ipsis dederent. Sic Augustus Romanis persuasit se ab Aenea, qui Veneris
20 filius et inter Deos credebatur, originem suam ducere; se templis et effigie numinum per flamines et sacerdotes coli voluit. Tac. Annal. lib. I. Alexander ut Jovis filius salutari voluit; quod quidem consilio, non autem ex superbia fecisse videtur, ut ejus responsio ad Hermolai invectivam indicat. *Illud*, inquit, *paene risu dignum fuit quod Hermolaus*
25 *postulabat me, ut aversarer Jovem, cujus oraculo agnoscor. An etiam* *quid Dii respondeant in mea potestate est? Obtulit nomen filii mihi: re-* *cipere* (N.B.) *ipsis rebus quas agimus haud alienum fuit. Utinam Indi* *quoque Deum esse me credant. Fama enim bella constant, et saepe quod falso* *creditum est veri vicem obtinuit.* Curtii lib. 8 § 8. Quibus paucis acute
30 rem simulatam ignaris persuadere pergit, et simul causam simulationis

7. *V–L libr. 8; I libr. VIII.*   16–17. *P putabant quod, si; I putabant, si.*
25. *B* (following Curtius) *postulabat a me.*   *B* (following Curtius) *agnoscor; I cognoscor.*

many solutions; yet they have never succeeded in ensuring that the state ran less risk from its citizens than from external enemies, and that its rulers feared the latter more than the former.[1] Witness the city of Rome, so invincible by its enemies, yet so often conquered and crushed most miserably by its own citizens, and especially during the civil war between Vespasian and Vitellius: on which see the start of Book IV of Tacitus' Histories,[2] where the melancholy appearance of the city is described. Alexander, as Curtius says at the end of Book 8,[3] was more generous in his praise of an enemy than of a fellow citizen, because he thought that his greatness might be destroyed by his own followers. It was in fear of this fate that he made the following request to his friends: 'Do you but keep me safe from internal treachery and the plots of my household, and I shall face undaunted the hazards of war and battle. Philip was safer in battle than in the theatre: he often evaded the blows of the enemy, but could not escape those of his countrymen. And if you consider the deaths of other kings, you will count more killed by their followers than by the enemy.' See Q. Curtius, Book 9, § 6.[4] It was then for this purpose, i.e. to render themselves secure, that kings who had usurped the throne in olden times tried to persuade men that they were descended from the immortal Gods; they thought, of course, that if only their subjects and men in general would regard them as Gods instead of as equals, they would be willing to accept their rule and ready to submit.[5] Thus Augustus persuaded the Romans that he traced his lineage to Aeneas, who was regarded as the son of Venus and a member of the pantheon; he wished to be worshipped with temples and statues befitting a god, and with rites performed by flamens and priests. Tacitus, Annals, Book I.[6] Alexander wished to be styled the son of Zeus, and this, it seems, from policy and not from vanity: witness his reply to the attack of Hermolaus. 'It was', he said, 'almost ludicrous for Hermolaus to ask me to decline recognition by the oracle of Zeus. Have I control even over the responses of the Gods? Zeus offered me the name of son: *to accept it was not inimical to our projects*. May the Indians too believe me to be a god; for wars are won by reputation, and a false belief has often served as well as truth.' Curtius, Book 8, § 8.[7] In these few words he proceeds—very cleverly— to make the ignorant believe the pretence, and at the same time he

[1] p. 149.
[2] Tacitus, *Histories*, IV, i.
[3] Curtius, *Historiae Alexandri Magni* VIII, xiv, 46.
[4] Curtius, op. cit. IX, vi, 24–25.
[5] *TT-P* v, p. 95.
[6] Tacitus, *Annals* I, x, 5.
[7] Curtius, op. cit. VIII, viii, 14–15.

innuit. Quod etiam Cleo in sua oratione qua Macedonibus conabatur persuadere ut regi assentarentur fecit; postquam enim laudes
Alexandri cum admiratione narrando ejusdemque merita recensendo
simulationi speciem veri dedit, ad rei utilitatem sic transit. *Persas*
5 *quidem non pie solum sed etiam prudenter reges suos inter Deos colere;*
majestatem enim imperii salutis esse tutelam. Et tandem concludit, *semet*
ipsum, cum rex inisset convivium, prostraturum humi corpus. Debere
idem facere caeteros, et imprimis sapientia praeditos. Vide ejusd. lib.
8 § 5. Sed prudentiores erant Macedones, nec homines, nisi prorsus
10 barbari sint, tam aperte falli et ex subditis inutiles sibi servi fieri
patiuntur. Alii autem facilius persuadere potuerunt majestatem sacram
esse, et vicem Dei in terra gerere, et a Deo, non autem ab hominum
suffragio et consensu, constitui, singularique providentia et auxilio
divino conservari atque defendi. Et ad hunc modum monarchae ad sui
15 imperii securitatem alia excogitaverunt: quae omnia missa facio, et ut
ad ea quae volo perveniam ea tantum, uti dixi, notabo et perpendam
quae in hunc finem olim divina revelatio Mosen docuit.

Diximus jam supra (Cap. V) quod postquam Hebraei Aegypto
exiverunt nullo alterius nationis jure amplius tenebantur, sed iis ad
20 lubitum nova jura instituere, et quas volebant terras occupare licebat.
Nam postquam ab intoleranda Aegyptiorum oppressione liberati, et
nulli mortalium ullo pacto addicti erant, jus suum naturale ad omnia
quae possent iterum adepti sunt; et unusquisque de integro deliberare
poterat num id retinere, an vero eodem cedere idque in alium transferre
25 volebat. Igitur in hoc statu naturali constituti, ex consilio Mosis, cui
omnes maximam fidem habebant, suum jus in neminem mortalium, sed
tantum in Deum transferre deliberaverunt: nec diu cunctati omnes
aeque uno clamore promiserunt Deo ad omnia ejus mandata absolute
obtemperare, nec aliud jus agnoscere nisi quod ipse revelatione pro-
30 phetica ut jus statueret. Atque haec promissio, sive juris in Deum
translatio, eodem modo facta est ac in communi societate supra concepimus fieri quando homines jure suo naturali cedere deliberant.
Expresso enim pacto (vide Exod. Cap. 24 vers. 7) et juramento jure

6. *B* (following Curtius) *majestatem enim imperii salutis esse tutelam;* *I Majestatis enim*
salutis esse tutelam; *IV Majestatem enim salutis esse tutelam.*
11. *Gf persuaderi.*

hints at the reason for it. Cleon did the same in the speech whereby he tried to persuade the Macedonians to kow-tow to their king. First he gives the pretence an appearance of truth by singing Alexander's praises and recounting his wonderful achievements: then he passes to its utility by saying that the Persians were prudent as well as pious to worship their kings as gods; for royalty was the pillar of a state's security. And he concludes by promising that he for his part would prostrate himself on the ground when the king entered the banquet; the others ought to do likewise, and especially those endowed with wisdom. Curtius, Book 8, § 5.[1] But the Macedonians were too sensible; and, unless they are ignorant savages, subjects do not allow themselves to be deceived so obviously, and to be turned into slaves useless to themselves. Still, others[2] have found it easier to persuade men that royalty is sacred, that it is God's representative on earth, that it is established by God and not by the votes and agreement of men, and that it is preserved and protected by a special divine providence and assistance. And kings have devised other means of the same kind to make their rule secure: but all these I pass over, and in order to reach the topic I wish to discuss I shall confine myself, as I said, to noting and considering the means which Moses learnt of old by divine revelation.

I have already said in Chapter V above[3] that after the exodus from Egypt the Jews were no longer bound by the law of another nation, but were free to establish new laws as they pleased and to occupy what lands they wished. For once they had been freed from the intolerable yoke of the Egyptians and were not bound by pact to any mortal man, they regained their natural right to do everything in their power; and each could decide afresh whether he would retain it or surrender and transfer it to another. Having thus reverted to the condition of nature, they took the advice of Moses, in whom they all had the greatest confidence, and decided to transfer their right to no mortal man, but to God alone; and without long delay they all promised equally, with one voice, to obey all God's commands implicitly, and to recognize as law only what he should declare to be such by prophetic revelation. This promise, or transference of right to God, was made in the same way as I conceived it to be made above in an ordinary society when men decide to surrender their natural right.[4] For it was by an explicit oath and covenant (see Exodus, Chapter 24, verse 7) that they surrendered

---

[1] Curtius, op. cit. VIII, v, 10–12.
[2] The advocates of the divine right of kings.
[3] pp. 95–97.   [4] Hobbes, *De Cive* xvi, 9.

suo naturali libere, non autem vi coacti neque minis territi, cesserunt et in Deum transtulerunt. Deinde ut pactum ratum fixumque esset et absque fraudis suspicione, nihil Deus cum ipsis pepigit nisi postquam experti sunt ejus admirandam potentiam, qua sola servati fuerant et qua 5 sola in posterum servari poterant (vide Exod. Cap. 19 vs. 4, 5). Nam hoc ipso quod se sola Dei potentia servari posse crediderunt omnem suam naturalem potentiam se conservandi, quam ex se habere antea forte putaverant, in Deum transtulerunt, et consequenter omne suum jus. Imperium ergo Hebraeorum Deus solus tenuit, quodque adeo solum 10 ex vi pacti Regnum Dei jure vocabatur, et Deus jure etiam Rex Hebraeorum: et consequenter hujus imperii hostes hostes Dei, et cives qui id usurpare vellent rei laesae divinae majestatis, et jura denique imperii jura et mandata Dei. Quare in hoc imperio jus civile et religio, quae, ut ostendimus, in sola obedientia erga Deum consistit, unum et 15 idem erant: videlicet religionis dogmata non documenta, sed jura et mandata erant; pietas justitia, impietas crimen et injustitia aestimabatur. Qui a religione deficiebat, civis esse desinebat, et eo solo hostis habebatur, et qui pro religione moriebatur, pro patria mori reputabatur; et absolute jus civile et religio nullo prorsus discrimine habebantur. Et hac de cáusa 20 hoc imperium theocratia vocari potuit, quandoquidem ejus cives nullo jure nisi a Deo revelato tenebantur. Verumenimvero haec omnia opinione magis quam re constabant; nam Hebraei revera jus imperii absolute retinuerunt, ut ex jam dicendis constabit, nempe ex modo et ratione qua hoc imperium administrabatur, et quam hic explicare 25 constitui.

Quandoquidem Hebraei suum jus in nullum alium transtulerunt, sed omnes aeque, ut in democratia, suo jure cesserunt, unoque ore clamaverunt *Quicquid Deus loquetur* (nullo expresso mediatore) *faciemus*, hinc sequitur omnes ab hoc pacto aequales prorsus mansisse, jusque Deum 30 consulendi legesque accipiendi et interpretandi omnibus aequale fuisse, et absolute omnem imperii administrationem omnes aeque tenuisse. Hac ergo de causa omnes aeque prima vice Deum adiverunt ut quae imperare vellet audirent; sed in hac prima salutatione adeo perterriti fuerunt et Deum loquentem adeo attoniti audiverunt ut supremum sibi

their natural right and transferred it to God; freely, and not through forcible constraint or terror at threats. Moreover, that the covenant should be permanently binding and free from any suspicion of duplicity, God made no promise to them until they had had proof of his marvellous power, which alone had saved them and alone could keep them safe in time to come. See Exodus, Chapter 19, verses 4 and 5. For it was precisely because they believed the power of God to be the only thing which could keep them safe that they transferred to him all their natural power to preserve themselves (which, I imagine, they had regarded as their own before),[1] and consequently all their right. The sovereignty of the Jews, then, was held by God alone; and it was the covenant alone which justified them in calling their state God's kingdom and God their king, and hence in calling the enemies of their state the enemies of God, citizens who aimed at usurping the sovereignty traitors to God, and, finally, their civil laws the laws and commandments of God. Thus in this state civil law and religion, which, as I have shown, lies wholly in obedience to God, were one and the same thing; by which I mean that the dogmas of religion were not precepts but laws and commands; piety was accounted justice, impiety crime and injustice. The man who forsook the faith ceased to be a citizen and was regarded as an enemy by the mere fact of his apostasy; while the man who died for the faith was thought to die for his country. In short, there was no distinction at all between civil law and religion.[2] This was why their state could be called a theocracy—because its citizens were only bound by laws revealed by God. Yet all this was based on belief rather than fact; for in fact the Jews retained their sovereignty completely, as will be clear from the manner and method in which their state was governed. This I now intend to describe.

Since the Jews transferred their right to no other man, but all made an equal surrender of their right as in a democracy, and cried with one voice 'Whatever God shall command we shall perform'[3] (without naming anyone as God's mouthpiece), the covenant left them all completely equal, and all had an equal right to consult God and to receive and interpret his laws; in short, they were all equally in charge of the whole administration of the state. This was why it was as equals that they first approached God to hear what he wished to command; but at this first approach they were so terrified and thunderstruck at hearing God speak that they thought their last hour was at hand.

---

[1] Falsely, on Spinoza's view: cf. *TT-P* xvi, p. 125; *TP* ii, 2–3, p. 267.
[2] *TT-P* vii, p. 109.   [3] *Exodus* 19, 8.

tempus adesse putaverint. Pleni igitur metu Mosen de novo sic adeunt: *Ecce Deum in igne loquentem audivimus, nec causa est cur mori velimus; hic certe ingens ignis nos vorabit; si iterum nobis vox Dei audienda est, certe moriemur. Tu igitur adi, et audi omnia Dei nostri dicta, et tu* (non 5 Deus) *nobis loqueris. Ad omne quod Deus tibi loquetur obediemus, idque exequemur.* His clare primum pactum aboleverunt, suumque jus Deum consulendi ejusque edicta interpretandi in Mosen absolute trans- tulerunt: non enim hic, ut antea, ad omnia quae Deus ipsis, sed quae Deus Mosi loqueretur obedire promiserunt. Vide Deuter. Cap. 5 post 10 decalog., et Cap. 18 vers. 15, 16. Moses ergo solus legum divinarum lator et interpres mansit, et consequenter etiam supremus judex, quem nemo judicare poterat, et qui solus apud Hebraeos vicem Dei, hoc est, supremam majestatem habuit; quandoquidem solus jus habebat Deum consulendi, et populo divina responsa dandi, ipsumque ad ea exequenda 15 cogendi. Solus, inquam; nam si quis vivente Mose nomine Dei praedicare aliquid volebat, quamvis verus propheta esset, reus tamen erat et supremi juris usurpator (vide Numer. Cap. 11 vers. 28).[36] Et hic notandum quod etsi Mosen populus elegerit, successorem tamen loco Mosis eligere jure non potuit. Nam simul ac jus suum Deum 20 consulendi in Mosen transtulerunt, et absolute promiserunt ipsum loco divini oraculi habere, omne jus plane amiserunt, et quem Moses successorem eligeret tanquam a Deo electum admittere debebant. Quod si talem elegisset qui, ut ipse, totam imperii administrationem haberet, nempe jus Deum in suo tentorio solus consulendi, et con- 25 sequenter authoritatem leges instituendi et abrogandi, de bello et pace decernendi, legatos mittendi, judices constituendi, successorem eli- gendi, et absolute summae potestatis omnia officia administrandi, im- perium mere monarchicum fuisset, nec ulla alia esset differentia nisi quod communiter monarchicum imperium ex Dei decreto ipsi etiam 30 monarchae occulto, Hebraeorum autem a Dei decreto monarchae tantum revelato certa ratione regatur, vel regi debuerit. Quae quidem differentia monarchae dominium et jus in omnes non minuit, sed contra auget. Caeterum, quod ad populum utriusque imperii, aeque uterque subjectus est et ignarus divini decreti: nam uterque ab ore 35 monarchae pendet, et quid fas nefasque sit ab eo solo intelligit; nec

So in utter panic they went to Moses again, saying: 'Behold we have heard God speaking in the fire, and why should we wish to die? This great fire will surely consume us; if we must hear the voice of God again we shall surely die. Go thou nigh therefore, and hear all the words of our God; and thou (not God) shalt speak unto us. Every command God shall give to thee we shall obediently perform.' By these words they obviously abolished the original covenant, transferring their right to consult God and to interpret his decrees to Moses without reserve; for what they now promised was not, as before, to obey all commands God should give to themselves, but all he should give to Moses. See Deuteronomy, Chapter 5 (the passage after the Decalogue),[1] and Chapter 18, verses 15 and 16. Thus Moses was left the sole legislator and interpreter of God's laws,[2] and hence also the supreme judge, whom no one could judge, and who alone held the place of God, or the supreme majesty, among the Jews; since he alone had the right to consult God, to give the divine responses to the people, and to compel it to carry them out. He alone, I say; for if anyone wished to proclaim anything in God's name during Moses' lifetime he was guilty of usurping the sovereignty, even although he was a true prophet. See Numbers, Chapter 11, verse 28.[3] And here we must note that although the people appointed Moses it had no right to appoint a successor to Moses. For as soon as the Jews transferred their right to consult God to Moses, and promised unreservedly to regard him as the divine mouth-piece, they lost all their right completely, and had to accept any successor chosen by Moses as chosen by God. Now if Moses had chosen such a successor, and had bequeathed to him his own control over the whole administration of the state, i.e. his right to consult God alone in his tent, and hence his authority to enact and repeal laws, to decide on war and peace, to send envoys, to appoint judges, to choose a successor, in short, to exercise all the functions of a sovereign, then the state would have been no more than a monarchy. The only difference would have been that whereas a monarchy is usually governed in accordance with a divine decree which is hidden even from the king, the Jewish monarchy would or should have been governed in a definite way in accordance with a divine decree revealed to the king alone. This, of course, increases the king's power and right over everyone, and does not diminish it. As for the people, it is equally subject and ignorant of the divine decree in both states; for in both it depends on the king's pronouncements, learning what is right and wrong from his lips

[1] *Deuteronomy* 5, 24–27.   [2] Hobbes, *De Cive* xvi, 13.   [3] n. 36, p. 251.

propterea quod populus credit monarcham nihil nisi ex Dei decreto ipsi revelato imperare, eidem minus, sed contra magis revera subjectus est. At Moses nullum talem successorem elegit, sed imperium ita administrandum successoribus reliquit ut nec populare, nec aristo-
5 craticum, nec monarchicum, sed theocraticum vocari potuerit. Nam jus leges interpretandi et Dei responsa communicandi penes unum, et jus et potestas imperium administrandi secundum leges jam explicatas et jam communicata responsa penes alium erat. Qua de re vide Num. Cap. 27 vers. 21.[37] Et ut haec melius intelligantur administrationem
10 totius imperii ordine exponam. Primo jussus est populus domum aedificare quae quasi Dei, hoc est, supremae illius imperii majestatis, aula esset. Atque haec non sumtibus unius, sed totius populi aedificanda fuit, ut domus ubi Deus consulendus erat communis esset juris. Regiae hujus divinae aulici et administratores Levitae electi sunt:
15 horum autem supremus et quasi a Rege Deo secundus electus est Aharon, frater Mosis, in cujus locum ejus filii legitime succedebant. Hic ergo, ut Deo proximus, summus legum divinarum interpres erat, et qui populo divini oraculi responsa dabat, et qui denique pro populo Deo supplicabat. Quod si cum his jus eadem imperandi haberet, nihil
20 restabat ut absolutus esset monarcha; sed eo privatus erat, et absolute tota tribus Levi communi imperio ita destituta fuit ut ne quidem partem cum reliquis tribubus habuerit quam jure possideret unde saltem vivere posset; sed ut a reliquo populo aleretur instituit, at ita ut semper maximo honore a communi plebe haberetur, utpote sola Deo
25 dicata. Deinde, militia ex reliquis duodecim tribubus formata, jussi sunt Canahanitarum imperium invadere, idque in duodecim partes dividere, et tribubus per sortes distribuere. Ad hoc ministerium electi sunt duodecim principes, ex unaquaque tribu unus, quibus simul cum Josua et summo pontifice Eleazaro jus datum est terras in aequales
30 duodecim partes dividere, et per sortes distribuere. Militiae autem summus imperator Josua electus est, qui solus in rebus novis jus

26. B *Canahanitarum*; I *Canahitarum.*   27. IV *distribuere*; I *destribuere.*

alone; and when a people believes that its king issues no command save by the decree of God revealed to him, this really gives him more control over it, and not less.[1] Moses, however, appointed no such successor,[2] but left the state to be so administered after his death that it could be called neither a democracy, nor an aristocracy, nor a monarchy, but only a theocracy: for while one man had the right to interpret the laws and to publish God's responses, another had the right and power to administer the state in accordance with the laws already expounded and the responses already made known. See Numbers, Chapter 27, verse 21.[3] That this may be better understood I shall describe the whole administration point by point. First the people was ordered to erect a building to serve as the palace of God, the sovereign of their state. This was to be built at the expense of the whole people, and not of one man, so that the building where God had to be consulted should be public property. The Levites were appointed courtiers and managers of this divine palace: while Aaron, the brother of Moses, was chosen as their head, next in rank, as it were, to God their king; and Aaron's sons succeeded him by hereditary right.[4] Since Aaron ranked next to God he was the supreme interpreter of the divine laws; he gave the people the responses of the divine oracle, and, finally, interceded with God for the people. Now if he had also held the right to issue these responses as commands, he would have had all the power of an absolute monarch; but that right he did not hold, and in general the whole tribe of Levi was excluded so completely from sharing in the state with the others that it did not even have its own portion of land to provide the bare necessities of life. Moses arranged that it should be maintained by the rest of the populace, but always held in high honour by the commons as the only tribe dedicated to God.[5] Next they were ordered to form an army from the remaining twelve tribes,[6] to attack the state of the Canaanites, to divide it into twelve parts, and to parcel it out among the tribes by lot.[7] For this task there were chosen twelve captains, one from each tribe, who, together with Joshua and the high priest Eleazar, were given the right to divide the land into twelve equal parts and to parcel it out by lot.[8] But Joshua was made the supreme commander of the army, and he alone had the right to consult

---

[1] Cf. Hobbes, *De Cive* vi, 11: 'nor is he less, but rather more a master, whom we believe we are to obey for fear of damnation, than he whom we obey for fear of temporal death.'

[2] Machiavelli advises that the legislator should not transmit his absolute authority to a successor (*Discourses* i, 9): a point frequently overlooked by interpreters of *The Prince*.

[3] n. 37, pp. 251–3. [4] *Exodus* 29, 9. [5] *Numbers* 18.
[6] *Numbers* 1. [7] *Numbers* 33, 52–54. [8] *Numbers* 34, 17 and ff.

habebat Deum consulendi, at non, ut Moses, solus in suo tentorio,
vel in tabernaculo, sed per summum pontificem, cui soli responsa Dei
dabantur: deinde Dei mandata per pontificem communicata statuendi,
et populum ad ea cogendi, media ad eadem exequenda excogitandi et
5 adhibendi, ex militia quot velit et quos velit eligendi, legatos suo
nomine mittendi, et absolute omne jus belli a solo ejus decreto pendebat. In ejus autem locum nemo legitime succedebat, nec ab aliquo nisi
a Deo immediate eligebatur, idque cogente universi populi necessitate:
alias omnia belli et pacis a principibus tribuum administrabantur, ut
10 mox ostendam. Denique omnes ab anno vigesimo aetatis usque ad
sexagesimum arma ad militandum capere jussit, et ex solo populo
exercitus formare, qui non in fidem imperatoris nec summi pontificis, sed religionis sive Dei jurabant: qui adeo exercitus sive ordines
Dei vocabantur, et Deus contra apud Hebraeos Deus exercituum. Et
15 hac de causa arca foederis in magnis proeliis, a quorum discrimine
totius populi vel victoria vel clades pendebat, in medio exercitu ibat,
ut populus Regem suum quasi praesentem videns extremis viribus
pugnaret. Ex his a Mose successoribus mandatis facile colligimus
ipsum administratores, non autem dominatores imperii elegisse. Nam
20 nemini jus dedit Deum solus et ubi vellet consulendi, et consequenter
nemini authoritatem dedit quam ipse habebat leges statuendi et abrogandi, de bello et pace discernendi, administratores tam templi quam
civitatum eligendi; quae omnia summum imperium tenentis officia
sunt. Summus enim pontifex jus quidem habebat leges interpretandi et
25 responsa Dei dandi, at non, ut Moses, quandocunque volebat, sed
tantum ab imperatore vel summo concilio vel similibus rogatus: et
contra, summus exercitus imperator et concilia Deum quando volebant
consulere poterant, at non nisi a summo pontifice Dei responsa accipere.
Quare Dei dicta in ore pontificis non decreta, ut in ore Mosis, sed
30 tantum responsa erant: a Josua autem et conciliis accepta tum demum
vim mandati et decreti habebant. Deinde hic summus pontifex, qui
Dei responsa a Deo accipiebat, militiam non habebat, nec imperium

7. *O autem*; *I antem.*   23. *I summt imperii tenentis.*

God about fresh matters; not as Moses did, alone in his tent or in the tabernacle, but through the medium of the high priest, to whom alone the responses of God were vouchsafed.[1] Moreover Joshua alone had the right to enact the commands of God passed on by the high priest, to compel the people to observe them, and to devise and apply means of carrying them out; the right to choose whom he wished from the armed forces without limit to number, to send envoys in his own name, and, in general, the whole authority in war. But to his position no one succeeded by hereditary right, nor was any successor chosen except by God's direct election, and then only when the need of the whole people required it: at other times all that concerned war and peace was handled by the captains of the tribes, as I shall presently show. Finally, Moses commanded that all between the ages of twenty and sixty should be trained for military service,[2] and that the armed forces should be recruited from the Jewish people alone. These armies did not swear allegiance to their general or the high priest, but to their religion, i.e. to their God: and so they were called the armies or hosts of God, and God in turn was called by the Jews the Lord of Hosts. This was why in great battles, where the fortunes of the whole people depended on the issue, the ark of the covenant was borne in the midst of the army, so that the people, seeing their King present symbolically among them, might fight to the utmost of their strength.[3] From the commands given by Moses to his successors we can readily see that it was ministers and not masters of the state whom he appointed. For to no one did he bequeath the right to consult God alone and wherever he pleased; to no one therefore did he transmit his own authority to establish and repeal laws, to decide between war and peace, and to choose officials for the temple and the cities—functions which all belong to the sovereign. The high priest had certainly the right to interpret the laws and to give God's responses; but only when asked by the commander-in-chief, the supreme council, or similar authorities, and not, like Moses, whenever he wished. The commander-in-chief and the councils could consult God when they wished; but receive his responses from the high priest alone. Hence the words of God in the mouth of the priest were not decrees, as they were in the mouth of Moses, but only responses; and only when accepted by Joshua and the councils did they have the force of commands and decrees. Again, the high priest who received the divine responses from God had no military

---

[1] *Numbers* 27, 18–23.   [2] *Numbers* 1, 2–3.
[3] *1 Samuel* 4, 3 and ff.; 14, 18; *2 Samuel* 11, 11.

jure possidebat: et contra, qui terras jure possidebant leges statuere jure non poterant. Summus deinde pontifex, tam Aharon quam filius ejus Eleazarus, uterque a Mose quidem electus fuit; mortuo autem Mose nemo jus eligendi pontificem habuit, sed filius patri legitime
5 succedebat. Imperator exercitus a Mose etiam electus fuit, et non ex jure summi pontificis, sed jure Mosis ipsi dato personam imperatoris induit: et ideo mortuo Josua pontifex neminem ejus loco elegit, nec principes de novo imperatore Deum consuluerunt, sed unusquisque in militiam suae tribus, et omnes simul in universam militiam jus
10 Josuae retinuerunt. Et videtur non opus fuisse summo imperatore nisi quando conjunctis viribus contra communem hostem pugnare debebant; quod quidem maxime locum habuit tempore Josuae, quo locum fixum nondum omnes habebant, et omnia communis juris erant. At postquam omnes tribus terras jure belli possessas, et quas adhuc possidere in
15 mandatis erat, inter se diviserunt, nec amplius omnia omnium erant, eo ipso ratio communis imperatoris cessavit, quandoquidem tribus diversae non tam concives quam confoederatae ab ea divisione reputari debuerunt. Respectu Dei et religionis concives quidem aestimari debuerunt; at respectu juris quod una in aliam habebat non nisi con-
20 foederatae, eodem fere modo (si templum commune demas) ac Praepotentes Confoederati Belgarum Ordines. Nam divisio rei communis in partes nihil aliud est quam quod unusquisque suam partem solus jam possideat, et reliqui jure quod in illam partem habebant cedant. Hac igitur de causa Moses principes tribuum elegit, ut post divisum im-
25 perium unusquisque curam suae partis haberet, nempe Deum per summum pontificem de rebus suae tribus consulendi, suae militiae imperandi, urbes condendi et muniendi, judices in unaquaque urbe constituendi, hostem sui singularis imperii invadendi, et absolute omnia belli et pacis administrandi. Nec alium judicem praeter Deum no-
30 scere tenebatur,[38] vel quem Deus prophetam expresse misisset: alias si a Deo defecisset, reliquae tribus ipsum non tanquam subditum judicare,

4. *O eligendi; I eilgendi.*

force, and did not hold the state by right; while those who held the land by right had no right to make laws. Once more, although two of the high priests, Aaron and his son Eleazar, were both appointed by Moses,[1] no one after Moses' death had the right to appoint a priest, but son succeeded father by hereditary right. The commander-in-chief was appointed by Moses also, and assumed his office by the right of Moses which was vested in him, and not by the right of the high priest. This was why the priest appointed no successor to Joshua after his death; nor did the captains consult God about a new commander-in-chief, but each retained Joshua's command over the forces of his own tribe, while they all retained collectively his command over the army as a whole. And it seems that a commander-in-chief was only necessary when the tribes had to join forces against a common enemy; as was very much the case in Joshua's time, when some tribes had still to acquire a fixed territory, and everything was held in common. But once they divided up among themselves the territories they had conquered, or were destined to conquer, and ceased to hold everything in common, they ceased to have any need for a common commander; for as a result of that distribution the different tribes had to be regarded as members of a federation rather than as parts of the same state. No doubt in respect of their God and religion they had to be regarded as parts of the same state; but in respect of the right which one had against another they were simply members of a federation, and (if you disregard the common temple) in much the same position as the High and Puissant Federated Estates of the Netherlands.[2] For the division of common property into shares simply means that each acquires exclusive possession of his own share and the others give up their right to it. This, then, was why Moses appointed captains over the tribes—that after the division of the state each captain should have control of his own part, i.e. the power to consult God through the high priest about the concerns of his own tribe, to command his own army, to found and fortify cities, to appoint judges in each, to attack the enemies of his particular realm, and, in short, to handle all matters concerning war and peace. He was not bound to recognize any judge other than God,[3] or a prophet sent expressly by God; if he forsook God the other tribes could not judge him as a subject, but had to attack him as an enemy

---

[1] *Exodus* 28, 3; *Numbers* 20, 28.

[2] Sir William Temple does not hesitate to speak of 'the sovereignty of the Provinces' (*Observations upon the United Provinces of the Netherlands*, with an Introduction by G. N. Clark, Cambridge, 1932, ch. ii, p. 57).

[3] n. 38, pp. 253-5.

sed tanquam hostem qui fidem contractus solverat invadere debebant.
Quorum exempla in Scriptura habemus. Mortuo enim Josua filii
Israëlis, non summus novus imperator, Deum consuluerunt; intellecto
autem quod tribus Judae omnium prima hostem suum invadere
5 debebat, ipsa sola cum Simeone contrahit ut junctis viribus utriusque
hostem invaderent. In quo contractu reliquae tribus non fuerunt com-
prehensae (vide Judic. Cap. 1 vers. 1, 2, 3), sed unaquaeque separatim
(ut in praedicto Cap. narratur) bellum contra suum hostem gerit, et
quem vult in ditionem et fidem accipit, etsi in mandatis esset nulli ulla
10 pacti conditione parcere, sed omnes exterminare: propter quod peccatum reprehenduntur quidem, a nemine autem in judicium vocantur.
Nec erat quod propterea bella contra invicem movere inciperent, et
rebus alterius alii se immiscerent: contra Benjaminitas, qui reliquos
offenderant, et pacis vinculum ita solverant ut nullus ex confoederatis
15 secure apud ipsos hospitium habere posset, hostiliter invadunt, et ter
proelio commisso tandem victores, omnes, nocentes et innocentes, jure
belli aeque trucidant; quod postea sera poenitentia lamentati sunt.

His exemplis quae de jure uniuscujusque tribus modo diximus plane
confirmantur. At forsan aliquis rogabit: Quisnam successorem prin-
20 cipis cujusque tribus eligebat? Verum de hac re nihil certi ex ipsa
Scriptura possum colligere: hoc tamen conjicio, quod quandoquidem
unaquaeque tribus in familias erat divisa, quarum capita ex senioribus
familiae eligebantur, ex his qui senior erat loco principis jure succedebat. Ex senioribus enim Moses septuaginta coadjutores qui cum ipso
25 supremum concilium formabant elegit; qui post mortem Josuae imperii administrationem habuerunt, senes in Scriptura vocantur; et
denique apud Hebraeos nihil frequentius quam per senes judices
intelligere, quod omnibus notum existimo. Sed ad nostrum propositum
parum refert hoc certo scire; sufficit quod ostenderim neminem post
30 mortem Mosis omnia summi imperatoris officia habuisse. Nam quandoquidem omnia non ab unius viri, neque unius concilii, neque populi
decreto pendebant, sed quaedam ab una tribu, alia a reliquis aequali
utriusque jure administrabantur, sequitur evidentissime imperium ab
obitu Mosis neque monarchicum, neque aristocraticum, neque populare

168

who had broken the promise made in the contract. This can be illustrated from Scripture. For example, after Joshua's death it was the children of Israel who consulted God, and not a new commander-in-chief; but once they learned that the tribe of Judah had to attack its enemy first, that tribe took action by itself and made a covenant with the tribe of Simeon to unite against their common enemies. In this covenant the other tribes were not included (see Judges, Chapter 1, verses 1, 2, and 3), but (as is described in that Chapter) each waged war separately against its own enemies, taking whom it pleased under its rule and protection, although one of God's commandments was that they should annihilate all their enemies and give them no quarter on any terms whatsoever. For such misdeeds tribes were no doubt blamed, but they were not called to account by anyone. Nor did such misdeeds give any cause for one tribe to make war on another or interfere in its affairs; whereas the tribe of Benjamin, which had offended the others and broken the bond of peace so completely that none of the allies could find safe lodging within it, was attacked as an enemy; and when the allies finally emerged victorious after three pitched battles they slew all who belonged to it, guilty and innocent alike, by the right of war[1]—a deed which they afterwards repented when it was too late.[2]

These instances fully confirm what I have just said about the right of each tribe. But perhaps someone will ask who appointed a successor to the captain of a tribe. Now on this point I can find no definite evidence in Scripture itself; but I should imagine that since each tribe was divided into families, and the head of a family was chosen from its elders, the eldest of these heads succeeded to the captaincy by right. For it was from the elders that Moses chose his seventy colleagues on the supreme council;[3] those who had charge of the administration of the state after Joshua's death are called elders in Scripture;[4] and, finally, nothing is commoner among the Jews than the use of 'elders' to mean judges—a point, I think, which is known to everyone. But it is hardly to my purpose to settle this question; it is enough to have shown that after Moses' death no one exercised all the functions of a sovereign. For since neither one man, nor one council, nor the people itself had the final decision on everything, but some affairs were managed by one tribe and others by the rest, each acting with equal right, it is obvious that on Moses' death the state was left neither a monarchy, nor an

---

[1] *Judges* 20.
[2] *Judges* 21 : for the expression see Curtius, op. cit. VIII, viii, 23.
[3] *Numbers* 11, 16–17.   [4] *Joshua* 24, 31.

mansisse, sed, uti diximus, theocraticum: I. quia imperii domus
regia templum erat, et sola ejus ratione, ut ostendimus, omnes tribus
concives erant; II. quia omnes cives in fidem Dei, supremi sui judicis,
jurare debebant, cui soli in omnibus absolute obedire promiserant; et
5 denique quia summus omnium imperator, quando eo opus erat, a
nemine nisi a solo Deo eligebatur. Quod Moses nomine Dei populo
expresse praedicit Deuter. Cap. 18 vers. 15, et re ipsa electio Gideonis,
Samsonis, et Samuëlis testatur; quare non dubitandum quin reliqui
fideles duces simili etiam modo electi fuerint, etsi id ex eorum historia
10 non constet.

His positis, tempus est ut videamus quantum haec ratio imperii
constituendi animos moderari poterat, et tam eos qui regebant quam
qui regebantur ita continere ut neque hi rebelles neque illi tyranni
fierent.

15   Qui imperium administrant vel qui id tenent, quicquid facinoris
committunt, id semper specie juris adumbrare, et populo id a se honeste
factum persuadere student; quod facile etiam obtinent quando tota juris
interpretatio ab iis solis pendet. Nam non dubium est quin eo ipso
maximam ad omnia quae volunt et eorum appetitus suadet libertatem
20 sumant, et contra magnam iisdem adimi si jus leges interpretandi apud
alium sit, et simul si vera earundem interpretatio omnibus ita pateat ut
nemo de eadem dubitare possit. Ex quo manifestum fit magnam Hebraeorum principibus causam facinorum sublatam fuisse eo quod jus
omne leges interpretandi Levitis datum fuerit (vide Deuteron. Cap.
25 21 vers. 5), qui nullam imperii administrationem nec partem cum
caeteris habebant, et quorum tota fortuna et honor a vera legum interpretatione pendebat; deinde quod universus populus jussus est singulis
septem annis certo in loco congregari ubi a pontifice leges edoceretur, et
praeterea ut unusquisque solus continuo et summa cum attentione
30 librum legis legeret et perlegeret. Vide Deuteron. Cap. 31 vers. 9 etc.
et Cap 6 vers. 7. Principes igitur maxime sui saltem causa curare
debebant ut omnia secundum leges praescriptas et omnibus satis per-
spectas administrarent si a populo maximo honore coli volebant, qui
tum eos utpote Dei imperii ministros et vicem Dei gerentes venerare-
35 tur; alias summum subditorum odium, quale theologicum esse solet,

4–5. *P et denique III.*   7. *B cap. 18; I Cap. 19.*

aristocracy, nor a democracy, but, as I have said, a theocracy; and for the following reasons. I. The state palace was the temple, and, as I have shown, it was only by virtue of the temple that all the tribes were parts of the same state. II. All the citizens had to swear allegiance to God, their supreme judge, to whom alone they had promised absolute obedience. Finally, when a commander-in-chief was needed he was appointed by God alone. Moses, speaking in God's name, foretold this to the people explicitly in Deuteronomy, Chapter 18, verse 15; and it is confirmed by the manner in which Gideon,[1] Samson,[2] and Samuel[3] were elected. Hence we must suppose that the other leaders who adhered to the faith were appointed in the same way, though the accounts of them do not make this clear.

My exposition being now complete, it is time to see how far these constitutional arrangements succeeded in controlling men's passions and restraining both rulers and ruled, i.e. in preventing the latter from becoming rebels and the former from becoming tyrants.

When those who govern or hold a state do anything wicked they always try to cover it up with a show of legality, and to persuade the people that they acted virtuously; which is easily done when they alone control the whole interpretation of the law. This in itself undoubtedly gives them the utmost freedom to indulge their desires and do everything they wish; but such freedom is largely removed if the right to interpret the laws is vested in another, and if, at the same time, their true meaning is so obvious to all that no one can be in any doubt about it. It plainly follows that the Jewish captains were saved from a great temptation to wickedness, first by the fact that the whole right to interpret the laws was vested in the Levites (see Deuteronomy, Chapter 21, verse 5), who had no share in either the administration or the territory of the state, and whose welfare and repute were wholly dependent on their interpreting the laws correctly; and also by the commandment that the whole people should assemble at a certain place every seven years to learn the laws from the priest, and that individuals should continually read and re-read the book of the law in private with the greatest attention. See Deuteronomy, Chapter 31, verse 9, etc. and Chapter 6, verse 7. Thus if the captains wished to be held in high honour by the people, they had—simply in their own interests—to be very careful to govern entirely by the written laws which were familiar to all. If they did so, they would be revered by the people as God's ministers and vicegerents; if they did otherwise, they inevitably

---

[1] *Judges* 6, 11 and ff.   [2] *Judges* 13.   [3] *1 Samuel* 3.

fugere non poterant. Ad haec, nempe ad effraenatam principum libidinem coercendam, aliud permagni momenti accessit, videlicet quod militia ex omnibus civibus (nullo a vigesimo usque ad sexagesimum aetatis annum excepto) formabatur, et quod principes nullum extraneum
5 militem mercede conducere poterant. Hoc, inquam, permagni fuit momenti: nam certum est principes sola militia cui stipendia solvunt populum opprimere posse; deinde eos nihil magis timere quam libertatem militum concivium quorum virtute, labore, et magno sui sanguinis impendio imperii libertas et gloria parta est. Ideo Alexander, cum
10 secundo contra Darium dimicandum erat, audito Parmenionis consilio, non ipsum qui consilium dedit, sed Polyperconta qui cum eodem stabat increpuit. Nam, ut ait Curtius lib. 4 § 13, Parmenionem nuper acrius quam vellet increpitum rursus castigare non sustinuit; nec Macedonum libertatem, quam maxime, ut jam diximus, timebat, opprimere potuit
15 nisi postquam numerum militum ex captivis longe supra Macedonas auxit: tum enim animo suo impotenti et diu civium optimorum libertate coercito morem gerere potuit. Si haec itaque militum concivium libertas humani imperii principes, qui soli totam laudem victoriarum usurpare solent, retinet, multo magis Hebraeorum principes coercere
20 debuit, quorum milites non pro principis sed pro Dei gloria pugnabant, et solo Dei responso accepto proelium committebant.

Accessit deinde quod omnes Hebraeorum principes solo religionis vinculo associati erant: quare, si aliquis ab eadem defecisset, jusque divinum uniuscujusque violare incepisset, eo hostis a reliquis haberi
25 potuerat et jure opprimi.

Accessit III. timor novi alicujus prophetae: modo enim probatae vitae aliquis receptis quibusdam signis ostenderet se prophetam esse, eo ipso jus summum imperandi habebat, nempe, sicuti Moses, Dei nomine ei soli revelati, et non tantum, ut principes, per pontificem
30 consulti. Et non dubium est quin tales populum oppressum facile ad se trahere poterant, et levibus signis quicquid vellent persuadere; cum

---

8. *O sanguinis; I sangninis.* 10. *O Darium; I darium.*

11. *Polyperconta.* Spinoza adopts the form used by Curtius. The Greek form is Πολυ-σπέρχων: hence P *Polysperconta.*

12. *O lib. 4. § 13; I lib. 4. 3. 13.* 22. *IV Accessit; I Accescit.* So also in l. 26.

aroused in their subjects the bitterness typical of religious hatred. And there were other factors which prevented the captains from freely indulging their whims. The first of these—and a very important one—was the fact that the army was recruited from all the citizens (nobody between the ages of twenty and sixty being exempt), and that the captains could not hire foreign troops.[1] This, I say, was a very important factor; for, of course, it is only by means of mercenary troops that rulers can oppress their peoples,[2] and there is nothing they fear more than the independence of citizen soldiers whose courage, energy, and readiness to shed their blood have won freedom and glory for their state. This explains why Alexander, when he had to fight a second battle against Darius, forebore to rebuke Parmenio for his advice and rebuked Parmenio's supporter Polypercon instead. For, as Curtius says in Book 4, § 13,[3] he had recently rebuked Parmenio more severely than he wished, and shrank from chiding him again; nor could he suppress the liberty of the Macedonians, which, as I have already said,[4] was what he feared most, until he had raised so many troops from prisoners of war that they far outnumbered the Macedonians. Only then could he indulge the reckless ambition that had been checked for so long by the freedom of the best citizens. Now if this freedom of citizen soldiers can restrain the rulers of a secular kingdom, who generally take the sole credit for victories, how much more must it have restrained the captains of the Jews, whose troops fought for the glory, not of their leader, but of God, and joined battle only when they had received God's response.

Another check was the fact that their religion was the only tie which bound all the captains of the Jews together:[5] so that if any of them had forsaken the faith, and begun to violate the religious rights of the individual, the others could have treated him as an enemy and put him down by right.[6]

A third check was the fear of a new prophet; for if anyone of proven righteousness could show that he was a prophet by certain accepted signs, he automatically had a supreme right to give commands in God's name,—commands based, like those of Moses, on private revelation, and not simply on priestly responses, like those of the captains. And there is no doubt that when the people was oppressed such prophets could easily attract its support, and persuade it by trifling

---

[1] p. 165. [2] *TP* vii, 17, p. 349.
[3] Curtius, op. cit. IV, xiii, 8. [4] Cf. pp. 155–7. [5] pp. 167–71.
[6] As they did to the tribe of Benjamin (p. 169).

contra, si res recte administrabantur, princeps in tempore providere poterat ut propheta prius ejus judicio stare deberet, ut ab eo examinaretur num probatae vitae esset, num certa et indubitata signa suae legationis haberet, et denique num id quod nomine Dei dicere volebat cum
5 recepta doctrina et communibus legibus patriae conveniret. Quod si nec signa satis responderent, vel doctrina nova esset, eum jure mortis damnare poterat: alias sola principis authoritate et testimonio recipiebatur.

Accessit IV. quod princeps reliquos nobilitate non excellebat, nec
10 jure sanguinis; sed tantum ratione aetatis et virtutis administratio imperii ei competebat.

Accessit denique quod principes et universa militia non magis desiderio belli quam pacis teneri poterant. Nam militia, uti diximus, ex solis civibus constabat; quare tam res belli quam pacis ab iisdem homini-
15 bus administrabantur. Qui igitur in castris miles, is in foro civis erat, et qui in castris dux, is in curia judex, et qui denique in castris imperator, princeps in civitate erat. Quare nemo bellum propter bellum sed propter pacem et ad tuendam libertatem desiderare poterat; et forte princeps ne summum pontificem adire teneretur, et
20 coram ipso praeter dignitatem stare, a rebus novis quantum poterat abstinebat. Haec de rationibus quae principes intra suos limites continebant.

Videndum jam qua ratione populus retinebatur: sed hanc etiam imperii fundamenta clarissime indicant. Si quis enim ad ea vel leviter
25 attendere velit, videbit statim haec amorem adeo singularem in civium animis parere debuisse ut nihil difficilius aliquis in mentem inducere potuerit quam patriam prodere, vel ab ea deficere: sed contra, omnes ita affecti esse debuerint ut extrema potius quam alienum imperium paterentur. Nam postquam suum jus in Deum transtulerunt, suumque
30 regnum Dei regnum esse, seque solos filios Dei, reliquas autem nationes Dei hostes esse crediderunt, in quas propterea odio infensissimo affecti erant (nam et hoc pium esse credebant, vide Psalm. 139 vers. 21, 22), nihil magis abhorrere potuerunt quam in fidem alicujus extranei

signs of anything they pleased; whereas if the administration was being properly conducted, the captain had time to take the precaution of making the prophet submit to his judgement first, and of examining him personally to see that he was of proven righteousness, that he had sure and unmistakable signs of his mission, and, finally, that what he wished to say in God's name was consistent with the accepted teaching and general laws of his country. If his signs were unsatisfactory, or his teaching strange, the captain could condemn him to death by right; while if he were accepted, it was only on the authority and testimony of the captain.

A fourth check was the fact that the captain did not excel the rest in nobility or right of birth, but was entrusted with the administration of the state only in virtue of his age and capacity.

A final check was the fact that the captains and the army as a whole had no reason for preferring war to peace. For the army, as I said, consisted of citizens alone; so the conduct of both war and peace lay in the same hands. The soldier in war was a citizen in the assembly, the officer in war was a judge in the council, and, finally, the general in war was a ruler in the commonwealth.[1] Thus no one could desire war for its own sake, but only to secure peace and safeguard freedom; and it was perhaps to avoid the need to consult the high priest, and to abase themselves before him, that the captains refrained from innovation as far as they could.[2] So much for the reasons which kept the captains within due bounds.

We must now see how the people was kept in check; although the basic principles of the state make this equally plain. For even a cursory examination will immediately show that they must have inspired such extraordinary devotion in the minds of the citizens that it would have been almost impossible for any of the latter to think of betraying or deserting his country, and they must all have been ready to suffer death rather than an alien yoke. For once they transferred their right to God, and believed that their kingdom was God's kingdom, and that they alone were God's children, the other nations being his enemies—and therefore the object of their implacable hatred (for such hatred too they regarded as piety, see Psalm 139, verses 21 and 22)—nothing could be more abhorrent to them than to swear allegiance and promise

---

[1] The point seems to be that war was not an avenue to political power in the Jewish state. For the tendency of successful generals to become tyrants cf. *TP* vii, 17, p. 349, and x, 10, p. 439.

[2] Even Joshua had to consult the high priest *in rebus novis* (pp. 163–5).

jurare, eique obedientiam promittere, nec majus flagitium nec quid magis execrandum excogitari apud ipsos poterat quam patriam, hoc est, ipsum regnum Dei quem adorabant, prodere. Imo aliquo extra patriam tantum habitatum ire pro flagitio habebatur, quia Dei cultus,
5 quo semper tenebantur, non nisi in patrio solo exerceri concedebatur, utpote quae sola tellus sancta, reliqua autem immunda et profana haberetur. Ideo David, quia exulare cogebatur, sic coram Saulo conqueritur: *Si qui te contra me instigant homines sunt, maledicti sunt, quia me secludunt ne spatier in Dei haereditate, sed dicunt 'Vade et Deos*
10 *alienos cole.'* Et hac etiam de causa nullus civis, quod hic apprime notandum, exilii damnabatur: nam qui peccat supplicio quidem dignus est, non autem flagitio. Amor ergo Hebraeorum erga patriam non simplex amor sed pietas erat, quae simul et odium in reliquas nationes ita quotidiano cultu fovebantur et alebantur ut in naturam verti debuerint.
15 Quotidianus enim cultus non tantum diversus omnino erat (quo fiebat ut omnino singulares, et a reliquis prorsus essent separati), sed etiam absolute contrarius. Quare ex quotidiana quadam exprobratione continuum odium oriri debuit, quo nullum firmius animis haerere potuit, utpote odium ex magna devotione seu pietate ortum, quodque pium
20 credebatur; quo sane nullum majus nec pertinacius dari potest. Nec causa communis deerat qua odium semper magis ac magis incenditur, nempe ejus reciprocatio; nam nationes eos contra odio infensissimo habere debuerunt. Quantum autem haec omnia, videlicet humani imperii libertas, erga patriam devotio, in omnes reliquos jus absolutum,
25 et odium non tantum licitum sed etiam pium, omnes infensos habere, morum et rituum singularitas, quantum, inquam, haec Hebraeorum animos firmare valuerint ad omnia singulari constantia et virtute pro patria tolerandum, ratio quam clarissime docet, et ipsa experientia testata est. Nunquam enim stante urbe sub alterius imperio durare
30 potuerunt, et ideo Hierosolymam rebellem civitatem vocitabant (vide Hezrae Cap. 4 vs. 12, 15). Secundum imperium (quod primi vix umbra fuit postquam pontifices jus etiam principatus usurpaverunt) difficillime a Romanis destrui potuit; quod ipse Tacitus lib. 2 Histor. his testatur. *Profligaverat bellum Judaicum Vespasianus, oppugnatione*

176

obedience to some foreigner, and they could conceive no greater or more execrable crime than to betray their country, the very kingdom of the God whom they worshipped. Indeed, even to emigrate from their country was regarded as outrageous; for the religious rites which they were always bound to practise could be performed only on their native soil, since it alone was thought to be holy ground, the rest of the world being unclean and profane. This is why David, on being forced to live in exile, complains to Saul in these words: 'If those who incite thee against me are men, they are accursed, for they shut me out from walking in the inheritance of the Lord, saying, "Go hence and worship alien Gods." '[1] This also explains the fact—especially worthy of notice here—that no citizen was condemned to exile; for although a wrong-doer deserves to be punished, he does not deserve to be outraged. Hence the patriotism of the Jews was not only patriotism but piety, and it was so fostered by their daily ritual that it must have become second nature. The same was true of their hatred for the Gentiles: for this daily ritual, which made them quite unique, and distinguished them completely from all other men, was not only radically different from, but also completely opposed to, that of the Gentiles. It therefore amounted to a daily reprobation of the latter; and this must have inspired in the Jews continual and ineradicable hatred, for a hatred which springs from great devotion or piety, and is itself believed to be pious, is undoubtedly greater and more persistent than any other. And the common reason for the continual growth of hatred, i.e. the fact that it is returned,[2] was also present; for the Gentiles must have regarded the Jews with the most bitter hatred. How greatly all this—their freedom from human government, their devotion to country, their absolute right against, and hatred for, the Gentiles (a hatred not only permitted but even regarded as pious), the hatred of the Gentiles for them, the uniqueness of their customs and rites—how greatly, I say, all this must have strengthened the minds of the Jews to endure every hardship for their country with remarkable constancy and courage, is obvious to reason and confirmed by actual experience. For never while their city stood could they remain for long under alien rule, and this was why Jerusalem used to be called the rebellious city. See Ezra, Chapter 4, verses 12 and 15. Even their second state (which was hardly a shadow of the first after the priests seized the right to govern) proved very difficult for the Romans to destroy; as Tacitus himself testifies in these words from Book II of his Histories:[3] 'Vespasian had concluded the

---

[1] *1 Samuel* 26, 19.   [2] *E* iii, 43.   [3] *Histories* ii, iv, 3.

Hierosolymorum reliqua, duro magis et arduo opere ob ingenium gentis et pervicaciam superstitionis quam quod satis virium obsessis ad tolerandas necessitates superesset. Verum praeter haec, quorum aestimatio a sola opinione pendet, aliud in hoc imperio, quod solidissimum est, singulare
5 fuit, quo cives maxime retineri debuerunt ne de defectione cogitarent, et ne unquam desiderio tenerentur deserendae patriae; nimirum ratio utilitatis, quae omnium humanarum actionum robur et vita est. Atque haec, inquam, in hoc imperio singularis erat. Nam cives nullibi majore jure bona sua possidebant quam hujus imperii subditi, qui cum principe
10 aequalem partem terrarum et agrorum habebant, et unusquisque suae partis aeternus dominus erat; nam si quis paupertate coactus fundum suum vel agrum vendiderat, adventante jubilaeo ei de integro restitui debebat, et ad hunc modum alia instituta erant ut nemo a fixis suis bonis alienari posset. Deinde paupertas nullibi tolerabilior esse poterat
15 quam ubi charitas erga proximum, hoc est, erga concivem, summa pietate coli debebat ut Deum, suum Regem, propitium haberent. Civibus igitur Hebraeis non nisi in sua patria bene esse poterat, extra eandem autem damnum maximum et dedecus. Deinde ad eosdem non tantum in patrio solo retinendum, sed ad bella etiam civilia vitandum et
20 causas contentionum tollendum, haec apprime conducebant: nempe quod nemo suo aequali, sed soli Deo serviebat, et quod charitas et amor erga concivem summa aestimabatur pietas, qui non parum fovebatur communi odio quo reliquas nationes, et hae eos contra habebant. Praeterea apprime conducebat summa obedientiae disciplina
25 qua educebantur, quod scilicet omnia ex determinato legis praescripto facere debebant. Non enim ad libitum arare licebat, sed certis temporibus et annis, et non nisi uno bestiarum genere simul: sic etiam non nisi certa ratione certoque tempore seminare et metere licebat, et absolute eorum vita continuus obedientiae cultus erat (qua de re vide
30 Cap. V circa usum caeremoniarum); quare eidem omnino assuefactis ipsa non amplius servitus sed libertas videri debuit. Unde sequi etiam

---

1–2. Modern editors of Tacitus read *montis* (for *gentis*) and *quo* (for *quod*). Spinoza quotes the text adopted by Justus Lipsius, whose edition (Antwerp, 1607) he had in his library. See A. J. Servaas van Rooijen, *La Bibliothèque de Bénédict Spinoza*, 1888, p. 122.

Jewish war except for the siege of Jerusalem. This was a hard and difficult task; not so much because the besieged had enough strength left to endure their privations, but because of the nature of the people and the stubbornness of their superstition.' But besides these factors, whose influence depends entirely on belief,[1] there was in this state another with an even firmer basis, which must have played a unique part in preventing the citizens from ever thinking of defection or desiring to desert their country; the motive of self-interest, which is the strength and life of all human actions. That, I say, played a unique part in this state. Nowhere did citizens hold their property with greater right, for the subjects of this state had an equal share with the captain in the lands and fields, and each held his own share in perpetuity; since if anyone was forced by poverty to sell his farm or his field, it had to be restored to him again when the jubilee came round, and there were other laws of the same kind to prevent anyone from losing the title to his estates.[2] Moreover, poverty could nowhere have been easier to bear than in a state whose subjects had to practise charity to their neighbours, i.e. their fellow citizens, with the greatest piety in order to keep the favour of God their king. Thus Jewish citizens could only be well off in their own country; abroad they were exposed to serious injury and opprobrium. These factors, then, helped to keep them on their native soil; others again also helped to prevent civil wars and to remove causes of dispute, in particular the following: no one was subordinated to his equal, but only to God; charity and love towards a fellow citizen was accounted the height of piety; and this love was fostered not a little by common hatred for the Gentiles, and of the Gentiles for them. Another vital factor was their thorough training in obedience—the fact that they had to do everything precisely as the law enjoined. For example, they were not allowed to plough when they pleased, but only at fixed times and seasons, and with only one kind of animal at once; similarly, they were not allowed to sow and reap save in a certain way and at a certain time.[3] In short, their life was a continual practice of obedience (for this see Chapter V on the utility of ceremonies); so that obedience became second nature, and must have seemed to them no longer servitude but freedom. Another result must have been that

---

[1] i.e. on the religious beliefs of the Jews. The importance of the factors mentioned is not a matter of opinion : on the contrary, Spinoza has said above that it is confirmed by both reason and experience. The real distinction is between *opinio* and *ratio utilitatis*. Though *opinio* is important and influential, it is not so deep-rooted in human nature (*solida*) as the motive of self-interest. See *TT-P* xvi, p. 129.

[2] *Leviticus* 25.

[3] *TT-P* v, p. 97 and nn.

debuit ut nemo negata, sed mandata cuperet; ad quod etiam non parum conduxisse videtur quod certis anni temporibus otio et laetitiae se dare tenebantur, non ut animo, sed ut Deo ex animo obtemperarent. Ter in anno Dei convivae erant (vide Deut. Cap. 16 vers. 16); septimo septi-
5 manae die ab omni opere cessare, seseque otio dare debebant; et praeter haec alia tempora signata erant quibus laetitiae actus honesti et convivia non quidem concedebantur sed mandabantur. Nec puto quod aliquid hoc efficacius ad hominum animos flectendos excogitari potest; nam nulla re magis capiuntur animi quam laetitia quae ex devotione, hoc
10 est, ex amore et admiratione simul, oritur. Nec facile fastidio rerum usitatarum capi poterant, nam cultus diebus festis destinatus rarus et varius erat. His accessit summa templi reverentia, quam propter singularem ejus cultum, et res quas tenebantur observare antequam alicui eo ire liceret, religiosissime semper servaverunt; atque adeo ut
15 hodierni adhuc non sine magno horrore illud Manassae flagitium legant, quod scilicet idolum in ipso templo ponere sustinuerit. Erga leges etiam quae in intimo sacrario religiosissime custodiebantur non minor erat populo reverentia. Quare populi rumores et praejudicia hic minime timenda erant. Nemo enim de rebus divinis judicium ferre audebat,
20 sed ad omnia quae ipsis imperabantur ex authoritate divini responsi in templo accepti, vel legis a Deo conditae, sine ulla rationis consultatione obtemperare debebant. Atque his me summam rationem hujus imperii, etsi breviter, satis tamen clare exposuisse puto.

Superest jam ut causas etiam inquiramus quare factum sit ut Hebraei
25 toties a lege defecerint, cur toties subacti fuerint, et cur tandem imperium omnino vastari potuerit. At forsan hic aliquis dicet id evenisse ex gentis contumacia: verum hoc puerile est. Nam cur haec natio reliquis contumacior fuit? An natura? Haec sane nationes non creat, sed individua, quae quidem in nationes non distinguuntur nisi ex
30 diversitate linguae, legum, et morum receptorum; et ex his duobus, legibus scilicet et moribus, tantum oriri potest quod unaquaeque natio singulare habeat ingenium, singularem conditionem, et denique singularia praejudicia. Si igitur concedendum esset quod Hebraei supra

---

4. *I Cap. 16*, omitting the verse.   19. *V–L audebat; I audet.*

everyone desired to do what was commanded, no one to do what was forbidden;[1] and it seems that an important cause of this result was the fact that they were required to give themselves up to rest and enjoyment at certain times of the year—not that they might indulge in pleasure, but that they might serve God with pleasure. Thrice a year they attended God's feasts (see Deuteronomy, Chapter 16, verse 16); on the seventh day of each week they had to cease all work and give themselves over to rest;[2] and there were other times assigned when innocent enjoyment and feasting were not only permitted but prescribed. This, I think, is the most effective means of influencing men's minds that can be devised; for nothing takes a greater hold on the mind than joy arising from devotion, i.e. from love and admiration together. Nor was it easy for them to take a distaste for familiar ritual, for the ceremonial appointed for holidays was unusual and varied. Then there was the profound reverence which they always felt for the temple on account of its peculiar ceremonial, and the rites which they had to perform before anyone could approach it; a reverence preserved so devoutly that the Jews of to-day still cannot read without great horror of the outrageous wickedness of Manasseh in daring to place an idol in its precincts.[3] For the laws which were devoutly guarded in the inmost shrine the reverence of the people was no less great. Hence popular murmurings and prejudgements were hardly to be feared in this state, for no one dared to pass judgement on matters of religion, but all had to yield unreasoning obedience to every command laid upon them, whether it had the authority of a divine response received in the temple, or of a law established by God. So much for the main principles of the Jewish state; though my account is brief, I think it is fairly clear.

It now remains to discover why the Jews forsook their law so often, why they were so often conquered, and why in the end their state could be utterly destroyed. Here, perhaps, it will be suggested that the cause of all this was the unruliness of the race; but this is a childish explanation. For what made this people more unruly than the others? Was it nature? But surely it is not peoples but individuals that nature creates, and individuals are only divided into peoples by diversity of language, laws, and customs;[4] and the two last, i.e. laws and customs, are the only factors which can give a people a particular temperament, a particular nature, and lastly particular beliefs. Thus if it were necessary to admit that the Jews were more unruly than the rest of mankind,

---

[1] Unlike the majority of men (cf. *TP* x, 5, p. 435).
[2] *Exodus* 20, 10.
[3] *2 Kings* 21, 7.
[4] *TT-P* iii, p. 57.

reliquos mortales contumaces fuerint, id vitio legum vel receptorum morum imputari deberet. Et sane hoc verum est, quod si Deus eorum imperium constantius voluisset aliter etiam jura et leges condidisset, aliamque rationem id administrandi instituisset. Quare quid aliud 5 dicere possumus nisi quod Deum suum iratum habuerint, non tantum, ut Jeremias Cap. 32 vers. 31 ait, ab urbe condita, sed jam inde a legibus conditis? Quod Ezechiël Cap. 20 vers. 25 etiam testatur, inquiens: *Ego etiam dedi ipsis statuta non bona, et jura quibus non viverent, eo quod impuravi ipsos muneribus suis remittendo omnem aperturam vul-* 10 *vae* (id est primogenitum) *ut eos vastarem, ut scirent quod ego sum Jehova.* Quae verba, et causa vastationis imperii, ut recte intelligantur, notandum quod primum intentum fuit totum sacrum ministerium primogenitis tradere, non Levitis (vide Numer. Cap. 8 vers. 17); sed postquam omnes praeter Levitas vitulum adoraverunt, repudiati et 15 impurati sunt primogeniti, et Levitae eorum loco electi (Deuteron. Cap. 10 vers. 8). Quae mutatio, quo eam magis ac magis considero, in verba Taciti me cogit erumpere: illo tempore non fuisse Deo curae securitatem illorum, fuisse ultionem. Nec satis mirari possum tantam animo coelesti fuisse iram, ut ipsas leges, quae semper solum universi 20 populi honorem, salutem, et securitatem intendunt, animo se vindicandi et ad populum puniendum condiderit; ita ut leges non leges, hoc est, populi salus, sed potius poenae et supplicia visae sint. Omnia enim munera quae Levitis et sacerdotibus dare tenebantur, ut etiam quod primogeniti redimi debebant, et argentum pro capite Levitis dare, et 25 denique quod Levitis solis ad sacra accedere concedebatur, eos continuo suae impuritatis et repudiationis arguebant. Habebant deinde Levitae quod iis continuo exprobrarent. Nam non dubium est quin inter tot millia multi importuni theologastri reperti fuerint: unde populo desiderium facta Levitarum, qui absque dubio homines erant, observandi, 30 et, ut fit, omnes ob unius delictum accusandi. Hinc continuo rumores: deinde fastidium homines otiosos et invisos, nec sanguine iis conjunctos, alendi, praecipue si annona cara erat. Quid igitur mirum si in otio,

23. *IV munera; I numera.*

we should have to attribute this to the defectiveness of their laws or customs. And, of course, it is true that if God had wished their state to be more stable he would have given it different laws and statutes, and established a different form of administration. So we can only say[1] that their God was angry with them, not only, as Jeremiah proclaims in Chapter 32, verse 31, from the foundation of their city, but right from the institution of their laws. Ezekiel actually confirms this in Chapter 20, verse 25, when he says: 'I gave them also statutes which were not good, and laws whereby they might not live, in that I made their own gifts a defilement by rejecting all that openeth the womb (i.e. the firstborn) so that I might destroy them: to the end that they should know that I am the Lord.' That these words, and the cause of the state's destruction, may be rightly understood, note that the original intention was to entrust the first-born, and not the Levites, with the whole administration of religion (see Numbers, Chapter 8, verse 17); but when everyone except the Levites worshipped the calf, the first-born were repudiated as unclean and the Levites appointed instead (Deuteronomy, Chapter 10, verse 8). The more I consider this change, the greater my urge to exclaim in the words of Tacitus, 'In those days God's purpose was vengeance, and not their security.'[2] Nor can I cease to marvel at God's anger against them,[3] an anger so fierce that even in framing the laws, whose sole aim is generally the glory, welfare, and security of the whole people, his purpose was to avenge himself and punish the people; so that their laws seemed penalties and punishments rather than laws, i.e. means to the people's welfare. For all the gifts they had to make to the Levites and priests, the fact that they had to redeem the first-born by paying the Levites for each, and, finally, the fact that the Levites alone were permitted to perform sacred rites,[4] were standing imputations of defilement and repudiation. Besides, the Levites had constant reason to upbraid them, since among so many thousands there must have been many troublesome dabblers in divinity; so the desire grew on the people to spy on the actions of the Levites—who were, of course, only human—and, as usually happens, to accuse them all because of the misdeeds of one. This immediately led to scandal, and ended in a reluctance to support men who were idle and unpopular, and not related to them by blood, especially when food was dear. What wonder then if in time of peace, when obvious miracles were ceasing,

---

[1] Speaking *more humano* (see *TT-P* iv, p. 81).   [2] *Histories* i, iii, 2.
[3] The expression is adapted from Virgil, *Aeneid* i, 11.
[4] *Numbers* 18.

quando manifesta miracula cessabant, nec homines exquisitissimae authoritatis dabantur, populi animus, irritatus et avarus, languescere inciperet, et tandem a cultu, quamvis divino, sibi tamen ignominioso et etiam suspecto deficeret, et novum cuperet: et quod principes, qui
5 semper ut jus summum imperii soli obtineant viam affectant, ut populum sibi alligarent et a pontifice averterent, omnia ei concederent novosque cultus introducerent? Quod si ex prima intentione respublica constituta fuisset, jus omnibus tribubus et honor aequalis semper fuisset, et omnia securissime sese habuissent. Nam quis jus sacrum suorum
10 consanguineorum violare vellet? Quid aliud mallent quam suos consanguineos, fratres et parentes, ex pietate religionis alere? Quam ab iisdem legum interpretationem edoceri? Et quam denique ab iisdem divina responsa expectare? Deinde hac ratione omnes tribus longe arctius invicem unitae mansissent, si nimirum omnibus aequale jus
15 fuisset sacra administrandi: quin imo nihil timendum esset si ipsa Levitarum electio aliam causam quam iram et vindictam habuisset. Sed, sicuti diximus, Deum suum iratum habuerunt, qui ipsos, ut verba Ezechiëlis iterum repetam, suis muneribus impuravit remittendo omnem aperturam vulvae, ut eosdem vastaret. Confirmantur haec praeterea
20 ipsis historiis. Simul ac populus in desertis otio abundare coepit, multi, et non de plebe viri, hanc electionem aegre ferre inceperunt, et hinc occasionem ceperunt credendi Mosen nihil ex mandato divino, sed ad libitum omnia instituere, quia scilicet suam tribum prae omnibus elegerit, et jus pontificatus in aeternum suo fratri dederit: quapropter
25 ipsum tumultu concitato adeunt clamantes omnes aeque sanctos esse, ipsumque supra omnes contra jus extolli. Nec eos ulla ratione sedare potuit, sed adhibito in signum fidei miraculo omnes extincti sunt. Unde nova et universalis populi totius seditio orta est, credentis scilicet eos non Deo judice, sed arte Mosis extinctos esse: qui tandem post
30 magnam cladem vel pestilentiam fessum sedavit, ast ita ut omnes mori mallent quam vivere. Quare tunc temporis seditio magis desierat quam

and men of the highest authority were no longer forthcoming, the people began to falter in its devotion through annoyance and greed; and if it finally forsook and wished to supersede a religion which, though divinely inspired, had become the object of its suspicion as well as the mark of its shame? And what wonder if its rulers, eager, like all rulers, to find ways of monopolizing sovereignty,[1] tried to alienate it from the priest and bind it to themselves by conceding all its demands and introducing new religions? Yet if the state had been organized as was originally intended, all the tribes would always have had the same right and status, and the whole structure would have been perfectly secure. For who would wish to violate the religious rights of his own kin? What more could men desire than to support their own kinsfolk, their fathers and brothers, out of religious piety, to learn from them the interpretation of the laws, and, finally, to await the divine responses from their lips? Besides, all the tribes would have remained much more closely united if they had all had an equal right to exercise religious functions; indeed, there would have been nothing to fear if the actual election of the Levites had not been inspired by anger and vengeance. But, as I said, their God was angry with them, and, to quote Ezekiel again, he made their own gifts a defilement by rejecting all that openeth the womb, so as to destroy them. These views, moreover, are confirmed by their actual history. As soon as the people began to have an easy time in the wilderness, many of them, and these by no means commoners, became dissatisfied with this election, and so began to believe that Moses was doing nothing by divine decree, but was settling everything to suit his own pleasure; for had he not chosen his own tribe before all, and given the right of priesthood to his brother in perpetuity? They therefore raised an uproar and assailed Moses with the cry that since all were equally holy he did wrong to exalt himself above everyone. And Moses found no means of pacifying them; but a miracle was performed to distinguish the faithful, and they were all wiped out.[2] This gave rise to a new and general revolt of the whole people,[3] for it thought that the men had not been destroyed by God's judgement, but by a trick on Moses' part; and although Moses restored peace eventually after it had been exhausted by a great disaster or plague, it was in such straits that everyone thought death more welcome than life.[4] Thus of that time it would be truer to say that rebellion had ceased than that

---

[1] *TP* viii, 2, p. 369.   [2] *Numbers* 16, 1–33.
[3] *Numbers* 16, 41 and ff.   [4] *Numbers* 20, 3.

concordia coeperat. Quod ita Scriptura testatur Deut. Cap. 31 vers.
21, ubi Deus Mosi, postquam ei praedixit populum post ejus mortem a
divino cultu defecturum, haec ait: *Novi enim ipsius appetitum et quid*
hodie machinatur, dum nondum eundem duxero ad terram quam juravi.
5 Et paulo post Moses ipsi populo: *Nam ego novi rebellionem tuam et*
contumaciam tuam. Si dum ego vobiscum vixi rebelles fuistis contra Deum,
multo magis eritis post mortem meam. Et revera sic etiam contigit, ut
notum. Unde magnae mutationes, magnaque ad omnia licentia, luxus,
et socordia, quibus omnia in deterius ire coeperunt, donec saepe subacti
10 jus divinum plane ruperunt, et regem mortalem voluerunt ut imperii
regia non templum, sed aula esset, et ut omnes tribus non amplius
juris divini et pontificatus, sed regum respectu concives manerent. At
hinc ingens materia novis seditionibus, ex quibus etiam tandem imperii
totius ruina sequuta est. Nam quid aliud reges minus ferre possunt quam
15 precario regnare et imperium in imperio pati? Qui primi ex privatis
electi sunt gradu dignitatis ad quem ascenderant contenti fuerunt;
at postquam filii jure successionis regno potiti sunt, omnia paulatim
mutare coeperunt ut omne jus imperii soli tenerent; quo maxima ex
parte carebant quamdiu jus legum ab iisdem non pendebat, sed a
20 pontifice qui eas in sacrario custodiebat, easque populo interpreta-
batur. Ideoque tanquam subditi legibus tenebantur, nec jure eas
abrogare poterant, vel novas aequali authoritate condere; deinde quia
jus Levitarum reges aeque ac subditos, ut profanos, sacra administrare
prohibebat; et denique quia tota sui imperii securitas a sola voluntate
25 unius, qui propheta videbatur, pendebat. Cujus rei exempla viderant:
nimirum quanta cum libertate Samuël Saulo omnia imperabat, et
quam facile unam ob noxam jus regnandi in Davidem transferre
potuerit. Quare et imperium in imperio habebant, et precario regna-
bant. Ad haec ergo superanda alia templa Diis dicare concesserunt, ut
30 nulla Levitis amplius consultatio esset; deinde plures qui nomine Dei

---

1. *B cap. 31; I Cap. 33.*   8. *O magnaque; I magnaquae.*
21. *I Adeoque.*

harmony had been established.[1] And Scripture confirms this in Deuteronomy, Chapter 31, verse 21, where, after foretelling to Moses that the people will abandon their religion after his death, God says: 'For I know its desire and what it is devising even to-day, before I have brought it to the land which I sware.' And a little later Moses says to the people itself: 'For I know thy rebellion and thy stiff neck. If while I have lived among you ye have been rebellious against God, much more shall ye be rebellious after my death.'[2] And his prophecy was fulfilled, as we know. The result was great changes, unbounded licence, self-indulgence, and lack of energy, which led to the decline of their country and its frequent subjugation; until finally they broke the divine law completely and sought for a human king,[3] so that his court should replace the temple as the seat of government, and the union of the tribes in one citizen body should no longer be based on the divine law and the priesthood but on common allegiance to a king. But this provided abundant matter for fresh disturbances, and these eventually led to the destruction of the whole state. For what can kings bear less than to rule by courtesy, and to have their power restricted by another's?[4] The early kings, who were appointed from a private station, were content with the high rank to which they had risen; but their sons, acquiring the kingdom by right of succession, began to make gradual changes everywhere so as to get all power into their own hands. For as long as the authority of the laws did not derive from themselves, but from the priest who guarded them in the shrine and interpreted them to the people, they lacked the main element of sovereignty. This was one reason why they were bound by the laws like subjects, and had no right to repeal them or to establish new ones of equal authority; another was that the right of the Levites prevented kings just as much as subjects—since both were profane—from handling religious affairs; and a third was that their tenure of office depended entirely on the will of one man, the man who appeared as a prophet. The last they had learnt from precedents; had not Samuel, for instance, given orders to Saul about everything without the least opposition, and been able with ease to transfer the sovereignty to David because of a single fault?[5] So not only was their power restricted by another's, but they ruled by courtesy. To overcome these limitations they allowed other temples to be dedicated to other Gods, so that the Levites might be consulted no

---

[1] The expression is adapted from Tacitus, *Histories* IV, i, 1 : *bellum magis desierat, quam pax coeperat.*　　　　　　　　　　　　　　　　　　[2] *Deuteronomy* 31, 27.

[3] *1 Samuel* 8, 4–5.　　　　[4] Cf. *TT-P* xviii, pp. 199–201.　　　　[5] *1 Samuel* 15–16.

prophetarent quaesiverunt, ut prophetas haberent quos veris opponerent. Sed quicquid conati sunt, nunquam voti compotes esse potuerunt. Prophetae enim, ad omnia parati, tempus opportunum expectabant, nempe imperium successoris, quod semper dum memoria
5 praecedentis viget precarium est: tum facile authoritate divina aliquem in regem infensum et virtute clarum inducere poterant ad jus divinum vindicandum, et imperium vel ejus partem jure possidendum. Verum nec prophetae aliquid hac ratione promovere poterant; nam etsi tyrannum e medio tollerent, manebant tamen causae; quare nihil
10 aliud faciebant quam novum tyrannum multo civium sanguine emere. Discordiis igitur bellisque civilibus finis nullus, causae autem jus divinum violandi semper eaedem, quae etiam non nisi simul cum toto imperio e medio tolli potuerunt.

His videmus quomodo religio in Hebraeorum rempublicam intro-
15 ducta fuerit, et qua ratione imperium aeternum esse potuerit si justa legislatoris ira in eodem persistere concessisset. Sed quia id fieri non potuit, tandem interire debuit. Atque hic de solo primo imperio locutus sum; nam secundum vix umbra fuit primi, quandoquidem jure Persarum, quorum subditi erant, tenebantur, et postquam libertatem
20 adepti sunt pontifices jus principatus usurpaverunt, quo imperium absolutum obtinuerunt; unde sacerdotibus regnandi et pontificatum simul adipiscendi ingens libido. Quare de hoc secundo minime opus fuit plura dicere. An vero primum, prout ipsum durabile concepimus, imitabile sit, vel pium id quoad ejus fieri potest imitari, id ex sequenti-
25 bus patebit. Hic tantum coronidis loco notari velim id quod jam supra innuimus, nempe ex his quae in hoc Capite ostendimus constare jus divinum sive religionis ex pacto oriri, sine quo nullum est nisi naturale; et ideo Hebraei nulla pietate erga gentes quae pacto non interfuerunt ex jussu religionis tenebantur, sed tantum in concives.

16. It is just possible that *concessasset* is the correct reading.
19. *O tenebantur; I tenebautur.*

more,[1] and tried to find other men to prophesy in God's name, so as to have champions against the true prophets.[2] But none of their schemes could ever achieve the end they desired. For the prophets, prepared for everything, would wait for their chance, i.e. the beginning of a new reign, which is always precarious as long as the memory of the previous king is fresh; when by their divine authority they could easily induce someone hostile to the king, and renowned for his prowess, to assert the divine law and take possession of the state, or a part of it, by right. Yet the prophets in their turn could make no headway by this means; for although they removed the tyrant the causes of tyranny remained, so they were merely purchasing a new tyrant at the cost of much citizen blood.[3] There was therefore no end to dissension and civil war, while the causes which led men to break the divine law were always the same, and could only disappear with the destruction of the whole state.

We have now seen how religion was introduced into the Jewish state, and how that state could have lasted for ever if the righteous anger of the legislator had allowed it to remain in its original condition. But since this was impossible it had to perish in the end. I have here confined my remarks to the first state; for the second[4] was hardly a shadow of the first, since its citizens were bound by the laws of the Persians, whose subjects they were, and after they achieved their freedom[5] the high priests usurped the right to govern, thus obtaining absolute sovereignty; so priests had a passionate desire to hold the reins of government and the high priesthood simultaneously. For these reasons there was little need to say more of the second state.[6] Whether the first in its durable form is a model which it would be profitable, or pious, to follow as closely as possible, will be shown in the following Chapters. Here, in conclusion, I merely wish to draw attention to a point already suggested above. It is clear from the findings of the present Chapter that divine or religious law[7] arises from a contract,[8] without which there is no law but natural law; and this is why the Jews were not bound by their religion to practise piety towards peoples who were not parties to the contract, but only towards fellow citizens.

---

[1] *1 Kings* 12, 26–33.   [2] *TT-P* xviii, p. 197.   [3] *TT-P* xviii, p. 201.

[4] For the beginning of 'the second state' in 537 B.C. see *Ezra* 1 (cf. *TT-P* iii, pp. 61–63).

[5] Under Simon, the last surviving brother of Judas Maccabaeus, in 143–2 B.C.

[6] The interesting feature of the first state was the division between secular and religious authority from Moses' death until the appointment of Saul.

[7] i.e. revealed divine law like the law of Moses (*TT-P* iv, p. 73). The statement is not true of natural divine law (ibid. p. 75).   [8] *TT-P* xix, p. 209.

CAPUT XVIII

Ex Hebraeorum republica et historiis quaedam dogmata politica concluduntur

QUAMVIS Hebraeorum imperium, quale ipsum in praecedenti Capite concepimus, aeternum esse potuerit, idem tamen nemo jam imitari 5 potest, nec etiam consultum est. Nam si qui suum jus in Deum transferre vellent, id cum Deo, sicuti Hebraei fecerunt, expresse pacisci deberent; adeoque non tantum voluntas jus transferentium, sed etiam Dei, in quem esset transferendum, requireretur. At Deus contra per Apostolos revelavit Dei pactum non amplius atramento nec in tabulis 10 lapideis, sed Dei spiritu in corde scribi. Deinde talis imperii forma iis forsan tantum utilis esse posset, qui sibi solis absque externo commercio vivere, seseque intra suos limites claudere et a reliquo orbe segregari velint, at minime iis quibus necesse est cum aliis commercium habere; quapropter talis imperii forma paucissimis tantum ex usu esse potest. 15 Verumenimvero, tametsi in omnibus imitabile non sit, multa tamen habuit dignissima saltem ut notarentur, et quae forsan imitari consultissimum esset. Attamen, quia mea intentio, ut jam monui, non est de republica ex professo agere, eorum pleraque missa faciam, et tantum ea quae ad meum scopum faciunt notabo: nempe quod contra Dei 20 regnum non pugnet summam majestatem eligere quae summum imperii jus habeat. Nam postquam Hebraei suum jus in Deum transtulerunt, jus summum imperandi Mosi tradiderunt; quique adeo solus authoritatem habuit leges Dei nomine condendi et abrogandi, sacrorum ministros eligendi, judicandi, docendi, et castigandi, et omnibus denique 25 omnia absolute imperandi. Deinde, quod quamvis sacrorum ministri legum interpretes fuerint, eorum tamen non erat cives judicare, nec aliquem excommunicare; hoc enim tantum judicibus et principibus ex populo electis competebat (vide Josuae Cap. 6 vers. 26, Judicum Cap. 21 vers. 18, et 1. Samuëlis Cap. 14 vers. 24).

30 Praeter haec, si etiam ad Hebraeorum successus et historias attendere velimus, alia digna etiam ut notentur reperiemus: videlicet, I. quod

CHAPTER XVIII

Some political lessons derived from the Jewish state and the history of the Jewish people

ALTHOUGH the Jewish state as conceived in the previous Chapter could have lasted for ever, it is neither advisable nor possible to copy it to-day. For if men wished to transfer their right to God, they would have to make an explicit covenant with God to that effect, just as the Jews did; and this would require God's willingness to receive their right as well as their own willingness to transfer it. God, however, has revealed through the Apostles that his covenant is no longer written with ink or graven on tablets of stone, but is imprinted by his spirit on men's hearts.[1] Besides, I suspect that this form of state could only be expedient for men who wanted to live their own lives behind their own frontiers, with no foreign trade or contact with the rest of the world, and not for men who must have dealings with others;[2] which means that it can only be of use to very few. Yet although it is not a model to be followed in all respects, it did have many features which were at least very noteworthy, and which it would perhaps be highly advisable to copy. Most of these I shall omit, for I have already said that it is not my intention to write a formal treatise on the state;[3] and I shall confine my attention to points which are relevant to my purpose. The first is that it is not inconsistent with the government of God to choose a supreme ruler to hold sovereignty in the state. The fact that the Jews transferred their right to God did not prevent them from giving sovereignty to Moses, who therefore had sole authority to establish and repeal laws in God's name, to choose priests, to judge, to teach, to punish, and, in short, to command all men in absolutely every sphere.[4] The second is that the priests, although the interpreters of the laws, had no right to judge citizens or excommunicate anyone;[5] for this right belonged only to the judges and captains chosen from the people. See Joshua, Chapter 6, verse 26; Judges, Chapter 21, verse 18; and 1 Samuel, Chapter 14, verse 24.

If we now extend our survey to the course of Jewish history, we shall discover other features which are also worthy of note. I. There

---

[1] *2 Corinthians* 3, 3.
[2] *TT-P* xvii, p. 177.
[3] *TT-P* xvii, p. 153.
[4] Hobbes, *De Cive* xvi, 13.
[5] Spinoza attacks priestly exercise of this power in *TT-P* xix, p. 205.

nullae in religione sectae fuerint nisi postquam pontifices in secundo imperio authoritatem habuerunt decretandi et negotia imperii tractandi; quae authoritas ut aeterna esset, jus sibi principatus usurpaverunt, et tandem reges appellari voluerunt. Ratio in promptu est; in primo
5 namque imperio nulla decretalia nomen a pontifice habere poterant, quandoquidem nullum jus decretandi habebant, sed tantum Dei responsa, a principibus vel conciliis rogati, dandi; ac propterea nulla tum iis libido esse potuit nova decretandi, sed tantum assueta et recepta administrandi et defendendi. Nam nulla alia ratione libertatem suam
10 invitis principibus conservare tuto poterant nisi leges incorruptas servando. At postquam potestatem etiam ad imperii negotia tractandum, jusque principatus juxta pontificatum adepti sunt, unusquisque tam in religione quam in reliquis sui nominis gloriam incepit quaerere, omnia scilicet pontificali authoritate determinando, et quotidie nova de
15 caeremoniis, de fide, et omnibus decretando; quae non minus sacra nec minoris authoritatis esse voluerunt quam leges Mosis. Ex quo factum ut religio in exitiabilem superstitionem declinaret, et legum verus sensus et interpretatio corrumperetur; ad quod etiam accessit quod, dum pontifices viam ad principatum in initio restaurationis
20 affectabant, omnia ut plebem ad se traherent assentabantur, plebis scilicet facta, etsi impia, approbando, et Scripturam pessimis ejus moribus accommodando. Quod quidem Malachias de iis conceptissimis verbis testatur; is enim, postquam sacerdotes sui temporis increpuit eos Dei nominis contemptores appellando, sic eos castigare pergit: *Labia*
25 *pontificis custodiunt scientiam, et lex ex ipsius ore quaeritur, quia Dei missarius est. At vos recessistis a via, fecistis ut lex multis esset offendiculo, pactum Levi corrupistis, ait Deus exercituum.* Et sic porro eos accusare pergit quod leges ad libitum interpretabantur, et nullam Dei rationem, sed tantum personarum habebant. At certum est pontifices haec
30 nunquam tam caute facere potuisse ut a prudentioribus non animadverterentur, qui proinde crescente audacia contenderunt nullas alias leges teneri debere quam quae scriptae erant; caeterum decreta quae decepti Pharisaei (qui, ut Josephus in Antiquitatibus habet, ex communi

---

20. *IV ad*; *I ab*.   30-31. *B animadverterentur*; *I animadverteretur*.

were no religious divisions among them until the high priests in the second state had authority to make decrees and handle public affairs. (It was to make this authority permanent that they usurped the right to govern and finally wanted to be styled kings.) The reason is not far to seek. In the first state no decree could bear the name of a high priest, for these priests had no right to make decrees, but could only give the responses of God when consulted by the captains or councils.[1] Under these circumstances they could have no desire to make new decrees, but only to administer and uphold the customary and accepted laws; for the only way in which they could safely preserve their privileges against the opposition of the captains was by keeping the laws inviolate. But once they also obtained the power to handle state affairs, and held not only the priesthood but the right to govern, each one of them, eager to make his name in religion no less than in government, began to subject all sacred matters to his pontifical authority, and to issue daily batches of new decrees about ritual, dogma, and everything; decrees which he wished to be just as sacred and authoritative as the laws of Moses. The result was that religion degenerated into pernicious superstition and the true meaning and interpretation of the laws was distorted. Besides, in paving their way to sovereignty at the start of the restoration[2] the high priests indulged every whim of the commons in an effort to gain its support, approving its actions, however impious, and perverting Scripture to excuse its depravity. Malachi testifies to their conduct in formal terms; he rebukes the priests of his day by calling them despisers of God's name, and then proceeds to chastise them as follows: 'The lips of the priest are the guardians of knowledge, and the law is sought from his mouth, because he is the messenger of God. But ye have turned aside from the way, ye have made the law a stumbling-block unto many, ye have corrupted the covenant of Levi, saith the Lord of Hosts.'[3] And so he goes on to accuse them of interpreting the laws as they pleased, and of paying no respect to God, but only to persons. Of course the high priests, however circumspect, could never conceal this from the more enlightened citizens; and the latter therefore maintained with increasing boldness that only the written laws should be observed, and that the decrees which the Pharisees (who, as Josephus affirms in his Antiquities,[4] were drawn mainly from the

---

[1] *TT-P* xvii, p. 165.   [2] *TT-P* iii, pp. 61–63; xvii, p. 189.
[3] *Malachi* 2, 7–8.
[4] The reference is probably to *Antiquitates* xiii, 297–8, though in that passage Josephus merely says that the Pharisees had the masses on their side.

plebe maxime constabant) traditiones patrum vocabant minime custo-
dienda esse. Quicquid fuerit, nullo modo possumus dubitare quin
pontificum adulatio, religionis et legum corruptio, harumque incredi-
bilis augmentatio magnam admodum et frequentem occasionem dederint
5 disputationibus et altercationibus quae nunquam componi potuerunt;
nam ubi homines ardore superstitionis, magistratu alterutram partem
adjuvante, litigare incipiunt, nequaquam sedari possunt, sed necessario
in sectas dividuntur.

II. Notatu dignum est quod prophetae, viri scilicet privati, libertate
10 sua monendi, increpandi, et exprobrandi homines magis irritaverunt
quam correxerunt; qui tamen a regibus moniti vel castigati facile
flectebantur. Imo regibus etiam piis saepe intolerabiles fuerunt propter
authoritatem quam habebant judicandi quid pie vel impie factum esset,
et vel reges ipsos castigandi si quod negotium publicum vel privatum
15 contra eorum judicium agere sustinebant. Rex Asa, qui ex testimonio
Scripturae pie regnavit, prophetam Hananiam in pistrinum dedit (vide
2. Paralip. Cap. 16) quia ipsum libere reprehendere et increpare sustinuit ob pactum cum Rege Aramaeae factum. Et praeter hoc alia
reperiuntur exempla quae ostendunt religionem plus detrimenti quam
20 incrementi ex tali libertate accepisse; ut jam taceam quod hinc etiam,
quod prophetae tantum sibi jus retinuerint, magna bella civilia orta
fuerint.

III. Dignum etiam ut notetur est quod quamdiu populus regnum
tenuit non nisi unum bellum civile habuerit; quod tamen absolute
25 extinctum fuit, et victores victorum ita miseriti sunt ut omnibus modis
curaverint eosdem in antiquam suam dignitatem et potentiam resti-
tuere. At postquam populus, regibus minime assuetus, imperii primam
formam in monarchicam mutavit, civilibus bellis nullus fere finis fuit,
et proelia adeo atrocia commiserunt ut omnium famam exuperaverint.
30 In uno enim proelio (quod fidem fere superat) quingenta millia Israëlitarum necati sunt a Judaeis; et in alio contra Israëlitae Judaeorum
multos trucidant (numerus in Scriptura non traditur), ipsum regem
capiunt, Hierosolymae murum fere demoliuntur, et ipsum templum
(ut irae nullum modum fuisse noscatur) omnino spoliant; et ingenti
35 fratrum praeda onusti, et sanguine satiati, acceptis obsidibus et rege
in jam fere vastato suo regno relicto, arma deponunt, non fide sed

18. *B Aramaeae*; *I Armeniae*.   33. *O Hierosolymae*; *I Hierusolymae*.

194

ignorant masses) wrongly called 'the traditions of our forefathers'[1] should be entirely ignored. However that may be, there is no possible doubt that the servility of the high priests, the corruption of religion and laws, and the incredible increase in the latter, gave great and frequent occasion for disputes and quarrels which could never be settled; for when men begin to wrangle through superstitious fervour, and the magistrate favours one side or the other, it is quite impossible to pacify them, and they inevitably divide into sects.[2]

II. It is noteworthy that, by their freedom to warn, rebuke, and denounce, the prophets, being private individuals, did more to provoke men than to correct them; though when subjects were warned or punished by the kings they were easily reformed. Indeed, even kings, and devout kings at that, often found the prophets insufferable because of their authority to decide what was pious or impious, and even to reprove the king himself if he dared to do anything, public or private, contrary to their will. Asa was a devout ruler, according to Scripture; yet he consigned the prophet Hanani to prison for being too free with his rebukes and reproaches over the treaty made with the King of Aramaea (see 2 Chronicles, Chapter 16). And there are other examples which show that such freedom did more harm than good to religion; to say nothing of the fact that the prophets' retention of so important a right was also the cause of great civil wars.[3]

III. It is noteworthy too that as long as the people held the king-dom there was only one civil war,[4] and it ended in the complete re-storation of peace, the victors having so much compassion on the vanquished that they spared no pains to restore them to their former position and power.[5] But after the people, though quite unused to kings, changed the state into a monarchy, there was almost no end to civil wars, and the battles they fought were of a fierceness unparalleled in history. In a single battle—and this almost passes belief—five hundred thousand Israelites were slain by the men of Judah;[6] in another the Israelites in turn slew many of the men of Judah[7] (the number is not recorded in Scripture), captured their king himself, practically razed the walls of Jerusalem, and even sacked the temple—a proof that their fury knew no bounds. Laden with enormous booty seized from their brethren, and glutted with their blood, they took hostages, and, leaving the king in his own kingdom, now almost

---

[1] See E. Bevan, *Jerusalem under the High Priests*, Arnold, 1904, ch. iv, pp. 121 and ff.
[2] *TT-P* xx, p. 237. [3] *TT-P* xvii, p. 189. [4] *TT-P* xvii, p. 169.
[5] *Judges* 21. [6] *2 Chronicles* 13, 17. [7] *2 Chronicles* 25, 21 and ff.

imbecillitate Judaeorum securi facti. Nam paucis post annis, Judaeorum viribus refectis, novum proelium rursus committunt, in quo iterum Israëlitae victores evadunt; centum et viginti millia Judaeorum trucidant, mulieres et liberos eorum usque ad ducenta millia captivos ducunt, 5 magnamque praedam iterum rapiunt. Atque his et aliis proeliis quae in historiis obiter narrantur consumpti, praeda tandem hostibus fuerunt. Deinde, si etiam tempora reputare velimus quibus absoluta pace frui licuit, magnam reperiemus discrepantiam; saepe enim ante reges quadraginta, et semel (quod omni opinione majus) octoginta annos sine 10 bello externo vel interno concorditer transegerunt. At postquam reges imperium adepti sunt, quia non amplius, ut antea, pro pace et libertate, sed pro gloria certandum erat, omnes praeter unum Salomonem (cujus virtus, sapientia scilicet, melius in pace quam in bello constare poterat) bella gessisse legimus. Accessit deinde exitiabilis regnandi libido, quae 15 plerisque iter ad regnum admodum cruentum fecit. Denique, leges durante populi regno incorruptae manserunt, et constantius observatae fuerunt. Nam ante reges paucissimi fuerunt prophetae qui populum monerent, post electum autem regem permulti simul fuerunt; Hobadias namque centum a caede liberavit, eosque abscondidit ne cum reliquis 20 occiderentur. Nec videmus quod populus ullis falsis prophetis deceptus fuit nisi postquam imperium regibus cessit, quibus plerique assentari student. Adde quod populus, cujus plerumque animus pro re nata magnus vel humilis est, facile se in calamitatibus corrigebat, et ad Deum convertebat, legesque restituebat, et hoc modo sese etiam omni 25 periculo expediebat: contra reges, quorum animi semper aeque elati sunt, nec flecti absque ignominia possunt, pertinaciter vitiis adhaeserunt usque ad supremum urbis excidium.

Ex his clarissime videmus:

I. Quam perniciosum et religioni et reipublicae sit sacrorum mini-30 stris jus aliquod decretandi vel imperii negotia tractandi concedere; et contra, omnia multo constantius sese habere si hi ita contineantur ut de

completely devastated, laid down their arms; relying on the weakness rather than the word of the men of Judah. For when the latter regained their strength a few years later, battle was joined again, and the Israelites again emerged victorious; they slew a hundred and twenty thousand of the men of Judah, led their wives and children captive to the number of two hundred thousand, and again seized vast quantities of booty.[1] These battles, and others described here and there in their history, exhausted them so much that they finally fell a prey to their enemies. If we also consider the periods of unbroken peace which they were allowed to enjoy under the two constitutions, we shall again find a great difference; for before the monarchy they often lived at peace for forty years at a time,[2] and once they had no foreign or civil war for the incredible period of eighty years.[3] But after the kings obtained sovereignty, the object of warfare ceased to be peace and freedom,[4] and became glory instead; accordingly, we learn that wars were waged by all the kings save Solomon, whose virtue, wisdom, could be better displayed in peace than in war. There was also a fatal lust for royal power, which usually made the path to the throne a very bloody one. Finally, as long as the people continued to rule, the laws remained uncorrupted and were observed with great constancy.[5] For before the monarchy very few prophets were sent to warn the people, but once kings were appointed a great many arose simultaneously; Obadiah, for example, rescued a hundred from execution, and hid them away lest they should be killed with the rest.[6] Nor do we hear of the people being deceived by false prophets until after the sovereignty was given to kings, whose favour most men are eager to win.[7] Moreover, the people, tending like all peoples to be elated or depressed according to the circumstances of the moment, found it easy to reform itself in the midst of calamities, to turn to God, to restore the laws, and so to extricate itself from every danger; whereas the kings, with the unvarying self-confidence of royalty, and its inability to give way without loss of face, persisted obstinately in their faults right down to the final destruction of the city.[8]

These points show very clearly:

I. How disastrous it is for both religion and the state to give ministers of religion any right to make decrees or to handle state affairs; and how greatly general stability is increased if these ministers

---

[1] *2 Chronicles* 28, 5 and ff.   [2] *Judges* 3, 11; 5, 31.   [3] *Judges* 3, 30.
[4] *TT-P* xvii, p. 175.   [5] *TT-P* xvii, pp. 171 and 181.
[6] *1 Kings* 18, 4 and 13.   [7] *TT-P* xvii, p. 189.   [8] By Nebuchadnezzar in 586 B.C.

nulla re nisi rogati respondeant, et ut interim recepta tantum et
maxime usitata doceant exerceantque.

II. Quam periculosum sit ad jus divinum referre res mere specula-
tivas, legesque de opinionibus condere de quibus homines disputare
5 solent vel possunt; ibi enim violentissime regnatur, ubi opiniones quae
uniuscujusque juris sunt quo nemo cedere potest pro crimine habentur.
Imo plebis ira, ubi hoc fit, maxime regnare solet; Pilatus namque, ut
Pharisaeorum irae concederet, Christum, quem innocentem noverat,
crucifigere jussit. Deinde, ut Pharisaei ditiores a suis dignitatibus
10 deturbarent, quaestiones de religione movere coeperunt, et Tsadu-
caeos impietatis accusare: et ad hoc Pharisaeorum exemplum pessimi
quique hypocritae, eadem rabie agitati—quam zelum juris divini
vocant—viros probitate insignes et virtute claros, et ob id plebi invisos, ubique persecuti sunt; eorum·scilicet opiniones publice detestando,
15 et saevam multitudinem ira in eosdem incendendo. Atque haec
procax licentia, quia specie religionis adumbratur, non facile coerceri
potest, praecipue ubi summae potestates sectam aliquam introduxerunt
cujus ipsae authores non sunt; quia tum non ut juris divini interpretes,
sed ut sectarii habentur, hoc est, ut qui sectae doctores juris divini
20 interpretes agnoscunt; et ideo magistratuum authoritas circa haec apud
plebem parum valere solet, at plurimum doctorum authoritas, quorum
interpretationibus vel reges submitti debere putant. Ad haec ergo mala
vitanda nihil reipublicae tutius excogitari potest quam pietatem et
religionis cultum in solis operibus, hoc est, in solo exercitio charitatis et
25 justitiae ponere, et de reliquis liberum unicuique judicium relinquere.
Sed de his postea fusius.

III. Videmus quam necesse sit tam reipublicae quam religioni summis potestatibus jus de eo quod fas nefasque sit discernendi concedere.
Nam si hoc jus de factis discernendi ipsis divinis prophetis concedi non
30 potuit nisi cum magno reipublicae et religionis damno, multo minus iis
concedendum erit qui nec futura praedicere sciunt nec miracula possunt facere. Verum de hoc in sequenti ex professo agam.

IV. Denique videmus quam exitiale sit populo qui sub regibus non
consuevit vivere, quique jam leges conditas habet, monarcham eligere.
35 Nam nec ipse tantum imperium sustinere, nec regia authoritas pati
poterit leges et jura populi ab alio minoris authoritatis instituta, et

are not allowed to give responses except when asked, and at other times must only teach and practise what is received and hallowed by custom.

II. How dangerous it is to apply religious law to matters purely speculative, and to legislate concerning beliefs about which it is common or possible for men to dispute; for tyranny is at its worst where the opinions to which everyone has an inalienable right are regarded as criminal. In fact, where this happens, the supreme tyrant is usually the anger of the mob;[1] for instance, it was to appease the anger of the Pharisees that Pilate ordered the crucifixion of Christ, whom he knew to be innocent. Again, it was to displace the rich from their high positions that the Pharisees began to instigate religious inquisitions, and to accuse the Sadducees of impiety; and all the worst hypocrites have followed their example. Impelled by the same fury—which they call zeal for God's law—they have everywhere persecuted those whose reputation for righteousness and virtue has incurred the envy of the masses, denouncing their opinions in public and inflaming the savage mob against them. Such shameless effrontery, being cloaked with a show of religion, is difficult to check, especially where sovereigns have introduced some sect which has been founded by others; for then they are not regarded as interpreters of religious law but as members of that sect, i.e. as men who accept the leaders of that sect as interpreters of religious law; so that in this field the mob generally sets little store by the authority of the magistrates and a great deal by the authority of the sect leaders, believing that even kings should bow to the interpretations of the latter.[2] The safest way to protect a state from these evils is to make piety and worship consist simply in works, i.e. simply in the practice of charity and justice, and otherwise to leave the individual his freedom of judgement. But more on this point later.[3]

III. How necessary it is both for the state and for religion to allow the sovereign the right to decide what is right and wrong. For if the right to judge actions could not be given to God's true prophets without great harm to the state and to religion,[4] still less should it be given to those who can neither foretell the future nor work miracles. But I shall deal formally with this point in my next Chapter.

IV. Finally, how fatal it is for a people unaccustomed to royal rule, and already possessed of established laws, to appoint a king.[5] For not only will the people be unable to tolerate his power: he in turn will be unable to tolerate democratic laws and rights instituted by an inferior

---

[1] *TT-P* xx, p. 237. [2] Cf. *TT-P* xix, p. 221. [3] *TT-P* xx.
[4] p. 195. [5] *TP* vii, 30, p. 363.

multo minus animum inducere ad easdem defendendum, praesertim quia in iis instituendis nulla ratio regis, sed tantum populi—vel concilii—qui regnum tenere putabat haberi potuit; atque adeo rex jura populi antiqua defendendo ejus potius servus quam dominus videretur.
5 Novus ergo monarcha summo studio novas leges statuere conabitur, et jura imperii in suum usum reformare, et populum eo redigere ut non tam facile regibus dignitatem adimere possit quam dare. At hic praeterire nequaquam possum non minus periculosum etiam esse monarcham e medio tollere, tametsi omnibus modis constet eundem
10 tyrannum esse. Nam populus regiae authoritati assuetus, eaque sola retentus, minorem contemnet et ludibrio habebit; ac proinde, si unum e medio tollat, necesse ipsi erit, ut olim prophetis, alium loco prioris eligere, qui non sponte sed necessario tyrannus erit. Nam qua ratione videre poterit civium manus caede regia cruentatas, eosque parricidio,
15 tanquam re bene gesta, gloriari, quod non nisi ad exemplum in ipsum solum statuendum commiserunt? Sane, si rex esse vult, nec populum regum judicem suumque dominum agnoscere, nec precario regnare, prioris mortem vindicare debet, et contra sui causa exemplum statuere ne populus iterum tale facinus committere audeat. At mortem tyranni
20 civium nece non facile vindicare poterit, nisi simul ejusdem prioris tyranni causam defendat, ejusque facta approbet, et consequenter omnia prioris tyranni vestigia sequatur. Hinc igitur factum ut populus saepe quidem tyrannum mutare, at nunquam tollere, nec imperium monarchicum in aliud alterius formae mutare potuerit. Hujus rei fatale exem-
25 plum populus Anglicanus dedit, qui causas quaesivit quibus specie juris monarcham e medio tolleret; at eo sublato nihil minus facere potuit quam formam imperii mutare. Sed post multum sanguinem effusum huc perventum est ut novus monarcha alio nomine salutaretur (quasi tota quaestio de solo nomine fuisset); qui nulla ratione persistere poterat
30 nisi stirpem regiam penitus delendo, regis amicos vel amicitia suspectos

---

2–3. *I populi, vel concilii, qui; Gf populi, vel concilii, quod.*

authority, and still less able to bring himself to defend them, especially as they were designed purely for the benefit of the people or assembly which envisaged possession of power, and could not possibly have taken any account of his interests; so that if he defended the ancient rights of the people he would seem to be its slave rather than its master. Hence a newly instituted king will do his best to establish new laws, to alter the rights of citizens for his own advantage, and so to weaken the power of the people that it cannot withdraw the royal authority as easily as it bestowed it. Here, however, I must point out that it is equally dangerous to remove a king, even although it is perfectly clear that he is a tyrant. For a people accustomed to royal rule, and kept in check by that alone, will despise and make a mockery of any lesser authority;[1] and so, if it removes one king, it will find it necessary, as the prophets did of old,[2] to replace him by another, and he will be a tyrant not by choice but by necessity. For what must he think as he sees the stains of royal blood on the hands of his citizens, and hears them boasting of their regicide as though it were a glorious deed—especially when it has been done solely as a warning to himself? Assuredly, if he wants to be a king, and does not want to recognize the people as his master and the judge of kings, or to rule by courtesy, he is bound to avenge the death of his predecessor, and to give a counter-warning on his own behalf that the people must not dare to perpetrate such an outrage again. But he will not find it easy to execute citizens in revenge for the tyrant's death without at the same time defending the cause of his predecessor, approving his actions, and thus following wholly in his footsteps. This is why peoples, though often able to change their tyrants, have never been able to abolish them and replace monarchy by a different form of constitution.[3] The English have provided a melancholy instance of this truth. They tried to find plausible legal grounds for removing their king;[4] but having removed him, they still found it quite impossible to change the form of the state. Indeed, after much bloodshed they got the length of calling their new king[5] by a different name (as though the name alone had been the whole question at issue!); and he could only maintain his position by extirpating the old royal family, killing the old king's friends and those suspected of

[1] For a shorter version of the following passage see *TP* v, 7, p. 313.

[2] *TT-P* xvii, p. 189.

[3] Van Hove, *Polityke Weegschaal*, 1661, I, iii, I, p. 188, quotes *mutatio tyranni non tyrannidis ablatio*. Spinoza holds that it is even dangerous to replace tyranny by constitutional monarchy (*TP* vii, 26, pp. 357–9).   [4] Charles I, executed in 1649.

[5] Oliver Cromwell, who adopted the title of Protector.

necando, et otium pacis rumoribus aptum bello disturbando, ut plebs,
novis rebus occupata et intenta, cogitationes de caede regia alio diver-
teret. Sero igitur animadvertit populus se pro salute patriae nihil aliud
fecisse quam jus legitimi regis violare, resque omnes in pejorem statum
5 mutare. Ergo gradum ubi licuit revocare decrevit, nec quievit donec
omnia in pristinum suum statum restaurata vidit. At forsan aliquis
exemplo populi Romani objiciet populum facile posse tyrannum e
medio tollere; sed ego eodem nostram sententiam omnino confirmari
existimo. Nam quamvis populus Romanus longe facilius tyrannum e
10 medio tollere, et formam imperii mutare potuerit, propterea quod jus
regem ejusque successorem eligendi penes ipsum populum erat, et
quod ipse (utpote ex seditiosis et flagitiosis hominibus conflatus) nondum regibus obedire consueverat—nam ex sex quos antea habuerat
tres interfecerat,—tamen nihil aliud fecit quam loco unius plures
15 tyrannos eligere; qui ipsum externo et interno bello misere conflictum
semper habuerunt, donec tandem imperium iterum in monarcham—
mutato etiam tantum, ut in Anglia, nomine—cessit. Quod autem ad
Ordines Hollandiae attinet, hi nunquam, quod scimus, reges habuerunt,
sed comites, in quos nunquam jus imperii translatum fuit. Nam, ut ipsi
20 Praepotentes Ordines Hollandiae in inductione tempore comitis Ley-
cestriae ab ipsis edita palam faciunt, sibi authoritatem semper reserva-
verunt ad eosdem comites sui officii monendum, et potestatem sibi
retinuerunt ad hanc suam authoritatem et civium libertatem defendendum, seseque de iisdem, si in tyrannos degenerarent, vindicandum, et
25 eos ita retinendum ut nihil nisi concedentibus et approbantibus Ordinibus efficere possent. Ex quibus sequitur jus supremae majestatis semper
penes Ordines fuisse; quod quidem ultimus comes conatus est usurpare.
Quare longe abest quod ab eo defecerint cum pristinum suum imperium
paene jam amissum restauraverunt. His igitur exemplis id quod diximus
30 omnino confirmatur, quod scilicet uniuscujusque imperii forma necessario retinenda est, nec absque periculo totalis ipsius ruinae mutari
potest. Et haec sunt quae hic operae pretium notare duxi.

---

6 Spinoza is anxious that his argument shall not be used to further the Orangist cause.
After the fall of the Republic in 1672 he appears to have recognized that sovereignty had lain
with the counts after all, and that the reversion to monarchy could only have been avoided
by a complete reorganization of the state (*TP* ix, 14, p. 427).

7 This seems to be the document mentioned by P. J. Blok, *A History of the People of the
Netherlands*, vol. iii, ch. vi, p. 232. 8 Philip II of Spain.

9 Spinoza turns the argument against the Orangists, echoing the conclusion of Van Hove
(op. cit. III, iii, 5, p. 567) that the existing form of government is the best.

being such, and shattering peace-time ease, which loosens censorious tongues, with a call to war,[1] so that the common people should have its attention occupied with new matters and forget the execution of its king.[2] Thus it was a long time before the people came to its senses; but it eventually realized that it had done nothing for the safety of the country but violate the right of its lawful king and change everything for the worse. It therefore decided to retrace its steps as soon as possible, and did not rest until it saw everything restored to its former state.[3] Here someone may cite the Romans to show that a people can easily abolish its tyrants: but, as I see it, this example entirely confirms my view. Admittedly the Roman people found it much easier than most to abolish tyrants and change the form of the state; for it not only had the right to choose its king and his successor,[4] but (being composed of rebels and criminals) it was not yet broken in to royal authority, having killed three kings out of the six who had ruled it. The fact remains that it did nothing but appoint several tyrants in place of one; and these kept it miserably embroiled in external and internal wars, until the government finally passed to a king again—the only difference being, as in England, a change of title.[5] As for Holland, its Estates never had a king, as far as we know, but only counts; and the latter were never vested with the sovereignty.[6] For as the High and Puissant Estates of Holland themselves make plain in the declaration they published in the time of Count Leicester,[7] they always kept the authority to remind the aforesaid counts of their duty, and retained the power not only to defend this authority, and the freedom of the citizens, but also to get rid of their counts should these degenerate into tyrants, and to curb them so that they could do nothing without the permission and approval of the Estates. Thus sovereignty was always held by the Estates, and it was their sovereignty that the last count[8] attempted to usurp. It is therefore quite wrong to suppose that they revolted from him; they simply reasserted their original sovereignty at a time when it had almost been lost. These examples, then, fully confirm my assertion that every state must necessarily preserve its own form, and cannot change it without risking complete destruction.[9] Such are the points I have thought worthy of note in this Chapter.

---

[1] The war against the Dutch, 1652–4.

[2] For Cromwell's policy cf. Machiavelli, *Prince* xxi.   [3] At the Restoration of 1660.

[4] Like the people of Aragon in early times (*TP* vii, 30, p. 363).

[5] The reference is probably to Augustus, who adopted the title of Princeps. If so, the 'several tyrants' would include men like Marius and Sulla; Pompey, Crassus, and Caesar; Antony, Lepidus, and Octavian. But the ease with which Spinoza dismisses the Roman Republic is astonishing.   6, 7, 8, 9. *See opposite page.*

CAPUT XIX

Ostenditur jus circa sacra penes summas potestates omnino esse, et religionis cultum externum reipublicae paci accommodari debere, si recte Deo obtemperare velimus

CUM supra dixi eos qui imperium tenent jus ad omnia solos habere, et
5 a solo eorum decreto jus omne pendere, non tantum civile intelligere
volui, sed etiam sacrum; nam hujus etiam et interpretes esse debent et
vindices. Atque hoc hic expresse notare volo, et de eo ex professo in
hoc Capite agere, quia plurimi sunt qui pernegant hoc jus, nempe circa
sacra, summis potestatibus competere, neque eas interpretes juris divini
10 agnoscere volunt; unde etiam licentiam sibi sumunt easdem accusandi
et traducendi, imo ab ecclesia (ut olim Ambrosius Theodosium
Caesarem) excommunicandi. Sed eos hac ratione imperium dividere,
imo viam ad imperium affectare, infra in hoc ipso Capite videbimus;
nam prius ostendere volo religionem vim juris accipere ex solo eorum
15 decreto qui jus imperandi habent, et Deum nullum singulare regnum in
homines habere nisi per eos qui imperium tenent; et praeterea quod
religionis cultus et pietatis exercitium reipublicae paci et utilitati
accommodari, et consequenter a solis summis potestatibus determinari
debet; quaeque adeo ejus etiam interpretes debent esse. Loquor ex-
20 presse de pietatis exercitio et externo religionis cultu; non autem de ipsa
pietate et Dei interno cultu, sive mediis quibus mens interne disponitur
ad Deum integritate animi colendum; internus enim Dei cultus et
ipsa pietas uniuscujusque juris est (ut in fine Cap. VII ostendimus)
quod in alium transferri non potest. Porro, quid hic per Dei regnum
25 intelligam ex Cap. XIV satis constare existimo; in eo enim ostendimus
eum legem Dei adimplere qui justitiam et charitatem ex Dei mandato
colit: unde sequitur illud regnum esse Dei in quo justitia et charitas
vim juris et mandati habent. Atque hic nullam agnosco differentiam
sive Deus verum justitiae et charitatis cultum lumine naturali sive

---

8. *O pernegant*; *I perneganr.*   9. *I eos.*

CHAPTER XIX

*That the sovereign has full right to control religion,[1]
and that our external acts of worship must be adapted
to the public peace if we wish to obey God properly*

WHEN I said above[2] that the sovereign had exclusive right over everything, and that all law depended entirely on his will, I was referring
to religious law as well as to civil; for he must also be the interpreter
and guardian of religious law. I now wish to draw particular attention
to this point, and to deal with it formally in this Chapter, because
many people flatly deny that the right to control religion belongs to the
sovereign, and refuse to recognize him as the interpreter of divine
law; hence they actually presume to accuse and traduce him, and even
to excommunicate him from the church, as Ambrose excommuni-
cated the Emperor Theodosius in days gone by.[3] By so doing they are
dividing the sovereign power, and in fact paving their way to supremacy;
but this will appear later in the Chapter.[4] What I want to show first is
that religion acquires the force of law only by the will of those who
have the right to command, and that God has no special kingdom over
men save through those who hold sovereignty; that religion and piety
must be adapted to the peace and welfare of the state, and hence
defined by the sovereign alone; and that in consequence he must also
be its interpreter. I am speaking expressly of external acts of piety and
worship; not of inward piety and the inward worship of God, i.e. of
the means by which the mind is inwardly led to worship God in purity
of spirit; for, as I have shown at the end of Chapter VII,[5] inward
worship and piety are part of the inalienable right of the individual.
Moreover, the meaning here given to 'the kingdom of God' is clear
enough, I think, from Chapter XIV,[6] where I showed that he who
practises justice and charity by God's command fulfils God's law
completely; from which it follows that God is king where justice and
charity have the force of law and command. And I recognize no
difference here whether it is by natural reason or by revelation that

---

[1] Spinoza here follows Hobbes, *De Cive*, 1642; Grotius, *De Imperio Summarum Potestatum circa Sacra*, 1647; and Lucius Antistius Constans, *De Jure Ecclesiasticorum Liber Singularis*, 1665. Note, however, that he is dealing only with 'outward religion', as he says below.

[2] *TT-P* xvi, pp. 133–5.

[3] After the massacre at Thessalonica in A.D. 390.

[4] p. 217.   [5] p. 109.   [6] p. 113.

revelatione doceat imperetque; nihil enim refert quomodo ille cultus
revelatus sit, modo summum jus obtineat summaque lex hominibus sit.
Si igitur jam ostendam justitiam et charitatem vim juris et mandati
non posse accipere nisi ex jure imperii, facile inde concludam (quando-
5 quidem jus imperii penes summas potestates tantum est) religionem vim
juris accipere ex solo eorum decreto qui jus imperandi habent, et Deum
nullum singulare regnum in homines habere nisi per eos qui imperium
tenent. At quod cultus justitiae et charitatis vim juris non accipit nisi
ex jure imperii, ex antecedentibus patet; ostendimus enim Cap. XVI
10 in statu naturali non plus juris rationi quam appetitui esse, sed tam eos
qui secundum leges appetitus quam eos qui secundum leges rationis
vivunt jus ad omnia quae possunt habere. Hac de causa in statu naturali
peccatum concipere non potuimus, nec Deum tanquam judicem homines
propter peccata punientem, sed omnia secundum leges universae naturae
15 communes fieri, et eundem casum (ut cum Salomone loquar) justo ac
impio, puro ac impuro etc. contingere, et nullum locum justitiae nec
charitati esse. At ut verae rationis documenta, hoc est (ut in Cap. IV
circa legem divinam ostendimus) ipsa divina documenta, vim juris
absolute haberent, necesse fuisse ut unusquisque jure suo naturali
20 cederet, et omnes idem in omnes, vel in aliquot, vel in unum trans-
ferrent; et tum demum nobis primum innotuit quid justitia, quid
injustitia, quid aequitas, quidque iniquitas esset. Justitia igitur, et
absolute omnia verae rationis documenta, et consequenter erga proximum charitas, a solo imperii jure, hoc est (per ea quae in eodem Cap.
25 ostendimus) a solo eorum decreto qui jus imperandi habent, vim juris
et mandati accipiunt: et quia (ut jam ostendi) in solo justitiae et charitatis sive verae religionis jure Dei regnum consistit, sequitur, ut vole-
bamus, Deum nullum regnum in homines habere nisi per eos qui
imperium tenent. Et perinde, inquam, est sive religionem lumine natu-
30 rali sive prophetico revelatam concipiamus; demonstratio enim universalis est, quandoquidem religio eadem est, et a Deo aeque revelata, sive
hoc sive illo modo hominibus innotuisse supponatur. Et ideo, ut etiam
religio prophetice revelata vim juris apud Hebraeos haberet, necesse
fuit ut unusquisque eorum jure suo naturali prius cederet, et omnes ex

15. *I ferri.*

God teaches and commands true justice and charity; for it does not
matter how they have been revealed as long as they have supreme
authority over men and are their supreme law. So if I now show that
justice and charity can acquire the force of law and command only
through the right of the state, then, since the right of the state is vested
in the sovereign alone, it will follow at once that religion acquires the
force of law only by the will of those who have the right to command,
and that God has no special kingdom over men save through those
who hold sovereignty. Now, that the practice of justice and charity
acquires the force of law only by the right of the state, is clear from our
previous discussion; for I showed in Chapter XVI[1] that in the state
of nature reason had no more authority than appetite, and that those
who were governed by appetite had as much right to do everything
they could as those who were governed by reason. This was why we
could not conceive of sin,[2] or of God as a judge punishing men for
their sins,[3] in the state of nature, where everything came to pass in
accordance with laws common to the whole of nature, the same fate—
to quote Solomon—befell the righteous and the wicked, the pure and
the impure,[4] and justice and charity had no place. The precepts of true
reason, which are (as I showed in discussing the divine law in Chapter
IV)[5] God's real precepts, could have the full force of law only if
everyone surrendered his natural right, and transferred it either to all,
or to a few, or to one man; not till then did the nature of justice and
injustice, of equity and iniquity, first dawn upon our minds.[6] Hence
justice, and absolutely all the precepts of true reason, and therefore
charity towards one's neighbour, acquire the force of law and command
only through the right of the state, i.e. (by our findings in the same
Chapter)[7] only by the will of those who have the right to command;
and since, as I have just shown, the kingdom of God is simply the rule
of justice and charity, i.e. of true religion, the desired conclusion follows that God has no kingdom over men save through those who hold
sovereignty. How we think religion was revealed does not matter; for
the proof is valid in all cases, since religion is the same, and equally
revealed by God, whether we suppose that men discovered it by the
light of nature or by prophecy. This explains why even when religion
was revealed by prophecy it could not have the force of law among the
Jews until they all surrendered their natural right, and all decided by

[1] pp. 125–7. [2] Loc. cit. (cf. p. 143). [3] Cf. *TT-P* iv, pp. 77–83.
[4] *Ecclesiastes* 9, 2. [5] pp. 71–73.
[6] *TP* ii, 23, p. 283; Machiavelli, *Discourses* i, 2. [7] *TT-P* xvi, pp. 133–7.

communi consensu statuerent iis tantum obedire quae ipsis a Deo
prophetice revelarentur; eodem prorsus modo ac in imperio democratico
fieri ostendimus, ubi omnes communi consensu deliberant ex solo
rationis dictamine vivere. Et quamvis Hebraei suum jus praeterea in
5 Deum transtulerint, hoc magis mente quam opera facere potuerunt:
nam re ipsa (ut supra vidimus) jus imperii absolute retinuerunt donec
ipsum in Mosen transtulerunt, qui etiam deinceps rex absolute mansit,
et per eum solum Deus Hebraeos regnavit. Porro hac etiam de causa
(quod scilicet religio ex solo jure imperii vim juris accipit) Moses nullo
10 eos supplicio afficere potuit qui ante pactum, et qui consequenter sui
adhuc juris erant, sabbatum violaverunt (vide Exodi Cap. 16 vers. 27),
sicuti post pactum (vide Num. Cap. 15 vers. 36), postquam scilicet
unusquisque jure suo naturali cessit, et sabbatum ex jure imperii vim
mandati accepit. Denique hac etiam de causa destructo Hebraeorum
15 imperio religio revelata vim juris habere desiit; nequaquam enim
dubitare possumus quin simul ac Hebraei jus suum in Babylonium
Regem transtulerunt, continuo regnum Dei jusque divinum cessaverit.
Nam eo ipso pactum quo promiserant omnibus quae Deus loqueretur
obedire, quodque Dei regni fundamentum fuerat, omnino sublatum
20 est; nec eo amplius stare poterant, quandoquidem ab eo tempore non
amplius sui juris (ut cum in desertis vel in patria essent), sed Regis
Babyloniae erant, cui in omnibus (ut Cap. XVI ostendimus) obedire
tenebantur. Quod etiam Jeremias eosdem Cap. 29 vers. 7 expresse
monet. *Consulite,* inquit, *paci civitatis ad quam vos captivos duxi; nam*
25 *ipsius incolumitate vobis erit incolumitas.* At incolumitati illius civitatis
consulere non poterant tanquam imperii ministri (captivi enim erant),
sed tanquam servi; se scilicet ad vitandas seditiones in omnibus obedientes
praestando, imperii jura et leges, tametsi a legibus quibus in patria
consueverant admodum diversa, observando etc. Ex quibus omnibus
30 evidentissime sequitur religionem apud Hebraeos vim juris a solo imperii jure accepisse, et eo destructo non amplius tanquam jussum
singularis imperii, sed catholicum rationis documentum haberi potuisse.
Rationis, inquam; nam catholica religio nondum ex revelatione inno-
tuerat. Absolute igitur concludimus religionem, sive ea lumine naturali

---

10. *O supplicio; I suplicio.*

11. *V–L (vide Exodi cap. 16. vs. 27.); B (vide Exodi cap. 16. vers. 27. sqq.); I (vide Exodi
Cap. 15. vers. 30.).*

16. *IV Babylonium; I Babilonium.*　　　　　　　　22. *Gf Babyloniae; I Babiloniae.*

common consent that they would obey only the commands of God revealed by prophecy; just as men do in a democracy, as I have shown, when they all decide by common consent to live only by the dictate of reason.[1] The Jews, of course, went farther, and transferred their right to God, but this transfer was imaginary rather than real; for in reality, as we saw above,[2] they remained in full possession of sovereignty until they transferred it to Moses. From then on Moses was an absolute monarch, and it was through him alone that God ruled over the Jews. The fact that religion acquires the force of law only by the right of the state also explains why Moses could not punish those who broke the sabbath before the covenant, when they were still in possession of their own right (see Exodus, Chapter 16, verse 27), as he could after the covenant (see Numbers, Chapter 15, verse 36), i.e. after each surrendered his natural right and sabbath observance acquired the force of a command by the right of the state. Finally, it also explains why on the destruction of the Jewish state revealed religion ceased to have the force of law; for we cannot doubt that the kingdom of God and the divine law came to an end as soon as the Jews transferred their right to the King of Babylon.[3] By so doing they completely annulled their covenant to obey all God's commands, which had been the basis of God's kingdom; they could abide by it no longer, since from that time on they were no longer autonomous (as they had been in the wilderness or in their own country), but subject to the King of Babylon, and bound to obey all his commands, as I have shown in Chapter XVI.[4] Indeed, Jeremiah expressly reminds them of this in Chapter 29, verse 7: 'Seek the peace of the city whither I have brought you captive; for in the safety thereof ye shall have safety.' Now, being captives, they could not seek the safety of that city as ministers of state, but only as slaves; that is, by rendering complete obedience in order to avoid civil strife, by observing the laws and statutes of the state—although these were very different from the laws to which they had been accustomed in their own country—and so on. From all this it obviously follows that religion among the Jews acquired the force of law only by the right of the state, and when their state was destroyed could no longer be regarded as the command of a particular state, but only as a universal precept of reason. I say 'of reason', because the universal religion had still to be revealed. I therefore conclude unreservedly that religion,

[1] *TT-P* xvi, p. 129; xvii, p. 159.   [2] *TT-P* xvii, p. 159; xviii, p. 191.
[3] The reference is to the first capture of Jerusalem by Nebuchadnezzar in 597 B.C.
[4] p. 147.

sive prophetico revelata sit, vim mandati accipere ex solo eorum decreto qui jus imperandi habent, et Deum nullum singulare regnum in homines habere nisi per eos qui imperium tenent. Sequitur hoc etiam, et clarius etiam intelligitur, ex dictis in Cap. IV: ibi enim ostendimus
5 Dei decreta aeternam veritatem et necessitatem omnia involvere, nec posse concipi Deum tanquam principem vel legislatorem leges hominibus ferentem. Quapropter divina documenta lumine naturali vel prophetico revelata vim mandati a Deo immediate non accipiunt, sed necessario ab iis, vel mediantibus iis, qui jus imperandi et decretandi
10 habent; adeoque non nisi mediantibus iisdem concipere possumus Deum in homines regnare, resque humanas secundum justitiam et aequitatem dirigere. Quod ipsa etiam experientia comprobatur. Nam nulla divinae justitiae vestigia reperiuntur nisi ubi justi regnant; alias (ut Salomonis verba iterum repetam) eundem casum justo ac injusto, puro ac impuro
15 contingere videmus: quod quidem plurimos qui Deum in homines immediate regnare, et totam naturam in eorum usum dirigere putabant, de divina providentia dubitare fecit. Cum itaque tam experientia quam ratione constet jus divinum a solo decreto summarum potestatum pendere, sequitur easdem etiam ejusdem esse interpretes. Qua autem
20 ratione, jam videbimus; nam tempus est ut ostendamus cultum religionis externum, et omne pietatis exercitium, reipublicae paci et conservationi debere accommodari si recte Deo obtemperare velimus. Hoc autem demonstrato facile intelligemus qua ratione summae potestates interpretes religionis et pietatis sint.

25 Certum est quod pietas erga patriam summa sit quam aliquis praestare potest; nam sublato imperio nihil boni potest consistere, sed omnia in discrimen veniunt, et sola ira et impietas maximo omnium metu regnat. Unde sequitur nihil proximo pium praestari posse, quod non impium sit si inde damnum totius reipublicae sequatur; et contra nihil
30 in eundem impium committi, quod pietati non tribuatur si propter reipublicae conservationem fiat. Ex. gr. pium est ei qui mecum contendit, et meam tunicam vult capere, pallium etiam dare; at ubi judicatur hoc reipublicae conservationi perniciosum esse, pium contra est eundem in

whether revealed by natural reason or by prophecy, acquires the force of a command only by the will of those who have the right to govern, and that God has no special kingdom over men save through those who hold sovereignty. This also follows, and is also understood more clearly, from what I have said in Chapter IV;[1] for I showed there that God's decrees involve eternal truth and necessity in every case, and that God cannot be conceived as a king or legislator who gives laws to men. Hence the divine precepts revealed by natural or prophetic insight do not acquire the force of commands from God directly, but must acquire it from those, or through the medium of those, who have the right to command and make decrees; so that it is only through their mediation that we can conceive God as ruling over men and directing their affairs in accordance with justice and equity. And this conclusion is confirmed by the facts of experience. For traces of divine justice are found only where just men rule; otherwise—to quote Solomon again —we see the same fate befalling righteous and unrighteous, pure and impure alike:[2] a fact which has caused many who thought that God ruled over men directly, and ordered the whole of nature for their advantage, to doubt of divine providence.[3] Reason and experience, then, both make it plain that divine law depends entirely on the will of the sovereign; and so he is also its interpreter. The sense in which he is so we shall see later; for it is now time to show that outward religion and the whole practice of piety must be adapted to the peace and preservation of the state if we wish to obey God properly. Once this has been shown we shall easily discover the sense in which the sovereign is the interpreter of religion and piety.

There is no doubt that devotion to country is the highest form of piety a man can show;[4] for once the state is destroyed nothing good can survive, but everything is put to hazard; anger and wickedness rule unchallenged and terror fills every heart. It follows that any act of piety towards a neighbour would become an act of impiety if it caused harm to the state as a whole; while any act of impiety towards him would be reckoned as piety if it were done for the state's preservation. For instance, when someone is at odds with me and wants to take my coat, it is a pious act to give him my cloak as well; but once it is decided that this is harmful to the state's preservation, it then becomes pious to

---

[1] pp. 77–83.
[2] *Ecclesiastes* 9, 2, quoted already on p. 207.
[3] In the ordinary sense. For Spinoza's conception see *TT-P* iii, pp. 53–55.
[4] *TP* iii, 10, p. 293.

judicium vocare, tametsi mortis damnandus sit. Hac de causa Manlius Torquatus celebratur, quod salus populi plus apud ipsum valuerit quam erga filium pietas. Cum hoc ita sit, sequitur salutem populi summam esse legem, cui omnes, tam humanae quam divinae, accommodari 5 debent. At cum solius summae potestatis officium sit determinare quid saluti totius populi et imperii securitati necesse sit, et quid necesse esse judicaverit imperare; hinc sequitur solius etiam summae potestatis officium esse determinare qua ratione unusquisque debet proximum pietate colere, hoc est, qua ratione unusquisque Deo obedire tenetur. 10 Ex his clare intelligimus qua ratione summae potestates interpretes religionis sint; deinde, quod nemo Deo recte obedire potest si cultum pietatis, qua unusquisque tenetur, publicae utilitati non accommodet, et consequenter, si omnibus summae potestatis decretis non obediat. Nam quandoquidem ex Dei mandato omnes (nullo excepto) pietate 15 colere tenemur, neminique damnum inferre, hinc sequitur nemini licere opem alicui cum alterius, et multo minus cum totius reipublicae damno ferre; adeoque neminem posse proximum pietate colere secundum Dei mandatum nisi pietatem et religionem publicae utilitati accommodet. At nullus privatus scire potest quid reipublicae utile sit 20 nisi ex decretis summarum potestatum, quarum tantum est negotia publica tractare; ergo nemo pietatem recte colere, nec Deo obedire potest, nisi omnibus summae potestatis decretis obtemperet. Atque hoc ipsa etiam praxi confirmatur. Quem enim, sive civem sive extraneum, privatum vel imperium in alios tenentem, summa potestas reum mortis 25 vel hostem judicavit, nemini subditorum eidem auxilium ferre licet. Sic etiam, quamvis Hebraeis dictum fuerit ut unusquisque socium tanquam se ipsum amaret (vide Levit. Cap. 19 vers. 17, 18), tenebantur tamen eum qui contra edicta legis aliquid commiserat judici indicare (vide Levit. Cap. 5 vers. 1, et Deut. Cap. 13 vers. 8, 9), et eundem, si 30 reus mortis judicabatur, interficere (vide Deut. Cap. 17 vers. 7). Deinde, ut Hebraei libertatem adeptam possent conservare, et terras quas occuparent imperio absoluto retinerent, necesse fuit, ut Cap. XVII ostendimus, ut religionem suo soli imperio accommodarent, seseque a reliquis nationibus separarent; et ideo iis dictum fuit, *Dilige* 35 *proximum tuum, et odio habe inimicum tuum* (vide Matth. Cap. 5 vs. 43).

32–33. P *necesse fuit, uti Cap. XVII. ostendimus, ut religionem*; I *necesse fuit, ut Cap. XVII. ostendimus, religionem.*

summon him to court, even although he must be condemned to death. This is why Manlius Torquatus[1] is renowned—because the people's welfare meant more to him than duty to his son. It follows, then, that the people's welfare is the highest law,[2] to which all other laws, both human and divine, must be adjusted. But since it is the function of the sovereign alone to decide what is necessary for the welfare of the whole people and the security of the state, and to command accordingly, it is also the function of the sovereign alone to decide how everyone should practise piety towards his neighbour, i.e. how everyone should obey God. This clearly explains the sense in which the sovereign is the interpreter of religion;[3] it also shows that no one can obey God properly unless he adjusts to the public good the acts which piety obliges everyone to perform, and in consequence obeys all the sovereign's decrees. For since by God's command we are bound to practise piety towards all without exception, and to harm no man, nobody is at liberty to help anyone by harming another, far less by harming the whole state; and so no one can practise piety towards his neighbour as God commands unless he adapts his piety and religion to the public good. But a private individual can know what is good for the state only through the decrees of the sovereign, who alone has the function of handling public affairs; therefore nobody can practise piety or obey God properly unless he obeys all the sovereign's decrees. And this is confirmed by actual practice. For no matter whether a man be a citizen or an alien, a private individual or one who holds command over others, if the sovereign condemns him to death or declares him an enemy none of the subjects may give him aid. Similarly, although the Jews were told that everyone should love his neighbour as himself (see Leviticus, Chapter 19, verses 17 and 18), they were bound to report to the judge anyone who had done anything illegal (see Leviticus, Chapter 5, verse 1, and Deuteronomy, Chapter 13, verses 8 and 9), and to kill him if he was condemned to death (see Deuteronomy, Chapter 17, verse 7). Again, the Jews could preserve the freedom they had won, and maintain complete control over the territories they held, only by adapting religion to the needs of their own state alone, and making a clean break with the rest of the world, as I have shown in Chapter XVII;[4] and this is why they were told, 'Love thy neighbour and hate thine enemy.' See Matthew, Chapter 5, verse 43. But once they lost their

---

[1] A Roman consul who is said to have had his son executed for disobeying orders during a battle against the Latins at the river Veseris in 340 B.C. (Livy VIII, vii).

[2] *TP* vii, 5, p. 339.   [3] Cf. Hobbes, *De Cive* xvii, 10.   [4] p. 177.

Postquam autem imperium amiserunt, et Babyloniam captivi ducti sunt, Jeremias eosdem docuit ut incolumitati (etiam) illius civitatis in quam captivi ducti erant consulerent; et postquam Christus eos per totum orbem dispersum iri vidit, docuit ut omnes absolute pietate
5 colerent: quae omnia evidentissime ostendunt religionem reipublicae utilitati accommodatam semper fuisse. Si quis autem jam quaerat, *Quo ergo jure Christi discipuli, viri scilicet privati, religionem praedicare poterant?*—eosdem id fecisse dico jure potestatis quam a Christo acceperant adversus spiritus impuros (vide Matth. Cap. 10 vers. 1).
10 Supra enim in fine Cap. XVI expresse monui omnes fidem tyranno etiam servare teneri, excepto eo cui Deus certa revelatione singulare contra tyrannum auxilium promiserit. Quare nemini inde exemplum sumere licet nisi etiam potestatem habeat ad facienda miracula; quod hinc etiam conspicuum fit, quod Christus discipulis etiam dixerit ne
15 metuerent eos qui occidunt corpora (vide Matth. Cap. 10 vers. 28). Quod si hoc unicuique dictum fuisset, frustra imperium statueretur, et illud Salomonis (Prov. Cap. 24 vers. 21), *Fili mi, time Deum et regem,* impie dictum fuisset: quod longe a vero abest. Atque adeo necessario fatendum authoritatem illam quam Christus discipulis dedit iis tantum
20 singulariter datam fuisse, nec inde exemplum aliis sumi posse. Caeterum adversariorum rationes quibus jus sacrum a jure civili separare volunt, et hoc tantum penes summas potestates, illud autem penes universam ecclesiam esse contendunt, nihil moror; adeo namque frivolae sunt ut nec refutari mereantur. Hoc unum silentio praeterire nequeo, quam
25 misere ipsi decipiantur quod ad hanc seditiosam opinionem (veniam verbo duriori precor) confirmandam exemplum sumant a summo Hebraeorum pontifice, penes quem olim jus sacra administrandi fuit; quasi pontifices illud jus a Mose non acceperint (qui, ut supra ostendimus, summum solus imperium retinuit), ex cujus etiam decreto eodem
30 privari poterant. Ipse enim non tantum Aharonem, sed etiam filium

---

1. *Gf Babyloniam; I Babiloniam.*   10. *O Cap. XVI; I Cap. 16.*

state and were led captive to Babylon, Jeremiah bade them seek the safety (even) of the city whereunto they were led captive;[1] and after Christ saw that they were going to be scattered over the whole world, he taught them to practise piety to all men without exception: which obviously shows that their religion was always adapted to the public good. If I am now asked by what right Christ's disciples, private individuals, were able to propagate religion, I reply that they did so by virtue of the power they had received from Christ against unclean spirits (see Matthew, Chapter 10, verse 1).[2] For I stated explicitly at the end of Chapter XVI[3] that everyone is bound to remain loyal even to a tyrant, except the man whom God has promised special aid against him by certain revelation. Nobody, then, may take an example from Christ's disciples unless he too has the power to work miracles. This is likewise shown by the fact that Christ also told his disciples not to fear those who kill the body (see Matthew, Chapter 10, verse 28); for had this command been laid on every man, it would be futile to organize a state, and Solomon's well-known saying (Proverbs, Chapter 24, verse 21), 'My son, fear God and the king', would have been impious: which is certainly not the case. We must therefore admit that the authority which Christ gave his disciples was given to them only, as a special gift, and that they cannot be taken as an example for others. As for the arguments by which my opponents[4] seek to separate religious right from civil, and contend that only the latter is vested in the sovereign, while the former belongs to the whole church, I shall waste no time on them; for they are so trivial as not to be worth refuting.[5] But one thing I cannot refrain from remarking upon; their lamentable error in citing the example of the Jewish high priest, who once had the right to administer religion, to confirm what the reader must pardon me for calling, rather bluntly, this seditious opinion.[6] As though the priests did not receive that right from Moses (who, as I have shown above,[7] alone had sovereign power), and could not also have been deprived of it by his decree! For it was Moses who appointed not only Aaron but Aaron's son Eleazar and his grandson

---

[1] *Jeremiah* 29, 7, quoted above on p. 209.　　[2] *TP* iii, 10, p. 293.　　[3] p. 147.

[4] The orthodox Calvinists (or Counter-Remonstrants), who agreed with the Roman Catholics in maintaining the independence of the spiritual authority (G. J. Renier, *The Dutch Nation*, Allen & Unwin, 1944, i, viii, p. 45).

[5] Grotius had already dealt with them in *De Imperio Summarum Potestatum circa Sacra*, caput iv.

[6] Hobbes's phrase; see *De Cive* xii.

[7] p. 209; cf. *TT-P* xvii, p. 161.

ejus Eleazarum et nepotem Pineham elegit, et authoritatem pontificatum administrandi dedit; quam postea pontifices ita retinuerunt ut
nihilominus Mosis, id est, summae potestatis substituti viderentur.
Nam, ut jam ostendimus, Moses nullum imperii successorem elegit,
5 sed ejus omnia officia ita distribuit ut posteri ejus vicarii visi fuerint,
qui imperium quasi rex absens esset, non mortuus, administrabant. In
secundo deinde imperio hoc jus absolute tenuerunt pontifices postquam
cum pontificatu jus principatus etiam adepti sunt. Quare jus pontificatus ex edicto summae potestatis semper dependit, nec pontifices id
10 unquam nisi cum principatu tenuerunt. Imo jus circa sacra penes reges
absolute fuit (ut ex mox dicendis in fine hujus Capitis patebit), praeter
hoc unum, quod manus sacris in templo administrandis admovere non
licebat, quia omnes qui suam genealogiam ex Aharone non ducebant
profani habebantur; quod sane in Christiano imperio locum nullum
15 habet. Atque ideo dubitare non possumus quin hodierna sacra (quorum
administratio singulares mores, non autem familiam, requirit—unde
nec ii qui imperium tenent tanquam profani ab eadem secluduntur)
solius juris summarum potestatum sint; et nemo nisi ex earum authoritate vel concessu jus potestatemque eadem administrandi, eorum mini-
20 stros eligendi, ecclesiae fundamenta ejusque doctrinam determinandi et
stabiliendi, de moribus et pietatis actionibus judicandi, aliquem excommunicandi vel in ecclesiam recipiendi, nec denique pauperibus
providendi habet. Atque haec non tantum demonstrantur (ut jam
fecimus) vera, sed etiam apprime necessaria tam ipsi religioni quam
25 reipublicae conservationi esse; norunt enim omnes quantum jus et
authoritas circa sacra apud populum valeat, et quantum unusquisque
ab ejus ore pendeat qui eandem habet; ita ut affirmare liceat eum
maxime in animos regnare cui haec authoritas competit. Si quis ergo
hanc summis potestatibus adimere vult, is imperium dividere studet;
30 ex quo necessario, ut olim inter Hebraeorum reges et pontifices, contentiones et discordiae oriri debebunt quae nunquam sedari possunt.
Imo, qui hanc authoritatem summis potestatibus adimere studet, is
viam (ut jam diximus) ad imperium affectat. Nam quid ipsae decernere
possunt si hoc iisdem jus denegatur? Nihil profecto, nec de bello, nec de
35 pace, nec de ullo quocunque negotio, si sententiam alterius expectare

---

10. Perhaps *absolute* should be inserted before *tenuerunt*.   18. I *eorum*.

Phinehas as well,[1] and gave them authority to perform their priestly duties; an authority which their successors retained only in so far as they were regarded as representatives of Moses, i.e. of the sovereign. For, as I have shown already,[2] Moses chose no one to succeed him as sovereign, but distributed all his offices among different people; so that those who followed him were regarded as his deputies, who governed the state as though the king were absent, not dead.[3] Then in the second state the high priests only had absolute possession of this right once they also acquired the right to govern. Thus the pontifical right always depended on the edict of the sovereign, and the high priests never held it absolutely except when they combined it with the right to govern. In fact, as I shall show presently at the end of this Chapter,[4] the kings had full possession of all religious rights save one; they were not allowed to perform sacred duties in the temple, because everyone not descended from Aaron was regarded as profane. This, of course, is not the case in a Christian state. Thus the control of present-day religion (which requires excellent morals, but not descent from a particular family, so that sovereigns are not debarred from it on the ground that they are profane) certainly belongs to the sovereign alone; and no one has the right and power to exercise it, to appoint pastors, to determine and establish the organization and doctrine of the church, to judge of morals and pious actions, to excommunicate or receive into communion,[5] and, finally, to provide for the poor, except by his authority or permission. Now clearly this doctrine is not only true, as I have just shown, but absolutely essential both for religion itself and for the preservation of the state. Everyone knows what a tremendous weight the right and authority in matters of religion carries with the people, and how all men hang on the lips of the person who has it; in fact he who has it may be said to have most control over their minds. Hence if anyone wants to take it from the sovereign he is seeking to divide the sovereignty; and this will inevitably cause disputes and quarrels which can never be settled, just as it did of old between the kings and priests of the Jews.[6] Indeed, the man who seeks to take this authority from the sovereign is paving his own way to sovereignty, as I have already said.[7] For what can sovereigns decide for themselves if this right is denied them? If they have to wait for another's decision to learn whether what they think to be beneficial

---

[1] In *TT-P* xvii, p. 167, Phinehas is omitted. [2] *TT-P* xvii, pp. 163–7.

[3] Hobbes held that after the death of Moses sovereignty resided in the High Priest (*De Cive* xvi, 14–15).

[4] pp. 223–5. [5] Hobbes, *De Cive* xvii, 26.

[6] *TT-P* xvii, pp. 187–9. [7] p. 205.

tenentur qui ipsas doceat num id quod utile judicant pium sit an impium; sed contra omnia potius ex illius decreto fient qui jus habet judicandi et decretandi quid pium vel impium, fas nefasque sit. Cujus rei exempla omnia viderunt saecula; quorum unum tantum, quod instar

5 omnium est, adferam. Quia Romano Pontifici hoc jus absolute concessum fuit, tandem omnes paulatim reges sub potestate habere incepit, donec etiam ad summum imperii fastigium ascenderit; et quicquid postea monarchae, et praecipue Germaniae Caesares, conati sunt ejus authoritatem vel tantillum diminuere, nihil promoverunt, sed contra

10 eandem eo ipso multis numeris auxerunt. Verum enim vero hoc idem, quod nullus monarcha nec ferro nec igne, ecclesiastici solo tantum calamo facere potuerunt; ut vel hinc tantum ejusdem vis et potentia facile dignoscatur, et praeterea quam necesse sit summis potestatibus hanc sibi authoritatem reservare. Quod si etiam ea quae in superiore

15 Capite notavimus considerare velimus, videbimus hoc ipsum religionis et pietatis incremento non parum etiam conducere. Vidimus enim supra ipsos prophetas, quamvis divina virtute praeditos, tamen, quia privati viri erant, libertate sua monendi, increpandi, et exprobrandi homines magis irritavisse quam correxisse; qui tamen a regibus moniti

20 vel castigati facile flectebantur. Deinde ipsos reges ob hoc tantum, quod ipsis hoc jus non absolute competebat, saepissime a religione descivisse, et cum ipsis fere totum populum; quod etiam in Christianis imperiis ob eandem causam saepissime contigisse constat. At hic forsan me aliquis rogabit, *Quisnam ergo, si ii qui imperium tenent impii esse*

25 *velint, pietatem jure vindicabit? An tum etiam iidem ejus interpretes habendi sunt?* Verum ego contra ipsum rogo, *Quid si ecclesiastici (qui etiam homines sunt, et privati quibus sua tantum negotia curare incumbit), vel alii penes quos jus circa sacra esse vult, impii esse velint? An tum etiam ejusdem interpretes habendi sunt?* Certum quidem est quod si ii qui

30 imperium tenent qua juvat ire velint, sive jus circa sacra habeant sive minus, omnia tam sacra quam profana in deterius ruent; at longe citius

31. *I et longe citius.*

is pious or impious, the answer is obviously nothing at all, either about war or peace or anything else; everything will be done by the will of the man who has the right to judge and decree what is pious or impious, right or wrong. There have been instances of this in every age; but I shall cite only one, which is worth all the others put together. It was because the Pope was allowed full possession of this right that in the end all the kings in Christendom began one by one to fall into his power, until he actually reached the height of temporal dominion; and although the kings, and particularly the Emperors of Germany, afterwards did all they could to achieve even the slightest diminution of his authority, they failed completely, and only multiplied his power by their efforts.[1] Yet what no king could do by fire or sword, churchmen[2] could do by the pen alone; which in itself clearly shows the tremendous power and influence of religious authority, and the need for sovereigns to keep it in their own hands. If the points made in the previous Chapter are considered as well, we shall see that by doing this they also make a considerable contribution to the growth of religion and piety. For I noted above[3] that although the prophets were endowed with divine virtue, yet, because they were private individuals, their freedom to warn, rebuke, and denounce did more to provoke men than to correct them; though when warned or punished by the kings men were easily reformed. Again, the mere fact that they did not have full possession of this right often caused the kings themselves, and with them the great mass of the people, to forsake their religion;[4] and it is common knowledge that the same cause has often had this effect even in Christian states.[5] But here perhaps someone will ask me, 'Then who will be the rightful guardian of piety if the sovereign chooses to be impious? Is he even then to be regarded as its interpreter?' I counter with another question—'What if churchmen (who are also human, and, indeed, private individuals who ought to confine themselves to their own affairs), or any others the objector wants to invest with religious authority, choose to be impious? Are they even then to be regarded as the interpreters of piety?' I grant that if sovereigns, whether in control of religion or not, choose to do as they please, all the interests of the state, spiritual as well as material, will suffer harm; but

---

[1] The submission of the Emperor Henry IV to Pope Gregory VII in 1077 paved the way for the culmination of papal power in the thirteenth century.

[2] e.g. Luther and Calvin.

[3] *TT-P* xviii, p. 195.

[4] *TT-P* xvii, p. 185.

[5] Spinoza is probably thinking of the change from Roman Catholicism to Protestantism in England and Northern Germany.

si qui viri privati seditiose jus divinum vindicare velint. Quapropter hoc iisdem jus denegando nihil absolute promovetur, sed contra malum magis augetur; nam hoc ipso fit ut necessario (sicuti Hebraeorum reges, quibus hoc jus non absolute concessum fuit) impii sint, et 5 consequenter ut totius reipublicae damnum et malum ex incerto et contingente certum et necessarium reddatur. Sive igitur rei veritatem, sive imperii securitatem, sive denique pietatis incrementum spectemus, statuere cogimur jus etiam divinum, sive jus circa sacra, a decreto summarum potestatum absolute pendere, easque ejusdem interpretes 10 esse et vindices; ex quibus sequitur illos Dei verbi ministros esse, qui populum ex authoritate summarum potestatum pietatem docent, prout ipsa ex earum decreto publicae utilitati accommodata est.

Superest jam causam etiam indicare cur semper in Christiano imperio de hoc jure disceptatum fuit, cum tamen Hebraei nunquam, quod 15 sciam, de eodem ambegerint. Sane monstro simile videri posset quod de re tam manifesta tamque necessaria quaestio semper fuerit, et quod summae potestates hoc jus nunquam absque controversia, imo nunquam nisi magno seditionum periculo et religionis detrimento habuerint. Profecto, si hujus rei nullam certam causam assignare possemus, facile 20 mihi persuaderem omnia quae in hoc Capite ostendi non nisi theoretica esse, sive ex earum speculationum genere quae nunquam ex usu esse possunt. Etenim ipsa primordia Christianae religionis consideranti hujus rei causa sese omnino manifestat. Christianam namque religionem non reges primi docuerunt, sed viri privati, qui, invitis iis qui imperium 25 tenebant et quorum subditi erant, privatis ecclesiis concionari, sacra officia instituere, administrare, et soli omnia ordinare et decretare, nulla imperii ratione habita, diu consueverunt. Cum autem multis jam elapsis annis religio in imperium introduci incepit, ecclesiastici eandem, sicuti ipsam determinaverant, ipsos imperatores docere debuerunt; ex 30 quo facile obtinere potuerunt ut ejus doctores et interpretes, et praeterea ecclesiae pastores, et quasi Dei vicarii agnoscerentur; et ne postea reges Christiani hanc sibi authoritatem capere possent optime sibi

disaster will come much more quickly if private individuals conceive the seditious desire to uphold religious law. Hence to deny this right to sovereigns serves no useful purpose whatsoever, but only aggravates the evil; for this is the very thing that inevitably makes them impious (as it did the Jewish kings, who were denied full possession of this right), and so makes the damage and harm to the whole state certain and necessary instead of uncertain and contingent. So whether we consider the truth of the matter, or the security of the state, or finally the increase of piety, we are forced to conclude that divine law, i.e. law concerning religion, also depends entirely on the will of the sovereign, and that he is its interpreter and guardian. It follows that those are the ministers of God's word who have the authority of the sovereign to teach the people piety in the form adapted to the public welfare by his decree.

It now remains to indicate the reason why there has always been controversy over this right in Christian states, although it was never, to my knowledge, called in question among the Jews. It would certainly seem monstrous that there has always been dispute about a right so obvious and so vital, and that sovereigns have never held it without controversy, or even without great danger of sedition and harm to religion. Indeed, if I could assign no definite reason for this, I should readily be convinced that everything I have shown in this Chapter is merely theoretical,[1] belongs, that is, to the kind of speculation which can never be of practical use. But in fact the reason for it becomes perfectly obvious when we consider the actual beginnings of the Christian religion. It was originally taught by private individuals, and not by kings; and these individuals were for long in the habit of opposing the will of their sovereign by preaching to private gatherings, establishing and performing sacred rites, and organizing and deciding everything on their own authority without paying any heed to the state. So when, many years later, their religion began to be adopted by the state,[2] even the emperors had to be taught it by churchmen, and in the form which churchmen had laid down. Thus it was easy for the latter to get themselves accepted, not only as its teachers and interpreters, but also as pastors of the church, and virtually representatives of God. And to prevent Christian kings from later assuming their authority, the churchmen adopted an excellent safeguard; they forbade

---

[1] *TT-P* xvii, p. 149.

[2] Constantine was converted to Christianity in A.D. 312, and Christians were granted religious freedom by the Edict of Milan in the following year.

caverunt ecclesiastici, prohibendo scilicet matrimonium supremis ecclesiae ministris summoque religionis interpreti. Ad quod praeterea
accessit quod religionis dogmata ad tam magnum numerum auxerant,
et cum philosophia ita confuderant, ut summus ejus interpres summus
5 philosophus et theologus esse, et plurimis inutilibus speculationibus
vacare deberet; quod tantum viris privatis et otio abundantibus contingere potest. At apud Hebraeos longe aliter res sese habuit. Nam
eorum ecclesia simul cum imperio incepit, et Moses, qui id absolute
tenebat, populum religionem docuit, sacra ministeria ordinavit, eorum-
10 que ministros elegit. Hinc igitur contra factum est ut authoritas regia
apud populum maxime valuerit, et ut jus circa sacra reges maxime
tenuerint. Nam quamvis post mortem Mosis nemo imperium absolute
tenuerit, jus tamen decretandi tam circa sacra quam circa reliqua penes
principem (ut jam ostendimus) erat; deinde, ut populus religionem et
15 pietatem edoceretur non magis pontificem quam supremum judicem
adire tenebatur (vide Deut. Cap. 17 vers. 9, 11). Reges denique
quamvis non aequale ac Moses jus habuerint, omnis tamen fere sacri
ministerii ordo et electio ab eorum decreto pendebat. David enim
fabricam templi totam concinnavit (vide Paralip. 1 Cap. 28 vers. 11,
20 12, etc.); ex omnibus deinde Levitis viginti quatuor millia elegit ad
psallendum, et sex millia ex quibus judices et praetores eligerentur,
quatuor deinde millia janitorum, et quatuor denique millia qui organis
canerent (vide ejusdem libri Cap. 23 vers. 4, 5). Porro eosdem in
cohortes (quarum etiam primarios elegit) divisit, ut unaquaeque suo
25 tempore, servatis vicibus, administraret (vide vers. 6 ejusdem Cap.).
Sacerdotes itidem in tot cohortes divisit. Sed ne omnia singulatim recensere tenear, lectorem refero ad lib. 2 Paralip. Cap. 8, ubi vers. scil.
13 dicitur *cultum Dei, sicuti eundem Moses instituerat, fuisse ex mandato
Salomonis in templo administratum,* et vers. 14, *quod ipse* (Salomon)
30 *cohortes sacerdotum in suis ministeriis et Levitarum etc. constituerit
secundum jussum viri divini Davidis.* Et versu denique 15 testatur

<hr />

25. *B vers. 6; I vers. 5.*

the chief ministers of the church and the supreme interpreter of religion to marry.[1] In addition, they had so increased the number of religious dogmas, and so confused them with philosophy,[2] that the supreme interpreter of religion had to be a master philosopher and theologian, and to have time for a host of useless speculations; conditions which can only be fulfilled by a private individual with plenty of leisure. But among the Jews the position was very different. Their church began at the same time as their state, and it was Moses, the absolute ruler of that state, who taught the people religion, organized sacred duties, and chose priests to perform them. This led to the opposite result; the royal authority had great influence among the people, and the kings a great deal of control over religion. For although no one was in full possession of the sovereignty after Moses' death, the captains, as I have already shown,[3] had the right to make decrees about religion as well as about other matters; besides, for instruction in religion and piety the people had to consult the supreme judge as well as the priest (see Deuteronomy, Chapter 17, verses 9 and 11). Finally, although the kings did not have as great a right as Moses, practically the whole organization of religious offices, and appointments to them, depended on their will. David, for example, organized the whole construction of the temple (see 1 Chronicles, Chapter 28, verses 11, 12 and ff.), and out of all the Levites chose twenty-four thousand to sing psalms, six thousand to be candidates for appointment as officers and judges, then four thousand door-keepers, and, finally, four thousand to play with instruments (see Chapter 23, verses 4 and 5, of the same book). Moreover he divided them into courses (whereof he also appointed the leaders), so that each course might officiate in turn (see verse 6 of the same Chapter). The priests he likewise divided into the same number of courses. But to obviate the need to recount all the details I refer the reader to 2 Chronicles, Chapter 8, where we are told in verse 13 that 'the worship of God, as established by Moses, was conducted in the temple by the command of Solomon'; and in verse 14 that 'he (Solomon) appointed the courses of the priests to their functions, and of the Levites to their charges, in accordance with the command of David, the man of God'. And finally

---

[1] By the end of the fourth century A.D. it had become customary to forbid marriage to those in holy orders.

[2] See *TT-P* xiv, p. 123. Hobbes also criticizes ecclesiastics for 'mixing with the Scripture . . . much of the vain and erroneous philosophy of the Greeks, especially of Aristotle' (*Leviathan* 44).

[3] *TT-P* xvii, pp. 165 and 175; xviii, p. 193.

Historicus *quod non recesserunt a praecepto regis imposito sacerdotibus et Levitis in nulla re, neque in aerariis administrandis.* Ex quibus omnibus, et aliis regum historiis, sequitur evidentissime totum religionis exercitium sacrumque ministerium a solo regum mandato dependisse. Cum autem supra dixi eosdem jus non habuisse, ut Moses, summum pontificem eligendi, Deum immediate consulendi, et prophetas qui ipsis viventibus prophetarent damnandi; nulla alia de causa id dixi quam quia prophetae ex authoritate quam habebant novum regem eligere poterant, et veniam parricidio dare, at non quod regem, si quid contra leges audebat, in judicium vocare liceret, et jure contra eundem agere.[39] Quapropter, si nulli fuissent prophetae qui singulari revelatione veniam parricidio tuto possent concedere, jus ad omnia absolute, tam sacra quam civilia, omnino habuissent. Quare hodiernae summae potestates, quae nec prophetas habent, nec recipere jure tenentur (Hebraeorum enim legibus addicti non sunt), hoc jus, tametsi caelibes non sint, absolute habent, et semper retinebunt modo tantum religionis dogmata neque in magnum numerum augeri, neque cum scientiis confundi sinant.

16–17. *B* dogmata *neque in magnum numerum augeri*; *G* dogmata *in magnum numerum non augeri*; *I* dogmata *in magnum numerum augeri.*

in verse 15 the Historian declares that 'they departed not from the precept of the king unto the priests and Levites in any matter, not even in the governance of the treasuries'. From all this, and from other accounts of the kings, it is abundantly plain that the whole practice of religion and every sacred office depended solely on their decree. My only reason for saying above that the kings did not have Moses' right to appoint a high priest, to consult God directly, and to condemn such prophets as might prophesy in their life-time, was that the authority possessed by the prophets enabled them to appoint a new king, and give absolution for regicide;[1] I did not mean that they were free to take the king to court, and to impeach him by right[2] if he dared to do anything illegal. So that if there had been no prophets with the power to pardon regicide with impunity by special revelation, the kings would have had full right to control everything without exception, religious as well as civil affairs. Hence modern sovereigns, who have no prophets, and are not bound by law to recognize any (for they are not bound by the laws of the Jews), possess this right in full even though they are not celibate, and will always retain it as long as they do not allow religious dogmas to be multiplied or confused with philosophy.

---

[1] *TT-P* xvii, p. 189.

[2] The note on this passage (n. 39, p. 255) refers the reader to the discussion of right in *TT-P* xvi. M. Francès (*Œuvres Complètes de Spinoza*, Gallimard, 1954, p. 952) makes the note refer to the account of the right of the sovereign; in which case Spinoza is pointing out that it would be inconsistent with the right of the king to attribute to the prophets a civil right to impeach him. But in his note Spinoza simply says *de jure* (not *de jure summarum potestatum*) and the text suggests that the reference is to the right of the prophets. If so, Spinoza is denying them not only the civil but the natural right to impeach the king: on the ground that when *A* can do *x* only by the consent of *B*, and *B* is bound to refuse his consent, *A* has no natural right to do *x*. Cf. *TP* iii, 8, pp. 289–91, and iv, 4, p. 303, where the same principle is applied to the sovereign.

CAPUT XX

Ostenditur in libera republica unicuique et sentire quae velit, et quae sentiat dicere licere

Si aeque facile esset animis ac linguis imperare, tuto unusquisque regnaret, et nullum imperium violentum foret: nam unusquisque ex
5 imperantium ingenio viveret, et ex solo eorum decreto quid verum vel falsum, bonum vel malum, aequum vel iniquum esset judicaret. Sed hoc, ut jam in initio Cap. XVII notavimus, fieri nequit, ut scilicet animus alterius juris absolute sit; quippe nemo jus suum naturale, sive
· facultatem suam libere ratiocinandi et de rebus quibuscunque judicandi,
10 in alium transferre, neque ad id cogi potest. Hinc ergo fit ut illud imperium violentum habeatur, quod in animos est, et ut summa majestas injuriam subditis facere, eorumque jus usurpare videatur, quando unicuique praescribere vult quid tanquam verum amplecti, et tanquam falsum rejicere, et quibus porro opinionibus uniuscujusque animus erga
15 Deum devotione moveri debeat; haec enim uniuscujusque juris sunt, quo nemo, etsi velit, cedere potest. Fateor judicium multis et paene incredibilibus modis praeoccupari posse, atque ita ut, quamvis sub alterius imperio directe non sit, tamen ab ore alterius ita pendeat ut merito eatenus ejus juris dici possit: verum quicquid ars hac in re
20 praestare potuerit, nunquam tamen eo perventum est ut homines unquam non experirentur unumquemque suo sensu abundare, totque capitum quam palatorum esse discrimina. Moses, qui non dolo sed divina virtute judicium sui populi maxime praeoccupaverat, utpote qui divinus credebatur, et divino afflatu dicere et facere omnia, ejus tamen
25 rumores et sinistras interpretationes fugere non potuit; et multo minus reliqui monarchae. At si hoc aliqua ratione posset concipi, conciperetur saltem in monarchico imperio, at minime in democratico quod omnes

26. I et si.   etsi si is also possible.

---

which all statesmen, knowing the diversity of human opinions, had considered necessary in order to maintain fraternal harmony.' See J. L. Motley, *The United Netherlands*, 1869, vol. ii, xv, p. 214. For the expression cf. Tacitus, *Histories* i, i, 4: *rara temporum felicitate, ubi sentire quae velis et quae sentias dicere licet.*

² *TT-P* xvii, p. 151.   ³ p. 149.
⁴ *TT-P* vii, p. 109.   ⁵ *TT-P* xvii, pp. 151–3; *TP* ii, 11, p. 275.
⁶ *TT-P* xvii, pp. 185–7.

CHAPTER XX

That in a free state everyone may think what he pleases, and say what he thinks[1]

COULD thought be controlled as easily as speech,[2] all governments would rule in safety, and none would be oppressive; for everyone would live as his rulers wanted, and his judgements of true and false, good and bad, fair and unfair, would be determined entirely by their will. However, as I have already noted at the start of Chapter XVII,[3] it is impossible for thought to be completely subject to another's control, because no one can give up to another his natural right to reason freely and form his own judgement about everything, nor can he be compelled to do so. This is why a government is regarded as oppressive if it tries to control men's minds, and why a sovereign is thought to wrong its subjects, and to usurp their right, if it seeks to tell them what they should embrace as true and reject as false, and to prescribe the beliefs which should inspire their minds with devotion to God; for in such matters an individual cannot alienate his right even if he wishes.[4] Admittedly a man's judgement can be influenced in many ways, some of them hardly credible; so much so, in fact, that though not directly under another's command it may depend entirely on his words, and thus in that respect can properly be called subject to his right.[5] Yet in spite of all that political skill has been able to achieve in this field, it has never been completely successful; men have always found that individuals were full of their own ideas, and that opinions varied as much as tastes. Even Moses, who by extraordinary ability, and not by deception, had so captivated the mind of his people that it regarded him as a superman, divinely inspired in everything he said and did, was not immune from its criticisms and misrepresentations;[6] and this is still more true of the other kings. Yet were such immunity conceivable at all it would be in a monarchy; not in a democracy where all

---

[1] The spirit of this chapter is concisely expressed in a declaration by the States-General in 1587. 'The nobles and cities constituting the States have been denounced to Lord Leicester as enemies of religion by the self-seeking mischief-makers who surround him. Why? Because they had refused the demand of certain preachers to call a general synod in defiance of the States-General, and to introduce a set of ordinances with a system of discipline according to *their arbitrary will*. This the late Prince of Orange and the States-General had always thought detrimental both to religion and polity. They respected the difference in religious opinions, and, leaving all churches in their freedom, they *chose to compel no man's conscience*—a course

[*footnotes contd. opposite*

vel magna populi pars collegialiter tenet; cujus rei causam omnibus patere existimo.

Quantumvis igitur summae potestates jus ad omnia habere, et juris et pietatis interpretes credantur, nunquam tamen facere poterunt ne
5 homines judicium de rebus quibuscunque ex proprio suo ingenio ferant, et ne eatenus hoc aut illo affectu afficiantur. Verum quidem est eas jure posse omnes qui cum iisdem in omnibus absolute non sentiunt pro hostibus habere; sed nos de ipsarum jure jam non disputamus, sed de eo quod utile est. Concedo enim easdem jure posse violentissime
10 regnare, et cives levissimis de causis ad necem ducere; at omnes negabunt haec salvo sanae rationis judicio fieri posse. Imo, quia haec non sine magno totius imperii periculo facere queunt, negare etiam possumus easdem absolutam potentiam ad haec et similia habere, et consequenter neque etiam absolutum jus; jus enim summarum potesta-
15 tum ab earum potentia determinari ostendimus.

Si itaque nemo libertate sua judicandi et sentiendi quae vult cedere potest, sed unusquisque maximo naturae jure dominus suarum cogitationum est, sequitur in republica nunquam nisi admodum infelici successu tentari posse ut homines, quamvis diversa et contraria sen
20 tientes, nihil tamen nisi ex praescripto summarum potestatum loquantur; nam nec peritissimi, ne dicam plebem, tacere sciunt. Hoc hominum commune vitium est, consilia sua, etsi tacito opus est, aliis credere: illud ergo imperium violentissimum erit, ubi unicuique libertas dicendi et docendi quae sentit negatur, et contra, id moderatum, ubi haec eadem
25 libertas unicuique conceditur. Verum enimvero nequaquam etiam negare possumus quin majestas tam verbis quam re laedi potest; atque adeo, si impossibile est hanc libertatem prorsus adimere subditis, perniciosissimum contra erit eandem omnino concedere. Quapropter nobis hic inquirere incumbit quousque unicuique haec libertas, salva
30 reipublicae pace, salvoque summarum potestatum jure, potest et debet concedi: quod hic, ut in initio Cap. XVI monui, praecipuum meum intentum fuit.

Ex fundamentis reipublicae supra explicatis evidentissime sequitur finem ejus ultimum non esse dominari, nec homines metu retinere et
35 alterius juris facere, sed contra, unumquemque metu liberare ut secure

26. *Gf possit.*

or most men are colleagues in the government. The reason for this, I think, is plain to everyone.

Thus no matter how completely a ruler has convinced his subjects that he has the right to do everything, and is the interpreter of law and piety, he will never be able to prevent them from passing their own individual judgements on everything, and from feeling different emotions accordingly. It is true that he has the right to treat as enemies all who are not in complete agreement with him on every point; but what I am discussing now is not his right, but the good of the state.[1] Admittedly he has the right to rule with the utmost violence, and to hale citizens off to execution on the most trivial pretexts; but everyone will deny that he can do so with the approval of sound reason. Indeed, just because he cannot do such things without great danger to the whole state, we may even deny that he has full power to do them, and hence deny that he has full right to do them either;[2] since, as I have shown, a sovereign's right is determined by its power.[3]

If no man, then, can surrender his freedom to judge and think as he pleases, and everyone is master of his own thoughts by perfect natural right, the attempt to make men speak only as the sovereign prescribes, no matter how different and opposed their ideas may be, must always meet with very little success in a state; for even men of great experience cannot hold their tongues, far less the mass of the people. It is a common human failing to confide one's plans to others even when secrecy is needed: hence government will be most oppressive where the individual is denied the freedom to express and communicate his opinions, and moderate where this freedom is allowed him. Yet it must also be admitted that words can be treasonable as well as deeds; and so, though it is impossible to deprive subjects of such freedom entirely, it will be quite disastrous to grant it to them in full. Hence we must now inquire how far it can and must be granted to everyone if the peace of the state and the right of the sovereign are to be preserved. This inquiry, as I said at the start of Chapter XVI, was the main object of the concluding Chapters.

It is abundantly clear from my previous account of the basis of the state[4] that its ultimate purpose is not to subject men to tyranny, or to restrain and enslave them through fear,[5] but rather to free everyone from fear so that he may live in all possible security, i.e. may preserve

---

[1] For the distinction see *TP* v, 1, p. 309.   [2] *TT-P* v, pp. 93–95.
[3] *TT-P* xvi, pp. 133 and 135.   [4] *TT-P* xvi, p. 129.
[5] Spinoza is here attacking Hobbes: cf. *TT-P* xvii, p. 151, and *TP* v, 4-6, p. 311.

quoad ejus fieri potest vivat, hoc est, ut jus suum naturale ad existendum et operandum absque suo et alterius damno optime retineat. Non, inquam, finis reipublicae est homines ex rationalibus bestias vel automata facere; sed contra, ut eorum mens et corpus tuto suis functionibus 5 fungantur, et ipsi libera ratione utantur, et ne odio, ira, vel dolo certent, nec animo iniquo invicem ferantur. Finis ergo reipublicae revera libertas est. Porro ad formandam rempublicam hoc unum necesse fuisse vidimus, nempe ut omnis decretandi potestas penes omnes, vel aliquot, vel penes unum esset: nam quandoquidem liberum hominum 10 judicium varium admodum est, et unusquisque solus omnia scire putat, nec fieri potest ut omnes aeque eadem sentiant et uno ore loquantur, pacifice vivere non poterant nisi unusquisque jure agendi ex solo decreto suae mentis cederet. Jure igitur agendi ex proprio decreto unusquisque tantum cessit, non autem ratiocinandi et judicandi; adeo-15 que salvo summarum potestatum jure nemo quidem contra earum decretum agere potest, at omnino sentire et judicare, et consequenter etiam dicere, modo simpliciter tantum dicat vel doceat, et sola ratione, non autem dolo, ira, odio, nec animo aliquid in rempublicam ex authoritate sui decreti introducendi, defendat. Ex. gr. si quis legem aliquam 20 sanae rationi repugnare ostendit, et propterea eandem abrogandam esse censet, si simul suam sententiam judicio summae potestatis (cujus tantum est leges condere et abrogare) submittit, et nihil interim contra illius legis praescriptum agit, bene sane de republica meretur, ut optimus quisque civis. Sed si contra id faciat ad magistratum iniquitatis accu-25 sandum, et vulgo odiosum reddendum, vel seditiose studeat invito magistratu legem illam abrogare, omnino perturbator est et rebellis. Videmus itaque qua ratione unusquisque, salvo jure et authoritate summarum potestatum, hoc est, salva reipublicae pace, ea quae sentit dicere et docere potest; nempe si decretum omnium rerum agendarum 30 iisdem relinquat, et nihil contra earum decretum agat, etiamsi saepe contra id quod bonum judicat et palam sentit agere debeat. Quod quidem salva justitia et pietate facere potest; imo debet, si se justum et pium praestare vult. Nam, ut jam ostendimus, justitia a solo summarum potestatum decreto pendet; adeoque nemo nisi qui secundum earum

his natural right to exist and act in the best possible way, without harm to himself or his neighbour. It is not, I say, the purpose of the state to change men from rational beings into brutes or puppets; but rather to enable them to exercise their mental and physical powers in safety and use their reason freely, and to prevent them from fighting and quarrelling through hatred, anger, bad faith, and mutual malice. Thus the purpose of the state is really freedom.[1] We also saw that to create a state the one thing needful was that all power to make decisions should be vested either in all collectively, or in a few, or in one man;[2] for the great diversity of men's free judgements, the claim of each to have a monopoly of wisdom, and their inability to think alike and speak with one voice made it impossible for men to live at peace unless everyone surrendered his right to act entirely as he pleased. Thus it was only his right to act as he pleased that everyone surrendered, and not his right to think and judge. This means that while a subject necessarily violates his sovereign's right by acting contrary to its decree, there is no violation whatever in his thinking and judging, and therefore also saying, that the decree is ill-advised; as long as he does no more than express or communicate his opinion, and only defends it out of honest rational conviction, and not out of anger, hatred, or a desire to introduce any change in the state on his own authority. For example, suppose a man shows that some law is contrary to sound reason, and thus maintains that it should be repealed; if he at the same time submits his opinion to the judgement of the sovereign (which alone is competent to pass and repeal laws), and meanwhile does nothing contrary to what that law commands, then, of course, he ranks with all good citizens as a benefactor of the state. But if he breaks the law in order to accuse the magistrate of injustice and to stir up mob hatred against him, or makes a seditious attempt to repeal the law against the magistrate's will, he is simply an agitator and a rebel. This shows how everyone can express and communicate his opinions without infringing the right and authority of the sovereign, i.e. without disturbing the peace of the state; he must leave the determination of all actions to the sovereign, and do nothing contrary to its decree, even though the actions required are frequently in conflict with what he thinks, and declares, to be good.[3] He can do this without violating justice and piety; indeed, he must do this if he wants to be just and pious. For justice, as I have already shown,[4] depends entirely on the sovereign's will; so no one can be just

---

[1] *TP* v, 2, p. 309, n. 3.   [2] *TT-P* xvi, pp. 133–7.
[3] *TP* iii, 6, p. 289.   [4] *TT-P* xix, pp. 207–11.

recepta decreta vivit justus esse potest. Pietas autem (per ea quae in praecedente Capite ostendimus) summa est quae circa pacem et tranquillitatem reipublicae exercetur; atqui haec conservari non potest si unicuique ex suae mentis arbitrio vivendum esset; adeoque impium 5 etiam est ex suo arbitrio aliquid contra decretum summae potestatis cujus subditus est facere, quandoquidem, si hoc unicuique liceret, imperii ruina inde necessario sequeretur. Quinimo nihil contra decretum et dictamen propriae rationis agere potest quamdiu juxta decreta summae potestatis agit; ipsa enim ratione suadente omnino decrevit jus 10 suum vivendi ex proprio suo judicio in eandem transferre. Atqui hoc ipsa etiam praxi confirmare possumus; in conciliis namque, tam summarum quam minorum potestatum, raro aliquid fit ex communi omnium membrorum suffragio, et tamen omnia ex communi omnium decreto, tam scilicet eorum qui *contra* quam qui *pro* suffragium tulerunt, 15 fiunt. Sed ad meum propositum revertor.

Qua ratione unusquisque judicii libertate salvo summarum potestatum jure uti potest, ex fundamentis reipublicae vidimus. At ex iis non minus facile determinare possumus quaenam opiniones in republica seditiosae sint; eae nimirum quae simul ac ponuntur, pactum quo 20 unusquisque jure agendi ex proprio suo arbitrio cessit tollitur. Ex. gr. si quis sentiat summam potestatem sui juris non esse, vel neminem promissis stare debere, vel oportere unumquemque ex suo arbitrio vivere, et alia hujusmodi quae praedicto pacto directe repugnant, is seditiosus est; non tam quidem propter judicium et opinionem, quam 25 propter factum quod talia judicia involvunt; videlicet, quia eo ipso quod tale quid sentit fidem summae potestati tacite vel expresse datam solvit. Ac proinde caeterae opiniones quae actum non involvunt, nempe ruptionem pacti, vindictam, iram, etc., seditiosae non sunt, nisi forte in republica aliqua ratione corrupta, ubi scilicet superstitiosi et ambitiosi,

---

15. *O revertor; I reverto.*

unless he lives by its published decrees. Piety (according to the previous Chapter)[1] attains its highest expression in the service of public peace and tranquillity; but peace could not be preserved if everyone were to follow his own will; so it is impious, as well as unjust, for a subject to follow his own will and contravene his sovereign's decree, for if this were universally permitted it would inevitably lead to the destruction of the state. He cannot even contravene the judgement and dictate of his own reason in carrying out the sovereign's decrees,[2] for it was with the full approval of his own reason that he decided to transfer his right to determine his actions to the sovereign.[3] But my main point[4] can be confirmed from actual practice; for at meetings of public authorities, both sovereign and subordinate, it is rare for anything to be done by the unanimous vote of all the members, yet everything *is* done by the common decision of all, of those, that is, who voted against the measure as well as of those who voted for it. However I must return to my subject.

A consideration of the basis of the state has shown us how everyone can exercise freedom of judgement without infringing the sovereign's right. It enables us to determine just as easily which beliefs are seditious;[5] they are those which, when accepted, immediately destroy the covenant whereby everyone surrendered the right to act as he pleased. For instance, if anyone believes that the sovereign does not have absolute right, or that nobody is bound to keep promises, or that everyone should live as he pleases, or holds other similar views which directly contradict the said covenant, he is seditious; not so much, to be sure, because of his judgement and opinion as because of the action which it involves; i.e. because merely by thinking in this way he breaks the promise he has given either tacitly or expressly to the sovereign. Hence other beliefs which do not involve action like the breaking of the covenant, the taking of vengeance, and the venting of anger, are not seditious; except perhaps in a state which is in some way corrupt, i.e. a state where superstitious and ambitious men,[6] who cannot tolerate

---

[1] p. 211; cf. *TP* iii, 10, p. 293.   [2] *TP* iii, 6, p. 289.   [3] *TT-P* xvi, p. 133.

[4] The main point is that a citizen infringes no right in arguing against the sovereign's decision as long as he does not refuse to accept and observe it.

[5] Spinoza's distinction between beliefs which necessarily involve sedition and beliefs which do not is derived from Hobbes, *De Cive* vi, 11, n. His attack, like Hobbes's in the passage cited, is directed equally against the Roman Catholics (who deny that the sovereign has absolute right) and the Protestant extremists. For the views of the latter see the words of Buffe-coate quoted on p. 2.

[6] The reference is mainly to the orthodox Calvinist clergy, who attempted to gain this position in the Netherlands.

qui ingenuos ferre nequeunt, ad tantam nominis famam pervenerunt ut apud plebem plus valeat eorum quam summarum potestatum authoritas. Nec tamen negamus quasdam praeterea esse sententias quae, quamvis simpliciter circa verum et falsum versari videantur,
5 iniquo tamen animo proponuntur et divulgantur. Verum has etiam Cap. XV jam determinavimus, at ita ut ratio nihilominus libera manserit. Quod si denique ad hoc etiam attendamus, quod fides uniuscujusque erga rempublicam, sicuti erga Deum, ex solis operibus cognosci potest, nempe ex charitate erga proximum, nequaquam dubitare poteri-
10 mus quin optima respublica unicuique eandem philosophandi libertatem concedat quam fidem unicuique concedere ostendimus. Equidem fateor ex tali libertate incommoda quaedam aliquando oriri; verum quid unquam tam sapienter institutum fuit ut nihil inde incommodi oriri potuerit? Qui omnia legibus determinare vult, vitia irritabit potius
15 quam corriget. Quae prohiberi nequeunt necessario concedenda sunt, tametsi inde saepe damnum sequatur. Quot enim mala ex luxu, invidia, avaritia, ebrietate, et aliis similibus oriuntur? Feruntur tamen haec quia imperio legum prohiberi nequeunt, quamvis revera vitia sint. Quare multo magis judicii libertas concedi debet, quae profecto virtus
20 est, nec opprimi potest. Adde quod nulla ex eadem incommoda oriuntur quae non possint (ut statim ostendam) authoritate magistratuum vitari; ut jam taceam quod haec libertas apprime necessaria est ad scientias et artes promovendum, nam hae ab iis tantum felici cum successu coluntur, qui judicium liberum et minime praeoccupatum
25 habent.

At ponatur hanc libertatem opprimi, et homines ita retineri posse ut nihil mutire audeant nisi ex praescripto summarum potestatum; hoc profecto nunquam fiet ut nihil etiam nisi quid ipsae velint cogitent. Atque adeo necessario sequeretur ut homines quotidie aliud sentirent,
30 aliud loquerentur, et consequenter ut fides, in republica apprime necessaria, corrumperetur, et abominanda adulatio et perfidia foverentur; unde doli et omnium bonarum artium corruptio. Verum longe abest ut id fieri possit, ut omnes scilicet praefinito loquantur: sed contra, quo magis libertas loquendi hominibus adimi curatur, eo contumacius
35 contra nituntur, non quidem avari, adulatores, et reliqui impotentes animi, quorum summa salus est nummos in arca contemplari et ventres

---

28. The correct reading may be *quod*.

liberal minds, have gained such a reputation that their authority has more weight with the masses than that of the sovereign. Admittedly there are also some beliefs which, although apparently purely theoretical, are advanced and disseminated from hostility to the sovereign; but I have already dealt with these in Chapter XV, and still left reason free.[1] Finally, if we reflect that a man's devotion to the state, like his devotion to God,[2] can only be known from his actions, i.e. from his charity towards his neighbour, we can have no doubt that a good state allows everyone the same freedom to philosophize as I have shown to be permitted by faith.[3] I grant that such freedom sometimes leads to trouble; but the same is true of any institution, no matter how wisely planned. He who seeks to determine everything by law will aggravate vices rather than correct them. We must necessarily permit what we cannot prevent, even though it often leads to harm. Things like extravagance, envy, greed, and drunkenness are a source of much evil; yet we put up with them because they cannot be prevented by legal enactment, vices though in fact they are.[4] Much more then must we allow independence of judgement; for it is certainly a virtue, and it cannot be suppressed. Besides, it leads to no trouble which cannot be forestalled by the influence of the magistrates (as I shall presently show);[5] to say nothing of the fact that it is quite indispensable for the advancement of the arts and sciences, for these are cultivated with success only by men whose judgement is free and unbiased.

But let us assume that such freedom can be suppressed, and that men can be so thoroughly coerced that they dare not whisper a word which is not prescribed by the sovereign. Will it ever come to pass that they also think nothing but what it wills? Assuredly not. Then the inevitable result will be this. Every day men will be saying one thing and thinking another; belief in another's word, a prime necessity in a state, will thus be undermined, nauseating sycophancy and deceitfulness encouraged; and hence will come frauds and the destruction of all honest dealing. In fact, however, the assumption that everyone can be made to speak to order is quite impossible. The more the sovereign tries to deprive men of freedom of speech, the more stubbornly is it opposed; not indeed by money-grubbers, sycophants, and the rest of the shallow crew, whose supreme happiness is to gloat over the coins in

---

[1] Spinoza is referring in particular to the belief that revelation is superior to reason. For the political consequences of this belief see p. 243.

[2] *TT-P* xiv, pp. 115 and ff.   [3] *TT-P* xiv, p. 123.

[4] For Spinoza's views on sumptuary legislation see *TP* x, 5–6, pp. 433–5.

[5] pp. 239 and ff. Spinoza follows Hobbes, *De Cive* vi, 11, n.

distentos habere, sed ii quos bona educatio, morum integritas, et virtus
liberiores fecit. Ita homines plerumque constituti sunt ut nihil magis
impatienter ferant quam quod opiniones quas veras esse credunt pro
crimine habeantur, et quod ipsis sceleri reputetur id quod ipsos ad
5 pietatem erga Deum et homines movet; ex quo fit ut leges detestari, et
quidvis in magistratum audeant, nec turpe, sed honestissimum putent
seditiones hac de causa movere, et quodvis facinus tentare. Cum itaque
humanam naturam sic comparatam esse constet, sequitur leges quae
de opinionibus conduntur non scelestos sed ingenuos respicere, nec ad
10 malignos coercendum, sed potius ad honestos irritandum condi, nec
sine magno imperii periculo defendi posse. Adde quod tales leges inutiles omnino sunt; nam qui opiniones quae legibus damnatae sunt
sanas esse credent, legibus parere non poterunt, qui contra easdem
tanquam falsas rejiciunt, leges quibus hae damnantur tanquam privi-
15 legia recipiunt, et iisdem ita triumphant ut magistratus easdem postea,
etsi velit, abrogare non valeat. His accedunt quae supra Cap. XVIII ex
historiis Hebraeorum N°. II deduximus. Et denique, quot schismata
in ecclesia ex hoc plerumque orta sunt, quod magistratus doctorum controversias legibus dirimere voluerunt? Nam ni homines spe teneren-
20 tur leges et magistratum ad se trahendi, et de suis adversariis communi
vulgi applausu triumphandi, et honores adipiscendi, nunquam tam
iniquo animo certarent, nec tantus furor eorum mentes agitaret. Atque
haec non tantum ratio, sed etiam experientia quotidianis exemplis
docet; nempe similes leges, quibus scilicet imperatur quid unicuique
25 credendum sit, et contra hanc aut illam opinionem aliquid dicere vel
scribere prohibetur, saepe institutas fuisse ad largiendum, vel potius
cedendum eorum irae qui libera ingenia ferre nequeunt, et torva
quadam authoritate seditiosae plebis devotionem facile in rabiem
mutare, et in quos volunt instigare possunt. At quanto satius foret vulgi
30 iram et furorem cohibere, quam leges inutiles statuere quae violari non
possunt nisi ab iis qui virtutes et artes amant, et rempublicam in tantam angustiam redigere ut viros ingenuos sustinere non possit? Quid

17. *IV schismata*; *I scismata*.

their coffers and to have their bellies well stuffed, but by those who, because of their culture, integrity, and ability, have some independence of mind. Ordinary human nature is such that men find nothing more irritating than to have the views which they hold to be true branded as criminal, and the beliefs which inspire them to piety towards God and man held up against them as wickedness; this encourages them to denounce the laws, and to go to all lengths against the magistrate, in the belief that it is not disgraceful but highly laudable to stir up sedition and attempt the most outrageous crimes in such a cause. Given, then, that human nature is such, it follows that laws which proscribe beliefs do not affect the wicked but the liberal-minded, that they are passed to annoy the good rather than to restrain the malicious, and that they cannot be upheld without great danger to the state. In any case, such laws are utterly useless; for those who regard the proscribed beliefs as sound will be unable to obey the laws which proscribe them,[1] while those who reject such beliefs as false welcome these laws as privileges, and are so proud of them that the magistrate can never repeal them even if he wishes. Then there are the dangers which I showed to follow from them in discussing my second lesson from Jewish history in Chapter XVIII above.[2] Finally, the readiness of magistrates to settle the disputes of scholars by legislation[3] has been the main source of innumerable divisions in the church; for were men not captivated by the hope of getting the laws and the magistrate on their side, of triumphing over their opponents amid the general applause of the mob, and of attaining high office, they would never quarrel with such spite or be driven by such frenzy. And these are the findings of experience as well as of reason; for each new day brings instances to show that laws which prescribe what everyone must believe, and forbid men to say or write anything against this or that opinion, are often passed to gratify, or rather, to appease the anger of those who cannot abide independent minds, but by their savage influence can easily change the fervour of an unruly people into frenzy, and direct it against anyone they please.[4] Yet how much better would it be to curb the furious anger of the mob, instead of passing useless laws which can only be broken by those who love the virtues and the arts, and reducing the state to such straits that it cannot support men of liberal

---

[1] p. 227; cf. *TP* iii, 8 pp. 289–91. [2] p. 199.

[3] Grotius, on the other hand, seems to have approved of this (op. cit. viii, 6).

[4] Spinoza himself was to suffer a certain amount of persecution from the Calvinist clergy: see *Ep.* lxviii and Freudenthal, *Lebensgeschichte*, pp. 121 and ff.

enim majus reipublicae malum excogitari potest quam quod viri
honesti, quia diversa sentiunt et simulare nesciunt, tanquam improbi in
exilium mittantur? Quid, inquam, magis perniciosum quam quod
homines ob nullum scelus neque facinus, sed quia liberalis ingenii sunt,
5 pro hostibus habeantur et ad necem ducantur; et quod catasta, malorum
formido, pulcherrimum fiat theatrum ad summum tolerantiae et virtutis exemplum cum insigni majestatis opprobrio ostentandum? Qui
enim se honestos norunt mortem ut scelesti non timent, nec supplicium
deprecantur; eorum quippe animus nulla turpis facti poenitentia angi-
10 tur: sed contra, honestum, non supplicium, putant pro bona causa
mori, et pro libertate gloriosum. Quid ergo talium nece exempli
statuitur, cujus causam inertes et animo impotentes ignorant, seditiosi
oderunt, et honesti amant? Nemo sane ex eadem exemplum capere
potest nisi ad imitandum, vel saltem ad adulandum.

15   Ne itaque assentatio, sed ut fides in pretio sit, et ut summae potestates
imperium optime retineant, nec seditiosis cedere cogantur, judicii
libertas necessario concedenda est, et homines ita regendi sunt ut,
quamvis diversa et contraria palam sentiant, concorditer tamen vivant.
Nec dubitare possumus quin haec ratio imperandi optima sit, et
20 minora patiatur incommoda; quandoquidem cum hominum natura
maxime convenit. In imperio enim democratico (quod maxime ad
statum naturalem accedit) omnes pacisci ostendimus ex communi
decreto agere, at non judicare et ratiocinari; hoc est, quia omnes
homines non possunt aeque eadem sentire, pacti sunt ut id vim
25 decreti haberet quod plurima haberet suffragia, retinendo interim
authoritatem eadem, ubi meliora viderint, abrogandi. Quo igitur
hominibus libertas judicandi minus conceditur, eo a statu maxime
naturali magis receditur, et consequenter violentius regnatur. Ut
autem porro constet ex hac libertate nulla oriri incommoda quae non
30 possint sola summae potestatis authoritate vitari, et hac sola homines,
etsi palam contraria sentientes, facile retineri ne invicem laedant,

---

14. The correct reading may be *vel saltem ad laudandum.*
17. *O necessario*; *I necessaro.*

views? What greater calamity to a state can be imagined than that good men should be sent into exile as malefactors because they hold unorthodox beliefs and cannot pretend otherwise? What, I say, is more disastrous than that men should be branded as public enemies and haled off to execution for no crime or misdeed, but simply because they have independent minds; and that the scaffold, the terror of the wicked, should become a glorious stage for presenting—to the signal disgrace of the sovereign—supreme examples of courage and endurance? For men whose consciences are clear do not fear death or beg for mercy like criminals, since their minds are not tormented by remorse for deeds of shame; they think it a merit, not a punishment, to die for a good cause, and an honour to die for freedom.[1] And since they give their lives for a cause that is beyond the ken of fainéants and fools, hateful to the unruly, and dear to the good, what are men taught by their death? Only to emulate them, or at least to hold them in reverence.[2]

If honesty, then, is to be valued above servility, and sovereigns are to retain full control, without being forced to yield to agitators, it is necessary to allow freedom of judgement, and so to govern men that they can express different and conflicting opinions without ceasing to live in harmony. This method of government is undoubtedly best, and least subject to inconveniences; for it is best suited to human nature. I have shown that in a democracy (which comes nearest to the natural condition)[3] all make a covenant to act, but not to judge and think, in accordance with the common decision;[4] that is, because all men cannot think alike, they agree that the proposal which gets the most votes shall have the force of a decree, but meanwhile retain the authority to revoke such decrees when they discover better. Thus the less freedom of judgement men are allowed, the greater is the departure from the most natural condition, and, in consequence, the more oppressive is the government. To show in addition that the sovereign's authority is sufficient to prevent all inconveniences arising from such freedom, and can easily restrain men from harming one another, no matter how openly their opinions are in conflict, we need not go far afield; for

[1] Here Spinoza has in mind not only the execution of Oldenbarneveldt and the exile of Grotius, but also the fate of the Jews under the Inquisition in Spain and Portugal.

[2] Elwes renders 'to flatter the persecutor', and most modern translators have followed him. But (*a*) it is difficult to supply different objects for *imitandum* and *adulandum*; (*b*) *saltem* is left untranslated; and (*c*) men of spirit are unlikely to be terrified into servility (cf. p. 243). I therefore suppose that *adulari* is used here in a good sense. Its similarity to *adorare* and *adolere* made this easy; Tertullian actually uses it as a synonym for *adorare*.   [3] *TT-P* xvi, p. 137.

[4] *TT-P* xvi, p. 133: but the distinction between acting and thinking is not explicitly drawn until *TT-P* xx, p. 231.

exempla praesto sunt, nec opus mihi est ea longe petere. Urbs Am-
stelodamum exemplo sit, quae tanto cum suo incremento, et omnium
nationum admiratione, hujus libertatis fructus experitur. In hac enim
florentissima republica et urbe praestantissima omnes cujuscunque
5 nationis et sectae homines summa cum concordia vivunt; et ut alicui
bona sua credant, id tantum scire curant, num dives an pauper sit, et
num bona fide an dolo solitus sit agere. Caeterum religio vel secta
nihil eos movet, quia haec coram judice ad justificandam vel damnan-
dam causam nihil juvat; et nulla omnino tam odiosa secta est cujus
10 sectarii (modo neminem laedant, et suum unicuique tribuant, honesteque vivant) publica magistratuum authoritate et praesidio non pro-
tegantur. Contra, cum olim Remonstrantium et Contraremonstrantium
controversia de religione a politicis et Ordinibus Provinciarum agitari
incepit, tandem in schisma abiit, et multis tum exemplis constitit leges
15 quae de religione conduntur, ad dirimendas scilicet controversias,
homines magis irritare quam corrigere; alios deinde infinitam ex iisdem
licentiam sumere; praeterea schismata non oriri ex magno veritatis
studio (fonte scilicet comitatis et mansuetudinis), sed ex magna libidine
regnandi. Ex quibus luce meridiana clarius constat eos potius schisma-
20 ticos esse qui aliorum scripta damnant, et vulgum petulantem in
scriptores seditiose instigant, quam scriptores ipsos, qui plerumque
doctis tantum scribunt, et solam rationem in auxilium vocant; deinde
eos revera perturbatores esse, qui in libera republica libertatem judicii,
quae non potest opprimi, tollere tamen volunt.

25 His ostendimus:—

I. Impossibile esse libertatem hominibus dicendi ea quae sentiunt
adimere.

II. Hanc libertatem salvo jure et authoritate summarum potestatum unicuique concedi, et eandem unumquemque servare posse, salvo
30 eodem jure, si nullam inde licentiam sumat ad aliquid in rempublicam
tanquam jus introducendum, vel aliquid contra receptas leges agendum.

21. *Gf ipsos; I ipsi.*

with the Counter-Remonstrant ministers. In 1617 Maurice of Orange espoused the cause of
the Counter-Remonstrants, and used their support to destroy Oldenbarneveldt in 1619. In
the same year the Remonstrants were expelled from the church by the national synod, and it
was only after the death of Maurice in 1625 that they began to be tolerated as a separate sect.
See Renier, *The Dutch Nation* I, viii–xi, pp. 41–76.

² Spinoza's sympathies are obviously with the Remonstrants, who, unlike their opponents,
admitted the right of public authorities to arbitrate in ecclesiastical matters (Renier, op. cit.
I, viii, p. 45).

examples are ready to hand. Take the city of Amsterdam, whose enjoyment of this freedom has made it great and admired by the whole world. In this flourishing state, this city without a peer, men of every race and sect live in the greatest harmony, and before they entrust their goods to anyone there are only two things they want to know: whether he is rich or poor, and whether he is honest or dishonest. His religion or sect does not matter, for it has no influence on the decision of lawsuits; and no sect whatsoever is so detested that its members (provided that they harm no one, give every man his own, and live decent lives) are refused the protection of the civil authorities. In the past, when statesmen and the Provincial Estates began to take sides in the religious controversy between the Remonstrants and the Counter-Remonstrants,[1] this was not the case. The result of their intervention was a division in the church; and that period provided abundant evidence that laws passed about religion, i.e. to settle religious disputes, are more apt to provoke men than to reform them, that they enable some to assume unbounded licence, and, finally, that the cause of schisms is not great zeal for the truth (which is, of course, the source of comradeship and sociability), but great ambition to rule.[2] From which it is clearer than noonday that the real disrupters are those who condemn the writings of others, and seditiously incite the insolent mob against their authors, rather than the authors themselves, who generally write for the learned only, appealing to reason alone; and furthermore, that the real disturbers of peace are those who seek to abolish freedom of judgement in a free state, although it cannot be suppressed.

I have thus shown:—

I. That it is impossible to deprive men of the freedom to say what they think.

II. That this freedom can be granted to everyone without infringing the right and authority of the sovereign; and that everyone can keep it without infringing that right as long as he does not use it as a licence to introduce anything into the state as a law, or to do anything contrary to the accepted laws.

[1] This controversy arose from a dispute between two professors of theology at Leiden, Arminius and Gomarus, at the start of the seventeenth century. Gomarus maintained the Calvinist doctrine of predestination in its extreme form, while Arminius left some scope for human free will. The Arminians became known as 'Remonstrants' because of the appeal or 'remonstrance' which they addressed to the Estates of Holland in 1610, and to which the Gomarists replied in a 'counter-remonstrance'. Oldenbarneveldt and the Estates of Holland intervened in the controversy in order to save the Remonstrants, who were in the minority, from persecution; but met with little success in Amsterdam, where the regents were in league

[*footnotes contd. opposite*

III. Hanc eandem libertatem unumquemque habere posse servata reipublicae pace; et nulla ex eadem incommoda oriri quae facile coerceri non possint.

IV. Eandem salva etiam pietate unumquemque habere posse.

V. Leges quae de rebus speculativis conduntur inutiles omnino esse.

VI. Denique ostendimus hanc libertatem non tantum servata reipublicae pace, pietate, et summarum potestatum jure posse, sed ad haec omnia conservandum etiam debere concedi. Nam ubi ex adverso eandem hominibus adimere laboratur, et discrepantium opiniones (non autem animi, qui soli peccare possunt) in judicium vocantur, ibi in honestos exempla eduntur quae potius martyria videntur, quaeque reliquos magis irritant, et ad misericordiam, si non ad vindictam, plus movent, quam terrent. Bonae deinde artes et fides corrumpuntur, adulatores et perfidi foventur, et adversarii triumphant quod eorum irae concessum sit, quodque imperium tenentes suae doctrinae—cujus interpretes habentur—sectatores fecerint. Ex quo fit ut eorum authoritatem et jus usurpare audeant, nec jactare erubescant se a Deo immediate electos, et sua decreta divina, summarum autem potestatum contra humana esse; quae propterea divinis, hoc est, suis decretis, ut cedant volunt. Quae omnia nemo ignorare potest reipublicae saluti omnino repugnare. Quapropter hic (ut supra Cap. XVIII) concludimus nihil reipublicae tutius quam ut pietas et religio in solo charitatis et aequitatis exercitio comprehendatur, et jus summarum potestatum, tam circa sacra quam profana, ad actiones tantum referatur; caeterum unicuique et sentire quae velit, et quae sentiat dicere concedatur.

His quae in hoc tractatu agere constitueram absolvi. Superest tantum expresse monere me nihil in eo scripsisse quod non libentissime examini et judicio summarum potestatum patriae meae subjiciam. Nam si quid horum quae dixi patriis legibus repugnare, vel communi saluti obesse judicabunt, id ego indictum volo. Scio me hominem esse, et errare potuisse; ne autem errarem sedulo curavi, et apprime, ut quicquid scriberem legibus patriae, pietati, bonisque moribus omnino responderet.

III. That it is no danger to the peace of the state; and that all troubles arising from it can easily be checked.

IV. That it is no danger to piety either.

V. That laws passed about speculative matters are utterly useless; and finally,

VI. That this freedom not only can be granted without danger to public peace, piety, and the right of the sovereign, but actually must be granted if they are all to be preserved. For where the opposite course is taken, and attempts are made to deprive men of it, and where the opinions of the dissenters—not their wills, which alone are capable of moral error—are called to account, the punishment inflicted on good men seems more like martyrdom than punishment, provokes instead of intimidating the rest, and moves them to pity, if not to vengeance. Good faith and honest dealing are undermined, lick-spittles and rascals encouraged, and opponents exult because concessions have been made to their anger, and they have converted the sovereign to a creed of which they are the recognized interpreters. They thus make bold to usurp its authority and right, and have the effrontery to boast that since they have been chosen by God directly their commands are divine; and to require that the sovereign's, which are merely human, should give way to the divine commands, i.e. to their own. No one can fail to see that all this is quite incompatible with the well-being of a state. I therefore conclude here, as I did above in Chapter XVIII,[1] that it is safest for a state to make piety and religion consist wholly in the practice of charity and equity; to confine the sovereign's right in the religious as well as in the secular sphere to the control of actions alone; and otherwise to allow everyone both to think what he pleases and to say what he thinks.

My treatise being now complete, it only remains to say expressly that it contains nothing which I would not willingly submit to the examination and judgement of my country's rulers. If anything I have written is in their judgement contrary to my country's laws or detrimental to the general welfare, I am ready to retract it. I know that, being human, I may have made errors; but I have taken great pains to avoid error, and, above all, to see that everything I wrote should be in complete accord with my country's laws, with piety, and with sound morals.[2]

---

[1] p. 199.

[2] In this final paragraph Spinoza repeats his remarks at the end of the Preface with some necessary alterations.

AUCTORIS ADNOTATIONES
AD
TRACTATUM THEOLOGICO-POLITICUM

SPINOZA'S NOTES
ON THE
TRACTATUS THEOLOGICO-POLITICUS

4 (p. 56). Genes. Cap. 15 narratur quod Deus Abrahamo dixerit se ipsius esse defensorem, et remunerationem daturum amplam admodum; ad quae Abrahamus, sibi nihil quod alicujus posset momenti esse expectandum, quia provecta jam senectute orbus erat.

5   5 (p. 58). Ad vitam aeternam non sufficere V.T. mandata observare, patet ex Marc. Cap. 10 vs. 21.

32 (p. 128). In statu civili, ubi communi jure decernitur quid bonum et quid malum sit, recte dolus distinguitur in bonum et malum. Sed in statu naturali, ubi unusquisque sui judex est, summumque jus habet leges sibi
10 praescribendi et interpretandi, imo etiam, prout sibi utilius judicat, abrogandi, ibi sane concipi non potest quemquam dolo malo agere.

33 (p. 134). In quacunque civitate homo sit, liber esse potest. Nam certe homo eatenus liber est, quatenus ratione ducitur. At (N.B. aliter Hobbesius) ratio pacem omnino suadet; haec autem obtineri nequit nisi communia civita-
15 tis jura inviolata serventur; ergo, quo homo ratione magis ducitur, id est, quo magis est liber, eo magis constanter civitatis jura servabit, et summae potestatis mandata, cujus subditus est, exequetur.

34 (p. 142). Quod Paulus ait homines esse sine effugio, more humano loquitur. Nam Cap. 9 vs. 18 ejusdem Epistolae expresse docet quod Deus
20 cujus vult miseretur, et quem vult indurat, et homines nulla de causa inexcusa-biles esse quam quia in Dei potestate ita sunt ut lutum in potestate figuli, qui ex eadem massa facit vasa, aliud ad decus, aliud ad dedecus, et non propterea quod praemoniti sunt. Quod autem ad legem divinam naturalem attinet, cujus summum praeceptum esse diximus Deum amare, eo sensu legem appel-
25 lavi quo philosophi communes naturae regulas, secundum quas omnia neces-sario fiunt, leges vocant. Amor enim Dei non obedientia, sed virtus est quae

---

7. *ML et*, which *Mr* omits.
9. *StG où chacun est de droit maistre de ses actions.*   10. *ML imo*; *Mr immo.*
11. *StG que la fraude puisse avoir lieu, ny qu'il s'y trouve de malice* (for *quemquam dolo malo agere*).
13. *ML est*; *Mr esse potest.*   19. *StG verset 18*; *Mr* and *ML* omit.
22–23. *StG et (par ce) que les avertissements ne servent de rien à leur salut, ou à leur perte* (for *et non . . . sunt*).
24–25. *Mr adpellavi*; *ML appellamus*; *StG elle s'appelle.*
25–26. *Mr* and *ML* omit *necessario*; *StG necessairement.*

4 (p. 57). In Genesis, Chapter 15, we are told that God promised to be Abraham's protector, and to give him a reward exceeding great; to which Abraham answered that, being childless at such an advanced age, he had nothing of any consequence left to hope for.

5 (p. 59). Mark, Chapter 10, verse 21, shows that observance of the commandments in the Old Testament is not enough to give men eternal life.

32 (p. 131). In the political condition, where what is moral and immoral is determined by the right of the community, it is correct to make a distinction between moral and immoral intent to deceive. But in the state of nature, where everyone is his own judge, and has a perfect right to prescribe laws for himself, to interpret them, and indeed even to discard them when he thinks it in his own interest, 'immoral intent to deceive' is quite inconceivable.[1]

33 (p. 135). A man can be free in any kind of state;[2] for, of course, a man is free in so far as he is guided by reason.[3] Now, pace Hobbes,[4] reason counsels peace unreservedly. But peace cannot be maintained unless the general laws of the state are kept inviolate; therefore, the more a man is guided by reason, in other words, the more free he is, the more consistently will he observe the laws of his state and carry out the commands of his sovereign.[5]

34 (p. 143). When Paul says that men are without excuse, he is speaking in popular terms.[6] For in Chapter 9, verse 18, of the same Epistle he teaches explicitly that God has mercy on whom he wills, and hardens whom he wills; and that the reason why men 'cannot be excused' is not that they have been forewarned, but simply that they are in the power of God like clay in the power of the potter, who from the same lump makes one vessel for honourable, another for dishonourable use.[7] As for the natural divine law, whose main precept I said was to love God,[8] I have called it a 'law' in the sense in which scientists apply the word to the universal rules of nature in accordance with which all things necessarily come to pass.[9] For love of God is a virtue which

---

[1] Spinoza is explaining why he says *dolo* (intent to deceive) and not *dolo malo* (immoral intent to deceive).

[2] As long as its constitution is based on 'sound reason'. Spinoza does not mean that a man can be free under a despotism (*TP* v, 6, p. 311, and vii, 22, p. 353), for a despotism hardly deserves the name of state (*TP* v, 4, p. 311); but that he can be free in a monarchy as well as in an aristocracy or democracy (*TP* vii, 31, p. 365).

[3] *TP* ii, 11, p. 275.

[4] J. Laird, *Hobbes*, p. 300, regards this as 'a very captious piece of exegesis'; but see *De Cive* i, 7, and iii, 27.

[5] Most of this note is reproduced with minor variations in *TP* iii, 6, p. 289.

[6] For Spinoza's interpretation of this statement see *T T-P* iv, p. 87.

[7] *Romans* 9, 21, quoted again in *TP* ii, 22, p. 281; *Epp.* lxxv and lxxviii.

[8] *T T-P* iv, p. 73.   [9] *T T-P* iv, p. 67; *TP* ii, 18, p. 279.

homini qui Deum recte novit necessario inest. At obedientia voluntatem imperantis, non rei necessitatem respicit et veritatem. Cum autem naturam Dei voluntatis ignoremus, et contra certi simus quidquid fit ex sola Dei potentia fieri, nequaquam nisi ex revelatione scire possumus an Deus aliquo honore coli
5 velit ab hominibus tanquam princeps. Adde quod jura divina nobis ut jura seu instituta videri ostenderimus quamdiu eorum causam ignoramus; hac autem cognita illico jura esse desinunt, atque eadem ut aeternas veritates, non ut jura, amplectimur; hoc est, obedientia illico in amorem transit, qui ex vera cognitione tam necessario oritur ut ex sole lumen. Ex rationis igitur ductu
10 Deum quidem amare, sed non obedire ei possumus, quandoquidem nec jura divina, quamdiu eorum causam ignoramus, ut divina amplecti, nec Deum jura ut principem constituentem concipere ratione possumus.

StG has preserved the second half of this note in a different form:

Car comme il nous est impossible (ainsi que nous l'avons fait voir au Chapitre 4) de concevoir Dieu comme un Prince qui fait dęs loix que nous pouvons violer, il est évident que nul homme qui n'a que la raison pour guide ne peut sçavoir qu'il soit obligé d'obeïr à Dieu. Davantage nous avons montré que les commandemens que Dieu a revelez ne nous obligent point, et qu'ils ne passent pour commandemens à nôtre égard, que tandis que nous en ignorons la cause, mais que dés là que nous la connoissons, ils cessent d'estre tels, et que nous ne les embrassons plus comme commandemens, mais comme veritez éternelles, et par consequent que l'obeïssance se convertit alors en amour, lequel est produit aussi necessairement d'une vraye connoissance que la lumiere est produite par le Soleil. D'où il s'ensuit que la raison nous enseigne à la verité à aimer Dieu, mais non pas à luy obeïr: puisque nous ne sçaurions recevoir les commandemens de Dieu entant que commandemens, c'est à dire tandis que nous ne les concevons pas comme veritez éternelles, que Dieu ne nous les ait expressément revelés.

---

asserts that the natural divine law is not a command at all, but a scientific truth. To say that our reason, or God as manifested in our reason, commands us to love God is to speak metaphorically: the truth is that our knowledge of God necessarily gives rise to love of him, and our use of the word 'commands' is a metaphorical way of expressing our awareness of this necessity. Having eliminated political metaphors from his rational theology Spinoza is now seeking to banish them from his moral philosophy. Cf. Kant, *Grundlegung*, p. 39: 'For a holy will there are no imperatives.'

He then proceeds to support it by adding two further points: (1) Since natural reason cannot conceive God as a legislator who lays down laws for men, it cannot acquaint us with the content of any such laws (the nature of God's will). (2) It is only through ignorance of God that we conceive his laws as commands; once reason reveals the true nature of God we see that his laws are not commands but eternal truths, and in consequence we no longer obey God, but love him.

necessarily belongs to the man who has a proper knowledge of God;[1] it is not obedience, which involves reference to the will of a commander, and not to the necessity of the activity or to the truth.[2] But we do not know the nature of God's will,[3] whereas we are certain that everything comes to pass by God's power alone; hence it is only through revelation that we can discover whether God wills to be honoured by men like a king. Besides, I have shown that we only regard the divine laws as commandments or statutes as long as we do not know their cause;[4] once their cause is known, they immediately cease to be commandments, and we embrace them as eternal truths instead; that is, obedience is at once transformed into love, which derives from true knowledge with the same necessity as light from the sun. Accordingly, although reason can lead us to love God, it cannot lead us to obey him; since reason can neither accept God's commandments as God's as long as their cause is unknown, nor conceive God as laying down statutes like a king.[5]

For since we cannot conceive God as a king who makes laws which we can break (as I have shown in Chapter 4), it is clear that a man who has nothing but reason to guide him cannot know that he is obliged to obey God. Besides, I have shown that the commandments revealed by God only impose obligations upon us, and are only regarded by us as commandments, as long as we do not know their cause; but that as soon as we know their cause they cease to be commandments, and we embrace them as eternal truths instead. The consequence is that obedience is then transformed into love, which is produced by true knowledge with the same necessity as light is produced by the sun. It follows that reason does indeed teach us to love God, but not to obey him; since we could not receive the commandments of God as commandments— I am speaking of the time when we do not conceive them as eternal truths— unless God had expressly revealed them to us.

[1] *E* v, 32 Cor.

[2] *TT-P* iv, p. 69; cf. the contrast between Moses and Christ, *TT-P* iv, pp. 79–81, and v, p. 91.

[3] Except in so far as it is equated with the laws of nature (*TT-P* iii, p. 53).

[4] *TT-P* iv, pp. 77–83.

[5] In this important but difficult note Spinoza first answers two objections to his statement in the text. (1) Paul's language in *Romans* 1, 20, suggests that men are without excuse because they have disobeyed divine commandments revealed to them by natural reason. But in view of his statements elsewhere Paul's assertion must not be taken too literally: men are 'without excuse', not for the reason suggested, but because 'the reward follows the work with the same necessity as it follows from the nature of a triangle that its angles are equal to two right angles' (*Ep.* xxi). (2) But Spinoza himself has spoken of a natural divine law discovered by natural reason (cf. *TT-P* v, p. 89); and this law not only contains a supreme *precept*, but also gives rise to subordinate precepts which may be called '*the commands of God*' (*TT-P* iv, p. 71). The obvious reply is that 'the commands of God' in Spinoza's sense are not the commands of an external legislator, of 'a king who lays down laws for men', but of a God who manifests himself in human reason; so that observance of these commands is not obedience but freedom (cf. *TP* ii, 20, p. 281). But instead of contenting himself with this answer Spinoza boldly

[*footnotes contd. opposite*

35 (p. 148). Suscepere duo manipulares imperium populi Romani transferendum, et transtulerunt. Tacit. 1 Histor. libro.

36 (p. 160). In hoc loco accusantur duo quod in castris prophetaverint, et
Josua illos asservandos censet; quod non fecisset, si unicuique injussu Mosis
5 divina responsa populo dare licuisset. At Mosi reos absolvere placuit, et
Josuam increpat quod ipsi suaderet jus suum regium persequi eo tempore,
quando ipsum tantum regnandi taedium tenebat ut maluerit mori quam solus
regnare, ut patet ex vs. 14 et 15 ejusdem Capitis. Sic enim Josuae respondit,
Excandescisne mea de causa? Utinam omnis Dei populus propheta esset, hoc est,
10 utinam ad id rediret jus Deum consulendi, ut regnum apud ipsum populum
esset. Josua itaque non jus, sed temporis rationem ignoravit, et ideo a Mose
castigatur, sicut Abisaeus a Davide, cum regem monuit ut Shimhgi, qui certe
reus majestatis erat, mortis damnaret; vid. 2. Sam. Cap. 19 vs. 22, 23.

37 (p. 162). Vs. 19 et 23 hujus (quos mihi videre contigit) male interpretes
15 vertunt. Nam vs. 19 et 23 non significat quod ei praecepta dedit, aut praeceptis
instruxit, sed quod Josuam principem creaverit seu constituerit; quod in
Scriptura frequens est, ut Exodi Cap. 18 vs. 23, 1. Sam. Cap. 13 vs. 14, Jos.
Cap. 1 vs. 9, et 1. Sam. Cap. 25 vs. 30, etc.

StG has a fuller version of this note:

Plus les interpretes s'efforcent de rendre mot à mot le verset 19 et le 23 de
ce Chapitre, moins ils le rendent intelligible, et je suis asseuré que tres peu de
personnes en entendent le veritable sens. Car la pluspart se figurent que Dieu
commande à Moyse au verset 19 d'instruire Josué en presence de l'Assemblée,
et au verset 23 qu'il luy imposa les mains et l'instruisit; ne prenant pas garde
que cette façon de parler est fort en usage chez les Hebreux pour declarer
que l'election du Prince est legitime, et qu'il est confirmé dans sa charge.
C'est ainsi que parle Jetro en conseillant à Moyse de choisir des Coadjuteurs
qui l'aidassent à juger le Peuple. *Si tu fais cecy*, dit-il, *alors Dieu te comman-
dera*; comme s'il disoit que son autorité sera ferme, et qu'il pourra subsister.
Touchant quoy voyez l'Exode Chapitre 18 verset 23, et le 1 liv. de Samuel
Chapitre 13 verset 14, et le Chapitre 25 verset 30; et sur tout le Chapitre 1

---

3. After *duo StG* adds *dont les noms sont escrits au verset 28* (? 26) *du chapitre 11 de ce livre*;
after *prophetaverint, la nouvelle en vint aussi-tôt à Moyse.*

4. After *fecisset StG* adds *et que l'on n'eût eu garde de rapporter à Moyse comme une action
criminelle.*

7. *ML tantum*; *Mr* omits.   8. *StG et 15*; *Mr* and *ML* omit.

9–11. After *hoc est, StG* reads *voudrois tu qu'il n'y eût que moy à regner? Pour moy, je
souhaitterois que le droit de consulter Dieu revint à chaque particulier, et par consequent qu'ils
regnassent tous ensemble, et me laissassent aller.*   11. After *jus StG* adds *et l'autorité.*

12. *ML Shimhgi*; *Mr Shimghi.*   17. *B c. 13. v. 14*; *Mr XIII, v. 15.*

35 (p. 149).[1] Two common soldiers undertook to transfer the Roman Empire, and did so. Tacitus, Histories, Book I.[2]

36 (p. 161). In this passage two men are accused of having prophesied in the camp, and Joshua advises their arrest; as he would not have done had everyone been free to prophesy to the people without Moses' permission. Moses, however, decided to pardon the accused, and rebuked Joshua for advising him to assert his royal authority; for at the time he was so weary of ruling that he preferred to die rather than to continue governing alone (see verses 14 and 15 of the same Chapter). So he replied to Joshua in these words: 'Art thou jealous for my sake? Would that all God's people were prophets', that is to say, 'Would that the right to consult God might revert to all, so that the people itself might hold the sovereignty.' Thus it was not Moses' right, but the circumstances at the time which Joshua misconstrued; accordingly, he was rebuked by Moses as Abishai was rebuked by David for his advice to pass sentence of death on Shimei, who was certainly guilty of treason. See 2 Samuel, Chapter 19, verses 22 and 23.

37 (p. 163). Verses 19 and 23 of this Chapter[3] are mistranslated in all the versions I have come across. Their meaning is not that he gave Joshua commands or instructions, but that he appointed or constituted him captain. The usage is common in Scripture; see, for example, Exodus, Chapter 18, verse 23, 1 Samuel, Chapter 13, verse 14, Joshua, Chapter 1, verse 9, and 1 Samuel, Chapter 25, verse 30, etc.

The more literally translators try to render verses 19 and 23 of this Chapter, the more unintelligible do they make it, and I am convinced that very few people understand its true meaning. Most people imagine that in verse 19 God is commanding Moses to give Joshua instructions in the presence of the congregation, and that in verse 23 Moses laid his hands upon him, and gave him instructions. In so doing they fail to notice that this form of words was very often used among the Jews to signify that the appointment of the captain was legitimate, and that he was confirmed in his office. It is the form used by Jethro in advising Moses to choose colleagues to help him judge the people: 'If thou shalt do this thing,' he says, 'then God will command thee', meaning that his authority would be secure, and that he would be able to maintain his power. On this point see Exodus, Chapter 18 verse 23: 1 Samuel, Chapter 13, verse 14: Chapter 25, verse 30: and especially Joshua, Chapter 1,

---

[1] This note seems to have no particular relevance to the words *ut nihil in posterum possent*, to which it is referred in the sources. Meijer is right in taking it as a note on the previous sentence, but he gives no good reason for regarding it as spurious.

[2] Tacitus, *Histories* I, xxv, 1.

[3] In *De Cive* xvi, 14, Hobbes uses the same passage to prove that Eleazar had not only the priesthood but the sovereignty after Moses' death. The object of this note is to dispose of any idea that Moses commanded Joshua to obey Eleazar.

de Josué au verset 9, où Dieu luy dit, *Ne t'ay-je pas commandé? Prends courage, et montre toy homme de cœur;* comme si Dieu luy disoit, *N'est ce pas moy qui t'ay constitué Prince? Ne t'espouvante donc de rien, car je seray par tout avec toy.*

38 (p. 166). Magnum quod vulgo vocant Sanhedrin fingunt Rabini a Mose fuisse institutum; nec Rabini soli, sed plurimi inter Christianos, qui cum Rabinis ineptiunt. Moses quidem sibi 70 coadjutores elegit qui cum ipso reipublicae curam haberent, quia solus sustinere non poterat onus totius
5 populi. Sed nullam legem unquam tulit de instituendo collegio septuaginta-virali, sed contra jussit ut unaquaeque tribus in urbibus quas Deus ipsi dederat judices constitueret, qui secundum leges ab ipso latas lites dirimerent; et, si contingeret ut ipsi judices de jure dubitarent, ad summum pontificem (qui scilicet legum summus interpres), vel judicem cui eo tempore subordinati
10 essent (nam is jus habebat pontificem consulendi) adirent, ut juxta pontificis explicationem litem dirimerent. Quod si contingeret ut subordinatus judex contenderet se non teneri ex mente summi pontificis, quam ab ipso vel summa ejus potestate accepit, sententiam ferre, mortis damnabatur; nempe a summo judice, qualis is eo tempore esset, a quo subordinatus judex constitutus fuerat;
15 vid. Deuter. Cap. 17 ex vs. 9. Videlicet vel ut Josua, totius populi Israëlitici summus imperator; vel ut unius tribus princeps, penes quem post factam divisionem jus fuit pontificem de rebus suae tribus consulendi, de bello et pace discernendi, urbes muniendi, judices constituendi, etc.; vel ut rex, in quem omnes vel aliquot tribus jus suum transtulerant. Ad hoc vero confirman-
20 dum plura adferre possem ex historiis testimonia, sed ex multis unum, quod praecipuum videtur, adferam. Cum propheta Silonita Jerobeamum regem elegit, eo ipso jus ipsi dedit pontificem consulendi, judices constituendi; et absolute omne jus quod Rehabeam in duas tribus retinuit, id omne Jerobeam in decem obtinuit. Quare eodem jure quo Jehosaphat Hierosolymae (vid. 2.
25 Paralip. Cap. 19 vs. 8 seqq.), Jerobeam in sua regia summum sui imperii concilium constituere poterat. Nam certum est quod Jerobeam, quatenus ex mandato Dei rex erat, et consequenter ejus subditi, non tenebantur ex lege

---

1. *StG Sanhedrin; Mr* and *ML Synedrium.*   2. *ML qui; Mr* omits.
6. *ML unaquaeque; Mr una quaequae.*
7. After *dirimerent StG* adds *et de punir les delinquants.*
8. *ML et si; Mr etsi.   ML ad; Mr an.*
15. *Mr* and *ML Cap. 17 vs. 9.   B vel ut; Mr* and *ML velut.*
18. After *constituendi StG* adds *dans ses villes, lesquels ne fussent subordonnez qu'à luy.*
21. *ML Jeroboamum; StG Jeroboam.*
23. *ML Reghabuam; StG Roboam; G Reghabaam.* But cf. p. 354, l. 15.
24. *ML Jehosaphat; Mr Josaphath; G Jehosaphath.* The form *Jehosaphat* is found in the text of the *TT-P.*

verse 9, where God says, 'Have I not commanded thee? Take courage, and show thyself a man of spirit'; in other words, 'Have not I myself made thee captain? Then fear naught, for I shall be with thee everywhere.'

38 (p. 167).[1] The Rabbis imagine that what is popularly known as the Grand Sanhedrin was established by Moses; a view accepted by the many Christians who share their absurd beliefs. It is true that Moses, being unable to support the burden of the whole people by himself, appointed seventy colleagues to assist him in administering the state.[2] But he never passed any law establishing a permanent college of seventy men; his orders were that each tribe should appoint judges in the cities which God had given it, and that these should decide lawsuits in accordance with his laws.[3] In cases where such judges were themselves in doubt about the law, they had to consult the high priest (the supreme interpreter of the laws), or the judge who was then their superior (for he had the right to consult the priest), in order to decide the suit in accordance with the priest's interpretation. If, however, a subordinate judge maintained that he was not bound to pass sentence in accordance with the high priest's interpretation, as received either from the priest himself or from his own superior, he was condemned to death by the person who was supreme judge at the time, and who had appointed him as a subordinate. See Deuteronomy, Chapter 17, verses 9 and ff. This person might be the commander-in-chief of the whole people of Israel, like Joshua; or the captain of a single tribe (for after the division was made it was he who had the right to consult the priest about the affairs of his own tribe, to decide between peace and war, to fortify cities, to appoint judges, etc.); or else the king to whom some or all of the tribes had transferred their right. I could produce many pieces of evidence from Jewish history to confirm this view, but I shall only quote the one which seems most important. By appointing Jeroboam as king,[4] the Shilonite prophet also gave him the right to consult the priest and to set up judges; in fact Jeroboam received in full absolutely every right over his ten tribes that Rehoboam retained over his two. Therefore Jeroboam had the same right to set up a supreme council of state in his capital as Jehoshaphat had to establish one at Jerusalem (see 2 Chronicles, Chapter 19, verses 8 and ff.). For, of course, in so far as Jeroboam was king by God's command, the law of Moses did not require either him or his subjects to submit to the jurisdiction

---

[1] This note is an attack on the belief that Moses' council survived his death and exercised control over the captains of the tribes.

[2] *Numbers* 11, 16–17.

[3] *Deuteronomy* 16, 18.

[4] *1 Kings* 11, 29 and ff.

Mosis coram Rehabeamo, cujus subditi non erant, judice stare, et multo minus judicio Hierosolymitano a Rehabeamo constituto, eique subordinato. Prout igitur Hebraeorum imperium divisum fuit, tot suprema concilia in eodem fuerunt. Qui vero ad varium Hebraeorum statum non attendunt, sed diversos
5 eorum status in unum confundunt, multis modis intricantur.

39 (p. 224). Hic apprime ad illa attendendum est quae Cap. XVI de jure diximus.

3. For *tot suprema concilia StG* has *autant de jurisdictions differentes, et independentes les unes des autres.*

of Rehoboam, who had no authority over them; and still less to the jurisdiction of the court at Jerusalem established by Rehoboam and subordinate to him. Thus each division of the Jewish state had its own supreme council, and there were as many councils as there were divisions. Those who disregard the changes in the Jewish state, and reduce its different forms to a single one, get involved in many difficulties.

39 (p. 225). The reader should here pay particular attention to my discussion of right in Chapter XVI.[1]

---

[1] See *TT-P* xix, p. 225, n. 2.

TRACTATUS POLITICUS,

In quo demonstratur quomodo
Societas ubi Imperium Monarchicum
locum habet, sicut et ea ubi Optimi im-
perant, debet institui, ne in Tyrannidem labatur, et ut Pax Liber-
tasque civium inviolata
maneat.

5

6–7. For *Libertas NS* has *Veiligheit* (*Securitas*). But the reading of *OP* is guaranteed by
p. 364, ll. 28–32; p. 366, ll. 1–4; p. 426, ll. 24–29; and p. 436, ll. 9–12. In any case
the account of the contents of the *TP* was probably composed by Spinoza's editors: see
M. Francès, *Œuvres Complètes de Spinoza*, Gallimard, 1954, pp. 1471–4.

A TREATISE ON POLITICS,

Wherein it is shown how a Monarchy
and an Aristocracy must be organized if
they are not to degenerate into Tyranny,
and if the Peace and Freedom of the
citizens is to remain intact.

Auctoris epistola ad Amicum, quae Praefationis loco huic Tractatui Politico apte praefigi et inservire poterit

AMICE DILECTE,

Grata tua mihi heri tradita est. Gratias pro cura tam diligenti quam
5 pro me geris ex animo ago. Hanc occasionem . . . non praetermitterem,
nisi in quadam re essem occupatus quam utiliorem judico, quaeque
tibi, ut credo, magis arridebit; nempe in Tractatu Politico concin-
nando quem ante aliquod tempus te auctore inchoavi. Hujus Tractatus
capita sex jam sunt absoluta. Primum ad ipsum opus introductionem
10 quasi continet; secundum tractat de jure naturali; tertium de jure
summarum potestatum; quartum quaenam negotia politica a summarum potestatum gubernatione pendeant; quintum quidnam sit illud
extremum et summum quod societas potest considerare; et sextum qua
ratione imperium monarchicum debeat institui ne in tyrannidem
15 labatur. Impraesentiarum caput septimum tracto, in quo omnia praecedentis sexti capitis membra ordinem bene ordinatae monarchiae
concernentia methodice demonstro. Postea ad aristocraticum et populare imperium, denique ad leges aliasque particulares quaestiones
politicam spectantes transibo. Hisce vale. . . .

20   Patet hinc Auctoris scopus; sed morbo impeditus et morte abreptus
hoc opus non ulterius quam ad finem Aristocratiae perducere valuit,
quemadmodum Lector ipse experietur.

11–12. *alleenlijk van de bestiering der Oppermachten afhangen,* i.e. *a sola summarum potestatum gubernatione pendeant.*

*A letter from the Author to a friend, which may
fittingly serve as a Preface to this Treatise on Politics*

DEAR FRIEND,

Your welcome letter was delivered to me yesterday, and I thank
you most sincerely for the kindly interest which you take in my welfare. I should not miss this opportunity of . . ., if I did not have something in hand which I think more useful, and which, I believe, will
please you more; I mean the composition of the Treatise on Politics
which I began some time ago at your suggestion. Of this Treatise
six chapters are already complete. The first is a sort of introduction to
the work itself; the second deals with natural right; the third with the
right of sovereign powers; the fourth with the political functions which
are subject to their control; the fifth with the best and highest aim that
a society can contemplate; and the sixth with the manner in which a
monarchy must be organized if it is not to degenerate into tyranny. At
the moment I am busy with the seventh chapter, in which I justify
point by point all the sections on the constitution of a well organized
monarchy in the previous chapter. This done, I shall turn to aristocracy and democracy; and shall conclude by discussing laws and other
particular questions relating to politics. Now I must say farewell. . . .

This letter shows the Author's design; but his illness and untimely
death prevented him from continuing this work beyond the end of the
chapters on Aristocracy, as the Reader will discover for himself.[1]

---

[1] The work in fact contains four sections on democracy (*TP* xi, pp. 441–5).

CAPUT I

1. Affectus quibus conflictamur concipiunt philosophi veluti vitia in quae homines sua culpa labuntur; quos propterea ridere, flere, carpere, vel (qui sanctiores videri volunt) detestari solent. Sic ergo se rem divinam facere, et sapientiae culmen attingere credunt, quando humanam 5 naturam quae nullibi est multis modis laudare, et eam quae revera est dictis lacessere norunt. Homines namque, non ut sunt, sed ut eosdem esse vellent, concipiunt: unde factum est ut plerumque pro ethica satyram scripserint, et ut nunquam politicam conceperint quae possit ad usum revocari; sed quae pro chimaera haberetur, vel quae in 10 Utopia, vel in illo poëtarum aureo saeculo, ubi scilicet minime necesse erat, institui potuisset. Cum igitur omnium scientiarum quae usum habent, tum maxime politices theoria ab ipsius praxi discrepare creditur, et regendae reipublicae nulli minus idonei aestimantur quam theoretici seu philosophi.

15 2. At politici contra hominibus magis insidiari quam consulere creduntur, et potius callidi quam sapientes aestimantur. Docuit nimirum eosdem experientia vitia fore donec homines. Humanam igitur malitiam praevenire dum student, idque iis artibus quas experientia longo usu docuit, et quas homines magis metu quam ratione ducti exercere 20 solent, religioni adversari videntur, theologis praecipue, qui credunt summas potestates debere negotia publica tractare secundum easdem pietatis regulas quibus vir privatus tenetur. Ipsos tamen politicos multo felicius de rebus politicis scripsisse quam philosophos dubitari non potest. Nam quoniam experientiam magistram habuerunt, nihil docuerunt 25 quod ab usu remotum esset.

---

5. *multis modis* not in *NS*.

6–7. *NS Want de menschen bevatten de hartstochten niet gelijk zy zijn, maar gelijk zy hen willen.* A mistranslation by which *Homines* is taken as the subject of *concipiunt* and *affectus* supplied as its object.

20. *NS zo schijnen zy tegen de Godsdienst gekant te wezen, en voornamelijk tegen de Godgeleerden.* I prefer to take *theologis* with *videntur*.

CHAPTER I

1. Philosophers regard the passions that torment us as vices into which we fall through our own fault; and so their habit is to deride, deplore, and revile them, or else, if they want to seem more pious than the rest, to denounce them in God's name. Such conduct they take to be godlike, and they think they have reached the acme of wisdom when they have learnt to sing the praises of a human nature nowhere to be found, and to rail at the sort which actually exists.[1] In fact they conceive men, not as they are, but as they would like them to be.[2] The result is that they have generally written satire instead of ethics, and have never conceived a political system which can be applied in practice;[3] but have produced either obvious fantasies, or schemes that could only have been put into effect in Utopia, or the poets' golden age, where, of course, there was no need of them at all.[4] Thus while theory is supposed to be at variance with practice in all the sciences which admit of application, this is held to be particularly true in the case of politics, and no men are regarded as less fit to govern a state than theorists or philosophers.[5]

2. Statesmen, on the other hand, are believed to plan men's undoing rather than their welfare, and have a greater reputation for cunning than for wisdom. No doubt experience has taught them that there will be vices so long as there are men.[6] They therefore try to forestall human wickedness; but since they do so by means of tricks which have been learnt from long practical experience, and which men usually employ out of fear rather than from rational motives, they are regarded as opponents of religion, especially by theologians, who believe that sovereigns ought to handle public affairs in accordance with the same moral rules as are binding on private individuals.[7] Yet there is no doubt that statesmen have written much more successfully about politics than philosophers; for since experience has been their guide, they have taught nothing which could not be put into practice.[8]

---

[1] *E* iii, Pref.; iv, 50 Sch; *Ep.* xxx.   [2] Aristotle, *Poetics* 1460ᵇ 33–34.

[3] Machiavelli, *Prince* xv.   [4] *TT-P* v, p. 93; *TP* vi, 3, p. 315.

[5] An allusion to Plato's philosopher-king.   [6] Tacitus, *Histories* IV, lxxiv, 2.

[7] Unlike Machiavelli, who held that 'una repubblica e un popolo si governa altrimenti che un privato' (quoted in L. A. Burd's edition of *The Prince*, p. 298).

[8] Spinoza agrees with Thomas Cromwell, who advised Cardinal Pole 'to fling aside dreamers like Plato, and read a new book by an ingenious Italian who treated the arts of government practically'. See Morley's essay on Machiavelli, pp. 5–6 (*Miscellanies*, 4th series, Macmillan, 1908).

3. Et sane mihi plane persuadeo experientiam omnia civitatum genera quae concipi possunt ut homines concorditer vivant, et simul media quibus multitudo dirigi, seu quibus intra certos limites contineri debeat, ostendisse: ita ut non credam nos posse aliquid, quod ab experien-
5 tia sive praxi non abhorreat, cogitatione de hac re assequi, quod nondum expertum compertumque sit. Nam homines ita comparati sunt ut extra commune aliquod jus vivere nequeant; jura autem communia et negotia publica a viris acutissimis, sive astutis sive callidis, instituta et tractata sunt; adeoque vix credibile est nos aliquid quod communi
10 societati ex usu esse queat posse concipere, quod occasio seu casus non obtulerit, quodque homines communibus negotiis intenti, suaeque securitati consulentes, non viderint.

4. Cum igitur animum ad politicam applicuerim, nihil quod novum vel inauditum est, sed tantum ea quae cum praxi optime conveniunt,
15 certa et indubitata ratione demonstrare, et ex ipsa humanae naturae conditione deducere intendi; et ut ea quae ad hanc scientiam spectant eadem animi libertate, qua res mathematicas solemus, inquirerem, sedulo curavi humanas actiones non ridere, non lugere, neque detestari, sed intelligere: atque adeo humanos affectus, ut sunt amor, odium, ira,
20 invidia, gloria, misericordia, et reliquae animi commotiones, non ut humanae naturae vitia, sed ut proprietates contemplatus sum, quae ad ipsam ita pertinent ut ad naturam aëris aestus, frigus, tempestas, tonitru, et alia hujusmodi; quae tametsi incommoda sunt, necessaria tamen sunt, certasque habent causas per quas eorum naturam intelligere
25 conamur, et mens eorum vera contemplatione aeque gaudet ac earum rerum cognitione quae sensibus gratae sunt.

5. Est enim hoc certum, et in nostra Ethica verum esse demonstravimus, homines necessario affectibus esse obnoxios; et ita constitutos esse ut eorum quibus male est misereantur, et quibus bene est invideant, et
30 ut ad vindictam magis quam ad misericordiam sint proni; et praeterea unumquemque appetere ut reliqui ex ipsius ingenio vivant, et ut probent quod ipse probat, et quod ipse repudiat repudient. Unde fit ut,

---

2. *ut homines concorditer vivant* not in *NS.*
15–16. *NS te betogen, en . . . af te leiden,* i.e. *demonstrare, et . . . deducere; OP aut.*
30. *NS en dieshalven willen en begeren,* i.e. *propterea.*

Chapter I

3. In fact, I am fully convinced that every form of commonwealth which can be devised to secure human concord, and all the means required to guide a people, or to keep it within definite bounds, have already been revealed by experience;[1] and so I do not believe that speculation on this matter can lead us to anything, not utterly at variance with practical experience, which has not been discovered and tried already. Human nature is such that men cannot live without some common system of law. Now such systems have been established, and public affairs conducted, by men of great acuteness—call them astute or cunning as you please; and so it is hardly credible that we can conceive anything for the benefit of an ordinary community which has not been suggested already by opportunity or chance, and which men intent on public business, and careful of their own safety, have not discovered for themselves.

4. Thus my object in applying my mind to politics is not to make any new or unheard of suggestions, but to establish by sound and conclusive reasoning, and to deduce from the real nature of man, nothing save the principles and institutions which accord best with practice. Moreover, in order to investigate the topics pertaining to this branch of knowledge with the same objectivity as we generally show in mathematical inquiries, I have taken great care to understand human actions, and not to deride, deplore, or denounce them. I have therefore regarded human passions like love, hate, anger, envy, pride, pity, and the other feelings that agitate the mind, not as vices of human nature, but as properties which belong to it in the same way as heat, cold, storm, thunder and the like belong to the nature of the atmosphere. Inconvenient though they be, such things are necessary properties; they have definite causes[2] through which we try to understand their nature, and a true understanding of them gives the mind as much satisfaction as the apprehension of things pleasing to the senses.[3]

5. I have taken this course because it is certainly true, and proved to be so in my Ethics, that men are necessarily subject to passions;[4] that by nature they pity the unfortunate, but envy the fortunate,[5] and incline more to vengeance than to compassion.[6] I have also shown that each man strives to make the others live as *he* pleases, approve what *he* approves, and reject what *he* rejects.[7] In consequence,

---

[1] But they may not have been properly combined: cf. Aristotle, *Politics* 1264ᵃ 1–5. Hence *TP* vi-xi.

[2] For Spinoza's account of the 'causes' of the passions see *E* iii.

[3] *E* iii, Pref.   [4] *E* iv, 4 Cor.   [5] *E* iii, 32 Sch.

[6] *E* iv, App. 13.   [7] *E* iii, 31 Cor.

cum omnes pariter appetant primi esse, in contentiones veniant, et quantum possunt nitantur se invicem opprimere; et qui victor evadit magis glorietur quod alteri obfuit quam quod sibi profuit. Et quamvis omnes persuasi sint religionem contra docere ut unusquisque proximum
5 tanquam se ipsum amet, hoc est, ut jus alterius perinde ac suum defendat, hanc tamen persuasionem in affectus parum posse ostendimus. Valet quidem in articulo mortis, quando scilicet morbus ipsos affectus vicit, et homo segnis jacet; vel in templis, ubi homines nullum exercent commercium; at minime in foro vel in aula, ubi maxime
10 necesse esset. Ostendimus praeterea rationem multum quidem posse affectus coërcere et moderari; sed simul vidimus viam quam ipsa ratio docet perarduam esse; ita ut qui sibi persuadent posse multitudinem, vel qui publicis negotiis distrahuntur, induci ut ex solo rationis praescripto vivant, saeculum poëtarum aureum seu fabulam somnient.

15 6. Imperium igitur cujus salus ab alicujus fide pendet, et cujus negotia non possunt recte curari nisi ii qui eadem tractant fide velint agere, minime stabile erit; sed, ut permanere possit, res ejus publicae ita ordinandae sunt ut qui easdem administrant, sive ratione ducantur sive affectu, induci nequeant ut male fidi sint seu prave agant. Nec ad
20 imperii securitatem refert quo animo homines inducantur ad res recte administrandum, modo res recte administrentur: animi enim libertas seu fortitudo privata virtus est; at imperii virtus securitas.

7. Denique, quia omnes homines, sive barbari sive culti sint, consuetudines ubique jungunt et statum aliquem civilem formant, ideo
25 imperii causae et fundamenta naturalia non ex rationis documentis petenda, sed ex hominum communi natura seu conditione deducenda sunt, quod in sequenti Capite facere constitui.

8. *NS overwint*, i.e. *vincit*.
19. *NS of qualijk te doen*, i.e. *seu*. So *P. OP ceu*.
25. *Gf causae; OP causas*. An obvious correction which has been overlooked by subsequent editors.

since all are equally bent on supremacy, they start to quarrel, and do their utmost to enslave one another; and he who comes off victorious prides himself more on having harmed his opponent than on having benefited himself.[1] All may know perfectly well that this is contrary to religion, which teaches that everyone should love his neighbour as himself, i.e. should defend the rights of another just as he does his own; but, as I have shown, this conviction is of little avail against the passions.[2] It is strong, no doubt, at the moment of death, when even the passions have been subdued by illness, and the man lies listless; or in churches, where men have no dealings one with another; but it has very little influence in courtroom or palace, where the need for it would seem to be greatest. I have also shown that reason can do a great deal to check and moderate the passions;[3] but at the same time we saw that the way prescribed by reason is very difficult;[4] so that those who believe that a people, or men divided over public business, can be induced to live by reason's dictate alone, are dreaming of the poets' golden age or of a fairy-tale.

6. Thus when the safety of a state depends on any man's good faith, and its affairs cannot be administered properly unless its rulers choose to act from good faith, it will be very unstable; if a state is to be capable of lasting, its administration must be so organized that it does not matter whether its rulers are led by reason or passion—they cannot be induced to break faith or act badly. In fact it makes no difference to the stability of a state what motive leads men to conduct its affairs properly, provided that they *are* conducted properly. For freedom or strength of mind is a private virtue; the virtue of a state is stability.

7. Finally, since all men, savage and civilized alike, everywhere enter into social relations and form some sort of civil order, the causes and natural foundations of the state are not to be sought in the precepts of reason,[5] but must be deduced from the common nature or constitution of men. And this is what I propose to do in the next Chapter.

---

[1] *E* iv, 58 Sch.   [2] *E* iv, 15; 62 Sch.
[3] *E* v, 4 Sch.   [4] *E* v, 42 Sch.
[5] *TP* vi, 1, p. 315. In denying that the state is a product of reason Spinoza abandons his original belief in an historical social contract (*TT-P* xvi, pp. 129–33). The only contract mentioned in the *TP* is a contract of government (*TP* iv, 6, p. 305).

1. In nostro Tractatu Theologico-politico de jure naturali et civili egimus, et in nostra Ethica explicuimus quid peccatum, quid meritum, quid justitia, quid injustitia, et quid denique humana libertas sit. Sed ne ii qui hunc tractatum legunt opus habeant ea quae ad hunc
5 ipsum tractatum maxime spectant in aliis quaerere, ea hic iterum explicare et apodictice demonstrare constitui.

2. Res quaecunque naturalis potest adaequate concipi, sive existat sive non existat. Ut igitur rerum naturalium existendi principium, sic earum in existendo perseverantia ex earum definitione non potest
10 concludi; nam earum essentia idealis eadem est postquam existere inceperunt quam antequam existerent. Ut ergo earum existendi principium ex earum essentia sequi nequit, sic nec earum in existendo perseverantia; sed eadem potentia, qua indigent ut existere incipiant, indigent ut existere pergant. Ex quo sequitur rerum naturalium poten-
15 tiam, qua existunt, et consequenter qua operantur, nullam aliam esse posse quam ipsam Dei aeternam potentiam: nam si quae alia creata esset, non posset seipsam, et consequenter neque res naturales conservare, sed ipsa etiam eadem potentia, qua indigeret ut crearetur, indigeret ut in existendo perseveraret.

20 3. Hinc igitur, quod scilicet rerum naturalium potentia, qua existunt et operantur, ipsissima Dei sit potentia, facile intelligimus quid jus naturae sit. Nam quoniam Deus jus ad omnia habet, et jus Dei nihil aliud est quam ipsa Dei potentia quatenus haec absolute libera consideratur, hinc sequitur unamquamque rem naturalem tantum juris ex
25 natura habere quantum potentiae habet ad existendum et operandum; quandoquidem uniuscujusque rei naturalis potentia, qua existit et operatur, nulla alia est quam ipsa Dei potentia quae absolute libera est.

4. Per jus itaque naturae intelligo ipsas naturae leges seu regulas secundum quas omnia fiunt, hoc est, ipsam naturae potentiam; atque

---

8–10. *M* brackets *Ut . . . concludi* as superfluous.
11. *NS als zy was*. The correct reading may be *quae*.
18. *NS 't welk het behoeft om geschapen te worden*, i.e. *qua indiget ut creetur*.

CHAPTER II

1. I have dealt in my Tractatus Theologico-Politicus with natural and civil right,[1] and have explained in my Ethics what is meant by sin, righteousness, justice, injustice,[2] and finally by human freedom.[3] But to save my readers the trouble of consulting other works for discussions which are particularly relevant to the present treatise, I have decided to explain my views again here and to give a formal proof of their validity.

2. Anything in nature can be conceived adequately whether it is actually in being or not.[4] Thus neither its coming into being nor its persistence in being can be deduced from its definition; for its essence in thought is the same after it has come into being as it was before it existed. Its persistence in being, then, cannot follow from its essence any more than its coming into being can; it needs the same power to continue in being as it needs to come into being.[5] It follows that the power by which things in nature exist, and by which, in consequence, they act, can be none other than *the eternal power of God*. For suppose it were some other power, created by God; then, not being able to preserve itself, it would not be able to preserve things in nature either, but would itself need the same power to persist in being as it needed to be created.

3. Now from the fact that the power of things in nature to exist and act is really *the power of God*,[6] we can easily see what the right of nature is. For since God has the right to do everything, and God's right is simply *God's power* conceived as completely free, it follows that each thing in nature has as much right from nature as it has power to exist and act; since the power by which it exists and acts is nothing but the completely free *power of God*.[7]

4. By the right of nature, then, I mean the actual laws or rules of nature in accordance with which all things come to be; that is, the

---

[1] With natural right in *TT-P* xvi, pp. 125–7: with civil right in *TT-P* xvi, p. 139.

[2] *E* iv, 37 Sch. 2.   [3] *E* v.   [4] *E* i, 24.

[5] *CPP* i, Ax. 10.   [6] *E* i, 34.

[7] *TT-P* xvi, pp. 125–7. Since power and right are identical in God, the identification of the power of nature with the power of God enables Spinoza to equate natural right with natural power. The assertion that God's right is simply God's power conceived as completely free enables him to identify natural right and natural law, since to conceive God's power as completely free is to conceive it as determined by the laws of its own nature alone (*E* i, 17). These laws, unlike the laws established by human legislators, are eternal and inviolable (*TP* ii, 18, p. 279).

adeo totius naturae et consequenter uniuscujusque individui naturale jus eo usque se extendit quo ejus potentia; et consequenter quicquid unusquisque homo ex legibus suae naturae agit, id summo naturae jure agit, tantumque in naturam habet juris quantum potentia valet.

5   5. Si igitur cum humana natura ita comparatum esset ut homines ex solo rationis praescripto viverent, nec aliud conarentur, tum naturae jus, quatenus humani generis proprium esse consideratur, sola rationis potentia determinaretur. Sed homines magis caeca cupiditate quam ratione ducuntur; ac proinde hominum naturalis potentia sive jus, non
10 ratione, sed quocunque appetitu quo ad agendum determinantur, quoque se conservare conantur, definiri debet. Equidem fateor cupiditates illas, quae ex ratione non oriuntur, non tam actiones quam passiones esse humanas. Verum quia hic de naturae universali potentia seu jure agimus, nullam hic agnoscere possumus differentiam inter cupiditates quae
15 ex ratione, et inter illas quae ex aliis causis in nobis ingenerantur; quandoquidem tam hae quam illae effectus naturae sunt, vimque naturalem explicant qua homo in suo esse perseverare conatur. Est enim homo, sive sapiens sive ignarus sit, naturae pars, et id omne ex quo unusquisque ad agendum determinatur ad naturae potentiam referri
20 debet, nempe quatenus haec per naturam hujus aut illius hominis definiri potest. Nihil namque homo, seu ratione seu sola cupiditate ductus, agit nisi secundum leges et regulas naturae, hoc est (per Art. 4 hujus Cap.), ex naturae jure.

6.   At plerique ignaros naturae ordinem magis perturbare quam sequi
25 credunt, et homines in natura veluti imperium in imperio concipiunt. Nam mentem humanam a nullis causis naturalibus statuunt produci, sed a Deo immediate creari, a reliquis rebus adeo independentem ut absolutam habeat potestatem sese determinandi et ratione recte utendi. Sed experientia satis superque docet quod in nostra potestate non magis sit
30 mentem sanam quam corpus sanum habere. Deinde, quandoquidem unaquaeque res quantum in se est suum esse conservare conatur, dubitare

---

1. *Gf individui*; *OP invidui*.

4. *OP potentiâ*; *NS als zijn vermogen vermag*.

10–11. *NS door de welke hy tot werken bepaalt word, en daar door hy poogt zich zelf te bewaren.*

24. For *naturae ordinem NS* has *de natuur*.

actual power of nature.[1] Thus the natural right of nature as a whole, and consequently the natural right of each individual, extends as far as its power. Hence everything a man does in accordance with the laws of his nature, he does by the sovereign right of nature, and he has as much right against other things in nature as he has power and strength.

5. If, then, human nature were such that men lived only as reason prescribed, and never tried to do anything else, the right of nature attributed to human beings would be restricted to the power to use reason.[2] But men are led more by blind desire than by reason; and so their natural power, or natural right, must not be defined in terms of reason, but must be held to cover every possible appetite by which they are determined to act, and by which they try to preserve themselves. Admittedly, the desires which are not based on reason are instances of human passivity rather than of human activity.[3] But since we are dealing at present with the power or right of nature which is common to everything, we can admit no distinction here between desires which are engendered in us by reason, and those which arise from other causes; since both are equally products of nature, and manifest the natural force by which man tries to preserve his own being.[4] For man, whether enlightened or unenlightened, is part of nature, and every motive which determines an individual to action must be attributed to a power of nature that is manifested equally in the natures of both kinds of man. For whether man is led by reason or by desire alone, he always acts in accordance with the laws and rules of nature, that is, by the right of nature (Section 4 of this Chapter).

6. Most men, however, believe that the unenlightened violate the order of nature rather than conform to it; they conceive men in nature as a state within a state.[5] They maintain, in fact, that the human mind is not produced by natural causes at all, but is the direct creation of God, and is so completely independent of every other thing that it has an absolute power to determine itself and use reason correctly.[6] But experience teaches us only too well that it is no more in our power to have a sound mind than to have a sound body. Moreover, since everything does all it *can* do to preserve its own being, we cannot have the

---

[1] Hobbes distinguishes natural right and natural law (*De Cive* xiv, 3), and regards natural law as prescriptive (*De Cive* ii, 1).

[2] In *De Cive* i, 7 Hobbes defines natural right in terms of right reason.

[3] *E* iii, 58–59.

[4] Man's *conatus sese conservandi* is his actual essence (*E* iii, 7), the source of both his 'actions' and his 'passions'. Cf. *E* v, 4 Sch.

[5] *E* iii, Pref.

[6] Contrast *E* iv, 4.

nequaquam possumus quin, si aeque in nostra potestate esset tam ex
rationis praescripto vivere quam caeca cupiditate duci, omnes ratione
ducerentur et vitam sapienter instituerent; quod minime fit. Nam trahit
sua quemque voluptas. Nec theologi hanc difficultatem tollunt, qui sci-
5 licet statuunt hujus impotentiae causam humanae naturae vitium seu
peccatum esse, quod originem a primi parentis lapsu traxerit. Nam
si etiam in primi hominis potestate fuit tam stare quam labi, et mentis compos erat et natura integra, quî fieri potuit ut sciens prudensque
lapsus fuerit? At dicunt eum a Diabolo deceptum fuisse. Verum quis
10 ille fuit qui ipsum Diabolum decepit,—quis, inquam, ipsum omnium
creaturarum intelligentium praestantissimum adeo amentem reddidit,
ut Deo major esse voluerit? Nonne enim se ipsum, qui mentem sanam
habebat, suumque esse quantum in se erat conservare conabatur?
Deinde quî fieri potuit ut ipse primus homo, qui mentis compos erat
15 et suae voluntatis dominus, seduceretur et mente pateretur capi? Nam
si potestatem habuit ratione recte utendi, decipi non potuit; nam quantum in se fuit conatus est necessario suum esse mentemque suam
sanam conservare. Atqui supponitur eum hoc in potestate habuisse:
ergo mentem suam sanam necessario conservavit, nec decipi potuit.
20 Quod ex ipsius historia falsum esse constat; ac proinde fatendum est
quod in primi hominis potestate non fuerit ratione recte uti, sed quod,
sicuti nos, affectibus fuerit obnoxius.

7. Quod autem homo, ut reliqua individua, suum esse quantum in
se est conservare conetur, negare nemo potest. Nam si hic aliqua con-
25 cipi posset differentia, inde oriri deberet quod homo voluntatem haberet
liberam. Sed quo homo a nobis magis liber conciperetur, eo magis
cogeremur statuere ipsum sese necessario debere conservare, et mentis
compotem esse; quod facile unusquisque qui libertatem cum contin-
gentia non confundit mihi concedet. Est namque libertas virtus seu
30 perfectio: quicquid igitur hominem impotentiae arguit, id ad ipsius
libertatem referri nequit. Quare homo minime potest dici liber propterea quod potest non existere, vel quod potest non uti ratione, sed
tantum quatenus potestatem habet existendi et operandi secundum
humanae naturae leges. Quo igitur hominem magis liberum esse con-
35 sideramus, eo minus dicere possumus quod possit ratione non uti, et

---

6. For *primi parentis NS* reads *van onze eerste Ouders.*

10–11. *NS* has a different punctuation: *Wie, zeg ik, heeft hem, de voortreffelijkste van
alle verstandelijke schepselen, zo dwaas gemaakt.*

slightest doubt that, if it *were* as much in our power to live by the precept of reason as it is to be led by blind desire, all men *would* be guided by reason, and *would* order their lives wisely; which is very far from being the case. For everyone is captivated by his own pleasure.[1] Nor do theologians dispose of this difficulty by their dogma that the cause of this weakness is the vice or sin which arose in human nature through the fall of our first ancestor. For if even the first man had as much power to stand as to fall, if his mind was sound and his nature uncorrupted, how, with his knowledge and foresight, could he possibly have fallen? Their answer is that he was deceived by the Devil.[2] Then who was it that deceived the Devil himself? Who, I ask, made the very foremost of all intelligent creatures so insane that he wished to be greater than God? For surely, if the Devil had a sound mind, he must have been doing all he could to preserve himself and his own being? Again, if the first man himself was sound in mind and master of his own will, how could he possibly have allowed himself to be seduced and tricked? If he had the power to use reason correctly, he could not have been deceived; for he must have done everything in his power to preserve his own being and his own sound mind. Now the hypothesis is that he did have the power to use reason correctly: therefore he must have preserved his sound mind, and could not have been deceived. This, however, is shown to be false by the story told about him; and so we must admit that the first man did not have it in his power to use reason correctly, but was subject to passions like ourselves.

7. But that man, like everything else in nature, does his utmost to preserve his own being, no one can deny. In fact, we could only conceive man to differ from other things in this respect if we assumed that he had free will. Yet the more free we conceived a man to be, the more should we be compelled to maintain that he must necessarily preserve himself and have a sound mind; as everyone who does not confuse freedom with chance will readily grant me. For freedom is virtue or perfection: and so nothing that betokens weakness in a man can be put down to his freedom.[3] In consequence, it is quite impossible to call a man free because he can fail to exist, or fail to use reason; he can be called free only in so far as he has the power to exist and act in accordance with the laws of human nature.[4] So the more free we conceive a man to be, the less we can say that he can fail to use reason, and choose

---

[1] Virgil, *Eclogues* ii, 65 (quoted also in *TT-P* xvi, p. 131).
[2] Spinoza has no need of this hypothesis: see *KV* ii, 25.
[3] See *E* iv, 66 Sch.   [4] *E* iv, 24.

mala prae bonis eligere; et ideo quod Deus, qui absolute liber existit, intelligit, et operatur, necessario etiam, nempe ex suae naturae necessitate, existit, intelligit, et operatur. Nam non dubium est quin Deus eadem qua existit libertate operetur: ut igitur ex ipsius naturae necessi-
5 tate existit, ex ipsius etiam naturae necessitate agit, hoc est, libere absolute agit.

8. Concludimus itaque in potestate uniuscujusque hominis non esse ratione semper uti et in summo humanae libertatis fastigio esse; et tamen unumquemque semper quantum in se est conari suum esse con-
10 servare, et (quia unusquisque tantum juris habet quantum potentia valet) quicquid unusquisque, sive sapiens sive ignarus, conatur et agit, id summo naturae jure conari et agere. Ex quibus sequitur jus et institutum naturae, sub quo omnes nascuntur homines et maxima ex parte vivunt, nihil nisi quod nemo cupit et quod nemo potest prohibere; non
15 contentiones, non odia, non iram, non dolos, nec absolute aliquid quod appetitus suadet aversari. Nec mirum; nam natura non legibus humanae rationis, quae non nisi hominum verum utile et conservationem intendunt, continetur, sed infinitis aliis quae totius naturae, cujus homo particula est, aeternum ordinem respiciunt; ex cujus sola necessitate
20 omnia individua certo modo determinantur ad existendum et operandum. Quicquid ergo nobis in natura ridiculum, absurdum, aut malum videtur, id inde est quod res tantum ex parte novimus, totiusque naturae ordinem et cohaerentiam maxima ex parte ignoramus, et quod omnia ex praescripto nostrae rationis ut dirigerentur volumus: cum tamen id
25 quod ratio malum esse dictat non malum sit respectu ordinis et legum universae naturae, sed tantum solius nostrae naturae legum respectu.

9. Praeterea sequitur unumquemque tamdiu alterius esse juris, quamdiu sub alterius potestate est, et eatenus sui juris, quatenus vim omnem repellere, damnumque sibi illatum ex sui animi sententia vin-
30 dicare, et absolute, quatenus ex suo ingenio vivere potest.

10. Is alterum sub potestate habet, quem ligatum tenet; vel cui arma et media sese defendendi aut evadendi ademit; vel cui metum

---

1. *OP et ideo Deus*; *NS Dieshalven God.* But Spinoza always argues from God to man, never from man to God.

12 ff. The passage from *Ex quibus* to the end of the Section is repeated practically word for word from *TT-P* xvi, pp. 126–8.   18. *NS door ontellijke andere dingen.*

30. *NS en volstrektelijk naar zijn zinnelijkheit leven.*

31–32. *NS of die hy van de wapenen, om zich te verdedigen . . . heeft berooft.*

evil in preference to good; and this because God, who exists, understands, and acts with complete freedom, also exists, understands, and acts by necessity; i.e. by the necessity of his own nature. For there is no doubt that God acts with the same freedom with which he exists: therefore, just as he exists by the necessity of his own nature, so he also acts by the necessity of his own nature, i.e. with complete freedom.[1]

8. I conclude, then, that it is not in a man's power to use reason always and to be always at the peak of human freedom; yet that he always does his best to preserve his own being, and, whether enlightened or unenlightened, attempts and does by the sovereign right of nature everything he attempts and does;[2] since he has as much right as he has power and strength. It follows that the right and law of nature, under which all men are born and for the most part live, forbids nothing but what nobody desires and nobody can do: it forbids neither strife, nor hatred, nor anger, nor deceit; in short, it is opposed to nothing that appetite can suggest. Nor is this surprising; for nature is not bounded by the laws of human reason, which aim only at men's true interest and preservation, but by other laws of infinite scope governing the eternal order of the whole of nature, in which man is a tiny part; and it is by the necessity of this order alone that all individual things are determined to exist and act in a definite way. Hence if anything in nature seems to us ridiculous, absurd, or bad, this is because we know things only in part, being almost entirely ignorant of how they are linked together in the universal system of nature;[3] and because we want everything to be directed in accordance with the precept of our own reason. Yet what reason declares to be bad is not bad in relation to the order and laws of nature as a whole, but only in relation to the laws of our nature in particular.

9. It also follows that one individual is subject to the right of another, or dependent upon him, for as long as he is subject to the other's power; and possessed of his own right, or free, in so far as he can repel all force, take what vengeance he pleases for harm done him, and, to speak generally, live as his own nature and judgement dictate.

10. One man has another in his power when he holds him in bonds; when he has disarmed him and deprived him of the means of self-defence or escape; when he has inspired him with fear; or when he has

---

[1] *E* i, Def. 7.

[2] But the enlightened man acts by the right of his own nature alone; as Spinoza says below, he is *omnino sui juris*.

[3] *T T-P* iv, pp. 67–69, and xvi, p. 127; *TP* ii, 22, p. 281; *Epp.* xxx and xxxii.

injecit; vel quem sibi beneficio ita devinxit ut ei potius quam sibi morem gerere, et potius ex ipsius quam ex sui animi sententia vivere velit. Qui primo vel secundo modo alterum in potestate habet, ejus tantum corpus, non mentem, tenet; tertio autem vel quarto tam ipsius mentem quam corpus sui juris fecit, sed non nisi durante metu vel spe; hac vero aut illo adempto manet alter sui juris.

11. Judicandi facultas eatenus etiam alterius juris esse potest, quatenus mens potest ab altero decipi: ex quo sequitur mentem eatenus sui juris omnino esse, quatenus recte uti potest ratione. Imo quia humana potentia non tam ex corporis robore quam ex mentis fortitudine aestimanda est, hinc sequitur illos maxime sui juris esse qui maxime ratione pollent, quique maxime eadem ducuntur. Atque adeo hominem eatenus liberum omnino voco, quatenus ratione ducitur, quia eatenus ex causis quae per solam ejus naturam possunt adaequate intelligi ad agendum determinatur, tametsi ex iis necessario ad agendum determinetur. Nam libertas (ut Art. 7 hujus Cap. ostendimus) agendi necessitatem non tollit, sed ponit.

12. Fides alicui data, qua aliquis solis verbis pollicitus est se hoc aut illud facturum quod pro suo jure omittere poterat, vel contra, tamdiu rata manet, quamdiu ejus qui fidem dedit non mutatur voluntas. Nam qui potestatem habet solvendi fidem, is revera suo jure non cessit, sed verba tantum dedit. Si igitur ipse, qui naturae jure sui judex est, judicaverit, seu recte seu prave (nam errare humanum est), ex fide data plus damni quam utilitatis sequi, ex suae mentis sententia fidem solvendam esse censet, et naturae jure (per Art. 9 hujus Cap.) eandem solvet.

13. Si duo simul conveniant et vires jungant, plus simul possunt, et consequenter plus juris in naturam simul habent, quam uterque solus; et quo plures necessitudines sic junxerint suas, eo omnes simul plus juris habebunt.

14. Quatenus homines ira, invidia, aut aliquo odii affectu conflictantur, eatenus diverse trahuntur et invicem contrarii sunt, et propterea eo plus timendi quo plus possunt, magisque callidi et astuti sunt, quam

---

1. *NS heeft . . . verwonnen,* i.e. *devicit.*

15–16. *tametsi . . . determinetur* not in *NS.*

21. *NS om de belofte te voldoen.* Perhaps *niet* has fallen out of the text: cf. the note on p. 298, l. 3.

22. *NS die . . . zijns zelfs recht is,* i.e. *sui juris.*

25. *NS zo ontslaat hy zich daar af,* i.e. *solvit.*

bound him so closely by a service that he would rather please his benefactor than himself, and rather be guided by his benefactor's judgement than by his own. The man who has another in his power in the first or second way holds his body only, not his mind; whereas he who controls another in the third or fourth way has made the mind as well as the body of the other subject to his right; but only while the fear or hope remains. Once the one or the other has been removed, the second man is left in possession of his own right.

11. One man's power of judgement can be subject to the right of a second in another way: the first man may be the dupe of the second.[1] This means that the mind is fully possessed of its own right, or completely free, in so far as it can use reason correctly. Indeed, since human power must be judged by strength of mind rather than by vigour of body, it means that those whose reason is most powerful, and who are most guided thereby, are also most fully possessed of their own right. And this is why I call a man completely free in so far as he is guided by reason, for then he is determined to action by causes which can be understood adequately through his own nature alone.[2] But he is necessarily determined to action by them; for freedom (as I have shown in Section 7 of this Chapter) does not remove the necessity of acting, but imposes it.

12. When a man has given a pledge to somebody, and made a purely verbal promise to do something or other which he had the right to refrain from doing, or vice versa, his pledge remains valid only as long as his will does not change. For a man who has the power to break his pledge has not really surrendered his right, but has given words only. Thus he is still his own judge by the right of nature; so if he judges that his pledge is causing him more loss than gain—and it makes no difference whether he judges truly or falsely, for to err is human— then, since it is the verdict of his own judgement that he should break it, he will break it by the right of nature (Section 9 of this Chapter).[3]

13. If two men unite and join forces, then together they have more power, and consequently more right against other things in nature, than either alone; and the more there be that unite in this way, the more right will they collectively possess.

14. In so far as men are tormented by anger, envy, or any passion involving hatred, they are divided and at odds with one another; and are the more to be feared because they are more powerful, more cunning

---

[1] *TT-P* xx, p. 227.   [2] *E* iv, App. 2.
[3] *TT-P* xvi, pp. 129-31.

reliqua animalia. Et quia homines ut plurimum (ut in Art. 5 praec.
Cap. diximus) his affectibus natura sunt obnoxii, sunt ergo homines ex
natura hostes. Nam is mihi maximus hostis qui mihi maxime timendus,
et a quo mihi maxime cavendum est.

5   15. Cum autem (per Art. 9 hujus Cap.) in statu naturali tamdiu
unusquisque sui juris sit, quamdiu sibi cavere potest ne ab alio opprimatur, et unus solus frustra ab omnibus sibi cavere conetur, hinc
sequitur, quamdiu jus humanum naturale uniuscujusque potentia
determinatur, et uniuscujusque est, tamdiu nullum esse, sed magis
10 opinione quam re constare, quandoquidem nulla ejus obtinendi est
securitas. Et certum est unumquemque tanto minus posse, et consequenter tanto minus juris habere, quanto majorem timendi causam
habet. His accedit quod homines vix absque mutuo auxilio vitam sus-
tentare et mentem colere possint. Atque adeo concludimus jus naturae
15 quod humani generis proprium est vix posse concipi nisi ubi homines
jura habent communia, qui simul terras quas habitare et colere possunt
sibi vindicare, seseque munire, vimque omnem repellere, et ex communi
omnium sententia vivere possunt. Nam (per Art. 13 hujus Cap.) quo
plures in unum sic conveniunt, eo omnes simul plus juris habent; et si
20 Scholastici hac de causa, quod scilicet homines in statu naturali vix sui
juris esse possunt, velint hominem animal sociale dicere, nihil habeo
quod ipsis contradicam.

16. Ubi homines jura communia habent, omnesque una veluti
mente ducuntur, certum est (per Art. 13 hujus Cap.) eorum unum-
25 quemque tanto minus habere juris quanto reliqui simul ipso potentiores
sunt, hoc est, illum revera jus nullum in naturam habere praeter id quod
ipsi commune concedit jus; caeterum quicquid ex communi consensu
ipsi imperatur teneri exequi, vel (per Art. 4 hujus Cap.) jure ad id cogi.

17. Hoc jus, quod multitudinis potentia definitur, imperium appellari solet. Atque hoc is absolute tenet qui curam reipublicae ex

27. *OP concedit jus. Caeterum* . . .; *NS toestaat: en voorts* . . .; *L concedit jus, caeterum* . . .

and astute, than other creatures.[1] But men are by nature subject to these passions in the highest degree (as I said in Section 5 of the previous Chapter); so men are by nature enemies. For he is my greatest enemy whom I have most need to fear, and against whom I have most need to guard myself.

15. Now (by Section 9 of this Chapter) a man in the state of nature is possessed of his own right, or free, only as long as he can protect himself from being subjugated by others; and his own unaided power is insufficient to protect him against all. Hence human natural right or freedom is a nonentity as long as it is an individual possession determined by individual power; it exists in imagination rather than in fact, since there is no certainty of making it good. Nor can it be disputed that the more cause for fear an individual has, the less power he has, and in consequence the less right he has. Besides, it is hardly possible for men to maintain life and cultivate the mind without mutual help.[2] I therefore conclude that the right of nature peculiar to human beings can scarcely be conceived save where men hold rights as a body, and thus have the power to defend their possession of territories which they can inhabit and cultivate, to protect themselves, to repel all force, and to live in accordance with the common judgement of all. For (by Section 13 of this Chapter) the more men there be that unite in this way, the more right they collectively possess; and if it is because men in the state of nature can hardly be possessed of their own right that the Schoolmen wish to call man a social animal, I have nothing to say against them.[3]

16. Where men hold rights as a body, and are all guided as if by one mind, then, of course, (by Section 13 of this Chapter) each of them has the less right the more the rest together exceed him in power; that is, his only real right against other things in nature is what the corporate right allows him. In other matters he must carry out every command laid upon him by the common decision; or (by Section 4 of this Chapter) be compelled to do so by right.

17. This corporate right, which is defined by the power of a people, is generally called sovereignty, and is entirely vested in those who by

---

[1] *E* iv, App. 10.

[2] Although man acts *summo naturae jure* in the state of nature he can scarcely be said to be *sui juris*. Even if a strong and cunning individual evades control by others, and is thus *sui juris* as the term is defined in Section 9, he is not *omnino sui juris* as defined in Section 11, since his conduct is largely determined by fear of his fellow-men. Thus a life guided by reason, and therefore characteristically human (*TP* v, 5, p. 311), is possible only in a state. The state of nature, conceived by Hobbes as a state of human freedom, is the negation of human freedom in Spinoza's sense of the term.

[3] *E* iv, 35 Sch.

communi consensu habet, nempe jura statuendi, interpretandi, et abolendi, urbes muniendi, de bello et pace decernendi, etc. Quod si haec cura ad concilium pertineat quod ex communi multitudine componitur, tum imperium democratia appellatur; si autem ex quibusdam tantum
5 selectis, aristocratia; et si denique reipublicae cura et consequenter imperium penes unum sit, tum monarchia appellatur.

18. Ex his quae in hoc Capite ostendimus perspicuum nobis fit in statu naturali non dari peccatum; vel, si quis peccat, is sibi, non alteri peccat: quandoquidem nemo jure naturae alteri, nisi velit, morem
10 gerere tenetur, nec aliquid bonum aut malum habere, nisi quod ipse ex suo ingenio bonum aut malum esse decernit; et nihil absolute naturae jure prohibetur, nisi quod nemo potest. Vid. Art. 5 et 8 hujus Cap. At peccatum actio est quae jure fieri nequit. Quod si homines ex naturae instituto tenerentur ratione duci, tum omnes necessario ratione duce-
15 rentur. Nam naturae instituta Dei instituta sunt (per Art. 2 et 3 hujus Cap.), quae Deus eadem qua existit libertate instituit, quaeque adeo ex naturae divinae necessitate consequuntur (vide Art. 7 hujus Cap.), et consequenter aeterna sunt, nec violari possunt. Sed homines maxime appetitu sine ratione ducuntur, nec tamen naturae ordinem perturbant,
20 sed necessario sequuntur; ac proinde ignarus et animo impotens non magis ex naturae jure tenetur vitam sapienter instituere quam aeger tenetur sano corpore esse.

19. Peccatum itaque non nisi in imperio concipi potest, ubi scilicet quid bonum et quid malum sit ex communi totius imperii jure decer-
25 nitur, et ubi nemo (per Art. 16 hujus Cap.) jure quicquam agit, nisi quod ex communi decreto vel consensu agit. Id enim (ut in praec. Art. diximus) peccatum est quod jure fieri nequit, sive quod jure prohibetur; obsequium autem est constans voluntas id exequendi quod jure bonum est, et ex communi decreto fieri debet.

30 20. Solemus tamen id etiam peccatum appellare quod contra sanae rationis dictamen fit, et obsequium constantem voluntatem moderandi appetitus ex rationis praescripto; quod omnino probarem si humana libertas in appetitus licentia, et servitus in rationis imperio consisteret.

13–15. *NS indien de menschen* ... *gehouden zijn* ... *geleid te worden, zo zullen zy* ... *geleid worden*, i.e. *tenentur* ... *ducentur*.

20. *NS een achteloze*, glossed *ignavus. G* illustrates the corruption by reference to *E* iv, 70, where the Dutch translator has made the same mistake.

25. *OP Art. 6*, corrected to *Art. 16* in the list of Errata; *NS het zestiende Lid.*

common consent manage the affairs of state, i.e. who make, interpret, and repeal laws, fortify cities, take decisions about war and peace, and so on. If such functions belong to a general assembly of the people, then the state is called a democracy; if to a council composed of certain persons only, who have been chosen as members, it is called an aristocracy; and if, finally, the management of state affairs, and consequently the sovereignty, is vested in a single man, then it is called a monarchy.

18. What I have proved in this Chapter makes it clear that there is no sin in the state of nature;[1] or rather, that if anyone sins, it is against himself, and not against others.[2] For the law of nature obliges nobody to do the will of another unless he so desires; it obliges nobody to count anything good or bad save what he himself decides to be such in accordance with his own nature and judgement; and it forbids absolutely nothing that is within human power. See Sections 5 and 8 of this Chapter. But sin is action contrary to law. If the law of nature bound men to be guided by reason, they would all necessarily be guided by reason; for the laws of nature are the laws of God (by Sections 2 and 3 of this Chapter), established by God with the same freedom wherewith he exists; which means that they follow from the necessity of the divine nature (see Section 7 of this Chapter), and are thus eternal and inviolable. But in fact men are mainly guided by irrational appetite; yet they do not violate the order of nature, but necessarily conform to it. Hence the law of nature no more obliges an unenlightened and weak-minded man to order his life wisely than it obliges a sick man to have a healthy body.[3]

19. It follows that sin is inconceivable except in a state, where what is good and bad is determined by civil laws which are common to all, and where (by Section 16 of this Chapter) nobody has a right to do anything but what he does by the common decree or consent. For (as I said in the previous Section) sin is conduct contrary to law, or forbidden by law; while obedience is the steadfast will to do what the law declares to be good, and the common decree requires.

20. However, in common usage the word 'sin' is also applied to transgression of the dictate of sound reason, and the word 'obedience' to the steadfast will to control the appetites as reason prescribes. Now of this I should entirely approve if human freedom consisted in freedom of appetite, and human servitude in the rule of reason. But since the

---

[1] *TT-P* xvi, p. 143; *E* iv, 37 Sch. 2.
[2] For the sense in which a man can sin against himself see *TP* iv, 4–5, pp. 301–5.
[3] *TT-P* xvi, p. 127.

Sed quia humana libertas eo major est, quo homo magis ratione duci et appetitus moderari potest, non possumus, nisi admodum improprie, vitam rationalem vocare obsequium, et peccatum id quod revera mentis impotentia, non autem contra se ipsam licentia est, et per quod homo
5 servus potius quam liber potest dici. Vide Art. 7 et 11 hujus Cap.

21. Verumenimvero, quia ratio pietatem exercere, et animo tranquillo et bono esse docet, quod non nisi in imperio fieri potest, et praeterea, quia fieri nequit ut multitudo una veluti mente ducatur, sicut in imperio requiritur, nisi jura habeat quae ex rationis praescripto instituta
10 sint, non ergo adeo improprie homines qui in imperio vivere consueverunt id peccatum vocant quod contra rationis dictamen fit, quandoquidem optimi imperii jura ex rationis dictamine institui debent. Cur autem dixerim (Art. 18 hujus Cap.) hominem in statu naturali sibi peccare, si quid peccat, de hoc vide Cap. 4 Art. 4 et 5, ubi ostenditur quo
15 sensu dicere possumus eum qui imperium tenet, et jure naturae potitur, legibus adstrictum esse et peccare posse.

22. Ad religionem quod attinet, certum etiam est hominem eo magis esse liberum, et sibi maxime obsequentem, quo Deum magis amat et animo magis integro colit. Verum quatenus non ad naturae ordinem,
20 quem ignoramus, sed ad sola rationis dictamina quae religionem concernunt attendimus, et simul consideramus eadem nobis a Deo, quasi in nobis ipsis loquente, revelari, vel etiam haec eadem Prophetis veluti jura fuisse revelata, eatenus, more humano loquendo, dicimus hominem Deo obsequi qui ipsum integro animo amat, et contra peccare qui caeca
25 cupiditate ducitur; sed interim memores esse debemus quod in Dei potestate sumus sicut lutum in potestate figuli, qui ex eadem massa alia vasa ad decus, alia ad dedecus facit; atque adeo quod homo contra haec Dei decreta quidem, quatenus in nostra vel in Prophetarum mente tanquam jura inscripta fuerunt, at non contra aeternum Dei decretum

---

1. *OP homo; NS zy.*

12. *OP* reads (*vide Art. 18 hujus Cap.*) between *jura* and *ex rationis dictamine. NS* has the same reference. But the laws of a good state are first mentioned in this section. I suppose that the reference stood between two lines in Spinoza's MS., and was wrongly incorporated in the upper as well as in the lower.

15. *OP possumus; B possimus.* But cf. p. 304, l. 3, *Videmus itaque quo sensu dicere possumus,* where *B* retains the original text.

18–19. *NS en oprechter van gemoed is.*

22–23. *NS of ook gelijk rechten door de Profeten geöpenbaart zijn.*

more man can be guided by reason and control his appetites, the greater human freedom is, we cannot without great impropriety call the rational life 'obedience',[1] and apply the word 'sin' to something which, far from involving a freedom of the mind to transgress its own dictates, is really a lack of mental power,[2] and gives us more warrant to call someone a slave than to call him a free man. See Sections 7 and 11 of this Chapter.

21. On the other hand, since reason teaches men to practise morality, and to be of a tranquil and friendly disposition, which is possible only in a state; and since, moreover, it is impossible for a people to be guided as if by one mind, as is required in a state, unless the state has laws that have been established in conformity with the precept of reason; men who are accustomed to living in a state commit no great impropriety in applying the word 'sin' to transgression of the dictate of reason, since in fact the laws of a good state must be based on the dictate of reason. As for my remark (in Section 18 of this Chapter) that a man in the state of nature sins against himself if he sins at all, the explanation of this will be found in Chapter 4 Sections 4 and 5, where it is shown in what sense we can say that the man who holds sovereign power, and is possessed of the right of nature, is bound by laws and capable of doing wrong.

22. Similarly, as regards religion, the more a man loves God, and the sounder the mind with which he worships him, the more free he is, and the more completely he obeys himself.[3] No doubt when we disregard the unknown ways in which things are connected in the system of nature, and, confining our attention to the dictates of reason which concern religion, regard them as revealed to us by the voice of God in our own hearts, or, indeed, as revealed to the Prophets in the form of laws; then, speaking in the manner of men, we say that a man 'obeys' God when he loves him with a sound mind, and 'sins' when he is led by blind desire.[4] But we must always remember that we are in the power of God like clay in the power of the potter, who from the same lump makes some vessels for honourable, and others for dishonourable use;[5] and hence that, although a man *can* transgress the decrees of God which have been written as laws upon *our* minds or the minds of the Prophets, he can in no wise transgress the eternal decree of God which

---

[1] *TT-P*, n. 34, pp. 247–9.   [2] *Ep.* xix.

[3] Just as the life of reason is not obedience, so the life of true religion (as opposed to that of faith) is not obedience either; and consequently failure to live these lives is not disobedience.

[4] Hobbes holds that men can sin against God in the state of nature (*De Cive* i, 10, n.).

[5] *Romans* 9, 21, quoted also in *TT-P*, n. 34, p. 247; *Epp.* lxxv and lxxviii.

quod in universa natura inscriptum est, quodque totius naturae ordinem respicit, quicquam agere potest.

23. Ut itaque peccatum et obsequium stricte sumptum, sic etiam justitia et injustitia non nisi in imperio possunt concipi. Nam nihil in natura datur quod jure posset dici hujus esse et non alterius; sed omnia omnium sunt, qui scilicet potestatem habent sibi eadem vindicandi. At in imperio, ubi communi jure decernitur quid hujus quidque illius sit, ille justus vocatur, cui constans est voluntas tribuendi unicuique suum; injustus autem, qui contra conatur id quod alterius est suum facere.

24. Caeterum laudem et vituperium affectus esse laetitiae et tristitiae, quos comitatur idea virtutis aut impotentiae humanae tanquam causa, explicuimus in nostra Ethica.

6. *Gf vindicandi*; *OP vendicandi.*

is written upon universal nature, and which has regard to the system of nature as a whole.[1]

23. Like sin and obedience in the strict sense, justice and injustice are inconceivable except in a state. For there is nothing in nature which could rightly be said to belong to one man and not to another; all things belong to all, to all, that is, who have the power to appropriate them for themselves.[2] But in a state, where the property of each individual is determined by common laws, a man is called just if he has a steadfast will to give everyone his own; unjust if he seeks to appropriate what belongs to another.

24. As for praise and blame, I have explained in my Ethics that they are feelings of joy and sorrow accompanied by the idea of human virtue or weakness as a cause.[3]

---

[1] See *TT-P*, n. 34, pp. 247–9. Men cannot break God's laws, and therefore cannot sin against God; God, in fact, is not a king who lays down laws which men can break (*TT-P* iv, pp. 77–83; *KV* ii, 24; *E* ii, 3 Sch.).

[2] *E* iv, 37 Sch. 2.

[3] The definitions given in *E* iii, 29 Sch. are different.

1. Imperii cujuscunque status dicitur civilis; imperii autem integrum corpus civitas appellatur, et communia imperii negotia, quae ab ejus qui imperium tenet directione pendent, respublica. Deinde homines quatenus ex jure civili omnibus civitatis commodis gaudent cives appel-
5 lamus, et subditos quatenus civitatis institutis seu legibus parere tenentur. Denique status civilis tria dari genera, nempe democraticum, aristocraticum, et monarchicum, in Art. 17 Cap. praeced. diximus. Jam antequam de unoquoque seorsim agere incipiam, illa prius demonstrabo quae ad statum civilem in genere pertinent; quorum ante omnia
10 considerandum venit summum civitatis seu summarum potestatum jus.

2. Ex Art. 15 praeced. Cap. patet imperii seu summarum potestatum jus nihil esse praeter ipsum naturae jus, quod potentia, non quidem uniuscujusque, sed multitudinis quae una veluti mente ducitur determinatur; hoc est, quod ut unusquisque in statu naturali, sic etiam totius
15 imperii corpus et mens tantum juris habet quantum potentia valet; atque adeo unusquisque civis seu subditus tanto minus juris habet, quanto ipsa civitas ipso potentior est (vid. Art. 16 praeced. Cap.), et consequenter unusquisque civis nihil jure agit nec habet praeter id quod communi civitatis decreto defendere potest.

20 3. Si civitas alicui concedat jus, et consequenter potestatem (nam alias per Art. 12 praeced. Cap. verba tantum dedit) vivendi ex suo ingenio, eo ipso suo jure cedit, et in eum transfert cui talem potestatem dedit. Si autem duobus aut pluribus hanc potestatem dedit, ut scilicet unusquisque ex suo ingenio vivat, eo ipso imperium divisit; et si deni-
25 que unicuique civium hanc eandem potestatem dedit, eo ipso sese destruxit, nec manet amplius civitas, sed redeunt omnia ad statum naturalem; quae omnia ex praecedentibus manifestissima fiunt. Atque adeo sequitur nulla ratione posse concipi quod unicuique civi ex civitatis instituto liceat ex suo ingenio vivere, et consequenter hoc jus

6. *OP dari*, altered to *dantur* in the list of Errata. But this change makes it necessary to insert *ut* before *in Art. 17*. The reading of *NS, gelijk wy . . . getoont hebben*, cannot be regarded as supporting these alterations, since it is not uncommon for the Dutch translator to render an accusative and infinitive construction in this way. Cf. p. 394, l. 8, where *quod neminem ignorare credo* is rendered by *daar af, gelijk ik geloof, niemant onkundig is.*

14. *Gf quod ut unusquisque*; *OP quod unusquisque*. *NS dat is, gelijk yder in de naturelijke stant, zo . . . ook.* Hence *L ut unusquisque* (omitting *quod*). *G quod sicuti unusquisque*, on the analogy of the passage on p. 288, ll. 23–26.

14–15. *NS het geheel lighaam, en de ziel van de Heerschappy*, i.e. *totum.*

17–18. *NS en by gevolg heeft yder Burger geen ander recht.*

CHAPTER III

1. The order maintained by any state is called political. When considered as a complete body, a state is called a commonwealth; and its common activities, which are directed by the holder of sovereignty, are called affairs of state. Again, I call men citizens in so far as they enjoy all the advantages of the commonwealth by civil right; and subjects in so far as they are bound to obey the ordinances or laws of the commonwealth. Finally, as I said in Section 17 of the previous Chapter, there are three kinds of political order, viz. democracy, aristocracy, and monarchy. But before starting to deal with each separately I shall establish the essential features of political order in general; and of these the supreme right of the commonwealth or of the sovereign must be considered first.

2. It is clear from Section 15 of the previous Chapter that the right of the state or of the sovereign is nothing but the right of nature itself, and as such determined by power; not however by the power of a single individual, but by that of a people which is guided as if by one mind. In other words, it is clear that what is true of each man in the state of nature is true likewise of the body and mind of the whole state—it has as much right as it has power and strength. Hence the more the commonwealth exceeds a citizen or subject in power, the less right he has[1] (see Section 16 of the previous Chapter); and consequently a citizen does nothing and possesses nothing by right unless he can defend it by the common decree of the commonwealth.

3. If a commonwealth gives anyone the right to live as his own judgement dictates, and consequently the power to do so (for otherwise, by Section 12 of the previous Chapter, it gives words only), it thereby surrenders its own right, and vests it in the man to whom it gives such power. If it gives this power to two men or more, and allows each of them to live in accordance with his own judgement, it thereby divides the sovereignty; and if, finally, it gives this same power to each of its citizens, it thereby destroys itself; it ceases to be a commonwealth, and everything reverts to the state of nature. All this emerges very clearly from what has been said above. It is therefore quite inconceivable that every citizen should be allowed by a law of the commonwealth to live as his own judgement dictates; accordingly, the natural

---

[1] *Ep.* l. Cf. Rousseau, *Social Contract* iii, 1.

naturale, quod scilicet unusquisque sui judex est, in statu civili necessario cessat. Dico expresse *ex civitatis instituto*; nam jus naturae uniuscujusque (si recte rem perpendamus) in statu civili non cessat. Homo
namque tam in statu naturali quam civili ex legibus suae naturae agit
5 suaeque utilitati consulit. Homo, inquam, in utroque statu spe aut metu
ducitur ad hoc aut illud agendum vel omittendum; sed praecipua inter
utrumque statum differentia est, quod in statu civili omnes eadem
metuant, et omnibus una eademque securitatis sit causa et vivendi ratio;
quod sane judicandi facultatem uniuscujusque non tollit. Qui enim
10 omnibus civitatis mandatis obtemperare constituit, sive ejus potentiam
metuit, vel quia tranquillitatem amat, is profecto suae securitati suaeque
utilitati ex suo ingenio consulit.

4. Praeterea concipere etiam non possumus quod unicuique civi
liceat civitatis decreta seu jura interpretari. Nam si hoc unicuique
15 liceret, eo ipso sui judex esset; quandoquidem unusquisque facta sua
specie juris nullo negotio excusare seu adornare posset, et consequenter
ex suo ingenio vitam institueret; quod (per Art. praeced.) est absurdum.

5. Videmus itaque unumquemque civem non sui sed civitatis juris
esse, cujus omnia mandata tenetur exequi, nec ullum habere jus decer-
20 nendi quid aequum, quid iniquum, quid pium, quidve impium sit: sed
contra, quia imperii corpus una veluti mente duci debet, et consequenter civitatis voluntas pro omnium voluntate habenda est, id quod
civitas justum et bonum esse decernit tanquam ab unoquoque decretum
esse censendum est; atque adeo, quamvis subditus civitatis decreta
25 iniqua esse censeat, tenetur nihilominus eadem exequi.

6. At objici potest: an non contra rationis dictamen est se alterius
judicio omnino subjicere? Et consequenter, an status civilis rationi non

---

10–11. *NS of om dat hy der zelfder macht vreest*, which suggests *sive quod* or *sive quia*.
22. *NS voor die van alle in 't gemeen*, i.e. *pro communi omnium voluntate*.

right of every man to be his own judge necessarily ceases in the political order. I say 'by a law of the commonwealth' expressly;[1] for, as proper consideration of the point will show, the individual's right of nature does not cease in the political order. The fact is that man acts in accordance with the laws of his own nature and pursues his own advantage in both the natural and the political order. In both conditions, I say, man is led by hope or fear either to do or to refrain from doing one thing or another. The chief difference between the two is that in the political order all fear the same things, and all have one and the same source of security, one and the same mode of life; but this, of course, does not deprive the individual of his power of judgement. For the man who decides to obey all the commands of the commonwealth, whether through fear of its power, or because he loves tranquillity, is certainly pursuing his own security and advantage in accordance with his own judgement.

4. It is also inconceivable that every citizen should be permitted to interpret the commonwealth's decrees or laws. For if everyone were permitted to do this, he would thereby be his own judge, since he could easily excuse or adorn his actions with a show of legality. He would thus arrange his life in accordance with his own judgement; and this (by the previous Section) is absurd.

5. It is clear, then, that a citizen is not in possession of his own right, but is subject to the right of the commonwealth, and is bound to carry out every one of its commands; clear also that he has no right to decide what is fair or unfair, moral or immoral.[2] On the contrary, since the body of the state must be guided as if by one mind,[3] and, in consequence, the will of the commonwealth be taken for the will of all, what the commonwealth decides to be just and good must be regarded as having been so decided by every citizen. Thus, no matter how unfair a subject considers the decrees of the commonwealth to be, he is bound to carry them out.

6. It may be objected that it is contrary to the dictate of reason for one man to subject himself entirely to the jurisdiction of another, and that the political order is therefore contrary to reason. This would

---

[1] Spinoza stresses these words because without them the previous sentence is false. We *can* conceive every citizen in a commonwealth being allowed to live as his own judgement dictates: every citizen does in fact live as his own judgement dictates in so far as he obeys the civil laws because he thinks it in his own interest to do so. What *is* inconceivable is a law of the commonwealth exempting citizens from obedience to law.

[2] Hobbes, *De Cive* xii, 1.

[3] Cf. Tacitus, *Annals* I, xii, 4: *unum esse rei publicae corpus atque unius animo regendum.*

repugnat? Ex quo sequeretur statum civilem irrationalem esse, nec posse creari nisi ab hominibus ratione destitutis, at minime ab iis qui ratione ducuntur. Sed quoniam ratio nihil contra naturam docet, non potest ergo sana ratio dictare ut unusquisque sui juris maneat quamdiu
5 homines affectibus sunt obnoxii (per Art. 5 Cap. 1), hoc est, (per Art. 15 praeced. Cap.) ratio hoc posse fieri negat. Adde quod ratio omnino docet pacem quaerere, quae quidem obtineri nequit nisi communia civitatis jura inviolata serventur; atque adeo, quo homo ratione magis ducitur, hoc est (per Art. 11 praeced. Cap.), quo magis liber est, eo
10 constantius civitatis jura servabit, et summae potestatis cujus subditus est mandata exequetur. Ad quod accedit quod status civilis naturaliter instituitur ad metum communem adimendum et communes miserias propellendum, ac proinde id maxime intendit quod unusquisque qui ratione ducitur in statu naturali conaretur; sed frustra (per Art. 15
15 praeced. Cap.). Quapropter si homini qui ratione ducitur id aliquando ex civitatis mandato faciendum est quod rationi repugnare novit, id damnum longe compensatur bono quod ex ipso statu civili haurit: nam rationis etiam lex est ut ex duobus malis minus eligatur. Ac proinde concludere possumus neminem quicquam contra suae rationis prae-
20 scriptum agere quatenus id agit quod jure civitatis faciendum est: quod nobis facilius unusquisque concedet, postquam explicuerimus quo usque civitatis potentia, et consequenter jus, se extendit.

7. Nam considerandum primum venit quod sicuti in statu naturali (per Art. 11 praeced. Cap.) ille homo maxime potens maximeque sui
25 juris est qui ratione ducitur, sic etiam illa civitas maxime erit potens et maxime sui juris quae ratione fundatur et dirigitur. Nam civitatis jus potentia multitudinis quae una veluti mente ducitur determinatur. At haec animorum unio concipi nulla ratione posset, nisi civitas id ipsum maxime intendat quod sana ratio omnibus hominibus utile esse
30 docet.

8. Secundo venit etiam considerandum quod subditi eatenus non sui sed civitatis juris sint, quatenus ejus potentiam seu minas metuunt, vel quatenus statum civilem amant (per Art. 10 praeced. Cap.). Ex quo sequitur quod ea omnia ad quae agenda nemo praemiis aut minis induci
35 potest ad jura civitatis non pertineant. Ex. gr. judicandi facultate nemo

---

5–6. *OP (per Art. 15 praeced. Cap.) hoc est, (per Art. 5 Cap. 1)* etc. So *NS.*
28. *Gf At haec; NS En deze vereeniging . . ., i.e. Ac haec; OP Adhaec.*

mean that the political order was irrational, and could be instituted only by men bereft of reason, not by men who were guided by it. However, since reason teaches nothing contrary to nature, it follows that, as long as men are subject to passions (by Section 5, Chapter 1), sound reason cannot dictate that everyone should retain his own right; i.e. reason says that this is impossible (by Section 15 of the previous Chapter). Secondly, the whole teaching of reason is that men should seek peace. But peace cannot be achieved unless the general laws of the state are kept inviolate; and so the more a man is guided by reason, i.e. (by Section 11 of the previous Chapter) the more free he is, the more stead-fastly will he observe the laws of the state and carry out his sovereign's commands.[1] Finally, the political order is naturally established to remove general fear and to dispel general suffering, and thus its chief aim is one which every rational man would try to promote in the state of nature; though his efforts in that state would be useless (by Section 15 of the previous Chapter). Hence if the rational man has sometimes, by order of the commonwealth, to do what he knows to be opposed to reason, this inconvenience is far outweighed by the advantage which he derives from the actual existence of the political order:[2] reason, we must remember, also bids us choose the lesser evil.[3] We may therefore conclude that no one does anything contrary to the precept of his reason in doing what the law of the commonwealth requires. But everyone will grant this more readily once I have explained how far the power, and consequently the right, of the commonwealth extends.

7. The first point to be considered is this. Just as in the state of nature the man who is guided by reason is most powerful and most fully possessed of his own right (by Section 11 of the previous Chapter), so also the commonwealth which is based on and directed by reason will be most powerful and most fully possessed of its own right. For the right of a commonwealth is determined by the power of a people guided as if by one mind; but this union of minds is quite inconceivable unless the commonwealth does its best to achieve those conditions which sound reason declares to be for the good of all men.

8. In the second place, we must remember that subjects are under the control of the commonwealth, and not possessed of their own right, only in so far as they fear its power or its threats, or in so far as they love the political order (by Section 10 of the previous Chapter). It follows that all actions which no one can be induced to do by rewards or threats fall outside the right of the commonwealth. For example, nobody

---

[1] *TT-P*, n. 33, p. 247.   [2] Hobbes, *De Cive* x, 1.   [3] *E* iv, 65.

cedere potest: quibus enim praemiis aut minis induci potest homo ut credat totum non esse sua parte majus, aut quod Deus non existat, aut quod corpus quod videt finitum ens infinitum esse credat, et absolute ut aliquid contra id quod sentit vel cogitat credat? Sic etiam quibus prae-
5 miis aut minis induci potest homo ut amet quem odit, vel ut odio habeat quem amat? Atque huc etiam illa referenda sunt, a quibus humana natura ita abhorret ut ipsa omni malo pejora habeat, ut quod homo testem contra se agat, ut se cruciet, ut parentes interficiat suos, ut mortem vitare non conetur, et similia, ad quae nemo praemiis nec
10 minis induci potest. Quod si tamen dicere velimus civitatem jus sive potestatem habere talia imperandi, id nullo alio sensu poterimus con- cipere, nisi quo quis diceret hominem jure posse insanire et delirare: quid enim aliud nisi delirium jus illud esset, cui nemo adstrictus esse potest? Atque hic de iis expresse loquor quae juris civitatis esse neque-
15 unt, et a quibus natura humana plerumque abhorret. Nam quod stul- tus aut vesanus nullis praemiis neque minis induci possit ad exequenda mandata, et quod unus aut alter, ex eo quod huic aut illi religioni ad- dictus sit, imperii jura omni malo pejora judicat, jura tamen civitatis irrita non sunt, quandoquidem iisdem plerique cives continentur; ac
20 proinde, quia ii qui nihil timent neque sperant eatenus sui juris sunt (per Art. 10 praeced. Cap.), sunt ergo (per Art. 14 praeced. Cap.) imperii hostes, quos jure cohibere licet.

9. Tertio denique considerandum venit ad civitatis jus ea minus pertinere quae plurimi indignantur. Nam certum est homines naturae
25 ductu in unum conspirare, vel propter communem metum, vel desi- derio damnum aliquod commune ulciscendi; et quia jus civitatis com- muni multitudinis potentia definitur, certum est potentiam civitatis et jus eatenus minui, quatenus ipsa causas praebet ut plures in unum conspirent. Habet certe civitas quaedam sibi metuenda, et sicut

---

1. *NS overgeven*; *B credere*.   18. *Gf judicet.*

can give up his power of judgement;[1] for by what rewards or threats can a man be led to believe that a whole is no greater than its part, or that God does not exist, or that a body which he sees to be finite is an infinite being;[2] and, in general, to believe anything contrary to what he perceives or thinks? Similarly, by what rewards or threats can a man be induced to love someone he hates, or to hate someone he loves? Among such actions we must also include those which are so repugnant to human nature that it considers them worse than any penalty; for example, bearing witness against oneself, torturing oneself, killing one's own parents, making no attempt to avoid death, and things of that sort, which no man can be induced by rewards or threats to do.[3] If we still wish to say that a commonwealth has the right or power to command such actions, we shall find it impossible to conceive of this right in any other sense than that in which it might be said that a man has a right to be a raving lunatic: for what else but raving lunacy would such a right be, when nobody can be bound by it? I am here speaking expressly of those actions which cannot fall under the right of the commonwealth, and which are repugnant to ordinary human nature. No doubt fools and madmen cannot be induced to carry out commands by any reward or threat; no doubt devotion to some religion may lead one or two men to regard obedience to the civil laws as worse than any penalty.[4] But this does not invalidate these laws, since most of the citizens are bound by them. It follows that, since those who have neither hopes nor fears are to that extent in possession of their own right (by Section 10 of the previous Chapter), they are enemies of the state (by Section 14 of the previous Chapter), and the state may restrain them by right.

9. My third and final point is that commands which arouse the indignation of a great number of subjects hardly fall within the right of the commonwealth. It is, of course, natural for men to conspire together, either through common fear, or desire to avenge some common injury; and since the right of a commonwealth is determined by the collective power of a people,[5] the greater the number of subjects who are given cause by a commonwealth to join in conspiracy against it, the more must its power and right be diminished. A commonwealth has certainly dangers to fear, and what is true of each citizen, or of each

[1] *TT-P* vii, p. 109, and xx, p. 229.
[2] *Ep.* lxxiii (the reference to the Incarnation).
[3] Hobbes, *De Cive* ii, 18–19 and vi, 13. But Hobbes does not deny the sovereign the right to command such actions; he merely allows the subject the right to refuse obedience.
[4] Spinoza may be thinking of the Mennonites, who were conscientious objectors.
[5] Hobbes, *De Cive* vi, 18.

unusquisque civis, sive homo in statu naturali, sic civitas eo minus sui juris est, quo majorem timendi causam habet. Atque haec de jure summarum potestatum in subditos: jam antequam de earundem in alios jure agam, solvenda videtur quaestio quae de religione moveri solet.

5   10. Nam objici nobis potest an status civilis, et subditorum obedientia qualem in statu civili requiri ostendimus, non tollat religionem qua Deum colere tenemur. Sed si rem ipsam perpendamus, nihil reperiemus quod possit scrupulum injicere. Mens enim, quatenus ratione utitur, non summarum potestatum sed sui juris est (per Art. 11 Cap.
10 praeced.). Atque adeo vera Dei cognitio et amor nullius imperio subjici potest, ut nec erga proximum charitas (per Art. 8 hujus Cap.); et si praeterea consideremus summum charitatis exercitium esse illud quod ad pacem tuendam et concordiam conciliandam fit, non dubitabimus illum revera suo officio functum esse, qui unicuique tantum auxilii fert
15 quantum jura civitatis, hoc est, concordia et tranquillitas, concedunt. Ad externos cultus quod attinet, certum est illos ad veram Dei cognitionem, et amorem qui ex ea necessario sequitur, nihil prorsus juvare nec nocere posse; atque adeo non tanti faciendi sunt ut propter ipsos pax et tranquillitas publica perturbari mereatur. Caeterum certum est
20 me jure naturae, hoc est (per Art. 3 praec. Cap.) ex divino decreto, non esse religionis vindicem. Nam nulla mihi est, ut olim Christi Discipulis, potestas ejiciendi spiritus immundos et faciendi miracula; quae sane potestas adeo necessaria est ad propagandam religionem in locis ubi interdicta est, ut sine ipsa non tantum oleum et opera, ut ajunt, per-
25 datur, sed plurimae insuper creentur molestiae. Cujus rei funestissima exempla omnia viderunt saecula. Unusquisque igitur, ubicunque sit, Deum potest vera religione colere, sibique prospicere, quod viri privati officium est. Caeterum cura religionis propagandae Deo vel summis potestatibus, quibus solis incumbit reipublicae habere curam,
30 committenda est. Sed ad propositum revertor.

---

6. *OP qualis,* corrected to *qualem* in the list of Errata.

19. *OP merentur,* corrected to *mereatur* in the list of Errata.

21–22. *OP ut olim Christi Discipulis potestas fuit, ejiciendi.* But the order and punctuation are awkward, and *NS* reads *want ik heb niet, gelijk eertijts Christus Leerlingen, de macht.* Hence *L ut olim Christi Discipulis fuit, potestas ejiciendi.* But *fuit* is really superfluous.

man in the state of nature, is true of a commonwealth also; the greater cause for fear it has, the less is it possessed of its own right. So much for the right of sovereigns against subjects. Before dealing with their right against others I had better remove a difficulty which is usually raised concerning religion.

10. The objection is that the political order, and such obedience as I have shown to be required of subjects in that order, does away with religion and our duty to worship God.[1] However, if we consider the actual facts, we shall find nothing which can give rise to any misgiving. For in so far as the mind uses reason, it is not subject to the right of the sovereign, but in possession of its own right (by Section 11 of the previous Chapter). Hence true knowledge and love of God cannot be subject to anyone's command,[2] any more than love of one's neighbour (by Section 8 of this Chapter). And if we also remember that love finds its supreme expression when directed to the preservation of peace and the promotion of concord,[3] we shall have no doubt that a man truly does his duty if he gives everyone as much help as is consistent with the laws of the commonwealth, i.e. with peace and concord. As for outward rites, we may take it as certain that they cannot help or hinder a man at all in reaching true knowledge of God,[4] and the love of him which is its necessary consequence;[5] hence they are not to be esteemed of such importance as to justify a breach of the public peace and quiet. But of course I am not by right of nature, i.e. (by Section 3 of the previous Chapter) by divine decree, a champion of religion. For I have no power, such as once belonged to Christ's Disciples, to cast out unclean spirits and work miracles;[6] and this power is obviously so indispensable for the propagation of a religion in places where it is proscribed, that without it men not only lose their labour, as the saying is, but provoke a host of troubles into the bargain. Of this every age has seen the most melancholy examples. Each man, then, wherever he may be, can worship God with true piety, and take care of himself; and that is the duty of a private individual. The duty of propagating religion should be left to God or to the sovereign, on whom alone the charge of public affairs is laid. But I must return to my subject.

---

[1] *TT-P* xvi, pp. 145–7.

[2] Spinoza, of course, is speaking of 'inward religion' (*TT-P* vii, p. 109, and xix, p. 205); 'outward religion' is under the control of the sovereign (*TT-P* xix, pp. 205–25).

[3] *TT-P* xix, pp. 211–13.   [4] *TT-P* v, p. 99.   [5] *TT-P* n. 34, pp. 247–9.

[6] *TT-P* xix, p. 215. Miracles, in the sense of events contrary to the laws of nature, are rejected by Spinoza (*TT-P* vi), but he would no doubt credit the Apostles with unusual powers.

11. Jure summarum potestatum in cives, et subditorum officio explicato, superest ut earum jus in reliqua consideremus; quod jam ex dictis facile cognoscitur. Nam quandoquidem (per Art. 2 hujus Cap.) jus summae potestatis nihil est praeter ipsum naturae jus, sequitur duo
5 imperia ad invicem sese habere ut duo homines in statu naturali, excepto hoc, quod civitas sibi cavere potest ne ab alia opprimatur, quod homo in statu naturali non potest; nimirum qui quotidie somno, saepe morbo aut animi aegritudine, et tandem senectute gravatur, et praeter haec aliis incommodis est obnoxius a quibus civitas securam se reddere
10 potest.

12. Civitas igitur eatenus sui juris est, quatenus sibi consulere et cavere potest ne ab alia opprimatur (per Art. 9 et 15 praec. Cap.), et (per Art. 10 et 15 praec. Cap.) eatenus alterius juris, quatenus alterius civitatis potentiam timet, vel quatenus ab ea impeditur quo minus id
15 quod vult exequatur, vel denique quatenus ipsius auxilio ad sui conservationem vel incrementum indiget; nam dubitare nequaquam possumus quin, si duae civitates invicem mutuum auxilium praestare volunt, ambae simul plus possint, et consequenter plus juris simul habeant quam alterutra sola. Vid. Art. 13 Cap. praec.

20 13. Haec autem clarius intelligi possunt, si consideremus quod duae civitates natura hostes sunt: homines enim (per Art. 14 praec. Cap.) in statu naturali hostes sunt; qui igitur jus naturae extra civitatem retinent, hostes manent. Si itaque altera civitas alteri bellum inferre et extrema adhibere media velit quo eam sui juris faciat, id ei jure tentare
25 licet, quandoquidem, ut bellum geratur, ei sufficit ejus rei habere voluntatem. At de pace nihil statuere potest nisi connivente alterius civitatis voluntate. Ex quo sequitur jura belli uniuscujusque civitatis esse; pacis autem non unius, sed duarum ad minimum civitatum esse jura, quae propterea confoederatae dicuntur.

30 14. Hoc foedus tamdiu fixum manet, quamdiu causa foederis pangendi, nempe metus damni seu lucri spes, in medio est; hac autem aut illo civitatum alterutri adempto, manet ipsa sui juris (per Art. 10

9. *est obnoxius* not in *NS*.

31–32. *NS Maar als d' oorzaak of het verbont*, wrongly referring *hac* to *causa* and *illo* to *foedus*.

11. Now that I have explained the right of the sovereign over citizens, and the duty of subjects, it remains to consider its right against the rest of the world; and in the light of what I have said above this is easily understood. For since (by Section 2 of this Chapter) the right of the sovereign is simply the right of nature itself, two states are in the same relation to one another as two men in the condition of nature; with this exception, that a commonwealth can guard itself against being subjugated by another, as a man in the state of nature cannot do. For, of course, a man is overcome by sleep every day, is often afflicted by disease of body or mind, and is finally prostrated by old age; in addition, he is subject to other troubles against which a commonwealth can make itself secure.[1]

12. A commonwealth, then, is possessed of its own right in so far as it can guard and protect itself against being subjugated by another (by Sections 9 and 15 of the previous Chapter): and (by Sections 10 and 15 of the previous Chapter) subject to the right of another in so far as it fears the power of the other commonwealth, or is prevented by it from doing what it wants, or, finally, requires the help of the other for its own preservation or growth. For if two commonwealths wish to give each other such mutual help, their combined power, and therefore their combined right, is obviously greater than the power and right of either by itself. See Section 13 of the previous Chapter.

13. All this can be understood more clearly if we reflect that two commonwealths are enemies by nature. For men in the state of nature are enemies (by Section 14 of the previous Chapter); and so all who retain the right of nature, and are not united in a single commonwealth, remain enemies. If, therefore, one commonwealth wishes to attack another and to use extreme measures in order to make it subject, it has the right to attempt this, since all it needs to wage war by right is the will to wage war. But any arrangement for peace requires the voluntary co-operation of the other commonwealth.[2] It follows that, whereas the right to make war belongs to each commonwealth separately, the right to maintain peaceful relations does not belong to one commonwealth, but to two or more commonwealths acting in concert. Such commonwealths are therefore said to be allies.

14. Their treaty of alliance remains in force as long as the motive for making it, i.e. fear of loss or hope of gain, continues to hold good; but as soon as either commonwealth loses its fear or hope it is left in

---

[1] Because of this difference commonwealths have less need to combine than individual men.
[2] It takes one to make a quarrel, but two to make peace.

praec. Cap.), et vinculum quo civitates invicem adstrictae erant sponte solvitur. Ac proinde unicuique civitati jus integrum est solvendi foedus quandocunque vult, nec dici potest quod dolo vel perfidia agat propterea quod fidem solvit simulatque metus vel spei causa sublata est; quia haec 5 conditio unicuique contrahentium aequalis fuit, ut scilicet quae prima extra metum esse posset, sui juris esset, eoque ex sui animi sententia uteretur: et praeterea quia nemo in futurum contrahit nisi positis praecedentibus circumstantiis; his autem mutatis totius status etiam mutatur ratio. Et hac de causa unaquaeque confoederatarum civitatum 10 jus retinet sibi consulendi, et unaquaeque propterea quantum potest conatur extra metum, et consequenter sui juris esse, et impedire quo minus altera potentior evadat. Si quae ergo civitas se deceptam esse queritur, ea sane non confoederatae civitatis fidem, sed suam tantummodo stultitiam damnare potest, quod scilicet salutem suam alteri, qui 15 sui juris, et cui sui imperii salus summa lex est, crediderit.

15. Civitatibus quae una pacem contraxerunt jus competit dirimendi quaestiones quae moveri possunt de pacis conditionibus seu legibus quibus sibi invicem fidem adstrinxerunt, quandoquidem pacis jura non unius civitatis, sed contrahentium simul sunt (per Art. 13 hujus Cap.); 20 quod si de iis convenire inter ipsas non potest, eo ipso ad belli statum redeunt.

16. Quo plures civitates simul pacem contrahunt, eo unaquaeque reliquis minus timenda, sive unicuique minor est potestas bellum inferendi; sed eo magis pacis tenetur conditiones servare, hoc est (per 25 Art. 13 hujus Cap.), eo minus sui juris est, sed eo magis communi foederatorum voluntati sese accommodare tenetur.

17. Caeterum fides, quam sana ratio et religio servandam docet, hic minime tollitur: nam nec ratio nec Scriptura omnem datam fidem servare docet. Cui enim pollicitus sum argentum ex. gr. quod mihi secreto 30 servandum dedit custodire, fidem praestare non teneor simulac noverim, aut scire crediderim, furtum esse quod mihi servandum dedit; sed rectius agam si dem operam ut suis restituatur. Sic etiam, si summa

---

7–8. *NS 't en zy de tegenwoordige omstandigheden plaats behouden,* which suggests *praesentibus circumstantiis.*   13. *Gf queritur*; *NS klaagt*; *OP quaeritur.*

14–15. *NS aan een ander, die zijn eige recht en macht heeft.* But the correct reading may be *quae.*

20. *G possunt.* But in vi, 25 (p. 326, ll. 22–23), *si . . . inter ipsos convenire non poterit,* and vii, 30 (p. 362, l. 2), *non satis inter eosdem conveniebat,* G retains the text of *OP*. *NS* has the personal construction in all three cases.

20–21. *NS zo neemt men daar door terstont zijn toevlucht weêr tot d' oorlog,* i.e. *ad bellum statim redeunt.*

26. *NS der Bontgenoten,* glossed *Confaederati.* Hence *G confoederatorum.* But see p. 45, n. 7.

possession of its own right (by Section 10 of the previous Chapter), and the tie which bound the commonwealths together breaks of its own accord. Hence each of them has full right to break the treaty whenever it wishes, and cannot be accused of treachery or perfidy because it breaks faith as soon as its reason for fear or hope is removed.[1] For in this respect each contracting party was on precisely the same footing; if it could be the first to free itself from fear it would gain possession of its own right, and would use it as its own judgement dictated. Besides, nobody makes a contract for the future except under given conditions; and once these change, the reason for the whole arrangement changes as well. So each of the allied commonwealths retains the right to look after itself, and each accordingly does its utmost not only to gain possession of its own right by freeing itself from fear, but also to prevent the other from becoming too powerful. Hence if a commonwealth complains that it has been duped, it certainly cannot blame the bad faith of its ally, but only its own folly in entrusting its safety to a foreign ruler who is possessed of his own right, and has no higher law than the safety of his own realm.[2]

15. The commonwealths which have made peace with one another have the right to settle disputes which may arise concerning the conditions or rules of peace by which they have sealed their alliance, since rights concerning peace do not belong to one commonwealth only, but to the contracting parties in common (by Section 13 of this Chapter). If, however, it proves impossible for them to agree about such matters, they automatically revert to a state of war.

16. The greater the number of commonwealths that make a treaty of peace together, the less is each to be feared by the rest, or, if you like, the less power each has of making war on the rest; each is more strictly bound to observe the conditions of peace, i.e. (by Section 13 of this Chapter) it is less in possession of its own right, and more obliged to comply with the common will of the allies.

17. I should add that these arguments imply no rejection of the good faith which sound reason and religion enjoin, for neither reason nor Scripture bids men keep every promise they have made. I may, for example, have promised someone to look after money which he has given me to keep for him in secret; but as soon as I know, or think I know, that he has entrusted me with stolen money, I am no longer bound to keep my promise to him, and shall act more honestly if I try to restore the money to its owners. Similarly, if one sovereign has

---

[1] Machiavelli, *Prince* xviii.   [2] *TT-P* xvi, pp. 139–41.

potestas aliquid alteri se facturam promisit, quod postea tempus seu ratio docuit, aut docere videbatur, communi subditorum saluti obesse, fidem sane solvere tenetur. Cum itaque Scriptura non nisi in genere doceat fidem servare, et casus singulares qui excipiendi sunt unius-
5 cujusque judicio relinquat, nihil ergo docet quod iis quae modo ostendimus repugnat.

18. Sed ne toties opus sit sermonis filum interrumpere et similes posthac objectiones solvere, monere volo me haec omnia ex naturae humanae quomodocunque consideratae necessitate demonstrasse, nempe
10 ex universali omnium hominum conatu sese conservandi, qui conatus omnibus hominibus inest, sive ignari sive sapientes sint; ac proinde quomodocunque homines, sive affectu sive ratione, duci considerentur, res eadem erit, quia demonstratio, ut diximus, universalis est.

---

2. *Gf videbitur*, perhaps a misprint.
3. *NS zo ben ik warelijk gehouden mijn belofte niet te voldoen*, i.e. *tenemur*.

promised another to do something, and then time or reason shows, or appears to show, that the thing in question is prejudicial to the general welfare of its subjects, it is certainly bound to break its promise. Since Scripture, then, teaches us to keep faith only as a general rule, and leaves the agent to decide in which particular cases exceptions must be made, it teaches nothing contrary to what I have just shown.

18. But in order that there may be henceforth less need to interrupt the thread of my argument with answers to similar objections, I would remind my readers that I have deduced all these doctrines from the essential nature of man, irrespective of how he is considered; i.e. from the universal urge of all men to preserve themselves. This urge is present in all men, whether they are enlightened or not;[1] and so, no matter how we consider men, whether we take them to be guided by passion or by reason, it will make no difference, since the proof, as I have said, is valid in all cases.

---

[1] But although men by nature break their promises when they think that this is to their advantage, the enlightened may see disadvantages in promise-breaking which the unenlightened fail to see.

CAPUT IV

1. Jus summarum potestatum, quod earum potentia determinatur, in praec. Cap. ostendimus, idque in hoc potissimum consistere vidimus, nempe quod imperii veluti mens sint qua omnes duci debent; adeoque solas jus habere decernendi quid bonum, quid malum, quid aequum, 5 quid iniquum, hoc est, quid singulis vel omnibus simul agendum vel omittendum sit; ac proinde vidimus iis solis jus competere leges condendi, easque, quando de iis quaestio est, in quocunque singulari casu interpretandi, et decernendi an datus casus contra vel secundum jus factus sit (vide Art. 3, 4, 5, praec. Cap.); deinde bellum inferendi, vel 10 pacis conditiones statuendi et offerendi, vel oblatas acceptandi. Vide Art. 12 et 13 praec. Cap.

2. Cum haec omnia, ac etiam media quae ad eadem exequenda requiruntur, omnia negotia sint quae ad integrum imperii corpus, hoc est, quae ad rempublicam spectant, hinc sequitur rempublicam ab ejus 15 solummodo directione pendere qui summum habet imperium. Ac proinde sequitur solius summae potestatis jus esse de factis uniuscujusque judicandi, de factis cujuscunque rationem exigendi, delinquentes poena mulctandi, et quaestiones inter cives de jure dirimendi, vel legum latarum peritos statuendi qui haec ejus loco administrent; deinde omnia 20 ad bellum et pacem media adhibendi et ordinandi, nempe urbes condendi et muniendi, milites conducendi, officia militaria distribuendi, et quid factum velit imperandi, et pacis causa legatos mittendi et audiendi, et denique sumptus ad haec omnia exigendi.

3. Quoniam itaque solius summae potestatis jus sit negotia publica 25 tractandi vel ministros ad eadem eligendi, sequitur subditum imperium affectare qui suo solo arbitrio, supremo concilio inscio, negotium aliquod publicum aggressus est, tametsi id quod intenderat agere civitati optimum fore crediderit.

4. Sed quaeri solet an summa potestas legibus adstricta sit, et conse-30 quenter an peccare possit. Verum quoniam legis et peccati nomina non tantum civitatis jura, sed etiam omnium rerum naturalium et apprime rationis communes regulas respicere solent, non possumus absolute

---

3. *NS dat de Heerschappijen gelijk een ziel, of een geest zijn*, i.e. *imperia . . . sint. sint* at any rate is correct. *OP sit.*

13. *omnia* not in *NS.*

21. *OP milites ducendi*, corrected to *milites conducendi* in the list of Errata. *NS krijgslieden te geleiden*, i.e. *ducendi.*

CHAPTER IV

1. The right of the sovereign, which is determined by its power, has been explained in the previous Chapter. Its right, as we saw, lay primarily in the fact that it was, so to speak, the mind of the state by which all its subjects had to be guided; and so it alone had the right to decide what was good, what bad, what fair, and what unfair, i.e. to decide what had to be done or not done either by particular individuals or by all alike. This meant that it alone had the right to make laws, to interpret them in particular cases when there was a dispute about their meaning, and to decide whether any given action was illegal or not (see Sections 3, 4, and 5 of the previous Chapter). In addition, it alone had the right to make war, to decide upon and offer conditions of peace, or to accept them when offered.[1] See Sections 12 and 13 of the previous Chapter.

2. Since these functions, and the means required to perform them, are the only matters which concern the state as a whole, i.e. which are affairs of state, the conduct of state affairs depends entirely on the guidance of the sovereign. It follows that the sovereign alone has the right to judge the actions of individuals, to demand an account of anyone's conduct, to punish wrong-doers, and to settle disputes between citizens over questions of right; or to appoint men versed in the established laws to perform these functions on its behalf. It also follows that the sovereign alone has the right to use and organize all the means necessary to war and peace, viz., the right to found and fortify cities, to collect troops, to allocate military duties, to order what it wishes done, to send envoys with a view to peace, to give them audience, and finally to levy money to meet all these expenses.

3. Since the sovereign alone has the right to handle public affairs or appoint ministers to do so, a subject commits treason if, unbeknown to the supreme council, he undertakes any public business on his own initiative; even though he believes that what he intends to do is in the best interests of the commonwealth.[2]

4. It is often asked whether a sovereign is bound by laws and so capable of doing wrong. Now since the words 'law' and 'wrong-doing' often refer to the common laws which apply to everything in nature, and particularly to the common rules of reason,[3] as well as to the laws

---

[1] Hobbes, *De Cive* vi, 18.   [2] For another account see *TT-P* xvi, pp. 141-3.
[3] *TP* ii, 21, p. 281.

dicere civitatem nullis adstrictam esse legibus, seu peccare non posse. Nam si civitas nullis legibus seu regulis, sine quibus civitas non esset civitas, adstricta esset, tum civitas non ut res naturalis sed ut chimaera esset contemplanda. Peccat ergo civitas quando ea agit, vel fieri patitur,

5 quae causa esse possunt ipsius ruinae; atque tum eandem eo sensu peccare dicimus quo philosophi vel medici naturam peccare dicunt; et hoc sensu dicere possumus civitatem peccare quando contra rationis dictamen aliquid agit. Est enim civitas tum maxime sui juris quando ex dictamine rationis agit (per Art. 7 praeced. Cap.); quatenus igitur

10 contra rationem agit, eatenus sibi deficit seu peccat. Atque haec clarius intelligi poterunt si consideremus quod, cum dicimus unumquemque posse de re quae sui juris est statuere quicquid velit, haec potestas non sola agentis potentia, sed etiam ipsius patientis aptitudine definiri debet. Si enim ex. gr. dico me jure posse de hac mensa quicquid velim facere,

15 non hercle intelligo quod jus habeam efficiendi ut haec mensa herbam comedat. Sic etiam, tametsi dicimus homines non sui sed civitatis juris esse, non intelligimus quod homines naturam humanam amittant et aliam induant, atque adeo quod civitas jus habeat efficiendi ut homines volent, vel, quod aeque impossibile est, ut homines cum honore ad-

20 spiciant ea quae risum movent vel nauseam: sed quod quaedam circumstantiae occurrant, quibus positis ponitur subditorum erga civitatem reverentia et metus, et quibus sublatis metus et reverentia et cum his civitas una tollitur. Civitas itaque, ut sui juris sit, metus et reverentiae causas servare tenetur, alias civitas esse desinit. Nam iis vel ei qui im-

25 perium tenet aeque impossibile est ebrium aut nudum cum scortis per plateas currere, histrionem agere, leges ab ipso latas aperte violare seu contemnere, et cum his majestatem servare, ac impossibile est simul esse et non esse; subditos deinde trucidare, spoliare, virgines rapere, et

---

5. *NS dat zy dan in een zelfde zin zondigt*, which suggests *eam eodem* or *eodem eam*.

of a commonwealth, we cannot say without qualification that a commonwealth is bound by no laws and that it cannot do wrong. For if a commonwealth were not bound by the laws or rules which make it a commonwealth, it would have to be regarded, not as a real thing in nature, but as a figment of the imagination. A commonwealth, then, does wrong when it does, or allows to be done, things that can be the cause of its own downfall. When it acts in this way, I say that it does wrong in the sense in which scientists or doctors say that nature does wrong;[1] and in this sense we can say that a commonwealth does wrong when it does something contrary to the dictate of reason.[2] For a commonwealth is most fully possessed of its own right when it acts in accordance with the dictate of reason (by Section 7 of the previous Chapter); in so far, then, as it acts against reason, it fails to realize its true nature, or does wrong. This will be understood more clearly if we consider the following point. When we say that a man has the power to do what he likes with something over which he has a right, this power is necessarily limited by the capacity of the object affected as well as by the power of the agent. For example, if I say that I have the right to do whatever I wish with this table, I certainly do not mean that I have a right to make this table eat grass. Similarly, although I say that men are not possessed of their own right, but subject to the right of their commonwealth, I do not mean that they lose their human nature and assume another, and that the commonwealth has thus a right to make them fly in the air, or, what is equally impossible, to make them regard with honour things which arouse their ridicule or disgust. I mean that there are certain conditions whose fulfilment gives rise to respect for and fear of the commonwealth on the part of its subjects, and that, when these conditions are not fulfilled, fear, respect, and the commonwealth all disappear together. Thus in order that a commonwealth may possess its own right, it is bound to maintain the conditions of fear and respect, otherwise it ceases to be a commonwealth. For it is as impossible for a sovereign to run drunk or naked through the streets with harlots, to act on the stage,[3] openly to break or hold in contempt laws which he himself has passed, and still to preserve his sovereignty, as it is to be and not be at the same time. Besides, to slaughter subjects, to despoil them, to abduct women, and conduct of that kind, turns fear

---

[1] Speaking 'in human fashion'; cf. *TP* ii, 22, pp. 281–3, and *E* iv, Pref.

[2] The reason of the political scientist.

[3] Like Nero (Tacitus, *Annals* xvi, iv). According to Machiavelli (*Prince* xix), a ruler must at all costs avoid arousing the contempt and hatred of his subjects.

similia, metum in indignationem, et consequenter statum civilem in statum hostilitatis vertunt.

5. Videmus itaque quo sensu dicere possumus civitatem legibus teneri et peccare posse. Verum si per legem intelligamus jus civile, quod 5 ipso jure civili vindicari potest, et peccatum id quod jure civili fieri prohibetur, hoc est, si haec nomina genuino sensu sumantur, nulla ratione dicere possumus civitatem legibus adstrictam esse aut posse peccare. Nam regulae et causae metus et reverentiae quas civitas sui causa servare tenetur, non ad jura civilia sed ad jus naturale spectant, quandoqui-
10 dem (per Art. praeced.) non jure civili sed jure belli vindicari possunt; et civitas nulla alia ratione iisdem tenetur quam homo in statu naturali, ut sui juris esse possit, sive ne sibi hostis sit, cavere tenetur ne se ipsum interficiat; quae sane cautio non obsequium, sed humanae naturae libertas est. At jura civilia pendent a solo civitatis decreto, atque haec
15 nemini nisi sibi, ut scilicet libera maneat, morem gerere tenetur, nec aliud bonum aut malum habere nisi quod ipsa sibi bonum aut malum esse decernit; ac proinde non tantum jus habet sese vindicandi, leges condendi et interpretandi, sed etiam easdem abrogandi, et reo cuicunque ex plenitudine potentiae condonandi.

20 6. Contractus seu leges quibus multitudo jus suum in unum concilium vel hominem transferunt, non dubium est quin violari debeant, quando communis salutis interest easdem violare. At judicium de hac re, an scilicet communis salutis intersit easdem violare an secus, nemo privatus, sed is tantum qui imperium tenet jure ferre potest (per Art. 3
25 hujus Cap.); ergo jure civili is solus qui imperium tenet earum legum interpres manet. Ad quod accedit quod nullus privatus easdem jure vindicare possit; atque adeo eum qui imperium tenet revera non obligant. Quod si tamen ejus naturae sint ut violari nequeant nisi simul civitatis robur debilitetur, hoc est, nisi simul plerorumque civium

---

14. *P atque*; *OP acque.*

18–19. *OP reum quemcunque*, corrected to *reo cuicunque* in the list of Errata.

20. *NS het verdrach*, i.e. *Contractus* (singular); *OP Contractûs*. The error is due to the original editors, who were responsible for most of the accents in Spinoza's text. Cf. *G*, vol. iv, p. 171, ll. 2 and 19.

into indignation, and, as a result, the political condition into a condition of war.

5. This, then, makes clear the sense in which we can say that a commonwealth is bound by laws and capable of doing wrong. But if by 'law' we mean civil law, enforceable purely by civil right,[1] and by 'wrong-doing' that which is forbidden by civil law, i.e. if these words are taken in their proper sense, it is quite impossible to say that a commonwealth is bound by laws and capable of doing wrong. For the rules and conditions of fear and respect which a commonwealth is bound in its own interest to observe are no part of civil law, but are part of the law of nature, since (by the previous Section) they are not enforceable by civil right, but only by the right of war. In any case a commonwealth is bound by them only in the sense that a man in the state of nature, in order to possess his own right, and not be his own enemy, 'is bound' to take care not to kill himself; and this, of course, is not an obligation imposed on man, but an exercise of his freedom.[2] Civil laws, on the other hand, depend entirely on the decree of the commonwealth, and in order to maintain its freedom a commonwealth is bound to please nobody but itself, and to regard nothing as good or bad but what it decides to be good or bad for itself; so it has not only the right to assert itself, to lay down and interpret laws, but also the right to repeal them, and to pardon any offender out of the plenitude of its power.

6. The contract or laws by which a people transfers its right to one man or an assembly[3] should certainly be broken when the general welfare so requires. But the right to decide whether the general welfare requires this or not cannot belong to any private individual, but only to the sovereign (by Section 3 of this Chapter); and so by civil right the sovereign is always the sole interpreter of these laws. Besides, no private individual has a right to enforce them; so in fact they are not binding on the sovereign. Nevertheless, if they are of such a nature that they cannot be broken without the commonwealth being weakened, i.e. without the common fear of the majority of citizens being at once

---

[1] By civil right a citizen can enforce civil law against another citizen, but not against the commonwealth itself.

[2] *TP* ii, 20, pp. 279–81.

[3] Spinoza follows Hobbes (*De Cive* vii, 5–12) in holding that democracy is the original form of constitution (*TP* viii, 12, p. 377; cf. *TT-P* xvii, p. 159). But he denies that the people transfers its sovereignty *unconditionally* (*TP* vii, 1, p. 335; cf. vii, 30, p. 363). The question at issue here is how far and in what sense a king, for instance, is bound by the contract he makes with his people to observe certain fundamental laws. This is the only kind of contract mentioned in the *TP*; contrast *TT-P* xvi, pp. 129–33.

communis metus in indignationem vertatur, eo ipso civitas dissolvitur et contractus cessat; qui propterea non jure civili, sed jure belli vindicatur. Atque adeo is qui imperium tenet nulla etiam alia de causa hujus contractus conditiones servare tenetur, quam homo in statu naturali,
5 ne sibi hostis sit, tenetur cavere ne se ipsum interficiat, ut in praeced. Art. diximus.

turned into indignation, then to break them is to destroy the commonwealth and to end the contract; so that breach of the contract is not
punished by civil right but by the right of war. It follows that in this
case a sovereign is bound to observe the conditions of the contract for
precisely the same reason as a man in the state of nature, in order that
he may not be his own enemy, is bound to take care not to kill himself,
as I said in the previous Section.

CAPUT V

1. In Art. 11 Cap. 2 ostendimus hominem tum maxime sui juris esse quando maxime ratione ducitur, et consequenter (vid. Art. 7 Cap. 3) civitatem illam maxime potentem maximeque sui juris esse quae ratione fundatur et dirigitur. Cum autem optima vivendi ratio ad
5 sese quantum fieri potest conservandum ea sit quae ex praescripto rationis instituitur, sequitur ergo id omne optimum esse quod homo vel civitas agit quatenus maxime sui juris est. Nam non id omne quod jure fieri dicimus, optime fieri affirmamus: aliud namque est agrum jure colere, aliud agrum optime colere; aliud, inquam, est sese jure defen-
10 dere, conservare, judicium ferre etc., aliud sese optime defendere, conservare, atque optimum judicium ferre; et consequenter aliud est jure imperare et reipublicae curam habere, aliud optime imperare et rempublicam optime gubernare. Postquam itaque de jure cujuscunque civitatis in genere egimus, tempus est ut de optimo cujuscunque imperii
15 statu agamus.

2. Qualis autem cujuscunque imperii optimus sit status facile ex fine status civilis cognoscitur: qui scilicet nullus alius est quam pax vitaeque securitas. Ac proinde illud imperium optimum est ubi homines concorditer vitam transigunt, et cujus jura inviolata servantur. Nam cer-
20 tum est quod seditiones, bella, legumque contemptio sive violatio, non tam subditorum malitiae quam pravo imperii statui imputanda sunt. Homines enim civiles non nascuntur, sed fiunt. Hominum praeterea naturales affectus ubique iidem sunt; si itaque in una civitate malitia magis regnat pluraque peccata committuntur quam in alia, certum est
25 id ex eo oriri, quod talis civitas non satis concordiae providerit, nec jura satis prudenter instituerit, et consequenter neque jus civitatis absolutum obtinuerit. Status enim civilis qui seditionum causas non abstulit, et ubi bellum continuo timendum, et ubi denique leges frequenter violantur, non multum ab ipso naturali statu differt, ubi unusquisque
30 ex suo ingenio magno vitae periculo vivit.

16. *NS Maar hoedanige stant van yder Heerschappy de beste is*; *OP Qualis autem cujuscunque imperii sit status*. As *L* saw, *optimus* has dropped out of the *OP* text. He inserted it before *cujuscunque*: I prefer to place it before *sit*.
28. *NS* omits the first *et*.

308

CHAPTER V

1. I have shown in Chapter 2, Section 11, that a man is most fully possessed of his own right when he is most guided by reason, and consequently (see Section 7, Chapter 3) that a commonwealth is most powerful, and most fully possessed of its own right, if it is based on and guided by reason. Now since the best way to preserve oneself as far as possible is to live as reason prescribes,[1] a man or a commonwealth always acts in the best way when it is most fully possessed of its own right. I do not assert that everything which I say is done by right is done in the best way. It is one thing to cultivate a field by right, and another to cultivate it in the best way; it is one thing, I say, to defend and preserve oneself, to give judgement and so on by right, another to defend and preserve oneself in the best way, and to give the best judgement. In consequence, it is one thing to rule and have charge of public affairs by right, another to rule and direct public affairs in the best way.[2] So now that I have dealt with the right of commonwealths in general, it is time for me to discuss their best condition.

2. The best condition of a commonwealth is easily discovered from the purpose of political order: which is simply peace and security of life.[3] Accordingly, the best commonwealth is one in which men live in harmony, and the laws are kept unbroken. Rebellions, wars, and contemptuous disregard for law must certainly be attributed to the corrupt condition of the commonwealth rather than to the wickedness of its subjects.[4] For citizens are not born, but made.[5] Besides, men's natural passions are the same everywhere; hence if wickedness is more dominant and crime more prevalent in one commonwealth than in another, this is certainly due to the fact that the first has not done enough to promote harmony, has not framed its laws with sufficient foresight, and so has failed to acquire its absolute right as a commonwealth. For a political order which has not removed the causes of civil strife, where war is a constant threat, and the laws are often broken, differs little from a veritable state of nature, where everyone lives as he pleases with great danger to his life.

[1] *TP* ii, 8, p. 273; *TT-P* xvi, p. 127; *E* iv, 24.
[2] Man always acts *jure naturae*; but seldom acts in full possession of his *own* right, i.e. with complete freedom or from the dictates of reason.
[3] In *TT-P* xx, p. 231, Spinoza says that the purpose of the state is freedom. But the inconsistency disappears when he explains his conception of peace below.
[4] Machiavelli, *Discourses* iii, 29.   [5] Hobbes, *De Cive* i, 2, n. 1.

3. At sicut subditorum vitia, nimiaque licentia et contumacia, civitati imputanda sunt, ita contra eorum virtus et constans legum observantia maxime civitatis virtuti et juri absoluto tribuenda est, ut patet ex Art. 15 Cap. 2. Unde Hannibali merito eximiae virtuti ducitur quod
5 in ipsius exercitu nulla unquam seditio orta fuerit.

4. Civitas cujus subditi metu territi arma non capiunt potius dicenda est quod sine bello sit quam quod pacem habeat. Pax enim non belli privatio, sed virtus est quae ex animi fortitudine oritur: est namque obsequium (per Art. 19 Cap. 2) constans voluntas id exequendi quod
10 ex communi civitatis decreto fieri debet. Illa praeterea civitas, cujus pax a subditorum inertia pendet, qui scilicet veluti pecora ducuntur ut tantum servire discant, rectius solitudo quam civitas dici potest.

5. Cum ergo dicimus illud imperium optimum esse ubi homines concorditer vitam transigunt, vitam humanam intelligo, quae non sola
15 sanguinis circulatione et aliis quae omnibus animalibus sunt communia, sed quae maxime ratione, vera mentis virtute et vita, definitur.

6. Sed notandum imperium quod in hunc finem institui dixi a me intelligi id quod multitudo libera instituit, non autem id quod in multitudinem jure belli acquiritur. Libera enim multitudo majori spe quam
20 metu, subacta autem majori metu quam spe ducitur; quippe illa vitam colere, haec autem mortem tantummodo vitare studet. Illa, inquam, sibi vivere studet, haec victoris esse cogitur; unde hanc servire, illam liberam esse dicimus. Finis itaque imperii quod aliquis jure belli adipiscitur est dominari, et servos potius quam subditos habere. Et quam-
25 vis inter imperium quod a libera multitudine creatur, et illud quod jure belli acquiritur, si ad utriusque jus in genere attendamus, nulla essentialis detur differentia, finem tamen, ut jam ostendimus, et praeterea media quibus unumquodque conservari debeat, admodum diversa habent.

12. *OP tantum*; *NS eindelijk*, i.e. *tandem.*
16. *NS door de ware reden, door de deucht, en door 't leven des gemoeds bepaalt word.*

3. But just as the vices of subjects, and their excessive lawlessness and perversity, must be attributed to the faults of the commonwealth, so conversely their virtues and steadfast observance of the laws must be chiefly credited to its excellence and absolute right, as is clear from Chapter 2, Section 15. This is why it is justly thought a remarkable virtue in Hannibal that no mutiny ever occurred in his army.[1]

4. A commonwealth whose subjects are restrained from revolting by fear must be said to be free from war rather than to enjoy peace. For peace is not the mere absence of war, but a virtue based on strength of mind;[2] since (by Chapter 2, Section 19) obedience is the steadfast will to do what the general decree of the commonwealth requires. Besides, a commonwealth whose peace depends on the apathy of its subjects, who are led like sheep so that they learn nothing but servility, may more properly be called a desert than a commonwealth.[3]

5. Thus when I say that the best state is one in which men live in harmony, I am speaking of a truly human existence, which is characterized, not by the mere circulation of blood and other vital processes common to all animals, but primarily by reason, the true virtue and life of the mind.[4]

6. When, however, I say that this is the end of the state the reader should note that I am referring to a state established by a free people, and not to a tyranny acquired over a people by the right of war.[5] A free people is led more by hope than by fear, a conquered people more by fear than by hope; for the former seeks to improve its life, the latter seeks only to avoid death. The former, I say, seeks to live for itself, the latter is compelled to belong to its conqueror; that is why I call the second enslaved and the first free. Thus the aim of a state acquired by the right of war is to oppress men, and to make them slaves rather than subjects. And although there is no essential difference in respect of their general right between a state created by a free people and a state acquired by the right of war,[6] their aims, as I have just shown, are very different;[7] and so too are the means required to preserve them.

---

[1] Machiavelli, *Prince* xvii; *Discourses* iii, 21.   [2] Contrast Hobbes, *De Cive* i, 12.

[3] Tacitus, *Agricola* 30, *ubi solitudinem faciunt, pacem appellant*; Locke, *Second Treatise of Civil Government*, § 228; Rousseau, *Social Contract* i, 4.

[4] *TT-P* xx, p. 231.

[5] Cf. Hobbes's distinction between institution and acquisition (*De Cive* v, 12).

[6] Hobbes, *De Cive* ix, 10.

[7] Aristotle (*Politics* 1279^{a-b}) distinguished between monarchy, where the ruler ruled in the common interest, and tyranny, where he ruled in his own. Hobbes rejected this distinction (*De Cive* vii, 3) on the ground that the interests of the ruler and of his subjects were inseparable (*De Cive* x, 2; cf. xiii, 4). But even if this is true the ruler may not realize it.

7. Quibus autem mediis princeps qui sola dominandi libidine fertur uti debet ut imperium stabilire et conservare possit, acutissimus Machiavellus prolixe ostendit: quem autem in finem non satis constare videtur. Si quem tamen bonum habuit, ut de viro sapiente credendum est,

5 fuisse videtur ut ostenderet quam imprudenter multi tyrannum e medio tollere conantur, cum tamen causae cur princeps sit tyrannus tolli nequeant, sed contra eo magis ponantur quo principi major timendi causa praebetur: quod fit quando multitudo exempla in principem edidit, et parricidio quasi re bene gesta gloriatur. Praeterea ostendere

10 forsan voluit quantum libera multitudo cavere debet ne salutem suam uni absolute credat, qui, nisi vanus sit, et omnibus se posse placere existimet, quotidie insidias timere debet; atque adeo sibi potius cavere, et multitudini contra insidiari magis quam consulere cogitur: et ad hoc de prudentissimo isto viro credendum magis adducor, quia pro libertate

15 fuisse constat, ad quam etiam tuendam saluberrima consilia dedit.

8–9. *NS voorbeelden . . . voortbrengt,* i.e. *edit.*
13–15. *et ad hoc . . . dedit* not in *NS.*

7. The means which a prince whose sole motive is lust for despotic power must employ to strengthen and preserve his state have been described at great length by that shrewd observer, Machiavelli; but there seems to be some uncertainty about the purpose of his account. If he had some good purpose, as we must believe of so wise a man, it was probably to show the folly of attempting—as many do—to remove a tyrant[1] when the causes which make a prince a tyrant cannot be removed, but become rooted more firmly as the prince is given more reason to be afraid; which happens when a people has made an example of its prince, and boasts of its regicide as though it were a glorious deed.[2] Perhaps he wished to show also how chary a free people should be of entrusting its welfare entirely to one man,[3] who, if he is not a vain fool who thinks that he can please everybody, must go in daily fear of plots; and thus is forced in self-defence to plot against his subjects rather than to further their interests. This interpretation of that wise statesman seems to me particularly attractive in view of the well-known fact that he was an advocate of freedom, and also gave some very sound advice for preserving it.

[1] Machiavelli held that 'a corrupt people' required a master (*Discourses* i, 55): hence his advocacy of a Prince for Italy.

[2] *TT-P* xviii, p. 201.

[3] This interpretation was adopted by Rousseau in *Social Contract* iii, 6. Some slight justification for it may perhaps be found in *Prince* xxiv; but when applied to the whole work it is quite indefensible.

CAPUT VI

1. Quia homines, uti diximus, magis affectu quam ratione ducuntur, sequitur multitudinem non ex rationis ductu, sed ex communi aliquo affectu naturaliter convenire et una veluti mente duci velle, nempe (ut Art. 9 Cap. 3 diximus) vel ex communi spe, vel metu, vel desiderio com-
5 mune aliquod damnum ulciscendi. Cum autem solitudinis metus omnibus hominibus insit, quia nemo in solitudine vires habet ut sese defendere et quae ad vitam necessaria sunt comparare possit, sequitur statum civilem homines natura appetere, nec fieri posse ut homines eundem unquam penitus dissolvant.

10 2. Ex discordiis igitur et seditionibus quae in civitate saepe concitantur nunquam fit ut cives civitatem dissolvant (ut in reliquis societatibus saepe evenit), sed ut ejusdem formam in aliam mutent, si nimirum contentiones sedari nequeunt servata civitatis facie. Quare media quae ad imperium conservandum requiri dixi, ea intelligo quae
15 ad imperii formam absque ulla ejus notabili mutatione conservandam necessaria sunt.

3. Quod si cum humana natura ita comparatum esset ut homines id quod maxime utile est maxime cuperent, nulla esset opus arte ad concordiam et fidem; sed quia longe aliter cum natura humana constitutum
20 esse constat, imperium necessario ita instituendum est ut omnes, tam qui regunt quam qui reguntur, velint nolint, id tamen agant quod communis salutis interest, hoc est, ut omnes sponte vel vi vel necessitate coacti sint ex rationis praescripto vivere; quod fit si imperii res ita ordinentur ut nihil quod ad communem salutem spectat ullius fidei
25 absolute committatur. Nemo enim tam vigilans est qui aliquando non dormitet, et nemo tam potenti tamque integro animo fuit qui aliquando, et praesertim quando maxime animi fortitudine opus est, non frangeretur ac pateretur vinci. Et sane stultitia est ab alio id exigere quod nemo a se ipso impetrare potest, nempe ut alteri potius quam sibi vigi-
30 let, ut avarus non sit, neque invidus, neque ambitiosus, etc., praesertim is qui omnium affectuum incitamenta maxima quotidie habet.

4. At experientia contra docere videtur pacis et concordiae interesse ut omnis potestas ad unum conferatur. Nam nullum imperium tamdiu

---

4–5. *NS of door een gemene begeerte van enige schade te wreken.* But in iii, 9 (p. 290, ll. 25–26) *NS has of uit begeerte van enige gemene schade te wreken.*

10. *NS uit de tweedracht*, i.e. *Ex discordia.*

CHAPTER VI

1. Since men, as I said, are led more by passion than by reason, their natural motive for uniting and being guided as if by one mind is not reason but some common passion;[1] common hope, or common fear, or a common desire to avenge some common injury (as I said in Chapter 3, Section 9). But since all men fear isolation, because no isolated individual has enough power to defend himself and procure the necessaries of life, they desire political society by nature,[2] and can never dissolve it entirely.

2. Thus the quarrels and rebellions which often arise in a commonwealth never lead the citizens to dissolve the commonwealth[3] (as often happens in other kinds of association); if their quarrels cannot be composed otherwise, they simply change its form. Hence by the means required to preserve a state I understand those which are necessary to preserve its form without any notable change.

3. Now if human nature were such that men desired most what was most to their advantage, there would be no need of artifice to promote loyalty and concord.[4] But since, as is well known, human nature is very different, it is necessary to organize the state so that all its members, rulers as well as ruled, do what the common welfare requires whether they wish to or not, that is to say, are compelled to live according to the precept of reason, if not by inclination, then by force or necessity—as happens when the administration is arranged so that nothing which concerns the common welfare is wholly entrusted to the good faith of any man.[5] For no one is so vigilant that he does not nod sometimes; even the most resolute and upright of men falter on occasion, and allow themselves to be overcome by their passions, especially when strength of mind is needed most. Now it is certainly foolish to make demands on another which no one can fulfil himself, to require him, for instance, to be more attentive to the interests of others than to his own, to eschew greed, envy, and ambition, and so forth; especially when the other is a man who has always the most powerful incentives to every kind of passion.

4. On the other hand, experience seems to teach that it makes for peace and harmony if all power is vested in one man. For no state has

---

[1] *TP* i, 7, p. 265.
[2] Hobbes, *De Cive* i, 2, n. 1.
[3] Locke, *Second Treatise of Civil Government*, § 211.
[4] *TT-P* v, p. 93; xvi, p. 131.
[5] *TP* i, 6, p. 265.

absque ulla notabili mutatione stetit quam Turcarum, et contra nulla minus diuturna quam popularia seu democratica fuerunt, nec ulla ubi tot seditiones moverentur. Sed si servitium, barbaries, et solitudo pax appellanda sit, nihil hominibus pace miserius. Plures sane et acerbiores
5 contentiones inter parentes et liberos quam inter dominos et servos moveri solent, nec tamen oeconomiae interest jus paternum in dominium mutare, et liberos perinde ac servos habere. Servitutis igitur, non pacis, interest omnem potestatem ad unum transferre: nam pax, ut jam diximus, non in belli privatione, sed in animorum unione sive con-
10 cordia consistit.

5. Et sane qui credunt posse fieri ut unus solus summum civitatis jus obtineat longe errant. Jus enim sola potentia determinatur, ut Capite 2 ostendimus: at unius hominis potentia longe impar est tantae moli sustinendae. Unde fit ut quem multitudo regem elegit, is sibi im-
15 peratores quaerat seu consiliarios seu amicos, quibus suam et omnium salutem committit, ita ut imperium quod absolute monarchicum esse creditur sit revera in praxi aristocraticum, non quidem manifestum, sed latens, et propterea pessimum. Ad quod accedit quod rex puer, aeger, aut senectute gravatus, precario rex sit, sed ii revera summam
20 potestatem habeant qui summa imperii negotia administrant, vel qui regi sunt proximi; ut jam taceam quod rex libidini obnoxius omnia saepe moderetur ex libidine unius aut alterius pellicis aut cinaedi. *Audieram*, inquit Orsines, *in Asia olim regnasse foeminas: hoc vero novum est, regnare castratum.* Curtius lib. X, Cap. 1.

25 6. Est praeterea hoc certum quod civitas semper magis propter cives quam propter hostes periclitetur: rari quippe boni. Ex quo sequitur quod is in quem totum imperii jus delatum est magis cives quam hostes semper timebit, et consequenter sibi cavere, et subditis non consulere sed insidiari conabitur, iis praecipue qui sapientia clari vel divitiis poten-
30 tiores sunt.

7. Accedit praeterea quod reges filios etiam plus timent quam amant,

---

2. *seu democratica* not in *NS*.
2–3. *NS daar in zo veel beroerten rijzen*, i.e. *moventur*.
4. *NS* adds *en niets minder te wenschen*.

stood so long without any notable change as that of the Turks, and, conversely, none have proved so short-lived and so liable to constant civil strife as popular or democratic states.[1] But if slavery, barbarism, and desolation are to be called peace, peace is the greatest misfortune that men can suffer. It is true that the quarrels which arise between parents and children are generally more frequent and more bitter than quarrels between masters and slaves, yet it is not conducive to good family management to make the father a master, and to treat children as slaves. So it is slavery, not peace, that is furthered by the transfer of all power to one man; for peace, as I have said already, is not mere absence of war, but a union or agreement of minds.

5. And, of course, those who believe that one man *can* hold the supreme right of a commonwealth by himself are greatly mistaken. For right is determined by power alone, as I have shown in Chapter 2; and the power of one man is far too small to bear so great a burden. The result is that the man whom the people has chosen as king looks for generals or counsellors or friends to help him,[2] and entrusts them with his own safety and the safety of all; so that the state which is believed to be a pure monarchy is really an aristocracy in practice, but a concealed and not an open one, and therefore of the very worst type. Besides, a king who is a boy, an invalid, or a man burdened by years, is king only by courtesy, and the sovereignty is really held by those who handle the most important affairs of state, or who are nearest to the king; not to mention that a king who is a prey to lust often manages everything to suit the whim of some concubine or catamite.[3] 'I had heard', said Orsines, 'of women once ruling in Asia: but for a eunuch to rule is something new.' Curtius, Book X, Chapter 1.[4]

6. It is also true that a commonwealth is always in greater danger from its citizens than from external enemies:[5] for loyal subjects are rare. In consequence, a man in whom the whole right of the state has been vested will always be more afraid of his citizens than of external enemies.[6] He will therefore try to protect himself from them; instead of furthering their interests he will plot against them; and especially against those who have a reputation for wisdom or are too powerful because of their wealth.

7. I may add that their sons too are more feared than loved by kings;

[1] Rousseau, *Social Contract* iii, 4. [2] Aristotle, *Politics* 1287^b 8–9.
[3] Van Hove, *Polityke Weegschaal*, 1661, i, i, 25 (p. 92).
[4] *Historiae Alexandri Magni* x, i, 37. [5] *TT-P* xvii, p. 155.
[6] Van Hove, op. cit. i, i, 10 (p. 41).

et eo magis quo pacis bellique artes magis callent et subditis ob virtutes dilectiores sunt. Unde fit ut eos ita educare studeant ut causa timendi absit. Qua in re officiarii promptissime regi obsequuntur, et studium adhibebunt summum ut regem successorem rudem habeant quem arte
5 tractare possint.

8. Ex quibus omnibus sequitur regem eo minus sui juris, et subditorum conditionem eo miseriorem esse, quo magis absolute civitatis jus in eundem transfertur. Atque adeo necesse est ad imperium monarchicum rite stabiliendum fundamenta jacere firma quibus super-
10 struatur: ex quibus monarchae securitas et multitudini pax sequatur; ac proinde ut monarcha tum maxime sui juris sit cum maxime multitudinis saluti consulit. Quaenam autem haec imperii monarchici fundamenta sint, primum breviter proponam, et deinde ordine ea ostendam.

9. Urbs una aut plures condendae et muniendae sunt, quarum omnes
15 cives, sive ii intra moenia sive extra propter agriculturam habitent, eodem civitatis jure gaudeant; ea tamen conditione, ut unaquaeque certum civium numerum ad sui et communem defensionem habeat. Quae autem id praestare nequit aliis conditionibus in ditione habenda.

10. Militia ex solis civibus nullo excepto formanda est, et ex nullis
20 aliis; atque adeo omnes arma habere teneantur, et nullus in civium numerum recipiatur, nisi postquam exercitium militare didicerit, illudque signatis anni temporibus exercere pollicitus fuerit. Deinde uniuscujusque familiae militia in cohortes et legiones divisa, nullius cohortis dux eligendus nisi qui architecturam militarem noverit. Porro cohor-
25 tium et legionum duces ad vitam quidem, sed qui unius familiae integrae militiae imperet in bello tantummodo eligendus, qui annum ad summum imperium habeat, nec continuari in imperio nec postea eligi possit. Atque hi eligendi sunt ex regis consiliariis (de quibus Art. 15 et seqq. dicendum), vel qui officio consiliarii functi sunt.

---

4. *NS om een ruw en ongeleert Koning . . . tot navolger in de heerschappy te hebben.* Perhaps *imperii* has dropped out of the Latin text between *successorem* and *rudem.*

12. *P Imperii Monarchici*; *NS van d'eenhoofdige Heerschappy,* glossed *Imperium monarchicum*; *OP Imperii Monarchi.*

18. *NS die dit niet willen doen.*

25. *NS van een enig geslacht,* which is, however, altered to *van de Heerschappy* in the list of Errata. In view of Spinoza's remark on p. 348, ll. 17–20, and the fact that the contingent from one tribe might form less than a six-hundredth part of the state's armed forces (p. 320, ll. 25–26), the alteration is not unreasonable.

especially if their sons are skilled in the arts of peace and war, and popular with the subjects because of their virtues. The result is that kings try to educate their sons so as to prevent any cause for alarm. In this matter ministers are very ready to comply with the king's wishes, and will make every effort to have a novice whom they can hoodwink for their next king.[1]

8. It follows from all this that the more completely the right of a commonwealth is transferred to one man, the less is he possessed of his own right, and the more wretched is the condition of his subjects. Thus to establish a monarchy properly it is necessary to ground it on strong foundations which will provide security for the king and peace for the people, and so ensure that the king is most fully possessed of his own right when he pays most attention to the people's welfare. I shall first set out briefly these foundations of monarchy, and then justify each of them in turn.

9. One or more cities must be founded and fortified, and every citizen of these, including farmers living outside their boundaries, should enjoy the same rights in the commonwealth; but only if his city can provide a certain number of citizens for the defence of itself and of the state. If it cannot fulfil this condition it must be held in subjection on different terms.

10. The army must be recruited *from the citizens alone*,[2] and no one must be exempted from military service. Thus all should be required to possess arms, and no one should be admitted to the citizen roll until he has been trained as a soldier,[3] and has promised to practise his duties at appointed times of the year. The contingent from each tribe must be divided into companies and regiments, and no one must be chosen as a company commander unless he has been trained in military engineering.[4] The commanders of companies and regiments must be appointed for life, but the commander of a tribe's whole contingent must be appointed in time of war only; he should hold his command for a year at most, without the possibility of extension or subsequent re-appointment. The latter commanders must be chosen from the king's counsellors (of whom I have to speak in Sections 15 and ff.), or from ex-counsellors.

---

[1] Van Hove, op. cit. i, i, 10 (p. 40), who quotes Tacitus, *Annals* ii, lxxxii, 3 : *displicent regnantibus civilia filiorum ingenia.*

[2] *TT-P* xvii, p. 173 ; cf. Machiavelli, *Prince* xii-xiii and *Discourses* ii, 20.

[3] A young man in ancient Athens was enrolled on the register of his father's deme at the age of eighteen, but only became a full citizen after two years' military training.

[4] In Spinoza's time war was largely a matter of besieging and defending fortresses and cities.

11. Omnium urbium incolae et agricolae, hoc est, omnes cives, in familias dividendi sunt, quae nomine et insigni aliquo distinguantur; et omnes ex aliqua harum familiarum geniti in civium numerum recipiantur, eorumque nomina in catalogum eorum familiae redigantur
5 simulac eo aetatis pervenerint ut arma ferre et officium suum noscere possint; iis tamen exceptis qui ob scelus aliquod infames, vel qui muti, vesani, vel famuli sunt qui servili aliquo officio vitam sustentant.

12. Agri et omne solum et, si fieri potest, domus etiam publici juris sint, nempe ejus qui jus civitatis habet, a quo annuo pretio civibus, sive
10 urbanis et agricolis, locentur; et praeterea omnes ab omni exactione tempore pacis liberi sive immunes sint. Atque hujus pretii alia pars ad civitatis munimenta, alia ad usum domesticum regis referenda est. Nam tempore pacis urbes tanquam ad bellum munire, et praeterea naves et reliqua instrumenta bellica parata necesse est habere.

15 13. Electo rege ex aliqua familia, nulli nobiles censendi nisi a rege oriundi, qui propterea insignibus regiis a sua et a reliquis familiis distinguantur.

14. Regis consanguinei nobiles masculi, qui ei qui regnàt gradu consanguinitatis tertio aut quarto propinqui sunt, uxorem ducere pro-
20 hibeantur, et si quos liberos procreaverint illi illegitimi habeantur et omni dignitate indigni, nec parentum haeredes agnoscantur, sed eorum bona ad regem redeant.

15. Regis praeterea consiliarii, qui ei proximi vel dignitate secundi sunt, plures esse debent et non nisi ex civibus eligendi; nempe ex una-
25 quaque familia tres aut quatuor, aut quinque (si familiae non plures quam sexcentae fuerint), qui simul unum hujus concilii membrum constituent; non ad vitam, sed in tres aut quatuor aut quinque annos, ita ut singulis annis eorum tertia, quarta, aut quinta pars nova eligatur: in qua electione tamen apprime observandum ut ex unaquaque familia
30 unus ad minimum juris peritus consiliarius eligatur.

16. Haec electio ab ipso rege fieri debet, cui constituto anni tempore, quo scilicet novi consiliarii eligendi sunt, unaquaeque familia omnium suorum civium nomina qui ad annum quinquagesimum aetatis

---

7. *NS of zot zijn, of die met enig dienstbaar ampt hun leven onderhouden*, i.e. *NS* omits *famuli* and suggests *vel*; *OP et.*

20. *NS en, indien zy kinderen telen, de zelfden voor onwettig houden*, i.e. *illi illegitimi habeantur*; *OP illegitimi habeantur, illegitimi* being divided between two lines and printed *il-legitimi.*

11. All the city-dwellers and farmers, that is to say, all the citizens, must be divided into tribes, which should be distinguished by some name and emblem. Everyone born into any of these tribes should be admitted to the citizen roll, and have his name inscribed on the roll of his tribe, as soon as he is old enough to bear arms and undergo military training; unless he is a convicted criminal, a mute, a lunatic, or a menial who supports himself by some servile occupation.

12. The fields and the whole territory—and, if possible, the houses also—should be owned by the state, i.e. by the sovereign; who should let them out at an annual rent to the citizens, i.e. to the city-dwellers and farmers. These should be subject to no other form of taxation in time of peace. Part of this rent should go to the king's privy purse, the rest to the defences of the commonwealth. For in time of peace it is necessary to fortify cities for war, and to keep ships and other weapons of war in trim.

13. Once the first king has been chosen from some tribe, only his descendants must be regarded as noblemen; they should therefore be distinguished by royal insignia both from their own tribe and from the others.

14. The male nobles who are blood relatives of the reigning king, and stand in the third or fourth degree of blood relationship to him, should be forbidden to marry. If they do have sons, the latter should be regarded as illegitimate and unworthy of any office; they should be debarred from inheriting their father's estate, which should revert to the king.

15. The king's counsellors, who are nearest or at least next to him in rank, should be numerous, and chosen from the citizens alone; three or four from each tribe, or even five if the number of tribes is less than six hundred. The counsellors from each tribe will together make up one section of this council; they will not serve for life, but for three, four, or five years, and a third, fourth, or fifth of them must be chosen afresh each year. Here it is most important that at least one lawyer should be appointed as counsellor from each tribe.[1]

16. The choice of counsellors must be made by the king himself. At the time of year appointed for the election of new counsellors each tribe must deliver to the king the names of all its citizens—aged fifty

---

[1] In addition to its deputies, each of the eighteen towns of Holland sent a lawyer, the Pensionary, to the Provincial Estates. See Sir William Temple, *Observations upon the United Provinces of the Netherlands*, with an Introduction by G. N. Clark, Cambridge, 1932, ch. ii, p. 65.

pervenerunt, et qui hujus officii candidati rite promoti fuerunt, tradere debet; ex quibus quem velit rex eliget. At eo anno quo alicujus familiae juris peritus alteri succedere debet, juris peritorum tantum nomina sunt regi tradenda. Qui statuto tempore officio hoc consiliarii functi sunt in
5 eodem continuari nequeant, nec ad catalogum eligendorum quinquennio aut amplius referri. Causa autem cur necesse sit singulis annis ex unaquaque familia unum eligere est ne concilium jam ex inexpertis novitiis, jam ex veteratis et rerum expertis componeretur; quod necessario fieret si omnes simul recederent et novi succederent. Sed si sin-
10 gulis annis ex unaquaque familia unus eligatur, tum non nisi quinta, quarta, aut ad summum tertia concilii pars ex novitiis erit. Praeterea si rex aliis negotiis impeditus, aut alia de causa, huic electioni vacare aliquamdiu non possit, tum ipsi consiliarii alios pro tempore eligant donec ipse rex vel alios eligat, vel quos concilium elegit probet.

15   17. Hujus concilii primarium officium sit imperii fundamentalia jura defendere, et consilia de rebus agendis dare ut rex quid in bonum publicum decernendum sit sciat; atque adeo ut regi nihil de aliqua re statuere liceat nisi intellecta prius hujus concilii sententia. Sed si concilio, ut plerumque fiet, non una mens fuerit, sed diversas habuerit
20 sententias etiam postquam bis aut ter quaestionem de eadem re habuerint, res in longius trahenda non est, sed discrepantes sententiae ad regem deferendae, ut Art. 25 hujus Capitis docebimus.

     18. Hujus praeterea concilii officium etiam sit regis instituta seu decreta promulgare, et quid in rempublicam decretum est curare,
25 totiusque administrationis imperii curam habere tanquam regis vicarii.

     19. Civibus nulli ad regem aditus pateant nisi per hoc concilium, cui omnes postulationes seu libelli supplices tradendi sunt ut regi offerantur. Legatis etiam aliarum civitatum non nisi intercedente hoc concilio veniam regem alloquendi impetrare liceat. Epistolae praeterea
30 quae ex aliis locis regi mittuntur ei ab hoc concilio tradi debent; et absolute rex censendus est veluti civitatis mens, hoc autem concilium

---

1–2. *OP Regi tradere debet.* But *Regi* is not in *NS*, and is redundant after *cui.*
8. *P. veteranis.*   9. *NS zou moeten geschieden*; *V–L fieret*; *OP fiet.*
16. *NS en bericht tot verhandeling van zaken te geven*; *OP consilia de rebus agendis dare.*
I insert *et* before *consilia.*
23. *praeterea* not in *NS.*

Chapter VI

or over—who have been duly proposed as candidates for this office; and from these the king will choose whom he wishes.[1] But in the year when a successor to the lawyer of a tribe is due to be chosen the names of its lawyers only must be submitted to the king. Those who have served as counsellors for the appointed time should be debarred from having their tenure extended, and from being replaced on the roll of candidates for five years or more. The reason for appointing one counsellor a year from each tribe is to prevent the council from being composed alternately of inexperienced new-comers and experienced veterans; as would be inevitable if all counsellors retired and took up office together. But if only one is appointed every year from each tribe, only a fifth, fourth, or at the very most a third of the council will be made up of new-comers. If the king is prevented from attending to these appointments for some length of time, either by pressure of business or for some other reason, the counsellors themselves should choose new members to hold office temporarily until the king himself chooses others, or approves those chosen by the council.

17. The chief duty of this council should be to maintain the fundamental laws of the state, and to give advice on the conduct of affairs so that the king may know what to decree for the public good; it being understood that the king is not allowed to make a decision about any matter without hearing the opinion of this council. But if it turns out, as it generally will, that the council is divided in opinion even after discussing the same matter two or three times, the different opinions must be submitted to the king without further delay. How this must be done I shall show in Section 25 of this Chapter.

18. It should also be the duty of this council to publish the king's ordinances or decrees, to attend to his decisions about public affairs, and to supervise in his name the whole administration of the state.

19. The citizens should have no access to the king except through this council, to which all requests or written petitions must be submitted for transmission. In like manner the ambassadors of other commonwealths should not be given permission to address the king except by application to this council. Letters sent to the king from foreign parts must also be transmitted through this council; in short, the king must be regarded as the mind of the commonwealth, and this council as the outer sense organs or body through which that mind

---

[1] The stadtholders had originally the right to appoint the magistrates of a town from a list of candidates presented by the town. See F. M. Janiçon, *État Présent de la République des Provinces-Unies*, 1755, vol. i, ch. x, p. 245. Cf. Temple, op. cit., ch. ii, pp. 60 and 82.

mentis sensus externi seu civitatis corpus, per quod mens civitatis statum concipit, et id agit quod sibi optimum esse decernit.

20. Cura filios regis educandi huic etiam concilio incumbat, et etiam tutela si rex successore infante seu puero relicto obiit. Sed ne 5 tamen concilium interea temporis sine rege sit, ex nobilibus civitatis senior eligendus, qui regis locum suppleat donec legitimus successor eo aetatis pervenerit quo imperii onus sustinere possit.

21. Hujus concilii candidati ii sint qui regimen, fundamenta, et statum seu conditionem civitatis cujus subditi sunt norint. At qui juris- 10 periti locum occupare vult, is praeter regimen et conditionem civitatis cujus subditus est, aliarum etiam cum quibus commercium aliquod intercedit scire debet. Sed nulli nisi qui ad quinquagesimum aetatis annum nullo convicti crimine pervenerint in catalogum eligendorum referendi sunt.

15 22. In hoc concilio nihil de rebus imperii concludendum nisi praesentibus omnibus membris: quod si aliquis morbi aut alia de causa adesse nequeat, aliquem ex eadem familia, qui eodem officio functus vel qui in catalogum eligendorum relatus est, in ipsius locum mittere debet. Quod si nec hoc fecerit, sed quod concilium propter ejus absentlam 20 rem aliquam consulendam in diem differre coactus fuerit, summa aliqua pecuniae sensibili mulctetur. Sed hoc intelligendum quando quaestio est de re quae integrum imperium spectat, videlicet de bello et pace, de jure aliquo abrogando vel instituendo, de commercio, etc. Sed si quaestio sit de re quae unam aut alteram urbem spectet, de libellis supplicibus, 25 etc., satis erit si major concilii pars adsit.

23. Ut inter familias aequalitas in omnibus, et ordo sedendi, proponendi, et dicendi habeatur, vices servandae sunt, ut singulae singulis sessionibus praesideant, et quae hac sessione prima, sequenti ultima sit. Sed eorum qui ejusdem familiae sunt is primus sit qui prior electus 30 fuerit.

24. Hoc concilium quater ad minimum in anno convocetur, ut rationem administrationis imperii a ministris exigant, ut rerum statum

---

1. *NS of als het lighaam der Burgerschap*; *Gf seu civitatis corpus*; *OP ceu*.

1–2. *NS daar door de ziel de Stant van de Burgerschap bevat, en het geen doet*; *OP per quod mens civitatis statum concipit, et per quod mens id agit*. I delete the second *per quod mens* as a duplication of the first.

27. *NS zo moet men in dier voegen beurten houden, dat* suggests *vices ita servandae sunt ut*. But cf. p. 332, ll. 1–2.

perceives the state of the commonwealth, and does what it decides to be best for itself.

20. Responsibility for educating the king's sons should also rest on this council, and likewise the duty of guardianship if the king dies and leaves a minor as his heir.[1] But the council must not be left without a king during the minority; and so the senior nobleman in the commonwealth must be appointed to act as king until the rightful successor is old enough to bear the burden of sovereignty.

21. Candidates for election to this council should be acquainted with the government, the fundamental laws, and the state or condition of their own commonwealth; but the man who aspires to serve on it as a lawyer must also be familiar with the government and condition of the other commonwealths which have any dealings with his own. But only men who have reached their fiftieth year without being convicted of any crime must be placed on the roll of candidates.

22. No decision must be taken in this council about affairs of state unless all its members are present. If through illness or some other cause a counsellor is unable to attend, he must send someone from the same tribe in his place, either an ex-counsellor or an accepted candidate for the office. If he fails to do so, and the council is forced to defer consideration of any matter on account of his absence, he should be heavily fined. But this, of course, applies only when a matter affecting the whole state is under discussion, i.e. when it is a question of war and peace, of repealing or passing some law, of commercial relations, etc. If the matter under discussion affects one or two cities only, if it concerns written petitions, etc., it will be sufficient if the greater part of the council is present.

23. In order that the tribes may have an order of sitting, making proposals, and speaking, and still remain completely equal, they must follow a system of rotation, so that one presides at one session and another at another, and the tribe which takes precedence at one session is last at the next. Among counsellors from the same tribe precedence should be given to the one who was appointed first.[2]

24. This council should be summoned at intervals—at least four times a year[3]—to ask the ministers for an account of their administration, to learn the condition of affairs, and to consider if any new

[1] The education of the future William III ('the child of the state') was entrusted to loyal republicans by Jan de Witt.

[2] In the States General each Province presided in turn under its senior deputy (Janiçon, op. cit., vol. i, ch. ii, pp. 76–77).

[3] The Estates of Holland met four times a year (Temple, op. cit., ch. ii, p. 65).

noscant, et si quid praeterea statuendum sit videant. Nam adeo magnum civium numerum negotiis publicis continuo vacare impossibile videtur. Sed quia negotia publica interim exerceri nihilominus debent, ideo ex hoc concilio quinquaginta aut plures eligendi sunt, qui soluto
5 concilio ejus vicem suppleant, quique quotidie congregari debeant in cubiculo quod regio sit proximum, atque adeo quotidie curam habeant aerarii, urbium munimentorum, educationis filii regis, et absolute eorum omnium magni concilii officiorum quae modo enumeravimus, praeterquam illud, quod de rebus novis de quibus nihil decretum est
10 consulere non possint.

25. Congregato concilio, antequam aliquid in eo proponatur, quinque aut sex aut plures jurisperiti ex familiis quae illa sessione ordine loci priores sunt, regem adeant, ut libellos supplices vel epistolas, si quas habent, tradant, ut rerum statum indicent, et denique ut ex ipso
15 intelligant quid in suo concilio proponere jubeat. Quo accepto concilium repetant, et qui ordine loci prior est rem consulendam aperiat. Nec de re suffragia statim colligenda quae aliquibus videtur alicujus esse momenti, sed in id tempus differenda quod rei necessitas concedit. Concilio igitur ad id statutum tempus soluto, poterunt interea unius-
20 cujusque familiae consiliarii de ipsa seorsum quaestionem habere, et, si res iis magni momenti videbitur, alios qui eodem officio functi vel qui ejusdem concilii candidati sunt consulere; et si intra constitutum tempus inter ipsos convenire non poterit, illa familia extra suffragium erit; nam unaquaeque familia unum tantum ferre suffragium poterit. Alias
25 ejus familiae jurisperitus instructus sententiam quam optimam judicaverint esse in ipso concilio ferat, et sic reliqui; et si majori parti visum fuerit post auditas cujusque sententiae rationes rem iterum perpendere, concilium iterum in tempus solvatur, ad quod unaquaeque familia quaenam ultima ejus sit sententia pronunciabit; et tum demum prae-
30 sente integro concilio suffragiis collectis ea irrita habeatur quae centum ad minimum suffragia non habuerit, reliquae autem ad regem deferantur

22–23. *NS en indien zy . . . niet met malkander konnen verdragen.* Cf. p. 296, l. 20.

decisions need to be made. For that such a large number of citizens should be constantly available for administrative duties seems quite impossible. But since continuous administration is in fact required, fifty or more members of this council must be appointed to carry on its work when it has adjourned.[1] These should meet every day in a chamber next to the king's, and so exercise a daily supervision over the treasury, the defences of the cities,[2] the education of the king's heir, and, in general, perform all the functions of the great council which I have just enumerated; with this exception, that they should have no power to deal with fresh matters on which no decision has been made.

25. When the council has assembled, no matter must be proposed for discussion until five or six or more lawyers from the tribes which are first in order of precedence at that session have had audience with the king, laid before him any written petitions or letters which they have received, informed him about the condition of affairs, and, finally, learnt from his own lips what business he requires them to bring up in his council. When they have received his instructions they should return to the council-chamber, and the first in order of precedence should explain the matter to be decided. If some of the members think it important, it must not be put to the vote at once, but deferred for such time as its urgency allows. The council must therefore be adjourned until the date fixed, and in the meantime the counsellors of each tribe will have an opportunity to discuss it among themselves, and, if they think it of vital importance, to consult ex-counsellors and candidates from their own tribe. If they cannot reach agreement among themselves within the time appointed, their tribe shall be debarred from voting, for each tribe shall be allowed to cast one vote only. Otherwise they shall brief their lawyer in the opinion which they all think best, and he shall present it in the actual assembly. The lawyers of the other tribes shall do likewise; and if, after hearing the reasons for each opinion, the majority decides to reconsider the matter, the council should be adjourned again until a later date, when each tribe shall deliver its final opinion; and only then, when the whole council is present, should the vote be taken. Any opinion which does not receive at least a hundred votes should be disregarded; the others

---

[1] In Holland day-to-day administration was carried on by the *Gecommitteerde Raden*, who represented the Estates of the Province when these were not in session. See Temple, op. cit., ch. ii, p. 65, and J. J. de la Bassecour Caan, *Schets van den Regeringsvorm van Nederland*, 1866, p. 156.

[2] These were also functions of the *Gecommitteerde Raden* (de la Bassecour Caan, op. cit., p. 157).

a jurisperitis omnibus qui concilio interfuerunt, ut ex iis, postquam uniuscujusque partis rationes intellexerit, quam velit eligat. Atque inde digressi ad concilium revertantur, ubi omnes regem ad constitutum ab ipso tempus exspectent, ut quam sententiam ex latis eligendam censet
5 omnes audiant, et quid faciendum ipse decernat.

26. Ad justitiam administrandam concilium aliud ex solis jurisperitis est formandum, quorum officium sit lites dirimere, et poenas ex delinquentibus sumere; sed ita ut omnes sententiae quas tulerint ab iis qui concilii magni vicem supplent probari debeant, num scilicet ser-
10 vato rite in judicando ordine prolatae fuerint et absque partium studio. Quod si quae pars, quae causa cecidit, ostendere poterit aliquem ex judicibus munere aliquo corruptum fuisse ab adversario, vel aliam communem causam amicitiae erga eundem, vel odii erga ipsum habere, vel denique quod communis judicandi ordo non fuerit servatus, ea in
15 integrum restituatur. Sed haec forsan observari non possent ab iis qui, quando quaestio de crimine est, non tam argumentis quam tormentis reum convincere solent. Verum nec ego hic alium in judicando ordinem concipio praeter eum qui cum optimo civitatis regimine convenit.

20 27. Hi judices magno etiam et impari numero esse debent, nempe sexaginta et unus aut quinquaginta et unus ad minimum; et ex una familia non nisi unus eligendus, nec tamen ad vitam, sed ut quotannis etiam aliqua ejus pars cedat, et alii totidem eligantur, qui ex aliis sint familiis, quique ad quadragesimum aetatis annum pervenerint.

25 28. In hoc concilio nulla sententia pronuncianda nisi praesentibus omnibus judicibus. Quod si aliquis morbi aut alterius rei causa diu concilio interesse non poterit, alius ad id tempus eligendus qui ipsius locum suppleat. In suffragiis autem ferendis debebit unusquisque sententiam suam non palam dicere, sed calculis indicare.

30 29. Hujus et praecedentis concilii vicariorum emolumenta sint primo bona eorum qui mortis damnati sunt ab ipsis, et etiam eorum qui summa

---

4. *NS die hem voorgedragen zijn.* Perhaps the correct reading is *delatis.*

11. *NS op dat,* i.e. *ut,* for *Quod.*   15–19. *Sed . . . convenit* not in *NS.*

24. *OP quadragesimum; NS en d' ouderdom van vijftig jaren bereikt hebben,* i.e. *quinquagesimum.*

30–31. *NS zullen zijn vooréerst de goederen; OP sint primo. V–L* saw that *bona* had dropped out, and inserted it before *primo.* But *NS* suggests *primo bona. Primo* is answered, not by *etiam* in l. 31, but by *Deinde* on p. 330, l. 1 : first the emoluments from criminal cases, then those from civil suits. Cf. p. 404, ll. 20–24, where the order is reversed.

should be submitted to the king by all the lawyers who have attended the council, so that he may hear the reasons of each party and decide which opinion he favours. The lawyers should then return to the council-chamber, where all should wait upon the king at a time fixed by himself, so that they may all hear which of the opinions presented he has decided to adopt, and he may decree in person the measures to be taken.[1]

26. To administer justice there must be another council composed entirely of lawyers. Its duty should be to decide lawsuits and to punish criminals; but all its verdicts must be confirmed by those who are acting as deputies for the great council, i.e. reviewed to see that they have been given with due regard to regular judicial procedure and without partiality. If a party who has lost his case shall be able to show that a judge has been bribed by his opponent, or that a judge has some general reason for friendship to his opponent, or for hatred against himself, or, finally, that the regular judicial procedure has not been observed, the judgement against him must be quashed. It may be that these regulations could not be observed by those who use torments instead of arguments to convict defendants on criminal charges; but I for my part am here considering no other judicial procedure than that which is consistent with the good government of a commonwealth.

27. The number of these judges should be not only large, like the number of counsellors, but also uneven, i.e. sixty-one or fifty-one at least. No more than one judge must be appointed from each tribe; he must not serve for life, but here again a certain proportion of the council should retire annually, and be succeeded by a like number of lawyers from other tribes who have reached their fortieth year.

28. No verdict must be pronounced in this council unless all the judges are present. If a judge is compelled by illness or other causes to absent himself from the council for a long period of time, another must be appointed for that time to take his place. In voting each judge shall be required to give his verdict by secret and not by open ballot.

29. The remuneration of this council and of the above-mentioned council of deputies should be as follows. First they should receive the goods of those they have condemned to death and the fines imposed on

---

[1] In the Estates of Holland each town, though it had several deputies, had only one vote (Temple, op. cit., ch. ii, pp. 63 and 65), and the lawyer or pensionary acted as spokesman for the deputies of his town (de la Bassecour Caan, op. cit., p. 142). Again, the Estates could be adjourned to allow deputies to return home for further consultations (Temple, op. cit., ch. ii, p. 66). But by basing representation on tribes and not on towns Spinoza gives the larger towns more votes than the smaller.

quadam argenti plectuntur. Deinde ex unaquaque sententia quam de rebus civilibus tulerint, ab eo qui causa cecidit pro ratione totius summae partem aliquotam accipiant, qua utrumque concilium gaudeat.

30. His conciliis alia subordinentur in unaquaque urbe, quorum 5 etiam membra ad vitam eligi non debent; sed etiam quotannis pars aliqua eligenda ex solis familiis quae in eadem habitant. Sed opus non est haec latius persequi.

31. Militiae stipendia nulla solvenda tempore pacis; tempore autem belli iis tantummodo quotidiana stipendia danda qui quotidiano opere 10 vitam sustentant. At duces et reliqui officiarii cohortium nulla alia emolumenta ex bello exspectanda habeant praeter hostium praedam.

32. Si quis peregrinus alicujus civis filiam in uxorem duxerit, ejus liberi sunt cives censendi et in catalogo familiae matris inscribendi. Qui autem ex peregrinis parentibus in ipso imperio nati et educati sunt, iis 15 constituto aliquo pretio jus civis ex chiliarchis alicujus familiae emere liceat, et in catalogum ejusdem familiae referantur. Nec imperio, tametsi chiliarchae lucri causa aliquem peregrinum infra constitutum pretium in numerum suorum civium receperint, aliquod inde detrimentum oriri potest; sed contra media excogitanda quibus facilius 20 civium augeri possit numerus, et magna hominum detur confluentia. At qui in catalogum civium non referuntur, aequum est ut tempore saltem belli otium suum labore aut exactione aliqua compensent.

33. Legati qui tempore pacis ad alias civitates pacis contrahendae vel conservandae causa mitti debent, ex solis nobilibus eligendi sunt, et 25 ex civitatis aerario sumptus iisdem suppeditandi, non autem ex regis domestico aerario. Sed tales speculatores eligendi sunt qui regi periti videbuntur.

34. Qui aulam frequentant, et regis domestici sunt, quibusque ex suo aerario domestico stipendia solvit, ab omni civitatis ministerio seu 30 officio secludendi sunt. Dico expresse *quibus rex ex aerario suo domestico stipendia solvit*, ut corporis custodes ab iisdem secludam. Nam corporis custodes nulli praeter cives ejusdem urbis in aula, servatis vicibus, vigilare pro rege ante fores debent.

35. Bellum non nisi pacis causa inferendum, ut eo finito arma cessent.

1–2. *NS van burgerlijke zaken, die 't lijf niet aangaan.*
26–27. *Sed ... videbuntur* not in *OP*. This is *L*'s translation of the *NS* text: *Maar men moet zodanige bespieders verkiezen, die aan de Koning bequaam zullen schijnen.*

offenders. Secondly, as a fee for every verdict given in civil suits, they should receive from the man who has lost his case a certain proportion of the whole sum involved, and this should be enjoyed by both councils.

30. Other councils subordinate to these should be appointed in each city, and their members should not be elected for life either; but here again a certain proportion must be chosen each year, exclusively from the tribes which inhabit the city in question. But there is no need to discuss this in greater detail.[1]

31. No payment for military service must be made in time of peace; in war-time a daily wage must be given only to those who support life by their daily toil. But commanders and other company officers should have no gain to expect from war but the booty they win from the enemy.

32. If an alien marries the daughter of a citizen, his children must be regarded as citizens and enrolled in their mother's tribe. Those who are of alien parentage on both sides, but have been born and brought up within the territory of the state, should be permitted to acquire citizen status by paying a fixed sum of money to the officers of some tribe, and should be enrolled in that tribe. Even if an alien does bribe these officers to admit him as a citizen at less than the appointed fee, this can do no harm whatever to the state; on the contrary, means must be devised so that the number of citizens may be more readily increased, and a great influx of population secured.[2] It is only fair, however, that those who are not inscribed on the citizen roll should, in war-time at any rate, make up for their exemption from military duties by performing some sort of service or paying some sort of tax.

33. Ambassadors who have to be sent to other commonwealths in time of peace, either to conclude peace or to maintain it, must be chosen exclusively from the nobles, and have their expenses provided from the treasury of the commonwealth, not from the king's privy purse. But secret agents must be chosen from such as appear suitable to the king.

34. Those who live at court, serve in the king's household, and are paid by the king from his own privy purse, must be debarred from holding any magistracy or office in the commonwealth. I say 'those who are paid by the king from his own privy purse' expressly, in order to exclude the king's body-guard. For none but citizens of the capital city must serve as his body-guard and take turns at keeping watch in the palace before the king's doors.

35. The sole object of warfare should be to secure peace, so that the

---

[1] Each town in Holland had a council and a law-court (Temple, op. cit., ch. ii, pp. 57–60).
[2] Machiavelli, *Discourses* i, 6 and ii, 3; Bacon, *Essay* xxix.

Urbibus igitur jure belli captis, et hoste subacto, pacis conditiones
instituendae sunt ut captae urbes nullo praesidio servari debeant; sed
vel ut hosti, pacis foedere accepto, potestas concedatur easdem pretio
redimendi, vel—si ea ratione timor semper a tergo maneat formidine
5 loci—prorsus delendae sunt, et incolae alio locorum ducendi.

36. Regi nullam extraneam matrimonio sibi jungere, sed tantum ex
consanguineis vel civibus aliquam in uxorem ducere liceat; ea tamen
conditione, si scilicet civem aliquam duxerit, ut qui uxori sanguine sint
proximi nullum civitatis officium administrare possint.

10 37. Imperium indivisibile esse debet. Si igitur rex plures liberos pro-
creaverit, illorum major natu jure succedat; minime autem concedendum ut imperium inter ipsos dividatur, nec ut indivisum omnibus vel
aliquibus tradatur, et multo minus ut partem imperii dotem filiae dare
liceat. Nam filias in haereditatem imperii venire nulla ratione con-
15 cedendum.

38. Si rex liberis masculis orbus obierit, ille qui ipsi sanguine proximus haeres imperii habendus, nisi forte uxorem extraneam duxerit
quam repudiare nolit.

39. Ad cives quod attinet, patet ex Art. 5 Cap. 3 eorum unumquem-
20 que ad omnia regis mandata sive edicta a concilio magno promulgata
(vide de hac conditione Art. 18 et 19 hujus Capitis) obtemperare debere,
tametsi eadem absurdissima credat, vel jure ad id cogi. Atque haec
imperii monarchici fundamenta sunt, quibus superstrui debet, ut stabile
sit, quemadmodum in seq. Cap. demonstrabimus.

25 40. Ad religionem quod attinet, nulla plane templa urbium sumptibus aedificanda, nec jura de opinionibus statuenda, nisi seditiosae sint
et civitatis fundamenta evertant. Ii igitur quibus religionem publice
exercere conceditur, templum, si velint, suis sumptibus aedificent. At
rex ad religionem cui addictus est exercendam templum in aula sibi
30 proprium habeat.

1–2. *NS zodanige voorwaarden van vrede* suggests *pacis conditiones ita instituendae sunt.*
But cf. p. 324, ll. 27–28.

4–5. *NS of indien men, uit vrees van de plaats, altijt in schrik zou blijven*, i.e. *si timor
semper maneat formidine loci.*

14. For *filias NS* has *een dochter.*

sword may be sheathed when the war is over. Thus when cities have been captured by the right of war, the terms which are arranged on the final defeat of the enemy should obviate the need to hold them by garrison; the enemy should either be allowed to redeem them for a money payment once he has accepted the peace treaty, or else—if their position is formidable, and this policy would therefore leave a constant threat in the rear—they must be utterly destroyed, and their inhabitants removed elsewhere.[1]

36. The king should not be allowed to marry an alien, but only a kinswoman or fellow citizen;[2] and his marriage to a citizen should debar his wife's nearest kinsmen from holding any office in the commonwealth.

37. The state must be indivisible. If, therefore, the king has more than one son, the eldest should succeed by right. What must not be permitted is that the state should be divided among them, or that it should be handed on undivided to all or some of them; and still less should the king be allowed to give part of the state to a daughter as a dowry. For daughters cannot possibly be permitted to succeed to the throne.

38. If the king dies without male issue, his nearest kinsman must be regarded as heir to the throne, unless he happens to have married an alien and refuses to divorce her.

39. As for the citizens, it is clear from Chapter 3, Section 5, that each of them is bound to obey all the commands or edicts of the king that have been published by the great council (for this condition see Sections 18 and 19 of this Chapter), even though he regards them as utterly foolish; or be compelled to do so by right. Such are the foundations on which a monarchy must rest if it is to be stable, as I shall show in the next Chapter.

40. As regards religion, no churches whatsoever are to be built at the cities' expense; nor should laws be passed against religious beliefs unless they are seditious and radically subversive.[3] Thus those who are permitted to practise their religion openly may, if they wish, build a church at their own expense.[4] That the king may practise the religion which he favours he should have a chapel of his own in the palace.

---

[1] Machiavelli, *Prince* iii; *Discourses* ii, 23.

[2] The Doges of Venice were subject to a similar restriction: see *Mémoires historiques et politiques sur la République de Venise*, 1795, vol. ii, ch. v, p. 197. But Spinoza probably has in mind the connexion between the House of Orange and the British House of Stuart, which had brought autocracy to the Netherlands under William II, who married the daughter of Charles I, and might bring Catholicism under William III, who in 1676 was suing for the hand of Mary, daughter of the future James II.

[3] *TT-P* xx, p. 233.   [4] Temple, op. cit., ch. v, p. 124.

1. Imperii monarchici fundamentis explicatis, eadem hic ordine demonstrare suscepi; ad quod apprime notandum est praxi nullo modo repugnare quod jura adeo firma constituantur quae nec ab ipso rege aboleri queant. Persae enim reges suos inter deos colere solebant, et ta-
5 men ipsi reges potestatem non habebant jura semel instituta revocandi, ut ex Dan. Cap. 6 patet; et nullibi, quod sciam, monarcha absolute eligitur, nullis expressis conditionibus. Imo nec rationi nec obedientiae absolutae quae regi debetur repugnat; nam fundamenta imperii veluti regis aeterna decreta habenda sunt, adeo ut ejus ministri ei
10 omnino obediant, si, quando aliquid imperat quod imperii fundamentis repugnat, mandata exequi velle negent. Quod exemplo Ulissis clare explicare possumus. Socii enim Ulissis ipsius mandatum exequebantur, quando navis malo alligatum et cantu Syrenum mente captum religare noluerunt, tametsi id modis multis minitando imperabat; et prudentiae
15 ejusdem imputatur quod postea sociis gratias egerit quod ex prima ipsius mente ipsi obtemperaverint. Et ad hoc Ulissis exemplum solent etiam reges judices instruere, ut scilicet justitiam exerceant, nec quenquam respiciant, nec ipsum regem, si quid singulari aliquo casu imperaverit quod contra institutum jus esse noverint. Reges enim non dii, sed
20 homines sunt, qui Syrenum capiuntur saepe cantu. Si igitur omnia ab inconstanti unius voluntate penderent, nihil fixum esset. Atque adeo imperium monarchicum, ut stabile sit, instituendum est ut omnia quidem ex solo regis decreto fiant, hoc est, ut omne jus sit regis explicata voluntas; at non ut omnis regis voluntas jus sit. De quo vide Art.
25 3, 5, et 6 praec. Cap.

2. Deinde notandum quod in jaciendis fundamentis maxime humanos affectus observare necesse est, nec ostendisse sufficit quid oporteat fieri, sed apprime quî fieri possit ut homines, sive affectu sive ratione ducantur, jura tamen rata fixaque habeant. Nam si imperii
30 jura, sive libertas publica, solo invalido legum auxilio nitatur, non tantum nulla ejus obtinendae erit civibus securitas, ut Art. 3 Cap.

4. *NS onder de Goden zelven*, i.e. *inter ipsos deos.*
6. *G Cap. 6*; *OP Cap. 5*; *NS uit Daniëls vijfde Hooftdeel. B* noted the false reference and read *ut ex Daniele patet.*
22. *NS moet . . . in dier voegen ingestelt worden.* Cf. p. 324, ll. 27–28, and p. 332, ll. 1–2.

CHAPTER VII

1. Having described the fundamental laws of monarchy, I must now fulfil my promise to justify them one by one. The main point to be noted is that it is by no means contrary to practice for laws to be so firmly established that even the king himself cannot repeal them. The Persians, for example, used to worship their kings as gods,[1] yet even their kings had no power to repeal laws that had once been established, as is clear from Daniel, Chapter 6; and nowhere, so far as I know, is a king appointed unconditionally, without any explicit terms.[2] This, in fact, is contrary neither to reason nor to the absolute obedience due to a king; for the fundamental laws of the state must be regarded as the king's permanent decrees, so that his ministers render him complete obedience in refusing to execute any command of his which contravenes them. We may clarify this point by reference to Ulysses, whose comrades did execute his command in refusing, in spite of all his orders and threats, to untie him from his ship's mast while he was enchanted by the Sirens' song;[3] and it is put down to his good sense that he thanked them afterwards for carrying out his original intention so obediently. Even kings follow the example of Ulysses; they usually instruct their judges to have no respect for persons in administering justice, not even for the king himself, if by some odd mischance he commands something which they know to contravene established law. For kings are not gods, but men, who are often enchanted by the Sirens' song. Accordingly, if everything depended on the inconstant will of one man, nothing would be stable.[4] Hence if a monarchy is to be stable it must be organized so that everything is done by the king's decree alone (i.e. every law is the king's declared will), but not everything the king wills is law. On this see Sections 3, 5, and 6 of the previous Chapter.

2. The second point to be noted is this. In laying down fundamental laws it is necessary to pay particular attention to human passions. To have shown what ought to be done is not enough; the main problem is to show how it can be done, i.e. how men, even when led by passion, may still have fixed and stable laws.[5] If civil right, or public liberty, has no basis but the slender support of legal prescriptions, it will not only be very difficult for the citizens to maintain, as I have shown in

---

[1] *TT-P* xvii, p. 157.
[3] *Odyssey* xii, 156 and ff.
[5] *TT-P* xvii, p. 153.
[2] *TP* iv, 6 and n. 3, p. 305.
[4] *TP* i, 6, p. 265.

praec. ostendimus, sed etiam exitio erit. Nam hoc certum est, nullam civitatis conditionem miseriorem esse quam optimae quae labascere incipit, nisi uno actu et ictu cadat et in servitutem ruat,—quod sane impossibile videtur esse; ac proinde subditis multo satius esset suum jus
5 absolute in unum transferre quam incertas et vanas, sive irritas libertatis conditiones stipulari, atque ita posteris iter ad servitutem crudelissimam parare. At si imperii monarchici fundamenta quae in praec. Cap. retuli firma esse ostendero, nec divelli posse nisi cum indignatione maximae partis armatae multitudinis, et ex iis regi et multitudini pacem
10 et securitatem sequi, atque haec ex communi hominum natura deduxero, dubitare nemo poterit eadem optima esse et vera, ut patet ex Art. 9 Cap. 3 et Art. 3 et 8 praec. Cap. Quod autem hujus illa naturae sint quam paucis potero ostendam.

3. Quod officium ejus qui imperium tenet sit imperii statum et
15 conditionem semper noscere, et communi omnium saluti vigilare, et id omne quod majori subditorum parti utile est efficere, apud omnes in confesso est. Cum autem unus solus omnia perlustrare nequeat, nec semper animum praesentem habere, et ad cogitandum instituere, et saepe morbo aut senectute aut aliis de causis rebus vacare publicis pro-
20 hibeatur, necesse ergo est ut monarcha consiliarios habeat qui rerum statum noscant, et regem consilio juvent, et ipsius locum saepe suppleant; atque adeo fiat ut imperium seu civitas una semper eademque mente constet.

4. Sed quia cum humana natura ita comparatum est ut unusquisque
25 suum privatum utile summo cum affectu quaerat, et illa jura aequissima esse judicet quae rei suae conservandae et augendae necessaria esse, et alterius causam eatenus defendat quatenus rem suam eo ipso stabilire credit, hinc sequitur consiliarios necessario debere eligi quorum privatae res et utilitas a communi omnium salute et pace pendeant.
30 Atque adeo patet quod, si ex unoquoque civium genere sive classe aliquot eligantur, id majori subditorum parti utile erit quod in hoc concilio plurima habuerit suffragia. Et quamvis hoc concilium, quod ex adeo magno civium numero componitur, frequentari necessario debeat a multis rudi admodum ingenio, hoc tamen certum est, unumquemque
35 in negotiis quae diu magno cum affectu exercuit satis callidum atque

---

10. *NS van de gemene natuur der menschen*, i.e. *ex communi hominum natura*; *OP ex communi natura*. For the order of words cf. p. 436, ll. 17–18, *communi hominum affectu*; see also ll. 15 and 29 below.

19. *P vacare*; *OP vocare*.

Section 3 of the previous Chapter, but will actually prove their undoing. For when a good commonwealth is beginning to decline, but
does not do the impossible by collapsing completely at the first blow and
throwing itself into its chains, its condition is certainly the most
wretched of all; and so it would be far better for subjects to transfer
their right to one man unconditionally than to insist upon untrust-
worthy and empty, i.e. useless guarantees of freedom, and thus prepare
the way for the brutal oppression of their descendants. But if I prove
that the foundations of monarchy described in the previous Chapter
are strong; that they cannot be destroyed without arousing indignation
in the bulk of an armed populace; that they provide peace and security
for both king and people; and deduce all this from the common nature
of men; then no one will be able to doubt that they are good and true
foundations, as is clear from Chapter 3, Section 9, and from Sections 3
and 8 of the previous Chapter. That they *are* of this nature I shall now
show as briefly as I can.

3. That it is the duty of the sovereign to acquaint himself constantly with the position and condition of the state, to watch over the
common welfare, and to do everything that is for the benefit of the
majority of his subjects, is universally admitted. But since one man cannot supervise everything by himself, cannot always have his wits about
him and apply himself to deliberation, but is often prevented from attending to public affairs by illness or age or other causes, a king needs
counsellors to find out the condition of affairs, to help him with advice,
and often to act as his deputies;[1] this that the policy of the state may
always be stable and consistent.

4. But human nature is such that everyone pursues his private
advantage with the greatest eagerness, regards the laws which he thinks
necessary for the preservation and promotion of his own interests as
entirely fair, and defends another's cause if—but only if—he believes
that by so doing he is strengthening his own position. It is therefore
necessary to appoint counsellors whose private interests and advantage
are bound up with the general welfare and the maintenance of peace.
So if some are chosen from each class or group of citizens, the measure
which receives most votes in their council will obviously be to the
advantage of the majority of the subjects. And although this council,
composed as it is of so large a number of citizens, must inevitably be
attended by many whose minds are very uncultivated, surely everyone
is fairly competent and shrewd in matters to which he has long applied

---

1 Aristotle, *Politics* 1287^b 8–9.

astutum esse. Quapropter si nulli alii eligantur nisi ii qui ad quinquagesimum aetatis annum usque negotia sua sine ignominia exercuerunt, satis apti erunt ut consilia res suas concernentia dare possint, praesertim si in rebus majoris ponderis tempus ad meditandum concedatur. Adde quod
5 longe abest ut concilium quod paucis constat a similibus non frequentetur. Nam contra maxima ejus pars ex hominibus ejusmodi constat, quandoquidem unusquisque ibi maxime conatur socios habere bardos qui ab ipsius ore pendeant; quod in magnis conciliis locum non habet.

5. Praeterea certum est unumquemque malle regere quam regi;
10 nemo enim volens imperium alteri concedit, ut habet Sallustius in prima ad Caesarem oratione. Ac proinde patet quod multitudo integra nunquam jus suum in paucos aut unum transferet, si inter ipsam convenire possit, nec ex controversiis quae plerumque in magnis conciliis excitantur in seditiones ire; atque adeo multitudo libere id tantummodo
15 in regem transfert quod absolute in potestate ipsa habere nequit, hoc est, controversiarum diremptionem et in decernendo expeditionem. Nam quod saepe etiam fit ut rex belli causa eligatur, quia scilicet bellum a regibus multo felicius geritur, inscitia sane est, nimirum quod, ut bellum felicius gerant, in pace servire velint; si quidem pax eo in imperio potest
20 concipi, cujus summa potestas sola belli causa in unum translata est, qui propterea virtutem suam et quid omnes in ipso uno habeant maxime in bello ostendere potest; cum contra imperium democraticum hoc praecipuum habeat quod ejus virtus multo magis in pace quam in bello valet. Sed quacunque de causa rex eligatur, ipse solus, ut jam diximus, quid
25 imperio utile sit scire nequit; sed ad hoc, ut in praec. Art. ostendimus, necesse est ut plures cives consiliarios habeat. Et quia concipere nequaquam possumus quod aliquid de re consulenda potest concipi quod tam magnum hominum numerum effugerit, sequitur quod praeter omnes hujus concilii sententias quae ad regem deferuntur, nulla poterit concipi ad populi salutem idonea. Atque adeo, quia populi salus suprema
30 cipi ad populi salutem idonea. Atque adeo, quia populi salus suprema lex, seu regis summum jus est, sequitur jus regis esse unam ex latis concilii sententiis eligere, non autem contra totius concilii mentem quicquam decernere vel sententiam ferre. Vide Art. 25 praeced. Cap.

7. *NS Jabroeders.*   10–11. *nemo . . . oratione* not in *NS*.
14. *NS en zo zy niet . . . tot beroerten uitbarst*; *M iret* or *irent*.
14–15. *NS de vrije menigte dit alleenlijk warelijk . . . overgeeft*, i.e. *multitudo libera id tantummodo . . . transfert*; *OP multitudo id libere tantummodo . . . transfert*.
20–21. *sola . . . propterea* not in *NS*.
31–32. *OP unam ex latis concilii sententiis eligere*; *NS een uit de gegeve gevoelens te verkiezen*, which suggests *unam ex datis sententiis eligere*. But cf. p. 362, l. 17, where *latas* is rendered by *gegeven*.

himself with enthusiasm. Hence if none are chosen but men who have practised their own trades without disgrace up to their fiftieth year, they will be well enough fitted to give advice about their own affairs, especially if they are allowed time to reflect in matters of greater importance. Besides, it is quite untrue that small councils are free from uneducated men. In fact they are largely composed of such men, for every member does his best to secure the appointment of slow-witted colleagues who will hang upon his lips. In large councils there is no opportunity for this.[1]

5. Again, it is certain that everyone would rather rule than be ruled; 'for nobody yields sovereignty to another willingly', as Sallust says in his first speech to Caesar.[2] Clearly, then, a whole people will never transfer its right to one man or a few if its members can agree among themselves and avoid falling into civil strife as a result of the controversies which often arise in large assemblies. Thus a people freely transfers to a king only what it cannot wholly command itself, viz., the power to settle disputes and to take rapid decisions. No doubt it is also common to appoint a king for purposes of war, on the ground that kings are far more successful in warfare. But surely it is foolish for men to embrace slavery in peace for the sake of better fortune in war; if, indeed, there can be any peace for a state where the sovereignty has been transferred to one man for purely military ends.[3] For it is in war that such a man can best display his prowess, and show what a unique asset he is to them all; whereas it is an outstanding feature of democracy that its merits are far greater in peace than in war. But whatever the reason for choosing a king, he cannot, as I have already said, know what is best for the state by himself; for this he must have a number of citizens as counsellors, as I have shown in the previous Section. And since it is quite impossible to imagine any conceivable opinion on a problem of policy being overlooked by so large a number of men, it will be impossible to imagine any opinion conducive to the people's welfare which is not included among those submitted to the king by this council. It follows that, since the people's welfare is the highest law, or the king's supreme right, the king's right is to choose one of the opinions presented in the council, and not to make any decree or pass any judgement contrary to the views of the entire council. See Section

[1] This is a reply to Hobbes's criticism of large councils in *De Cive* x, 10.

[2] Pseudo-Sallust, *Ad Caesarem Senem de Re Publica Oratio* i, 4 (quoted again in viii, 12, p. 379).

[3] *TT-P* xviii, p. 197. Spinoza rejects Hobbes's argument in *De Cive* x, 17: that kings make the best generals is an argument for peace rather than for monarchy.

Sed si omnes sententiae in concilio latae ad regem deferendae essent, fieri posset ut rex parvis urbibus, quae pauciora habent suffragia, semper faveret. Nam quamvis ex lege concilii statutum sit ut sententiae non indicatis earum authoribus deferantur, nunquam tamen tam bene cavere
5 poterunt ut non aliqua effluat; ac proinde necessario statuendum est ut illa sententia quae centum ad minimum suffragia non habuerit irrita habeatur; quod quidem jus majores urbes summa vi defendere debebunt.

6. Atque hic, nisi brevitati studerem, magnas hujus concilii utilitates alias ostenderem; unam tamen quae maximi videtur esse momenti
10 adducam, nempe quod nullum majus ad virtutem incitamentum dari potest hac communi spe summum hunc honorem adipiscendi. Nam gloria maxime ducimur omnes, ut in nostra Ethica fuse ostendimus.

7. Quin majori hujus concilii parti nunquam animus gerendi bellum, sed magnum pacis studium et amor semper futurus sit, dubitari non
15 potest. Nam praeterquam quod ex bello ipsis timor semper erit bona sua cum libertate amittendi, accedit quod ad bellum novi sumptus requirantur quos suppeditare debent, ac etiam quod ipsorum liberi et affines, curis domesticis intenti, studium ad arma in bello applicare et militatum ire cogentur; unde domum nihil praeter gratuitas cicatrices
20 referre poterunt. Nam, uti Art. 31 praeced. Cap. diximus, militiae stipendia nulla solvenda, et Art. 10 ejusdem Cap. ipsa ex solis civibus et ex nullis aliis formanda.

8. Ad pacem et concordiam aliud praeterea, quod etiam magni est momenti, accedit, nempe quod nullus civis bona fixa habeat. Vid. Art.
25 12 praeced. Cap. Unde omnibus ex bello par propemodum periculum est: nam omnes lucri causa mercaturam exercere, vel argentum suum invicem credere—si, ut olim ab Atheniensibus, lex lata sit qua prohibeatur unicuique argentum suum foenere aliis quam incolis dare,—atque adeo negotia tractare debebunt quae vel invicem intricata sunt,

19. *OP domum.* So Curtius VIII, vii, 11. *V-L donum* (perhaps a misprint).
20. B *Art. 31;* OP *Art. 30;* NS *in 't dartigste Lid.*
21. B *Art. 10;* OP *Art 11;* NS *volgens het elfde Lid.*

25 of the previous Chapter. Yet if every opinion presented in the council had to be submitted to the king, he might always favour the small cities, which have fewest votes.[1] For although it is laid down in the constitution of the council that opinions should be submitted without indication of their authors, it will never be possible to take such strict precautions that none whatever leaks out; and so there must be a law that any opinion which does not receive at least a hundred votes shall be disregarded; a law which the larger cities will necessarily uphold with all their power.

6. Were it not my aim to be brief, I should now point out other great advantages of this council; but I shall mention only the one which I regard as most important, namely, that no greater incentive to virtue can be provided than the general hope of attaining this high office.[2] For ambition is the main motive of man, as I have shown at length in my Ethics.[3]

7. That the majority in this council will never be enthusiastic for war, but will always have a great desire and love for peace, is not open to doubt. For not only will war always inspire in them the fear of losing both their goods and their freedom; it will also lay extra financial burdens upon them, and, in addition, compel their children and relatives, now busy with their private concerns, to apply their energies to arms and to go on campaigns; from which they can bring home nothing but unprofitable scars.[4] For, as I have said in Section 31 of the previous Chapter, no payment is to be made to the army, and, by Section 10 of the same Chapter, it must be composed of citizens alone.

8. Another thing which is of great importance in promoting peace and concord is the fact that no citizen is to have any real estate. See Section 12 of the previous Chapter. This means that the danger from war is practically the same for all; for if there is a law—like the one once passed by the Athenians[5]—forbidding them to lend money outside the country, their only means of gain will be to engage in trade[6] or make loans to their fellow subjects, and so they will have to deal with interests which are either interdependent or require the same

---

[1] The stadtholder could neutralize the votes of the larger cities of Holland by winning over the smaller (Temple, *Observations*, ch. ii, pp. 63–64). In Spinoza's monarchy a large city has more votes than a small one; but it is still necessary to prevent the king from accepting the proposal of a tiny minority.

[2] *TP* vii, 10, p. 343; viii, 30, p. 393. [3] *E* iii, App. 44.

[4] Curtius, *Historiae Alexandri Magni* VIII, vii, 11.

[5] Van Hove, *Polityke Weegschaal* III, ii, 1, p. 505.

[6] By making his model monarchy a commercial state like the Dutch Republic Spinoza gives it an additional bias towards peace (cf. *TP* vii, 28, p. 361).

vel quae eadem media ut promoveantur requirunt. Atque adeo hujus concilii maximae parti circa res communes et pacis artes una plerumque eademque erit mens; nam, ut Art. 4 hujus Cap. diximus, unusquisque alterius causam eatenus defendit quatenus eo ipso rem suam stabilire 5 credit.

9. Quod nemo unquam in animum inducet hoc concilium muneribus corrumpere dubitari non potest. Si enim aliquis ex tam magno hominum numero unum aut alterum ad se trahat, sane nihil promovebit; nam, uti diximus, sententia quae centum ad minimum suffragia 10 non habuerit irrita est.

10. Quod praeterea hujus concilii semel stabiliti membra ad minorem numerum redigi non poterunt, facile videbimus si hominum communes affectus consideremus. Omnes enim gloria maxime ducuntur, et nullus est qui sano corpore vivit qui non speret in longam senectutem vitam 15 trahere. Si itaque calculum ineamus eorum qui revera annum quinquagesimum aut sexagesimum aetatis attigerunt, et rationem praeterea habeamus magni istius concilii numeri qui quotannis eligitur, videbimus vix aliquem eorum qui arma ferunt dari posse qui non magna spe teneatur huc dignitatis ascendere; atque adeo omnes hoc concilii jus 20 quantum poterunt defendent. Nam notandum quod corruptio, nisi paulatim irrepat, facile praevenitur; at quia facilius concipi potest, et minori invidia fieri, ut ex unaquaque familia quam ut ex paucis minor numerus eligatur, aut ut una aut alia secludatur, ergo (per Art. 15 praeced. Cap.) consiliariorum numerus non potest ad alium minorem 25 redigi nisi simul ab eo una tertia, quarta, aut quinta pars auferatur; quae sane mutatio admodum magna est, et consequenter a communi praxi omnino abhorrens. Nec mora praeterea sive in eligendo negligentia timenda est, quia haec ab ipso concilio suppletur. Vid. Art. 16 praeced. Cap.

30 11. Rex igitur, sive multitudinis metu ductus, vel ut sibi armatae multitudinis majorem partem devinciat, sive animi generositate ductus, ut scilicet utilitati publicae consulat, illam semper sententiam quae plurima suffragia habuerit, hoc est (per Art. 5 hujus Cap.), quae imperii majori parti est utilior, firmabit, aut discrepantes sententias quae 35 ad ipsum delatae sunt, si fieri potest, conciliare studebit, ut omnes ad se

---

9. *NS dat gevoelen, 't welk ten minsten geen hondert stemmen had;* OP *sententia quae ad summum centum ad minimum suffragia non habuerit.* L *and* G *rightly delete* ad summum.

23. B *per Art.* 15; OP *per Art.* 14; NS *volgens het veertiende Lid.*

28. *NS dewijl zulks van de Raatvergadering zelve goed gemaakt en uitgevoert zal worden.*

34. *NS of.* Hence M aut. OP et.

means for their furtherance.[1] Hence the majority of this council will generally be in agreement about their common concerns and activities in time of peace; for, as I said in Section 4 of this Chapter, one man defends the cause of another if he believes that by so doing he is strengthening his own position.

9. No one, it is certain, will ever think to bribe this council. For if anyone does win over one or two men out of so large a number, it will not help him in the least, since, as I said, an opinion which does not receive at least a hundred votes is disregarded.

10. When this council has once been established it will be impossible to reduce the number of its members; as we shall easily see by considering the common passions of men. Ambition is the chief motive of all men, and everyone in good bodily health looks forward to a long span of years. If, then, we calculate the number of men who actually reach their fiftieth or sixtieth year, and also consider the large proportion of this council which is appointed annually, we shall hardly find anyone among those who bear arms who is not possessed by high hopes of rising to this position; so they will all do their utmost to maintain the law governing election to the council.[2] Notice that if corruption does not creep in gradually it is easily prevented. Now a violation of this law which reduces the quota of every tribe is more probable, and will cause less ill-feeling, than one which reduces or abolishes the quota of a few tribes only. It follows (by Section 15 of the previous Chapter) that the number of counsellors can only be reduced by the immediate removal of a third, fourth, or fifth of the council; a change which is obviously very great, and so wholly repugnant to current practice. And there is no need to fear delay or remissness in making appointments, since these are provided for by the council itself. See Section 16 of the previous Chapter.

11. The king, then, whether his motive for promoting the public interest is fear of the people, or desire to win over the bulk of the armed populace, or nobility of soul, will always do one of two things. Either he will ratify the opinion which has received most votes in the council, and is thus (by Section 5 of this Chapter) most advantageous to the majority; or he will try, if possible, to reconcile the different opinions submitted to him, in order to win everyone's support—his main

---

[1] This use of economic motives to secure harmony prompted Vico's sneer in *Scienza Nuova*, Book I, par. 335 : 'Benedict Spinoza speaks of the commonwealth as of a society of shop-keepers.'

[2] *TP* viii, 30, p. 393.

trahat—qua in re nervos intendet suos,—et ut tam in pace quam in bello experiantur quid in ipso uno habeant; atque adeo tum maxime sui juris erit et imperium maxime habebit, quando maxime communi multitudinis saluti consulit.

5   12. Nam rex solus omnes metu continere nequit; sed ipsius potentia, ut diximus, nititur militum numero, et praecipue eorundem virtute et fide; quae semper inter homines tamdiu constans erit quamdiu indigentia, sive haec honesta, sive turpis sit, copulantur. Unde fit ut reges incitare saepius milites quam coercere, et magis eorum vitia quam vir-
10 tutes dissimulare soleant, et plerumque, ut optimos premant, inertes et luxu perditos inquirere, agnoscere, pecunia aut gratia juvare, prehensare manus, jacere oscula, et omnia servilia pro dominatione agere. Ut itaque cives a rege prae omnibus agnoscantur, et quantum status civilis sive aequitas concedit sui juris maneant, necesse est ut militia ex solis
15 civibus componatur, et ut ipsi a consiliis sint; et contra eos omnino subactos esse, et aeterni belli fundamenta jacere, simulatque milites auxiliares conduci patiuntur; quorum mercatura bellum est, et quibus in discordiis et seditionibus plurima vis.

13. Quod regis consiliarii ad vitam eligi non debeant, sed in tres,
20 quatuor, vel quinque ad summum annos, patet tam ex Art. 10 hujus Capitis quam ex iis quae in Art. 9 hujus etiam Capitis diximus. Nam si ad vitam eligerentur, praeterquam quod maxima civium pars vix ullam spem posset concipere eum honorem adipiscendi, atque adeo magna inde inter cives inaequalitas, unde invidia et continui rumores et tan-
25 dem seditiones orirentur—quae sane regibus dominandi avidis non ingratae essent,—magnam praeterea ad omnia licentiam (sublato scilicet succedentium metu) sumerent, rege minime adversante. Nam quo civibus magis invisi, eo magis regi adhaerebunt, eique ad adulandum magis proni erunt. Imo quinque annorum intervallum nimium adhuc vide-
30 tur, quia eo temporis spatio non adeo impossibile factu videtur ut magna admodum concilii (quam etiam magnum sit) pars muneribus aut gratia corrumpatur. Atque adeo longe securius res sese habebit si

---

1. *et* not in *NS*.   4. *NS zal zorgen,* i.e. *consulet.*
7–8. *NS door zekere gemene behoeftigheit,* i.e. *indigentia aliqua communi.*
17. *NS zo haast als zy lijden dat men hulpbenden aanncemt,* i.e. *conduci;* OP *duci.*
27. *NS zo zouden zy . . . aan zich nemen.* Hence *L sumerent.* OP *sument.*

endeavour[1]—and prove his value to his subjects in peace as well as in war. He will thus be most fully possessed of his own right, and most firmly seated on his throne, when he gives most heed to the general welfare of his people.

12. For a king cannot keep all in awe by himself; his power, as I said, is based on the number of his troops, and, in particular, on their courage and loyalty; which will never last longer among men than the mutual need, whether honourable or base, which binds them together.[2] This is why it is more usual for kings to spur on than to check their troops, and to overlook their faults than to conceal their merits;[3] very often, to oppress the good, they seek out idlers and wastrels for recognition, helping them with money or influence, clasping their hands, throwing them kisses, and, in general, licking their boots as the price of despotic power.[4] Thus to ensure that citizens stand higher than any others in their king's regard, and retain their own right as far as political order or justice permits, it is necessary that they alone should be his soldiers and his counsellors; whereas slavery and perpetual warfare are their inevitable lot as soon as they allow the king to engage mercenary troops; for war is the trade of such men, and their power is greatest amid discord and rebellion.[5]

13. That the king's counsellors should not be appointed for life, but for three, four, or five years at the most, is clear both from Section 10 and from my remarks in Section 9 of this Chapter. If they were appointed for life, most of the citizens could have very little hope of attaining this office,[6] and so there would arise great inequality among them, leading in turn to jealousy and continual murmurings and finally to revolts—which, of course, would not be unwelcome to kings eager for tyranny. Besides, the counsellors, being no longer restrained by fear of successors,[7] would assume a large measure of arbitrary power over everything, and this with little or no opposition from the king. For the more they are hated by the citizens, the more will they cling to the king, and the more subservient to him will they tend to become. In fact, even a five years' term of office appears to be rather long, since it does not seem completely impossible for a very great part of the council, however large, to be corrupted by bribes or favours in that space of time. Hence it will be much safer if two members from each tribe are

---

[1] Terence, *Eunuchus* 312.
[2] *TT-P* xvi, p. 131 (the binding force of contracts); cf. *TP* iii, 14, pp. 295–7.
[3] Tacitus, *Histories* II, lxxxii, 1.   [4] Tacitus, *Histories* I, xxxvi, 2–3.
[5] Tacitus, *Histories* IV, i, 3.   [6] *TP* viii, 30, p. 393.   [7] *TP* vii, 21, p. 353.

quotannis ex unaquaque familia duo cedant et totidem iisdem succedant (si nimirum ex unaquaque familia quinque consiliarii habendi
sunt), praeterquam eo anno quo juris prudens alicujus familiae cedit et
novus ejus loco eligitur.

5   14. Rex praeterea nullus majorem sibi securitatem polliceri potest
quam qui in hujusmodi civitate regnat. Nam praeterquam quod cito
perit quem sui milites salvum esse nolunt, certum est regibus summum
semper periculum esse ab iis qui eis proximi sunt. Quo igitur consiliarii
numero pauciores, et consequenter potentiores sunt, eo regi majus ab
10 ipsis periculum est ne imperium in alium transferant. Nihil sane Davidem
magis terruit quam quod ipsius consiliarius Achitophel partes Absolomi
elegerat. Huc accedit, si omnis potestas in unum absolute translata
fuerit, quod tum longe facilius ex uno in alium transferri potest.
Suscepere enim duo manipulares imperium Romanum transferre, et
15 transtulerunt (Tacit. Hist. lib. 1). Omitto artes et astus callidos consiliariorum, quibus sibi cavere debent ne invidiae immolentur, quia
nimis noti sunt, et nemo qui historias legit ignorare potest consiliariis
fidem plerumque exitio fuisse; atque adeo, ut sibi caveant, eosdem
callidos non fidos esse oportet. Sed si consiliarii plures numero quam ut
20 in eodem scelere convenire possint, et omnes inter se aequales sint, nec
ultra quadriennium eo officio fungantur, regi nequaquam formido-
losi esse queunt nisi libertatem iis adimere tentet, quo omnes cives
pariter offendet. Nam (ut Ant. Perezius optime notat) imperio absoluto
uti principi admodum periculosum, subditis admodum odiosum, et
25 institutis tam divinis quam humanis adversum, ut innumera ostendunt
exempla.

    15. Praeter haec alia fundamenta in praec. Cap. jecimus, ex quibus
regi magna imperii, et civibus libertatis ac pacis obtinendae securitas
oritur, quae suis locis ostendemus. Nam quae ad supremum concilium
30 spectant, quaeque maximi ponderis sunt, ante omnia demonstrare
volui; jam reliqua eo quo ipsa proposui ordine persequar.

    16. Quod cives eo potentiores, et consequenter magis sui juris sint,

6–7. *NS behalven dat hy eindelijk vergaat.*

12–13. *NS Hier koomt noch by, dat, zo alle de macht volstrektelijk aan een alleen opgedragen
word, zy dan zeer gemakkelijk van d' een aan d' ander overgevoert kan worden.* This suggests
quod; *OP* quae.

21. Since the system proposed in § 13 does not apply where there are four counsellors
to a tribe, my emendation of *ultra quadriennium* to *ultra quam triennium* (see *Œuvres Complètes de Spinoza*, Gallimard, 1954, p. 1486) was mistaken.

30. *quaeque . . . sunt* not in *NS*.

replaced every year—assuming that each tribe is to have five counsellors—except in the year when the lawyer of a tribe retires and a new
one is chosen to succeed him.

14. No king can promise himself greater security than one who
rules in a commonwealth of this kind. For, of course, if we disregard
the obvious fact that a king is soon destroyed if his soldiers do not wish
his safety, the greatest danger to kings always comes from those who
are nearest to them. Thus the fewer in number, and, in consequence,
the more powerful the counsellors are, the greater the danger for the
king that they may transfer the sovereignty to another. Certainly,
nothing terrified David more than the fact that his own counsellor
Ahithophel had sided with Absalom.[1] Besides, if the whole power has
been entirely vested in one man it is all the easier to transfer to another.
Two privates undertook to transfer the Roman Empire, and did so
(Tacitus, Histories, Book I).[2] I say nothing of the trickery and guile
which counsellors must practise to save themselves from becoming the
victims of jealousy, because it is known only too well, and no reader of
history can be unaware that counsellors have very often been destroyed
by their loyalty; thus to protect themselves they have to be deceitful
rather than loyal. But if counsellors are too numerous to be able to
agree upon the same misdeed, if they are all equals, and do not hold
office for more than four years, they cannot possibly be a danger to the
king unless he tries to deprive them of their prerogatives, a course
which will be equally obnoxious to every citizen.[3] For (as Antonio
Perez well remarks)[4] the exercise of absolute power by a prince is most
dangerous to himself, most offensive to his subjects, and contrary to
the laws of God and man alike, as countless instances show.

15. In the previous Chapter I have laid down other fundamental
laws which do much to secure sovereignty for the king and freedom
and peace for the citizens. These I shall explain in due course; for I
wished to justify first the fundamental laws concerning the supreme
council, which are the most important. I shall now go on to deal with
the others in the order in which they were set out.

16. Citizens are undoubtedly more powerful, and therefore more

---

[1] 2 Samuel, 15, 31.

[2] Tacitus, Histories I, xxv, 1 (quoted also in T T-P, n. 35, p. 251). Sovereignty was transferred from Galba to Otho.

[3] Spinoza may have in mind the arrest of six members of the Estates of Holland by William II in 1650. See G. J. Renier, The Dutch Nation II, iv, p. 111.

[4] In his Relaçiones (Paris, 1598, p. 133). Perez, at one time Secretary of State to Philip II
of Spain, wrote this book to justify his own conduct by exposing that of his former master.

quo majores urbes et magis munitas habent, dubio caret: quo enim locus
in quo sunt tutior est, eo libertatem suam melius tueri, sive hostem
externum vel internum minus timere possunt; et certum est homines
naturaliter securitati suae eo magis consulere, quo divitiis potentiores
5 sunt. Quae autem urbes alterius potentia ut conserventur indigent,
aequale jus cum eo non habent; sed eatenus alterius sunt juris, quatenus alterius potentia indigent. Jus enim sola potentia definiri in 2
Cap. ostendimus.

17. Hac eadem etiam de causa, ut cives scilicet sui juris maneant
10 et libertatem tueantur, militia ex solis civibus nullo excepto constare
debet. Etenim homo armatus magis quam inermis sui juris (vide Art.
12 hujus Cap.), et ii cives suum jus in alterum absolute transferunt,
ejusdemque fidei omnino committunt, cui arma dederunt et urbium
munimenta crediderunt. Huc accedit humana avaritia, qua plerique
15 maxime ducuntur: fieri enim non potest ut auxiliarius miles sine magnis
sumptibus conducatur, et cives vix pati possunt exactiones quae susten-
tandae otiosae militiae requiruntur. Quod autem nullus qui integrae
militiae vel magnae ejus parti imperet nisi cogente necessitate in annum
ad summum eligendus sit, norunt omnes qui historias tam sacras quam
20 profanas legerunt. Ratio autem nihil hoc clarius docet. Nam sane imperii robur ei omnino creditur, cui satis temporis conceditur ut militarem gloriam occupet, ipsiusque nomen supra regis attollatur, vel fidum
sibi exercitum faciat obsequio, liberalitate, et reliquis artibus ducibus
assuetis quibus alienum servitium et sibi dominationem quaerunt.
25 Denique ad majorem totius imperii securitatem addidi quod hi militiae
imperatores eligendi sunt ex regis consiliariis, vel qui eodem officio
functi sunt, hoc est, viris qui eo aetatis pervenerunt qua homines
plerumque vetera et tuta quam nova et periculosa malint.

18. Cives inter se familiis distinguendos esse dixi, et ex unaquaque
30 aequalem consiliariorum numerum eligendum, ut majores urbes plures
haberent pro numero civium consiliarios, et plura, ut aequum est, adferre possent suffragia. Nam imperii potentia et consequenter jus ex
civium numero aestimanda est; nec credo quod ad hanc inter cives

19. *P quam; OP quas.*
22. *NS en zijn naam boven die van de Koning te verheffen*, which suggests *attollat*; but the
passive is used in Tacitus, *Agricola* 39, and Spinoza has that passage in mind here.
27. *NS uit mannen*, i.e. *ex viris.*

fully possessed of their own right, in proportion as their cities are larger and better fortified. For the more secure the place in which they live, the better can they defend their freedom, i.e. the less have they to fear from enemies at home or abroad; and, of course, the wealthier men are, the more provision they naturally make for their security. But cities which need another's help to survive are not his equals in right, being in fact subject to his right in so far as they require his power. For right is determined by power alone, as I have shown in Chapter 2.

17. It is also to ensure that the citizens retain possession of their own right, and preserve their freedom, that they alone must form the army, and none of them be exempted from military service.[1] For an armed man is more fully possessed of his own right than one who is unarmed (see Section 12 of this Chapter), and citizens transfer their right to another completely, and commit it entirely to his good faith, as soon as they give him arms and entrust him with the defence of their cities. The prevailing avarice of men is another reason for my plan; for the hire of mercenaries is bound to be expensive, and citizens find the exactions needed to maintain an idle soldiery very hard to bear. And the fact that no one should be appointed to command the whole of the armed forces, or a large part of them, except in time of urgent need, and then only for a year at the most, is known to all who have read history, either sacred or profane. Besides, reason teaches nothing more clearly. For it is obvious that the power of the state is wholly committed to the man who is given sufficient time to eclipse the king by achieving military glory, or to win over the army by indulgence, liberality, and all the favourite tricks of generals who are intent on slavery for others and despotism for themselves.[2] My last provision, that such army commanders should be chosen from the king's counsellors or ex-counsellors, i.e. from those who have reached an age to prefer the safety of tradition to the dangers of innovation,[3] is designed to provide greater security for the entire state.

18. I laid down that the citizen body was to be divided into tribes, and that an equal number of counsellors was to be appointed from each, to ensure that the larger cities should have more counsellors, and therefore, as is fair, more votes, in proportion to their greater number of citizens.[4] For the power of a city, and in consequence its right, depends on its number of citizens; and I believe it impossible to devise any

---

[1] *TT-P* xvii, p. 173.　　　　[2] Machiavelli, *Discourses* iii, 24.
[3] *TP* x, 2, p. 431. The phrase is adapted from Tacitus, *Annals* i, ii, 1.
[4] p. 329, n. 1.

aequalitatem servandam aliud medium aptius excogitari potest, quia
omnes natura ita comparati sunt ut unusquisque generi suo adscribi
velit et stirpe a reliquis internosci.

19. Praeterea in statu naturali unusquisque nihil minus sibi vindi-
5 care et sui juris facere potest quam solum, et quicquid solo ita adhaeret
ut id nusquam abscondere nec portare quo velit possit. Solum igitur,
et quicquid ei ea qua diximus conditione adhaeret, apprime communis
civitatis juris est, nempe eorum omnium qui junctis viribus, vel ejus
cui omnes potestatem dederunt qua id sibi vindicare possit. Et conse-
10 quenter solum, et quicquid ei adhaeret, tanti valere apud cives debet,
quantum necesse est ut pedem eo in loco figere et commune jus seu
libertatem tueri possint. Caeterum utilitates quas civitas hinc necesse
est ut capiat ostendimus Art. 8 hujus Capitis.

20. Ut cives quantum fieri potest aequales sint, quod in civitate
15 apprime necessarium est, nulli nisi a rege oriundi nobiles censendi sunt.
At si omnibus ex rege oriundis uxorem ducere seu liberos procreare
liceret, successu temporis in magnum admodum numerum crescerent,
et regi et omnibus non tantum oneri, sed formidolosissimi insuper
essent. Homines enim qui otio abundant scelera plerumque meditan-
20 tur; unde fit ut reges maxime nobilium causa inducantur bellum gerere,
quia regibus nobilibus stipatis major ex bello quam ex pace securitas et
quies. Sed haec, utpote satis nota, relinquo, ut et quae ex Art. 15
usque ad 27 in praec. Capite dixi: nam praecipua in hoc Cap.
demonstrata, et reliqua per se manifesta sunt.

25 21. Quod judices plures numero esse debeant quam ut a viro privato magna ejus pars possit muneribus corrumpi, ut et quod suffragia
non palam sed clam ferre debeant, et quod vacationis praemium mereantur, omnibus etiam notum. Sed solent ubique annuum habere stipendium; unde fit ut non admodum festinent lites dirimere, et saepe ut
30 quaestionibus nullus sit finis. Deinde ubi bonorum publicatio regum
emolumenta sunt, ibi saepe non jus aut verum in cognitionibus, sed
magnitudo opum spectatur; passim delationes, et locupletissimus quisque in praedam correpti; quae gravia et intoleranda, sed necessitate

---

1–2. *NS om dat wy alle van natuur in dier voegen gestelt zijn*, i.e. *quia omnes natura ita
comparati sumus*; OP *qui . . . comparati sunt*. I accept *quia*, and suppose that the Dutch translator changed the person in order to make it clear that this is a statement about human nature
in general.

4–5. *Gf vindicare*; OP *vendicare*.   6. *Gf possit*; OP *potest*.

8. *NS die met samengevoegde krachten, of.* Though the relative clause is incomplete, the
text here is probably sound. Understand *id sibi vindicare possunt* after *viribus*.

9. *Gf vindicare*; OP *vendicare*.   13. *P capiat*; OP *capia*.

18. *P formidolosissimi*; OP *formidolossimi*.

28. *NS Aan allen is ook genoegsamelijk bekent* suggests *omnibus etiam satis notum*.

better means of maintaining equality of representation among the citizens, for everyone has a natural desire to be ascribed to his own family and to be distinguished by lineage from the rest.

19. Again, if there is one thing which an individual in the condition of nature cannot appropriate and make his own, it is land and other real estate. Thus the land and other real estate is essentially the public property of the commonwealth, i.e. it belongs by right to all who have united and are therefore able to protect it, or to the man whom they have all empowered to protect it for them. In consequence it must be valued very highly among the citizens, since they need it as a base from which to defend their corporate right or freedom. The advantages which the commonwealth necessarily derives from this arrangement have been shown in Section 8 of this Chapter.

20. That the citizens may enjoy as much equality as possible[1]—a prime necessity in a commonwealth—none but those of royal descent must be regarded as noblemen.[2] But if all of royal descent were allowed to marry or beget children, they would eventually become very numerous, and not only a burden, but a formidable threat to the king and all his subjects.[3] For the Devil finds work for idle hands to do; hence it is largely to occupy their nobles that kings make war, since when surrounded by nobles they get more security and tranquillity from war than from peace. But since this is quite well known I can pass it by, and likewise what I said in Sections 15 to 27 of the previous Chapter; for the main points have been established in this Chapter, and the others are self-evident.

21. That the number of judges should be too great to make it possible for a private individual to bribe a large proportion of them, that they should not vote openly, but by secret ballot, and that they deserve remuneration for their services, is also known to everyone. But if they are paid an annual salary, as is the universal custom, they make no great haste to settle lawsuits, and in many cases disputes never reach a decision. Again, where confiscated goods are made over to the king, it is common for trials to be conducted with more attention to the size of the defendant's fortune than to justice or truth; denunciations are made on every side, and all the richest men are seized as a prey; practices which, though oppressive and intolerable, are excused by a plea of

---

[1] Though Spinoza's monarch is to possess all the land, his state lacks the hierarchical structure of a feudal monarchy.

[2] There were very few nobles in Holland (Temple, op. cit., ch. ii, p. 64). Machiavelli regarded feudal nobles as enemies of all civil government (*Discourses* i, 55).

[3] Bacon, *Essay* xiv.

armorum excusata etiam in pace manent. At judicum avaritia, qui scilicet in duos aut tres annos ad summum constituuntur, metu succedentium temperatur; ut jam taceam quod judices bona fixa nulla habere possunt, sed quod argentum suum lucri causa concivibus credere
5 debeant; atque adeo iis magis consulere quam insidiari coguntur, praesertim si ipsi judices magno, uti diximus, numero sint.

22. At militiae nullum decernendum esse stipendium diximus: nam summum militiae praemium libertas est. In statu enim naturali nititur unusquisque sola libertatis causa sese quantum potest defendere, nec
10 aliud bellicae virtutis praemium exspectat quam ut suus sit. In statu autem civili omnes simul cives considerandi perinde ac homo in statu naturali, qui propterea, dum omnes pro eo statu militant, sibi cavent sibique vacant. At consiliarii, judices, praetores, etc., plus aliis quam sibi vacant; quare iis vacationis praemium decerni aequum est. Accedit
15 quod in bello nullum honestius nec majus victoriae incitamentum esse potest quam libertatis imago. Sed si contra civium aliqua pars militiae designetur, qua de causa necesse etiam erit iisdem certum stipendium decernere, rex necessario eosdem prae reliquis agnoscet (ut Art. 12 hujus Cap. ostendimus), homines scilicet qui belli artes tantummodo
20 norunt, et in pace propter nimium otium luxu corrumpuntur, et tandem propter inopiam rei familiaris nihil praeter rapinas, discordias civiles, et bella meditantur. Atque adeo affirmare possumus imperium monarchicum hujusmodi revera statum belli esse, et solam militiam libertate gaudere, reliquos autem servire.

25 23. Quae de peregrinis in civium numerum recipiendis Art. 32 praeced. Cap. diximus, per se nota esse credo. Praeterea neminem dubitare existimo quod ii qui regi sanguine propinqui sunt procul ab eo esse debeant, et non belli sed pacis negotiis distrahi, ex quibus ipsis decus et imperio quies sequatur; quamvis nec hoc quidem Turcarum tyrannis
30 satis tutum visum fuerit, quibus propterea religio est fratres omnes necare. Nec mirum; nam quo magis absolute imperii jus in unum

---

26–27. *OP dubitari*, corrected to *dubitare* in the list of Errata.

military necessity, and continued even in time of peace.[1] But the avarice of judges who are appointed, as we saw, for two or three years at the most, is restrained by fear of their successors; not to mention that they are not allowed to possess real estate, but must lend to their fellow citizens in order to make money, and are therefore forced to help rather than to ensnare them. This is particularly true if, as I said, these judges are numerous.

22. Soldiers on the other hand were to be assigned no wages;[2] for the supreme reward for military service is freedom. In the state of nature it is solely to maintain his freedom that an individual does his best to protect himself, and he expects no other reward for prowess in war than that of being his own master. Now in the political order the whole body of citizens must be viewed as an individual in the state of nature; hence when all of them fight to defend the political order they are protecting and working for themselves. But counsellors, judges, sheriffs, etc. work more for others than for themselves, and so it is fair to assign them a reward for their services. Besides, in time of war there can be no greater or nobler incentive to victory than the thought of freedom. If, on the other hand, only some of the citizens are detailed for military service—which will also make it necessary to assign them a fixed wage—the king will inevitably favour them more than the rest (as I have shown in Section 12 of this Chapter), though they are men who, having no profession but arms, ruin themselves by extravagance in peace because they have too little to do, and are finally led by their poverty to think of nothing but looting, sedition, and war.[3] We can therefore assert that a monarchy of this kind is really a state of war; that the soldiers alone enjoy freedom, and the rest are slaves.

23. The regulations concerning the naturalization of aliens set out in Section 32 of the previous Chapter seem to me self-evident. Again, I do not think anyone doubts that near kinsmen of the king should be sent abroad,[4] and kept busy, not with military duties,[5] but with peaceful missions which will bring honour to themselves and tranquillity to the state. It is true that the tyrants of Turkey have thought even this insufficient to ensure their own safety; that is why they religiously kill all their brothers.[6] And no wonder; for the more completely sovereignty

---

[1] Tacitus, *Histories* II, lxxxiv, 1–2.

[2] *TP* vi, 31, p. 331. Evidently Spinoza regards the payment to the rank and file in wartime as a subsistence allowance rather than as a wage.

[3] This passage owes something to Sallust, *Catiline* 5.

[4] *TP* vi, 33, p. 331.   [5] *TP* vi, 10, p. 319.

[6] Van Hove, op. cit. I, ii, 4 (p. 147).

translatum est, eo facilius ipsum (ut Art. 14 hujus Cap. exemplo ostendimus) ex uno in alium transferri potest. At imperium monarchicum
quale hic concipimus, in quo scilicet mercenarius miles nullus est, satis
hoc quo diximus modo regis saluti cautum fore, extra dubium est.

5   24. De iis etiam quae Art. 34 et 35 praeced. Cap. diximus ambigere
nemo potest. Quod autem rex extraneam in uxorem ducere non debet,
facile demonstratur. Nam praeterquam quod duae civitates, quanquam
foedere inter se sociatae, in statu tamen hostilitatis sunt (per Art. 14 Cap.
3), apprime cavendum est ne bellum propter regis res domesticas con-
10 citetur; et quia controversiae et dissensiones ex societate praecipue quae
ex matrimonio fit oriuntur, et quae inter duas civitates quaestiones
sunt jure belli plerumque dirimuntur, hinc sequitur imperio exitiale
esse arctam societatem cum alio inire. Hujus rei fatale exemplum in
Scriptura legimus: mortuo enim Salomone, qui filiam regis Aegypti
15 sibi matrimonio junxerat, filius ejus Rehabeam bellum cum Susaco
Aegyptiorum rege infelicissime gessit, a quo omnino subactus est.
Matrimonium praeterea Ludovici XIV, Regis Galliarum, cum filia
Philippi IV novi belli semen fuit; et praeter haec plurima exempla in
historiis leguntur.

20   25. Imperii facies una eademque servari, et consequenter rex unus
et ejusdem sexus, et imperium indivisibile esse debet. Quod autem
dixerim ut filius regis natu major patri jure succedat, vel (si nulli sint
liberi) qui regi sanguine proximus est, patet tam ex Artic. 13 praeced.
Cap. quam quia regis electio, quae a multitudine fit, aeterna, si fieri
25 potest, esse debet; alias necessario fiet ut summa imperii potestas saepe
ad multitudinem transeat, quae mutatio summa est et consequenter
periculosissima. Qui autem statuunt regem, ex eo quod imperii dominus
est, idque jure absoluto tenet, posse cui velit idem tradere, et successorem quem velit eligere, atque adeo regis filium imperii haeredem jure
30 esse, falluntur sane. Nam regis voluntas tamdiu vim juris habet quamdiu civitatis gladium tenet; imperii namque jus sola potentia definitur.
Rex igitur regno cedere quidem potest, sed non imperium alteri tradere

2–4. *NS Maar d' eenhoofdige Heerschappy ... zal zonder twijffel op deze wijze ... voor de welstant van de Koning zorgen.*

15. *B Susaco; NS Susak; OP Susano.*   17. *OP Ludovici 14.*

18. *OP Philippi quarti.* After *van Filippus de vierde NS* reads *Koning van Spanjen.*

28. *NS dien 't hem zal believen,* i.e. *velit; OP vellet.*

has been vested in one man, the more easily can it be transferred to another (as I have shown by the example in Section 14 of this Chapter). But in the kind of monarchy I am envisaging here, i.e. one in which there is not a single mercenary soldier, the measure I have prescribed will certainly be a sufficient safeguard for the king.

24. There can be no doubt either about the measures I have proposed in Sections 34 and 35 of the previous Chapter. Furthermore, that the king must not marry an alien is easily shown. For quite apart from the fact that two commonwealths remain in a state of hostility even when united by treaty (by Chapter 3, Section 14), it needs the utmost care to prevent the king's family concerns from leading to war; and since quarrels and disputes are particularly apt to arise from an alliance based on marriage, and differences between two commonwealths are generally settled by the right of war, it is fatal for a state to enter into so close an alliance with another. There is a dire example of this in Scripture: for on the death of Solomon, who had married the daughter of the king of Egypt, his son Rehoboam waged a disastrous war against Shishak, the Egyptian king, and was completely overthrown.[1] Again, the marriage of Louis XIV of France to the daughter of Philip IV sowed the seeds of a new war;[2] and history provides many other examples of the same thing.

25. The form of the state must be preserved unchanged; so there must be but one ruler, always of the male sex, and the state must be indivisible. Furthermore, that the king's eldest son should succeed by right, or (if there is no male issue) the king's nearest kinsman, is obvious not only from Section 13 of the previous Chapter, but also because the election of the king by the people must be, if possible, for all time; otherwise the sovereignty will often have to revert to the people, a change which is very great, and consequently very dangerous. But those who maintain that because a king is master of his state, and holds it by absolute right, he can give it to whom he pleases, and appoint any successor he chooses, and that this is why the king's son is heir to the state by right, are certainly mistaken.[3] For a king's will has the force of right only as long as he holds the sword of the commonwealth; since the right of a state is determined by power alone. Thus though a king can abdicate, he cannot give the state to another without the acquiescence

[1] *2 Chronicles* 8, 11, and 12, 2–9.

[2] The War of Succession for the possession of the Spanish Netherlands, 1667–8.

[3] Hobbes maintained (*a*) that it was best for subjects to be the inheritance of their king (*De Cive* x, 18); (*b*) that the king could give or sell his sovereignty to another (*De Cive* ix, 13); and (*c*) that he could bequeath it to anyone he pleased (*De Cive* vii, 15, and ix, 12).

nisi connivente multitudine vel parte ejus validiore. Quod ut clarius intelligatur, venit notandum quod liberi non jure naturali sed civili parentum haeredes sunt: nam sola civitatis potentia fit ut unusquisque quorundam bonorum sit dominus. Quare eadem potentia sive jure,
5 quo fit ut voluntas alicujus qua de suis bonis statuit rata sit, eodem fit ut eadem voluntas etiam post ipsius mortem rata maneat quamdiu civitas permanet; et hac ratione unusquisque in statu civili idem jus quod dum in vivis est etiam post mortem obtinet, quia, uti diximus, non tam sua quam civitatis potentia, quae aeterna est, de suis bonis quic-
10 quam statuere potest. At regis alia prorsus est ratio: nam regis voluntas ipsum jus civile est, et rex ipsa civitas; mortuo igitur rege obiit quodammodo civitas, et status civilis ad naturalem, et consequenter summa potestas ad multitudinem naturaliter redit; quae propterea jure potest leges novas condere et veteres abrogare. Atque adeo apparet neminem
15 regi jure succedere nisi quem multitudo successorem vult, vel in theocratia, qualis Hebraeorum civitas olim fuit, quem Deus per Prophetam elegerit. Possemus praeterea haec inde deducere, quod regis gladius sive jus sit revera ipsius multitudinis sive validioris ejus partis voluntas; vel etiam ex eo, quod homines ratione praediti nunquam suo jure ita
20 cedunt ut homines esse desinant, et perinde ac pecudes habeantur. Sed haec ulterius persequi non est opus.

26. Caeterum religionis sive Deum colendi jus nemo in alium transferre potest. Sed de hoc in duobus ultimis capitibus Tractatus Theologico-Politici prolixe egimus, quae hic repetere superfluum est.
25 Atque his me optimi imperii monarchici fundamenta satis clare, quamvis breviter, demonstrasse autumo. Eorum autem cohaerentiam sive imperii analogiam facile unusquisque observabit, qui eadem simul aliqua cum attentione contemplari velit. Superest tantum monere me hic imperium monarchicum concipere quod a libera multitudine insti-
30 tuitur, cui solummodo haec ex usu esse possunt; nam multitudo quae

of the people or its stronger part. We shall see this more clearly if we observe that children inherit from their parents by civil right, and not by natural; for it is due solely to the power of the commonwealth that anyone has definite property. Thus the same power or right which ensures that a man's decision about his property is valid, also ensures that his decision shall remain valid even after his death, for as long as the commonwealth lasts; and this is why everyone in the political condition retains even after his death the same right as he had while alive, because, as I said, it is by the continuing power of the commonwealth, rather than by his own, that he is able to make any effective decision about his property. But the case of the king is quite different: for the king's will is the civil law itself, and the king the commonwealth itself.[1] Thus in a sense the death of the king involves the death of the commonwealth, and causes a return from the political to the natural condition; so sovereignty naturally reverts to the people, which has therefore the right to make new laws and repeal the old.[2] This shows that nobody succeeds a king by right except the man whom the people wishes to be his successor, or, in a theocracy like the ancient Jewish commonwealth, the man whom God has appointed through his Prophet.[3] We could also infer this from the fact that the king's sword, or right, is really the will of the people itself, or of its stronger part; or indeed from the fact that men endowed with reason never renounce their right so completely that they cease to be men and can be treated like sheep.[4] But there is no need to pursue this farther.

26. Finally, religious right, or the right to worship God, is something which no one can transfer to another. But this right has been dealt with at length in the two concluding chapters of the Tractatus Theologico-Politicus, which it is unnecessary to reproduce here. I now claim that I have justified briefly, but with sufficient clarity, the fundamental laws required by a good monarchy. That they combine to produce a well-balanced state will easily be seen by anyone who is prepared to consider them together with a little attention.[5] It only remains to remind readers that I am envisaging here a monarchy established by a free people,[6] and that only to such a people can my proposals be of service; for a people accustomed to another form of

---

[1] Cf. Hobbes's definition of a commonwealth (*De Cive* v, 9).

[2] This means that the 'eternal election' of the king is always to some extent fictitious (cf. viii, 3, p. 371), and that the original democratic sovereign is always lurking in the background : views which have more in common with Locke than with Hobbes.

[3] *TT-P* xvii, p. 187.

[4] *TT-P* xvii, p. 149.

[5] *TP* i, 3, p. 263, n. 1.

[6] *TP* v, 6, p. 311.

alii imperii formae assuevit non poterit sine magno eversionis periculo totius imperii recepta fundamenta evellere, et totius imperii fabricam mutare.

27. Atqui haec quae scripsimus risu forsan excipientur ab iis qui
5 vitia, quae omnibus mortalibus insunt, ad solam plebem restringunt; nempe quod in vulgo nihil modicum, terrere ni paveant, et quod plebs aut humiliter servit aut superbe dominatur, nec ei veritas aut judicium, etc. At natura una et communis omnium est. Sed potentia et cultu decipimur, unde est ut duo cum idem faciant, saepe dicamus 'Hoc licet
10 impune facere huic, illi non licet', non quod dissimilis res sit, sed qui facit. Dominantibus propria est superbia. Superbiunt homines annua designatione: quid nobiles qui honores in aeternum agitant? Sed eorum arrogantia fastu, luxu, prodigalitate, certoque vitiorum concentu et docta quadam insipientia et turpitudinis elegantia adornatur, ita ut vitia
15 quorum singula seorsim spectata, quia tum maxime eminent, faeda et turpia sunt, honesta et decora imperitis et ignaris videantur. Nihil praeterea in vulgo modicum, terrere nisi paveant: nam libertas et servitium haud facile miscentur. Denique quod plebi nulla veritas neque judicium sit, mirum non est, quando praecipua imperii negotia clam ipsa
20 agitantur, et non nisi ex paucis quae celari nequeunt conjecturam facit. Judicium enim suspendere rara est virtus. Velle igitur clam civibus omnia agere, et ne de iisdem prava judicia ferant, neque ut res omnes sinistre interpretentur, summa est inscitia. Nam si plebs sese temperare, et de rebus parum cognitis judicium suspendere, vel ex paucis prae-
25 cognitis recte de rebus judicare posset, dignior sane esset ut regeret quam ut regeretur. Sed, uti diximus, natura omnibus eadem est; superbiunt omnes dominatione, terrent nisi paveant, et ubique veritas plerumque infringitur ab infensis vel obnoxiis, praesertim ubi unus vel pauci dominantur, qui non jus aut verum in cognitionibus sed magnitudinem
30 opum spectant.

---

4. *NS Doch*, i.e. *Atqui*; *OP Atque*. Cf. *Ep.* xii (*G*, vol. iv, p. 62, l. 2) where *OP* has *atque*, *NS maar*, and Leibniz's copy *atqui*.

21. For *rara NS* has *wonderlijke*, i.e. *mira*.   28. *NS een of twee*.

government will not be able to uproot the accepted foundations of their whole state, and to change its entire construction, without great danger of destroying it completely.

27. Those who confine to the common people the vices which exist in all human beings will perhaps greet my contentions with ridicule, on the ground that 'there is no moderation in the masses, they terrorize unless they are afraid',[1] that 'the common people is either an obsequious servant or a domineering master',[2] that 'it has no truth or judgement in it',[3] and so on. But all men have one and the same nature: it is power and culture which mislead us. Hence 'when two men do the same thing we often say that the one may do it with impunity but not the other; not because the thing, but because the person who does it, is different'.[4] Pride is characteristic of rulers. If men are puffed up by appointment for a year, what can we expect of nobles who hold office without end? But *their* arrogance is adorned with refinement, magnificence, lavishness, with an harmonious blend of vices, a sophisticated folly, and an elegant depravity; so that faults which when viewed singly and in isolation are base and ugly, because then most obvious, seem honourable and becoming to the ignorant and inexperienced. Again, 'there is no moderation in the masses, they terrorize unless they are afraid' because freedom and slavery are not easily combined. Finally, that 'there is no truth or judgement in the common people' is not surprising, when they are kept in ignorance of the main affairs of state, and merely guess at the facts from the little that cannot be concealed. For to suspend judgement is a rare virtue. Thus to keep all the work of government a secret from the citizens, and then to expect them not to misjudge it and put the worst construction on everything, is the height of folly.[5] For if the common people could practise self-restraint, and suspend judgement when the evidence is insufficient, or could make correct judgements about public affairs with little information to go on, they would certainly be more worthy to rule than to be ruled. However, as I said, all men have the same nature; all are puffed up by rule, they terrorize when they are not afraid, and it is everywhere common for truth to be disregarded by bitter enemies or servile followers,[6] especially when one man or a few have despotic power, and pay more attention at trials to the size of the defendant's fortune than to justice or truth.

---

[1] Tacitus, *Annals* I, xxix, 3.
[2] Livy XXIV, xxv, 8.
[3] Tacitus, *Histories* I, xxxii, 1.
[4] Terence, *Adelphi* 823–5.
[5] *TT-P* xx, p. 227.
[6] Tacitus, *Histories* I, i, 1.

28. Milites deinde stipendiarii, militari scilicet disciplinae assueti, algoris et inediae patientes, civium turbam contemnere solent, utpote ad expugnationes vel aperto marte dimicandum longe inferiorem. Sed quod imperium ea de causa infelicius sit aut minus constans, nullus cui 5 mens sana est affirmabit. Sed contra unusquisque aequus rerum aestimator illud imperium omnium constantius esse non negabit, quod parta tantum tueri nec aliena appetere potest, quodque propterea bellum omnibus modis declinare et pacem tueri summo studio conatur.

29. Caeterum fateor hujus imperii consilia celari vix posse. Sed unus-
10 quisque mecum etiam fatebitur multo satius esse ut recta imperii consilia hostibus pateant quam ut prava tyrannorum arcana clam civibus habeantur. Qui imperii negotia secreto agitare possunt idem absolute in potestate habent, et, ut hosti in bello, ita civibus in pace insidiantur. Quod silentium imperio saepe ex usu sit, negare nemo potest; sed
15 quod absque eodem idem imperium subsistere nequeat, nemo unquam probabit. At contra rempublicam alicui absolute credere, et simul libertatem obtinere, fieri nequaquam potest; atque adeo inscitia est parvum damnum summo malo vitare velle. Verum eorum qui sibi imperium absolutum concupiscunt haec unica fuit cantilena, civitatis omnino
20 interesse ut ipsius negotia secreto agitentur, et alia hujusmodi, quae quanto magis utilitatis imagine teguntur, tanto ad infensius servitium erumpunt.

30. Denique, quamvis nullum, quod sciam, imperium his omnibus, quas diximus, conditionibus institutum fuerit, poterimus tamen ipsa
25 etiam experientia ostendere hanc monarchici imperii formam optimam esse, si causas conservationis cujuscunque imperii non barbari, et ejusdem eversionis, considerare velimus. Sed hoc non sine magno lectoris taedio hic facere possem. Attamen unum exemplum, quod memoria dignum videtur, silentio praeterire nolo; nempe Arragonen-
30 sium imperium, qui singulari erga suos reges fide affecti et pari constantia regni instituta inviolata servaverunt. Nam hi, simulatque servile

---

12–14. *NS hebben volstrektelijk in hun macht dat zy zo wel de burgers in vrede, als de vijant in d' oorlog, konnen belagen,* i.e. *NS* omits *idem,* and suggests *absolute in potestate habent ut, ut hosti in bello, ita civibus in pace insidientur.*

17. *NS zo groot is d' onkunde;* M *esset.*

28. Mercenary troops, being accustomed to military discipline, and inured to cold and want, commonly despise the mass of citizens as far inferior to themselves at taking cities by storm or fighting in the open field; but no one in his senses will assert that this makes a state any less stable or successful. On the contrary, no state is more stable to the impartial eye than one which is just powerful enough to preserve its own possessions, without being able to covet those of others, and which therefore does its utmost to avoid war and maintain peace.[1]

29. I agree that the policies of this state can hardly be concealed;[2] but everyone will also agree that it is much better for the honest policies of a state to be obvious to its enemies than for the guilty secrets of tyrants to be kept hidden from its citizens. Those who can handle the affairs of a state in secret have it completely in their power, and plot against the citizens in peace no less than against the enemy in war. That secrecy is often useful to a state no one can deny; yet no one will ever prove that the same state cannot maintain itself without it. But to give someone absolute control of public affairs without losing one's freedom is quite impossible; so it is foolish to seek to avoid a small inconvenience by incurring a great calamity. Of course, it has always been the sole theme of would-be tyrants that secrecy in the conduct of affairs and the like are absolutely necessary in the interests of the commonwealth; but the better their proposals are disguised by a show of utility, the more swiftly do they issue in slavery and oppression.[3]

30. Finally, although there is no state, as far as I know, which incorporates all the constitutional provisions described above, we can confirm from actual experience that this form of monarchy is the best by surveying every civilized state and examining the causes of its preservation and downfall. But to do this here would be extremely tedious for the reader. Yet there is one memorable case which I cannot pass over in silence; I mean the kingdom of the Aragonese,[4] whose remarkable loyalty to their kings was combined with an equal steadfastness in defending their free institutions. No sooner had they thrown

---

[1] Although Spinoza conceives commonwealths to be mutual enemies (*TP* iii, 13, p. 295), he does not draw the conclusion that they should be organized for conquest. On the contrary he does his best to give the governments of his model states a bias towards peace (cf. *TP* vii, 7, p. 341, and viii, 31, p. 395). He obviously favours the unaggressive state existing in an inter-state equilibrium as described by Machiavelli in *Discourses* i, 6.

[2] Hobbes, *De Cive* x, 14–15.   [3] Tacitus, *Annals* i, lxxxi, 3.

[4] Spinoza's account of the history and institutions of Aragon is derived from the *Relaçiones* of Antonio Perez (Paris, 1598, pp. 90 and ff.). Perez fled to Aragon to escape the anger of Philip II, and involved that kingdom in his ruin.

Maurorum jugum a cervicibus dejecerant, regem sibi eligere statuerunt; quibus autem conditionibus non satis inter eosdem conveniebat, et hac de causa summum Pontificem Romanum de ea re consulere constitu- erunt. Hic, Christi profecto vicarium hac in re se gerens, eos castigavit
5 quod non satis Hebraeorum exemplo moniti regem adeo obfirmato animo petere voluerint; sed si sententiam mutare nollent, suasit ne regem eligerent nisi institutis prius ritibus satis aequis et ingenio gentis consentaneis, et apprime ut supremum aliquod concilium crearent, quod regibus, ut Lacedaemoniorum Ephori, opponeretur, et jus absolutum
10 haberet lites dirimendi quae inter regem et cives orirentur. Hoc igitur consilium sequuti jura quae ipsis omnium aequissima visa sunt insti- tuerunt, quorum summus interpres, et consequenter supremus judex, non rex sed concilium esset quod Septendecim vocant, et cujus praeses Justitia appellatur. Hic igitur Justitia et hi Septendecim, nullis suf-
15 fragiis sed sorte ad vitam electi, jus absolutum habent omnes sententias in civem quemcunque ab aliis conciliis, tam politicis quam ecclesiasti- cis, vel ab ipso rege latas revocandi et damnandi; ita ut quilibet civis jus haberet ipsum etiam regem coram hoc judicio vocandi. Praeterea olim jus etiam habuerunt regem eligendi et potestate privandi; sed multis
20 post elapsis annis Rex Don Pedro, qui dicitur Pugio, ambiendo, largi- endo, pollicitando, omniumque officiorum genere, tandem effecit ut hoc jus rescinderetur (quod simulac obtinuit, manum pugione coram omnibus amputavit, vel, quod facilius crediderim, laesit, addens non sine sanguinis regii impendio licere subditis regem eligere) ea tamen
25 conditione: *ut potuerint et possint arma capere contra vim quamcunque, qua aliquis imperium ingredi in ipsorum damnum velit, imo contra ipsum regem et principem futurum haeredem si hoc modo (imperium) ingrediatur.* Qua sane conditione praecedens illud jus non tam aboleverunt quam cor- rexerunt. Nam, ut Art. 5 et 6 Cap. 4 ostendimus, rex non jure civili sed
30 jure belli dominandi potentia privari potest, vel ipsius vim vi solummodo

---

17. For *latas* NS has *gegeven*.
24. OP *sanguinis regii*; NS *van koninklijk bloet*; Gf *sanguinis regis*.

off the Moorish yoke than they decided to choose themselves a king; but since they could not agree about the conditions on which he should be appointed, they resolved to consult the Pope.[1] He, acting like a true vicar of Christ on this occasion, told them reproachfully that they should have been warned by the example of the Jews not to set their hearts so firmly on a king;[2] but advised them, if they would not change their minds, to make no appointment until they had created equitable institutions suited to their racial character; and, in particular, a supreme council to counterbalance their kings as the Ephors did in Sparta, and to have full right to decide any disputes arising between king and citizens. On this advice, then, they established the laws which they thought most equitable, and ordained that their supreme interpreter, and consequently the highest judge, should not be the king but the council which they call 'The Seventeen', and whose president is called 'The Justice'. So this Justice and these Seventeen, appointed for life not by vote but by lot, had full right to review and annul all judgements made against any citizen by any other council, whether political or ecclesiastical, and even by the king himself; which meant that any citizen had the right to call even the king before this tribunal. What is more, they also had for many years the right to appoint and depose their kings; until by solicitations, bribes, promises, and favours of every kind, King Peter the Dagger[3] finally secured its abolition. (The story goes that as soon as he achieved his aim he hacked off, or—as seems to me more probable—cut[4] his hand with a dagger in the presence of all, observing as he did so that the right of subjects to appoint a king was bound to result in the shedding of royal blood.[5]) But it was abolished only on this condition: 'that they may, as heretofore, take arms against any force wherewith any man purposes to enter the realm to do them hurt, yea, even against the king himself, and the heir to the throne, if he enters (the realm) in this manner.' This condition, of course, amended rather than abolished the right in question. For, as I have shown in Sections 5 and 6 of Chapter 4, a king cannot be deprived of sovereignty by civil right, but only by the right of war; i.e. his subjects can repel his

---

[1] Gregory VII.　　　[2] *TT-P* xviii, pp. 199–201.　　　[3] Pedro IV (1336–87).

[4] Spinoza wrongly takes *se cortò la mano* (Perez, op. cit., p. 95) to mean 'cut off his hand'.

[5] Perez writes: *Que tal fuero, y fuero de poder eligir Rey los vassallos, sangre de Rey avia de costar*. The anonymous English translation of the *Relaçiones* (1715) has, 'That the abolishing of such a privilege, as for Subjects to be allowed to chuse a King, ought to cost the blood of a King'. This makes Pedro declare that he sheds his blood in exchange for the abolition of the privilege, which is the usual tradition. Spinoza interprets Perez differently, and more correctly. He regards such a privilege as dangerous to the king (cf. *TP* vii, 25, p. 355).

repellere subditis licet. Praeter hanc alias stipulati sunt conditiones, quae ad nostrum scopum non faciunt. Hi ritus ex omnium sententia instructi incredibili temporis spatio inviolati manserunt, pari semper fide regum erga subditos ac subditorum erga regem. Sed post-
5 quam regnum Castellae Ferdinando, qui omnium primus Catholicus nuncupatus fuit, haereditate cessit, incepit haec Arragonensium libertas Castellanis esse invisa; qui propterea ipsum Ferdinandum suadere non cessabant ut jura illa rescinderet. At ille, nondum imperio absoluto assuetus, nihil tentare ausus consiliariis haec respondit: *praeterquam quod*
10 *Arragonensium regnum iis quas noverant conditionibus acceperit, quodque easdem servare sanctissime juraverit, et praeterquam quod inhumanum sit fidem datam solvere, se in animum induxisse suum regnum stabile fore quamdiu securitatis ratio non major regi quam subditis esset, ita ut nec rex subditis, nec contra subditi regi praeponderarent: nam si alterutra pars*
15 *potentior evadat, pars debilior non tantum pristinam aequalitatem recuperare, sed dolore accepti damni in alteram contra referre conabitur; unde vel alterutrius vel utriusque ruina sequeretur.* Quae sane sapientia verba non satis mirari possem si prolata fuissent a rege qui servis, non liberis hominibus, imperare consuevisset. Retinuerunt igitur Arra-
20 gonenses post Ferdinandum libertatem, non jam jure sed regum potentiorum gratia, usque ad Philippum II, qui eosdem feliciori quidem fato, sed non minori saevitia quam Confoederatorum Provincias oppressit. Et quamvis Philippus III omnia in integrum restituisse videatur, Arragonenses tamen, quorum plerique cupidine potentioribus assen-
25 tandi ducti sunt (nam inscitia est contra stimulos calces mittere), et reliqui metu territi, nihil praeter libertatis speciosa vocabula et inanes ritus retinuerunt.

31. Concludimus itaque multitudinem satis amplam libertatem sub rege servare posse, modo efficiat ut regis potentia sola ipsius multi-
30 tudinis potentia determinetur, et ipsius multitudinis praesidio servetur. Atque haec unica fuit regula quam in jaciendis imperii monarchici fundamentis sequutus sum.

2–3. *NS Deze wetten en gewoonten, . . . opgerecht, wierden . . . onderhouden,* hence *G Hi ritus . . . instructi . . . inviolati manserunt*; *OP His ritibus . . . instructi . . . inviolati manserunt*; *M His ritibus . . . instructis . . . inviolati manserunt.* The *NS* reading is supported by *instituta inviolata servaverunt* earlier in this Section, and by the passage in Spinoza's source, the *Relaçiones* of Antonio Perez.

16. *NS maar door smarte van de gelede schade het ander deel ook schade aan te doen (zou pogen).* Hence *G* suggests the insertion of *damnum* before *referre.*

21. *OP Philippum secundum.*

22. *NS maar met geen minder dienstbaarheid,* i.e. *sed non minori servitio.*

23. *OP Philippus tertius.*

24–25. *NS van de welken veel door begeerte van de machtigen te believen gedreven wierden.* Hence I insert *ducti sunt* after *assentandi.*

force by force alone. They laid down other conditions as well,[1] which it is not to my purpose to discuss. These institutions, established with the agreement of all, remained intact for an incredible length of time, the kings supporting their subjects and the subjects their kings with equal loyalty always. But after Ferdinand, the first king to be styled 'The Catholic', inherited the realm of Castile,[2] the Castilians began to be envious of the liberty of the Aragonese; and so they never stopped urging Ferdinand to abolish these rights. But being still unaccustomed to absolute power he was afraid to do anything, and answered his advisers as follows: 'He had received the realm of Aragon on the terms which they knew, had sworn most faithfully to observe them, and it was barbarous to break a pledged word. Moreover, he had come to believe that his kingdom would only be stable as long as the king had no greater measure of security than the subjects had, so that the king was no stronger than the subjects nor the subjects than the king; for if either party were to get the upper hand, the weaker would try, not only to recover its former equality, but, through resentment at the damage it had suffered, to damage the other in turn; and hence would follow the ruin of one or of both.' These are wise words indeed, and had they been uttered by a king accustomed to rule over slaves, and not over free men, I could not admire them enough. Thus the Aragonese retained their freedom after Ferdinand's death—though now more as a favour from kings who surpassed them in power than as a right—up to the time of Philip II; who oppressed them with more success but with no less cruelty than he oppressed the United Provinces. And although Philip III appears to have restored the *status quo* completely, the Aragonese, of whom most were inspired by a desire to fawn on the powerful (for it is folly to kick against the pricks),[3] and the rest stricken by fear, have in fact retained nothing but the fine titles and empty forms of freedom.[4]

31. I conclude, then, that a people can maintain a fair amount of freedom under a king as long as it ensures that the king's power is determined by its power alone, and preserved only by its support. And this has been the one and only rule I have followed in laying the foundations of monarchy.

---

[1] In particular the king had to take an oath to maintain the rights, freedom, and customs of Aragon before being crowned.

[2] Ferdinand of Aragon (1479–1516) became regent of Castile by the testament of his wife Isabella, who died in 1504.

[3] Terence, *Phormio* 77–78.   [4] Tacitus, *Annals* 1, lxxxi, 3.

CAPUT VIII

Quod imperium aristocraticum magno patriciorum numero constare debet: de ejus praestantia, et quod ad absolutum magis quam monarchicum accedat, et hac de causa libertati conservandae aptius sit

5   1. Huc usque de imperio monarchico. Qua autem ratione aristocraticum instituendum sit ut permanere possit, hic jam dicemus. Aristocraticum imperium illud esse diximus, quod non unus sed quidam ex multitudine selecti tenent, quos imposterum patricios appellabimus. Dico expresse *quod quidam selecti tenent.* Nam haec praecipua est dif-
10 ferentia inter hoc et democraticum imperium, quod scilicet in imperio aristocratico gubernandi jus a sola electione pendeat, in democratico autem maxime a jure quodam innato vel fortuna adepto (ut suo loco dicemus), atque adeo, tametsi imperii alicujus integra multitudo in numerum patriciorum recipiatur, modo illud jus haereditarium non sit
15 nec lege aliqua communi ad alios descendat, imperium tamen aristocraticum omnino erit, quandoquidem nulli nisi expresse electi in numerum patriciorum recipiuntur. At si hi duo tantummodo fuerint, alter altero potior esse conabitur, et imperium facile ob nimiam uniuscujusque potentiam in duas partes dividetur, aut in tres, aut quatuor, aut quinque,
20 si tres, aut quatuor, aut quinque id tenuerint: sed partes eo debiliores erunt quo in plures ipsum imperium delatum fuerit. Ex quo sequitur in imperio aristocratico, ut stabile sit, ad minimum patriciorum numerum determinandum necessario habendam esse rationem magnitudinis ipsius imperii.

25   2. Ponatur itaque pro mediocris imperii magnitudine satis esse ut

---

3. *NS dan aan d' eenhoofdige Heerschappy koomt,* i.e. *quam ad monarchicum accedat.* But cf. p. 372, ll. 20–21: *magis quam monarchicum . . . ad absolutum accedit.*

9–17. *Dico expresse . . . recipiuntur* not in *NS.*

17–18. *OP altero potior; NS boven d' ander.* The correct reading may be *potentior.*

18. *P uniuscujusque; OP unicujusque.*

19. *NS of in drie, vier, of vijf (delen),* which suggests *aut in tres, aut quatuor, aut quinque;* *OP et in tres.*

That an aristocracy should consist of a large number of patricians: that it is a better and more absolute form of government than monarchy, and therefore more suitable for the preservation of freedom[1]

1. I now turn to aristocracy, and in this Chapter I shall describe how an aristocracy must be organized if it is to be capable of lasting. Aristocracy, as I said, is the form of government where power is held, not by one man, but by certain men chosen from the people, whom I shall henceforth call patricians. I say expressly 'where power is held by certain chosen men'; for the chief difference between aristocracy and democracy is this, that in an aristocracy the right to govern is entirely dependent on co-optation,[2] whereas in a democracy it depends mainly on a kind of innate right, or a right acquired by fortune, as I shall explain in due course.[3] Thus, even though the whole population of a state is admitted to the patriciate, nevertheless, as long as the right of entry is not hereditary and is not transmitted to others by virtue of some general law, the government will be entirely aristocratic, since none but those expressly chosen are admitted. But if there are only two such men, the one will try to get the better of the other, and because of the excessive power of each the state will be apt to split up into two factions, or into three, four, or five factions according as the sovereignty is held by three, four, or five men:[4] whereas the greater the number of men in whom the actual sovereignty is vested, the weaker the factions will be. It follows that, if an aristocracy is to be stable, the number of patricians must not fall below a certain limit, and this limit must necessarily be determined by reference to the size of the state.

2. Let us suppose, then, that for a state of moderate size it is

---

[1] M. Francès regards this heading as the work of one of Spinoza's editors (*Œuvres Complètes de Spinoza*, Gallimard, 1954, pp. 1486–7). In this she may be right. But I cannot agree that the heading is tendentious: on the contrary, it seems to me to give a fair summary of the contents of the chapter.

[2] The town council of Amsterdam was recruited by co-optation, 'which makes the Government a sort of *Oligarchy*, and very different from a popular Government' (Temple, *Observations*, ch. ii, p. 58).

[3] *TP* xi, 1–2, p. 441.

[4] Van Hove cites factions as a great defect of aristocracies (*Polityke Weegschaal* ii, ii, 5, p. 286).

centum optimi viri dentur in quos summa imperii potestas delata sit, et quibus consequenter jus competat collegas patricios eligendi quando eorum aliquis vita excessit. Hi sane omni modo conabuntur ut eorum liberi vel qui iis sanguine proximi sunt sibi succedant: unde fiet ut
5 summa imperii potestas semper penes eos erit quos fortuna patriciis liberos aut consanguineos dedit. Et quia ex centum hominibus qui fortunae causa ad honores ascendunt vix tres reperiuntur qui arte et consilio pollent vigentque, fiet ergo ut imperii potestas non penes centum, sed penes duos tantummodo aut tres sit qui animi virtute pollent, qui-
10 que facile omnia ad se trahere, et unusquisque more humanae cupidinis viam ad monarchiam sternere poterit. Atque adeo, si recte calculum ineamus, necesse est ut summa potestas imperii, cujus magnitudinis ratio centum optimates ad minimum exigit, in quinquies mille ad minimum patricios deferatur. Hac enim ratione nunquam deerit quin centum
15 reperiantur animi virtute excellentes, posito scilicet quod ex quinquaginta qui honores ambiunt, eosque adipiscuntur, unus semper reperiatur optimis non inferior, praeter alios qui optimorum virtutes aemulantur, quique propterea digni etiam sunt qui regant.

3. Solent frequentius patricii cives esse unius urbis quae caput totius
20 imperii est, ita ut civitas sive respublica ex eadem habeat vocabulum, ut olim Romana, hodie Veneta, Genuensis, etc. At Hollandorum respublica nomen ex integra provincia habet; ex quo oritur ut hujus imperii subditi majori libertate gaudeant. Jam antequam fundamenta quibus hoc imperium aristocraticum niti debet determinare possimus,
25 notanda est differentia inter imperium quod in unum et id quod in satis magnum concilium transfertur; quae sane permagna est. Nam primo unius hominis potentia integro imperio sustinendo (ut Art. 5 Cap. 6 diximus) longe impar est, quod sine manifesto aliquo absurdo de concilio satis magno enunciare nemo potest: qui enim concilium satis
30 magnum esse affirmat, simul negat idem imperio sustinendo esse impar. Rex igitur consiliariis omnino indiget, concilium autem hujusmodi minime. Deinde reges mortales sunt, concilia contra aeterna: atque adeo imperii potentia quae semel in concilium satis magnum translata

---

4. *OP unde fiet ut*; *NS Dit zal dan veröorzaken dat*; *P*, *Gf*, and *B* omit *fiet ut*.

10. *OP trahere*; *P*, *Gf*, and *B trahent*; *NS zullen konnen trekken*, which suggests *trahere poterunt*. But *poterunt* can be understood from *poterit* in the following line.

13. *Gf optimates*; *OP optimatum*.   14. *P patricios*; *OP parricios*.

21. *Genuensis* not in *NS*.

25. *OP et in id*; *NS en de gene*, hence *V–L et id*; *Gf et inter id*. There is little to choose between these two corrections. *et inter id* is supported by p. 268, ll. 14–15, and *E* ii, 17 Sch., but in both these places *tusschen* is repeated in the Dutch.

sufficient that there should be a hundred outstanding men vested with the sovereign power, and therefore possessed of the right to appoint colleagues in the patriciate when any of their number die. These, of course, will do their utmost to ensure that their children or nearest kinsmen succeed them: consequently the sovereignty will always be vested in those whom fortune has made the children or kinsmen of patricians. Now since out of a hundred men who rise to office by the favour of fortune it is hard to find three who excel in skill and wisdom, this will mean that the sovereignty will be vested, not in a hundred, but solely in the two or three men who excel in mental ability; who will find it easy to concentrate all business in their own hands, and, inspired by human ambition in the usual way, to smooth their several paths to monarchy. Thus if I calculate correctly, it is necessary that a state which requires at least a hundred outstanding men on account of its size should have its sovereignty vested in at least five thousand patricians.[1] In this way there will always be found a hundred men of surpassing mental ability; it being assumed that out of fifty who seek and obtain office one man will always be found who is equal to the best, as well as some who try to emulate the virtues of the best and are therefore also worthy to rule.

3. The patricians are usually citizens of one city which is the capital of the whole state, so that the commonwealth or republic takes its name from that city, like the ancient republic of Rome, and the modern republics of Venice, Genoa, etc. But the republic of Holland takes its name from the whole province, and the result is that the subjects of this state enjoy greater freedom.[2] Now before we can determine the foundations on which aristocracy must rest, we must notice the difference between government by one man and government by a council of sufficient size—a difference which is certainly very great. In the first place, as I said in Section 5, Chapter 6, the power of one man is quite unequal to bearing the whole burden of government, but no one can say this about a council of sufficient size without manifest absurdity; for to assert that a council is sufficiently large is to deny that it is unequal to bearing the burden of government. Counsellors, then, are quite indispensable to a king, but unnecessary to a council of this kind. Secondly, kings are mortal, whereas councils last for ever; and so sovereign power which has once been vested in a council of sufficient

---

[1] Van Hove (op. cit. III, iii, 4, p. 566) notes Thucydides' approval of the government of the Five Thousand at Athens in 411 B.C. (*History of the Peloponnesian War* viii, 97).

[2] *TP* ix, 14, p. 425, and 15, p. 427.

est nunquam ad multitudinem redit; quod in imperio monarchico locum non habet, ut Art. 25 Cap. praeced. ostendimus. Tertio regis imperium vel ob ejus pueritiam, aegritudinem, senectutem, vel aliis de causis saepe precarium est; hujusmodi autem concilii potentia econtra una eademque semper manet. Quarto unius hominis voluntas varia admodum et inconstans est: et hac de causa imperii monarchici omne quidem jus est regis explicata voluntas (ut in Art. 1 Cap. praeced. diximus), at non omnis regis voluntas jus esse debet; quod de voluntate concilii satis magni dici nequit. Nam quandoquidem ipsum concilium (ut modo ostendimus) nullis consiliariis indiget, debet necessario omnis ejus explicata voluntas jus esse. Ac proinde concludimus imperium quod in concilium satis magnum transfertur absolutum esse, vel ad absolutum maxime accedere. Nam si quod imperium absolutum datur, illud revera est quod integra multitudo tenet.

4. Attamen quatenus hoc imperium aristocraticum nunquam (ut modo ostensum) ad multitudinem redit, nec ulla in eo multitudini consultatio, sed absolute omnis ejusdem concilii voluntas jus est, debet omnino ut absolutum considerari; et consequenter ejus fundamenta sola ejusdem concilii voluntate et judicio niti debent, non autem multitudinis vigilantia, quandoquidem ipsa tam a consiliis quam suffragiis ferendis arcetur. Causa igitur cur in praxi imperium absolutum non sit, nulla alia esse potest quam quia multitudo imperantibus formidolosa est; quae propterea aliquam sibi libertatem obtinet, quam, si non expressa lege, tacite tamen sibi vindicat obtinetque.

5. Apparet itaque hujus imperii conditionem optimam fore si ita institutum fuerit ut ad absolutum maxime accedat, hoc est, ut multitudo quantum fieri potest minus timenda sit, nullamque libertatem obtineat nisi quae ex ipsius imperii constitutione ipsi necessario tribui debet, quaeque adeo non tam multitudinis quam totius imperii jus sit, quod soli optimates ut suum vindicant conservantque. Hoc enim modo praxis cum theoria maxime conveniet, ut ex Art. praeced. patet, et per se etiam manifestum est: nam dubitare non possumus imperium eo minus penes patricios esse quo plura sibi plebs jura

---

20–21. *NS zo wel van de beradingen, als van stem te geven,* which is glossed *a suffragiis ferendis.* But cf. p. 376, ll. 2–3.

24. *Gf vindicat; OP vendicat.*   30. *Gf vindicant; OP vendicant.*

size never reverts to the people; which is not the case in a monarchy, as I have shown in Section 25 of the previous Chapter. Thirdly, the rule of a king is often made precarious by his youth, ill health, senility, or other causes; whereas the power of a council of this kind remains always at one and the same level. Fourthly, the will of one man is extremely variable and inconstant, and this is why, although every law in a monarchy is the king's declared will (as I said in Section 1 of the previous Chapter), not everything the king wills should be law; but this cannot be said about the will of a council which is sufficiently large. For since, as I have just shown, the council itself needs no counsellors, its declared will must necessarily be law in every case. I therefore conclude that the sovereignty which is vested in a council of sufficient size is absolute, or nearly so. For absolute sovereignty, if any such thing exists, is really the sovereignty held by a whole people.[1]

4. Still, in so far as sovereignty of this aristocratic kind never reverts to the people (as has just been shown), and the people is not consulted in any way, but everything the council wills is law, without exception, we must certainly regard aristocracy as absolute. In consequence, its fundamental laws must be based exclusively on the will and judgement of the council, and not on the vigilance of the people, since the latter is debarred both from giving advice and from voting. So the only possible reason why the government is not absolute in practice is that the people is an object of fear to its rulers, and therefore retains a certain amount of freedom for itself, enforcing and preserving it, if not by express law, at least by tacit agreement.

5. It is clear then that the condition of this kind of state will be best if it is organized so as to approach most closely to the absolute, i.e. so that the people is as little to be feared as possible, and retains no freedom save that which must necessarily be allowed it by the constitution of the state itself, and which is therefore not so much a right of the people as a right of the whole state, enforced and preserved by the patricians as their own exclusive concern. For this will bring practice into the closest possible agreement with theory,[2] as is clear from the previous Section, and indeed is self-evident: since we cannot doubt that the more rights the people vindicates for itself—I am thinking of the sort of rights commonly possessed in Lower Germany[3] by the associations of

---

[1] For Hobbes all sovereigns are equally absolute, though not equally powerful (*De Cive* vi, 13, n.): for Spinoza they are not equally absolute because not equally powerful.

[2] *TT-P* xvii, p. 149.

[3] A strip of territory on the left bank of the Rhine, once a Roman province, and including what are to-day parts of Belgium, the Netherlands, and the German Rhineland.

vindicat, qualia solent in inferiori Germania opificum collegia, *Gilden* vulgo dicta, habere.

6. Neque hinc, quod scilicet imperium in concilium absolute delatum est, ullum ab eodem infensi servitii periculum plebi metuendum. Nam concilii adeo magni voluntas non tam a libidine quam a ratione determinari potest; quippe homines ex malo affectu diversi trahuntur, nec una veluti mente duci possunt nisi quatenus honesta appetunt, vel saltem quae speciem honesti habent.

7. In determinandis igitur imperii aristocratici fundamentis apprime observandum est ut eadem sola voluntate et potentia supremi ejusdem concilii nitantur; ita ut ipsum concilium quantum fieri potest sui juris sit, nullumque a multitudine periculum habeat. Ad haec fundamenta, quae scilicet sola supremi concilii voluntate et potentia nitantur, determinandum, fundamenta pacis quae imperii monarchici propria et ab hoc imperio aliena sunt videamus. Nam si his alia aequipollentia fundamenta imperio aristocratico idonea substituerimus, et reliqua ut jam jacta sunt reliquerimus, omnes absque dubio seditionum causae sublatae erunt, vel saltem hoc imperium non minus securum quam monarchicum, sed contra eo magis securum, et ipsius conditio eo melior erit, quo magis quam monarchicum absque pacis et libertatis detrimento (vid. Art. 3 et 6 hujus Cap.) ad absolutum accedit; nam quo jus summae potestatis majus est, eo imperii forma cum rationis dictamine magis convenit (per Art. 5 Cap. 3), et consequenter paci et libertati conservandae aptior est. Percurramus igitur quae Cap. 6 ex Art. 9 diximus, ut illa quae ab hoc aliena sunt rejiciamus, et quae ei congrua sunt videamus.

8. Quod primo necesse sit urbem unam aut plures condere et munire nemo dubitare potest. Sed illa praecipue munienda est quae totius imperii est caput, et praeterea illae quae in limitibus imperii sunt. Illa enim quae totius imperii caput est, jusque summum habet, omnibus potentior esse debet. Caeterum in hoc imperio superfluum omnino est ut incolae omnes in familias dividantur.

9. Ad militiam quod attinet, quoniam in hoc imperio non inter omnes sed tantum inter patricios aequalitas quaerenda est, et praecipue quod patriciorum potentia major est quam plebis, certum est ad

---

1. *P vindicat*; *OP vendicat.*

6. *NS verscheidelijk getrokken* ... *worden.* Hence *G diverse trahuntur.* But the reading *diversi trahuntur* also occurs in *E* iv, 37 Sch. 2; and there *G* retains it, although *NS* gives the same rendering as here.

24–25. *NS uit het negende Lid*, i.e. *ex Art. 9*; *OP Art 9.* Cf. p. 350, ll. 22–23, *ex Art. 15 usque ad 27.*   34–35. *NS en voornamelijk dat*, i.e. *et praecipue quod*; *OP et praecipue.*

artisans popularly known as Gilds[1]—the less is sovereignty in the hands of the patricians.

6. And the fact that sovereignty has been entirely vested in the council need give the common people no cause to fear any danger of slavery and oppression. For the will of so large a council must be determined by reason rather than by caprice; since evil passions draw men in different directions, and they can be guided as if by one mind only in so far as they aim at ends which are honourable, or at any rate appear to be so.

7. Thus in determining the fundamental laws of aristocracy we must make sure above all that they rest solely on the will and power of the supreme council; so that that council is in the fullest possible possession of its own right and has no danger to fear from the people. In order to determine these fundamental laws, which, as I said, are to rest exclusively on the will and power of the supreme council, let us consider the basic laws of civil peace which are peculiar to monarchy and unsuited to this kind of state. If we substitute for these other basic laws of equal effectiveness adapted to aristocracy, and leave the rest as they have been already laid down, then undoubtedly all causes of civil strife will have been removed, or at any rate this kind of state will be just as stable as monarchy. Indeed it will be more stable, and its condition will be better, in so far as it is more absolute than monarchy without endangering peace and freedom (see Sections 3 and 6 of this Chapter); for the greater the right of the sovereign the more does the form of the state agree with the dictate of reason (by Section 5, Chapter 3), and hence the more suitable it is for the preservation of peace and freedom. Let us therefore run through what we have said in Chapter 6 from Section 9 onwards, in order to reject the measures unsuited to aristocracy and discover those which are consistent with it.

8. First, that it is necessary to found and fortify one or more cities nobody can doubt. But it is necessary to fortify in particular the city which is the capital of the whole state, and, in addition, those which are situated on the frontiers. For the city which is the capital of the whole state, and holds the supreme right, should be more powerful than all the rest. However, in this kind of state it is quite unnecessary for all the inhabitants to be divided into tribes.

9. As for the armed forces, since in this kind of state it is not equality among all, but only among the patricians, that must be the aim, and since in particular the power of the patricians is greater than

---

[1] In addition to their economic powers the Gilds had considerable influence in the town councils of these districts.

leges seu jura fundamentalia hujus imperii non pertinere ut militia ex nullis aliis quam ex subditis formetur. Sed hoc apprime necesse est, ut nullus in patriciorum numerum recipiatur nisi qui artem militarem recte noverit. Subditos autem extra militiam esse, ut quidam volunt,
5 inscitia sane est. Nam praeterquam quod militiae stipendium quod subditis solvitur in ipso regno manet, cum contra id quod militi extraneo solvitur omne pereat, accedit quod maximum imperii robur debilitaretur. Nam certum est illos singulari animi virtute certare qui pro aris et focis certant. Unde etiam apparet illos etiam non minus errare,
10 qui belli duces, tribunos, centuriones, etc. ex solis patriciis eligendos statuunt. Nam qua virtute ii milites certabunt quibus omnis gloriam et honores adipiscendi spes adimitur? Verum contra legem stabilire ne patriciis militem extraneum liceat conducere quando res postulat, vel ad sui defensionem et seditiones coercendas, vel ob alias quascunque
15 causas, praeterquam quod inconsultum est, repugnaret etiam summo patriciorum juri; de quo vide Ar. 3, 4, et 5 huj. Cap. Caeterum unius exercitus vel totius militiae dux in bello tantummodo et ex solis patriciis eligendus, qui annum ad summum imperium habeat, nec continuari in imperio nec postea eligi possit; quod jus cum in monarchico tum
20 maxime in hoc imperio necessarium est. Nam quamvis multo facilius, ut supra jam diximus, imperium ex uno in alium quam ex libero concilio in unum hominem transferri possit, fit tamen saepe ut patricii a suis ducibus opprimantur, idque multo majori reipublicae damno; quippe quando monarcha e medio tollitur non imperii sed tantummodo
25 tyranni mutatio fit. At in imperio aristocratico fieri id nequit absque eversione imperii et maximorum virorum clade. Cujus rei funestissima exempla Roma dedit. Caeterum ratio cur in imperio monarchico

---

1–2. *NS dat de krijgsordening uit geen anderen, dan uit d' eige onderzaten, opgerecht zou worden.* Hence *M ex nullis aliis* (cf. p. 318, ll. 19–20); *OP ex ullis aliis.*

7–8. *NS verzwakt word*, i.e. *debilitatur.*

11. *B gloriam*, which is confirmed by the *NS* reading, *alle hoop, om eer en ampten te verkrijgen*; *OP gloriae.*

that of the common people, it is obviously no part of the laws or constitution of this kind of state that the armed forces should be composed of subjects alone: what *is* of fundamental importance is that no one should be admitted to the patriciate unless he has a thorough knowledge of the art of war. But to debar the subjects from military service, as some wish to do,[1] is certainly foolish. For money paid for military service to subjects remains within the state, while payment made to foreign troops is a dead loss; what is more, such a measure would sap the greatest source of the state's strength, since there is no doubt that men who fight for hearth and home fight with extraordinary courage. By the same argument, those who maintain that generals, colonels, captains, etc. should be chosen exclusively from the patricians are equally mistaken. For what courage in battle can we expect from soldiers who are denied all hope of winning glory and promotion? On the other hand, to establish a law forbidding the patricians to engage foreign troops when the situation requires it,[2] either for their own protection and the suppression of civil disorders, or for any other reason, is not only imprudent, but would contravene the supreme right of the patricians as I have described it in Sections 3, 4, and 5 of this Chapter. But a law prescribing that the commander of an army or of all the armed forces should be chosen only in time of war, from the patricians alone, and should hold his command for a year at most, without the possibility of extension or subsequent re-appointment, is even more necessary in an aristocracy than it is in a monarchy. For although it is much easier, as I have already said above,[3] for sovereignty to be transferred from one man to another than from a free council to one man, it is quite common for patricians to be enslaved by their own commanders, and with much greater damage to the common weal; for when a king is removed there is no change in the form of the state, but only in the identity of the tyrant.[4] In an aristocracy, however, the transfer of sovereignty inevitably involves the overthrow of the state and the destruction of its greatest men. The history of Rome provides melancholy examples of this.[5] On the other hand, my reason for recommending that the armed

---

[1] The Venetian aristocracy did not employ the commons in its armies (Machiavelli, *Discourses* i, 6). This made it strong internally, but weak against external enemies.

[2] In times of crisis (e.g. in 1617) the regents of Dutch towns engaged professional troops, called *waardgelders*, for their own protection (Renier, *The Dutch Nation* i, x, pp. 60 and ff.). In spite of his general dislike of mercenaries (vi, 10 and n. 2, p. 319), Spinoza is prepared to allow this in his aristocracy.   [3] *TP* vii, 14, p. 347.

[4] *TT-P* xviii, pp. 201–3. Van Hove (op. cit. i, iii, 1, p. 188) quotes *mutatio tyranni non tyrannidis ablatio.*

[5] Machiavelli, *Discourses* iii, 24.

diximus quod militia sine stipendio servire debeat locum in hujusmodi imperio non habet. Nam quandoquidem subditi tam a consiliis quam suffragiis ferendis arcentur, perinde ac peregrini censendi sunt, qui propterea non iniquiore conditione ac peregrini ad militandum condu-
5 cendi sunt. Neque hic periculum est ut a concilio prae reliquis agnoscantur. Quinimo ne unusquisque suorum factorum iniquus, ut fit, aestimator sit, consultius est ut patricii certum praemium militibus pro servitio decernant.

10. Praeterea hac etiam de causa, quod omnes praeter patricios pere-
10 grini sunt, fieri non potest absque totius imperii periculo ut agri et domus et omne solum publici juris maneant, et ut incolis annuo pretio locentur. Nam subditi qui nullam in imperio partem habent facile omnes in adversis urbes desererent, si bona quae possident portare quo vellent liceret. Quare agri et fundi hujus imperii subditis non locandi
15 sed vendendi sunt, ea tamen conditione, ut etiam ex annuo proventu partem aliquotam singulis annis numerent etc., ut in Hollandia fit.

11. His consideratis, ad fundamenta quibus supremum concilium niti et firmari debet pergo. Hujus concilii membra in mediocri imperio quinque circiter millia esse debere ostendimus Art. 2 hujus Cap. Atque
20 adeo ratio quaerenda est qua fiat ne paulatim ad pauciores deveniat imperium, sed contra ut pro ratione incrementi ipsius imperii eorum augeatur numerus; deinde ut inter patricios aequalitas quantum fieri potest servetur; ut praeterea in conciliis celeris detur expeditio; ut communi bono consulatur; et denique ut patriciorum seu concilii major
25 sit quam multitudinis potentia, sed ita ut nihil inde multitudo detrimenti patiatur.

12. Ad primum autem obtinendum maxima oritur difficultas ex invidia. Sunt enim homines, ut diximus, natura hostes; ita ut, quamvis legibus copulentur adstringanturque, retineant tamen naturam. Atque
30 hinc fieri existimo ut imperia democratica in aristocratica, et haec tandem in monarchica mutentur. Nam plane mihi persuadeo pleraque aristocratica imperia democratica prius fuisse, quod scilicet quaedam

---

13–14. *NS zullen ... verlaten, indien zy ... willen ... konnen voeren*, i.e. *deserent, si ... velint ... licet.*

forces should serve without pay in a monarchy does not hold good in a state of this kind. For since the subjects are debarred both from giving advice and from voting, they must be regarded as aliens, and therefore engaged on the same terms. Nor is there any danger here that those who serve will be favoured by the council above the rest. The danger is rather that each man will, as usual, set an exaggerated value on his own services; and to prevent this it is as well for the patricians to establish a fixed payment for the performance of military duties.

10. The fact that all save the patricians are aliens is also the reason why the fields and houses and the whole territory cannot possibly remain public property, and be let out to the inhabitants at an annual rent, without danger to the whole state. For subjects who have no share in the state would be apt to leave the cities *en masse* in time of danger, if they could carry their possessions wherever they wished. Hence the fields and farms in this state must be sold, not rented, to the subjects; but they should also pay over a certain proportion of their annual return each year, and have other burdens, as is the case in Holland.[1]

11. I now turn to the fundamental laws required to support and strengthen the supreme council.[2] I have shown in Section 2 of this Chapter that in a state of moderate size the members of this council should number about five thousand. We have therefore to look for means which will ensure that, so far from the sovereignty passing gradually into fewer hands, the number of patricians is proportionately increased as the state grows larger;[3] that the greatest possible equality is maintained among the patricians; that business is speedily transacted in the assemblies; that attention is paid to the common good; and, finally, that the power of the patricians or council is greater than that of the people, but without this causing any harm to the latter.

12. The main obstacle to the achievement of the first aim is caused by jealousy. For men, as I said, are enemies by nature; so much so that they still retain their nature even when joined and bound together by laws. This, I think, is why democracies change into aristocracies, and the latter in the end into monarchies. I am fully convinced that most aristocracies were originally democracies,[4] for when a people has sought,

---

[1] Temple, op. cit., ch. vii, pp. 154–5.

[2] This council is partly modelled on the Grand Council of Venice.

[3] Van Hove regards *dominatio paucorum* as one of the great faults of aristocracy, and criticizes the towns of Holland in particular for failing to enlarge their councils as they increased in population (op. cit. ii, ii, 6, pp. 290–1).

[4] *TP* iv, 6, p. 305, n. 3.

multitudo novas sedes quaerens, iisque inventis et cultis, imperandi aequale jus integra retinuit, quia nemo imperium alteri dat volens. Sed quamvis eorum unusquisque aequum esse censeat ut idem jus, quod alteri in ipsum est, ipsi etiam in alterum sit, iniquum tamen esse putat ut pere-
5 grinis, qui ad ipsos confluunt, aequale cum ipsis jus sit in imperio quod sibi labore quaesierant, et sui sanguinis impendio occupaverant. Quod nec ipsi peregrini renuunt; qui nimirum non ad imperandum, sed ad res suas privatas curandum eo migrant, et satis sibi concedi putant si modo ipsis libertas concedatur res suas cum securitate agendi. Sed in-
10 terim multitudo ex peregrinorum confluentia augetur, qui paulatim illius gentis mores induunt, donec demum nulla alia diversitate dignoscuntur quam hoc solo quod adipiscendorum honorum jure careant; et dum horum numerus quotidie crescit, civium contra multis de causis minuitur; quippe saepe familiae extinguuntur, alii ob scelera exclusi,
15 et plerique ob rei domesticae angustiam rempublicam negligunt, dum interea potentiores nihil studeant quam soli regnare; et sic paulatim imperium ad paucos, et tandem ob factionem ad unum redigitur. Atque his alias causas quae hujusmodi imperia destruunt adjungere possemus; sed quia satis notae sunt iisdem supersedeo, et leges quibus
20 hoc imperium de quo agimus conservari debet ordine jam ostendam.

13. Primaria hujus imperii lex esse debet qua determinatur ratio numeri patriciorum ad multitudinem. Ratio enim (per Art. 1 hujus Cap.) inter hanc et illos habenda est ita ut pro incremento multitudinis patriciorum numerus augeatur. Atque haec (per illa quae Art. 2 hujus
25 Cap. diximus) debet esse circiter ut 1 ad 50, hoc est, ut inaequalitas numeri patriciorum ad multitudinem nunquam major sit. Nam (per Art. 1 hujus Cap.) servata imperii forma numerus patriciorum multo major esse potest numero multitudinis. Sed in sola eorum paucitate periculum est. Qua autem ratione cavendum sit ut haec lex inviolata
30 servetur, suo loco mox ostendam.

14. Patricii ex quibusdam tantummodo familiis aliquibus in locis

---

1. *OP iisque*; *NS en de zelfden*; *P, Gf,* and *B iis.*
2. *NS volkomentlijk*, which suggests *integre.*
6. *NS gezocht, en . . . verkregen hebben.* Hence the correct reading may be *quaesierunt . . . occupaverunt.*
17. *NS door de samenspanningen*, which is glossed *factiones.* Hence *L factiones.*
19. *NS dewijl zy* (i.e. *oorzaken*) *genoech bekent zijn*; *OP nota.*
22. *OP per Art. 1*; *NS volgens het eerste Lid.* But the doctrine, although implied in Section 1, is not explicitly stated until Section 11. Hence the correct reading may be *per Art. 11.*
28. *NS naar het getal.* Hence *L pro numero.* But wrongly, as the reference shows.

found, and cultivated new territories, it always retains the right to govern as a corporate right in which each of its members has an equal share, since no one willingly yields sovereignty to another.[1] But while each member thinks it fair that he should have against another member the same right as the other has against him, he thinks it unfair that the aliens who flock to join them should have equal rights in a state which they have won for themselves by their labours, and carved out at the cost of their blood. The new-comers, for their part, make no objection to this; since it is not to be rulers, but to further their own private interests, that they join the settlement, and they are quite content as long as they are given freedom to conduct their own business in security.[2] Meanwhile the population is constantly growing through the influx of aliens, who gradually adopt the manners and customs of the original settlers, until finally the only thing which distinguishes them is the fact that they lack the right to hold office; and while they daily grow more numerous, the citizens grow fewer. There are many reasons for this; families often die out, some men are expelled because of their crimes, and many neglect public affairs through lack of private means. In the meantime the sole ambition of the powerful is to rule by themselves; and so sovereignty is gradually concentrated in the hands of a few men, and finally, through civil strife, in the hands of one. I could add other causes which destroy states of this kind,[3] but since they are quite well known I pass them over in silence, and shall now describe in their order of importance the laws required to preserve the kind of state we are discussing.

13. The principal law of this kind of state must be that which determines the ratio of patricians to people; for (by Section 1 of this Chapter) there should be a fixed ratio between them, so that as the population increases the number of patricians is raised proportionately. This ratio (according to our statement in Section 2 of this Chapter) should be about one to fifty, by which I mean that the proportion of patricians to people should never be lower. It *can* be higher; for (by Section 1 of this Chapter) the patricians can greatly outnumber the commons, and the state still remain an aristocracy; it is only in their fewness that danger lies. The means of ensuring that this law is kept inviolate I shall presently describe in their place.

14. In some places the patricians are chosen from certain families

---

[1] *TP* vii, 5 and n. 2, p. 339.

[2] Machiavelli, *Discourses* i, 6.

[3] These are discussed by Aristotle in *Politics* 1305^b–1307^b.

eliguntur. Sed hoc expresso jure statuere perniciosum est. Nam praeterquam quod familiae saepe extinguuntur, et quod nunquam reliquae
absque ignominia excluduntur, accedit quod hujus imperii formae repugnat ut patricia dignitas haereditaria sit, per Art. 1 hujus Cap. Sed
5 imperium hac ratione democraticum potius videretur quale in Art. 12
hujus Cap. descripsimus, quod scilicet paucissimi tenent cives. Attamen contra cavere ne patricii filios suos et consanguineos eligant, et
consequenter ne imperandi jus in quibusdam familiis maneat, impossibile est, imo absurdum, ut Art. 39 hujus Cap. ostendam. Verum,
10 modo id nullo expresso jure obtineant, nec reliqui (qui scilicet in imperio nati sunt, et patrio sermone utuntur, nec uxorem peregrinam
habent, nec infames sunt, nec serviunt, nec denique servili aliquo
officio vitam sustentant—inter quos etiam oenopolae et cerevisiarii et
alii hujusmodi numerandi sunt) excludantur, retinebitur nihilominus
15 imperii forma, et ratio inter patricios et multitudinem servari semper
poterit.

15. Quod si praeterea lege statuatur ut nulli juniores eligantur,
nunquam fiet ut paucae familiae jus imperandi retineant; atque adeo
lege statuendum ut nullus nisi qui ad annum aetatis trigesimum per-
20 venit in catalogum eligendorum referri possit.

16. Tertio deinde statuendum est ut patricii omnes in quodam urbis
loco statutis certis temporibus congregari debeant, et qui, nisi morbo
aut publico aliquo negotio impeditus, concilio non interfuerit, sensibili aliqua pecuniae poena mulctetur. Nam ni hoc fieret, plurimi, ob
25 rei domesticae curam, publicam negligerent.

17. Hujus concilii officium sit leges condere et abrogare, collegas
patricios et omnes imperii ministros eligere. Non enim fieri potest ut
is qui supremum jus habet, ut hoc concilium habere statuimus, alicui
potestatem det leges condendi et abrogandi, quin simul jure suo cedat,
30 et in illum id transferat cui illam potestatem dedit; quippe qui vel uno

---

3–4. *NS* punctuates *accedit (quod . . . repugnat) ut.*
5. *NS* *zou . . . schijnen,* i.e. *videretur*; *OP* *videtur.*
12. *P nec serviunt*; *NS en niet onëerlijk noch dienstbaar zijn*; *OP nunc serviunt.*
13–14. *OP oenopolae et cerevisiarii*; *NS de kroeghouders, tappers en andere dïergelijken.*
I therefore insert *et alii hujusmodi.*

only:[1] but to lay down a definite law to this effect is disastrous. For families often die out; those which are excluded always feel disgraced; what is more, it is contrary to the nature of aristocracy for patrician status to be hereditary, by Section 1 of this Chapter. In fact, this regulation would make the state more like a democracy such as we have described in Section 12 of this Chapter, where sovereignty is vested in very few citizens. On the other hand, to prevent the right to rule from remaining in the hands of certain families by preventing the patricians from appointing their own sons and kinsmen is not only impossible but absurd, as I shall show in Section 39 of this Chapter. However, as long as there is no explicit law giving some families the right to rule and excluding the rest (by the rest I mean those who have been born in the state and speak the mother tongue, are not married to aliens, have no criminal record, are not servants, and, finally, do not support life by any menial occupation—a condition which will exclude ale-house-keepers, tapsters, and the like[2]), the form of the state will be preserved, and it will always be possible to maintain the ratio of patricians to people.

15. Besides, if there is a law that no young men may be appointed, it will never be possible for a few families to monopolize the right to rule; and so a law must be made that only those who have reached their thirtieth year can be placed on the roll of candidates.[3]

16. Thirdly, all the patricians must be required by law to assemble at a particular place in the city at certain fixed times, and any man who does not attend the council—those prevented by illness or some public business excepted—should be heavily fined. Otherwise most patricians would neglect public affairs to attend to their private concerns.

17. The duty of this council should be to make and repeal laws, to co-opt to the patriciate, and to appoint all the ministers of state.[4] For he who holds sovereignty—as by my account this council does—cannot possibly give anyone the power to make and repeal laws without at once renouncing his own right and transferring it to the person to whom he gives that power; since anyone who has power to make and

---

[1] Venice and Genoa kept rolls of their noble families (the *Libro d'Oro* and the *Liber Civitatis* respectively), and membership of their Grand Councils was confined to men whose names were on these rolls.

[2] Van Hove excludes the same classes (op. cit. III, iii, 4, pp. 564–5).

[3] At Venice a noble became a member of the Grand Council on reaching the age of twenty-five.

[4] These were also functions of the Grand Council of Venice, which could confer nobility, but exercised this right very sparingly.

solo die potestatem habet leges condendi et abrogandi, ille totam imperii formam mutare potest. At quotidiana imperii negotia aliis ad tempus secundum constituta jura administranda tradere, retento supremo suo jure, potest. Praeterea, si imperii ministri ab alio quam ab hoc concilio 5 eligerentur, tum hujus concilii membra pupilli potius quam patricii appellandi essent.

18. Huic concilio solent quidam rectorem seu principem creare, vel ad vitam, ut Veneti, vel ad tempus, ut Genuenses, sed tanta cum cautione ut satis appareat id non sine magno imperii periculo fieri. Et 10 sane dubitare non possumus quin imperium hac ratione ad monarchicum accedat; et, quantum ex eorum historiis conjicere possumus, nulla alia de causa id factum est quam quia ante constituta haec concilia sub rectore vel duce veluti sub rege fuerant; atque adeo rectoris creatio gentis quidem, sed non imperii aristocratici absolute considerati 15 requisitum necessarium est.

19. Attamen quia summa hujus imperii potestas penes universum hoc concilium, non autem penes unumquodque ejusdem membrum est (nam alias coetus esset inordinatae multitudinis), necesse ergo est ut patricii omnes legibus ita astringantur ut unum veluti corpus quod 20 una regitur mente componant. At leges per se solae invalidae sunt, et facile franguntur ubi earum vindices ii ipsi sunt qui peccare possunt, quique soli exemplum ex supplicio capere debent, et collegas ea de causa punire ut suum appetitum ejusdem supplicii metu frenent; quod magnum est absurdum. Atque adeo medium quaerendum est quo 25 supremi hujus concilii ordo et imperii jura inviolata serventur, ita tamen ut inter patricios aequalitas quanta dari potest sit.

20. Cum autem ex uno rectore vel principe, qui etiam in conciliis suffragium ferre potest, magna necessario oriri debeat inaequalitas, praesertim ob potentiam quae ipsi necessario concedi debet ut suo

7. *OP Huic*; *NS over deze Raatvergadering*; *P* and *B Hinc.*
13. *NS hebben geweest.*

repeal laws even for a single day is in a position to change the whole form of the state. What the sovereign *can* do without renouncing his right is to entrust others temporarily with the duty of handling the daily business of the state in accordance with the laws established. Besides, if the ministers of state were appointed by any other council, the members of this council would deserve to be called bejants rather than regents.

18. Some are wont to appoint a governor or president over this council, either for life, like the Venetians, or for a definite time, like the Genoese;[1] but they do so with such circumspection as to make it quite clear that the practice necessarily involves great danger to the constitution.[2] Indeed, we cannot doubt that it brings the state very close to monarchy; and as far as I can gather from their history, the only reason for it is that before the institution of their councils they were subject to a governor or doge who ruled them like a king. Thus while the appointment of a governor meets a need of the race, it is not an indispensable requirement of aristocracy as such.

19. Nevertheless, since the sovereignty in this type of state is vested in this council as a whole, and not in each of its members separately (for otherwise it would be the gathering of a disorderly mob), it is necessary that all the patricians should be bound together so closely by laws that they form one body directed by one mind. But laws in themselves are weak, and are easily broken when their guardians are precisely the men who are in a position to break them, and the only men who must take a lesson from the punishment; for then they have to chastise their colleagues in order to curb their own ambition by fear of the same penalty, and this is quite absurd. We therefore need a means of keeping the organization of this supreme council and the laws of the state intact, while still ensuring the greatest possible equality among the patricians.

20. Now the creation of a single governor or president, who has also the right to vote at meetings of the assembly, must inevitably lead to great inequality, primarily because of the power which must necessarily

---

[1] At Venice the Doge was appointed for life: at Genoa for two years.

[2] Spinoza is thinking partly of the elaborate process, designed to make favouritism impossible, by which a Venetian Doge was elected; and partly of *i cinque correttori alla promission ducale*, a commission of five men appointed on the death of each Doge to review the powers of the office in the interests of public freedom. The recommendations of this commission, if accepted by the Grand Council, were binding on the new Doge, and in this way the ducal powers came to be more and more strictly defined. See *Mémoires historiques et politiques sur la République de Venise*, vol. i, ch. v, pp. 95–110.

officio securius fungi possit, nihil ergo, si omnia recte perpendamus, communi saluti utilius institui potest quam quod huic supremo concilio aliud subordinetur ex quibusdam patriciis, quorum officium solummodo sit observare ut imperii jura quae concilia et imperii ministros con-
5 cernunt inviolata serventur; qui propterea potestatem habeant delinquentem quemcunque imperii ministrum, qui scilicet contra jura quae ipsius ministerium concernunt peccavit, coram suo judicio vocandi, et secundum constituta jura damnandi: atque hos imposterum syndicos appellabimus.

10 21. Atque hi ad vitam eligendi sunt. Nam si ad tempus eligerentur, ita ut postea ad alia imperii officia vocari possent, in absurdum quod Art. 19 hujus Cap. modo ostendimus incideremus. Sed ne longa admodum dominatione nimium superbiant, nulli ad hoc ministerium eligendi sunt nisi qui ad annum aetatis sexagesimum aut ultra per-
15 venerunt, et senatorio officio (de quo infra) functi sunt.

22. Horum praeterea numerum facile determinabimus, si consideremus hos syndicos ad patricios sese habere ut omnes simul patricii ad multitudinem, quam regere nequeunt si justo numero pauciores sunt; ac proinde syndicorum numerus ad patriciorum numerum debet
20 esse ut horum numerus ad numerum multitudinis, hoc est (per Art. 13 hujus Cap.) ut 1 ad 50.

23. Praeterea, ut hoc concilium secure suo officio fungi possit, militiae pars aliqua eidem decernenda est, cui imperare quid velit possit.

24. Syndicis vel cuicunque status ministro stipendium nullum, sed
25 emolumenta decernenda sunt talia ut non possint sine magno suo damno rempublicam prave administrare. Nam quod hujus imperii ministris aequum sit vacationis praemium decerni dubitare non possumus, quia major hujus imperii pars plebs est, cujus securitati patricii invigilant, dum ipsa nullam rei publicae sed tantum privatae curam habet.
30 Verum quia contra nemo (ut Art. 4 Cap. 7 diximus) alterius causam

10–12. *NS verkiest . . . beroepen konnen worden . . . zullen vervallen. V–L possent*; *OP possint.*

12–13. *NS op dat zy...niet al te verwaant zouden worden.* Hence *L nimium. OP nimirum.*

27. *L vacationis*; *OP vocationis.* Cf. p. 350, l. 27, and p. 352, l. 14, where *OP* has *vacationis* in both cases. *NS vergelding voor hun bezigheit.*

29. *P rei publicae*; *OP Reip.*; *G Reipublicae.*

be given him if he is to perform his functions in comparative safety. Thus, if we weigh up all the considerations correctly, the means most conducive to the general welfare is to establish another council, subordinate to the supreme council I have described above, and composed of several patricians, whose sole duty should be to see that the state laws concerning the assemblies and ministers are kept unbroken; and who should therefore have the power to summon before their tribunal, and to condemn in accordance with the laws established, any minister of state who is guilty of transgressing the regulations concerning his office. These in future I shall call syndics.[1]

21. These syndics should be appointed for life; for if they were appointed for a certain period, and thus could be elected later to other offices of state, we should fall into the absurdity which I have just pointed out in Section 19 of this Chapter. But to prevent their becoming too arrogant through a very long term of rule, none must be appointed to this office save ex-senators (see below) who have reached their sixtieth year or beyond.

22. The number of these syndics will easily be determined if we consider that they stand to the patricians as the whole body of patricians stands to the commons, which the patricians cannot control if they fall below the requisite number; so the ratio of syndics to patricians must be the same as the ratio of patricians to commons, that is (by Section 13 of this Chapter) one to fifty.

23. Moreover, to ensure that this council may be able to perform its functions in safety, a part of the armed forces must be assigned to it and put entirely at its disposal.[2]

24. Syndics and ministers of state should not be paid a fixed salary, but assigned such sources of income that they cannot maladminister public affairs without great loss to themselves. That justice requires the ministers of this state to be assigned a reward for their services we cannot doubt; for while the patricians devote their attention to the security of the commons, who in this case make up the greater part of the state, the latter have no public duties, but only their private affairs to look after. Since, however, men only defend the cause of others in so far as they think that it serves their own interests to do so (as I said in

---

[1] The Areopagites of ancient Athens had similar supervisory and judicial powers, and were also appointed for life; but Spinoza probably has in mind the *Dieci* and *Avogadori di commun* of Venice (*Mémoires*, vol. i, ch. iv, pp. 72–94, and ch. vi, pp. 118–22), though these magistrates were not appointed for life. In their possession of the *dictatoria potestas* (*TP* x, 2, p. 431) his syndics resemble the *Dieci*: in other respects the *Avogadori*.

[2] The *Dieci* had a military guard.

defendit nisi quatenus rem suam eo ipso stabilire credit, res necessario ita ordinandae sunt ut ministri qui reipublicae curam habent tum maxime sibi consulant, cum maxime communi bono invigilant.

25. Syndicis igitur, quorum officium, uti diximus, est observare ut imperii jura inviolata serventur, haec emolumenta decernenda sunt: 5 videlicet ut unusquisque paterfamilias qui in aliquo imperii loco habitat quotannis nummum parvi valoris, nempe argenti unciae quartam partem, solvere teneatur syndicis; ut inde numerum inhabitantium cognoscere possint, atque adeo observare quotam ejus partem patricii 10 efficiant. Deinde, ut unusquisque patricius tyro, ut electus est, syndicis numerare debeat summam aliquam magnam, ex. gr. viginti aut viginti quinque argenti libras. Praeterea pecunia illa, qua absentes patricii (qui scilicet convocato concilio non interfuerunt) condemnantur, syndicis etiam decernenda est, et insuper ut pars bonorum delinquentium 15 ministrorum, qui eorum judicio stare tenentur, et qui certa pecuniae summa mulctantur, vel quorum bona proscribuntur, iisdem dedicetur; non quidem omnibus, sed iis tantummodo qui quotidie sedent, et quorum officium est syndicorum concilium convocare, de quibus vide Art. 28 hujus Cap. Ut autem syndicorum concilium suo semper 20 numero constet, ante omnia in supremo concilio solito tempore convocato de eo quaestio habenda est. Quod si a syndicis neglectum fuerit, ut tum ei qui senatui (de quo mox erit nobis dicendi locus) praeest supremum concilium ea de re monere incumbat, et a syndicorum praeside silentii habiti causam exigere, et quid de ea supremi concilii 25 sententia sit inquirere. Quod si is etiam tacuerit, ut causa ab eo qui supremo judicio praeest, vel eo etiam tacente ab alio quocunque patricio suscipiatur, qui tam a syndicorum quam senatus et judicum praeside silentii rationem exigat. Denique, ut lex illa qua juniores secluduntur stricte etiam observetur, statuendum est ut omnes qui ad annum 30 aetatis trigesimum pervenerunt, quique expresso jure a regimine non secluduntur, suum nomen in catalogo coram syndicis inscribi curent, et accepti honoris signum quoddam statuto aliquo pretio ab iisdem accipere,

Section 4, Chapter 7), the administration must necessarily be organized so that ministers in charge of public affairs take most care of their own interests when they pay most heed to the common good.

25. Thus the syndics, whose duty, as I said, is to see that the laws of the state are kept unbroken, must be assigned the following remuneration. Every family head who lives in any part of the state should be bound to pay a small coin, say a quarter of an ounce of silver, to the syndics each year; the latter will thus be able to discover the number of the inhabitants, and to note what proportion thereof is made up by patricians. Next, each new patrician must pay the syndics a large sum on his election, e.g. twenty or twenty-five pounds of silver.[1] In addition, the money fines imposed on absent patricians (i.e. on those who have absented themselves from a meeting of the council) must also be assigned to the syndics, and part of the goods of offending ministers—who, on submitting (as they must) to the syndics' jurisdiction, are condemned to pay a fine or to have their possessions confiscated—should be made over to them as well;[2] not, indeed, to all of them, but only to those who are sitting every day,[3] and whose duty it is to summon the council of syndics. For these see Section 28 of this Chapter. To ensure that the council of syndics always contains its proper complement of members, their number must be the first point raised at each regular meeting of the supreme council. If the syndics neglect this duty, it should then fall to the president of the senate (of which we shall have to speak presently) to raise the point in the supreme council, to demand from the president of the syndics an explanation of his silence, and to ask the supreme council for its opinion on the matter. If he says nothing either, the question should be taken up by the president of the supreme court, or, failing him, by any other patrician; who should demand an explanation of their silence from the presidents of the senate and court as well as from the president of the syndics. Next, to ensure that the law by which young men are excluded is also strictly observed, it must be laid down that all who have reached their thirtieth year, and are not debarred by explicit law from a share in the government, should see that their names are inscribed on a roll kept by the syndics, and procure from them, for a fixed sum of money, some token of the status they have acquired; this will allow them to assume a

---

[1] At Venice the *Avogadori* had charge of the *Libro d'Oro* (*Mémoires*, vol. i, ch. i, p. 12).

[2] The *Avogadori* received part of the fines imposed on offenders (op. cit., ch. vi, p. 121).

[3] At Venice the three *Capi di Dieci* met daily in a room in the ducal palace (op. cit., ch. iv, p. 77).

ut ipsis liceat certum ornatum iis tantummodo concessum induere, quo dignoscantur et in honore a reliquis habeantur. Et interim jure constitutum sit ut in electionibus nulli patricio quenquam nominare liceat nisi cujus nomen in communi catalogo inscriptum est, idque sub
5 gravi poena; et praeterea ne cuiquam liceat officium sive munus ad quod subeundum eligitur recusare. Denique, ut omnia absolute fundamentalia imperii jura aeterna sint, statuendum est, si quis in supremo concilio quaestionem de jure aliquo fundamentali moverit, utpote de prolonganda alicujus ducis exercitus dominatione, vel de numero
10 patriciorum minuendo, et similibus, ut reus majestatis sit, et non tantum mortis damnetur, ejusque bona proscribantur, sed ut supplicii aliquod signum in aeternam rei memoriam in publico emineat. Ad reliqua vero communia imperii jura stabiliendum sufficit si modo statuatur ut lex nulla abrogari nec nova condi possit nisi prius syndi-
15 corum concilium, et deinde supremi concilii tres quartae aut quatuor quintae partes in eo convenerint.

26. Jus praeterea supremum concilium convocandi resque decernendas in eodem proponendi penes syndicos sit, quibus etiam primus locus in concilio concedatur, sed sine jure suffragii. Verum antequam
20 sedeant, jurare debent per salutem supremi illius concilii, perque libertatem publicam, se summo studio conaturos ut jura patria inviolata serventur et communi bono consulatur; quo facto res proponendas ordine aperiant per ministrum qui ipsis a secretis est.

27. Ut autem in decernendo et in eligendis imperii ministris omni-
25 bus patriciis aequa sit potestas, et celeris expeditio in omnibus detur, omnino probandus est ordo quem Veneti observant, qui scilicet ad nominandos imperii ministros aliquot e concilio sorte eligunt, et, ab his ordine ministris eligendis nominatis, unusquisque patricius sententiam suam qua propositum ministrum eligendum probat vel reprobat
30 indicat calculis, ita ut postea ignoretur quisnam hujus aut illius sententiae fuerit auctor. Quo fit non tantum ut omnium patriciorum in

---

2. *NS boven d' anderen*, which suggests *prae reliquis*.
10. *NS of van andere diergelijke dingen*, which suggests *vel similibus*.

certain dress granted to them alone, to distinguish them from the rest and give them a higher standing. Meanwhile it must be laid down by law that at election times no patrician may nominate anyone whose name is not entered on the general roll, except under a heavy penalty; and also that none may refuse a post or duty which he is appointed to undertake.[1] Finally, that all the laws of the state which are absolutely fundamental may remain in force for ever, it must be laid down that if anyone calls in question any fundamental law in the supreme council —moves, for example, that the command of some general should be extended, or that the number of patricians should be diminished, or the like—he should be arraigned for high treason; and not only be condemned to death and the loss of his possessions, but have a record of his punishment prominently displayed in a public place to perpetuate the memory of his crime. But to strengthen the other general laws of the state it is enough to enact that no law can be repealed, or a new one made, unless first the council of syndics, and then three-fourths or four-fifths of the supreme council have agreed to it.

26. The right to summon the supreme council, and to bring up matters for its decision, should be vested in the syndics,[2] who should also be given the place of honour in the assembly, but without the right to vote. Before they take their seats, however, they must swear by the safety of the supreme council, and by public liberty, to do their utmost to keep the laws of their fathers inviolate and promote the common welfare; after which they should, through their secretary, set out in order the matters to be brought up for discussion.

27. As a means of ensuring that all the patricians have equal influence in the making of decisions and the appointment of ministers of state, and that all business is dealt with quickly, the system followed by the Venetians deserves our full approval. To nominate ministers of state they appoint some members of the council by lot;[3] and when these have nominated the candidates in order, every patrician votes for or against each nominee by secret ballot, so that nobody knows afterwards who has been the author of any particular vote. This ensures not only

---

[1] Refusal of some Venetian magistracies was punishable by a fine (*Mémoires*, vol. i, ch. vii, p. 138).

[2] Meetings of the Grand Council of Venice were regularly summoned by the *Signoria* (i.e. the Doge, his six councillors, and the three *Capi Superiori*), which presided in the assembly (op. cit., ch. i, p. 9). But the *Avogadori* could summon extraordinary meetings of any council in the state (op. cit., ch. vi, p. 121).

[3] Thirty-six, divided into four groups of nine. When there were nine offices to be filled each member of each group nominated a candidate for one office (op. cit., ch. i, pp. 20–26; Van Hove, *Polityke Weegschaal* ii, iv, 2, pp. 317 and ff.).

decernendo auctoritas aequalis sit, et ut negotia cito expediantur, sed etiam ut unusquisque absolutam libertatem, quod in conciliis apprime necessarium est, habeat suam sententiam absque ullo invidiae periculo proferendi.

5   28. In syndicorum etiam et reliquis conciliis idem ordo observandus est, ut scilicet suffragia calculis ferantur. Jus autem syndicorum concilium convocandi, resque in eodem decernendas proponendi, penes eorundem praesidem esse oportet, qui cum aliis decem aut pluribus syndicis quotidie sedeat ad plebis de ministris querelas et secretas
10 accusationes audiendum, et accusatos, si res postulat, asservandos, et concilium convocandum etiam ante constitutum tempus quo congregari solet, si in mora periculum esse eorum aliquis judicaverit. At hic praeses et qui cum ipso quotidie congregantur a supremo concilio eligi, et quidem ex syndicorum numero debent, non quidem ad vitam, sed in
15 sex menses, nec continuari nisi post tres aut quatuor annos: atque his, ut supra diximus, proscripta bona et pecuniarum mulctae vel eorum pars aliqua decernenda est. Reliqua quae syndicos spectant suis in locis dicemus.

29. Secundum concilium quod supremo subordinandum est sena-
20 tum appellavimus; cujus officium sit publica negotia agere, ex. gr. imperii jura promulgare, urbium munimenta secundum jura ordinare, diplomata militiae dare, tributa subditis imponere, eaque collocare, externis legatis respondere, et quo legati mittendi sunt decernere. Sed ipsos legatos eligere supremi concilii officium sit; nam id apprime obser-
25 vandum est ne patricius ad aliquod imperii ministerium vocari possit nisi ab ipso supremo concilio, ne ipsi patricii senatus gratiam aucupari studeant. Deinde illa omnia ad supremum concilium deferenda sunt quae praesentem rerum statum aliqua ratione mutant, uti sunt belli et pacis decreta; quare senatus decreta de bello et pace, ut rata sint, supremi

---

10. *NS de beschuldigden te beschutten.* Hence *G accusatos asservandos. OP accusatores asservandos. G* holds that the Dutch translator mistranslated *asservandos*, which means 'to arrest' as on p. 250, l. 4: *Josua illos asservandos censet.* If the *OP* text is right, *asservare* must mean 'to take into protective custody'; but there seems no need for protective custody if the accusations are secret.

15. *NS zonder in hun ampt verlangt te worden, en het zelfde weêr te konnen bedienen. G,* who refers to p. 322, ll. 4–6, and p. 374, ll. 18–19, suggests that something has fallen out of the *OP* text; but the Dutch is simply an expansion of *continuari,* which on p. 392, l. 8 is translated by *weêr verkozen worden.* So is *continuari iterum* on p. 392, l. 15.

20. *OP appellabimus; NS zullen wy . . . noemen.* But Spinoza has already referred to the senate by name on p. 386, l. 22. I therefore read *appellavimus.* Spinoza's handwriting encourages this sort of corruption: see, for example, how he writes *festinavit* in n. 14 as preserved on p. 117 of the Königsberg copy of the *TT-P.* Cf. also p. 408, l. 22, where *OP* has the true reading *observavimus,* but *NS wy . . . zullen waarneemen.*

that all the patricians have equal authority in the making of decisions, and that business is dealt with quickly, but also that each one of them is absolutely free to cast his vote without any danger of unpopularity: which is the main essential in assemblies.

28. In the council of syndics and the other councils the same system must be followed, i.e. votes must be cast by secret ballot. But the right to summon the council of syndics, and to bring up matters for its decision, should be vested in their own president, who should sit every day with at least ten other syndics to hear the complaints and secret accusations made against ministers by the common people,[1] to take the accused into custody if necessary, and to summon his council even before the time laid down for its regular session if he or any of his colleagues thinks that delay is dangerous. This president, and those who meet with him every day, must be chosen by the supreme council, and, of course, from the syndics, not for life, but for six months; and they must not have their term extended, or be re-appointed except after an interval of three or four years. It is to these, as I said above, that the confiscated goods and money fines, or at least a part of them, must be assigned. The other laws concerning the syndics I shall set out in their place.

29. The second council to be created under the supreme council I have called the senate.[2] Its duty should be to handle public affairs, e.g. to publish state laws, to organize the defence of the cities in accordance with the laws, to give commissions to the armed forces, to impose taxes on the subjects, to expend them, to reply to foreign envoys, and to decide where envoys must be sent. But to appoint the actual envoys should be the function of the supreme council;[3] for the utmost care must be taken to ensure that no patrician can be appointed to an office of state save by the supreme council, lest the patricians themselves try to curry favour with the senate. Moreover all decisions which in any way alter the existing state of affairs, e.g. decisions about war and peace, must be referred to the supreme council; hence the decisions of the senate about war and peace must be confirmed by the authority of the

---

[1] At Venice anyone could denounce a citizen to the *Capi di Dieci* by placing a signed accusation in the mouth of the Lion of St. Mark (W. C. Hazlitt, *The Venetian Republic*, Black, London, 1900, vol. ii, ch. 52, p. 543).

[2] Spinoza's senate resembles both the Council of State of the Netherlands and the Senate of Venice.

[3] But he will not allow his senate the right to appoint ambassadors possessed by the Venetian Senate (Hazlitt, op. cit., ch. 48, pp. 438–9).

concilii auctoritate firmanda sunt: et hac de causa judicarem ad solum supremum concilium, non ad senatum, pertinere nova tributa imponere.

30. Ad senatorum numerum determinandum haec consideranda
5 veniunt: primo ut omnibus patriciis spes aeque magna sit ordinem senatorium recipiendi; deinde ut nihilominus iidem senatores, quorum tempus in quod electi fuerant elapsum est, non magno post intervallo continuari possint, ut sic imperium a viris peritis et expertis semper regatur; et denique ut inter senatores plures reperiantur sapientia et
10 virtute clari. Ad has autem omnes conditiones obtinendas nihil aliud excogitari potest, quam quod lege institutum sit ut nullus nisi qui ad annum aetatis quinquagesimum pervenit in ordinem senatorium recipiatur, et ut quadringenti, hoc est, ut patriciorum una circiter duodecima pars in annum eligatur, quo elapso post biennium iidem
15 continuari iterum possint. Hoc namque modo semper patriciorum una circiter quarta pars brevibus tantummodo interpositis intervallis munus senatorium subibit; qui sane numerus una cum illo quem syndici conficiunt non multum superabitur a numero patriciorum qui annum aetatis quinquagesimum attigerunt. Atque adeo omnibus patriciis
20 magna semper erit spes senatorum aut syndicorum ordinem adipiscendi, et nihilominus iidem patricii, interpositis tantummodo, uti diximus, brevibus intervallis, senatorium ordinem semper tenebunt, et (per illa quae Art. 2 hujus Cap. diximus) nunquam in senatu deerunt viri praestantissimi qui consilio et arte pollent. Et quia haec lex frangi non
25 potest absque magna multorum patriciorum invidia, nulla alia cautione ut valida semper sit opus est quam ut unusquisque patricius, qui eo quo diximus aetatis pervenit, syndicis ejus rei testimonium ostendat, qui ipsius nomen in catalogum eorum qui senatoriis muneribus adipiscendis destinantur reponent, et in supremo concilio legent, ut locum in hoc
30 supremo concilio similibus dicatum, et qui senatorum loco proximus sit, cum reliquis ejusdem ordinis occupet.

31. Senatorum emolumenta talia esse debent ut iis major utilitas

---

15–16. *NS omtrent een vierde deel*, i.e. *una circiter quarta pars*; *OP una circiter duodecima pars*. Sense requires *quarta*; in practice, senatorial rank is to be confined to 1,200 men who serve in groups of 400, each group resuming office after an interval of two years. The reading *duodecima* has been foisted in from the previous sentence.

18. *OP superabitur*; *NS overtroffen zal worden*; *Gf separabitur*.

supreme council if they are to be valid.[1] For the same reason I should say that it is for the supreme council alone, and not for the senate, to impose new taxes.[2]

30. To determine the number of the senators we must consider the following points: first, all the patricians must have an equal hope of attaining senatorial rank; yet, secondly, senators whose term of office has expired must be eligible for re-appointment after a short interval, so that the state may always be directed by men of skill and experience; and finally, many of the senators must be men who are noted for wisdom and ability. Now the only means that can be devised to satisfy all these conditions is to establish by law that only those who have reached their fiftieth year should be admitted to senatorial rank; that four hundred, i.e. about a twelfth of the patricians, should be appointed for a year;[3] and that when their term has elapsed the same men should be eligible for re-appointment after an interval of two years. In this way there will always be roughly a fourth of the patricians serving as senators, with only short intervals between their periods of office; a number which, when added to that made up by the syndics, will certainly not be greatly exceeded by the number of patricians who have reached their fiftieth year. Thus every patrician will always have high hopes of attaining the position of senator or syndic, yet the position of senator will always be held by the same patricians, with only short intervals, as I said, between their periods of service; and (according to what I said in Section 2 of this Chapter) the senate will never lack outstanding men of great wisdom and skill. And since this law cannot be broken without arousing great jealousy in a large number of patricians, the only safeguard required to ensure that it shall always be maintained is that every patrician who has reached the age laid down should give proof of this fact to the syndics, who will enter his name on the roll of those destined to attain senatorial office, and read it out in the supreme council, so that he may acquire the seat in that council which is assigned to such persons, next to the seats of the senators, and take his place with others of the same status.

31. The remuneration of senators must be such that they derive

---

[1] Nor will he give it the Venetian Senate's right to make war and peace (*Mémoires*, vol. i, ch. i, p. 13).

[2] The Venetian Senate could not impose new taxes without the authority of the Grand Council (op. cit., ch. i, p. 14).

[3] Venetian senators were also appointed for a year, but could be re-appointed immediately (op. cit., ch. i, p. 11; Van Hove, *Polityke Weegschaal* ii, iv, 5, p. 331).

ex pace quam ex bello sit; atque adeo ex mercibus quae ex imperio in alias regiones, vel quae ex aliis regionibus in imperium portantur, una centesima aut quinquagesima pars ipsis decernatur. Nam dubitare non possumus quin hac ratione pacem quantum poterunt tuebuntur, et
5 bellum nunquam protrahere studebunt. Nec ab hoc vectigali solvendo ipsi senatores, si eorum aliqui mercatores fuerint, immunes esse debent: nam talis immunitas non sine magna commercii jactura concedi potest, quod neminem ignorare credo. Porro contra statuendum lege est ut senator, vel qui senatoris officio functus est, nullo militiae munere
10 fungi possit; et praeterea ut nullum ducem vel praetorem, quos tempore belli tantummodo exercitui praebendos diximus Art. 9 hujus Capitis, renunciare liceat ex iis quorum pater vel avus senator est, vel senatoriam dignitatem intra biennium habuit. Nec dubitare possumus quin patricii qui extra senatum sunt haec jura summa vi
15 defendant; atque adeo fiet ut senatoribus majus semper emolumentum ex pace quam ex bello sit; qui propterea bellum nunquam nisi summa imperii necessitate cogente suadebunt. At objici nobis potest quod hac ratione, si scilicet syndicis et senatoribus adeo magna emolumenta decernenda sunt, imperium aristocraticum non
20 minus onerosum subditis erit quam quodcunque monarchicum. Sed praeterquam quod regiae aulae majores sumptus requirunt, qui tamen ad pacem tutandam non praebentur, et quod pax nunquam nimis caro pretio emi possit, accedit primo quod id omne quod in monarchico imperio in unum aut paucos, in hoc in plurimos confertur. Deinde
25 reges eorumque ministri onera imperii cum subditis non ferunt, quod in hoc contra accidit; nam patricii, qui semper ex ditioribus eliguntur, maximam partem reipublicae conferunt. Denique imperii monarchici onera non tam ex regiis sumptibus quam ex ejusdem arcanis oriuntur. Onera enim imperii quae pacis et libertatis tutandae causa civibus
30 imponuntur, quamvis magna sint, sustinentur tamen et pacis utilitate feruntur. Quae gens unquam tot tamque gravia vectigalia pendere debuit ut Hollandica? Atqui haec non tantum non exhausta, quin contra opibus adeo potens fuit ut ejus fortunam omnes inviderent. Si itaque imperii monarchici onera pacis causa imponerentur, cives non

---

11. *NS over 't heir gestelt moeten worden*, which suggests *exercitui praeficiendos*.

21. *Gf qui*; *OP quae*; *NS de welken echter zich niet genegen tonen om de vrede te verdedigen*. Evidently the translator could only make sense of *quae* by mistranslating the rest of the clause. *qui* is supported by *Si itaque imperii monarchici onera pacis causa imponerentur* in ll. 33–34.

27. *NS maken het grootste deel van de gemene Staat*, which suggests *conficiunt*. But we have already been told on p. 384, l. 28 that *major hujus imperii pars plebs est*.

32. *NS en echter*, i.e. *Atqui*; *OP Atque*. See the note on p. 358, l. 4.

greater advantage from peace than from war;[1] so they should be assigned the proceeds of a duty of one or two per cent. on imports and exports. For we cannot doubt that they will then do their utmost to maintain peace, and will never seek to prolong a war. Nor should senators themselves, supposing that some of them are traders, be exempt from the payment of this duty; for such exemption—as, I think, is universally known—cannot be granted without great damage to commerce. On the other hand it must be laid down by law that no senator or ex-senator can perform any military duty; and, furthermore, that no one whose father or grandfather is a senator, or has held the position of senator within the previous two years, may be appointed commander-in-chief or field-commander, officers who, as I said in Section 9 of this Chapter, must be provided for the army only in time of war. We cannot doubt that the patricians who are not members of the senate will defend these regulations with all their power; so the senators will always have more to gain from peace than from war, and thus will never advise war unless the vital interests of the state force them to do so. It may however be objected that this measure of mine, by assigning such large rewards to the syndics and senators, will make aristocracy as burdensome to the subjects as any monarchy. But besides the fact that the cost of a royal court is greater, though no contribution to the preservation of peace, and that peace can never be bought too dearly, I have these further points in my favour. First, everything that falls in a monarchy to one man or a few is here shared by a great many. Next, kings and their ministers do not bear the burdens of the state along with their subjects, but in this case the opposite happens; for the patricians, who are always chosen from the wealthier classes, bear most of the burdens of the state. Finally, the burdensome nature of monarchy is due less to royal expenditure than to the secret aims of its government. For when state burdens are imposed on citizens to preserve peace and freedom, their weight does not matter; they are borne, and the benefits of peace make it possible to support them. What nation ever had to pay so many heavy taxes as the Dutch?[2] Yet these, so far from being exhausted, became so wealthy that their prosperity was the envy of all. Thus if the burdens of monarchy were imposed for the sake of peace they would not crush the citizens; as I have said,

---

[1] In order that members of the Netherlands Council of State should not make a profit from war they were forbidden on oath to engage in the provision of military stores (Janiçon, *État présent*, ch. iii, pp. 190–1).

[2] Temple, *Observations*, ch. iv, p. 102.

premerent; sed, uti dixi, ex hujusmodi imperii arcanis fit ut subditi oneri succumbant; nempe quia regum virtus magis in bello quam in pace valet, et quod iiʹqui soli regnare volunt summopere conari debent ut subditos inopes habeant; ut jam alia taceam quae prudentissimus Belga 5 V. H. olim notavit, quia ad meum institutum, quod solummodo est imperii cujuscunque optimum statum describere, non spectant.

32. In senatu aliqui ex syndicis, a supremo concilio electi, sedere debent, sed sine suffragii jure; nempe ut observent num jura quae illud concilium spectant recte serventur, et ut supremum concilium convo-10 cari curent quando ex senatu ad ipsum supremum concilium aliquid deferendum est. Nam jus supremum hoc concilium convocandi resque in eo decernendas proponendi penes syndicos, ut jam diximus, est. Sed antequam de similibus suffragia colligantur, qui senatui tum praesidet rerum statum, et quaenam de re proposita ipsius senatus sit sententia, 15 et quibus de causis, docebit; quo facto suffragia solito ordine colligenda erunt.

33. Integer senatus non quotidie, sed, ut omnia magna concilia, statuto quodam tempore congregari debet. Sed quia interim imperii negotia exercenda sunt, opus est ergo ut senatorum aliqua pars eligatur 20 quae dimisso senatu ejus vicem suppleat; cujus officium sit ipsum sena-tum quando eo opus est convocare, ejusque decreta de republica exsequi, epistolas senatui supremoque concilio scriptas legere, et denique de rebus in senatu proponendis consulere. Sed ut haec omnia, et universi hujus concilii ordo facilius concipiatur, rem totam accuratius describam. 25 34. Senatores in annum, ut jam diximus, eligendi, in quatuor aut sex ordines dividendi suɲt; quorum primus primis tribus vel duobus

---

7. *OP electis; NS Enigen uit de Wetverdedigers, door d' opperste Raat verkozen*, which suggests *electi*. Of course all the syndics are elected by the supreme council (p. 380, ll. 26–27); but we are here concerned with their representatives on the senate.

14–15. *NS zal . . . de staat der zaken vertonen, en met enen aanwijzen wat het gevoelen . . . is.* It is just possible that *indicabit* or some such word has fallen out of the *OP* text after *statum*.

it is the secret aims of such governments which cause the subjects to fall beneath their load. For the prowess of kings has greater scope in war than in peace,[1] and those who wish to be sole rulers must do their utmost to keep their subjects poor.[2] I omit here the other points noted some time ago by that shrewd Dutchman V. H.,[3] because they are irrelevant to my purpose, which is merely to describe the best condition of each kind of state.

32. Some of the syndics must be appointed by the supreme council to sit on the senate, but without having the right to vote;[4] to see whether the laws relating to the senate are duly observed, and to provide for the summoning of the supreme council when something has to be referred to it from the senate. For, as I have already said, the right to summon the supreme council and to submit matters for its decision is vested in the syndics. But before the supreme council votes on such matters, the current president of the senate will explain the position of affairs, announce the decision of the senate on the matter in question, and give the reasons for it; whereupon the vote should be taken in the usual way.

33. The whole senate should not meet every day, but, like all large councils, at certain appointed times.[5] However, since the administration of the state must be carried on in the intervals, it is necessary to appoint a certain number of senators to act on behalf of the senate when it is not in session; and their duties should be to summon the full senate when need arises, to execute its decisions about state affairs, to read the letters addressed to the senate and supreme council, and, finally, to discuss what business is to be brought up in the senate.[6] But that all this, and the organization of the council as a whole, may be easier to grasp, I shall describe the whole thing more precisely.

34. The senators, who must be appointed for a year, as I have already said, should be divided up into four or six sections;[7] the first of which should preside over the senate for the first few months, three or

---

[1] *TP* vii, 5, p. 339; *TT-P* xviii, p. 197.

[2] Spinoza would agree with Hobbes (*De Cive* x, 2) that such conduct was not in the ruler's interest; but rulers sometimes fail to see where their own interest lies.

[3] Van Hove, *Polityke Weegschaal* I, i, 10–34, pp. 39–136.

[4] At Venice the *Dieci* and *Avogadori* were members of the Senate ex officio (*Mémoires*, vol. i, ch. i, p. 8).

[5] The Venetian Senate met twice weekly (op. cit., ch. i, pp. 10–11), but was smaller than Spinoza's.

[6] The *Collegio* performed similar functions for the Venetian Senate (op. cit., ch. ii, pp. 49–54).

[7] These 'sections' owe something to the *prytaneis* of the ancient Athenian *boule*.

mensibus in senatu praesideat. Quibus elapsis secundus ordo locum primi occupet; et sic porro servatis vicibus unusquisque ordo eodem temporis intervallo primum locum in senatu teneat, ita ut qui primis mensibus primus, is secundis ultimus sit. Praeterea quot ordines, totidem

5 praesides, totidemque eorundem vicarii, qui ipsorum vicem quando opus est suppleant, eligendi sunt, hoc est, ex quocunque ordine duo eligendi sunt, quorum alter praeses, alter vicarius ejusdem ordinis sit; et qui primi ordinis praeses est, primis etiam mensibus senatui praesideat, vel, si absit, ejus vicarius ipsius vicem gerat; et sic porro reliqui, servato ut

10 supra ordine. Deinde ex primo ordine aliqui sorte vel suffragio eligendi sunt, qui cum praeside et vicario ejusdem ordinis senatus vicem, postquam dimissus est, suppleant, idque eodem temporis intervallo quo idem eorum ordo primum locum in senatu tenet: quippe eo elapso ex secundo ordine totidem iterum sorte vel suffragio eligendi

15 sunt, qui cum suo praeside et vicario primi ordinis locum occupent, vicemque senatus suppleant; et sic porro reliqui. Nec opus est ut horum electio, quos scilicet sorte vel suffragio singulis tribus vel duobus mensibus eligendos dixi, et quos imposterum consules appellabimus, a supremo concilio fiat. Nam ratio quam in Art. 29 hujus Cap. dedimus locum hic

20 non habet, et multo minus illa Art. 17. Sufficiet igitur si a senatu et syndicis qui praesentes sunt eligantur.

35. Horum autem numerum determinare non ita accurate possum. Attamen hoc certum est, plures esse debere quam ut facile corrumpi possint. Nam tametsi de republica nihil soli decernant, possunt tamen

25 senatum protrahere, vel, quod pessimum esset, ipsum deludere proponendo illa quae nullius, et illa reticendo quae majoris momenti essent: ut jam taceam quod si nimis pauci essent sola unius aut alterius absentia moram publicis negotiis adferre posset. Sed quoniam contra hi consules ideo creantur quia magna concilia publicis negotiis quotidie

30 vacare nequeunt, medium necessario hic quaerendum est, et defectus numeri temporis brevitate supplendus. Atque adeo, si modo triginta aut circiter in duos aut tres menses eligantur, plures erunt quam ut hoc brevi tempore corrumpi possint; et hac de causa etiam monui ut ii qui

1. M *praesideat*; OP *sedeat*; NS *zal zitten.*
1-2. NS *d' eerste plaats*, i.e. *locum primum.*
21. NS *die tegenwoordig zijn*; OP *qui praesentes adsunt.*
33. NS *Om deze oorzaak zal het ook dienstig zijn*, i.e. *etiam utile erit.*

two as the case may be. When this period has elapsed the second section should succeed the first; and so they should continue, each section holding the presidency of the senate in its turn for the same space of time, so that the one which holds the first place in the first period comes last in the second period. Next, for each section there must be elected a president and a vice-president to take his place when necessary, i.e. two men must be appointed from each section, one to be its president, the other its vice-president; and the president of the first section, or, failing him, his deputy, should also preside over the senate in the first period of months; being followed by the other presidents and vice-presidents, each presiding in turn as described above. Next, some senators from the first section must be appointed by lot or vote to deputize for the senate when it has adjourned, serving with the president and vice-president of their section for as long as it holds the presidency of the senate: for when its term has expired, the same number of men must again be appointed by lot or vote from the second section, so that with their president and vice-president they may succeed the first section in deputizing for the senate; and similarly with the rest. But there is no need for these men, who are, as I have said, to be appointed by lot or vote for single periods of two or three months, and whom I shall henceforth call consuls, to be appointed by the supreme council. For the reason for the latter proceeding given in Section 29 of this Chapter is here inapplicable, and that given in Section 17 is still more so. It will therefore suffice if they are appointed by the senate and the syndics who attend its meetings.

35. About their number I cannot be so precise; but they must certainly be too numerous to be corrupted easily. For although they make no decisions about state affairs on their own sole authority, they can nevertheless put off meetings of the senate, or, worst of all, mislead it by bringing up trifles for discussion and keeping back matters of greater importance: not to mention that if there were too few of them the mere absence of one or two could hold up the conduct of public business. Yet since these consuls are appointed just because large councils cannot give daily attention to public business, it is necessary to seek a compromise here, and to compensate for lack of numbers by a short term of office. Thus if thirty or so are appointed for two or three months,[1] they will be too numerous to be corrupted in that short space of time. This is why I also recommended that their successors should never be

---

[1] The *Collegio* of Venice consisted of twenty-six members, but some of these held office for a year, and the Doge was president for life (*Mémoires*, vol. i, ch. ii, p. 49).

in eorum locum succedunt, nullo modo eligendi sint nisi eo tempore quo ipsi succedunt et alii discedunt.

36. Horum praeterea officium esse diximus senatum quando eorum aliqui, licet pauci sint, opus esse judicaverint convocare, resque in 5 eodem decernendas proponere, senatum dimittere, ejusque de negotiis publicis decreta exequi. Quo autem id fieri ordine debeat ne res inutilibus quaestionibus diu protrahantur, paucis jam dicam. Nempe consules de re in senatu proponenda, et quid factu opus sit consulant, et si de eo omnibus una fuerit mens, tum convocato senatu et quaestione 10 ordine exposita quaenam eorum sit sententia doceant, nec alterius sententia exspectata suffragia ordine colligant. Sed si consules plures quam unam sententiam foverint, tum in senatu illa de quaestione proposita sententia prior dicenda erit quae a majori consulum numero defendebatur; et si eadem a majori senatus et consulum parte non fuerit pro- 15 bata, sed quod numerus dubitantium et negantium simul major fuerit —quod ex calculis, ut jam monuimus, constare debet—tum alteram sententiam, quae pauciora quam prior habuerit inter consules suffragia, doceant; et sic porro reliquas. Quod si nulla a majori totius senatus parte probata fuerit, senatus in sequentem diem aut in tempus breve 20 dimittendus, ut consules interim videant num alia media quae magis possint placere queant invenire. Quod si nulla alia invenerint, vel si quae invenerint senatus major pars non probaverit, tum senatoris cujusque sententia audienda est. In quam si etiam major senatus pars non iverit, tum de unaquaque sententia iterum suffragia ferenda; et 25 non tantum affirmantium, ut huc usque factum, sed dubitantium etiam et negantium calculi numerandi sunt. Et si plures reperientur affirmantes quam dubitantes aut negantes, ut tum sententia rata maneat; et contra irrita, si plures invenientur negantes quam dubitantes aut affirmantes. Sed si de omnibus sententiis major dubitantium quam 30 negantium aut affirmantium fuerit numerus, ut tum syndicorum concilium senatui adjungatur, qui simul cum senatoribus suffragia ferant, calculis solummodo affirmantibus aut negantibus, omissis iis qui animum ambiguum indicant. Circa res quae ad supremum concilium a senatu deferuntur idem ordo tenendus est. Haec de senatu.

appointed until they are due to take over the duties which the others lay down.

36. Their duties, as I said, are to summon the senate whenever any of them, however few, think this to be necessary; to bring up matters for its decision; to adjourn it; and to carry out its decisions about public affairs. How all this must be done if business is not to be held up by useless discussion I shall now briefly describe. The consuls should deliberate on the matter to be brought up in the senate, and consider what course should be taken. They should then summon the senate, duly explain the matter to be decided, and, if unanimous, announce their own view, putting it to the vote in the regular way without waiting to hear any other. But if they are divided in opinion, the view held by the majority of them must be put to the senate first; and if this is not ratified by a majority of the senate and consuls, the total of indecisive and negative votes—discovered by secret ballot, as I have already advised—outnumbering the affirmative, they should then put forward the second view, which got less votes among them than the first; and, if necessary, proceed to the others in the same way. But if none of these views is ratified by a majority of the whole senate, it must be adjourned until the following day, or for a short period, to give the consuls time to see if they can discover other measures more acceptable. If they can find no others, or if those which they do find are not ratified by a majority of the senate, suggestions should be invited from any senator.[1] But if these too fail to win a majority, a second vote must be taken on each view; and the indecisive and negative votes counted separately, not only the affirmative, as hitherto. If there are more affirmative than either indecisive or negative votes the opinion should be taken as carried; while if there are more negative than either indecisive or affirmative votes it should be regarded as null and void. But if in every case there are more indecisive than either negative or affirmative votes, the council of syndics should meet in joint session with the senate, and vote with the senators in a straight ballot for or against, the counters which indicate indecision being discarded. In referring matters from the senate to the supreme council the same procedure must be followed. So much for the senate.

---

[1] So far the procedure is similar to that of the Venetian Senate as described by Van Hove (op. cit. II, iv, 5, pp. 329–30). But in Venice the various proposals were voted upon simultaneously, and when none of them received more than half the votes the one which had fewest was eliminated, and another vote taken on the remainder. If a continuation of this process did not produce an absolute majority in favour of any proposal, the *Collegio* had to deliberate afresh, and any senator was allowed to submit a new proposal.

37. Ad forum quod attinet sive tribunal, non potest iisdem fundamentis niti quibus illud quod sub monarcha est, ut illud in Cap. 6 Art. 26 et seq. descripsimus. Nam (per Art. 14 hujus Cap.) cum fundamentis hujus imperii non convenit ut ulla ratio stirpium sive 5 familiarum habeatur. Deinde quia judices ex solis patriciis electi metu quidem succedentium patriciorum contineri possent ne in eorum aliquem iniquam aliquam sententiam pronuncient, et forte ut neque eos secundum merita punire sustineant; sed contra in plebeios omnia auderent, et locupletes quotidie in praedam raperent. Scio hac de causa 10 Genuensium consilium a multis probari, quod scilicet non ex patriciis sed ex peregrinis judices eligant; sed hoc mihi rem abstracte consideranti absurde institutum videtur, ut peregrini et non patricii ad leges interpretandas vocentur. Nam quid aliud judices sunt nisi legum interpretes? Quare mihi persuadeo Genuenses in hoc etiam negotio magis 15 suae gentis ingenium quam ipsam hujus imperii naturam respexisse. Nobis igitur rem abstracte considerantibus media excogitanda sunt quae cum hujus regiminis forma optime conveniunt.

38. Sed ad judicum numerum quod attinet, nullum singularem hujus status ratio exigit; sed ut in imperio monarchico ita etiam in hoc 20 apprime observari debet ut plures sint quam ut a viro privato corrumpi possint. Nam eorum officium solummodo est providere ne quisquam privatus alteri injuriam faciat, atque adeo quaestiones inter privatos tam patricios quam plebeios dirimere, et poenas delinquentibus, etiam ex patriciis, syndicis, et senatoribus, quatenus contra jura quibus omnes 25 tenentur deliquerunt, sumere. Caeterum quaestiones quae inter urbes quae sub imperio sunt moveri possunt in supremo concilio dirimendae sunt.

39. Temporis praeterea in quod eligendi sunt ratio est eadem in quocunque imperio, et etiam ut quotannis aliqua eorum pars cedat; 30 et denique, quamvis non opus sit ut unusquisque ex diversa sit familia, necesse tamen est ne duo sanguine propinqui simul in subselliis locum occupent. Quod in reliquis conciliis observandum est, praeterquam in supremo, in quo sufficit si modo in electionibus lege cautum sit ne cuiquam propinquum nominare, nec de eo si ab alio nominatus sit suf- 35 fragium ferre liceat, et praeterea ne ad imperii ministrum quemcunque

---

5. *OP Deinde quia judices; NS Wijders, de Rechters,* which may point to *Deinde, judices.*
15. *NS dan het volk op de natuur van deze Heerschappy,* wrongly referring *ipsam* to *gentis.*

37. As for the court of justice, it cannot rest on the same basis as the one in a monarchy (described in Chapter 6, Sections 26 and ff.). For to take any account of tribes or families is contrary to the fundamental laws of this kind of state (by Section 14 of this Chapter). Moreover, if the judges were appointed exclusively from patrician families they would doubtless be restrained by fear of their patrician successors from pronouncing an unjust verdict against a member of their own class, and perhaps even from punishing him as he deserved, but they might persecute the commons with unbounded audacity and continually prey upon rich plebeians. This, I know, is the reason why the Genoese policy of appointing judges from the resident aliens and not from the patricians is widely approved;[1] but considered in the abstract it seems to me an absurd arrangement for resident aliens and not patricians to be called upon to interpret the laws. For what *are* judges but interpreters of the laws? Thus I think that here again the Genoese have been guided by the bent of their race rather than by the actual nature of this kind of state. We must therefore consider the matter in the abstract if we are to discover the measures best suited to this form of government.

38. The size of the court, however, cannot be determined in this way, since the principles of this state do not require any particular number of judges; the main thing, as in monarchy, is to make sure that they are too numerous to be corrupted by a private individual. For their duty is simply to see that no private individual does wrong to another, so they have only to settle disputes between private individuals, patricians as well as plebeians, and to punish offenders, including patricians, syndics, and senators, if they transgress the laws which are binding on all. The disputes which may arise between subject cities must be settled in the supreme council.

39. Furthermore, the length of their appointment is based on a principle which is the same in every state, and so is the regulation that a certain proportion of them should retire every year. Finally, although there is no need for each judge to come from a different tribe, it *is* necessary that no two kinsmen should sit on the bench at the same time. The only assembly in which this rule should not be observed is the supreme council, where it is enough if there is a law to prevent anyone from nominating a kinsman at elections, or from voting on him if he is nominated by another, and also to debar two kinsmen from drawing

[1] Van Hove, op. cit. II, v, 8, pp. 363-4.

nominandum duo propinqui sortem ex urna tollant. Hoc, inquam, sufficit in concilio quod ex tam magno hominum numero componitur, et cui nulla singularia emolumenta decernuntur. Atque adeo imperio inde nihil erit detrimenti, ut absurdum sit legem ferre qua omnium
5 patriciorum propinqui a supremo concilio secludantur, ut Art. 14 hujus Cap. diximus. Quod autem id absurdum sit, patet. Nam jus illud ab ipsis patriciis institui non posset quin eo ipso omnes absolute suo jure eatenus cederent, ac proinde ejusdem juris vindices non ipsi patricii sed plebs esset; quod iis directe repugnat quae in Art. 5 et 6 hujus
10 Cap. ostendimus. Lex autem illa imperii, qua statuitur ut una eademque ratio inter numerum patriciorum et multitudinis servetur, id maxime respicit ut patriciorum jus et potentia conservetur, ne scilicet pauciores sint quam ut multitudinem possint regere.

40. Caeterum judices a supremo concilio ex ipsis patriciis, hoc est
15 (per Art. 17 hujus Cap.) ex ipsis legum conditoribus eligendi sunt, et sententiae quas tulerunt tam de rebus civilibus quam criminalibus ratae erunt si servato ordine et absque partium studio prolatae fuerint; de qua re syndicis lege permissum erit cognoscere, judicare, et statuere.

41. Judicum emolumenta eadem esse debent quae Art. 29 Cap. 6
20 diximus; nempe ut ex unaquaque sententia quam de rebus civilibus tulerint, ab eo qui causa cecidit pro ratione totius summae partem aliquotam accipiant. At circa sententias de rebus criminalibus haec sola hic differentia sit, ut bona ab ipsis proscripta, et quaecunque summa qua minora crimina mulctantur, ipsis solis designetur; ea tamen conditione,
25 ut nunquam iis liceat quenquam tormentis cogere quippiam confiteri. Et hoc modo satis cautum erit ne iniqui in plebeios sint, et ne metus causa nimium patriciis faveant. Nam praeterquam quod hic metus sola avaritia, eaque specioso justitiae nomine adumbrata, temperetur, accedit quod plures sint numero, et quod suffragia non palam sed cal-
30 culis ferantur; ita ut si quis ob damnatam suam causam stomachetur, nihil tamen habeat quod uni imputare possit. Porro ne iniquam, aut

lots from the urn for the duty of nominating any minister of state.[1]
No more, I say, is needed in a council which is composed of such a
large number of men, and whose members are assigned no remuneration as such. Thus the state will suffer no harm from this arrangement,
and so it is absurd, as I said in Section 14 of this Chapter, to pass a law
excluding all kinsmen of patricians from the supreme council. In any
case it is obvious that this would be absurd. For since the patricians
could not establish such a law themselves without completely surrender-
ing so much of their own right in the process, the upholders of the said
law would not be the patricians but the commons; which directly contradicts my conclusions in Sections 5 and 6 of this Chapter. This is not
true of the law providing that one and the same ratio shall always be
maintained between the patricians and the commons, for the main
object of that is to preserve the right and power of the patricians by
ensuring that they are not too few to be able to govern the commons.

40. But the nature of aristocracy does require that the judges should
be chosen by the supreme council from the patricians, i.e. (by Section
17 of this Chapter) from the actual law-makers. The verdicts of these
judges will be binding in both civil and criminal cases if given without
partiality and with due regard to procedure. To hear evidence, decide,
and pronounce judgement upon the last point will be legally the prerogative of the syndics.[2]

41. The remuneration of the judges should be the same as is laid
down in Section 29, Chapter 6; that is, as a fee for every verdict given
in civil suits they should receive from the man who has lost his case a
certain proportion of the whole sum involved. As for verdicts given in
criminal cases, the only difference here should be this, that goods which
they have confiscated, and all fines exacted for minor offences, should
be assigned to them alone; but on the same condition as in monarchy,
that they are never allowed to use torture to make anyone confess anything. These measures will be sufficient to prevent them from being
unjust to the commons and from being led by fear to show too much
favour to the patricians. For avarice alone, especially when camouflaged
by the fair name of justice, is sufficient to check this fear; in addition,
they are numerous, and do not vote openly but by secret ballot, so that
if anyone takes offence at the loss of his case, he has no reason to blame
any particular judge. Besides, their respect for the syndics will ensure

---

[1] Similar regulations were enforced at elections in the Grand Council of Venice (Van
Hove, op. cit. II, iv, 2, pp. 319–20).

[2] Judges in Venice were appointed by the Grand Council (*Mémoires*, vol. i, ch. iii, p. 56),
and their verdicts were subject to review by the *Avogadori* (loc. cit., p. 64).

saltem ne absurdam aliquam sententiam pronuncient, et ne eorum quispiam dolo quicquam faciat, syndicorum reverentia prohibebit; praeterquam quod in tam magno judicum numero unus semper aut alter reperietur quem iniqui formident. Ad plebeios denique quod attinet, 5 satis iis etiam cavebitur si ad syndicos iisdem appellare liceat, quibus, uti dixi, jure permissum sit de judicum rebus cognoscere, judicare, et statuere. Nam certum est quod syndici multorum patriciorum odium vitare non poterunt, et plebi contra gratissimi semper erunt, cujus applausum quantum ipsi etiam poterunt captare studebunt. Quem in 10 finem data occasione non omittent sententias contra leges fori prolatas revocare, et quemcunque judicem examinare, et poenas ex iniquis sumere; nihil enim hoc magis multitudinis animos movet. Nec obstat quod similia exempla raro contingere possint; sed contra maxime prodest. Nam praeterquam quod illa civitas prave constituta sit ubi quo-
15 tidie exempla in delinquentes eduntur (ut Cap. 5 Art. 2 ostendimus), illa profecto rarissima esse debent fama quae maxime celebrantur.

42. Qui in urbes vel provincias proconsules mittuntur ex ordine senatorio eligendi essent, quia senatorum officium est de urbium munimentis, aerario, militia, etc. curam habere. Sed qui in regiones aliquan-
20 tulum remotas mitterentur senatum frequentare non possent, et hac de causa ii tantummodo ex ipso senatu vocandi sunt qui urbibus in patrio solo conditis destinantur; at quos ad magis remota loca mittere volunt ex iis eligendi sunt quorum aetas a senatorio gradu non abest. Sed neque hac ratione paci totius imperii satis cautum fore existimo, si 25 nimirum urbes circumvicinae jure suffragii omnino prohibeantur, nisi adeo impotentes omnes sint ut palam contemni possint; quod sane concipi nequit. Atque adeo necesse est ut urbes circumvicinae jure civitatis donentur, et ex unaquaque viginti, triginta, aut quadraginta (nam numerus pro magnitudine urbis major aut minor esse debet) cives 30 electi in numerum patriciorum adscribantur; ex quibus tres, quatuor, aut quinque quotannis eligi debent qui ex senatu sint, et unus ad vitam syndicus. Atque hi qui ex senatu sunt proconsules in urbem ex qua electi sunt mittantur una cum syndico.

43. Caeterum judices in unaquaque urbe constituendi ex patriciis

4. *NS die de gerechtigheit bemint, en voor de welk zy ontsach zullen hebben*; literally, *qui justitiam amet et quem formident.*

17–18. *NS zullen uit de Staat der Staatsraden* (glossed *Senatores*) *moeten wezen.*

23. *OP non abest*; *NS niet . . . verschilt*; *M non multum abest.*

that they do not pronounce any unjust, or at any rate any ridiculous verdicts, and that none of them does anything underhand; not to mention that out of such a large number of judges there will always be found one or two men to inspire the unjust with fear. Finally, the common people too will be sufficiently protected if they are allowed to appeal to the syndics,[1] who, as I have said, should be permitted by law to hear evidence, decide, and pronounce judgement on the proceedings of the judges. For there is no doubt that while the syndics will be unable to avoid the hatred of many patricians, they will always be very popular with the common people, and will do everything they possibly can to win its applause. Thus they will not fail, when occasion offers, to nullify verdicts which violate the rules of the court, to inquire into the conduct of judges, and to punish those who are unjust; for nothing impresses the people more. That such examples can seldom be made is no drawback, but a great advantage. For if examples are to be widely reported and acclaimed they must of course be very rare; and in any case a commonwealth where examples are continually being made of offenders is badly organized (as I said in Chapter 5, Section 2).

42. It would appear that governors of cities or districts should be drawn from the ranks of the senators, since the senate has to supervise the defence of the cities, the treasury, the armed forces, and so on. But in that case governors of territories some distance away would be unable to attend the senate regularly. Hence only those appointed to cities in the fatherland should be drawn from the senate itself; those whom they wish to send to places more remote should be drawn from men of senatorial age. Yet even this measure, I think, will be insufficient to safeguard the peace of the whole state if the adjacent cities are entirely excluded from the right to vote; unless they are all so weak that they can be openly disregarded, which is quite inconceivable. Hence it is necessary that the adjacent cities should be granted political rights, twenty, thirty, or forty men from each—for the number must vary with the size of the city—being made citizens and added to the roll of patricians. Of these, three, four, or five must be appointed every year to serve on the senate, and one made a syndic for life. And those who are senators should be sent with the syndic as governors of the city from which they have been chosen.

43. The judges to be appointed in each city should also be chosen

---

[1] In their role of defenders of the commons Spinoza's syndics resemble the *tribuni plebis* of ancient Rome; but their powers are greater (*TP* x, 3, p. 433).

ejusdem urbis eligendi sunt. Sed de his non necesse judico prolixius agere, quia ad singularis hujus imperii fundamenta non pertinent.

44. Qui in quocunque concilio a secretis sunt, et alii ejusmodi ministri, quia suffragii jus non habent, eligendi sunt ex plebe. Sed quia
5 hi diuturna negotiorum tractatione maximam rerum agendarum notitiam habent, fit saepe ut eorum consilio plus quam par est deferatur, et ut status totius imperii ab eorum directione maxime pendeat; quae res Hollandis exitio fuit. Nam id sine magna multorum optimorum invidia fieri nequit. Et sane dubitare non possumus quin senatus cujus
10 prudentia non a senatorum sed ab administrorum consilio derivatur maxime ab inertibus frequentetur; et hujus imperii conditio non multo melior erit quam imperii monarchici quod pauci regis consiliarii regunt, de quo vide Cap. 6 Art. 5, 6, et 7. Verumenimvero imperium prout recte vel prave institutum fuerit, eo minus aut magis erit huic malo
15 obnoxium. Nam imperii libertas quae non satis firma· habet fundamenta nunquam sine periculo defenditur; quod patricii ne subeant, ministros gloriae cupidos ex plebe eligunt, qui postea vertentibus rebus veluti hostiae caeduntur ad placandam eorum iram qui libertati insidiantur. At ubi libertatis fundamenta satis firma sunt, ibi patricii ipsi
20 ejusdem tutandae gloriam sibi expetunt, studentque ut rerum agendarum prudentia ab eorum tantummodo consilio derivetur. Quae duo in jaciendis hujus imperii fundamentis apprime observavimus, nempe ut plebs tam a consiliis quam a suffragiis ferendis arceretur (vid. Art. 3 et 4 hujus Cap.), atque adeo ut suprema imperii potestas penes omnes
25 patricios, auctoritas autem penes syndicos et senatum, et jus denique senatum convocandi, resque ad communem salutem pertinentes proponendi, disserendi, et tractandi, penes consules ex ipso senatu electos esset. Quod si praeterea statuatur ut qui a secretis in senatu vel in aliis

26–28. *NS en van de zaken*, . . . *behorende, daar in voor te stellen, en daar af te spreken en te handelen by de Hoofden van de Staatsraat . . . zou wezen*; *Gf resque . . . pertinentes proponendi penes consules . . . esset*; *OP resque . . . pertinentes penes consules . . . esset*.

408

from the local patricians. But since these arrangements are not peculiar to this particular state it seems unnecessary to discuss them more fully.

44. Since they do not possess the right to vote, secretaries and similar officials in the various councils should be chosen from the common people. But because long experience in transacting business gives such men a very thorough knowledge of affairs, it often happens that undue weight is attached to their advice, and that the condition of the entire state largely depends on their guidance;[1] a situation which was the ruin of Holland.[2] For this is bound to arouse a great deal of jealousy in many of the nobles. And in truth we cannot doubt that if a senate derives its wisdom from the advice of its officials there is little energy among its members; in which case the condition of the state will be little better than that of a monarchy ruled by a few counsellors of the king; for which see Chapter 6, Sections 5, 6, and 7. But it is really the goodness or badness of a state's constitution which determines the degree to which it will be subject to this malady. For when public liberty is based on insecure foundations it is never defended without risk; and to avoid running this risk the patricians choose as officials ambitious commoners, who, when revolution eventually comes, are slaughtered like sacrificial animals to appease the anger of the enemies of freedom.[3] But where the foundations of freedom are sufficiently secure, the patricians claim for themselves the glory of preserving it, and try to see that wisdom in the conduct of affairs is due to their advice alone. Now the two main rules which I have followed in laying the foundations of this state are these: that the common people should be debarred both from giving advice and from voting (see Sections 3 and 4 of this Chapter); and hence that sovereignty should be held by the whole body of patricians, authority by the syndics and senators, and, finally, the right to summon the senate, and to bring up, explain, and handle matters concerning the general welfare, by consuls chosen from the senate itself. If we now add that the secretary of the senate or of any other council

---

[1] As the sequel shows, Spinoza is thinking primarily of Oldenbarneveldt and De Witt. It is strange to find such men classed as commoners; yet they did not belong to the old nobility (Motley, *The United Netherlands*, vol. ii, ch. xii, p. 119), and although certainly members of the bourgeois aristocracy, were also, in theory at least, its servants. Both started their political careers as town pensionaries, who, like our town clerks, were legal advisers to their town councils, but had no right to vote at their meetings; and even when they attained the position of pensionary of Holland they were still in theory merely the servants of the province, and inferior in status to the deputies (Temple, *Observations*, ch. ii, p. 64).

[2] In 1672.

[3] Oldenbarneveldt was executed by the stadtholder Maurice in 1619, De Witt was murdered at the Hague in 1672 by supporters of the Orangist cause.

conciliis est, in quatuor aut quinque ad summum annos eligatur, atque
ei secundus, qui a secretis in idem tempus designatus sit, adjungatur,
qui interim laboris partem ferat, vel si in senatu non unus sed plures
a secretis sint, quorum alius his, alius aliis negotiis detinetur, nunquam
5 fiet ut administrorum potentia alicujus sit momenti.

45. Aerarii tribuni ex plebe etiam eligendi sunt, qui ejus rationem
non tantum senatui sed etiam syndicis reddere teneantur.

46. Ad religionem quae spectant satis prolixe ostendimus in Tract.
Theologico-Politico. Quaedam tamen tum omisimus de quibus ibi non
10 erat agendi locus; nempe quod omnes patricii ejusdem religionis, simplicissimae scilicet et maxime catholicae, qualem in eodem tractatu
descripsimus, esse debeant. Nam apprime cavendum est ne ipsi patricii
in sectas dividantur, et ne alii his, alii aliis plus faveant, et deinde ne
superstitione capti libertatem subditis dicendi ea quae sentiunt adi-
15 mere studeant. Deinde quamvis unicuique libertas dicendi ea quae
sentit danda est, magni tamen conventus prohibendi sunt: atque adeo
iis qui alii religioni addicti sunt concedendum quidem est tot quot
velint templa aedificare, sed parva, et certae cujusdam mensurae, et
in locis aliquantulum ab invicem dissitis. At templa quae patriae reli-
20 gioni dicantur multum refert ut magna et sumptuosa sint, et ut prae-
cipuo ipsius cultui solis patriciis vel senatoribus manus admovere liceat;
atque adeo ut solis patriciis liceat baptizare, matrimonium consecrare,
manus imponere, et absolute ut templorum veluti sacerdotes, patriaeque
religionis vindices et interpretes agnoscantur. Ad concionandum
25 autem, et ecclesiae aerario ejusque quotidianis negotiis administrandis
aliqui ex plebe ab ipso senatu eligendi sunt, qui senatus quasi vicarii
sint; cui propterea rationem omnium reddere teneantur.

47. Atque haec illa sunt quae hujus imperii fundamenta spectant;
quibus pauca alia, minus quidem principalia sed magni tamen momenti,
30 addam: nempe ut patricii veste quadam seu habitu singulari quo
dignoscantur incedant, et ut singulari quodam titulo salutentur, et

---

4. *NS geschikt word.* As *schikken* is the regular rendering of *destinare*, the correct reading
may be *destinetur* or *destinatur*.
10–11. *P simplicissimae; OP sumplicissimae.*

should be appointed for four or five years at the most, and given an assistant, appointed for the same period, to take part of the work off his shoulders, or that several secretaries to the senate should be appointed instead of one, and each kept occupied with different business, the power of officials will never be of any consequence.

45. Treasury officials should also be chosen from the common people, and should be accountable to the syndics as well as to the senate for their administration.

46. My views on religion have been fully expounded in the Tractatus Theologico-Politicus, and it only remains to add one or two points which were beyond the scope of that work. The first is that all the patricians should be of the same faith, the very simple universal faith set out in the treatise referred to.[1] For it is vitally important to prevent the patricians in particular not only from splitting up into sects and favouring different religious groups, but also from becoming a prey to superstition and seeking to deprive their subjects of the freedom to voice their beliefs. Secondly, although everyone should be given freedom to voice his beliefs, large congregations should be forbidden; and so, while dissenters should be allowed to build as many churches as they wish, these churches must be small, of fixed dimensions, and situated some distance apart.[2] On the other hand it is most important that churches dedicated to the state religion should be large and magnificent, and that only patricians or senators should be permitted to perform its principal rites. Thus only patricians should be allowed to baptize, to solemnize marriages, and to lay on hands; in short, they alone should be recognized as the ministers of churches, and as the guardians and interpreters of the state religion. But preachers and officials to deal with the treasury and everyday business of the church may be drawn from the common people. These should be appointed by the senate itself, to act, so to speak, as its deputies, and should therefore be responsible to it for all that they do.

47. Such then are the measures which form the basis of this kind of state; and to them I shall add a few others, no doubt less fundamental, but still of great importance. For instance, the patricians should go about in a special form of clothing or dress to distinguish them from the rest; they should be greeted by a special title; all commoners should

---

[1] *TT-P* xiv, pp. 119–21.

[2] Religious toleration was practised both in Venice (Hazlitt, *The Venetian Republic*, vol. ii, ch. 45, p. 397), and the Netherlands (Temple, *Observations*, ch. v, pp. 122 and ff.; cf. *TT-P* xx, p. 227, n. 1).

unusquisque ex plebe iis loco cedat; et si aliquis patricius bona sua aliquo infortunio quod vitari nequit amiserit, idque liquido docere poterit, ut in integrum ex publicis bonis restituatur. Sed si contra constet eundem largitate, fastu, ludo, scortis, etc. eadem consumpsisse, vel quod abso-
5 lute plus debet quam est solvendo, ut dignitate cedat, et omni honore officioque indignus habeatur. Qui enim seipsum resque suas privatas regere nequit, multo minus publicis consulere poterit.

48. Quos lex jurare cogit a perjurio multo magis cavebunt si per salutem patriae et libertatem, perque supremum concilium, quam si per
10 Deum jurare jubeantur. Nam qui per Deum jurat privatum bonum interponit cujus ille aestimator est: at qui jurejurando libertatem patriaeque salutem interponit, is per commune omnium bonum cujus ille aestimator non est jurat, et, si pejerat, eo ipso se patriae hostem declarat.

15 49. Academiae quae sumptibus reipublicae fundantur non tam ad ingenia colenda quam ad eadem coercenda instituuntur. Sed in libera republica tum scientiae et artes optime excolentur, si unicuique veniam petenti concedatur publice docere, idque suis sumptibus suaeque famae periculo. Sed haec et similia ad alium locum reservo: nam hic de iis
20 solummodo agere constitueram quae ad solum imperium aristocraticum pertinent.

---

11. *NS van 't welk hy zelf de schatter is*, i.e. *cujus ipse aestimator est.*
13–14. *NS zo verklaart hy zich daar door vijant van 't Vaderlant.* Hence *G eo ipso. OP eo ipse.*

give way to them; and any patrician who has lost his possessions by some unavoidable mischance, and can prove this conclusively, should be compensated in full out of public funds.[1] But if it is shown that he has wasted his money through extravagance, luxury, gambling, debauchery, and so on, or that he is hopelessly in debt, he should be deprived of his status and regarded as unworthy of any office or appointment. For a man who cannot manage himself and his own private concerns will be much less able to advise on public affairs.

48. Those whom the law compels to take an oath will be much more careful to avoid perjury if they are told to swear by the safety and freedom of their country, and by its supreme council, than if they are told to swear by God. For he who swears by God stakes a private good, whose value is determined by *him*;[2] but he who stakes in his oath the freedom and safety of his country swears by the common good of all, whose value is not determined by him; and, if he swears falsely, thereby declares himself an enemy of his country.

49. Seats of learning founded at the public expense are established to fetter talent rather than to foster it: in a free republic the arts and sciences will flourish best when everyone who asks permission is allowed to teach openly, at his own expense, and at the risk of his own reputation.[3] But such topics I shall keep for another occasion, for my intention here was to confine myself to matters concerning aristocracy alone.

---

[1] Spinoza wishes to avoid the great inequalities of wealth which existed among the Venetian nobility, and made the poor nobles dependent upon the rich (*Mémoires*, vol. i, ch. x, pp. 183–4).

[2] And he may not believe in the God by whom he is required to swear (Hobbes, *De Cive* ii, 21).

[3] *TT-P* xx, p. 235.

1. Huc usque hoc imperium consideravimus quatenus ab una sola urbe, quae totius imperii caput est, nomen habet. Tempus jam est ut de eo agamus quod plures urbes tenent, quodque ego praecedenti praeferendum existimo. Sed ut utriusque differentiam et praestantiam noscamus, singula praecedentis imperii fundamenta perlustrabimus, et quae ab hoc aliena sunt rejiciemus, et alia quibus niti debeat eorum loco jaciemus.

2. Urbes itaque quae civitatis jure gaudent ita conditae et munitae esse debent ut unaquaeque sola sine reliquis subsistere quidem non possit, sed contra etiam ut a reliquis deficere nequeat absque magno totius imperii detrimento; hoc enim modo semper unitae manebunt. At quae ita constitutae sunt ut nec se conservare nec reliquis formidini esse queant, eae sane non sui sed reliquarum juris absolute sunt.

3. Quae autem Art. 9 et 10 praec. Cap. ostendimus ex communi imperii aristocratici natura deducuntur, ut et ratio numeri patriciorum ad numerum multitudinis, et qualis eorum aetas et conditio esse debeat qui patricii sunt creandi; ita ut nulla circa haec oriri possit differentia sive imperium una sive plures urbes teneant. At supremi concilii alia hic debet esse ratio. Nam si quae imperii urbs supremo huic concilio congregando destinaretur, illa revera ipsius imperii caput esset; atque adeo vel vices servandae essent, vel talis locus huic concilio esset designandus qui civitatis jus non habeat, quique ad omnes aeque pertineat. Sed tam hoc quam illud, ut dictu facile, ita factu difficile est, ut scilicet tot hominum millia extra urbes saepe ire, vel ut jam hoc, jam alio in loco convenire debeant.

---

3. NS *die in meer Steden bestaat,* i.e. *tenet* or *continet.*

9–10. NS *dat yder alleen niet alleenlijk zonder d' anderen kan bestaan,* which would be a literal rendering of *ut unaquaeque sola non solum sine reliquis subsistere possit.*

18. NS *'t zy dat deze Heerschappy een enige, of meer steden onder zich heeft,* i.e. *sive impertum unam sive plures urbes teneat.*

CHAPTER IX

1. So far I have been considering an aristocracy which takes its name from one city, the capital of the whole state. Now it is time to deal with the kind where sovereignty is vested in several cities;[1] and this I regard as superior to the former. To discover where the difference and the superiority lie, I shall survey the fundamental laws of the former one by one, rejecting those which are alien to the present type, and laying down others in their place to form the basis it requires.

2. The cities which enjoy political rights must be founded and fortified in such a way that while none of them is strong enough to maintain itself alone without the help of the rest, none is so weak that its secession would do little damage to the state as a whole; for under these conditions they will always remain united. But cities which can neither preserve themselves nor imperil the others are certainly not possessed of their own right, but are completely subject to the control of the rest.

3. Now the regulations explained in Sections 9 and 10 of the previous Chapter, like the law maintaining the ratio of patricians to commons, and the law prescribing the age and status of candidates for the patriciate, are all derived from the general nature of aristocracy; so that as far as these points are concerned it can make no difference whether the sovereignty is vested in one city or in several. But in the case of the supreme council there must be a difference in this second type. For if any city in the state were appointed as the meeting-place of this council, that city would really be the capital of the state; and to avoid this it would be necessary either to follow a system of rotation, or else to appoint for meetings of this council a place which did not possess political rights and belonged equally to all.[2] But both these suggestions are as difficult to follow as they are easy to make, for it is impracticable to require so many thousands of men to leave their cities so often, or to meet at different places in turn.[3]

[1] For this type of aristocracy Spinoza's chief model is the province of Holland (*TP* viii, 3, p. 369, and ix, 14, p. 427); but several features are taken from the Dutch Republic as a whole.

[2] Originally the Estates of Holland, like the States General, met in different places at different times; but about 1593 the Hague, which lacked political rights, became the meeting-place of both bodies (de la Bassecour Caan, *Schets van den Regeringsvorm van Nederland*, pp. 119 and 142).

[3] In the Netherlands this difficulty was overcome by a system of representation: the provinces sent deputies to the States General as the towns sent deputies to the Provincial Estates (Temple, *Observations*, ch. ii, pp. 67–69).

4. Verum ut recte quid in hac re fieri oporteat, et qua ratione hujus imperii concilia instituenda sint, ex ipsius natura et conditione concludere possimus, haec consideranda sunt: nempe quod unaquaeque urbs tanto plus juris quam vir privatus habeat quanto viro privato potentior 5 est (per Art. 4 Cap. 2); et consequenter unaquaeque hujus imperii urbs (vide Art. 2 hujus Cap.) tantum juris intra moenia seu suae jurisdictionis limites habeat quantum potest. Deinde quod omnes urbes non ut confoederatae, sed ut unum imperium constituentes invicem sociatae et unitae sint, sed ita ut unaquaeque urbs tanto plus juris in imperium 10 quam reliquae obtineat quanto reliquis est potentior; nam qui inter inaequales aequalitatem quaerit, absurdum quid quaerit. Cives quidem aequales merito aestimantur, quia uniuscujusque potentia cum potentia totius imperii comparata nullius est considerationis. At urbis cujuscunque potentia magnam partem potentiae ipsius imperii constituit, et 15 eo majorem quo ipsa urbs major est; ac proinde omnes urbes aequales haberi nequeunt, sed ut uniuscujusque potentia, ita etiam ejusdem jus ex ipsius magnitudine aestimari debet. Vincula vero, quibus adstringi debent ut unum imperium componant, apprime sunt (per Art. 1 Cap. 4) senatus et forum. Quomodo autem eae omnes his vinculis ita copu-20 landae sunt ut earum tamen unaquaeque sui juris, quantum fieri potest, maneat, breviter hic ostendam.

5. Nempe uniuscujusque urbis patricios, qui pro magnitudine urbis (per Art. 3 hujus Cap.) plures aut pauciores esse debent, summum in suam urbem jus habere concipio, eosque in concilio quod illius urbis 25 supremum est summam habere potestatem urbem muniendi, ejusque moenia dilatandi, vectigalia imponendi, leges condendi et abrogandi, et omnia absolute agendi quae ad suae urbis conservationem et incrementum necessaria esse judicant. Ad communia autem imperii negotia tractanda senatus creandus est iis omnino conditionibus quas in praeced. 30 Cap. diximus; ita ut inter hunc senatum et illum nulla alia sit differentia quam quod hic authoritatem etiam habeat dirimendi quaestiones

---

9. *NS in de Heerschappy*, which suggests *in imperio*. Cf. the parallel passage on p. 418, ll. 21–22. But cf. also ll. 23–24 below.
18–19. *NS zijn voornamelijk de Staatsraad, en de Rechtbank*, omitting the reference.
23–24. *NS in hun stat*, which suggests *in sua urbe*.

---

arising between the provinces. It was better fitted to perform this function than the States General, for while the deputies to the latter were bound to push the interests of their respective provinces the members of the Council of State took an oath to promote the good of the whole Republic (de la Bassecour Caan, op. cit., p. 170).

4. To discover the correct solution of this problem, and the right way to organize the councils of this kind of state, we must start from its nature and constitution and consider the following points. First, since the right of a city over a private individual is measured by its power over him (by Section 4, Chapter 2), each city in this state has as much right within its walls or the limits of its jurisdiction as it has power (see Section 2 of this Chapter). Secondly, all the cities are joined and bound together, not as allied states, but as constituent parts of one state; yet in such a way that one has more right in the government than the rest in proportion as it exceeds them in power; for to demand equality between unequals is to demand the absurd.[1] Citizens no doubt are rightly regarded as equal, since the power of an individual citizen is of no consequence when compared with the power of the state as a whole. But the power of a city constitutes a great part of the power of the state itself, and the larger the city, the greater its contribution to the power of the state; hence the cities cannot all be regarded as equal, but the right of each, like its power, must be determined by its size. The ties by which they must be bound together so as to form a single state are mainly the senate and the law-court[2] (see Section 1, Chapter 4). How they are all to be united by these ties so that each still remains in possession of its own right as far as possible, I shall now briefly explain.

5. I assume, then, that the patricians of each city, who (by Section 3 of this Chapter) are to be more or less numerous in proportion to the city's size, have supreme authority over their own city, and that as the supreme council of that city they have full power to fortify it,[3] to extend its boundaries, to impose taxes, to pass and repeal laws, in short, to do everything they think necessary for the preservation and growth of their city.[4] To handle the common concerns of the state, however, it is necessary to create a senate on precisely the same lines as I laid down in the previous Chapter; so that the sole difference between this senate and the former is that this has also authority to settle any disputes which may arise between the cities.[5]

[1] Each town represented in the Estates of Holland, and each province represented in the States General, had one vote only. Thus the tiny town of Purmerend had 'an equal voice' with Amsterdam, and the small province Overijssel 'an equal voice' with Holland (Temple, loc. cit., p. 63). See *TP* vi, 25, p. 329, n. 1.

[2] There were provincial courts in the Netherlands, but no supreme court for the country as a whole.

[3] See Bynkershoek, *Quaestiones Juris Publici*, Book II, ch. xiv.

[4] For the powers of the towns of Holland see Temple, op. cit., ch. ii, pp. 56 and ff.

[5] In 1588 the Council of State of the Netherlands was given the power to settle disputes

[*footnotes contd. opposite*

quae inter urbes oriri possunt. Nam hoc in hoc imperio, cujus nulla urbs caput est, non potest, ut in illo, a supremo concilio fieri. Vide Art. 38 praec. Cap.

6. Caeterum in hoc imperio supremum concilium convocandum 5 non est nisi opus sit ipsum imperium reformare, vel in arduo aliquo negotio ad quod peragendum senatores se impares esse credent; atque adeo raro admodum fiet ut omnes patricii in concilium vocentur. Nam praecipuum supremi concilii officium esse diximus (Art. 17 praec. Cap.) leges condere et abrogare, et deinde imperii ministros eligere. At 10 leges sive communia totius imperii jura, simulatque instituta sunt, immutari non debent. Quod si tamen tempus et occasio ferat ut novum aliquod jus instituendum sit, aut jam statutum mutandum, potest prius de eodem quaestio in senatu haberi; et postquam senatus in eo convenerit, tum deinde legati ad urbes ab ipso senatu mittantur, qui 15 uniuscujusque urbis patricios senatus sententiam doceant; et si denique major urbium pars in sententiam senatus iverit, ut tum ipsa rata maneat, alias irrita. Atque hic idem ordo in eligendis ducibus exercitus, et legatis in alia regna mittendis, ut et circa decreta de bello inferendo et pacis conditionibus acceptandis teneri potest. Sed in reliquis imperii ministris 20 eligendis, quia (ut in Art. 4 hujus Cap. ostendimus) unaquaeque urbs, quantum fieri potest, sui juris manere debet, et in imperio tanto plus juris obtinere quanto reliquis est potentior, hic ordo necessario servandus est. Nempe senatores a patriciis uniuscujusque urbis eligendi sunt; videlicet unius urbis patricii in suo concilio certum senatorum 25 numerum ex suis civibus collegis eligent, qui ad numerum patriciorum ejusdem urbis se habeat (vide Art. 30 praeced. Cap.) ut 1 ad 12; et quos primi, secundi, tertii, etc. ordinis esse volunt designabunt. Et sic reliquarum urbium patricii pro magnitudine sui numeri plures paucioresve senatores eligent, et in tot ordines distribuent in quot senatum

---

2. *NS kan dit niet anders, dan van d' opperste Raatvergadering, gedaan worden.*
18. *NS gelijk ook*; hence *L ut et. OP ut.*
29. *NS en in zo veel ordeningen (zullen) verdeelen*; *V-L et in tot ordines distribuent*; *OP et in ordines distribuent.*

---

of State, Gelderland, Zeeland, and Friesland two each, Utrecht, Overijssel, and Groningen one each. Since each deputy had a vote the leading position of Holland was to some extent recognized in this council (de la Bassecour Caan, op. cit., p. 166).

For in a state which has no capital city this cannot be done by the supreme council, as it was in the first type of aristocracy. See Section 38 of the previous Chapter.

6. Moreover in this state the supreme council[1] should not be summoned unless it is necessary to reorganize the state itself, or for some difficult task which the senators regard as beyond their power; and so it will be very rare for all the patricians to be summoned to meet as a body. For the chief duties of the supreme council are, as I said in Section 17 of the previous Chapter, first to make and repeal laws, and then to appoint ministers of state. But the laws or general ordinances of the whole state should not be altered as soon as they have been made. On the other hand time and circumstances may make it necessary to lay down some new law, or to change one which already exists. If so, the matter can first be discussed in the senate; once it has reached agreement, it should send official envoys to announce its decision to the patricians of each city; and if a majority of cities then agrees with the senate's decision, that decision should be valid—but otherwise null and void. This same procedure can be followed in appointing army commanders, and ambassadors to foreign states, and likewise in making decisions to wage war or to accept conditions of peace.[2] But in appointing the other ministers of state it is necessary to follow a different method, since (as I have shown in Section 4 of this Chapter) each city must remain in possession of its own right as far as possible, and must have more right in the government in proportion as it exceeds the others in power. Senators, for instance, should be chosen by the patricians of each city; i.e. the patricians of one city will appoint in their council a certain number of senators from their citizen colleagues, and this number should stand to the number of patricians in that city in the ratio of one to twelve. See Section 30 of the previous Chapter. Furthermore they will name those whom they wish to serve on each section, the first, the second, the third, and so on. In the same way the patricians of the other cities will appoint a greater or smaller number of senators in proportion to their own number,[3] and will divide them up among as many sections as I said should constitute the senate. See

[1] A model for Spinoza's supreme council may be found in the full States General, of which the ordinary States General was simply a representative (Temple, op. cit., ch. ii, pp. 67–69). The functions of the ordinary States General are performed by Spinoza's senate.

[2] The ordinary States General had to obtain the approval of the Provincial Estates, and the Provincial Estates that of the town councils, before decisions on such matters were valid; but the approval had usually to be unanimous (Temple, op. cit., ch. ii, pp. 70–72).

[3] *TP* vi, 25, p. 329, n. 1, and vii, 5, p. 341, n. 1. Holland sent three deputies to the Council

[*footnotes contd. opposite*

dividendum esse diximus (vid. Art. 34 praeced. Cap.): quo fiet ut in unoquoque senatorum ordine pro magnitudine cujuscunque urbis plures paucioresve ejusdem senatores reperiantur. At ordinum praesides eorumque vicarii, quorum numerus minor est urbium numero, a senatu ex 5 consulibus electis sorte eligendi sunt. In judicibus praeterea supremis imperii eligendis idem ordo retinendus est, scilicet ut uniuscujusque urbis patricii ex suis collegis pro magnitudine sui numeri plures aut pauciores judices eligant. Atque adeo fiet ut unaquaeque urbs in eligendis ministris sui juris quantum fieri potest sit, et ut unaquaeque quo 10 potentior est, eo etiam plus juris tam in senatu quam in foro obtineat; posito scilicet quod senatus et fori ordo in decernendis imperii rebus et quaestionibus dirimendis talis omnino sit qualem Art. 33 et 34 praec. Cap. descripsimus.

7. Cohortium deinde duces et militiae tribuni a patriciis etiam eli- 15 gendi sunt. Nam quia aequum est ut unaquaeque urbs pro ratione suae magnitudinis certum militum numerum ad communem totius imperii securitatem conducere teneatur, aequum etiam est ut patriciis uniuscujusque urbis, pro numero legionum quas alere tenentur, tot tribunos, duces, signiferos, etc. eligere liceat quot ad illam militiae partem quam 20 imperio suppeditant ordinandam requiruntur.

8. Vectigalia nulla etiam a senatu subditis imponenda; sed ad sumptus qui ad negotia publica peragenda ex senatus decreto requiruntur, non subditi sed urbes ipsae ab ipso senatu ad censum vocandae sunt, ita ut unaquaeque urbs pro ratione suae magnitudinis sumptuum partem 25 majorem vel minorem ferre debeat; quam quidem partem ejusdem urbis patricii a suis urbanis ea qua velint via exigent, eos scilicet vel ad censum trahendo, vel, quod multo aequius est, iisdem vectigalia imponendo.

9. Porro quamvis omnes hujus imperii urbes maritimae non sint, 30 nec senatores ex solis urbibus maritimis vocentur, possunt tamen iisdem eadem emolumenta decerni quae Art. 31 praec. Cap. diximus; quem

12. *P dirimendis*; *OP derimendis*.
14. *NS van de Keurraden*, i.e. *a patriciis*; *OP e patriciis*. I prefer the *NS* reading because (1) Spinoza, as the context shows, is contrasting the appointments which are made directly by the patricians of each city with those made by the senate, and (2) the *OP* reading, by suggesting that subordinate officers are to be appointed from the patricians alone, contradicts the statement on p. 374, ll. 9–12.
17–19. *NS dat de Keurraden . . . mogen verkiezen*; *OP ut e patriciis . . . eligere liceat.* See the previous note.

Section 34 of the previous Chapter. The result will be that in each section of the senate every city will have a greater or smaller number of senators according to its size. But the presidents and vice-presidents of the sections, whose number is less than the number of cities, should be chosen by lot by the senate from those who have been appointed consuls. The supreme judges of the state should be elected in the same way as the senators; i.e., the patricians of each city should choose from their colleagues more or fewer judges according to their own number.[1] This will ensure that each city has as much independence as possible in the appointment of ministers, and that each has as much right in both the senate and the law-court as is proportionate to its power; provided, of course, that in deciding state policy and settling disputes the senate and court follow exactly the same procedure as I described in Sections 33 and 34 of the previous Chapter.

7. Company commanders and colonels should also be appointed by the patricians. For since it is just that each city should be bound to engage for the common defence of the whole state a certain number of troops in proportion to its size, it is also just that the patricians of each city, in accordance with the number of regiments which they are bound to maintain, should be allowed to appoint as many colonels, captains, ensigns, etc., as are required to officer that portion of the armed forces which they provide for the state.[2]

8. Nor should the senate impose any taxes on the subjects. To meet the expenditure required to carry out public undertakings in accordance with its decree, it should assess, not individual subjects, but the cities themselves, binding each city to defray a greater or smaller part of the expenditure according to its size. The patricians of each city will collect this sum from their townsfolk in the way they think best,[3] i.e. either by direct or by indirect taxation, the latter being much the more equitable method.

9. Although the senators are not drawn exclusively from coastal cities—not all the cities of this state being on the coast—they can still be assigned the same remuneration as I have laid down in Section 31 of the previous Chapter; and to achieve this it will be possible to devise

---

[1] The Netherlands had no supreme court of justice, but Holland and Zeeland had a common court of twelve judges, nine from Holland and three from Zeeland (Temple, op. cit., ch. ii, p. 67).

[2] In 1651 'the States-Provincial (assumed) the disposal of all Military Commands in those Troops which their share was to pay' (Temple, op. cit., ch. ii, p. 82).

[3] Temple, op. cit., ch. ii, pp. 73–74.

in finem pro imperii constitutione media excogitari poterunt quibus urbes invicem arctius copulentur. Caeterum reliqua ad senatum et forum, et absolute ad universum imperium spectantia, quae in praec. Cap. tradidi, huic etiam imperio applicanda sunt. Atque adeo videmus
5 quod in imperio quod plures urbes tenent non necesse sit supremo concilio convocando certum tempus aut locum designare: at senatui et foro locus dicandus est in pago vel in urbe quae suffragii jus non habet. Sed ad illa quae ad singulas urbes spectant revertor.

10. Ordo supremi concilii unius urbis in eligendis urbis et imperii
10 ministris, et in rebus decernendis, idem ille quem Art. 27 et 36 praec. Cap. tradidi esse debet. Nam eadem hic quam illic est ratio. Deinde syndicorum concilium huic subordinandum est, quod ad urbis concilium se habeat ut illud syndicorum praeced. Cap. ad concilium totius imperii, et cujus officium intra limites jurisdictionis urbis idem etiam sit, iis-
15 demque emolumentis gaudeat. Quod si urbs et consequenter patriciorum numerus adeo exiguus fuerit ut non nisi unum aut duos syndicos creare possit, qui duo concilium facere nequeunt, tum syndicis in cognitionibus pro re nata judices a supremo urbis concilio designandi sunt, vel quaestio ad supremum syndicorum concilium deferenda. Nam
20 ex unaquaque urbe aliqui etiam ex syndicis in locum ubi senatus residet mittendi sunt, qui prospiciant ut jura universi imperii inviolata serventur, quique in senatu absque jure suffragii sedeant.

11. Urbium consules a patriciis etiam ejusdem urbis eligendi sunt, qui veluti senatum illius urbis constituant. Horum autem numerum
25 determinare non possum, nec etiam necesse esse existimo, quandoquidem ejusdem urbis negotia quae magni ponderis sunt a supremo ejusdem concilio, et quae ad universum imperium spectant a magno senatu peraguntur. Caeterum si pauci fuerint, necesse erit ut in suo concilio palam suffragia ferant, non autem calculis, ut in magnis con-
30 ciliis. In parvis enim conciliis ubi suffragia clam indicantur, qui aliquanto callidior est facile cujusque suffragii auctorem noscere, et minus attentiores multis modis eludere potest.

12. In unaquaque praeterea urbe judices a supremo ejusdem concilio constituendi sunt, a quorum tamen sententia supremum imperii

5. *NS daar in veel steden zijn*, i.e. *quod plures urbes tenet* (or *continet*).
9. *urbis et* not in *NS*.
30–31. *NS die in schalkheit d' anderen overtreft*, i.e. *qui reliquis callidior est*.

means, appropriate to the constitution of the state, which will bind the cities more closely together. The remaining regulations laid down for the senate and court, and, in general, for the whole state, are also applicable here. Thus we see that in a state where sovereignty is vested in several cities it is unnecessary to appoint a fixed time or place for meetings of the supreme council; the senate and law-court, however, should be assigned a meeting-place in a country district or a city which has no right of voting. But I must return to points concerning individual cities.

10. In appointing city officials and ministers of State, and in making decisions, the supreme council of a city must follow the same procedure as I have described in Sections 27 and 36 of the previous Chapter; for the same reasons apply in both cases. Furthermore, there should be a council of syndics under this council, and these should bear the same proportion to the city council as the council of syndics in the previous Chapter bears to the supreme council of the whole State. Their duties —within the limits of the city's jurisdiction—should also be the same, and they should enjoy the same remuneration. But if the city and consequently the number of patricians is so small that it is unable to appoint more than one or two syndics, then—since these two cannot constitute a council—the supreme council of the city should either nominate judges as occasion arises to assist the syndics in their inquiries, or else refer the matter to the supreme council of syndics. For every city should also send syndics to the place where the senate holds its sessions, to see that the laws of the whole state are kept inviolate, and to sit on the senate without the right to vote.

11. The patricians of a city should also appoint the city consuls,[1] who should form as it were the senate of that city. The number of these consuls I am unable to determine, nor indeed do I think it necessary to do so, since the main affairs of the city are handled by its supreme council, and those which concern the state as a whole by the grand senate. However, if they are few in number it will be necessary for them to vote openly in their assembly, and not, as in large councils, by secret ballot. For when votes are given in secret in small councils the man who is a little more cunning than the rest can easily discover the author of each vote, and outwit less attentive members in many ways.

12. Every city should also have judges appointed by its supreme council; but defendants should be allowed to appeal from their verdicts

---

[1] These are equivalent to the Burgomasters of Dutch towns.

judicium appellare liceat, praeterquam reo palam convicto et confitenti debitori. Sed haec ulterius persequi non est opus.

13. Superest igitur ut de urbibus quae sui juris non sunt loquamur.
Hae, si in ipsa imperii provincia vel regione conditae, et earum incolae
5 ejusdem nationis et linguae sint, debent necessario, sicuti pagi, veluti
urbium vicinarum partes censeri, ita ut earum unaquaeque sub regimine hujus aut illius urbis quae sui juris est esse debeat. Cujus rei ratio
est quod patricii non a supremo hujus imperii sed a supremo uniuscujusque urbis concilio eligantur, qui in unaquaque urbe pro numero
10 incolarum intra limites jurisdictionis ejusdem urbis plures paucioresve
sunt (per Art. 5 hujus Cap.). Atque adeo necesse est ut multitudo urbis
quae sui juris non est ad censum multitudinis alterius quae sui juris sit
referatur, et ab ejus directione pendeat. At urbes jure belli captae et
quae imperio accesserunt veluti imperii sociae habendae, et beneficio
15 victae obligandae; vel coloniae quae jure civitatis gaudeant eo mittendae, et gens alio ducenda; vel omnino delendae sunt.

14. Atque haec sunt quae ad hujus imperii fundamenta spectant.
Quod autem ejus conditio melior sit quam illius quod nomen ab una
urbe sola habet, hinc concludo: quod scilicet uniuscujusque urbis
20 patricii, more humanae cupidinis, suum jus tam in urbe quam in senatu
retinere, et, si fieri potest, augere studebunt, atque adeo quantum
poterunt conabuntur multitudinem ad se trahere, et consequenter
imperium beneficiis magis quam metu agitare, suumque numerum
augere; quippe quo plures numero fuerint, eo plures (per Art. 6 hujus
25 Cap.) ex suo concilio senatores eligent, et consequenter (per Art. eundem) plus juris in imperio obtinebunt. Nec obstat quod, dum unaquaeque urbs sibi consulit reliquisque invidet, saepius inter se discordent et
tempus disputando consumant. Nam si dum Romani deliberant perit
Sagunthus, dum contra pauci ex solo suo affectu omnia decernunt perit

---

12. *NS tot de schatting van een andere menigte*—a mistranslation.

16. *NS of (men moet) de plaatsen gantschelijk uitroejen*; *OP vel omnino delenda est.* But
genocide seems an extreme measure for Spinoza to advocate; even Machiavelli, on whom the
end of this Section is based, contents himself with the destruction of the ruling house.
Furthermore, the parallel passage on p. 332, ll. 1–5, suggests that it is the cities, not their
inhabitants, which are to be destroyed. Hence *G* reads *vel urbs omnino delenda est.* But the
change to the singular is awkward, and *NS* suggests a plural.

24. *OP per Art. 16*, which is corrected to *per Art. 6* in the list of Errata; *NS volgens het
zeste Lid.*

to the supreme court of the state, except when their guilt has been clearly proven or they confess their debt.[1] However there is no need to pursue this farther.

13. It remains, then, to speak of the cities which are not possessed of their own right. If these are situated in the actual lands or territories of the state, and their inhabitants belong to the same race and speak the same tongue, they must necessarily be regarded as parts of the neighbouring cities, just like the country districts; so that each must be under the control of some city or other which is possessed of its own right. The reason for this is that patricians are not co-opted here by the supreme council of the state but by the supreme council of each city, and their number in each city depends on the number of inhabitants within the limits of that city's jurisdiction (by Section 5 of this Chapter). This makes it necessary for the population of a city which is not possessed of its own right to be added to the population roll of another which is, and to be subject to its control. But cities which have been taken by the right of war, and annexed to the state, should be regarded as allies who must be won over and bound by kindness; or their population should be transplanted elsewhere and replaced by colonies which enjoy political rights; or they should be completely destroyed.[2]

14. These, then, are the laws which form the basis of this kind of state. That it is superior to an aristocracy which takes its name from one city only, I conclude from the following facts. The patricians of each city, inspired by normal human ambition, will be eager to maintain and, if possible, extend their right both in the city and in the senate. They will therefore do their utmost to attract population to their city by ruling more by kindness than by fear,[3] and to increase their own numbers; for the more numerous they are, the more members of their own council will they elect to the Senate (by Section 6 of this Chapter), and consequently the more right will they have in the state (by the same Section). To say that when every city is intent on its own advantage and jealous of the others they quarrel more frequently and waste time in argument is not a decisive objection to my view. No doubt 'Saguntum perishes while the Romans deliberate';[4] but liberty and the common

---

[1] In Holland no appeal was allowed from town court to provincial court in criminal cases (Temple, op. cit., ch. ii, pp. 56 and 60).

[2] Machiavelli, *Prince*, iii and v; *Discourses* ii, 23.

[3] Hence greater freedom for the subjects (*TP* viii, 3, p. 369).

[4] A proverb based on Livy xxi, vii, 1. Van Hove quotes it several times (e.g. *Polityke Weegschaal*, pp. 38 and 271) in pointing out that though a king can make speedy decisions, a council must often waste time and opportunity in discussing conflicting opinions.

libertas communeque bonum. Sunt namque humana ingenia hebetiora quam ut omnia statim penetrare possint; sed consulendo, audiendo, et disputando acuuntur, et dum omnia tentant media ea quae volunt tandem inveniunt, quae omnes probant et de quibus nemo antea cogitasset.
5 Cujus rei in Hollandia multa vidimus exempla. Quod si quis regerat hoc Hollandorum imperium non diu absque comite, vel vicario qui vicem comitis suppleret, stetisse, hoc sibi responsum habeat, quod Hollandi ad obtinendam libertatem satis sibi putaverunt comitem deserere, et imperii corpus capite obtruncare, nec de eodem reformando cogi-
10 tarunt, sed omnia ejus membra uti antea constituta fuerant reliquerunt, ita ut Hollandia comitatus sine comite, veluti corpus sine capite, ipsumque imperium sine nomine manserit. Atque adeo minime mirum quod subditi plerique ignoraverint penes quos summa esset imperii potestas. Et quamvis hoc non esset, ii tamen qui imperium revera tenebant longe
15 pauciores erant quam ut multitudinem regere et potentes adversarios opprimere possent. Unde factum ut hi saepe impune iis insidiari, et tandem evertere potuerint. Subita itaque ejusdem reipublicae eversio non ex eo orta est, quod tempus in deliberationibus inutiliter consumeretur, sed ex deformi ejusdem imperii statu et paucitate regentium.
20 15. Est praeterea hoc aristocraticum imperium quod plures urbes tenent alteri praeferendum, quia non opus est, ut in praecedenti, cavere ne universum supremum ejus concilium subito impetu opprimatur, quandoquidem (per Art. 9 hujus Cap.) eidem convocando nullum tempus nec locus designatur. Sunt praeterea potentes cives in hoc imperio
25 minus timendi. Nam ubi plures urbes libertate gaudent, non sufficit ei qui viam ad imperium affectat urbem unam occupare, ut imperium in reliquas obtineat. Est denique in hoc imperio libertas pluribus communis. Nam ubi una sola urbs regnat, eatenus reliquarum bono consulitur quatenus regnanti huic urbi expedit.

4–5. NS en op de welken te voren niemant gedacht had; daar af wy in Hollant veel voorbeelden gezien hebben. OP has no equivalent for *daar af . . . hebben,* although *hoc* in the following sentence suggests that some reference to Holland should precede. *Cujus rei in Hollandia multa vidimus exempla* is L's rendering of the Dutch.

6. *P, Gf,* and *B* delete *hoc,* not suspecting the lacuna; *NS deze.*

11. *NS in voegen dat Hollant een Graafschap zonder Graaf . . . gebleven is; OP ita ut Hollandiae comitatus sine comite . . . manserit.* The OP reading misses the point: which is, not that the county of Holland has been left without a count, but that Holland has been left a *county* without a count.   17. *NS De haastige omwerping,* i.e. *Subita; OP Subitâ.*

20–21. *NS die veel steden onder zich heeft,* i.e. *quod plures urbes tenet.* Cf. Sections 1, 3, and 9. The consistency with which this variant occurs suggests that these passages were revised by Spinoza, and that the *NS* text reflects an earlier version.

21. *NS (gelijk in 't voorgaande Lid gezegt is)*—a mistranslation.

29. *NS als het dienstig voor de genen is, die deze stat bestieren*—another mistranslation.

good perish when a few men decide everything to suit their own whims. The fact is that human wits are too blunt to get to the heart of all problems immediately; but they are sharpened by the give and take of discussion and debate, and by exploring every possible course men eventually discover the measures they wish, measures which all approve and which no one would have thought of before the discussion. Of this we have seen many instances in Holland.[1] And if anyone objects that the state of Holland has not maintained itself for long without a count, or a lieutenant to act in his place,[2] my reply is this. The people of Holland thought that to gain their freedom they had only to secede from their count[3] and cut off the head of the body politic; they never thought of reorganizing their state, but left all its other parts in their original form; and so Holland has been left a county without a count, like a body without a head, and the real government has been left without a name. Small wonder then that most of the subjects did not know in whose hands the sovereignty lay.[4] And even if this had not been so, those who actually held the sovereignty were far too few to be capable of governing the people and crushing their powerful opponents;[5] hence the latter have been able to plot against them, often without penalty, and finally to overthrow them. So the sudden overthrow of this republic[6] was not due to time wasted on deliberations, but to its defective condition and the fewness of its rulers.[7]

15. Another reason why an aristocracy where sovereignty is vested in several cities is superior is that, unlike the first type, it needs no safeguards to prevent its whole supreme council from being overthrown by a sudden attack; since that council has no time or place appointed for its meetings (by Section 9 of this Chapter).[8] Moreover, powerful citizens are less dangerous in this type of state; for where freedom is enjoyed by several cities it is not sufficient for the man who is aiming at sovereignty to seize one city in order to gain control over the rest. Finally, freedom is common to more of the members. For where one city alone holds sway the good of the others is considered only if it serves the interest of the ruling city.

---

1 Temple, op. cit., ch. ii, pp. 65–66.   2 i.e. a stadtholder.   3 Philip II of Spain.

4 The effect of Spinoza's proposals would be to confer it on a general assembly of the regents of the towns.

5 The Orangists.   6 In 1672.

7 Van Hove was perturbed by the disproportion between regents and commoners, especially in Holland, and foresaw a revolution (op. cit. II, ii, 6, p. 291).

8 Van Hove had pointed out that an enemy who captured the assembly-place of a republic had that republic in his power (op. cit. II, i, 3, p. 267).

CAPUT X

1. Imperii utriusque aristocratici fundamentis explicatis et ostensis, superest ut inquiramus an aliqua causa culpabili possint dissolvi aut in aliam formam mutari. Primaria causa unde hujusmodi imperia dissolvuntur illa est quam acutissimus Florentinus Disc. 1 lib. 3 in Tit.

5 Livium observat, videlicet quod *imperio, sicuti humano corpori, quotidie aggregatur aliquid quod quandoque indiget curatione.* Atque adeo necesse esse ait ut aliquando aliquid accidat quo imperium ad suum principium, quo stabiliri incepit, redigatur. Quod si intra debitum tempus non acciderit, vitia eo usque crescent ut tolli nequeant nisi cum ipso imperio.

10 Atque hoc, inquit, vel casu contingere potest, vel consilio, et prudentia legum aut viri eximiae virtutis. Nec dubitare possumus quin haec res maximi sit ponderis, et quod, ubi huic incommodo provisum non sit, non poterit imperium sua virtute, sed sola fortuna permanere; et contra, ubi huic malo remedium idoneum adhibitum fuerit, non poterit ipsum

15 suo vitio, sed solummodo inevitabili aliquo fato cadere, ut mox clarius docebimus. Primum quod huic malo remedium occurrebat, hoc fuit, ut scilicet singulis lustris supremus aliquis dictator in mensem unum aut duos crearetur, cui jus esset de senatorum et cujuscunque ministri factis cognoscendi, judicandi, et statuendi, et consequenter imperium

20 ad suum principium restituendi. Sed qui imperii incommoda vitare studet, remedia adhibere debet quae cum imperii natura conveniant, et quae ex ipsius fundamentis deduci queant; alias in Scyllam incidet cupiens vitare Charybdin. Est quidem hoc verum, quod omnes, tam qui regunt quam qui reguntur, metu supplicii aut damni contineri

25 debeant, ne impune vel cum lucro peccare liceat; sed contra certum etiam est, quod si hic metus bonis et malis hominibus communis fuerit, versetur necessario imperium in summo periculo. Cum igitur dictatoria potestas absoluta sit, non potest non esse omnibus formidabilis, praesertim si statuto tempore, ut requiritur, dictator crearetur;

30 quia tum unusquisque gloriae cupidus eum honorem summo studio ambiret, et certum est quod in pace non tam virtus quam opulentia spectatur, ita ut quo quisque superbior, eo facilius honores adipiscatur.

---

5. Whereas *OP* prints *sicuti humano corpori* in ordinary type, *NS* makes *gelijk aan een menschelijk lighaam* part of the quotation. Rightly, since Machiavelli himself draws the comparison.

17–18. *NS voor een maant, voor een jaar, of voor twee jaren.* Probably the translator misread *unum* as *annum.* 18. *V–L crearetur; OP creetur.*

29. *NS verkozen word,* i.e. *creetur.* 31. *NS naar deze eer zal trachten,* i.e. *ambiet.*

CHAPTER X

1. Now that I have set out and explained the fundamental laws of both aristocracies, it remains to inquire whether such states have any avoidable defect which is capable of destroying them or altering their form. The primary cause of their destruction is the one noted by the shrewd Florentine in the first Discourse of his third Book on Livy, when he says that 'a state, like a human body, is subject to daily accretions which occasionally require treatment'.[1] It is therefore necessary, he goes on, that something should happen from time to time to restore the state to its proper basis, the source of its original strength; for if this does not happen within the necessary time its defects will grow to such a pitch that they cannot be removed without destroying the state itself. The restoration, he tells us, can come about either by chance or by design; and either through wise laws or the wisdom of an outstanding man. Now we cannot doubt that this is a matter of vital importance, and that where no steps have been taken to deal with this malady the state will not be able to survive through its own strength, but only by good fortune; whereas if a proper remedy has been provided it will be impossible for the state to fall through any defect of its own, but only by some unavoidable mischance, as I shall presently show more clearly. The first remedy which suggested itself was to appoint a dictator, with supreme power for one or two months, every five years,[2] and to give him the right to examine, judge, and pronounce upon the conduct of the senators and all the ministers, and hence to restore the state to its original basis. But he who seeks to avoid the troubles which afflict a state should use remedies consistent with the nature of that state, and deducible from its fundamental laws; otherwise the cure will be worse than the disease. It is true that all men, rulers as well as ruled, must be restrained by fear of punishment or loss from doing wrong with impunity or profit; but it is also true that if this fear is common to good and bad men alike the state will inevitably find itself in very great danger. Now since dictatorial power is absolute, it cannot fail to inspire fear in everyone, especially if the dictator is appointed, as is necessary, at a fixed time; for in that case every man of ambition will canvass for the position with the greatest eagerness, and since in time of peace more attention is certainly paid to wealth than to ability, office tends

---

[1] Machiavelli, *Discourses* iii, 1. Cf. Aristotle, *Politics* 1307^b 1–6.
[2] I have not been able to trace the source of this suggestion.

Et forte hac de causa Romani nullo constituto tempore, sed fortuita quadam necessitate coacti, dictatorem facere consueverant. At nihilominus rumor dictatoris, ut Ciceronis verba referam, bonis injucundus fuit. Et sane, quandoquidem haec dictatoria potestas regia absolute est, 5 potest non absque magno reipublicae periculo imperium aliquando in monarchicum mutari, tametsi in tempus quantumvis breve id fiat. Adde quod, si ad creandum dictatorem nullum certum tempus designatum sit, ratio tum nulla temporis intercedentis ab uno ad alium, quam maxime servandam esse diximus, haberetur; et quod res etiam 10 vaga admodum esset, ut facile negligeretur. Nisi itaque haec dictatoria potestas aeterna sit et stabilis, quae servata imperii forma in unum deferri nequit, erit ergo ipsa, et consequenter reipublicae salus et conservatio, admodum incerta.

2. At contra dubitare nequaquam possumus (per Art. 3 Cap. 6) quod 15 si possit servata imperii forma dictatoris gladius perpetuus, et malis tantummodo formidini esse, nunquam eo usque vitia invalescere poterunt ut tolli aut emendari nequeant. Ut igitur has omnes conditiones obtineamus, syndicorum concilium concilio supremo subordinandum diximus, ut scilicet dictatorius ille gladius perpetuus esset non penes per- 20 sonam aliquam naturalem, sed civilem, cujus membra plura sint quam ut imperium inter se possint dividere (per Art. 1 et 2 Cap. 8), vel in scelere aliquo convenire. Ad quod accedit quod a reliquis imperii muneribus subeundis prohibeantur, quod militiae stipendia non solvant, et quod denique ejus aetatis sint ut praesentia ac tuta quam nova 25 et periculosa malint. Quare imperio nullum ab iis periculum, et consequenter non bonis sed malis tantummodo formidini esse queunt; et revera erunt. Nam ut ad scelera peragenda debiliores, ita ad malitiam coercendam potentiores sunt: nam praeterquam quod principiis obstare possunt (quia concilium aeternum est), sunt praeterea numero satis

---

3. *OP tumor dictatoris*; *NS d' opgeblazentheit van d' Oppervoocht. V–L*'s emendation *rumor* is based on the text of Cicero (*Epp. ad Quintum fratrem* III, 8, 4), which gives no support whatever for *tumor*. Though it is possible that Spinoza misquoted Cicero, it is more probable that his editors and translator mistook his *r* for a *t*. For (in spite of *opulentia* and *superbior* above) the context requires *rumor*; Spinoza is saying that although the Romans may have avoided dictators who were *opum magnitudine tumidi* (see p. 436, ll. 6–7) by appointing to the office only in emergencies, talk of a dictator (and it was *rumor* just because a Roman dictator was not appointed *constituto tempore*) was still displeasing to loyal citizens because his power was dangerous to the republican constitution.

9. *NS daar op men voornamelijk te zien had, gelijk wy gezegt hebben*, which suggests *observandam.*

19–20. *NS niet by enig man alleen, maar by verscheiden te zamen.*

21. *V–L Cap. 8; OP praec. Cap; NS van 't voorgaande Hooftdeel.*

to go to the richest and most arrogant. This perhaps is why the Romans used to appoint a dictator at no fixed time, but only when compelled by some chance need. Even so, to quote the words of Cicero, talk of a dictator was displeasing to loyal citizens. And obviously, since this dictatorial power is essentially regal, it is only with great risk to its republican constitution that a state can become a monarchy from time to time, however short the period for which it does so.[1] Besides, if no fixed time were assigned for the appointment of a dictator, no reckoning would be kept of the length of time between one dictator and the next, although, as I said, a careful reckoning is required; what is more, the whole thing would be so indefinite that it might easily be overlooked altogether. Thus unless this dictatorial power is permanent and stable—in which case it cannot be vested in one man without destroying the form of the state—its very existence, and hence the safety and preservation of the commonwealth, will be very much a matter of chance.

2. Yet in the light of Section 3, Chapter 6, it is impossible to doubt that if a dictatorial sword can be permanent without destroying the form of the state, and a threat to the wicked only, vices will never be able to increase to such a pitch that they cannot be removed or corrected. Now it was to satisfy all these conditions that we advised the creation of a council of syndics subordinate to the supreme council; so that the dictatorial sword might be permanently vested, not in any natural person, but in a civil person[2] whose members are too numerous to be capable of dividing the state among themselves (by Sections 1 and 2 of Chapter 8), or of agreeing on any crime. In addition, they are debarred from holding any other office in the state, they do not pay the armed forces, and, lastly, are of such an age as to prefer the safety of the status quo to the dangers of innovation. For these reasons the state has no danger to fear from them, so it is not to the good but only to the wicked that they can be a threat; and this, in fact, they will be. Indeed, the less power they have to perpetrate crimes, the more they have to suppress wickedness; for—apart from the fact that they can nip it in the bud[3] (since their council is permanent)—their numbers

---

[1] The Roman dictator was appointed to deal with an emergency, and held office for six months or less. Machiavelli maintained that this institution was highly beneficial to Rome (*Discourses* i, 34); Spinoza follows Van Hove, who pointed out that it later became a danger to freedom (*Polityke Weegschaal* ii, vi, 2, p. 377).

[2] Machiavelli is aware that the *dictatoria potestas* may be vested in a permanent council, and in *Discourses* i, 34 refers to the *Dieci* of Venice.

[3] Ovid, *Remedia Amoris*, 91 : *Principiis obsta.*

magno ut sine invidiae timore potentem unum aut alterum accusare et damnare audeant; praesertim quia suffragia calculis feruntur, et sententia nomine totius concilii pronunciatur.

3. At Romae plebis tribuni perpetui etiam erant: verum impares ut
5 Scipionis alicujus potentiam premerent; et praeterea id quod salutare esse judicabant ad ipsum senatum deferre debebant, a quo etiam saepe eludebantur, efficiendo scilicet ut plebs ei magis faveret quem ipsi senatores minus timebant. Ad quod accedit quod tribunorum contra patricios auctoritas plebis favore defenderetur, et quotiescunque ipsi
10 plebem vocabant seditionem potius movere quam concilium convocare viderentur. Quae sane incommoda in imperio quod in praecedd. duob. Capp. descripsimus locum non habent.

4. Verum enim vero haec syndicorum auctoritas hoc solummodo praestare poterit, ut imperii forma servetur; atque adeo prohibere ne
15 leges infringantur, et ne cuiquam cum lucro peccare liceat; sed nequaquam efficere poterit ne vitia quae lege prohiberi nequeunt gliscant, ut sunt illa in quae homines otio abundantes incidunt, et ex quibus imperii ruina non raro sequitur. Homines enim in pace deposito metu paulatim ex ferocibus et barbaris civiles seu humani, et ex humanis molles et
20 inertes fiunt, nec alius alium virtute, sed fastu et luxu excellere studet; unde patrios mores fastidire, alienos induere, hoc est, servire incipiunt.

5. Ad haec mala vitandum multi conati sunt leges sumptuarias condere; sed frustra. Nam omnia jura quae absque ulla alterius injuria

---

12. *OP habet*, which is corrected to *habent* in the list of Errata; *NS geen plaats heeft.*

19. *NS in plaats van woest en onbezuist.* Hence *L ex ferocibus et barbaris. OP ex ferocibus barbaris.*

21. *NS zy de vaderlijke zeden beginnen te verächten, en daar af te walgen, en de vreemden aan te wennen.* It is possible that *et* has fallen out before *alienos* in the *OP* text.

are large enough to embolden them to accuse and condemn powerful individuals without any fear of unpopularity; especially as the voting is by secret ballot, and the verdict is pronounced in the name of the council as a whole.

3. It may be said that at Rome the tribunes of the people[1] were also standing officials. But they were too weak to suppress the power of a Scipio;[2] besides, they had to lay any measure which they thought salutary before the senate itself, and that body could often frustrate their efforts by ensuring that a tribune whom the senators themselves feared less found greater support among the people.[3] In addition, their authority against the patricians was maintained by popular support, and whenever they called a meeting of the people on their own initiative it looked as if they were fomenting a revolt rather than convoking an assembly. Such defects, of course, have no place in the kind of state described in the last two Chapters.[4]

4. However, the authority of the syndics will be able to ensure no more than the preservation of the constitution. It will thus be able to prevent anyone from breaking the law, and from finding profit in wrong-doing; but it will be quite incapable of preventing the spread of the vices which cannot be forbidden by law, those, for instance, which arise from a life of ease, and which lead quite often to the downfall of the state. The fact is that in time of peace men lay aside their fear; savages and barbarians gradually become civilized or cultured, and culture in turn gives rise to softness and laziness; men no longer strive to surpass one another in courage, but in pride and extravagance; they thus begin to disdain the ways of their ancestors, to adopt foreign customs, in a word, to be slaves.[5]

5. Many have tried to prevent these ills by passing sumptuary laws; but without success.[6] For any law which can be broken without

---

[1] The *tribuni plebis* were appointed to protect the plebeians against the patricians (Machiavelli, *Discourses* i, 3). This function they share with Spinoza's syndics (*TP* viii, 28, p. 391, and viii, 41, p. 407); but they cannot be taken as an adequate model. It is necessary to make this clear since Machiavelli had mentioned the institution of tribunes as one of the things which brought the Roman Republic back to its original principles (*Discourses* iii, 1).

[2] Here Spinoza follows Van Hove (op. cit. ii, vi, 2, p. 377). Scipio Africanus successfully defended his brother and himself against tribunician attacks in 189 and 185 B.C.

[3] Machiavelli, *Discourses* iii, 11.

[4] The tribunes convoked, and were appointed by, the *concilium plebis*. Naturally no such assembly can exist in Spinoza's aristocracy (*TP* viii, 4–5, pp. 371–3).

[5] Machiavelli notices the enervating effects of peace in *Discourses* i, 6; cf. Bacon, *Essay* xxix.

[6] *TT-P* xx, p. 235. Sumptuary regulations had recently been devised for Amsterdam (Temple, *Observations*, ch. vi, p. 150).

violari possunt ludibrio habentur, et tantum abest ut hominum cupiditates et libidines frenent, quin contra easdem intendant: nam nitimur
in vetitum semper, cupimusque negata. Nec unquam hominibus otiosis
ingenium deest ad eludenda jura quae instituuntur de rebus quae
5 absolute prohiberi nequeunt, ut sunt convivia, ludi, ornatus, et alia
hujusmodi, quorum tantummodo excessus malus, et ex uniuscujusque
fortuna aestimandus est, ita ut lege nulla universali determinari queat.

6. Concludo itaque communia illa pacis vitia, de quibus hic loqui-
mur, nunquam directe, sed indirecte prohibenda esse, talia scilicet
10 imperii fundamenta jaciendo quibus fiat ut plerique, non quidem
sapienter vivere studeant—nam hoc impossibile est,—sed ut iis ducantur affectibus ex quibus reipublicae major sit utilitas. Atque adeo huic
rei maxime studendum, ut divites, si non parci, avari tamen sint. Nam
non dubium est quin, si hic avaritiae affectus, qui universalis est et con-
15 stans, gloriae cupidine foveatur, plerique rei suae sine ignominia augendae summum ponant studium, quo honores adipiscantur et summum
dedecus vitent.

7. Si itaque ad fundamenta utriusque imperii aristocratici quae
praeced. duobus Capp. explicui attendamus, hoc ipsum ex iisdem sequi
20 videbimus. Numerus enim regentium in utroque adeo magnus est ut
divitum maximae parti aditus ad regimen pateat et ad imperii honores
adipiscendos. Quod si praeterea (uti diximus Art. 47 Cap. 8) statuatur
ut patricii qui plus debent quam sunt solvendo ordine patricio detur-
bentur, et qui bona sua infortunio perdiderunt ut in integrum restituan-
25 tur, non dubium est quin omnes quantum poterunt conabuntur bona
sua conservare. Peregrinos praeterea habitus nunquam concupiscent
nec patrios fastidient, si lege constituatur ut patricii, et qui honores
ambiunt, singulari veste dignoscantur: de quo vide Art. 25 et 47 Cap. 8.
Et praeter haec alia in quocunque imperio cum natura loci et gentis
30 ingenio consentanea excogitari possunt, et in eo apprime vigilari ut
subditi magis sponte quam lege coacti suum officium faciant.

8. Nam imperium quod nihil aliud prospicit quam ut homines metu
ducantur, magis sine vitiis erit quam cum virtute. Sed homines ita
ducendi sunt, ut non duci sed ex suo ingenio et libero suo decreto vivere

---

1–2. *NS de lusten en begeerlijkheden*, i.e. *cupiditates et libidines*; *OP cupiditates et libidinem.*
18. *OP* makes no break in the text to indicate Section 7, but passes directly from Section 6
to Section 8. *NS* commences Section 7 here: *B* at *Quod si praeterea* below.

injustice to another person is regarded with derision, and intensifies the desires and lusts of men instead of restraining them; since we always strive for what is forbidden, and desire what is denied.[1] Besides, men of leisure never lack the wit to get round laws which are framed to deal with things which cannot be forbidden absolutely, things like feasting, gambling, personal adornment, and so forth, which are bad only in excess, and must be judged as excessive or otherwise in relation to the wealth of each individual, so that no general law can determine what is excessive and what is not.

6. I therefore conclude that the common peace-time vices which we are here discussing should be prevented indirectly and never directly; that is, by basing the state on such laws as will cause the majority, not indeed to seek to live wisely—for that is impossible—but at any rate to be governed by those passions which are most useful to the commonwealth. Thus every attempt must be made to ensure that the rich, if they cannot be thrifty, are at any rate greedy for gain. For if this passion for gain, which is universal and constant, is reinforced by the desire for glory, most men will certainly make every effort to increase their wealth by honourable means so as to obtain office and avoid great disgrace.

7. Now if we consider the fundamental laws of both aristocracies as set out in the last two Chapters, we shall see that they produce this very result. For in both the number of rulers is so large that most of the rich have access to the government and the offices of state. And if it is also laid down that patricians whose debts exceed their assets should be expelled from the patrician order, while those who have lost their possessions through misfortune should be compensated in full (as I recommended in Section 47, Chapter 8), everyone will certainly do his utmost to preserve his property. Moreover, they will never take a fancy to foreign fashions, and disdain their native garb, if there is a law prescribing that patricians and candidates for promotion should be distinguished from the rest by a particular dress: for this see Sections 25 and 47 of Chapter 8. And further measures can be devised in each state to suit the nature of its territory and the character of its people, their main object being to ensure that the subjects do their duty willingly rather than by legal constraint.[2]

8. For a state whose sole aim is to govern men by fear will be free from faults rather than possessed of merits. Men should really be governed in such a way that they do not regard themselves as being

[1] Ovid, *Amores* III, iv, 17.   [2] *TT-P* v, pp. 95–97; *TP* v, 4–6, p. 311.

435

sibi videantur; atque adeo ut solo libertatis amore, et rei augendae studio, speque imperii honores adipiscendi retineantur. Caeterum imagines, triumphi, et alia virtutis incitamenta magis servitutis quam libertatis sunt signa. Servis enim, non liberis, virtutis praemia decernun-
5 tur. Fateor quidem homines his stimulis maxime incitari; sed ut haec in initio viris magnis, ita postea crescente invidia ignavis et opum magnitudine tumidis decernuntur, magna omnium bonorum indignatione. Deinde qui parentum triumphos et imagines ostentant injuriam sibi fieri credunt ni reliquis praeferantur. Denique, ut alia taceam, hoc
10 certum est, quod aequalitas, qua semel exuta communis libertas necessario perit, conservari nullo modo possit simulatque alicui viro virtute claro singulares honores jure publico decernuntur.

9. His positis, videamus jam an hujusmodi imperia culpabili aliqua causa possint destrui. Verum si quod imperium aeternum esse potest,
15 illud necessario erit cujus semel recte instituta jura inviolata manent. Anima enim imperii jura sunt: his igitur servatis servatur necessario imperium. At jura invicta esse nequeunt nisi et ratione et communi hominum affectu defendantur; alias, si scilicet solo rationis auxilio nituntur, invalidae sane sunt, facileque vincuntur. Cum itaque utriusque
20 imperii aristocratici jura fundamentalia cum ratione et communi hominum affectu convenire ostenderimus, possumus ergo affirmare, si quae ulla imperia, haec necessario aeterna fore, vel nulla culpabili causa sed fato tantummodo aliquo inevitabili posse destrui.

10. At objici nobis adhuc potest quod, quamvis imperii jura in
25 praeced. ostensa ratione et communi hominum affectu defendantur, possint nihilominus aliquando vinci. Nam nullus affectus est qui aliquando a fortiori et contrario affectu non vincatur. Timorem namque mortis a cupidine rei alienae saepe vinci videmus. Qui hostem metu

---

1-2. *OP et rei augendae studio*; *NS en door d' yver van hun middelen te vermeerderen. P, Gf,* and *B* omit *et.*
27-28. *NS dewijl wy zien dat hy, door vrees van de doot, dikwijls van de begeerte van enig vreemd ding word verwonnen.*

Chapter X

governed, but as following their own bent and their own free choice
in their manner of life; in such a way, then, that they are restrained
only by love of freedom, desire to increase their possessions, and the
hope of obtaining offices of state. Statues, triumphs, and similar incentives to virtue,[1] however, are symbols of slavery rather than of freedom;
for it is slaves, not free men, who are assigned rewards for virtue.
Admittedly, such inducements are a very powerful stimulus; but while
at first they are assigned to the great, later, when envy rears its head,
they are given to purse-proud nonentities, much to the indignation of
all good citizens. Moreover, those who point with pride to the triumphs
and statues of their ancestors imagine that they are being wronged if
they are not given preference over the rest. Finally, to omit other
points, there is no doubt that once equality is abandoned[2] the loss of
general freedom inevitably follows, and that equality is doomed as soon
as extraordinary appointments are conferred by public decree on some
man of renowned ability.

9. Let us now consider in the light of this whether the states we
have described possess any avoidable defect which is capable of destroying them. Clearly, if any state can last for ever it must be the state whose
constitution, once established on correct principles, is kept intact. For
the constitution is the soul of a state:[3] so that to maintain the constitution is necessarily to maintain the state. But a constitution cannot be
kept intact unless it is supported both by reason and by the common
passions of men; otherwise, of course, i.e. if it depends on the support of
reason only, it is weak and easily overthrown.[4] Now I have shown that
the constitutions of my two aristocracies conform with both reason and
the common passions of men. I can therefore assert that if any state is
everlasting these will necessarily be so; in other words they cannot be
destroyed by any defect for which I can be held responsible, but only
by some unavoidable mischance.

10. However, an objection can still be brought against me. Although,
it may be said, the constitutions described above are supported by reason
and the common passions of men, there are times when they can still
be overthrown. For there is no passion that is not overcome at times by
a stronger and contrary passion. For instance, we can often see fear of
death being overcome by greed for another's possessions. Or take those

[1] Machiavelli seems to have approved of these devices (*Discourses* iii, 28); Bacon certainly
did (*Essay* xxix).
[2] Tacitus, *Annals* iii, xxvi, 3 (quoted by Van Hove in *Polityke Weegschaal* iii, i, 3, p. 437).
Spinoza has this chapter of Tacitus in mind when he rejects *praemia virtutis* above.
[3] Aristotle, *Politics* 1295ª 40.   [4] *TP* vii, 2, pp. 335–7, and viii, 19, p. 383.

territi fugiunt nullo alterius rei metu detineri possunt, sed sese in flu-
mina praecipitant, vel in ignem ruunt, ut hostium ferrum fugiant.
Quantumvis igitur civitas recte ordinata et jura optime instituta sint,
in maximis tamen imperii angustiis, quando omnes, ut fit, terrore
5 quodam panico capiuntur, tum omnes id solum quod praesens metus
suadet, nulla futuri neque legum habita ratione, probant; omnium ora
in virum victoriis clarum vertuntur, eundemque legibus solvunt,
atque ipsi imperium—pessimo exemplo—continuant, totamque rempublicam ipsius fidei committunt: quae res sane Romani imperii exitii
10 fuit causa. Sed ut huic objectioni respondeam, dico primo, quod in
recte constituta republica similis terror non oritur nisi ex justa causa;
atque adeo is terror, et confusio ex eo orta, nulli causae quae prudentia
humana vitari poterat adscribi potest. Deinde notandum quod in republica qualem in praeced. descripsimus fieri non potest (per Art. 9 et
15 25 Cap. 8) ut unus aut alter virtutis fama ita excellat ut omnium ora in
se vertat: sed necesse est ut plures habeat aemulos quibus plures alii
faveant. Quamvis itaque ex terrore confusio aliqua in republica oriatur,
leges tamen fraudare atque aliquem contra jus ad imperium militare
renunciare nemo poterit quin statim contentio aliorum petentium
20 oriatur; quae ut dirimatur necesse tandem erit ad semel statuta et ab
omnibus probata jura recurrere, atque res imperii secundum leges latas
ordinare. Possum igitur absolute affirmare, cum imperium quod una
sola urbs, tum praecipue illud quod plures urbes tenent aeternum esse,
sive nulla interna causa posse dissolvi aut in aliam formam mutari.

---

5. *NS alle de burgers,* glossed *cives;* which suggests *omnes cives.* But cf. l. 15, where
omnium is rendered *van alle de burgers.*

19. *NS of daar zal terstont twist tusschen anderen, die meê daar naar trachten, rijzen.* This
confirms *P*'s correction *aliorum petentium. OP alios petentium.*

22–23. *NS dat die Heerschappy, de welke in een enige Stat bestaat, en voornamelijk de gene,
die veel steden onder zich heeft, eeuwig is,* i.e. *cum imperium quod unam solam urbem, tum
praecipue illud quod plures urbes tenet* (or *continet*) *aeternum esse.*

who flee in terror from the enemy; they cannot be restrained by fear of anything else, but hurl themselves into rivers or rush into flames to get away from the swords of their foes. It does not matter, then, I shall be told, how correctly a commonwealth has been organized, and how well its laws have been framed; when the state is in desperate straits, and everyone, as often happens, is seized with panic, the citizens will take no account of the future or the laws, but will follow only the promptings of their immediate fear; they will all turn to the man who is renowned for his victories, release him from the laws,[1] create a disastrous precedent by prolonging his command,[2] and entrust the entire commonwealth to his good faith. This, in fact, was the cause of the overthrow of the Roman state. The above objection I answer as follows. First, in a well-organized commonwealth a panic like this does not arise without good reason; and so it, and the disturbance to which it leads, can be attributed to no cause which could have been avoided by human foresight. Secondly, it must be noted that in a commonwealth such as I have described above it is impossible for any single man to have such an outstanding reputation for ability that he turns everyone's eyes upon himself (by Sections 9 and 25 of Chapter 8): he must inevitably have numerous rivals, each with a considerable following. Thus even though panic does cause some disturbance in the commonwealth, no one will be able to get round the laws and appoint someone illegally to a military command without arousing the immediate opposition of other candidates; and to settle the dispute it will be necessary in the end to revert to the laws once established and approved by all, and to arrange such matters in accordance with the existing constitution. I can therefore assert without qualification that while both aristocracies are everlasting, this is particularly true of the one governed by several cities; that is, it cannot be destroyed or changed to another form by any internal cause.

---

[1] Spinoza is thinking of the panic of 1672, during which William III was appointed stadholder in spite of the Perpetual Edict of 1667.

[2] Machiavelli held that the prolongation of military commands caused Rome the loss of her liberty (*Discourses* iii, 24).

1. Transeo tandem ad tertium et omnino absolutum imperium quod democraticum appellamus. Hujus ab aristocratico differentiam in hoc potissimum consistere diximus, quod in eo a sola supremi concilii voluntate et libera electione pendeat ut hic aut ille patricius creetur; 5 ita ut nemo jus suffragii et munera imperii subeundi haereditarium habeat, nemoque id jus sibi poscere jure possit, ut in hoc, de quo jam agimus, imperio fit. Nam omnes qui ex parentibus civibus, vel qui in patrio illo solo nati, vel qui de republica bene meriti sunt, vel ob alias causas ob quas lex alicui jus civis dare jubet, ii, inquam, omnes jus 10 suffragii in supremo concilio muneraque imperii subeundi jure sibi poscunt; nec denegare iis licet nisi ob crimen aut infamiam.

2. Si igitur jure institutum sit ut seniores tantummodo qui ad certum aetatis annum pervenerunt, vel ut soli primogeniti simulatque per aetatem licet, vel qui certam pecuniae summam reipublicae contri- 15 buunt, jus suffragii in supremo concilio et imperii negotia tractandi habeant, quamvis hac ratione fieri posset ut supremum concilium ex paucioribus civibus componeretur quam illud imperii aristocratici de quo supra egimus, erunt nihilominus hujusmodi imperia democratica appellanda, quoniam eorum cives qui ad regendam rempublicam desti- 20 nantur, non a supremo concilio, ut optimi, eliguntur, sed lege ad id destinantur. Et quamvis hac ratione hujusmodi imperia, ubi scilicet non qui optimi, sed qui forte fortuna divites vel qui primi nati sunt ad regi- men destinantur, imperio aristocratico cedere videantur, tamen, si praxin seu communem hominum conditionem spectemus, res eodem 25 redibit. Nam patriciis ii semper optimi videbuntur, qui divites, vel ipsis sanguine proximi, vel amicitia conjuncti sunt. Et sane, si cum patriciis ita comparatum esset ut liberi ab omni affectu, et solo studio publicae salutis ducti, collegas patricios eligerent, nullum esset im- perium cum aristocratico comparandum. Sed rem contra omnino sese 30 habere satis superque ipsa experientia docuit, praesertim in oligarchiis, ubi patriciorum voluntas ob defectum aemulantium maxime lege soluta

---

10. *OP subeunda.* But cf. l. 5 above.

14–15. *NS of om dat zy zekere hoop gelts aan de gemene Staat verschaffen,* i.e. *vel quia.*

25. *OP videbantur,* corrected to *videbuntur* in the list of Errata; *NS zullen . . . schijnen.*

CHAPTER XI

1. I come at length to the third and completely absolute state[1] which we call democracy. The main difference between this state and aristocracy has been mentioned already:[2] in aristocracy the appointment of a particular individual to the patriciate depends entirely on the will and free choice of the supreme council, so that the right to vote and undertake offices of state is in no case an hereditary possession, and no one can demand that right for himself by law; but in the state I am now discussing the opposite is true. For here all who are of citizen parentage, or who have been born within the fatherland, or who have done good service to the commonwealth, or who qualify on other grounds recognized by law as entitling a man to civic rights, all these, I say, can legally claim the right to vote in the supreme council and to undertake offices of state; and it cannot be denied them unless they are criminals or persons of ill repute.

2. Thus if it is laid down in the constitution of a state that only older men who have reached a certain age, or eldest sons as soon as they attain their majority, or those who contribute a certain sum of money to the exchequer, shall have the right to vote in the supreme council and to handle public affairs, then, although such provisions would make it possible for its supreme council to be smaller than that of the aristocracy I have dealt with above, the state will still have to be called a democracy,[3] since those of its citizens who are appointed to govern the commonwealth are not selected by the supreme council as the best, but are assigned this function by law. This appears to make such a state inferior to an aristocracy, since it is not the best, but those who happen to be rich, or eldest sons, who are appointed to govern; but if we consider actual practice, or ordinary human nature, we shall find little to choose between them. For patricians will always regard as the best those who are rich or closely united to themselves by blood or friendship. Of course, if patricians were such that they could divest themselves of all partiality in choosing their colleagues, and be guided only by zeal for the public welfare, there would be no state to compare with aristocracy. But the very opposite is the case, as actual experience has amply shown; especially in oligarchies, where, since the patricians have no rivals, their will is completely free from legal restraint.

---

[1] *TP* viii, 3, p. 371.   [2] *TP* viii, 1, p. 367.
[3] *TP* viii, 12, p. 379, and 14, p. 381.

est. Ibi enim studio optimos a concilio arcent patricii, et eos sibi socios in concilio quaerunt qui ab eorum ore pendent; ita ut in simili imperio multo infelicius res ejus sese habeant, propterea quod patriciorum electio ab absoluta quorundam libera sive omni lege soluta voluntate
5 pendeat. Sed ad inceptum redeo.

3. Ex dictis in praeced. Art. patet nos posse imperii democratici diversa genera concipere. Sed meum institutum non est de unoquoque, sed de eo solummodo agere in quo omnes absolute qui solis legibus patriis tenentur, et praeterea sui juris sunt, honesteque vivunt, jus
10 suffragii in supremo concilio habent muneraque imperii subeundi. Dico expresse *qui solis legibus patriis tenentur*, ut peregrinos secludam, qui sub alterius imperio esse censentur. Addidi praeterea quod *praeterquam quod legibus imperii teneantur, in reliquis sui juris sint*, ut mulieres et servos secluderem, qui in potestate virorum et dominorum, ac etiam
15 liberos et pupillos, quamdiu sub potestate parentum et tutorum sunt. Dixi denique *honesteque vivunt*, ut ii apprime secluderentur qui ob crimen aut aliquod turpe vitae genus infames sunt.

4. Sed forsan rogabit aliquis num foeminae ex natura an ex instituto sub potestate virorum sint. Nam si ex solo instituto id factum est, nulla
20 ergo ratio nos coegit foeminas a regimine secludere. Sed si ipsam experientiam consulamus, id ex earum imbecillitate oriri videbimus. Nam nullibi factum est ut viri et foeminae simul regnarent; sed ubicunque terrarum viri et foeminae reperiuntur, ibi viros regnare et foeminas regi videmus, et hac ratione utrumque sexum concorditer vivere. Sed
25 contra Amazonae, quas olim regnasse fama proditum est, viros in patrio solo morari non patiebantur, sed foeminas tantummodo alebant, mares autem quos pepererant necabant. Quod si ex natura foeminae viris aequales essent, et animi fortitudine et ingenio, in quo maxime humana potentia et consequenter jus consistit, aeque pollerent, sane
30 inter tot tamque diversas nationes quaedam reperirentur ubi uterque sexus pariter regeret, et aliae ubi a foeminis viri regerentur, atque ita educarentur ut ingenio minus possent. Quod cum nullibi factum sit, affirmare omnino licet foeminas ex natura non aequale cum viris habere

---

4. *OP absolutâ. NS van de volstrekte vrije wil van enigen, die van alle wetten ontslagen zijn. de volstrekte vrije wil* is glossed *Voluntas absoluta libera.* Contrast p. 266, l. 27 : *potentia quae absolute libera est.*   10. *P supremo; OP suppremo.*
    11. *OP* commences the quotation at *solis* : *NS* rightly at *die (qui)*.
    12. Both *OP* and *NS* wrongly commence the quotation at *quod (dat)*.

For there they take every precaution to exclude the best men from the council, and seek as their colleagues upon it men who will hang on their lips; so that such states are actually in a far worse condition than democracy, since the selection of patricians depends on the arbitrary choice of a few men, i.e. on a will released from all legal restraint. But I must return to my subject.

3. It is clear from my remarks in the previous Section that we can conceive different kinds of democracy. My purpose, however, is not to discuss them all, but to confine myself to the type in which absolutely everyone who is bound only by the laws of his country, and is otherwise independent, and who leads a decent life, has the right to vote in the supreme council and to undertake offices of state. I say expressly 'who is bound only by the laws of his country', in order to exclude aliens, who are regarded as the subjects of another government. I added 'and is otherwise independent', to exclude women and servants, who are subject to their husbands and masters, and also children and wards, as long as they are under the control of their parents and guardians. I said lastly 'and who leads a decent life', primarily to exclude those who have gained a bad reputation through crime or some dishonourable mode of living.

4. But perhaps someone will ask whether it is by nature or by convention that women are subject to men.[1] For if this is due solely to convention, I have excluded women from the government without any reasonable cause. However, if we consult actual experience, we shall see that it is due to their weakness. For nowhere has there been any instance of men and women ruling together; but wherever we find men and women, we find that the men rule and the women are ruled, and that on this basis both sexes live in harmony. (The Amazons, who are said by legend to have ruled in days gone by, are no exception to this statement; for they would not allow men to stay in their native land, but used to rear females only and to kill the males they had borne.) Yet if nature had made women equal to men, and had given them equal strength of mind and intellectual ability, in which human power and therefore human right mainly consists, surely among so many different nations some would be found where both sexes ruled on equal terms, and others where the men were ruled by the women and brought up in such a manner that they had less ability. But since this has nowhere happened, I am fully entitled to assert that women have

---

[1] Lipsius, *Monita et Exempla Politica*, ii, ii. Cf. Van Hove, *Polityke Weegschaal* i, i, 16, who quotes from Tacitus, *Annals* iii, xxxiii.

jus, sed eas viris necessario cedere; atque adeo fieri non posse ut uterque sexus pariter regat, et multo minus ut viri a foeminis regantur.
Quod si praeterea humanos affectus consideremus, quod scilicet viri
plerumque ex solo libidinis affectu foeminas ament, et earum ingenium
5 et sapientiam tanti aestiment quantum ipsae pulchritudine pollent, et
praeterea quod viri aegerrime ferant ut foeminae quas amant aliis aliquo modo faveant, et id genus alia, levi negotio videbimus non posse
absque magno pacis detrimento fieri ut viri et foeminae pariter regant.
Sed de his satis.

Reliqua desiderantur

not the same right as men by nature, but are necessarily inferior to them; so that it is not possible for both sexes to rule on equal terms, and still less for men to be ruled by women. If we also consider human passions, and reflect that men generally love women out of mere lust, judge their ability and wisdom by their beauty, are highly indignant if the women they love show the slightest favour to others, and so on, we shall easily see that it is impossible for men and women to govern on equal terms without great damage to peace. But I have said enough on this topic.

Unfinished

INDEX OF REFERENCES TO SCRIPTURE

GENERAL INDEX

(All references to the *TT-P* and *TP* are to the pages of the English translation.)

Aaron, 163, 167, 215, 217.

Abimelech, 61 n. 1.

Abishai, 251.

Abraham, 247.

Absalom, 103, 347.

action: acting by right and acting in the best way distinguished, 309; acting from love of good and acting from fear of evil distinguished, 69, 73, 83; many actions not subject to state control, 149.

Adam, 75, 77–79, 83.

Aeneas, 155.

affairs of state, defined, 285.

affections of the human body, 6 ff.

Ahithophel, 103, 347.

Alexander the Great, 155–7, 173.

aliens, 331, 333, 353, 377, 379, 403, 443.

allies, 139–41, 295–7.

Amazons, the, 443.

ambassadors, 301, 331, 391 and n. 3, 419.

ambition: cause of schisms, 115 n. 1, 241; harnessed to support the constitutions of the model states, 41, 341, 343, 393; in a technical sense, 8.

Ambrose, 205.

Amsterdam, 35 n. 3, 42, 241 and n. 1, 367 n. 2, 417 n. 1, 433 n. 6.

angels, 79.

Antiochus Epiphanes, 147 n. 3.

Antony, 203 n. 5.

Apostles, the, 99, 191, 293 n. 6.

Appuhn, Ch., 47 and n. 1.

Aragon, 203 n. 4, 361 n. 4, 365 and nn. 1 and 2.

Aragonese, the, 361–5.

Aramaea, 195.

aristocracy: defined, 279, 367; differences between aristocracy and democracy, 367, 371, 441; differences between aristocracy and monarchy, 367, 369–71, 373; federal and unitary aristocracies, 369, 415; most aristocracies originally democracies, 377–9; must be broadly based in order to be stable, 367–9; primary

causes of the destruction of, 429–39; reason why not absolute in practice, 371–3.

model constitution for a unitary aristocracy:

aims, 371–3, 377.

institutions: law-court, 403–7; senate, 391–401 (consuls, 397–401); supreme council, 377–83, 389–91, 397; syndics, 385–91, 405–7, 431–3.

organization: armed forces, 373–7; cities, 373, 407; property, 377; religion, 34, 411; secretaries and officials, 409–11; subsidiary regulations, 411–13; taxation, 377.

model constitution for a federal aristocracy:

aims, 415, 417, 421.

institutions, city: law-court, 423–5; senate (consuls), 423; supreme council, 417–25 *passim*; syndics, 423.

institutions, federal: law-court, 421, 423, 425; senate, 417, 419–23 (consuls, 421); supreme council, 419, 423, 427; syndics, 423, 431–3.

organization: armed forces, 419, 421; cities, 415–27 *passim*; powers of city councils, 417–23 *passim*; powers of federal senate, 417–21 *passim*; taxation, 421.

superiority of federal to unitary constitution, 415, 425–7.

Aristotle, 24, 31, 107, 223 n. 2; *Ethics*, 105 n. 2, 107; *Poetics*, 261 n. 2; *Politics*, 40 n. 2, 41 n. 1, 263 n. 1, 311 n. 7, 317 n. 2, 337 n. 1, 379 n. 3, 429 n. 1, 437 n. 3.

Arminians, 241 n. 1.

army, professional: a threat to freedom, 353; does not make a state more stable, 361.

Asa, 195.

Athenians, the, 341.

Athens, 319 n. 3, 369 n. 1; Areopagites of, 385 n. 1; *boule* of, 397 n. 7.

General Index

subjects (*cont.*)

of due to the faults and virtues of the state, 309–11; obligation of to obey the sovereign, 28–31, 36, 129–35, 139, 145–53, 211–15, 231–3, 277, 285–93, 303–7, 333.

submission to the sovereign not contrary to reason, 133–5, 233, 247, 287–9.

succession: in a monarchy, 27, 355–7; in a Jewish tribe, 169.

Sulla, 203 n. 5.

sumptuary laws, 433–5, cf. 235.

superstition, 115 n. 1, 147, 193, 233, 411.

supreme good, the, 71–75.

Syriac text, the (of the New Testament), 87 and n. 1.

Tacitus: *Agricola*, 311 n. 3, 348 n.; *Annals*, 155 and n. 6, 287 n. 3, 303 n. 3, 319 n. 1, 349 n. 3, 359 n. 1, 361 n. 3, 365 n. 4, 437 n. 2, 443 n. 1; *Histories*, 155 and n. 2, 177 and n. 3, 183 and n. 2, 187 n. 1, 227 n. 1, 251 and n. 2, 261 n. 6, 345 nn. 3, 4, and 5, 347 and n. 2, 359 nn. 3 and 6.

Tartars, the, 65 and n. 1.

taxation, 321, 331, 377, 395, 421.

Taylor, A. E., 18 and n. 5, 29 n. 2.

Temple, Sir William, *Observations upon the United Provinces of the Netherlands*, 47, 167 n. 2, 321 n. 1, 323 n. 1, 325 n. 3, 327 n. 1, 329 n. 1, 331 n. 1, 333 n. 4, 341 n. 1, 351 n. 2, 367 n. 2, 377 n. 1, 395 n. 2, 409 n. 1, 411 n. 2, 415 n. 3, 417 nn. 1 and 4, 419 nn. 1 and 2, 421 nn. 1, 2, and 3, 425 n. 1, 427 n. 1, 433 n. 6.

temple, the, of the Jews, 61–63, 163, 165, 171, 181, 187, 223.

Terence: *Adelphi*, 359 n. 4; *Andria*, 153 n. 3; *Eunuchus*, 345 n. 1; *Phormio*, 365 n. 3.

Tertullian, 239 n. 2.

theocracy, 157–71.

Theodosius, 205.

theologians, 89, 183, 261, 271.

theology, 5; in the sense of faith or religion, 123.

theory and practice, 149, 221, 261–3, 371.

Thessalonica, 205 n. 3.

thought: attribute of, 9; freedom of, 22, 123, 199, 227–43.

Thucydides, 369 n. 1.

toleration, in the Netherlands, 3, 227 n. 1, 241, 411 n. 2.

Torah, the, 105 n. 2.

torture, 329, 405.

Tractatus Theologico-Politicus, 267, 357, 411.

trade, 35, 191, 325, 341 and n. 6, 395.

transference, law of, 7.

treason, 29 n. 5, 141–3, 229, 301; *see also* sedition.

treasury, 225, 327, 331, 411.

treaties, binding force of, 139–41, 295–7.

treaty between the Dutch and the Japanese, 99, 147.

Tremellius, E., 87 and n. 1.

tribunes, Roman, 407 n. 1, 433 and nn. 1, 2, and 4.

triumphs, 437.

truths, eternal, contrasted with commands, 10, 77–83, 249.

Turkey, tyrants of, 353.

Turks, the, 37 and n. 6, 147, 317.

tyranny, 30, 31–32, 93–95, 135, 149, 199, 201 n. 3, 227, 229, 235 ff., 257, 259, 303–5, 311–13, 317–19.

tyrants, 29 ff., 147, 171, 175 n. 1, 199, 201–3, 215, 313, 361.

Ulysses, 335.

understanding or intellect, 9 and n. 3, 71–87 *passim*, 99–101; and will of God, 77.

uniformity of worship, 1–3, 34–35.

United Provinces, the, 365; *see also* Dutch Republic, Netherlands.

unity, concord, or harmony, 31 ff., 38, 40, 135, 179, 239, 241, 263, 289, 293, 309, 311, 315, 317, 383, 443.

utility, *see* interest.

Utopia, 261.

utopianism, 11, 39, 261, 265.

Utrecht, 419 n. 3; Union of, 3.

Vaughan, C. E., 26 n. 3.

Venetians, the, 383, 389.

Venice, 369, 375 n. 1, 381 nn. 1 and 3, 383 n. 1, 387 nn. 1 and 3, 391 n. 1, 397 n. 4, 401 n. 1, 411 n. 2. *Avogadori di commun* of, 385 n. 1,

PRINTED IN GREAT BRITAIN
AT THE UNIVERSITY PRESS, OXFORD
BY VIVIAN RIDLER
PRINTER TO THE UNIVERSITY